Abortion
The Supreme Court Decisions

Abortion
The Supreme Court Decisions
1965–2022

Fourth Edition

Edited, with an Introduction, by
Ian Shapiro and Alicia Steinmetz

Hackett Publishing Company, Inc.
Indianapolis/Cambridge

Copyright © 2023 by Hackett Publishing Company, Inc.

All rights reserved
Printed in the United States of America

26 25 24 23   1 2 3 4 5 6 7

For further information, please address
    Hackett Publishing Company, Inc.
    P.O. Box 44937
    Indianapolis, Indiana 46244-0937

    www.hackettpublishing.com

Cover design by E. L. Wilson
Composition by Aptara, Inc.

Library of Congress Control Number: 2022946685

ISBN-13: 978-1-64792-121-7 (pbk.)
ISBN-13: 978-1-64792-122-4 (PDF ebook)

The paper used in this publication meets the minimum requirements of American National Standard for Information Sciences—Permanence of Paper for Printed Library Materials, ANSI Z39.48–1984.

CONTENTS

Preface   vii

Introduction   xi

Cases

Griswold v. Connecticut (1965)   1

Eisenstadt v. Baird (1972)   16

Roe v. Wade (1973)   19

Doe v. Bolton (1973)   42

Planned Parenthood of Central Missouri v. Danforth (1976)   50

Singleton v. Wulff (1976)   62

Beal v. Doe (1977)   66

Maher v. Roe (1977)   70

Poelker v. Doe (1977)   77

Colautti v. Franklin (1979)   80

Bellotti v. Baird (1979)   87

Harris v. McRae (1980)   95

H. L. v. Matheson (1981)   103

City of Akron v. Akron Center for Reproductive Health (1983)   111

Planned Parenthood Association of Kansas City, Missouri v. Ashcroft (1983)   128

Simopoulos v. Virginia (1983)   130

Thornburgh v. American College of Obstetricians and Gynecologists (1986)   132

Webster v. Reproductive Health Services (1989)   138

Ohio v. Akron Center for Reproductive Health (1990)   154

Hodgson v. Minnesota (1990)   160

Planned Parenthood of Southeastern Pennsylvania v. *Casey* (1992)   166

Stenberg v. *Carhart* (2000)   212

Gonzales v. *Carhart* (2007)   242

Whole Woman's Health v. *Hellerstedt, Texas Department of State Health Services* (2016)   260

Kristina Box v. *Planned Parenthood of Indiana and Kentucky* (2019)   271

June Medical Services v. *Russo* (2020)   275

Whole Woman's Health v. *Austin Reeve Jackson* (2021)   281

United States v. *Texas* (2021)   284

Whole Woman's Health v. *Jackson* (2021)   286

Dobbs v. *Jackson Women's Health Organization* (2022)   291

Index   343

Relevant Supreme Court decisions that postdate publication of this book will be posted on this book's title support page at www.hackettpublishing.com/abortion-4e-resources.

PREFACE

The United States Supreme Court is the American constitutional court of last resort. It has the final say in interpreting the Constitution, and—curiously in a modern democracy—its members are not elected: they are appointed with life tenure that can be revoked only in exceptional circumstances. Few other courts in the world match the American Supreme Court in their authority of constitutional interpretation, and none has exercised this authority for as long or enjoyed the same level of influence. The Court's appropriate place in the American political order has been the subject of much debate, and this will likely continue to be so for as long as the republic endures. Critics see the Court as an anachronistic throwback to predemocratic times and are skeptical that it does much to guard human liberties.[1] For defenders, by contrast, the Court protects democracy from itself in a variety of indispensable ways. It insulates us from the expedient passions of the moment that govern electoral politics, it guards individual rights against the excesses of majority tyranny, and it is a cornerstone of the separation of constitutional powers that is the lifeblood of modern republican government.[2]

The Court captivates insiders and fascinates outsiders. Whereas other American public officials are generally held in low public esteem, Supreme Court Justices are often greatly revered. There is, indeed, no more distinguished achievement for a lawyer than to be named to the nation's highest judicial bench. The quality of debate on the Court also

---

1. Perhaps the most persistent critic of both the justification for, and effectiveness of, judicial review was Robert Dahl. See, *How Democratic Is the American Constitution?* (New Haven, CT: Yale University Press, 2001); *A Preface to Democratic Theory* (Chicago: University of Chicago Press, 1956), pp. 105–112; and *Democracy and Its Critics* (New Haven, CT: Yale University Press, 1989), pp. 188–192. See also Michael Walzer, "Philosophy and Democracy," *Political Theory* 9, no. 3 (August 1981); Jeremy Waldron, "The Core of the Case Against Judicial Review," *Yale Law Journal* 115, no. 6 (April 2006), pp. 1346–1406; and Erwin Chemerinsky, *The Case Against the Supreme Court* (New York: Penguin Books, 2014).

2. For a sampling of different views of the Court's appropriate role, see Alexander M. Bickel, *The Least Dangerous Branch* (New Haven, CT: Yale University Press, 1962); John Hart Ely, *Democracy and Distrust: A Theory of Judicial Review* (Cambridge, MA: Harvard University Press, 1980); Michael Perry, *The Constitution, the Courts, and Human Rights* (New Haven, CT: Yale University Press, 1982); Rogers M. Smith, *Liberalism and American Constitutional Law* (Cambridge, MA: Harvard University Press, 1985); Ronald Dworkin, *Law's Empire* (Cambridge, MA: Harvard University Press, 1986); Bruce Ackerman, *We the People: Foundations* (Cambridge, MA: Harvard University Press, 1991); Robert A. Burt, *The Constitution in Conflict* (Cambridge, MA: Harvard University Press, 1992); Christopher L. Eisgruber, *Constitutional Self-Government* (Cambridge, MA: Harvard University Press, 2001); and Lawrence G. Sager, *Justice in Plainclothes: A Theory of American Constitutional Practice* (New Haven, CT: Yale University Press, 2004).

sets it apart from other American public institutions. In stark contrast to the cliché-ridden sound bites of electoral politics, argument on the Court—while often no less divisive or ideologically charged than political debate—is generally carried on at an exceedingly high intellectual level. Most Justices are persons of considerable intellectual ability and training. They probe one another's arguments with great acuity, and their deliberations exhibit a degree of thoroughness and rigor that are seldom found elsewhere in American public life.

The Supreme Court is a complex institution, and its operations and decisions can sometimes be opaque to outsiders. The Court's powers are set out in Article III of the U.S. Constitution. Apart from a small class of limited exceptions, it is a court of appellate, rather than original, jurisdiction. This means that the Supreme Court may only review decisions of lower courts and may consider only the issues that have been litigated below. Unlike appellate courts elsewhere in the world, the U.S. Supreme Court is not supposed to venture beyond these confines or issue advisory opinions about the validity of laws and statutes before they are tested by particular litigants who are engaged in actual disputes. Although the Supreme Court differs from lower courts in that it can reverse itself and alter its precedents, it has historically done this rarely. The doctrine of *stare decisis* (discussed in the introduction) creates a presumption of continuity in the law that further limits what the Court may do in a given case. Justices are often accused—and accuse one another— of exceeding the scope of their proper authority, but in theory, at least, this authority is comparatively limited.

Much of the controversy over the Court's unique role in the American political system issues from its power of judicial review, by which it is authorized to invalidate legislation or executive actions that the Court considers to be in conflict with the Constitution or other relevant statutes. Judicial review—the authority to determine what the law says, and therefore what the law is—while not explicitly mentioned in Article III, has been viewed as an essential power for fulfilling the Court's oath to uphold the Constitution. The Court exercises substantial discretion in deciding which cases to hear, selecting only about 100– 150 out of the 7,000–8,000 civil and criminal cases filed each year from state and federal courts. When the Court agrees to hear a case, Justices consider a variety of factors to reach a judgment. Precisely which factors to consider or emphasize, and to what degree, has been an issue of persistent debate within the Court. Former Justice Antonin Scalia, for instance, has referred to a "great divide" in constitutional interpretation in our era as being between originalists, who think the primary or sole consideration the Court should use in reaching judgments is the original intent of drafters or ratifiers of the Constitution, its amendments, or other relevant legislation, and non-originalists, who think additional considerations should be used, such as current meanings and values, pragmatic concerns relating to the authority and legitimacy of the judiciary, and the real-world consequences of each case.[3]

---

3. See Antonin Scalia, "Common-Law Courts in a Civil-Law System: The Role of United States Federal Courts in Interpreting the Constitution and Laws," in *A Matter of Interpretation: Federal Courts and the Law*, ed. Amy Gutmann (Princeton, NJ: Princeton University Press, 2018), pp. 3–48.

Although the Court's decisions are governed by strict majority rule, the five members needed for a majority when the Court is at full complement may reach the same result by different reasoning, or they may agree with one another in part only. In either instance, Justices may issue plurality or concurring opinions in order to explain their differences and the reasons for them, rather than sign a single majority opinion.[4] Justices who disagree with a decision may write dissenting opinions. These have a number of purposes. They may be simple expressions of outrage or anger, they may be designed to limit the majority holding as much as possible, they may be intended as signals to future litigants about how best to present an issue, and, perhaps most important, they sometimes provide conceptual resources for future majorities on the Court who might see an issue differently.[5] If the Court's decision is arrived at by an argument over the merits of a particular case, it is thus always somewhat more than merely that: it is an argument that extends backward and forward in time, engaging the present generation of Justices with their predecessors and successors. Nowhere is this more clearly evident than in the evolution of the constitutional law of abortion.

The present volume contains all the U.S. Supreme Court cases on abortion from the handing down of *Roe* v. *Wade* on January 22, 1973, through *Dobbs* v. *Jackson Women's Health Organization*, decided on June 24, 2022. It also contains *Griswold* v. *Connecticut* (1965) and *Eisenstadt* v. *Baird* (1972), the decisions that provided the often commented upon jurisprudential foundations for Justice Harry Blackmun's majority opinion in *Roe*. The cases deal with the nature of a woman's right to abortion, its evolving grounds and limits, informed consent and waiting periods, definitions of fetal viability, the rights of physicians, husbands, parents, and the state in the making of abortion decisions, abortion funding, and a host of related issues. The only cases that have been excluded are those arising out of conflicts surrounding demonstrations outside abortion clinics. Despite the attention they often receive in the media when the topic of abortion comes up, they turn on freedom of speech matters rooted in the First Amendment; they actually have nothing to do with the constitutional law of abortion.

In the Preface to the first edition of this book published in 1995, Ian Shapiro noted that the Court's membership at the time exhibited entrenched majority support for the

---

4. A plurality opinion is an opinion that commands the largest number of votes on the winning side when there is no majority opinion. The author of a concurrence "in the result" or "in judgment" accepts the conclusion in the majority or plurality opinion, but reaches it by different reasoning. However, a concurring opinion might not actually reject the reasoning in the majority or plurality opinion. Its author may merely want to express arguments or reservations that he or she thinks have not been adequately dealt with in the other opinions.

5. Concurrences and dissents can be complete or partial. That is, their authors may reject the majority or plurality opinion completely, or only aspects of it. Partial dissents and concurrences can be a source of considerable confusion as to what the Court has actually held. See the *Webster* decision in this volume.

changes in abortion jurisprudence that *Planned Parenthood* v. *Casey* had codified three years earlier with the requirement that states may regulate abortion so long as these regulations do not impose "undue burdens" on pregnant women, and therefore it seemed likely "that the main contours of the constitutional law of abortion are now set for some time to come." That basic prediction held true through 2007, when the Court upheld Congress's Partial-Birth Abortion Ban Act, thereby allowing the federal government to pass a nationwide abortion restriction for the first time while affirming its undue burden criterion. The Court continued to protect the constitutional right to abortion prior to viability, first established in *Roe* and reaffirmed in *Casey* thereafter, even if more conservative majorities on the Court began interpreting "undue burden" in increasingly restrictive ways. Indeed, Shapiro's prediction held true even as late as 2020, when the Court deployed "undue burden" to strike down a Louisiana law that would have caused the closure of state abortion clinics through medically unnecessary regulations in *June Medical Services, LLC* v. *Russo*. It was only in 2021, when a new Court membership with a majority of Justices known to be hostile to *Roe* agreed to review the constitutionality of a fifteen-week abortion ban in Mississippi, that it looked like the constitutional law of abortion was about to undergo a significant transformation. And it was not until the Court issued its official ruling in *Dobbs* v. *Jackson* in the summer of 2022, overturning *Roe* and *Casey* and declaring that the Constitution does not protect a right to abortion, that it became clear how radical this transformation would be. Even so, nothing on the Supreme Court is ever set in stone, and *Dobbs* is unlikely to be the final episode in the story of the constitutional law of abortion in the United States.

The cases have been edited for use in undergraduate and graduate courses in a variety of disciplines. We have included many dissenting opinions as well as majority and plurality ones in order to convey something of the flavor of argument on the Court and the manner in which constitutional doctrine evolves out of that argument over time. The principal cases, *Griswold* v. *Connecticut* (1965), *Roe* v. *Wade* (1973), *Webster* v. *Reproductive Health Services* (1989), *Planned Parenthood of Southern Pennsylvania* v. *Casey* (1992), *Gonzales* v. *Carhart* (2007), and *Dobbs* v. *Jackson Women's Health Organization*, have been less heavily edited than the others. They are also the principal focus of our discussion in the Introduction. We have tried, there, to set these cases in political, historical, and philosophical contexts, and to give the reader a sense of what the main issues in the constitutional law of abortion are likely to be in the future. The footnotes to the Introduction refer the reader to literatures in philosophy, law, history, and the social sciences that deal with the subject of abortion; they should be a useful starting point for further study.

For Supreme Court decisions on abortion that postdate the current edition of this book, please see the title support page for this volume, which appears at www.hackettpublishing.com/abortion-4e-resources.

INTRODUCTION

Abortion is one of the most intractable issues in American politics. Passionate and determined advocates argue and strategize relentlessly on multiple sides, each viewing the question as speaking to their most fundamental attitudes about society and morality. It has been portrayed as an issue of states' rights, human rights, and women's rights, as well as part and parcel of a constitutional right to privacy. Religious convictions which hold that the fetus is a person with rights from the moment of conception, and therefore, that abortion is murder, run headlong into rival views that personhood begins at birth. Many feel strongly that people are entitled to sovereign control over their bodies and that no one should be forced to give birth. Others are convinced that the state's interest in potential life outweighs bodily autonomy arguments, and that pregnancy, however unwelcome it might be, imposes the responsibility of carrying the fetus to term. Protest, vandalism, and even murder have seemed to some to be justified actions in pursuit of preventing abortions. Indeed, the one thing advocates on all sides often share is the belief that abortion is a matter of life and death.

In 1973, when the Supreme Court's landmark decision in *Roe* v. *Wade* established abortion as a constitutionally guaranteed right in the early stages of pregnancy, the seven Justices who authorized the decision hoped that *Roe* would resolve the issue "by constitutional measurement, free of emotion and of predilection."[1] But far from settling the issue, the Court's abortion rulings have played into the intense politicization of abortion law and funding debates, motivating a wide variety of governmental actions at local, state, and national levels designed either to further entrench abortion access or else to hinder or even nullify the Court's rulings. "No judicial decision in our time," Ronald Dworkin wrote of the 1973 decision, "has aroused as much sustained public outrage, emotion, and physical violence, or as much intemperate professional criticism."[2]

Indeed, some have claimed that the Supreme Court's attempt to put an end to the abortion debate in *Roe* had the opposite effect, transforming what had mainly been a state-level and bipartisan debate into a national and fiercely partisan one. Jurists and legal theorists as varied as Antonin Scalia[3] and Ruth Bader Ginsburg[4] criticized *Roe* for improperly intervening in an ongoing majoritarian political process, fueling the narrative that the Court's involvement may have actually stopped an otherwise growing momentum

---

1. *Roe* v. *Wade*, 410 U.S. 113 (1973), at p. 116.
2. Ronald Dworkin, "The Great Abortion Case," *New York Review of Books*, June 29, 1989, p. 49.
3. *Planned Parenthood of Southeastern Pa* v. *Casey*, 505 U.S. 833 (1992), at pp. 995–996.
4. Ruth Bader Ginsburg, "Some Thoughts on Autonomy and Equality in Relation to *Roe v. Wade*," *North Carolina Law Review* 63 (1985): 375–386, at p. 385.

toward political compromise over abortion. Others challenged this portrayal, claiming that "abortion became a wedge issue well before the Court intervened,"[5] and that even after *Roe*, there were attempts at middle-ground solutions at least up until the 1980s so that the Court is only one part of a larger story involving political realignment, movement building, and social change. They see the abortion fight as a product of polarization rather than its cause. Certainly, the Court's decision to overturn *Roe* in *Dobbs* v. *Jackson* forty-nine years later did nothing to diminish the partisan rancor over abortion.[6]

Despite the polarization and whatever its causes, much debate on the Court during the half century of *Roe*'s life span proceeded on the assumption that resolution is possible. Those who are convinced of this often point to public opinion polls, suggesting that in contrast to the extremes represented by activists and interest groups, public opinion data have shown a surprising stability in ambivalent feelings about abortion. For instance, a 1989 *Los Angeles Times* national poll found that 74 percent of Americans thought that "abortion is a decision that has to be made by every woman for herself," even though 57 percent considered abortion to be equivalent to murder.[7] Similarly, a 2022 survey conducted by the Pew Research Center found that 72 percent of Americans supported the statement that "the decision about whether to have an abortion should belong solely to the pregnant woman," while 56 percent supported the statement that "human life begins at conception, so a fetus is a person with rights."[8] This ambivalence underscores the reality that although abortion adds motivating fuel to activist-led single-issue campaigns, most Americans do not see the issue in similarly stark terms.

Abortion has also become involved in other contentious debates over racial and gender equality and justice, medical and scientific authority, disability rights, and the role of courts in democratic governance. This was not always the case. There was a time in American politics when abortion was not considered to be an issue of public concern. As recently as the 1970s, it would have been unthinkable to ask a politician or nominee for the Court what their position on abortion was. Even to mention it in public would have been considered impolite or irrelevant. Throughout the century following the Civil War, when abortion was illegal but nonetheless widely performed, it "was far from an everyday subject of public policy debate."[9] And even two years after *Roe*, in his 1975 Senate confirmation hearing, Justice John Paul Stevens was not asked a single question about abortion.

---

5. Mary Ziegler, *Abortion and the Law in America: Roe v. Wade to the Present* (Cambridge: Cambridge University Press, 2020), p. 209.

6. *Dobbs* v. *Jackson Women's Health Organization*, 597 U.S. ___ (2022).

7. Reported in Dworkin, "The Great Abortion Case," p. 49.

8. "America's Abortion Quandary," Pew Research Center, Washington, DC, May 6, 2022.

9. Gilbert Y. Steiner, "Introduction: Abortion Policy and the Potential for Mischief," in *The Abortion Dispute and the American System*, ed. Gilbert Y. Steiner (Washington, DC: Brookings Institution, 1983), pp. 2–3.

But we live in a different world today, in which abortion has become a galvanizing issue for activists who lobby politicians and often dominate primary campaigns. This reality should throw cold water on the hope that public opinion data will spontaneously produce a decisive resolution to the abortion question, at least as long as it remains as fiercely and pervasively politicized as it has become.

Yet it is clear that most Americans think that abortion should be legal in some but not all circumstances. And despite a partisan gap that has widened slightly over the last two decades, mostly due to increasing support for legal abortion among Democrats, this majority support holds across racial, gender, and ethnic lines, with the notable exception of white evangelical Protestants, nearly three-quarters of whom believe that abortion should be illegal in most or all cases. When asked in 2022, before the Court overturned *Roe*, whether this would be good or bad, 63 percent said that it would be bad.[10] But the same poll showed that most Americans support abortion restrictions that increase with the duration of pregnancy. For instance, 67 percent think abortion should be legal in the first trimester, 36 percent think the same during the second trimester, and just 20 percent think abortion should be legal in the third trimester.[11] (*Roe* had protected abortion until viability, then around twenty-three to twenty-four weeks). In addition, most Americans think abortion should be legal if pregnancy threatens the life or health of the pregnant individual, including a majority (62 percent) of Republicans; and most also think abortion should be legal in cases of rape (with 56 percent support among Republics, and 83 percent among Democrats).[12] In short, most Americans regard abortion as a complex and weighty issue.

Part of the evolution in the Court's understanding of the right to abortion reflects changes in its personnel. In 1973, Justices William H. Rehnquist and Byron White were the only dissenters from the majority opinion authored by Justice Harry Blackmun. Within two decades Rehnquist was Chief Justice, and most of the original *Roe* majority had departed. Warren E. Burger, William O. Douglas, William J. Brennan, Potter Stewart, Thurgood Marshall, Lewis F. Powell, and Blackmun had all retired (as had the other dissenter from *Roe*, Justice White). They had been replaced by Justices John Paul Stevens, Antonin Scalia, Sandra Day O'Connor, Anthony Kennedy, David Souter, Clarence Thomas, Ruth Bader Ginsburg, and Stephen Breyer. All the replacements other than Ginsburg and Breyer (appointed by President Clinton in 1993 and 1994) were Republican appointees who were in varying degrees uncomfortable with the reasoning, outcome, or both in *Roe*. Indeed, even Ginsburg was known to be uncomfortable with aspects of the reasoning. As we explain below, the result was that while a majority on the Rehnquist Court continued to support the constitutional protection of a woman's right to abortion,

---

10. "Abortion," *The Gallup Poll Briefing*, Washington, DC: Gallup Organization, 2022.
11. *Ibid.*
12. "America's Abortion Quandary," Pew Research Center.

starting with *Planned Parenthood* v. *Casey* in 1992 they replaced *Roe*'s underlying legal rationale and began altering its scope in fundamental ways.[13]

This group of Justices served together for over a decade until the summer of 2005 when Justice O'Connor announced her retirement and Chief Justice Rehnquist passed away. President George W. Bush filled these new openings with Justice Samuel A. Alito and Chief Justice John Roberts. When Justice Souter and Justice Stevens retired, respectively, in 2009 and 2010 (and their places were filled by President Barack Obama with the nominations of Justice Sonia Sotomayor and Justice Elena Kagan), the only member of the *Casey* plurality remaining on the court was Justice Kennedy. When Justices Scalia and Ginsburg died in 2016 and 2020, and Justice Kennedy retired in 2018, all three spots were filled by President Donald Trump, who had campaigned in the 2016 election on the promise to appoint Justices who would overturn *Roe*.

Roe was overturned in 2022, when the Court ruled in *Dobbs* v. *Jackson Women's Health Organization* that the Constitution does not confer a right to abortion. Justice Alito, joined by all three Trump appointees, Justice Neil Gorsuch, Justice Brett Kavanaugh, and Justice Amy Coney Barrett, in addition to Justice Clarence Thomas, penned the majority decision. In it, he declared that *Roe* had been "egregiously wrong" and "on a collision course with the Constitution from the day it was decided," and that subsequent cases had perpetuated *Roe*'s error, "calling both sides of the national controversy to resolve their debate, but in doing so . . . necessarily declared a winning side."[14] In overturning these cases, and nearly fifty years of the Court's own precedent on abortion, *Dobbs* returned the constitutional law of abortion to the pre-*Roe* status quo ante, when states were permitted to pass any abortion laws—including outright prohibition—so long as they are "rationally related" to a "legitimate state interest." This means that, going forward, abortion regulations will be subject to the Court's lowest tier of constitutional scrutiny. Continuing the Court's trend of shifting jurisprudential reasoning informing its abortion decisions, *Dobbs* employs an originalist approach to constitutional interpretation and draws on a test established in *Washington* v. *Glucksberg* in which the Court held that rights not explicitly mentioned in the Constitution can be recognized as constitutionally protected only when they are deeply rooted in history and tradition and implicit in the concept of ordered liberty, standards radically different from those used in *Roe*.[15]

Alasdair MacIntyre once remarked that the most striking feature of the modern abortion debate has been its interminable character. The views that are pitted against one another are "conceptually incommensurable" in that although they are internally consistent, they rest on rival premises which "are such that we possess no rational way of

---

13. *Planned Parenthood of Southeastern Pennsylvania* v. *Casey* 505 U.S. 833 (1992).

14. *Dobbs* v. *Jackson Women's Health Organization* 597 U.S. ____ (2022), p. 44.

15. *Washington* v. *Glucksberg*, 521 U.S. 702 (1997).

weighing the claims of one as against the other."[16] Much of the evolution of the constitutional debate over abortion since *Roe* has been driven by attempts by various members of the Court to prove him wrong; to reconcile the apparently irreconcilable and find a middle ground that could satisfy at least some of the contending parties who have sought to influence the Court's handling of the abortion issue. Several Justices have struggled mightily in this regard. The *Dobbs* decision appears to have announced an end to that search as it has operated since *Roe*, at least for the foreseeable future. Whether that end signals the Court's intention to stay out of the abortion rights debate as a constitutional matter moving forward, or whether instead it might signal an openness to taking a radically different approach to constitutional abortion law in the coming years, remains to be seen. These possibilities are considered below. First, we sketch the evolution of the right to abortion, the Court's rejection of that right in *Dobbs*, and the political and jurisprudential issues that are at stake in the ongoing abortion controversy.

History of the Constitutional Right to Abortion

Much of the debate about constitutional protection for abortion rights on the Supreme Court has proceeded at some distance from the public abortion debate. The slogans and protests at demonstrations outside of abortion clinics, at rallies for and against *Roe*, and in much of the discussion in the media might reasonably lead one to assume that the central constitutional question at issue is whether or not a fetus is a person. Kristin Luker is surely correct when she says of the public abortion debate that it is fundamentally "a debate about personhood."[17] There is no doubt that this is the central issue in the view of the anti-abortion movement, which, from its pre-*Roe* and initially mostly Catholic inception has articulated their concern for fetal life "in the language of both 'inalienable' human rights and constitutional rights . . . rooted in the Declaration of Independence and the Fourteenth Amendment."[18] Yet no Justice on the Supreme Court has ever openly contended that the Constitution should regard the fetus as a person. In the early 1970s, when the lawyers representing the state of Texas argued *Roe v. Wade* before the Court, they claimed that the fetus is a person, and therefore entitled to all the protections guaranteed by the Fourteenth Amendment.[19] In *Roe*, the Court explicitly rejected this reasoning.

---

16. Alasdair MacIntyre, *After Virtue: A Study in Moral Theory*, 2nd ed. (Notre Dame, IN: University of Notre Dame Press, 1984), pp. 6–8.

17. Kristin Luker, *Abortion and the Politics of Motherhood* (Los Angeles: University of California Press, 1984), p. 5.

18. Daniel K. Williams, *Defenders of the Unborn: The Pro-life Movement Before Roe v. Wade* (Oxford: Oxford University Press, 2016), p. 5.

19. During the oral arguments for *Roe*, Robert C. Flowers, representing Texas, put it starkly: "Gentlemen, we feel that the concept of a fetus being within the concept of a person, within the

"The word 'person,' as used in the Fourteenth Amendment," Justice Blackmun wrote, "does not include the unborn."[20] To date, no subsequent abortion decision, opinion, or dissent on the Court has taken the contrary position.

By contrast, the Court has been much more comfortable with recognizing the fetus as falling under the category of "potential human life," and since *Roe*, this status has been one of the two primary foundations upon which the state has been seen as having a legitimate interest in regulating abortion in the first place, along with its legitimate interest in protecting the health of pregnant women. (Since *Gonzales* v. *Carhart*, additional legitimate state interests have also been recognized, including an interest in drawing "a bright line that clearly distinguishes abortion and infanticide,"[21] and an interest in preserving the integrity of the medical profession. *Dobbs* also added mitigation of fetal pain and preventing discrimination on the basis of race, sex, or disability to this list.) Even the Court's opinion in *Dobbs*, which criticizes the view that "the Constitution requires the states to regard a fetus as lacking even the most basic human right—to live—at least until an arbitrary point in a pregnancy has passed,"[22] also explicitly states that the decision to overturn *Roe* and *Casey* is not based on any position about if and when prenatal life is entitled to any of the rights the Constitution guarantees to a person after birth.

If the Court were ever to declare the fetus or embryo to be included under the meaning of "person" for constitutional purposes, the implications would be more radical than even the most ardent opponents of *Roe* appear to realize.[23] They would reach far beyond

---

framework of the Unites States Constitution and the Texas Constitution, is an extremely fundamental thing. . . . We feel that this is the only question, really, that this Court has to answer." In response, one Justice asked, "Do you think the case is over for you? You've lost your case, then, if the fetus or the embryo is not a person, is that it?" To which Flowers answered, "Yes, sir, I would say so." *Roe* v. *Wade* #70-18, argued December 13, 1971 (Washington, DC: Hoover Reporting Company), pp. 1–50, at pp. 29–30.

20. 410 U.S. 113 (1973), at p. 158.

21. *Gonzales* v. *Carhart*, 550 U.S. 124 (2007), at pp. 157–160.

22. 597 U.S. ____ (2022), at p. 38.

23. Judith Jarvis Thompson has famously argued that the common perception that whether or not one is in favor of abortion depends on whether or not one thinks a fetus is a person is false. She argues that if a woman awoke one day to discover that a brilliant but sick violinist had been attached by tubes to her kidneys and that the attachment must be maintained for nine months if the violinist was not to die, the woman would have no moral obligation to maintain the attachment against her will. "A Defense of Abortion," *Philosophy and Public Affairs* 1, no. 1 (Fall 1971): 47–66. Ronald Dworkin points out that Thompson's argument, although influential among philosophers, is not legally dispositive because "abortion normally requires a physical attack on a fetus, not just a failure to aid it, and, in any case, parents are invariably made an exception to the general doctrine [that one ordinarily has no affirmative legal duty to save a stranger] because they have a legal duty to care for their children." *Life's Dominion: An Argument about Abortion, Euthanasia, and Individual*

the regulation of abortion as a medical procedure, potentially opening the door to states trying to pass a much more expansive set of laws regulating pregnant women, or even, although it seems less likely at present, the embryo prior to implantation.[24] Moreover, a declaration that the fetus or embryo is a person with rights might be held to generate a federal constitutional obligation to *proscribe* abortion—at least in a large class of circumstances. Almost all jurists and legal commentators who have argued that the decision in *Roe* was unconstitutional and that it should be overturned have not been partisans of that view.[25] Rather, they have been advocates of restoring the status quo ante that existed before *Roe*'s passage, when the law of abortion was regulated differently in different states—sometimes by state legislatures and sometimes as a matter of state constitutional law. Opposition to *Roe* has therefore not been tantamount to opposition to abortion rights as such. But that could change. Congress entered the fray in 2003 by enacting the Partial-Birth Abortion Ban Act which ruled out certain abortion procedures, a law that the Supreme Court upheld four years later.[26] This means that part of the law on abortion is already constitutionally sanctioned federal law. Now that *Roe* has been reversed, states are no longer hindered from passing more restrictive abortion laws or even outright bans on the grounds that a fetus is a person. Dozens of states have already done so. It is not a large leap from there to the claim that the fetal person should be protected as a matter of federal law, and perhaps even federal constitutional law. That would involve a new tectonic shift in the constitutional battle over reproductive rights, but it is not one that can be ruled out.

The idea that the government should regulate or limit abortion in order to protect the fetus is relatively recent in American law and politics. Historically its emergence seems to have been linked to the increase in abortions sought by white, Protestant, married middle- and upper-class women in the mid- to late nineteenth century, and the threat to the existing social order that these developments implied.[27] Until then, early abortion seems

---

Freedom (New York: Knopf, 1993), p. 111. For a more elaborate discussion of the legal implications of Thompson's argument, see Donald Regan, "Rewriting *Roe v. Wade*," *Michigan Law Review* 77, no. 7 (1979): 1569–1646.

24. As of 2022, none of the eighty-three bills introduced or passed by states since 2010 that mention both abortion and in vitro fertilization (IVF) have explicitly sought to ban IVF, and forty-five of these bills explicitly exempt reproductive technologies from abortion restrictions.

25. See, for example, Justice Rehnquist's dissent in *Roe*, in which he concedes that he has "little doubt" that statutes proscribing abortion in all circumstances would not survive constitutional scrutiny. 410 U.S. 113 (1973), at p. 173.

26. Nothing in that legislation, or in the Court's 2007 upholding of it in *Gonzales* v. *Carhart* 550 U.S. 124 (2007), raises Supremacy Clause issues beyond the federal proscription of this rare abortion procedure.

27. See James Mohr, *Abortion in America: The Origins and Evolution of National Policy* (Oxford: Oxford University Press, 1978), especially chapters 3 and 4.

to have been widely tolerated, and "many ordinary Americans at the turn of the [nineteenth] century had not adopted the idea that there was a rigid dividing line between menstruation and conception, but continued to think of menstruation and early pregnancy as related."[28] When the first statutes governing abortion appeared in the 1820s and 1830s, they were essentially poison control measures meant to regulate the sale of abortifacient drugs that often killed the women who took them. For instance, the first law to criminalize abortion, passed in Connecticut in 1821, made it a crime to perform an abortion by poison after quickening (defined as the first movement of the fetus, as reported by the pregnant woman).[29] During the century preceding *Roe*, abortion restrictions were typically based on the rationale of protecting maternal health because abortion was a dangerous procedure often leading to infection and death.

Beginning in the middle of the twentieth century, abortion became much safer, as medical advancements such as the development of antibiotics significantly reduced the risk of infection. In 1955, the mortality rate for women who got abortions was one hundred out of every one hundred thousand. By 1972, it had dropped to three out of every one hundred thousand.[30] Meanwhile, the fight for contraceptive access had gained an important victory in 1965, when the Supreme Court's decision in *Griswold v. Connecticut* effectively legalized the distribution and use of birth control for married people.[31] In a seven-to-two decision, the majority opinion authored by Justice Douglas ruled that, although the Constitution does not explicitly protect a general right to privacy, several amendments contained in the Bill of Rights create "penumbras," "formed by emanations from those guarantees that help give them life and substance," including a penumbral right to privacy in the marriage relationship. In the late 1960s, state courts started overturning anti-abortion laws, some on the grounds that patients have a right to privacy

---

28. Leslie J. Reagan, *When Abortion Was a Crime: Women, Medicine, and Law in the United States, 1867–1973* (Berkeley: University of California Press, 1997), p. 20. Even Catholics during this period considered there to be gradations in the moral permissibility of the practice, considering abortion only to be equivalent to homicide after ensoulment, although this changed in 1869 when Pope Pius IX declared even early abortions to be "anticipated homicide." Jean Reith Schroedel, *Is the Fetus a Person? A Comparison of Policies Across the Fifty States* (New York: Cornell University Press, 2000), pp. 19–20.

29. See Melody Rose, *Abortion: A Documentary and Reference Guide* (Westport, CT: Greenwood Press, 2008), p. 5.

30. See Laurie Collier Hillstrom, *Roe v. Wade* (Detroit, MI: Omnigraphics, 2008), p. 19.

31. *Griswold v. Connecticut* 381 U.S. 479 (1965). A subsequent case, *Eisenstadt v. Baird* 405 U.S. 438 (1972), then also legalized the use of birth control by unmarried people, but instead of basing the decision on *Griswold*'s reasoning that the Constitution contains a right to privacy, the Court relied on the Fourteenth Amendment's Equal Protection Clause. That is, since married individuals were entitled to contraception under *Griswold*, the Court reasoned that the same right could not be denied to unmarried individuals.

in reproductive decisions; in 1967, twenty-eight state legislatures debated abortion reform measures, twelve of which were adopted over the next few years. In 1970, Hawaii became the first state to legalize abortion prior to viability, followed by New York, which passed a law by referendum allowing abortion within the first twenty-four weeks of pregnancy. At the same time, pro-life advocates also picked up their efforts to oppose abortion reform, successfully getting states to vote down abortion legalization proposals in the early 1970s.[32]

These developments set the context for the Court's analysis of the right to abortion in *Roe* in which a Texas statute that had made it a crime to "procure an abortion" unless the life of the mother is threatened by continuing the pregnancy, was held unconstitutional. For reasons that are taken up later, such statutes were held to violate the Due Process Clause of the Fourteenth Amendment.[33] First, let us get clear on the holding. Blackmun's majority opinion deals with abortion differently during the three trimesters of a normal pregnancy:

(a) For the stage prior to approximately the end of the first trimester, the abortion decision and its effectuation must be left to the medical judgment of the pregnant woman's attending physician.

(b) For the stage subsequent to approximately the end of the first trimester, the State, in promoting its interest in the health of the mother, may, if it chooses, regulate the abortion procedure in ways that are reasonably related to maternal health.

(c) For the stage subsequent to viability the State, in promoting its interest in the potentiality of human life, may, if it chooses, regulate, and even proscribe, abortion except where it is necessary, in appropriate medical judgment, for the preservation of the life or health of the mother.[34]

This trimester-based test greatly limited the power of states to regulate abortion. Before the end of the first trimester abortion could no longer be regulated at all; prior to the point of viability, it could only be regulated in the interests of the health of the mother; and even after viability if a state chose to regulate or proscribe abortion acting on its interest "in the potentiality of human life," this could be trumped if the attending physician made an "appropriate" judgment that this was necessary for the "life or health" of the mother. In the years following *Roe*, various modifications to the constitutional right that it created were added by the evolving majority on the Court.

---

32. Hillstrom, *Roe v. Wade*, pp. 30–36.

33. The Due Process Clause states: "No state shall . . . deprive any person of life, liberty or property, without due process of law."

34. 410 U.S. 113 (1973), at pp. 164–165.

In a number of respects the right recognized in *Roe* was secured and expanded. In *Doe v. Bolton*, also decided in 1973, the Court struck down restrictions on places that could be used to perform abortions, giving rise to the modern abortion clinic.[35] Three years later, in *Planned Parenthood* v. *Danforth*, the Court denied states the authority to give husbands veto power over their wives' decisions to abort pregnancies, and it also held that parents of unwed minor girls could not be given an absolute veto over abortions.[36] In 1979, in *Colautti* v. *Franklin*, the Court affirmed its intention to give physicians broad discretion to determine when a fetus can live outside the womb.[37] The Justices said that although a state may seek to protect a viable fetus, the determination of viability must be left to doctors. In 1983, the Court placed additional limits on the types of regulations that states may place on abortion. In a trio of decisions, *City of Akron* v. *Akron Center for Reproductive Health*, *Planned Parenthood of Kansas City* v. *Ashcroft*, and *Simopoulos* v. *Virginia*, by a six-to-three vote a majority on the Court denied states and local communities the power to require that women more than three months pregnant have their abortions in a hospital and struck down regulations that, among other things, imposed a twenty-four-hour waiting period between the signing of an abortion consent form and the medical procedure.[38] Three years later (this time by a five-to-four vote that reflected the conservative drift on the Court that was by then well underway), a bare majority struck down Pennsylvania regulations that had required doctors to inform women seeking abortions about potential risks and about available benefits for prenatal care and childbirth.[39] In 1987, the Justices split four-to-four in *Hartigan* v. *Zbaraz*, thereby letting stand a decision below invalidating an Illinois law that might have restricted access to abortions for some teenagers.[40]

Despite the elaboration and deepening of the woman's constitutional right to abortion brought about by these decisions, the Court had also begun to limit that right in various ways long before the *Roe* majority started to erode. One important area of constraint concerned abortion funding. In 1977, the Court ruled, in *Maher* v. *Roe*, that states have no constitutional obligation to pay for "non-therapeutic" abortions,[41] and three years later a five-to-four majority held, in *Harris* v. *McRae*, that, even for medically necessary abortions sought by women on welfare, neither states nor the federal government are under any constitutional obligation to provide public funding.[42] In 1979, in the first of what was

---

35. *Doe* v. *Bolton*, 410 U.S. 179 (1973).

36. *Planned Parenthood* v. *Danforth*, 428 U.S. 52 (1976).

37. *Colautti* v. *Franklin*, 439 U.S. 379 (1979).

38. *City of Akron* v. *Akron Center for Reproductive Health*, 462 U.S. 416 (1983); *Planned Parenthood of Kansas City* v. *Ashcroft*, 462 U.S. 476 (1983); and *Simopoulos* v. *Virginia*, 462 U.S. 506 (1983).

39. *Thornburgh* v. *American College of Obstetricians and Gynecologists*, 476 U.S. 747 (1986).

40. *Hartigan* v. *Zbaraz*, 484 U.S. 171 (1987).

41. *Maher* v. *Roe*, 432 U.S. 464 (1977).

42. *Harris* v. *McRae*, 448 U.S. 297 (1980).

to turn out to be a string of decisions regulating the rights of dependent minors to abortion, an eight-to-one majority on the Court held in *Bellotti* v. *Baird* that states may be able to require a pregnant, unmarried minor to obtain parental consent to an abortion so long as the state provides a "bypass" procedure, such as allowing the minor to seek a judge's permission instead.[43] In 1981, a six-to-three majority held, in *H. L.* v. *Matheson*, that states may require physicians approached by some girls who are still dependent on their parents and too "immature" to decide such matters for themselves to try to inform parents before performing abortions.[44] Two 1990 decisions, *Hodgson* v. *Minnesota* and *Ohio* v. *Akron Center for Reproductive Health*, further elaborated the law of parental notification.[45] In the Ohio case, a six-to-three majority upheld the state law requiring notification of at least one parent so long as it provided a judicial bypass, although in the Minnesota case a five-to-four majority made it clear that statutes requiring both parents to be informed before a minor can have an abortion would not survive in the future.

By the time of the 1990 decisions, much of the reasoning underlying *Roe* had been compromised by the watershed decision in *Webster* v. *Reproductive Health Services*, handed down by a multiply divided Court eleven months earlier.[46] With that decision, majority support for *Roe* on the Court seemed finally to have evaporated—as Justice Blackmun acknowledged in a bitter dissent. In its controlling opinion, the *Webster* Court upheld a Missouri statute requiring that before a physician performs an abortion on a woman whom he has reason to believe is twenty or more weeks pregnant, he shall first determine whether the unborn child is viable. More important than this comparatively minor new restriction of a woman's right to an abortion was that the plurality launched a frontal assault on *Roe*'s trimester-based framework of analysis that had been law for the preceding decade and a half.

Justice Blackmun's throwaway remark in *Roe* that the state has an interest in "the potentiality of human life" had come back to haunt him. In Chief Justice Rehnquist's hands, it became a stake that he seemed poised to drive into *Roe*'s heart. In an opinion also signed by Justices Kennedy and White, Rehnquist flatly rejected *Roe*'s "rigid" framework as "hardly consistent with the notion of a Constitution cast in general terms, as ours is, and usually speaking in general principles." Rehnquist went on to say that the plurality did "not see why the State's interest in protecting potential human life should come into existence only at the point of viability, and that there should therefore be a rigid line allowing state regulation after viability but prohibiting it before viability."[47]

---

43. *Bellotti* v. *Baird*, 443 U.S. 622 (1979).

44. *H. L.* v. *Matheson*, 450 U.S. 398 (1981).

45. *Hodgson* v. *Minnesota*, 497 U.S. 417 (1990); *Ohio* v. *Akron Center for Reproductive Health*, 497 U.S. 502 (1990).

46. *Webster* v. *Reproductive Health Services*, 492 U.S. 490 (1989).

47. 492 U.S. 490 (1989), at 518–519.

Justice O'Connor had announced her opposition to *Roe*'s trimester framework as early as 1985[48] and Justice Scalia's only objection to the plurality opinion in *Webster* was that it should have gone further and done explicitly what he insisted it did implicitly, namely overrule *Roe*. This appeared to mean that there were now five votes in favor of overruling *Roe*, even if the five Justices in question were not yet all prepared to reach that matter on the grounds that the Missouri statute in question did not in fact try to regulate abortions prior to viability. The principle had been conceded, even if what Scalia dismissed as the Court's "newly contracted abstemiousness" meant that "the mansion of constitutionalized abortion-law, constructed overnight in *Roe v. Wade*, must be disassembled doorjamb by doorjamb."[49] No more impressed than Scalia by what he saw as the plurality's "feigned restraint," Justice Blackmun writing in dissent (also for Brennan and Marshall) declared that it "implicitly invites every state legislature to enact more and more restrictive abortion regulations in order to provoke more and more test cases, in the hope that sometime down the line the Court will return the law of procreative freedom to the severe limitations that generally prevailed in this country before January 22, 1973." Thus, "not with a bang, but a whimper," Blackmun concluded, "the plurality discards a landmark case of the last generation, and casts into darkness the hopes and visions of every woman in this country who had come to believe that the Constitution guaranteed her right to exercise some control over her unique ability to bear children."[50]

That some of Blackmun's own formulations in *Roe* could be used to undermine its result in *Webster* is characteristic of the haphazard way in which constitutional interpretation often evolves over time. Perhaps this very fact should have alerted Blackmun to the possibility that all was not lost from his point of view. Although *Roe*'s trimester framework had been jettisoned and a majority on the Court had embraced the idea that states may assert an interest in protecting "potential" human life even before the point at which a fetus is viable, this did not necessarily mean that the constitutional protection of a woman's right to an abortion would soon follow the trimester framework into the annals of constitutional history. Everything would now turn on what the nature of states' interest in potential life would turn out to be. Until that was determined, just what the impact of *Webster* would be on a woman's constitutionally protected right to an abortion could not be known. This would remain unclear for almost three years.

In retrospect, we can say that there were clues dating back to the 1970s. In *Maher v. Roe* the Court had declared that the right recognized in *Roe* "protects the woman from unduly burdensome interference with her freedom to decide whether to terminate her

---

48. See her dissenting opinion in *Thornburgh v. American College of Obstetricians and Gynecologists*, 476 U.S. 747 (1985), at p. 828.

49. 492 U.S. 490 (1989), at p. 537.

50. *Ibid.*, pp. 538, 557.

pregnancy."[51] This notion that state interference with a woman's right to an abortion must not be "unduly burdensome" had first appeared in 1976 in *Bellotti v. Baird*, in which the Court had held that states may not "impose undue burdens upon a minor capable of giving informed consent."[52] Since that time, various members of the Court, including several majorities, had held that no state may "unduly burden the right to seek an abortion,"[53] that the constitutional right affirmed in *Roe* "protects the woman from unduly burdensome interference with her freedom to decide whether to terminate her pregnancy,"[54] and that the state interest in protecting human life "does not, at least until the third trimester, become sufficiently compelling to justify unduly burdensome state interference."[55] In 1982, Justice O'Connor made it clear in her dissent in *City of Akron v. Akron Center for Reproductive Health* that, for her at least, the issue of abortion revolved around finding restrictions that do not "infringe substantially" or impose "unduly burdensome" interference on the woman's right to an abortion,[56] a view that she reasserted in *Hodgson v. Minnesota* in the course of arguing that only when a state regulation imposes an "undue burden" on a woman's ability to make the abortion decision does the power of the state reach into the heart of the liberty protected by the Due Process Clause.[57]

In view of these formulations, it should perhaps not come as a surprise that Justices O'Connor and Kennedy—who had declined Justice Scalia's invitation to overrule *Roe* in *Webster*—would be part of a centrist bloc on the Court (the other member being Souter) committed to reformulating the constitutional right to abortion by reference to an "undue burden" standard rooted in the Due Process Clause of the Fourteenth Amendment. This was the step taken in *Planned Parenthood v. Casey*, handed down in June 1992, in which a once more multiply divided Court reaffirmed *Roe*'s basic holding while detaching it from Blackmun's now defunct trimester-based framework of analysis, and tethering it instead to the notion of undue burden.[58] The *Casey* decision left many matters unresolved. But two fundamental matters about which *Webster* had generated considerable confusion were now clarified. The first was that "the essential holding of *Roe v. Wade* should be retained and once again reaffirmed."[59] This meant not only that the Constitution guarantees women a right to abortion that no legislature has the power to destroy, but also that the

---

51. 432 U.S. 464 (1977), at pp. 473–474.

52. *Bellotti v. Baird*, 482 U.S. 132 (1976), at p. 147.

53. *Bellotti v. Baird*, 433 U.S. 622 (1979), at p. 640.

54. *Maher v. Roe*, 432 U.S. 464 (1977), at pp. 473–474.

55. *Beal v. Doe*, 432 U.S. 438 (1977), at p. 446.

56. 462 U.S. 416 (1982), at pp. 461–462.

57. 497 U.S. 417 (1990), at pp. 458–459.

58. 505 U.S. 833 (1992).

59. *Ibid.*, p. 846.

Court decided not completely to reject Blackmun's original reasoning that had located the constitutional protection in question in a right to privacy thought to be entailed by the Due Process Clause. This was a notable development because Blackmun's reasoning had been much criticized in the academic literature, and several of the newer appointees to the Court—not to mention Chief Justice Rehnquist—were on record as being unimpressed by it. This was perhaps the main reason that *Webster* was thought by so many to be the beginning of the end of *Roe*, prompting the introduction of legislation intended to reverse *Webster* in Congress and turning abortion into a lightning-rod political issue in the run-up to the 1992 presidential election.

Declaring that "liberty finds no refuge in a jurisprudence of doubt,"[60] the *Casey* plurality invoked the doctrine of *stare decisis*. This doctrine rests on the notion that "no judicial system could do society's work if it eyed each issue afresh in every case that raised it," and that consequently once a decision has become part of the law on which people have come to rely, it should not lightly be overturned. *Stare decisis* is not an "inexorable command" to uphold every precedent, and it might reasonably be ignored if a rule has "proved to be intolerable simply in defying practical workability," if it is "subject to a kind of reliance that would lend a special hardship to the consequences of overruling and add inequity to the cost of repudiation," or if "facts have so changed or come to be seen so differently, as to have robbed the old rule of significant application or justification."[61] But the plurality held that none of these considerations applied in the case of *Roe*, so that it should be upheld, even though "[w]e do not need to say whether each of us, had we been Members of the Court when the valuation of the State interest [in protecting potential life] came before it . . . would have concluded, as the *Roe* Court did, that its weight is insufficient to justify a ban on abortions prior to viability even when it is subject to certain exceptions."[62] By appeal to this reasoning, the plurality in *Casey* held that a woman does have a constitutionally protected right to an abortion until the point of viability, and that after that point states have the power to "restrict abortions," provided the law contains "exceptions for pregnancies which endanger a woman's life or health."[63]

The *Casey* decision was a compromise in that neither *Roe*'s defenders nor *Roe*'s critics got precisely what they wanted; it was seen by many as politically vulnerable and highly ambiguous in what it allowed.[64] Yet some on the pro-choice side were surprised that the *Casey* majority upheld *Roe* at all after *Webster*, and they saw this very ambiguity as a source of strength. Indeed, the second matter resolved by *Casey* was that the state's interest

---

60. *Ibid.*, p. 844.

61. *Ibid.*, p. 855.

62. *Ibid.*, p. 871.

63. *Ibid.*, p. 846.

64. N. E. H. Hull, *Roe v. Wade: The Abortion Rights Controversy in American History* (Lawrence: University Press of Kansas, 2001), p. 258.

in protecting potential life would be seen as subordinate to the woman's constitutionally protected right to an abortion. The plurality's discussion of this issue did not amount to a definitive account of the status of the state's interest or of the woman's, but it set some limits on what states may do in regulating abortions. Following the point of viability, threats to the woman's life or health could trump legitimate abortion restrictions rooted in the state's interest in protecting potential life. Depending on how broadly "health" was defined (in particular whether it includes psychological well-being), and bearing in mind that it would generally be a physician of the patient's choosing who decides whether the woman's health is threatened, this might place substantial constraints on the state's power even after the point of viability. In any case, *Casey* appeared to foreclose the possibility of an outright repudiation of *Roe* until the makeup of the Court changed. That seemed unlikely after the 1992 election brought pro-choice president Bill Clinton to the White House, and the battle over *Roe*'s survival cooled down.

Casey amounted to a rejection of *Roe*'s underlying logic not only because the trimester-based analysis was explicitly abandoned, but also because the state's interest in potential life was held unequivocally to begin before the point at which the fetus is viable. Under *Casey*, the state's interest was conceived of as strengthening as the fetus develops, justifying gradual increases in interference by the state with the constitutionally protected rights of pregnant women over the course of their pregnancies. Before the point of viability, the Court's "undue burden" test ruled out "[u]necessary health regulations that have the purpose or effect of presenting a substantial obstacle to a woman seeking an abortion."[65] This did not render the state powerless to try to influence a woman's decision to abort in the early stages of pregnancy. "What is at stake," the *Casey* plurality insisted, "is the woman's right to make the ultimate decision, not a right to be insulated from all others in doing so."[66] From the onset of a pregnancy, states "may enact rules and regulations designed to encourage [a woman] to know that there are philosophic and social arguments of great weight that can be brought to bear in favor of continuing the pregnancy."[67] So long as neither the purpose nor effect of the regulations in question was to place an "undue burden" on women by imposing "substantial obstacles" on their choice in favor of abortion, states could try to get women to reflect on that choice and encourage them to consider alternatives.[68]

Just what would count as an undue burden in particular cases was by no means clear and was bound to invite further litigation, as the dissenters in *Casey* were quick to point out. In *Casey* itself, the Court held that a Pennsylvania statute placed an undue burden by requiring a married woman seeking an abortion to sign a statement that she had notified

---

65. 505 U.S. 833 (1992), at p. 878.

66. *Ibid.*, p. 877.

67. *Ibid.*, p. 872.

68. *Ibid.*

her husband, but that a variety of the Pennsylvania statute's other provisions could survive the test. These included provisions designed to ensure that the woman was giving informed consent to the procedure by requiring that she receive certain information at least twenty-four hours before undergoing the abortion procedure, that for a minor to undergo an abortion there must be informed consent from at least one parent at least twenty-four hours before the procedure (with provisions for a judicial bypass procedure), and that abortion clinics could be obliged to comply with a variety of reporting requirements. The spousal notification requirement was thought to differ from the others in that although most women would tell their husbands voluntarily what their intentions were, women who are victims of physical and psychological spousal abuse "may have very good reasons for not wishing to inform their husbands of their decision to obtain an abortion."[69] If the Court was clear that this tipped the scale of undue burden while the twenty-four-hour waiting period did not, the reasoning behind the distinction was less than entirely lucid. In particular, the Court seemed to have run together the quite different considerations of trying to ensure that the woman makes a well-thought-out decision (in the sense of not being one that *she* would subsequently come to regret) and the state's right to further *its* interest in potential life by regulating the woman's abortion choice. For this and other reasons *Casey* raised as many questions as it settled, as subsequent litigation soon began to reveal.[70]

For the next eight years the Court was silent on the abortion question, apparently content to wait for litigation under the new regime to play out in the lower courts. Then the Supreme Court Justices revisited the subject in *Stenberg v. Carhart*, taking up the highly charged procedure that had become labeled by its critics as "partial birth abortion."[71] This comparatively rare procedure was defined in the Nebraska statute that banned it as "intentionally delivering into the vagina a living unborn child, or a substantial portion thereof, for the purpose of performing a procedure that the [abortionist] knows will kill the . . . child and does kill the . . . child." Comparable statutes had been enacted in thirty state legislatures. The challenged Nebraska statute made it a felony to conduct a partial birth abortion unless it was necessary to save the life of the mother. Conviction would lead to automatic revocation of a doctor's license to practice medicine. The Eighth Circuit Court of Appeals had upheld the District Court's finding that the statute was unconstitutional, and the Supreme Court affirmed this result in a contentious five-to-four decision.

Justice Kennedy, who had been part of the plurality in *Casey*, now voted with the dissenters.[72] Justice O'Connor, the main architect of *Casey*'s undue burden test, made it

---

69. *Ibid.*, p. 893.

70. See *Fargo Women's Health Organization v. Schafer* 113 S.Ct. 1668 (1993) and *Planned Parenthood v. Casey II* 114 S.Ct. 909 (1994).

71. *Stenberg v. Carhart*, 530 U.S. 914 (2000).

72. This did not affect the outcome because Byron White, who had dissented in *Casey*, had been replaced by Ruth Bader Ginsburg, who endorsed *Casey*'s application in *Stenberg*, in the interim.

plain that although she was voting to strike down the challenged Nebraska statute, this was because it was overbroad and lacked an exception for the health (in addition to the life) of the mother. Otherwise she would have held it constitutional, which, given Kennedy's stance, suggested that a five-to-four majority on the Court might be willing to uphold a more restrictive partial abortion statute with an exception for the mother's health. Much turned, therefore, on why the majority thought the Nebraska statute overinclusive, and on just what would be needed to ensure protection of the mother's health.

The two issues are distinct. The least controversial part of the decision was about the language of the challenged Nebraska statute. Even though Nebraska never sought to outlaw the "dilation and evacuation" (D&E) procedures commonly used in previability second trimester abortions, but only the rare "dilation and extraction" (D&X) method, typically used after sixteen weeks, the statute could be construed to include both. The majority and dissenters were divided on whether the Court should have construed the statute more narrowly to render it constitutional or strike it down and in effect require Nebraska to enact a more narrowly drawn statute. The more contentious question dividing the Justices was about the comparative dangers of different abortion procedures. The D&X procedure involves the doctor pulling the fetal body through the cervix (hence the term "partial birth") after collapsing the skull. The procedure was defended at trial as safer than the alternatives for the woman in circumstances involving nonviable fetuses, for women with prior uterine scars, or for women for whom induced labor would be particularly dangerous. The majority accepted the evidence that D&X was safer in some circumstances, and therefore they found that the lack of a health exception rendered the Nebraska statute unconstitutional.

The dissenters objected. *Roe* had insisted on the inclusion of such an exception when states regulate abortion procedures, and *Casey* had affirmed that there must be exceptions when abortion is "necessary, in appropriate medical judgment, for the preservation of the life or health of the mother."[73] But what constitutes appropriate medical judgment? It had long been a criticism of *Roe* that this escape clause created abortion on demand. "Appropriate medical judgment" had been interpreted as the judgment of the attending physician, and there would always be a physician willing to say that carrying a pregnancy to term would in some way be harmful to a woman's physical or psychological health. Part of the opposition to *Casey* had derived from its limitation of this escape clause by holding that states may regulate abortion so long as this does not burden women unduly. The dissenters in *Stenberg* differed among themselves as to whether the *Casey* rule should have been adopted. They were united, however, in insisting that *Stenberg* rendered the *Casey* rule meaningless because the interpretation of "appropriate medical judgment" seemed sufficiently capacious to re-create abortion on demand by creating an attending physician's veto over all abortion regulation.

---

73. 505 U.S., 833 (1992), at p. 879.

The objection here was not to the proposition that part of the idea of an undue burden includes the notion that a woman should not be required to endure a less safe procedure when a safer one is available. Whatever else it might mean, undue burden includes that idea. Rather, the objection goes to the question: who should decide safety? Dissenting Justice Kennedy objected that the majority had deferred to the judgment of the attending physician, re-creating abortion on demand and so rendering *Casey*'s modification of *Roe* meaningless. Justice Thomas added that the majority did not substantiate its assertion that a "substantial body" of medical opinion supports the proposition that the D&X procedure is safer than the alternative in any circumstances. By what logic or authority, he asked, should the Supreme Court second-guess the judgment of the Nebraska state legislature on this factual question? And in an "I told you so" mood, Justice Scalia insisted that "those who believe that a 5-to-4 vote on a policy matter by unelected lawyers should not overcome the judgment of 30 state legislatures have a problem, not with the *application* of *Casey*, but with its *existence. Casey* must be overruled."[74]

In 1994, the Republicans had taken control of both houses of Congress for the first time in a generation. This led to the opening of a new front in the battle over abortion rights in national politics. There had been skirmishes even before *Stenberg* was handed down, but the decision galvanized pro-life forces to craft a national ban on partial birth abortion that could pass muster on the Court. The House and Senate had passed partial birth abortion bans in 1996 and 1997, but these had been vetoed by President Clinton. When George W. Bush took office in January of 2001, the stars were aligned for enactment of a nationwide ban. This occurred on November 5, 2003, when President Bush signed the Partial-Birth Abortion Ban Act, which had been passed by both houses of Congress, into law.

The new federal statute addressed some infirmities that the Court had identified in the Nebraska law struck down in *Stenberg*. Congress responded to the overbreadth problem by explicitly excluding D&E abortions as well as inadvertent D&X extractions—where the physician ends up performing a partial birth abortion that was not intended. The politicians responded to the women's health issue by holding hearings on the relative safety of the D&X procedure and then declaring in the statute that a "moral, medical, and ethical consensus exists" to the effect that partial birth abortion "is a gruesome and inhumane procedure that is never medically necessary and should be prohibited."[75]

In the litigation that inevitably followed, the lower federal courts revealed that they were unimpressed. The partial birth abortion ban was struck down by district courts in California and Nebraska. Their decisions were upheld by the Eighth and Ninth Circuit appellate courts in 2005 and 2006. But the Supreme Court granted certiorari, and in April of 2007 it handed down a new decision sustaining the constitutionality of the federal Partial-Birth Abortion Ban Act, overturning the lower court decisions and all but reversing the Court's own precedent that had been set seven years earlier in *Stenberg*.

---

74. 530 U.S. 914 (2000), at p. 955.

75. 18 U.S.C. § 1531 (2000 ed., Supp. IV), p. 767.

The new decision, *Gonzales* v. *Carhart*, partly reflected the changed Court.[76] Justices Rehnquist and O'Connor had by then been replaced by Roberts and Alito. Both had been artfully imprecise about their views on the constitutionality of abortion during their Senate confirmation hearings, but both were well-known as Catholic conservatives, and few Court-watchers were surprised when the five-to-four majority that had upheld the constitutionality of the D&X procedure in *Stenberg* was replaced, in *Gonzales*, by a five-to-four majority that took the opposite view.

Chief Justice Rehnquist's replacement by John Roberts had left the abortion arithmetic on the Court unaffected, but Sandra Day O'Connor had been both the architect of *Casey*'s undue burden standard and the swing vote in its application in *Stenberg*. Justice Alito now joined a majority opinion penned by Justice Kennedy in which the Court held that Congress had indeed solved the overbreadth problem by exempting the D&E procedure and indemnifying physicians who performed D&X abortions inadvertently. Moreover, the lack of a health exception was held to have been cured by the congressional finding that the D&X procedure is never medically necessary.

The Court's basis for deferring to the congressional finding was not entirely clear. As Justice Ginsburg noted in her stinging dissent, the *Congressional Record* was replete with testimony contradicting the finding in the act that the D&X procedure is never safer than the alternative—not to mention evidence from other professional sources such as the College of Obstetricians and Gynecologists. The act incorrectly asserted that no medical schools teach the D&X procedure when in fact many of the leading ones do. Moreover, as if to underscore the cursory and result-driven nature of the hearings, none of the physicians who testified that the D&X procedure is never medically indicated had in fact performed it.[77] The federal courts have a long history of refusing to defer to manifestly implausible legislative findings, and the lower courts followed that precedent in this case. But the new majority on the Supreme Court did not, holding instead that in the face of professional disagreement over the medical merits of the procedure, Congress was free to take the position it did.

Gonzales v. *Carhart* was the first time since *Roe* that the Court ruled that an abortion restriction is constitutional despite the lack of a health exception, as well as the first time that the Court declared constitutional a federal statute banning a specific abortion method. Indeed, some observers were surprised that Justice Thomas signed on to the majority opinion, given that he had been outspoken in his belief that abortion law should be left to the states.[78] The decision also marked a departure from the Court's previous approach to

---

76. *Gonzales* v. *Carhart* 550 U.S. 124 (2007).

77. *Ibid.*, p. 175.

78. He did however also write a separate concurring opinion, expressing his view that the Court's abortion jurisprudence—including *Casey* and *Roe*—has no constitutional basis, and questioning Congress's power to enact the legislation under its Commerce Clause authority, but since the parties did not raise or brief this second issue, "it is outside the question presented." *Ibid.*, p. 169.

evaluating the constitutionality of laws restricting abortion under *Casey*'s "undue burden" standard by recognizing new state interests other than the traditional two of protecting potential life and protecting the health of the pregnant individual. Drawing on the ruling in *Glucksberg* v. *Washington* (1997), which had declared constitutional state laws prohibiting assisted suicide, Justice Kennedy's majority opinion recognized legitimate state interests in drawing boundaries to prevent practices extinguishing life that are close to actions that are condemned, and in protecting the integrity and ethics of the medical profession. More nebulously, the Court suggested that the state had an interest in protecting the pregnant woman from the emotional consequences of knowledge about what it considers barbaric medical practices, emphasized by the graphic description of the outlawed procedure with which Kennedy opened his opinion, as well as his appeal to the possible future emotional consequences for the individual who undergoes an abortion in this manner. "It is self-evident," he wrote, "that a mother who comes to regret her choice to abort must struggle with grief more anguished and sorrow more profound when she learns, only after the event, what she once did not know: that she allowed a doctor to pierce the skull and vacuum the fast-developing brain of her unborn child, a child assuming the human form."[79]

Abortion played a relatively minor role in the 2008 election. Republicans had performed poorly in the 2006 midterm elections, with Democrats winning control of both houses of Congress. In the 2008 election, Barack Obama won the presidency and Democrats not only retained their control of Congress but also gained seats in both houses. In the first few days of his presidency, Obama signed an executive order repealing the global gag rule, which had banned the distribution of federal funds to organizations that offer abortions. Abortion opponents feared that the Democrats would now move to pass the Freedom of Choice Act, which would have codified *Roe* by prohibiting federal, state, or local governments from denying a woman the right to terminate pregnancy prior to fetal viability, as well as after viability when necessary to protect her life or health. The bill never made it out of committee, and in 2009, Obama admitted that pursuing the act was not the highest legislative priority.[80] To many at the time, the law of abortion seemed to have found a relatively stable equilibrium.

In 2009, law professor Neal Devins claimed that despite superficial similarities to earlier abortion battles, the post-*Casey* conflicts bore "no meaningful resemblance to battles of the 1987–1992 era."[81] While the intensity of the positions voiced by pro-life and pro-choice interest groups had not softened, and state legislatures continued to pass laws aimed at restricting abortion access, Devins argued that this was the expected, and relatively stable, outcome of the *Casey* compromise. By providing a template and parameters by which states could determine which abortion regulations were constitutionally

---

79. *Ibid.*, p. 159.

80. The White House, "News Conference by the President, 4/29/2009," April 30, 2009, https://obamawhitehouse.archives.gov/the-press-office/news-conference-president-4292009.

81. Neal Devins, "How Planned Parenthood v. Casey (Pretty Much) Settled the Abortion Wars," *The Yale Law Journal* 118, no. 7 (2009): 1318–1354, at p. 1322.

viable, states could satisfy their pro-life constituents' desires for restricting abortion without unleashing the pro-choice backlash that would follow from overturning *Roe*, thereby giving neither side the political incentive to reverse the *Casey* decision moving forward. In 2016, however, Devins took a very different position, arguing that changing political conditions had rendered the indeterminate standards established by *Casey* inadequate for protecting even limited abortion rights.[82] He argued that *Casey*'s indeterminate standard was only workable in political conditions where discourse on divisive social issues was possible. The 2010s, however, had proved to be a decade of rapid party polarization and political gerrymandering.

The year 2010 saw a number of developments that would lead to significant transformations and realignments in U.S. party politics. First, the Supreme Court held in a five-to-four majority decision in *Citizens United* v. *Federal Election Commission* that the Free Speech Clause of the First Amendment prohibits the government from restricting independent expenditures by corporations on political campaigns.[83] This opened the door for ultraconservative issue-oriented organizations to outspend the Republican party establishment, shifting power to social conservatives who were able to be competitive in primaries against the candidates of the party establishment.[84] Second, in March 2010, the Obama administration won a major legislative victory with the passage of the Affordable Care Act. In order to pass the act, Democrats needed to include guarantees that would allow states to restrict abortion coverage in private insurance sold within their state, and President Obama agreed to issue an executive order ensuring that no federal funds would be used for abortions. In the midterm elections that fall, dozens of Tea Party–affiliated candidates won the Republican nominations for U.S. Senate, House, and gubernatorial races. Republicans took control of the House and reduced the Democratic majority in the Senate. In addition, Democrats went from controlling twenty-seven state legislatures before 2010 to controlling sixteen after the election, and Republicans went from controlling fourteen state legislatures to controlling twenty-five.

At the time *Roe* was decided, the party that controlled state governments was not a strong predictor of the policies that a state would adopt. This changed after 2000, when there was a rapid increase in policy polarization, and whether a state was controlled by Democrats or Republicans increasingly began to be a strong predictor of state policy.[85] In this new age of red states and blue states, 2010 did not merely sweep Republicans

---

82. Neal Devins, "Rethinking Judicial Minimalism: Abortion Politics, Party Polarization, and the Consequences of Returning the Constitution to Elected Government," *Vanderbilt Law Review* 69, no. 4 (2019): 935–990.

83. *Citizens United* v. *Federal Election Commission*, 558 U.S. 310 (2010).

84. See Mary Ziegler, *Dollars for Life: The Anti-Abortion Movement and the Fall of the Republican Establishment* (New Haven, CT: Yale University Press, 2022).

85. See Jacob M. Grumbach, "From Backwaters to Major Policymakers: Policy Polarization in the States, 1970–2014," *Perspectives on Politics* 16, no. 2 (2018): 416–435.

into state legislatures, it also introduced a radically different breed of Republican. The years after the 2010 elections saw over two hundred anti-abortion laws passed across the country. A 2012 report by the Guttmacher Institute described "a seismic shift" in abortion restrictions at the state level, marked by a considerable decrease in supportive and middle-ground states and a rise in hostile states.[86] The 2012 presidential election passed without party control shifting in Congress, but the effects of *Citizens United* were already becoming evident, as the election saw a 594 percent increase in independent expenditures on campaigning.[87] In the 2014 midterm elections, Republicans gained control of the Senate and retained control of the House, while state elections put Republicans in control of sixty-seven out of ninety-nine state legislative chambers nationwide.

The first sign that the *Casey* equilibrium was starting to shift occurred in June of 2016, when the Supreme Court ruled in *Whole Woman's Health* v. *Hellerstedt* that a Texas law designed to shut down most of the state's abortion clinics by requiring medically unnecessary restrictions was unconstitutional.[88] In one way, the decision further entrenched the *Casey* framework as the five-to-three majority decision held that the Texas law violated the undue burden test by placing a substantial burden on women seeking abortions without advancing the state's interest in protecting women's health. But as Justice Thomas's dissent observed, the *Whole Woman's Health* majority also significantly reconceived the undue burden test in three ways. First, the Court held that *Casey* required consideration of both the benefits and the burdens created by a law regulating abortion. Second, it told lower courts that whenever a law's justifications are medically uncertain, they could not defer to legislatures but must instead "assess medical justifications for abortion restrictions by scrutinizing the record themselves," a guideline which seems to be at odds with the more deferential approach used in *Gonzales*. And third, the Court required meaningful proof that a law claiming to protect women's health actually did so. Thomas objected that this new approach to the undue burden test amounted to requiring strict scrutiny in assessing laws regulating abortion. "The State's burden has been ratcheted to a level that has not applied for a quarter century," he wrote, "[a]fter disregarding significant aspects of the Court's prior jurisprudence, the majority applies the undue-burden standard in a way that will surely mystify lower courts for years to come."[89] Observers agreed with Thomas's assessment of the significance and ambiguities of the decision, noting that while *Whole Woman's Health* "put teeth" into *Casey*'s undue burden test by making it harder for states to

---

86. Rachel Benson Gold and Elizabeth Nash, "Troubling Trend: More States Hostile to Abortion Rights as Middle Ground Shrinks," *Guttmacher Policy Review* 15, no. 1 (Winter 2012).

87. Wendy L. Hansen, Michael S. Rocca, Brittany Leigh Ortiz, "The Effects of Citizens United on Corporate Spending in the 2012 Presidential Election," *Journal of Politics* 77, no. 2 (2015): 535–545.

88. *Whole Woman's Health* v. *Hellerstedt*, 579 U.S. 582 (2016).

89. *Whole Woman's Health* v. *Hellerstedt*, 579 U.S. ____ (2016), at p. 9 (Thomas, J., dissenting).

pass medically unnecessary abortion regulations, it had also "set the stage for fact-intensive litigation about the benefits and burdens of measures restricting access to abortion."[90]

Justice Scalia died in February of 2016, and before President Obama announced his nominee to fill the vacant seat, Senate Majority Leader Mitch McConnell made the unprecedented declaration that any appointment by the sitting president would be null and void, and that the new Justice should be chosen by the next president. It was the first time since 1895 that a Democratic president had made a court appointment while Republicans held the Senate. When President Donald Trump won the election that fall, and Republicans retained control of Congress, he announced the nomination of Neil Gorsuch eleven days after being sworn into office. Justice Kennedy, the last remaining member of the *Casey* plurality, retired two years later and was replaced by Brett Kavanaugh after highly politicized Senate hearings surrounding Kavanaugh's alleged sexual assault of Christine Blasey Ford in the early 1980s. The appointment and hearing occurred in the midst of the #MeToo movement, which saw waves of people publicizing their experiences of sexual abuse or harassment on social media. The 2018 elections saw the highest voter turnout in a midterm election since 1914 and gave Democrats back control of the House.

Box v. *Planned Parenthood*, decided in 2019, garnered national attention as the first major abortion-related case to be taken up by the Supreme Court after Justice Kennedy's retirement.[91] The case concerned an Indiana law that sought to ban abortions performed solely on the basis of the fetus's gender, race, ethnicity, or disabilities. The law also required the disposal of aborted fetuses through burial or cremation. Lower courts had blocked both parts of the law. With its unsigned decision, the Court overturned the lower courts' proscription of the fetal disposal part of the law, but left unchallenged the nondiscrimination provision. In separate opinions, Justice Thomas and Justice Ginsburg took sharply opposing stances on the decision, with the former comparing abortion practices and birth control to eugenics and arguing that *Roe* should be reexamined for the scope of what it allowed, and the latter arguing that the Indiana law should have been blocked in its entirety under *Casey*'s "undue burden" standard. The case had no impact on the constitutional status of abortion rights, but observers noted that it had revealed the new battle lines over abortion of the now fully post-*Casey* Court.

A Louisiana law almost identical to the Texas law struck down in *Whole Woman's Health* came before the Court in *June Medical Services, LLC* v. *Russo* in 2020, and the Court again determined the law to be unconstitutional, but this time by a thinner five-to-four margin. Chief Justice Roberts joined the four liberal members of the Court, concurring with the judgment out of deference to the precedent set in *Whole Woman's Health*, but upholding his position of dissent from the previous case. A dissent by Justice Alito, and joined in whole or part by Justices Gorsuch, Thomas, and Kavanaugh, objected to

---

90. See Mary Ziegler, "Substantial Uncertainty: *Whole Woman's Health v. Hellerstedt* and the Future of Abortion Law," *The Supreme Court Review* 2016 (2017).

91. *Box* v. *Planned Parenthood*, 587 U.S. ____ (2019).

the decision on the grounds that it went even further than *Whole Woman's Health* had in hindering the ability of states to pass laws under the rationale of protecting women's health when a law could have the effect of limiting abortion access. Alito argued that third-party abortion providers should not be able to invoke a woman's right to abortion in challenging laws that are facially directed at protecting women's health. "This case features a blatant conflict of interest between an abortion provider and its patients," he wrote, "but an abortion provider's ability to assert the rights of women when it challenges ostensible safety regulations should not turn on the merits of its claim."[92]

On September 18, 2020, Justice Ginsburg died six weeks before the presidential election. Mitch McConnell succeeded in pushing through President Trump's nomination of Amy Coney Barrett, and she was confirmed in late October, just days before the election saw Democrats regain control of the presidency and both houses of Congress. This meant that since 1968, Republicans had appointed nineteen members to the Supreme Court while Democrats had appointed four (President Biden would appoint Ketanji Brown Jackson in June of 2022), reflecting their demographic advantage in the Senate and Electoral College. All three Trump appointees had been approved by the Federalist Society, bringing to six the number of sitting Justices with ties to the conservative group.[93] The Court, which had been deadlocked with four liberal Justices and four conservative Justices before the Trump presidency, now had a six-to-three conservative majority, so that it could overturn *Roe* once a new case presented the opportunity. The question was, Would it?

Buoyed by the changed composition of the Court, conservative state legislators raced to enact new abortion restrictions. By the end of 2021, 108 such restrictions had been enacted in nineteen states, the highest number in any year since 1973. Liberal state legislatures also started to pass laws expanding abortion access in their state. In May of 2021, the Court granted the petition for a writ of certiorari in reviewing a 2018 Mississippi law, the Gestational Age Act, which banned abortion after the first fifteen weeks of pregnancy, with exceptions for medical emergencies or severe fetal abnormality but no exception for cases of rape or incest. The Court limited its review to the question of "[w]hether all previability prohibitions on elective abortions are unconstitutional." At the time of Mississippi's petition to the Supreme Court to review the case, the state had only asked the Court to revisit the viability standard as established in *Roe* and reaffirmed in *Casey*. By the time oral arguments began, however, Mississippi had changed its appeal, arguing that the Court should overturn *Roe* and *Casey* on the grounds that they had proved unworkable and that new facts about when fetuses begin to feel pain had been established since they were decided—a switch that Chief Justice Roberts bitterly noted in his concurring opinion in *Dobbs*, writing that the Court had rewarded Mississippi's "gambit."[94]

---

92. *June Medical Services, LLC v. Russo*, 591 U.S. ____ (2020), at pp. 25–26 (Alito, J., dissenting).

93. Noah Feldman, *TAKEOVER: How a Conservative Student Club Captured the Supreme Court* (New York: Pushkin, 2021).

94. 597 U.S. ____ (2022), at p. 6 (Roberts, J., concurring).

Meanwhile, the Texas Heartbeat Act, which bans abortion at six weeks of pregnancy, went into effect in September 2021. Normally, the Texas law would clearly have been unconstitutional according to both *Roe* and *Casey*, but the law's designers employed the unique and novel strategy of placing enforcement of the law into the hands of private individuals rather than state officials. The act allows any member of the public to sue anyone who performs or facilitates an illegal abortion with a minimum of $10,000 in statutory damages if they win the civil suit. After denying a request from Texas abortion providers and abortion rights advocates seeking emergency relief, the act became the first previability abortion ban allowed to go into effect since *Roe* was decided, and later that year, the Court issued a five-to-four decision in *Whole Woman's Health* v. *Jackson* ruling that abortion providers could not sue state judges, court clerks, or the attorney general to stop the filing of private civil-enforcement lawsuits.[95] In his partial dissent joined by Justices Breyer, Sotomayor, and Kagan, Chief Justice Roberts wrote that the Texas law had "the clear purpose and actual effect" of nullifying Supreme Court rulings, and that, regardless of "the nature of the federal right infringed," the decision to allow the Texas law to go into effect jeopardizes "the role of the Supreme Court in our constitutional system."[96]

The reality that many people were now openly questioning the Supreme Court's authority and legitimacy was clearly on display as meetings began for the Presidential Commission on the Supreme Court of the United States, established by President Joe Biden to investigate opinions for Court reform. Biden had created the commission in response to pressure from his Democratic base to expand the Court on the grounds that the Republican Senate had refused to confirm President Obama's nomination of Merrick Garland nine months before a presidential election but had confirmed Amy Coney Barrett a few days before one. Linda Greenhouse notes that the liberal and younger members of the commission showed little faith in the Supreme Court. They recognized that the progressive rulings of the Warren Court had been a historical aberration, and that "across the span of American history, the Supreme Court has most often been the obstacle to progress."[97] Perhaps unsurprisingly, the commission failed to agree on recommendations for reform. President Biden and conservative Senate Democrats made it clear that they opposed changing the Court's size, making change all but impossible for the moment.

The Court's authority took another unexpected and unprecedented hit when *Politico* released a draft of Justice Alito's majority *Dobbs* opinion in May 2022 and the Supreme Court confirmed the draft's authenticity. The leak led to an immediate response by pro-choice protestors and pro-life counterprotestors who gathered outside the Supreme Court and outside of the homes of conservative Justices, launched marches and protests across the country, and motivated a failed attempt by Democrats in Congress to pass the

---

95. *Whole Woman's Health* v. *Jackson*, 595 U.S. ____ (2021).
96. 595 U.S. ____ (2021), at p. 4 (Roberts, J., partial dissenting/partial concurring).
97. Linda Greenhouse, "Should We Reform the Court?" *New York Review of Books*, April 7, 2022.

Women's Health Protection Act and to codify *Roe* and *Casey* before *Dobbs* was decided. A Gallup poll conducted after the leak showed just 25 percent of U.S. adults reporting confidence in the Supreme Court, the lowest since Gallup began collecting data on the question in 1973.[98]

Few were surprised when the Court's official ruling was released that summer, Alito's final majority opinion was little changed from the draft version. The Court had at last overruled *Roe* and *Casey* in holding that the Constitution does not protect a right to abortion. It confirmed what many had already sensed—that Chief Justice Roberts had lost the power to hold a moderate center in his Court. And along with the loss of a moderate approach went Roberts' philosophy of incrementalism, with strong respect for *stare decisis*, in revising constitutional abortion law. In the majority decision, Justice Alito claimed that *Casey*, in skipping a review of the reasoning behind *Roe* and reaffirming it solely on the basis of *stare decisis*, had failed to apply *stare decisis* properly. He identified five factors in considering whether to overturn Court precedent, relying in part on his own opinion in *Janus* v. *AFSCME* which had articulated a weaker form of *stare decisis* that focuses on the "quality of reasoning" behind earlier decisions in addition to issues such as reliance and workability.[99] In *Dobbs*, the five factors that the Court considered in overruling its own precedent on abortion, were that *Roe* and *Casey* (1) "short-circuited the democratic process"; (2) lacked grounding in constitutional text, history, or precedent; (3) established rules that were not workable; (4) caused distortion in law in other areas; and (5) that they could be overruled without upending concrete reliance interests.

The Court argued that *Roe* had failed to specify the "exact location" in the Constitution that guaranteed the right to abortion, relying instead on a vague sense that the Fourteenth Amendment provided support for the finding, and that *Casey*, rather than "defend[ing] this unfocused analysis," had based its decision on a flawed approach to evaluating unenumerated substantive due process claims. Substantive due process is the doctrine that courts can enjoin the government from depriving people of fundamental rights to "life, liberty, or property without due process of law," even if these rights are not enumerated in the Constitution. Originally enunciated by the Court in 1905 in *Lochner* v. *New York* to protect freedom of contract and other economic rights in the face of state efforts to regulate employment relations and enforce minimum wages, substantive due process provided the foundation for the right to privacy that the Court affirmed in *Griswold* and which the majority opinion relied on in *Roe*.[100] In *Casey*, the Court had

---

98. Jeffery M. Jones, "Confidence in U.S. Supreme Court Sinks to Historic Low," *Gallup*, June 23, 2022, accessed July 12, 2022, https://news.gallup.com/poll/394103/confidence-supreme-court-sinks-historic-low.aspx.

99. *Janus* v. *American Federation of State, County, and Municipal Employees, Council 31*, 585 U.S. _____ (2018).

100. *Lochner* v. *New York* 18 U.S. 45 (1905). The Due Process Clause of the Fifth Amendment was invoked to enjoin relevant deprivations by the federal government while the Fourteenth Amendment

based its evaluation of abortion as protected under substantive due process on "reasoned judgment." Under this approach, "the Court itself evaluates the liberty interest of the individual and weighs it against competing governmental concerns, determining on this basis whether the liberty interest deserves protection as a constitutional right."[101] Reasoned judgment allows for a comparatively expansive understanding of what protections can be covered under substantive due process, based on the idea that the historical tradition encapsulated in the Constitution "is a living thing"[102] not reducible to exact formulas.

The *Dobbs* majority argued, by contrast, that the Court should adjudicate claims by evaluating whether the protection in question is "fundamental to our scheme of ordered liberty" or "deeply rooted in this Nation's history and tradition," a test articulated in cases like *Glucksberg* v. *Washington*, *McDonald* v. *Chicago*, and *Timbs* v. *Indiana*.[103] In evaluating whether abortion is protected using the *Glucksberg* test, Alito interpreted the task then to be to answer what the Fourteenth Amendment means by the term "liberty" by looking at "how the States regulated abortion"[104] in 1868. He argued that if the amendment was meant to protect the right to an abortion at a time when the procedure was widely illegal, then its authors would have explicitly said so. And in turning to the historical record, which the opinion of the Court did at great length in an appendix listing every state statute criminalizing abortion on the books in 1868, one finds that abortion was widely criminalized in the nineteenth century. Thus, a purported constitutional right to abortion failed his test.

To these points, the *Dobbs* majority opinion added that *Roe* lacked a convincing account of why viability should mark the moment when the state's interest in fetal life begins to outweigh the interest of the woman seeking an abortion. The Court also ruled that *Casey*'s undue burden standard had proven unworkable, both because it had failed to settle the issue and because the Court had continued to change its conception of how to determine what is an "undue burden" or "substantial obstacle" or "unnecessary health regulation" when confronted with new cases. Such standards "call on courts to examine a law's effect on women," Justice Alito wrote, "but a regulation may have a very different impact on different women for variety of reasons" and therefore, "in order to determine whether a regulation presents a substantial obstacle to women, a court needs to know

---

was held to apply to state actions such as the Connecticut law outlawing contraception in *Griswold* and the Texas abortion statute struck down in *Roe*.

101. Daniel O. Conkle, "Three Theories of Substantive Due Process," *Articles by Maurer Faculty* 166 (2006): 63–148, at pp. 66–67.

102. 505 U.S. 833 (1992), at p. 850 (quoting Justice Harlan, *Poe* v. *Ullman*, 367 U.S. 497 (1961), at p. 542).

103. *Glucksberg* v. *Washington* 521 U.S. 702 (1997); *McDonald* v. *Chicago* 561 U.S. 742 (2010); and *Timbs* v. *Indiana* 586 U.S. ____ (2019).

104. 597 U.S. ____ (2022), at p. 47.

which set of women it should have in mind and how many of the women in this set must find that an obstacle is 'substantial.'"[105]

Finally, *Dobbs* rejected the claim that a protected right to abortion was necessary for reasons having to do with *reliance*, the notion that women have come to depend on the availability of abortion in organizing their lives for so long that it would be too disruptive to allow states to outlaw it now. The majority held that *Casey* had embraced an intangible form of reliance that depends on empirical questions that courts are in no position to assess, "namely, the effect of the abortion right on society and in particular on the lives of women."[106] The Court reasoned that since women are not "without electoral or political power," and in fact the percentage of women who cast ballots in elections is now consistently higher than the percentage of men, it is particularly inappropriate for courts to speculate on the impact of abortion rights and restrictions on a population that can speak for itself through the political process.

Since *Dobbs* found that there is no fundamental constitutional right to abortion, Justice Alito announced that the standard for evaluating state abortion regulations moving forward on the Court would be rational-basis review. This means that state laws regulating abortion will be entitled to a "strong presumption of validity," and in reviewing future laws that come under constitutional challenge, the Court will uphold the law as long as "the legislature could have thought that it would serve legitimate state interests."[107] Such legitimate interests can include "respect for and preservation of prenatal life at all stages of development," maternal health, the prevention of barbaric medical procedures, the integrity of the medical profession, mitigation of fetal pain, and preventing discrimination on the basis of race, sex, or disability.[108]

Abortion Jurisprudence

Much of the heat generated by the abortion controversy stems from its symbolic role in American politics; arguments over "life" versus "choice" serve as proxies for conflicts over the role of women in American society, the controversial status of "traditional" and "family" values, and the place of religion in American politics.[109] However, part of the jurisprudential heat has been internally generated, by the manner in which the Court's major abortion rulings—particularly *Roe* and *Dobbs*—were decided and the arguments

---

105. *Ibid.*, at p. 58.

106. *Ibid.*, at p. 65.

107. *Ibid.*, at p. 77.

108. *Ibid.*, at p. 78.

109. An excellent treatment of this subject is found in Luker, *Abortion and the Politics of Motherhood*, especially chapters 3–7.

informing these decisions. In *Roe*, this controversy stemmed partly from the sweeping nature of the holding, and partly from the fact that the right of privacy on which Justice Blackmun based his argument is not explicitly mentioned in the Constitution. In *Dobbs*, it came mainly from the Court's approach to *stare decisis* on the one hand, and to interpreting the Fourteenth Amendment's Due Process Clause on the other, both because the decision told Americans they no longer had a constitutionally guaranteed right they had enjoyed for half a century and because of the possible implications for other substantive due process rights relating to privacy and autonomy moving forward.

There is no doubt that *Roe* was a sweeping decision. Overnight, and at a time when most states outlawed abortion except when it was necessary to protect the life of the woman, the Court's decision made abortion legal across the United States. Thirty-one strict abortion laws were immediately invalidated, fifteen more moderate laws had to be considerably rewritten, and even the four states with the most permissive abortion legislation had to broaden the language of their laws following *Roe*.[110] Critics of the decision accused the Court of judicial activism reminiscent of the Warren Court (authors of the once-controversial *Brown v. Board of Education* decision). Comparisons between *Brown* and *Roe* were also made in the *Dobbs* decision, with the majority comparing *Roe* to *Plessy v. Ferguson*, which *Brown* had overturned.

In fact, the two cases generated quite different political responses. *Brown* was certainly controversial when it was decided, but it became broadly accepted a few years later—particularly following the passage of the Civil Rights Act in 1964. *Roe*, by contrast, was not nearly as controversial at the time it was decided as it became in subsequent years, particularly following the passage of the Hyde Amendment in 1976, which barred federal funding for abortion except to save the life of the mother or in pregnancies resulting from rape or incest.

One way that the very different trajectories of *Brown* and *Roe* have been understood is rooted in the sympathetic critique of *Roe* articulated by Justice Ginsburg[111] and Robert Burt.[112] Whatever the jurisprudential basis for the right to abortion, it is arguable that it was the manner in which *Roe* was decided—as much as the content of the decision—that was to render its legitimacy suspect. After all, in *Roe* the Court did a good deal more than strike down a Texas abortion statute. The majority opinion laid out a detailed test to determine the conditions under which any abortion statute could be expected to pass muster; in effect Justice Blackmun authored a federal abortion statute of his own. Ginsburg argued that decisions of this kind tend to undermine the Court's legitimacy. She thought that it is sometimes necessary for the Court to step "ahead" of the political

---

110. David Granfield, "The Legal Impact of the *Roe* and *Doe* Decisions," *The Jurist* 33 (1973): 113–122, at p. 116.

111. Ruth Bader Ginsburg, "Speaking in a Judicial Voice," Madison Lecture, New York University Law School, March 9, 1993, *mimeo*.

112. Robert A. Burt, *The Constitution in Conflict* (Harvard University Press, 1992), pp. 344–352.

process to achieve reforms that the Constitution requires, but if it gets too far ahead it can produce a backlash and provoke charges that it is overreaching its appropriate place in a democratic constitutional order.[113]

Contrasting the Court's handling of the abortion question with its approach in the school desegregation cases of the 1950s, Burt pointed out that the Justices in *Brown* declared the doctrine of "separate but equal" to be an unconstitutional violation of the Equal Protection Clause,[114] but they did not describe schooling conditions that would be acceptable. Rather, they turned the problem back to Southern state legislatures, requiring them to fashion acceptable remedies themselves.[115] These remedies came before the Court as a result of subsequent litigation, were evaluated when they did, and were often found to be wanting.[116] But the Court avoided designing the remedy itself, and with it the charge that it was usurping the legislative function. In *Roe*, by contrast, as Ginsburg put it, the Court "invited no dialogue with legislators. Instead, it seemed entirely to remove the ball from the legislators' court" by wiping out virtually every form of abortion regulation then in existence.[117]

Following the *Brown* model, the Court might have struck down the Texas abortion statute in *Roe* (whether by appeal to Blackmun's privacy argument or to the equality argument favored by Ginsburg and others) without going on to develop and apply Blackmun's trimester framework. This would have set some limits on what legislatures might do in the matter of regulating abortion without involving the Court directly in designing that regulation. On the Ginsburg-Burt view, this would have left space for democratic resolution of the conflict, ensuring the survival of the right to abortion while at the same time preserving the legitimacy of the Court's role in a democratic constitutional order.[118]

Yet another account of the very different trajectories of *Brown* and *Roe*, offered by Gerald Rosenberg, warns that it is a mistake to put too much explanatory power on the Court's actions without taking into account the actions of other branches of government. Rosenberg claims that U.S. courts are almost never effective producers of social reform on their own, and "at best, they can second the social reform acts of the other branches of government."[119] On this view, those who claim that overturning *Roe* will produce moderation in the abortion controversy might well be disappointed, depending on what the wider political response to *Dobbs* is in coming years. It seems likely that a new series of political battles, not only over abortion rights, but also over the Supreme Court's structure

---

113. Ginsburg, Madison Lecture, pp. 30–38.

114. *Brown v. Board of Education I*, 347 U.S. 483 (1954).

115. *Brown v. Board of Education II*, 349 U.S. 294 (1955).

116. Burt, *Constitution in Conflict*, pp. 271–310.

117. Ginsburg, Madison Lecture, p. 32.

118. Burt, *Constitution in Conflict*, pp. 349–352.

119. Gerald N. Rosenberg, *The Hollow Hope: Can Courts Bring About Social Change?* (Chicago: University of Chicago Press, 1991), p. 338.

and function in American government, are just starting to heat up; the Ginsburg-Burt view that sweeping holdings diminish the Court's democratic legitimacy (a view formulated in critique of *Roe*) may now feature in debates precipitated by *Dobbs*.

Indeed, in the immediate wake of *Dobbs*, claims of judicial activism were again rampant, with some accusing the Court of making a naked power play. "It is now clear that politics has triumphed over law," one *Washington Post* opinion piece claimed. "All that matters now is who can muster five votes, long-standing precedent (and confirmation hearing commitments to abide by them) be damned."[120] In response, defenders of *Dobbs* argued it was the original *Roe* decision that was the egregious example of judicial activism and that *Roe* had distorted the public perception of the Court's role in the American system by putting it at the center of a controversy that it was in no position to resolve. By overturning that decision, they maintain, the Court was actually enacting a "course correction."

"Judicial activism" is a contested term, and over the last few decades, it has taken on sufficiently negative connotations that neither *Dobbs*'s nor *Roe*'s defenders are likely to want to claim it as characteristic of their position.[121] On the one hand, critics of *Roe* are surely right that abortion battles have only intensified since that decision was made, placing the Court's legitimacy into question for those who would like to advocate, by legislative process, for more restrictive abortion laws in their states. On the other hand, critics of *Dobbs*, whatever else they might think about *Roe*, are also surely correct to worry about the impact of the Court's taking away, essentially overnight, a constitutional right it had recognized for nearly fifty years.

As Chief Justice Roberts's concurring opinion in *Dobbs* reveals, the implications of enacting such a sharp reversal of precedent on abortion was a key point of contention within the Court leading up to the decision. Roberts, in the interest of protecting the Court's institutional legitimacy, has favored incremental changes to constitutional law and rejected dramatic shifts and reversals. While not staunchly opposed to reconsidering past precedents, he had previously said it should only be done in exceptional circumstances, with due recognition to the fact that judges operate "within a system of precedent shaped by other judges equally striving to live up to the judicial oath."[122] In the oral arguments

---

120. Barry Friedman, Dahlia Lithwick, Stephen I. Vladeck, "Supreme Court Leak Signals the Triumph of Politics over Law," *Washington Post*, May 3, 2022, accessed July 10, 2022, https://www.washingtonpost.com/opinions/2022/05/03/supreme-court-abortion-leak-politics-law-overturn-roe/.

121. According to *Black's Law Dictionary*, judicial activism is "a philosophy of judicial decision-making whereby judges allow their personal views about public policy, among other factors, to guide their decisions, usually with the suggestion that adherents of this philosophy tend to find constitutional violations and are willing to ignore precedent." Eighth edition, ed. Bryan A. Garner (Eagan, MN: Thompson West, 2004), p. 2473.

122. *Confirmation Hearing on the Nomination of John G. Roberts, Jr. to Be Chief Justice of the United States before the Senate Committee on the Judiciary, September 12–15, 2005* (Washington, DC: U.S. Government Printing Office, 2005), p. 55.

for *Dobbs*, Roberts suggested that the first issue to consider with respect to *stare decisis* was whether *Roe* was wrongly decided, but he showed uncertainty about how the "wrongness" of a previous decision should be evaluated: "Is it wrongly decided based on legal principles and doctrine when it was decided or—or in retrospect?"[123] If the principles the Court used to decide *Roe* in the first place or to reaffirm it in *Casey* were markedly different from the principles used to overturn *Roe*, Roberts worried, then the Court could be opening a proverbial can of *stare decisis* worms in the future.

Dobbs in fact did rely on an approach to *stare decisis* radically different from *Casey*'s as we have seen. Indeed, it applied a test that did not exist at the time *Casey* had reaffirmed *Roe* (the *Glucksberg* test). Roberts wanted a more moderate opinion, in which the Court would have rejected *Roe* and *Casey*'s viability line, while upholding a constitutional right to abortion extending only "far enough to ensure a reasonable opportunity to choose."[124] The Chief Justice reasoned that this resolution to *Dobbs* would have been more in keeping with a principle of judicial restraint, where "[i]f it is not necessary to decide more to dispose of a case, then it is necessary *not* to decide more."[125] Since the Mississippi Gestational Age Act only restricted abortion at fifteen weeks, Chief Justice Roberts argued, that was all the Court should have affirmed, which would have involved overturning *Roe* and *Casey* only in part.

The *Dobbs* majority rejected Roberts's approach, in part because they claimed that a standard of "reasonable opportunity" would suffer from the same exact defects as the viability standard, and in part because they rightly recognized that finding in favor of Mississippi's fifteen-week ban, while not overturning *Roe*, would invite additional constitutional challenge from states trying to pass more restrictive laws (e.g., at twelve or six weeks) under the new ambiguous standard. Thus, Roberts's approach, Justice Alito wrote, "would only put off the day when we would be forced to confront the question we now decide."[126]

Yet the swiftness and completeness with which *Roe* was overturned raises questions beyond abortion rights, potentially also touching the controversial "right to privacy" on which the *Roe* majority originally based their finding. The idea that there is a right to privacy protected under the Due Process Clause of the Fourteenth Amendment stems from a 1965 decision in *Griswold* v. *Connecticut*.[127] *Griswold* was the culmination of a fifty-year battle to organize formal opposition to birth control statutes.[128] By a seven-

---

123. *Dobbs v. Jackson Women's Health Organization* #19–1392, Argued December 1, 2021 (Washington, DC: Hoover Reporting Company), pp. 1–114, at p. 39.

124. 597 U.S. ____ (2022), at p. 1 (Roberts, J., concurring).

125. *Ibid.*, at p. 2 (Roberts, J., concurring).

126. 597 U.S. ____ (2022), at p. 76.

127. 381 U.S. 479 (1965)

128. For an account of this history, see David J. Garrow, *The Right to Privacy and the Making of Roe v. Wade* (New York: Lisa Drew Books, 1993).

to-two majority, the Court struck down an 1879 statute that had made it illegal "to use any drug or article to prevent conception," holding that a zone of privacy encompasses the marital relationship that outweighs any legitimate state interest in preventing sexual immorality.[129] This decision provided part of the logical foundation for Justice Blackmun's reasoning in *Roe*, in which he maintained that the zone of privacy encompasses decisions about abortion as well as contraception. But *Griswold* applied to married couples only; by itself this could not generate the right to *individual* privacy on which *Roe* rests. The bridging argument was supplied in *Eisenstadt* v. *Baird* in 1972 when Justice Brennan, writing for the majority, observed of the contraception cases that if "the right of privacy means anything, it is the right of the *individual*, married or single, to be free from unwanted governmental intrusions into matters so fundamentally affecting a person as the decision whether to bear or beget a child."[130]

The *Griswold* result has often been criticized as a poor piece of constitutional jurisprudence, and Blackmun's extension of it to *Roe* was controversial from the moment it was decided. But commentators have generally viewed *Griswold* itself as fairly secure ever since Judge Robert Bork's failed Senate confirmation hearing to replace Justice Lewis Powell on the Supreme Court in 1987. Before the hearings, Bork had been outspoken in his criticism of *Griswold* as an unprincipled usurpation of democratic authority unsupported by the text of the Constitution. Bork argued that "substantive due process, revived by the *Griswold* case, is and always has been an improper doctrine."[131] After an infamous exchange during the widely televised hearings, in which then-senator Joe Biden questioned Bork repeatedly on his constitutional views about privacy, Bork's nomination was rejected by a vote of fifty-eight to forty-two. Reva Siegel has argued that the showdown over privacy that took place during the Bork hearings played a key role in entrenching *Griswold*, for "after this great conflict, subsequent nominees concluded that *Griswold*, like *Brown*, was part of the constitutional canon—accepted as mainstream."[132] Indeed, President Ronald Reagan's next nominee, Anthony Kennedy, did not repeat Bork's mistake. Commenting on Kennedy's successful confirmation, Linda Greenhouse noted that "it was his eloquent statement in support of the constitutional right to privacy at his confirmation hearing that, as much as any other factor, made him acceptable to the Senators who had found Judge Bork unacceptable."[133]

---

129. 381 U.S. 479–84 (1965).

130. *Eisenstadt* v. *Baird*, 405 U.S. 453 (1972), emphasis in original.

131. Robert Bork, "Neutral Principles and Some First Amendment Problems," *Indiana Law Journal* 47, no. 1 (1971): 1–35, at p. 11.

132. Reva B. Siegel, "How Conflict Entrenched the Right to Privacy," *Yale Law Journal Forum*, March 2, 2015, pp. 316–323, at p. 321.

133. Linda Greenhouse, "THE LAW; Echo of '87 Bork Uproar Rings Softly in Abortion Debate," *New York Times*, April 28, 1989, sec. B, p. 12.

Will the *Dobbs* decision reopen the privacy debate? The *Dobbs* majority opinion suggests that it need not, explicitly stating that "our decision concerns the constitutional right to abortion and no other right."[134] But other concurring and dissenting opinions show considerable disagreement among current members of the Court about how far the implications of *Dobbs* might stretch. After all, if the test used in *Dobbs* requires turning to nineteenth-century law as the central guide in evaluating whether a substantive due process protection not explicitly mentioned in the Constitution is nonetheless implied by it, then it is not only abortion that would likely fail this test. As the dissenting opinion joined by Justices Breyer, Sotomayor, and Kagan points out, the right to abortion arose out of the right to use contraception and both rights have been closely connected to rights of same-sex intimacy and marriage established in *Lawrence* v. *Texas*[135] and *Obergefell* v. *Hodges*.[136] Like abortion, none of these other rights is explicitly listed in the Constitution. Perhaps rightly anticipating that the Court will be more circumspect in revisiting such broadly popular rights as contraception and same-sex marriage, the dissent accuses the *Dobbs* majority of blatant hypocrisy, arguing that "one of two things must be true. Either the majority does not really believe in its own reasoning. Or if it does, all rights that have no history stretching back to the mid-19th century are insecure."[137]

In fact, the majority does provide a possible rationale for overturning *Roe* and *Casey* without impacting *Griswold* or other related cases. Primarily, what makes it legitimate to single out abortion for special treatment—"as even the *Casey* plurality recognized"—is that abortion involves the termination of "potential life," whereas cases like *Griswold*, *Lawrence*, and *Obergefell* do not. Unlike the choice to marry another willing adult or the choice to use contraception, the choice to have an abortion involves the destruction of a fetus. If a given state declares an interest in protecting the right of a fetus to life, then there is a clash between that interest and the right to privacy of the person seeking an abortion. Since the other substantiative due process rights the Court has recognized do not have this character, the majority states, it is neither legitimate to justify a right to abortion by purported analogy to those rights, nor is it legitimate to infer that in rejecting constitutional protections for abortion, the Court is *ipso facto* placing other privacy rights on the chopping block.

But Justice Thomas's concurring opinion makes a very different claim. Thomas agrees with the majority's claim that the right to abortion is unique among other privacy rights, but he nonetheless asserts that the Court should reconsider all its substantive due process precedents—explicitly naming *Griswold*, *Lawrence*, and *Obergefell* as cases the Court should overturn. Like Bork, he argues that the very idea of substantive due process rights

---

134. 597 U.S. ____ (2022), at p. 7.

135. *Lawrence* v. *Texas*, 539 U.S. 558 (2003).

136. *Obergefell* v. *Hodges*, 576 U.S. 644 (2015).

137. 597 U.S. ____ (2022), at p. 5 (Breyer, Sotomayor, and Kagan, JJ., dissenting).

is fundamentally mistaken because the Due Process Clause does not secure any substantive rights at all—it only secures *process*. "After overruling these demonstrably erroneous decisions," he writes, "the question would remain whether other constitutional provisions guarantee the myriad rights that our substantive due process cases have generated," noting that the Privileges and Immunities Clause might be able to justify some of the unenumerated rights that he would find unprotected under the Due Process Clause. However, he goes on to clarify, abortion would not be one of them "under any plausible interpretive approach."[138]

Justice Thomas's willingness to take on *Griswold* directly notwithstanding, few critics of *Griswold* would want to live with the full implications of abandoning the notion that there is a constitutionally protected right to privacy. But there is another way in which the wider network of privacy rights and abortion intersect, one that might involve the Court in future constitutional challenges to *Griswold* whether or not it wants to be. As Ronald Dworkin—perhaps the most articulate defender of *Griswold* and its extension to *Roe*—has noted, it is difficult to discern a principled basis for marking off abortion completely from contraception. Once *Griswold* is accepted, it seems inevitably to lead to *Roe*, partly because the technologies of contraception and abortion overlap (and may do so increasingly over time),[139] and partly because it is difficult to articulate compelling grounds for distinguishing the two cases from one another.

The Court's reasoning in *Griswold* was that decisions affecting marriage and childbirth are so intimate and personal that people must be free to make the decisions for themselves. As Dworkin notes, decisions regarding abortion are at least as private as those concerning contraception. Indeed, in one respect they are more so because the abortion decision "involves a woman's control not just of her sexual relations but of changes within her own body, and the Supreme Court has recognized in various ways the importance of physical integrity."[140] This is likely even more true now than when Dworkin originally made this argument. After all, medical advances since *Roe* have made it so that enforcing laws restricting or banning abortion will involve more significant interference with bodily integrity and privacy than did the crackdowns on abortion before the 1970s.[141] The morning-after pill and the copper IUD are both forms of birth control that significantly blur the line between contraception and abortion, as is the use of mifepristone and misoprostol abortion pills, which can eliminate a pregnancy for up to ten weeks in the privacy of one's own home without ever having to step into a doctor's office.

---

138. 597 U.S. ____ (2022), at pp. 3–4 (Thomas, J., concurring).

139. Some intrauterine devices and many popular birth control pills destroy fertilized ova if they fail to prevent fertilization.

140. Dworkin, *Life's Dominion*, p. 107.

141. See Jia Tolentino, "We're Not Going Back to the Time before Roe. We're Going Somewhere Worse," *New Yorker*, July 4, 2022.

According to the Guttmacher Institute, medication abortion already accounts for more than half of all abortions performed in the United States, a trend that will likely increase in coming years. Mailed pills are considerably more challenging to police than are abortion clinics. Still, this has not stopped states from trying to limit or ban medication abortion, and experts expect that battle over medication abortion will escalate. "The political environment threatens to pit state against state," one *Washington Post* article reports, noting that at the time of writing, Republican lawmakers in Missouri were considering a proposal to criminalize abortions that take place out of state while Democratic lawmakers in California were advancing a bill that would protect patients and health-care providers from civil penalties from states that ban abortion.[142] If anti-abortion states continue to mount efforts to ban travel for abortion, or try to prosecute women who receive abortions outside of their jurisdiction, it might open challenges to the long-established right to interstate travel, another right not explicitly mentioned in the Constitution.

In any case, it is clear that the battle over abortion rights is far from over, and that overturning *Roe* may enable arguments that have previously been peripheral in debates over constitutional protections for abortion and contraception to gain traction. On the left, for instance, the *Griswold* doctrine has long been criticized by radical feminists as male ideology that contributes to the subjugation of women.[143] Indeed, in other contexts—such as in arguing for the passage of marital rape statutes—feminists have worked to weaken the common law presumption that the marital relationship shields "intimate" behavior from the criminal law.[144] Partly for these reasons, some advocates of the right to abortion have developed a defense of it that jettisons the privacy argument altogether and relies instead on the constitutional commitment to equal protection of the laws, explicit in the Fourteenth Amendment, and implied in the Due Process Clause of the Fifth Amendment. This equality argument is usually presented in terms of the claim that restrictions on abortion discriminate against women by placing constraints on their freedom that men do not have to bear.

---

142. Christopher Rowland, Laurie McGinley, Jacob Bogage, "Abortion Pills by Mail Pose Challenge for Officials in Red States," *Washington Post*, May 4, 2022, accessed June 30, 2022, https://www.washingtonpost.com/business/2022/05/04/abortion-pills-online-telemedicine.

143. See Catherine McKinnon, *Feminism Unmodified: Discourses on Life and Law* (Cambridge, MA: Harvard University Press, 1987), pp. 93–102; and Robin West, "Jurisprudence and Gender," *University of Chicago Law Review* 55, no. 1 (1988): 67–70.

144. On the changing law of marital rape in the United States, see Michael Freeman, "But If You Can't Rape Your Wife, Who[m] Can You Rape? The Marital Rape Exemption Re-examined," *Family Law Quarterly* 15, no. 1 (Spring 1981): 1–29; Deborah Rhode, *Justice and Gender* (Cambridge, MA: Harvard University Press, 1989), pp. 249–251; Rene I. Augustine, "Marriage: The Safe Haven for Rapists," *The Journal of Family Law* 29, no. 3 (1990–91): 559–590; and Sandra Ryder and Sheryl Kuzmenka, "Legal Rape: The Marital Exemption," *John Marshall Law Review* 24, no. 2 (1991): 393–421. On the English evolution of the exception, see P. M. Bromley and N. V. Lowe, *Family Law*, 7th ed. (London: Butterworths, 1987), pp. 109–112.

Introduction xlvii

This was the view defended by then federal Appellate Court judge Ruth Bader Ginsburg in her 1993 Madison Lecture at New York University, which prompted some sharp questioning in her confirmation hearings for the Supreme Court because it revealed her discomfort with *Roe*'s privacy doctrine.[145] On Ginsburg's account, abortion regulations affect "a woman's autonomous charge of her full life's course—her ability to stand in relation to man, society, and the state as an independent, self-sustaining citizen."[146] In her view the *Roe* Court should have "homed in more precisely on the woman's equality dimension of the issue," enabling it to argue that "disadvantageous treatment of a woman because of her pregnancy and reproductive choice is a paradigm case of discrimination on the basis of sex."[147] In the very term *Roe* was decided, Ginsburg pointed out, the Supreme Court had a case on its calendar that could have served as a bridge, "linking reproductive choice to disadvantageous treatment of women on the basis of their sex."[148] Accordingly, she saw the decision to opt for the *Griswold* reasoning in *Roe* as a missed opportunity to place the right to abortion on a firmer conceptual and constitutional footing.[149]

Since *Roe*, the Court has recognized equality concerns to some extent in its subsequent abortion jurisprudence. The *stare decisis* passage in *Casey*, for instance, emphasized that a reason to reaffirm *Roe* is that "[t]he ability of women to participate equally in the economic and social life of the Nation has been facilitated by their ability to control their reproductive lives."[150] And in Justice Blackmun's separate opinion, he wrote that by restricting the right to abortion, "the State conscripts women's bodies into its service" based on the assumption "that women can simply be forced to accept the 'natural' status and incidents of motherhood"—an assumption which "appears to rest upon a conception of women's role that has triggered the protection of the Equal Protection Clause."[151] Eight years after *Casey* there were other signs that egalitarian considerations were shaping the

---

145. Ginsburg, Madison Lecture. For the hearings, see "Nomination of Ruth Bader Ginsburg to Be an Associate Justice of the United States Supreme Court: Report Together with Additional Views," Exec Report. 103-6-93-1, United States Senate, pp. 17–19.

146. "Nomination of Ruth Bader Ginsburg," p. 17.

147. Ginsburg, Madison Lecture, pp. 24, 28. For a more elaborate defense of the equality-based view, see Sylvia A. Law, "Rethinking Sex and the Constitution," *University of Pennsylvania Law Review* 132, no. 2 (1983–84): 1002–1013.

148. Ginsburg, Madison Lecture, p. 24. The case, *Struck* v. *Secretary of Defense* 409 U.S. 947 (1973), was remanded for consideration of mootness.

149. It is of course possible that Blackmun canvassed this possibility and could not find support for it among his brethren on the Court, though—given his failure even to mention it—it seems more likely that, as Ronald Dworkin suggests, Blackmun simply thought *Griswold* compelling.

150. 505 U.S. 833 (1992), at 856.

151. 505 U.S. 833 (1992), at 928 (Blackmun, J., concurring in part, concurring in the judgment in part, and dissenting in part).

Court's abortion jurisprudence. The opening paragraph of Justice Stephen Breyer's majority opinion in *Stenberg* v. *Carhart* notes that millions "fear that a law that forbids abortion would condemn many American women to lives that lack dignity, depriving them of equal liberty and leading those with the least resources to undergo illegal abortions with the attendant risks of death and suffering."[152] The decision in *Gonzales* v. *Carhart*, which reversed the *Stenberg* outcome, did not repudiate this egalitarian logic.

But these arguments have remained largely peripheral, and the primary foundation for abortion protections has remained rooted in the Due Process Clause. As a result, the *Dobbs* decision devotes one paragraph to considering the Equal Protection Clause as an alternative basis for abortion protections, arguing that "neither *Roe* nor *Casey* saw fit to invoke this theory" and that "it is squarely foreclosed by our precedents" because "the regulation of a medical procedure that only one sex can undergo does not trigger heightened constitutional scrutiny" unless the regulation has discriminatory intent.[153]

Equality arguments about abortion rights tend to focus on two distinct, but related issues. The first is the rationale behind state laws that restrict abortion: are abortion regulations based solely on the state's interest in protecting potential life, or are they rooted in constitutionally suspect judgments about women? Advocates of this type of argument point out that historically, laws limiting abortion or contraception have often espoused explicit or implicit ideological beliefs about women's proper role in society as mothers above all else. They also argue that states that seek to restrict abortion but do not simultaneously introduce laws to provide support and protection for women's economic prospects or health after they have given birth might be hiding rationales reflecting traditional sex-role stereotypes. An *amicus* brief authored by law professors Serena Mayeri, Melissa Murray, and Reva Siegel in support of Jackson Women's Health in the *Dobbs* case points out that the nineteenth-century laws that proved decisive in the majority's opinion were based on arguments that "banning abortion would protect fetal life, protect a woman's health, enforce wives' marital duties, and control the relative birthrates of 'native' and immigrant populations, in order to preserve the demographic character of the nation."[154] It is precisely because of this history, they argue, that any regulation directed at women's role in reproduction should demand exacting scrutiny to make sure that it is not based in discriminatory sex-role stereotypes or being used to generate or enforce the legal, social, and economic inferiority of women.[155]

---

152. 530 U.S. 914 (2000), at p. 920, emphasis supplied.

153. 597 U.S. ___ (2022), at pp. 10–11.

154. Brief of Equal Protection, Constitutional Law Scholars Serena Mayeri, Melissa Murray, and Reva Siegel as *Amici Curiae* in Support of Respondents (September 20, 2021), p. 13.

155. See Reva Siegel, "Reasoning from the Body: A Historical Perspective on Abortion Regulation and Questions of Equal Protection," *Stanford Law Review* 44, no. 2 (1992): 261–381.

The other main issue that proponents of equality arguments emphasize is the gendered impact of abortion restrictions. Since abortion restrictions hinder the ability of women to choose whether and when to become mothers, they also play a role in exacerbating inequalities between men and women in economic and political achievement. For instance, Diana Greene Foster's Turnaway Study, which recruited women who sought abortions and continued interviewing them over several years, found that women who succeeded in getting a desired abortion were less likely to be on public assistance and less likely to report inability to pay for food, housing, and transportation than women who were denied an abortion. The study also found women who had been in a physically abusive relationship at the time they sought an abortion were less likely to have remained in that relationship if they succeeded in terminating their pregnancy than those who were turned away. This underscores the wider connection between abortion rights and economic and social inequalities: the availability of abortion affects women's personal, social, and economic options, and with them the power women have in society relative to men.

Equality advocates have also pointed out that abortion restrictions can extend beyond gender inequality, exacerbating racial, ethnic, and income inequalities. Since the 1990s, women of color have responded to what they see as the limitations of an individual choice-based framework to abortion rights by advocating "reproductive justice," which treats abortion rights as part of a larger constellation of intersectional concerns and disparities in health and maternal welfare. A successful approach along these lines was seen in Colombia in 2022, when its Constitutional Court legalized abortion during the first twenty-four weeks of pregnancy in response to claims that the criminalization of abortion had excessively harmful consequences for migrant women who are at high risk of sexual violence. These women enjoy less access to contraception and maternal health services than do other women, factors that render them more vulnerable to high-risk pregnancies. Following Colombia's example would offer a novel equality-based approach to evaluating abortion restrictions. By focusing on their impact on vulnerable groups, this approach would depend neither on *Griswold*'s privacy-based rationale nor on sex-based classifications that trigger heightened scrutiny from the current majority on the U.S. Supreme Court.

The Future of the Abortion Rights

Dobbs is unlikely to be the Court's final word on abortion, but even if it is, the larger political battle over abortion rights will continue. For the moment, it will be fought out state by state and in conflicts between states, as some states seek to enforce restrictions or bans, and others try to secure and expand access for their residents or for those who travel to their state to undergo abortions. With states now unhindered by federal constitutional protections of the right to abortion, the issue may become a new motivating factor in how Americans vote. Indeed, abortion has for years now been a key and unifying issue in the electoral strategy and messaging for social conservatives and the Republican party more generally. Democratic voters and candidates, who may have long taken *Roe* for granted as settled precedent, might now begin organizing around abortion rights and articulating novel arguments in state and federal elections. Meanwhile, Republicans might find themselves on the defensive, particularly in the wake of some states having passed abortion restrictions or bans that do not contain exceptions for when pregnancy imperils the life or health of the woman, or for pregnancies resulting from rape or incest—provisions that are widely popular even among Republican voters.

As this volume goes to press it is too early to tell how overturning *Roe* will impact the political landscape. There are signs that powerful shifts are occurring. In August of 2022, Kansas voters delivered an unexpected victory for abortion rights by rejecting a proposed amendment that would have eliminated protection for abortion in their state constitution. Commenting on the surprising decisiveness of the vote, decided by a 59–41 percent margin in a firmly Republican state, Nate Cohn of the *New York Times* remarked, "The political winds are now at the backs of abortion rights supporters," estimating that voters would reject similar initiatives in more than forty of the fifty states.[156] A few days later, the Indiana legislature passed the first new abortion ban since *Dobbs* was decided, allowing for abortion only in cases of rape, incest, lethal fetal abnormality, or when continued pregnancy poses severe health risks to the mother. Perhaps Republican-controlled state legislatures will continue enacting restrictive abortion legislation and Democrats will continue pushing for ballot initiatives that put the issue directly before voters, as Michigan, Vermont, and California are already planning to do in the coming year. But there are many other possibilities.

Throughout history women have found ways to take control of their reproductive futures, whether through legal or illegal, safe or unsafe means, as abortion rights advocates have long pointed out. There are many who will work in various ways, directly political or otherwise, to help them do so safely. And with the advances in abortion medication, which studies have shown to be both safe and effective in eliminating unwanted pregnancies, it will become increasingly difficult, if not impossible, for states completely to enforce effective bans. Thus, one way in which post-*Dobbs* America might mirror pre-*Roe* America is in the spottiness of enforcement and prosecution, the optics of which may look different in an age of mass media and social media than they did in the late nineteenth and early twentieth centuries. Anti-abortion advocates have tended to be squeamish in the past about imposing criminal penalties directly on the women seeking abortions, who, in contrast to narratives that paint abortion-seekers as flippant or irresponsible about the procedure, are often in reality facing difficult, and sometimes desperate, circumstances. However, with the closure of abortion clinics in many states, and with the difficulty of preventing the transfer of abortion medication through the mail, states looking to enforce

---

156. Nate Cohn, "Kansas Result Suggests 4 Out of 5 States Would Back Abortion Rights in Similar Vote," *New York Times*, August 4, 2022, https://www.nytimes.com/2022/08/04/upshot/kansas-abortion-vote-analysis.html.

restrictions might discover that they have little choice other than to target pregnant people themselves, as well as any friends and family members who might try to help them. That, in turn, might trigger significant political backlash from people who supported overruling *Roe*.

There are other reasons why long-time critics of *Roe* who feel vindicated and satisfied that *Dobbs* has returned abortion to state legislatures might not get what they want. Many anti-abortion activists who believe that the fetus is a person from the moment of conception and therefore that abortion at any stage of pregnancy is murder will not be pacified by this result. They often liken their battle to the struggle against slavery. They will be no more willing to tolerate abortion in pro-choice states than abolitionists were willing to tolerate slavery in the American South. They will want federal action. Given that *Dobbs* affirms the possibility that states may invoke the claim that a fetus is a person in vindicating abortion restrictions, they will see obvious parallels in the history of the slavery battle in fighting to get other states to be required to recognize those claims, and eventually for the federal government to recognize them as well. By affirming the constitutionality of the Partial-Birth Abortion Ban Act in *Gonzales*, the Court has acknowledged that Congress can enter the field. On the day *Dobbs* was handed down House Republican leader Kevin McCarthy declared that "encouraging as today's decision is, our work is far from done" and that he would support a nationwide fifteen-week abortion ban.[157]

Anti-abortion activists can be expected to push for such legislation. To be sure, it would be difficult to pass and to retain if it could be enacted. Partly for that reason, some anti-abortion activists will not be satisfied with legislation. Likening their struggle to the crusade to overturn *Dred Scott*, they will want to get the Court to recognize the fetus as a human being who is entitled to Constitutional protection as an unborn person.[158] That seems far-fetched today, but life has more imagination than us. Few would have predicted the Court's stance in *Dobbs* five years ago. Particularly if state legislatures, and perhaps Congress, were to declare that a fetus is a person, the possibility that the Court would eventually do so as well cannot be ruled out. Indeed, Georgia may soon become a test case for such questions if its 2019 Living Infants Fairness and Equality Act goes into effect. The law, previously placed on hold pending the outcome of *Dobbs*, considers fetuses with a detectable heart rate as full people for civil liability purposes, counts them as part of the population in census surveys, and allows people to claim them as dependents worth $3,000 in tax credits. Critics, some of whom are Republicans, worry that the law will have

---

157. Justin Tasolides, "'Our Work Is Far from Done': McCarthy Suggests GOP Will Propose Anti-abortion Legislation If They Retake House," Spectrum News New York, June 24, 2022, https://www.ny1.com/nyc/all-boroughs/news/2022/06/24/republican-mccarthy-congress-abortion-roe-v-wade.

158. In 1857, the Court held in *Dred Scott* v. *Sandford* 60 U.S. (19 How.) that people of African descent are not citizens. It was effectively overruled by the passage of the Thirteenth and Fourteenth Amendments in 1865 and 1868, respectively.

a much wider impact than on abortion, affecting criminal, tort, and immigration law as well.[159]

"For God's sake, there's an election in November. Vote! Vote! Vote! Vote!" President Biden said, shortly before signing an executive order designed to ensure access to abortion medication and emergency contraception two weeks after the *Dobbs* decision.[160] It seems likely that *Roe*'s demise will indeed spur more national political debate and activism over abortion, but it would be foolhardy to try to predict the forms it will take or the results it will produce. As law professors Ryan D. Doerfler and Samuel Moyn remarked days after the Biden's Commission on the Supreme Court released its report, "Ideas that were once fringe have now moved to the center of Court discourse."[161] Following his retirement from the Court Justice Blackmun, author of the majority opinion in *Roe*, reflected that "I feel as though I have been a cork on a fast-moving stream propelled by forces over which I had little control."[162] It is possible that the authors of the *Dobbs* decision will someday look back in a similar way. In any case, the future of the abortion debate in America is likely to provide further ballast for Mary Ziegler's statement that the legal history of abortion has told and will continue to tell "a story about what kind of country the United States has been and will become."[163]

---

159. Ross Williams and Jill Nolin, "Georgia's Strict Abortion Law Could Take Effect Soon. Here's What the Law Does." *Georgia Recorder*, June 27, 2022, https://georgiarecorder.com/2022/06/27/georgias-strict-abortion-law-could-take-effect-soon-heres-what-the-law-does/.

160. Michael D. Shear and Sheryl Gay Stolberg, "Under Pressure, Biden Issues Executive Order on Abortion," *New York Times*, July 8, 2022, https://www.nytimes.com/2022/07/08/us/politics/biden-abortion-executive-order.html.

161. Ryan D. Doerfler and Samuel Moyn, "Court Reform Is Dead! Long Live Court Reform!" *The Atlantic*, December 12, 2021, https://www.theatlantic.com/ideas/archive/2021/12/commission-supreme-court-may-revive-reform/620969/.

162. Quoted from Linda Greenhouse, "The Blackmun Papers," *Proceedings of the American Philosophical Society* 148, no. 3 (2004): 332–357, at p. 334.

163. Ziegler, *Abortion and the Law in America*, p. 212.

GRISWOLD ET AL. *v.* CONNECTICUT

APPEAL FROM THE SUPREME COURT OF ERRORS OF CONNECTICUT

No. 496. Argued March 29–30, 1965.—Decided June 7, 1965

Douglas, J. delivered the opinion of the Court. Goldberg, J., and Brennan, J., filed concurring opinions. Black, J., and Stewart, J., filed dissenting opinions.

Mr. Justice Douglas delivered the opinion of the Court.

Appellant Griswold is Executive Director of the Planned Parenthood League of Connecticut. Appellant Buxton is a licensed physician and a professor at the Yale Medical School who served as Medical Director for the League at its Center in New Haven—a center open and operating from November 1 to November 10, 1961, when appellants were arrested.

They gave information, instruction, and medical advice to *married persons* as to the means of preventing conception. They examined the wife and prescribed the best contraceptive device or material for her use. Fees were usually charged, although some couples were serviced free.

The statutes whose constitutionality is involved in this appeal are §§ 53–32 and 54–196 of the General Statutes of Connecticut (1958 rev.). The former provides:

> "Any person who uses any drug, medicinal article or instrument for the purpose of preventing conception shall be fined not less than fifty dollars or imprisoned not less than sixty days nor more than one year or be both fined and imprisoned."

Section 54–196 provides:

> "Any person who assists, abets, counsels, causes, hires or commands another to commit any offense may be prosecuted and punished as if he were the principal offender."

The appellants were found guilty as accessories and fined $100 each, against the claim that the accessory statute as so applied violated the Fourteenth Amendment. The Appellate Division of the Circuit Court affirmed. The Supreme Court of Errors affirmed that judgment. 151 Conn. 544, 200 A. 2d 479. We noted probable jurisdiction. 379 U.S. 926.

We think that appellants have standing to raise the constitutional rights of the married people with whom they had a professional relationship. *Tileston* v. *Ullman*, 318 U.S.

44, is different, for there the plaintiff seeking to represent others asked for a declaratory judgment. In that situation we thought that the requirements of standing should be strict, lest the standards of "case or controversy" in Article III of the Constitution become blurred. Here those doubts are removed by reason of a criminal conviction for serving married couples in violation of an aiding-and-abetting statute. Certainly the accessory should have standing to assert that the offense which he is charged with assisting is not, or cannot constitutionally be, a crime.

This case is more akin to *Truax* v. *Raich*, 239 U.S. 33, where an employee was permitted to assert the rights of his employer; to *Pierce* v. *Society of Sisters*, 268 U.S. 510, where the owners of private schools were entitled to assert the rights of potential pupils and their parents; and to *Barrows* v. *Jackson*, 346 U.S. 249, where a white defendant, party to a racially restrictive covenant, who was being sued for damages by the covenantors because she had conveyed her property to Negroes, was allowed to raise the issue that enforcement of the covenant violated the rights of prospective Negro purchasers to equal protection, although no Negro was a party to the suit. And see *Meyer* v. *Nebraska*, 262 U.S. 390; *Adler* v. *Board of Education*, 342 U.S. 485; *NAACP* v. *Alabama*, 357 U.S. 449; *NAACP* v. *Button*, 371 U.S. 415. The rights of husband and wife, pressed here, are likely to be diluted or adversely affected unless those rights are considered in a suit involving those who have this kind of confidential relation to them.

Coming to the merits, we are met with a wide range of questions that implicate the Due Process Clause of the Fourteenth Amendment. Overtones of some arguments suggest that *Lochner* v. *New York*, 198 U.S. 45, should be our guide. But we decline that invitation. . . . We do not sit as a superlegislature to determine the wisdom, need, and propriety of laws that touch economic problems, business affairs, or social conditions. This law, however, operates directly on an intimate relation of husband and wife and their physician's role in one aspect of that relation.

The association of people is not mentioned in the Constitution nor in the Bill of Rights. The right to educate a child in a school of the parents' choice—whether public or private or parochial—is also not mentioned. Nor is the right to study any particular subject or any foreign language. Yet the First Amendment has been construed to include certain of those rights.

By *Pierce* v. *Society of Sisters*, *supra*, the right to educate one's children as one chooses is made applicable to the States by the force of the First and Fourteenth Amendments. By *Meyer* v. *Nebraska*, *supra*, the same dignity is given the right to study the German language in a private school. In other words, the State may not, consistently with the spirit of the First Amendment, contract the spectrum of available knowledge. The right of freedom of speech and press includes not only the right to utter or to print, but the right to distribute, the right to receive, the right to read (*Martin* v. *Struthers*, 319 U.S. 141, 143) and freedom of inquiry, freedom of thought, and freedom to teach (see *Wieman* v. *Updegraff*, 344 U.S. 183, 195)—indeed the freedom of the entire university community. *Sweezy* v. *New Hampshire*, 354 U.S. 234, 249–250, 261–263; *Barenblatt*. v. *United States*, 360 U.S. 109, 112; *Baggett* v. *Bullitt*, 377 U.S. 360, 369. Without those peripheral rights the specific rights would be less secure. And so we reaffirm the principle of the *Pierce* and the *Meyer* cases.

In *NAACP* v. *Alabama*, 357 U.S. 449, 462, we protected the "freedom to associate and privacy in one's associations," noting that freedom of association was a peripheral First Amendment right. Disclosure of membership lists of a constitutionally valid association, we held, was invalid "as entailing the likelihood of a substantial restraint upon the exercise by petitioner's members of their right to freedom of association." *Ibid*. In other words, the First Amendment has a penumbra where privacy is protected from governmental intrusion. In like context, we have protected forms of "association" that are not political in the customary sense but pertain to the social, legal, and economic benefit of the members. *NAACP* v. *Button*, 371 U.S. 415, 430–431. In *Schware* v. *Board of Bar Examiners*, 353 U.S. 232, we held it not permissible to bar a lawyer from practice, because he had once been a member of the Communist Party. The man's "association with that Party" was not shown to be "anything more than a political faith in a political party" (*id*., at 244) and was not action of a kind proving bad moral character. *Id*., at 245–246.

Those cases involved more than the "right of assembly"—a right that extends to all irrespective of their race or ideology. *De Jonge* v. *Oregon*, 299 U.S. 353. The right of "association," like the right of belief (*Board of Education* v. *Barnette*, 319 U.S. 624), is more than the right to attend a meeting; it includes the right to express one's attitudes or philosophies by membership in a group or by affiliation with it or by other lawful means. Association in that context is a form of expression of opinion; and while it is not expressly included in the First Amendment its existence is necessary in making the express guarantees fully meaningful.

The foregoing cases suggest that specific guarantees in the Bill of Rights have penumbras, formed by emanations from those guarantees that help give them life and substance. See *Poe* v. *Ullman*, 367 U.S. 497, 516–522 (dissenting opinion). Various guarantees create zones of privacy. The right of association contained in the penumbra of the First Amendment is one, as we have seen. The Third Amendment in its prohibition against the quartering of soldiers "in any house" in time of peace without the consent of the owner is another facet of that privacy. The Fourth Amendment explicitly affirms the "right of the people to be secure in their persons, houses, papers, and effects, against unreasonable searches and seizures." The Fifth Amendment in its Self-Incrimination Clause enables the citizen to create a zone of privacy which government may not force him to surrender to his detriment. The Ninth Amendment provides: "The enumeration in the Constitution, of certain rights, shall not be construed to deny or disparage others retained by the people."

The Fourth and Fifth Amendments were described in *Boyd* v. *United States*, 116 U.S. 616, 630, as protection against all governmental invasions "of the sanctity of a man's home and the privacies of life."* We recently referred in *Mapp* v. *Ohio*, 367 U.S. 643, 656, to the Fourth Amendment as creating a "right to privacy, no less important than any other right carefully and particularly reserved to the people." See Beaney, The Constitutional Right to Privacy, 1962 Sup. Ct. Rev. 212; Griswold, The Right to be Let Alone, 55 Nw. U. L. Rev. 216 (1960).

We have had many controversies over these penumbral rights of "privacy and repose." See, *e.g.*, *Breard* v. *Alexandria*, 341 U.S. 622, 626, 644; *Public Utilities Comm'n* v. *Pollak*, 343 U.S. 451; *Monroe* v. *Pape*, 365 U.S. 167; *Lanza* v. *New York*, 370 U.S. 139; *Frank* v. *Maryland*, 359 U.S. 360; *Skinner* v. *Oklahoma*, 316 U.S. 535, 541. These cases bear witness that the right of privacy which presses for recognition here is a legitimate one.

The present case, then, concerns a relationship lying within the zone of privacy created by several fundamental constitutional guarantees. And it concerns a law which, in forbidding the *use* of contraceptives rather than regulating their manufacture or sale, seeks to achieve its goals by means having a maximum destructive impact upon that relationship. Such a law cannot stand in light of the familiar principle, so often applied by this Court, that a "governmental purpose to control or prevent activities constitutionally subject to state regulation may not be achieved by means which sweep unnecessarily broadly and thereby invade the area of protected freedoms" *NAACP* v. *Alabama*, 377 U.S. 288, 307. Would we allow the police to search the sacred precincts of marital bedrooms for telltale signs of the use of contraceptives? The very idea is repulsive to the notions of privacy surrounding the marriage relationship.

We deal with a right of privacy older than the Bill of Rights—older than our political parties, older than our school system. Marriage is a coming together for better or worse, hopefully enduring, and intimate to the degree of being sacred. It is an association that promotes a way of life, not causes; a harmony in living, not political faiths; a bilateral loyalty, not commercial or social projects. Yet it is an association for as noble a purpose as any involved in our prior decisions.

Reversed.

---

*The Court said in full about this right of privacy:

"The principles laid down in this opinion [by Lord Camden in *Entick* v. *Carrington*, 19 How. St. Tr. 1029] affect the very essence of constitutional liberty and security. They reach farther than the concrete form of the case then before the court, with its adventitious circumstances; they apply to all invasions on the part of the government and its employees of the sanctity of a man's home and the privacies of life. It is not the breaking of his doors, and the rummaging of his drawers, that constitutes the essence of the offence; but it is the invasion of his indefeasible right of personal security, personal liberty and private property, where that right has never been forfeited by his conviction of some public offence—it is the invasion of this sacred right which underlies and constitutes the essence of Lord Camden's judgment. Breaking into a house and opening boxes and drawers are circumstances of aggravation; but any forcible and compulsory extortion of a man's own testimony or of his private papers to be used as evidence to convict him of crime or to forfeit his goods, is within the condemnation of that judgment. In this regard the Fourth and Fifth Amendments run almost into each other." 116 U.S., at 630.

MR. JUSTICE GOLDBERG, whom THE CHIEF JUSTICE and MR. JUSTICE BRENNAN join, concurring.

I agree with the Court that Connecticut's birth-control law unconstitutionally intrudes upon the right of marital privacy, and I join in its opinion and judgment. Although I have not accepted the view that "due process" as used in the Fourteenth Amendment incorporates all of the first eight Amendments (see my concurring opinion in *Pointer* v. *Texas*, 380 U.S. 400, 410, and the dissenting opinion of MR. JUSTICE BRENNAN in *Cohen* v. *Hurley*, 366 U.S. 117, 154), I do agree that the concept of liberty protects those personal rights that are fundamental, and is not confined to the specific terms of the Bill of Rights. My conclusion that the concept of liberty is not so restricted and that it embraces the right of marital privacy though that right is not mentioned explicitly in the Constitution[1] is supported both by numerous decisions of this Court, referred to in the Court's opinion, and by the language and history of the Ninth Amendment. In reaching the conclusion that the right of marital privacy is protected, as being within the protected penumbra of specific guarantees of the Bill of Rights, the Court refers to the Ninth Amendment, *ante*, at 484. I add these words to emphasize the relevance of that Amendment to the Court's holding.

The Court stated many years ago that the Due Process Clause protects those liberties that are "so rooted in the traditions and conscience of our people as to be ranked as fundamental." *Snyder* v. *Massachusetts*, 291 U.S. 97, 105. In *Gitlow* v. *New York*, 268 U.S. 652, 666, the Court said:

> "For present purposes we may and do assume that freedom of speech and of the press—which are protected by the First Amendment from abridgment by Congress—are among the *fundamental* personal rights and 'liberties' protected by the due process clause of the Fourteenth Amendment from impairment by the States." (Emphasis added.)

---

1. My Brother STEWART dissents on the ground that he "can find no . . . general right of privacy in the Bill of Rights, in any other part of the Constitution, or in any case ever before decided by this Court." *Post*, at 530. He would require a more explicit guarantee than the one which the Court derives from several constitutional amendments. This Court, however, has never held that the Bill of Rights or the Fourteenth Amendment protects only those rights that the Constitution specifically mentions by name. See, *e.g.*, *Bolling* v. *Sharpe*, 347 U.S. 497; *Aptheker* v. *Secretary of State*, 378 U.S. 500; *Kent* v. *Dulles*, 357 U.S. 116; *Carrington* v. *Rash*, 380 U.S. 89, 96; *Schware* v. *Board of Bar Examiners*, 353 U.S. 232; *NAACP* v. *Alabama*, 360 U.S. 240; *Pierce* v. *Society of Sisters*, 268 U.S. 510; *Meyer* v. *Nebraska*, 262 U.S. 390. To the contrary, this Court, for example, in *Bolling* v. *Sharpe*, *supra*, while recognizing that the Fifth Amendment does not contain the "explicit safeguard" of an equal protection clause, *id.*, at 499, nevertheless derived an equal protection principle from that Amendment's Due Process Clause. And in *Schware* v. *Board of Bar Examiners*, *supra*, the Court held that the Fourteenth Amendment protects from arbitrary state action the right to pursue an occupation, such as the practice of law.

And, in *Meyer* v. *Nebraska*, 262 U.S. 390, 399, the Court, referring to the Fourteenth Amendment, stated:

> "While this Court has not attempted to define with exactness the liberty thus guaranteed, the term has received much consideration and some of the included things have been definitely stated. Without doubt, it denotes not merely freedom from bodily restraint but also [for example,] the right . . . to marry, establish a home and bring up children. . . ."

This Court, in a series of decisions, has held that the Fourteenth Amendment absorbs and applies to the States those specifics of the first eight amendments which express fundamental personal rights.[2] The language and history of the Ninth Amendment reveal that the Framers of the Constitution believed that there are additional fundamental rights, protected from governmental infringement, which exist alongside those fundamental rights specifically mentioned in the first eight constitutional amendments.

The Ninth Amendment reads, "The enumeration in the Constitution, of certain rights, shall not be construed to deny or disparage others retained by the people." The Amendment is almost entirely the work of James Madison. It was introduced in Congress by him and passed the House and Senate with little or no debate and virtually no change in language. It was proffered to quiet expressed fears that a bill of specifically enumerated rights[3] could not be sufficiently broad to cover all essential rights and that the specific mention of certain rights would be interpreted as a denial that others were protected.[4]

---

2. See, *e.g., Chicago, B. & Q. R. Co.* v. *Chicago*, 166 U.S. 226; *Gitlow* v. *New York, supra; Cantwell* v. *Connecticut*, 310 U.S. 296; *Wolf* v. *Colorado*, 338 U.S. 25; *Robinson* v. *California*, 370 U.S. 660; *Gideon* v. *Wainwright*, 372 U.S. 335; *Malloy* v. *Hogan*, 378 U.S. 1; *Pointer* v. *Texas, supra; Griffin* v. *California*, 380 U.S. 609.

3. Madison himself had previously pointed out the dangers of inaccuracy resulting from the fact that "no language is so copious as to supply words and phrases for every complex idea." The Federalist, No. 37 (Cooke ed. 1961), at 236.

4. Alexander Hamilton was opposed to a bill of rights on the ground that it was unnecessary because the Federal Government was a government of delegated powers and it was not granted the power to intrude upon fundamental personal rights. The Federalist, No. 84 (Cooke ed. 1961), at 578–579. He also argued,

"I go further, and affirm that bills of rights, in the sense and in the extent in which they are contended for, are not only unnecessary in the proposed constitution, but would even be dangerous. They would contain various exceptions to powers which are not granted; and on this very account, would afford a colourable pretext to claim more than were granted. For why declare that things shall not be done which there is no power to do? Why for instance, should it be said, that the liberty of the press shall not be restrained, when no power is given by which restrictions may be imposed? I will not contend that such a provision would confer a regulating power; but it is evident that it would furnish, to men disposed to usurp, a plausible pretence for claiming that power." *Id.*, at 579.

In presenting the proposed Amendment, Madison said:

"It has been objected also against a bill of rights, that, by enumerating particular exceptions to the grant of power, it would disparage those rights which were not placed in that enumeration; and it might follow by implication, that those rights which were not singled out, were intended to be assigned into the hands of the General Government, and were consequently insecure. This is one of the most plausible arguments I have ever heard urged against the admission of a bill of rights into this system; but, I conceive, that it may be guarded against. I have attempted it, as gentlemen may see by turning to the last clause of the fourth resolution [the Ninth Amendment]." I Annals of Congress 439 (Gales and Seaton ed. 1834).

Mr. Justice Story wrote of this argument against a bill of rights and the meaning of the Ninth Amendment:

"In regard to . . . [a] suggestion, that the affirmance of certain rights might disparage others, or might lead to argumentative implications in favor of other powers, it might be sufficient to say that such a course of reasoning could never be sustained upon any solid basis. . . . But a conclusive answer is, that such an attempt may be interdicted (as it has been) by a positive declaration in such a bill of rights that the enumeration of certain rights shall not be construed to deny or disparage others retained by the people." II Story, Commentaries on the Constitution of the United States 626–627 (5th ed. 1891).

He further stated, referring to the Ninth Amendment:

"This clause was manifestly introduced to prevent any perverse or ingenious misapplication of the well-known maxim, that an affirmation in particular cases implies a negation in all others; and, *e converso*, that a negation in particular cases implies an affirmation in all others." *Id.*, at 651.

These statements of Madison and Story make clear that the Framers did not intend that the first eight amendments be construed to exhaust the basic and fundamental rights which the Constitution guaranteed to the people.[5]

The Ninth Amendment and the Tenth Amendment, which provides, "The powers not delegated to the United States by the Constitution, nor prohibited by it to the States, are reserved to the States respectively, or to the people," were apparently also designed in part to meet the above-quoted argument of Hamilton.

5. The Tenth Amendment similarly made clear that the States and the people retained all those powers not expressly delegated to the Federal Government.

While this Court has had little occasion to interpret the Ninth Amendment,[6] "[i]t cannot be presumed that any clause in the constitution is intended to be without effect." *Marbury* v. *Madison*, 1 Cranch 137, 174. In interpreting the Constitution, "real effect should be given to all the words it uses." *Myers* v. *United States*, 272 U.S. 52, 151. The Ninth Amendment to the Constitution may be regarded by some as a recent discovery and may be forgotten by others, but since 1791 it has been a basic part of the Constitution which we are sworn to uphold. To hold that a right so basic and fundamental and so deep-rooted in our society as the right of privacy in marriage may be infringed because that right is not guaranteed in so many words by the first eight amendments to the Constitution is to ignore the Ninth Amendment and to give it no effect whatsoever. Moreover, a judicial construction that this fundamental right is not protected by the Constitution because it is not mentioned in explicit terms by one of the first eight amendments or elsewhere in the Constitution would violate the Ninth Amendment, which specifically states that "[t]he enumeration in the Constitution, of certain rights, shall not be *construed* to deny or disparage others retained by the people." (Emphasis added.) . . .

Mr. Justice Harlan, concurring in the judgment.

I fully agree with the judgment of reversal, but find myself unable to join the Court's opinion. The reason is that it seems to me to evince an approach to this case very much like that taken by my Brothers Black and Stewart in dissent, namely: the Due Process Clause of the Fourteenth Amendment does not touch this Connecticut statute unless the enactment is found to violate some right assured by the letter or penumbra of the Bill of Rights.

In other words, what I find implicit in the Court's opinion is that the "incorporation" doctrine may be used to *restrict* the reach of Fourteenth Amendment Due Process. For

---

6. This Amendment has been referred to as "The Forgotten Ninth Amendment," in a book with that title by Bennett B. Patterson (1955). Other commentary on the Ninth Amendment includes Redlich, Are There "Certain Rights . . . Retained by the People"? 37 N. Y. U. L. Rev. 787 (1962), and Kelsey, The Ninth Amendment of the Federal Constitution, 11 Ind. L. J. 309 (1936). As far as I am aware, until today this Court has referred to the Ninth Amendment only in *United Public Workers* v. *Mitchell*, 330 U.S. 75, 94–95; *Tennessee Electric Power Co.* v. *TVA*, 306 U.S. 118, 143–144; and *Ashwander* v. *TVA*, 297 U.S. 288, 330–331. See also *Calder* v. *Bull*, 3 Dall. 386, 388; *Loan Assn.* v. *Topeka*, 20 Wall. 655, 662–663.

In *United Public Workers* v. *Mitchell, supra,* at 94–95, the Court stated: "We accept appellants' contention that the nature of political rights reserved to the people by the Ninth and Tenth Amendments [is] involved. The right claimed as inviolate may be stated as the right of a citizen to act as a party official or worker to further his own political views. Thus we have a measure of interference by the Hatch Act and the Rules with what otherwise would be the freedom of the civil servant under the First, Ninth and Tenth Amendments. And, if we look upon due process as a guarantee of freedom in those fields, there is a corresponding impairment of that right under the Fifth Amendment."

me this is just as unacceptable constitutional doctrine as is the use of the "incorporation" approach to *impose* upon the States all the requirements of the Bill of Rights as found in the provisions of the first eight amendments and in the decisions of this Court interpreting them. See, *e.g.*, my concurring opinions in *Pointer* v. *Texas*, 380 U.S. 400, 408, and *Griffin* v. *California*, 380 U.S. 609, 615, and my dissenting opinion in *Poe* v. *Ullman*, 367 U.S. 497, 522, at pp. 539–545.

In my view, the proper constitutional inquiry in this case is whether this Connecticut statute infringes the Due Process Clause of the Fourteenth Amendment because the enactment violates basic values "implicit in the concept of ordered liberty," *Palko* v. *Connecticut*, 302 U.S. 319, 325. For reasons stated at length in my dissenting opinion in *Poe* v. *Ullman*, *supra*, I believe that it does. While the relevant inquiry may be aided by resort to one or more of the provisions of the Bill of Rights, it is not dependent on them or any of their radiations. The Due Process Clause of the Fourteenth Amendment stands, in my opinion, on its own bottom.

A further observation seems in order respecting the justification of my Brothers BLACK and STEWART for their "incorporation" approach to this case. Their approach does not rest on historical reasons, which are of course wholly lacking (see Fairman, Does the Fourteenth Amendment Incorporate the Bill of Rights? The Original Understanding, 2 Stan. L. Rev. 5 (1949)), but on the thesis that by limiting the content of the Due Process Clause of the Fourteenth Amendment to the protection of rights which can be found elsewhere in the Constitution, in this instance in the Bill of Rights, judges will thus be confined to "interpretation" of specific constitutional provisions, and will thereby be restrained from introducing their own notions of constitutional right and wrong into the "vague contours of the Due Process Clause." *Rochin* v. *California*, 342 U.S. 165, 170.

While I could not more heartily agree that judicial "self restraint" is an indispensable ingredient of sound constitutional adjudication, I do submit that the formula suggested for achieving it is more hollow than real. "Specific" provisions of the Constitution, no less than "due process," lend themselves as readily to "personal" interpretations by judges whose constitutional outlook is simply to keep the Constitution in supposed "tune with the times" (*post*, p. 522). Need one go further than to recall last Term's reapportionment cases, *Wesberry* v. *Sanders*, 376 U.S. 1, and *Reynolds* v. *Sims*, 377 U.S. 533, where a majority of the Court "interpreted" "by the People" (Art. I, § 2) and "equal protection" (Amdt. 14) to command "one person, one vote," an interpretation that was made in the face of irrefutable and still unanswered history to the contrary? See my dissenting opinions in those cases, 376 U.S., at 20; 377 U.S., at 589.

Judicial self-restraint will not, I suggest, be brought about in the "due process" area by the historically unfounded incorporation formula long advanced by my Brother BLACK, and now in part espoused by my Brother STEWART. It will be achieved in this area, as in other constitutional areas, only by continual insistence upon respect for the teachings of history, solid recognition of the basic values that underlie our society, and wise appreciation of the great roles that the doctrines of federalism and separation of powers have played in establishing and preserving American freedoms. See *Adamson* v. *California*, 332 U.S. 46, 59 (Mr. Justice Frankfurter, concurring). Adherence to these principles will not, of course, obviate all constitutional differences of opinion among judges, nor should it. Their continued recognition will, however, go farther toward keeping most judges from roaming at large in the constitutional field than will the interpolation into the Constitution of an artificial and largely illusory restriction on the content of the Due Process Clause.*

MR. JUSTICE WHITE, concurring in the judgment.

In my view this Connecticut law as applied to married couples deprives them of "liberty" without due process of law, as that concept is used in the Fourteenth Amendment. I therefore concur in the judgment of the Court reversing these convictions under Connecticut's aiding and abetting statute.

It would be unduly repetitious, and belaboring the obvious, to expound on the impact of this statute on the liberty guaranteed by the Fourteenth Amendment against arbitrary or capricious denials or on the nature of this liberty. Suffice it to say that this is not the first time this Court has had occasion to articulate that the liberty entitled to protection under the Fourteenth Amendment includes the right "to marry, establish a home and bring up children," *Meyer* v. *Nebraska*, 262 U.S. 390, 399, and "the liberty . . . to direct the upbringing and education of children," *Pierce* v. *Society of Sisters*, 268 U.S. 510, 534–535, and that these are among "the basic civil rights of man." *Skinner* v. *Oklahoma*, 316 U.S. 535, 541. These decisions affirm that there is a "realm of family life which the state cannot enter" without substantial justification. *Prince* v. *Massachusetts*, 321 U.S. 158, 166. Surely the right invoked in this case, to be free of regulation of the intimacies of the marriage relationship, "come[s] to this Court with a momentum for respect lacking when appeal is made to liberties which derive merely from shifting economic arrangements." *Kovacs* v. *Cooper*, 336 U.S. 77, 95 (opinion of Frankfurter, J.).

The Connecticut anti-contraceptive statute deals rather substantially with this relationship. For it forbids all married persons the right to use birth-control devices, regardless of whether their use is dictated by considerations of family planning, *Trubek* v. *Ullman*, 147 Conn. 633, 165 A. 2d 158, health, or indeed even of life itself. *Buxton* v. *Ullman*, 147 Conn. 48, 156 A. 2d 508. The anti-use statute, together with the general aiding and abetting statute, prohibits doctors from affording advice to married persons on proper and effective methods of birth control. *Tileston* v. *Ullman*, 129 Conn. 84, 26 A. 2d 582. And the clear effect of these statutes, as enforced, is to deny disadvantaged citizens of Connecticut, those without either adequate knowledge or resources to obtain private counseling,

---

*Indeed, my Brother BLACK, in arguing his thesis, is forced to lay aside a host of cases in which the Court has recognized fundamental rights in the Fourteenth Amendment without specific reliance upon the Bill of Rights.

access to medical assistance and up-to-date information in respect to proper methods of birth control. *State* v. *Nelson*, 126 Conn. 412, 11 A. 2d 856; *State* v. *Griswold*, 151 Conn. 544, 200 A. 2d 479. In my view, a statute with these effects bears a substantial burden of justification when attacked under the Fourteenth Amendment. *Yick Wo* v. *Hopkins*, 118 U.S. 365; *Skinner* v. *Oklahoma*, 316 U.S. 535; *Schware* v. *Board of Bar Examiners*, 353 U.S. 232; *McLaughlin* v. *Florida*, 379 U.S. 184, 192.

An examination of the justification offered, however, cannot be avoided by saying that the Connecticut anti-use statute invades a protected area of privacy and association or that it demeans the marriage relationship. The nature of the right invaded is pertinent, to be sure, for statutes regulating sensitive areas of liberty do, under the cases of this Court, require "strict scrutiny," *Skinner* v. *Oklahoma*, 316 U.S. 535, 541, and "must be viewed in the light of less drastic means for achieving the same basic purpose." *Shelton* v. *Tucker*, 364 U.S. 479, 488. "Where there is a significant encroachment upon personal liberty, the State may prevail only upon showing a subordinating interest which is compelling." *Bates* v. *Little Rock*, 361 U.S. 516, 524. See also *McLaughlin* v. *Florida*, 379 U.S. 184. But such statutes, if reasonably necessary for the effectuation of a legitimate and substantial state interest, and not arbitrary or capricious in application, are not invalid under the Due Process Clause. *Zemel* v. *Rusk*, 381 U.S. 1. . . .

MR. JUSTICE BLACK, with whom MR. JUSTICE STEWART joins, dissenting.

I agree with my Brother STEWART's dissenting opinion. And like him I do not to any extent whatever base my view that this Connecticut law is constitutional on a belief that the law is wise or that its policy is a good one. In order that there may be no room at all to doubt why I vote as I do, I feel constrained to add that the law is every bit as offensive to me as it is to my Brethren of the majority and my Brothers HARLAN, WHITE and GOLDBERG who, reciting reasons why it is offensive to them, hold it unconstitutional. There is no single one of the graphic and eloquent strictures and criticisms fired at the policy of this Connecticut law either by the Court's opinion or by those of my concurring Brethren to which I cannot subscribe—except their conclusion that the evil qualities they see in the law make it unconstitutional.

Had the doctor defendant here, or even the nondoctor defendant, been convicted for doing nothing more than expressing opinions to persons coming to the clinic that certain contraceptive devices, medicines or practices would do them good and would be desirable, or for telling people how devices could be used, I can think of no reasons at this time why their expressions of views would not be protected by the First and Fourteenth Amendments, which guarantee freedom of speech. Cf. *Brotherhood of Railroad Trainmen* v. *Virginia ex rel. Virginia State Bar*, 377 U.S. 1; *NAACP* v. *Button*, 371 U.S. 415. But speech is one thing; conduct and physical activities are quite another. See, *e.g.*, *Cox* v. *Louisiana*, 379 U.S. 536, 554–555; *Cox* v. *Louisiana*, 379 U.S. 559, 563–564; *id.* 575–584 (concurring opinion); *Giboney* v. *Empire Storage & Ice Co.*, 336 U.S. 490; cf. *Reynolds* v.

United States, 98 U.S. 145, 163–164. The two defendants here were active participants in an organization which gave physical examinations to women, advised them what kind of contraceptive devices or medicines would most likely be satisfactory for them, and then supplied the devices themselves, all for a graduated scale of fees, based on the family income. Thus these defendants admittedly engaged with others in a planned course of conduct to help people violate the Connecticut law. Merely because some speech was used in carrying on that conduct—just as in ordinary life some speech accompanies most kinds of conduct—we are not in my view justified in holding that the First Amendment forbids the State to punish their conduct. Strongly as I desire to protect all First Amendment freedoms, I am unable to stretch the Amendment so as to afford protection to the conduct of these defendants in violating the Connecticut law. What would be the constitutional fate of the law if hereafter applied to punish nothing but speech is, as I have said, quite another matter.

The Court talks about a constitutional "right of privacy" as though there is some constitutional provision or provisions forbidding any law ever to be passed which might abridge the "privacy" of individuals. But there is not. There are, of course, guarantees in certain specific constitutional provisions which are designed in part to protect privacy at certain times and places with respect to certain activities. Such, for example, is the Fourth Amendment's guarantee against "unreasonable searches and seizures." But I think it belittles that Amendment to talk about it as though it protects nothing but "privacy." To treat it that way is to give it a niggardly interpretation, not the kind of liberal reading I think any Bill of Rights provision should be given. The average man would very likely not have his feelings soothed any more by having his property seized openly than by having it seized privately and by stealth. He simply wants his property left alone. And a person can be just as much, if not more, irritated, annoyed and injured by an unceremonious public arrest by a policeman as he is by a seizure in the privacy of his office or home.

One of the most effective ways of diluting or expanding a constitutionally guaranteed right is to substitute for the crucial word or words of a constitutional guarantee another word or words, more or less flexible and more or less restricted in meaning. This fact is well illustrated by the use of the term "right of privacy" as a comprehensive substitute for the Fourth Amendment's guarantee against "unreasonable searches and seizures." "Privacy" is a broad, abstract and ambiguous concept which can easily be shrunken in meaning but which can also, on the other hand, easily be interpreted as a constitutional ban against many things other than searches and seizures. I have expressed the view many times that First Amendment freedoms, for example, have suffered from a failure of the courts to stick to the simple language of the First Amendment in construing it, instead of invoking multitudes of words substituted for those the Framers used. See, *e.g., New York Times Co.* v. *Sullivan*, 376 U.S. 254, 293 (concurring opinion); cases collected in *City of El Paso* v. *Simmons*, 379 U.S. 497, 517, n. 1 (dissenting opinion); Black, The Bill of Rights, 35 N. Y. U. L. Rev. 865. For these reasons I get nowhere in this case by talk about a constitutional "right of privacy" as an emanation from one or more constitutional provisions.[1] I like my privacy as well as the next one, but I am nevertheless compelled to admit that government has a right to invade it unless prohibited by some specific constitutional provision. For these reasons I cannot agree with the Court's judgment and the reasons it gives for holding this Connecticut law unconstitutional. . . .

Mr. Justice Stewart, whom Mr. Justice Black joins, dissenting.

Since 1879 Connecticut has had on its books a law which forbids the use of contraceptives by anyone. I think this is an uncommonly silly law. As a practical matter, the law is obviously unenforceable, except in the oblique context of the present case. As a philosophical matter, I believe the use of contraceptives in the relationship of marriage should be left to personal and private choice, based upon each individual's moral, ethical, and religious beliefs. As a matter of social policy, I think professional counsel about methods of birth control should be available to all, so that each individual's choice can be meaningfully made. But we are not asked in this case to say whether we think this law is unwise, or even asinine. We are asked to hold that it violates the United States Constitution. And that I cannot do.

In the course of its opinion the Court refers to no less than six Amendments to the Constitution: the First, the Third, the Fourth, the Fifth, the Ninth, and the Fourteenth. But the Court does not say which of these Amendments, if any, it thinks is infringed by this Connecticut law.

We *are* told that the Due Process Clause of the Fourteenth Amendment is not, as such, the "guide" in this case. With that much I agree. There is no claim that this law, duly enacted by the Connecticut Legislature, is unconstitutionally vague. There is no claim that the appellants were denied any of the elements of procedural due process at their trial, so

---

1. The phrase "right to privacy" appears first to have gained currency from an article written by Messrs. Warren and (later Mr. Justice) Brandeis in 1890 which urged that States should give some form of tort relief to persons whose private affairs were exploited by others. The Right to Privacy, 4 Harv. L. Rev. 193. Largely as a result of this article, some States have passed statutes creating such a cause of action, and in others state courts have done the same thing by exercising their powers as courts of common law. See generally 41 Am. Jur. 926–927. Thus the Supreme Court of Georgia, in granting a cause of action for damages to a man whose picture had been used in a newspaper advertisement without his consent, said that "A right of privacy in matters purely private is . . . derived from natural law" and that "The conclusion reached by us seems to be . . . thoroughly in accord with natural justice, with the principles of the law of every civilized nation, and especially with the elastic principles of the common law. . . ." Pavesich v. *New England Life Ins. Co.*, 122 Ga. 190, 194, 218, 50 S. E. 68, 70, 80. Observing that "the right of privacy . . . presses for recognition here," today this Court, which I did not understand to have power to sit as a court of common law, now appears to be exalting a phrase which Warren and Brandeis used in discussing grounds for tort relief, to the level of a constitutional rule which prevents state legislatures from passing any law deemed by this Court to interfere with "privacy."

as to make their convictions constitutionally invalid. And, as the Court says, the day has long passed since the Due Process Clause was regarded as a proper instrument for determining "the wisdom, need, and propriety" of state laws. Compare *Lochner* v. *New York*, 198 U.S. 45, with *Ferguson* v. *Skrupa*, 372 U.S. 726. My Brothers HARLAN and WHITE to the contrary, "[w]e have returned to the original constitutional proposition that courts do not substitute their social and economic beliefs for the judgment of legislative bodies, who are elected to pass laws." *Ferguson* v. *Skrupa, supra*, at 730.

As to the First, Third, Fourth, and Fifth Amendments, I can find nothing in any of them to invalidate this Connecticut law, even assuming that all those Amendments are fully applicable against the States.[1] It has not even been argued that this is a law "respecting an establishment of religion, or prohibiting the free exercise thereof."[2] And surely, unless the solemn process of constitutional adjudication is to descend to the level of a play on words, there is not involved here any abridgment of "the freedom of speech, or of the press; or the right of the people peaceably to assemble, and to petition the Government for a redress of grievances."[3] No soldier has been quartered in any house.[4] There has been no search, and no seizure.[5] Nobody has been compelled to be a witness against himself.[6]

The Court also quotes the Ninth Amendment, and my Brother GOLDBERG's concurring opinion relies heavily upon it. But to say that the Ninth Amendment has anything to do with this case is to turn somersaults with history. The Ninth Amendment, like its companion the Tenth, which this Court held "states but a truism that all is retained which has not been surrendered," *United States* v. *Darby*, 312 U.S. 100, 124, was framed by

---

1. The Amendments in question were, as everyone knows, originally adopted as limitations upon the power of the newly created Federal Government, not as limitations upon the powers of the individual States. But the Court has held that many of the provisions of the first eight amendments are fully embraced by the Fourteenth Amendment as limitations upon state action, and some Members of the Court have held the view that the adoption of the Fourteenth Amendment made every provision of the first eight amendments fully applicable against the States. See *Adamson* v. *California*, 332 U.S. 46, 68 (dissenting opinion of MR. JUSTICE BLACK).

2. U.S. Constitution, Amendment I. To be sure, the injunction contained in the Connecticut statute coincides with the doctrine of certain religious faiths. But if that were enough to invalidate a law under the provisions of the First Amendment relating to religion, then most criminal laws would be invalidated. See, *e.g.*, the Ten Commandments. The Bible, Exodus 20:2–17 (King James).

3. U.S. Constitution, Amendment I. If all the appellants had done was to advise people that they thought the use of contraceptives was desirable, or even to counsel their use, the appellants would, of course, have a substantial First Amendment claim. But their activities went far beyond mere advocacy. They prescribed specific contraceptive devices and furnished patients with the prescribed contraceptive materials.

4. U.S. Constitution, Amendment III.

5. U.S. Constitution, Amendment IV.

6. U.S. Constitution, Amendment V.

James Madison and adopted by the States simply to make clear that the adoption of the Bill of Rights did not alter the plan that the *Federal* Government was to be a government of express and limited powers, and that all rights and powers not delegated to it were retained by the people and the individual States. Until today no member of this Court has ever suggested that the Ninth Amendment meant anything else, and the idea that a federal court could ever use the Ninth Amendment to annul a law passed by the elected representatives of the people of the State of Connecticut would have caused James Madison no little wonder.

What provision of the Constitution, then, does make this state law invalid? The Court says it is the right of privacy "created by several fundamental constitutional guarantees." With all deference, I can find no such general right of privacy in the Bill of Rights, in any other part of the Constitution, or in any case ever before decided by this Court.[7]

At the oral argument in this case we were told that the Connecticut law does not "conform to current community standards." But it is not the function of this Court to decide cases on the basis of community standards. We are here to decide cases "agreeably to the Constitution and laws of the United States." It is the essence of judicial duty to subordinate our own personal views, our own ideas of what legislation is wise and what is not. If, as I should surely hope, the law before us does not reflect the standards of the people of Connecticut, the people of Connecticut can freely exercise their true Ninth and Tenth Amendment rights to persuade their elected representatives to repeal it. That is the constitutional way to take this law off the books.[8]

---

7. Cases like *Shelton* v. *Tucker*, 364 U.S. 479 and *Bates* v. *Little Rock*, 361 U.S. 516, relied upon in the concurring opinions today, dealt with true First Amendment rights of association and are wholly inapposite here. See also, *e.g.*, *NAACP* v. *Alabama*, 357 U.S. 449; *Edwards* v. *South Carolina*, 372 U.S. 229. Our decision in *McLaughlin* v. *Florida*, 379 U.S. 184, is equally far afield. That case held invalid under the Equal Protection Clause, a state criminal law which discriminated against Negroes.

The Court does not say how far the new constitutional right of privacy announced today extends. See, *e.g.*, Mueller, Legal Regulation of Sexual Conduct, at 127; Ploscowe, Sex and the Law, at 189. I suppose, however, that even after today a State can constitutionally still punish at least some offenses which are not committed in public.

8. See *Reynolds* v. *Sims*, 377 U.S. 533, 562. The Connecticut House of Representatives recently passed a bill (House Bill No. 2462) repealing the birth control law. The State Senate has apparently not yet acted on the measure, and today is relieved of that responsibility by the Court. New Haven Journal-Courier, Wed., May 19, 1965, p. 1, col. 4, and p. 13, col. 7.

EISENSTADT, SHERIFF *v.* BAIRD

APPEAL FROM THE UNITED STATES COURT OF APPEALS FOR THE FIRST CIRCUIT

No. 70–17. Argued November 17–18, 1971—Decided March 22, 1972

BRENNAN, J., delivered the opinion of the Court, in which DOUGLAS, STEWART, and MARSHALL, JJ., joined. DOUGLAS, J., filed a concurring opinion. WHITE, J., filed an opinion concurring in the result, in which BLACKMUN, J., joined. BURGER, C. J., filed a dissenting opinion. POWELL and REHNQUIST, JJ., took no part in the consideration or decision of the case.

MR. JUSTICE BRENNAN delivered the opinion of the Court.

Appellee William Baird was convicted at a bench trial in the Massachusetts Superior Court under Massachusetts General Laws Ann., c. 272, § 21, first, for exhibiting contraceptive articles in the course of delivering a lecture on contraception to a group of students at Boston University and, second, for giving a young woman a package of Emko vaginal foam at the close of his address. . . . The Massachusetts Supreme Judicial Court unanimously set aside the conviction for exhibiting contraceptives on the ground that it violated Baird's First Amendment rights, but by a four-to-three vote sustained the conviction for giving away the foam. *Commonwealth* v. *Baird*, 355 Mass. 746, 247 N. E. 2d 574 (1969). Baird subsequently filed a petition for a federal writ of habeas corpus, which the District Court dismissed. 310 F. Supp. 951 (1970). On appeal, however, the Court of Appeals for the First Circuit vacated the dismissal and remanded the action with directions to grant the writ discharging Baird. 429 F. 2d 1398 (1970). This appeal by the Sheriff of Suffolk County, Massachusetts, followed, and we noted probable jurisdiction. 401 U.S. 934 (1971). We affirm.

Massachusetts General Laws Ann., c. 272, § 21, under which Baird was convicted, provides a maximum five-year term of imprisonment for "whoever . . . gives away . . . any drug, medicine, instrument or article whatever for the prevention of conception," except as authorized in § 21A. Under § 21A, "[a] registered physician may administer to or prescribe for any married person drugs or articles intended for the prevention of pregnancy or conception. [And a] registered pharmacist actually engaged in the business of pharmacy may furnish such drugs or articles to any married person presenting a prescription from a registered physician." . . . As interpreted by the State Supreme Judicial Court, these provisions make it a felony for anyone, other than a registered physician or pharmacist acting in accordance with the terms of § 21A, to dispense any article with the intention that it be used for the prevention of conception. The statutory scheme distinguishes among three distinct classes of distributees—*first*, married persons may obtain contraceptives to prevent pregnancy, but only from doctors or druggists on prescription; *second,* single persons may not obtain contraceptives from anyone to prevent pregnancy; and, *third,* married or single persons may obtain contraceptives from anyone to prevent, not pregnancy, but the spread of disease. This construction of state law is, of course, binding on us. *E.g., Groppi* v. *Wisconsin,* 400 U.S. 505, 507 (1971). . . .

The basic principles governing application of the Equal Protection Clause of the Fourteenth Amendment are familiar. As THE CHIEF JUSTICE only recently explained in *Reed* v. *Reed,* 404 U.S. 71, 75–76 (1971):

> "In applying that clause, this Court has consistently recognized that the Fourteenth Amendment does not deny to States the power to treat different classes of persons in different ways. *Barbier* v. *Connolly,* 113 U.S. 27 (1885); *Lindsley* v. *Natural Carbonic Gas Co.,* 220 U.S. 61 (1911); *Railway Express Agency* v. *New York,* 336 U.S. 106 (1949); *McDonald* v. *Board of Election Commissioners,* 394 U.S. 802 (1969). The Equal Protection Clause of that amendment does, however, deny to States the power to legislate that different treatment be accorded to persons placed by a statute into different classes on the basis of criteria wholly unrelated to the objective of that statute. A classification 'must be reasonable, not arbitrary, and must rest upon some ground of difference having a fair and substantial relation to the object of the legislation, so that all persons similarly circumstanced shall be treated alike.' *Royster Guano Co.* v. *Virginia,* 253 U.S. 412, 415 (1920)."

The question for our determination in this case is whether there is some ground of difference that rationally explains the different treatment accorded married and unmarried persons under Massachusetts General Laws Ann., c. 272, §§ 21 and 21A.[1] For the reasons that follow, we conclude that no such ground exists.

First. Section 21 stems from Mass. Stat. 1879, c. 159, § 1, which prohibited, without exception, distribution of articles intended to be used as contraceptives. In *Commonwealth* v. *Allison,* 227 Mass. 57, 62, 116 N. E. 265, 266 (1917), the Massachusetts Supreme Judicial Court explained that the law's "plain purpose is to protect purity, to preserve chastity, to encourage continence and self-restraint, to defend the sanctity of the home, and thus to engender in the State and nation a virile and virtuous race of men and women." Although the State clearly abandoned that purpose with the enactment of § 21A, at least insofar as the illicit sexual activities of married persons are concerned, see n. 3, *supra,* the court

---

1. Of course, if we were to conclude that the Massachusetts statute impinges upon fundamental freedoms under *Griswold,* the statutory classification would have to be not merely *rationally related* to a valid public purpose but *necessary* to the achievement of a *compelling* state interest. *E.g., Shapiro* v. *Thompson,* 394 U.S. 618 (1969); *Loving* v. *Virginia,* 388 U.S. 1 (1967). But just as in *Reed* v. *Reed,* 404 U.S. 71 (1971), we do not have to address the statute's validity under that test because the law fails to satisfy even the more lenient equal protection standard.

reiterated in *Sturgis* v. *Attorney General, supra*, that the object of the legislation is to discourage premarital sexual intercourse. Conceding that the State could, consistently with the Equal Protection Clause, regard the problems of extramarital and premarital sexual relations as "[e]vils . . . of different dimensions and proportions, requiring different remedies," *Williamson* v. *Lee Optical Co.*, 348 U.S. 483, 489 (1955), we cannot agree that the deterrence of premarital sex may reasonably be regarded as the purpose of the Massachusetts law.

It would be plainly unreasonable to assume that Massachusetts has prescribed pregnancy and the birth of an unwanted child as punishment for fornication, which is a misdemeanor under Massachusetts General Laws Ann., c. 272, § 18. Aside from the scheme of values that assumption would attribute to the State, it is abundantly clear that the effect of the ban on distribution of contraceptives to unmarried persons has at best a marginal relation to the proffered objective. What Mr. Justice Goldberg said in *Griswold* v. *Connecticut, supra*, at 498 (concurring opinion), concerning the effect of Connecticut's prohibition on the use of contraceptives in discouraging extramarital sexual relations, is equally applicable here. "The rationality of this justification is dubious, particularly in light of the admitted widespread availability to all persons in the State of Connecticut, unmarried as well as married, of birth-control devices for the prevention of disease, as distinguished from the prevention of conception." See also *id.*, at 505–507 (WHITE, J., concurring in judgment). Like Connecticut's laws, §§ 21 and 21A do not at all regulate the distribution of contraceptives when they are to be used to prevent, not pregnancy, but the spread of disease. *Commonwealth* v. *Corbett*, 307 Mass. 7, 29 N. E. 2d 151 (1940), cited with approval in *Commonwealth* v. *Baird*, 355 Mass., at 754, 247 N. E. 2d, at 579. Nor, in making contraceptives available to married persons without regard to their intended use, does Massachusetts attempt to deter married persons from engaging in illicit sexual relations with unmarried persons. Even on the assumption that the fear of pregnancy operates as a deterrent to fornication, the Massachusetts statute is thus so riddled with exceptions that deterrence of premarital sex cannot reasonably be regarded as its aim. . . .

If under *Griswold* the distribution of contraceptives to married persons cannot be prohibited, a ban on distribution to unmarried persons would be equally impermissible. It is true that in *Griswold* the right of privacy in question inhered in the marital relationship. Yet the marital couple is not an independent entity with a mind and heart of its own, but an association of two individuals each with a separate intellectual and emotional makeup. If the right of privacy means anything, it is the right of the *individual*, married or single, to be free from unwarranted governmental intrusion into matters so fundamentally affecting a person as the decision whether to bear or beget a child. See *Stanley* v. *Georgia*, 394 U.S. 557 (1969). . . . See also *Skinner* v. *Oklahoma*, 316 U.S. 535 (1942); *Jacobson* v. *Massachusetts*, 197 U.S. 11, 29 (1905).

On the other hand, if *Griswold* is no bar to a prohibition on the distribution of contraceptives, the State could not, consistently with the Equal Protection Clause, outlaw distribution to unmarried but not to married persons. In each case the evil, as perceived by the State, would be identical, and the underinclusion would be invidious. . . .

ROE ET AL. *v.* WADE, DISTRICT ATTORNEY OF DALLAS COUNTY

APPEAL FROM THE UNITED STATES DISTRICT COURT FOR THE NORTHERN DISTRICT OF TEXAS

No. 70–18. Argued December 13, 1971—Reargued October 11, 1972—Decided January 22, 1973

BLACKMUN, J., delivered the opinion of the Court, in which BURGER, C. J., and DOUGLAS, BRENNAN, STEWART, MARSHALL, and POWELL, JJ., joined. BURGER, C. J., DOUGLAS, J., and STEWART, J., filed concurring opinions. WHITE, J., filed a dissenting opinion, in which REHNQUIST, J., joined. REHNQUIST, J., filed a dissenting opinion.

MR. JUSTICE BLACKMUN delivered the opinion of the Court.

This Texas federal appeal and its Georgia companion, *Doe* v. *Bolton*, present constitutional challenges to state criminal abortion legislation. The Texas statutes under attack here are typical of those that have been in effect in many States for approximately a century. The Georgia statutes, in contrast, have a modern cast and are a legislative product that, to an extent at least, obviously reflect the influences of recent attitudinal change, of advancing medical knowledge and techniques, and of new thinking about an old issue.

We forthwith acknowledge our awareness of the sensitive and emotional nature of the abortion controversy, of the vigorous opposing views, even among physicians, and of the deep and seemingly absolute convictions that the subject inspires. One's philosophy, one's experiences, one's exposure to the raw edges of human existence, one's religious training, one's attitudes toward life and family and their values, and the moral standards one establishes and seeks to observe, are all likely to influence and to color one's thinking and conclusions about abortion.

In addition, population growth, pollution, poverty, and racial overtones tend to complicate and not to simplify the problem.

Our task, of course, is to resolve the issue by constitutional measurement, free of emotion and of predilection. We seek earnestly to do this, and, because we do, we have inquired into, and in this opinion place some emphasis upon, medical and medical-legal history and what that history reveals about man's attitudes toward the abortion procedure over the centuries. We bear in mind, too, Mr. Justice Holmes' admonition in his now vindicated dissent in *Lochner* v. *New York*, 198 U.S. 45, 76 (1905):

"[The Constitution] is made for people of fundamentally differing views, and the accident of our finding certain opinions natural and familiar or novel and even shocking ought not to conclude our judgment upon the question whether statutes embodying them conflict with the Constitution of the United States."

I

The Texas statutes that concern us here are Arts. 1191–1194 and 1196 of the State's Penal Code.[1] These make it a crime to "procure an abortion," as therein defined, or to attempt one, except with respect to "an abortion procured or attempted by medical advice for the purpose of saving the life of the mother." Similar statutes are in existence in a majority of the States. . . .

Texas first enacted a criminal abortion statute in 1854. Texas Laws 1854, c. 49, § 1, set forth in 3 H. Gammel, Laws of Texas 1502 (1898). This was soon modified into language that has remained substantially unchanged to the present time. See Texas Penal Code of 1857, c. 7, Arts. 531–536; G. Paschal, Laws of Texas, Arts. 2192–2197 (1866); Texas Rev. Stat., c. 8, Arts. 536–541 (1879); Texas Rev. Crim. Stat., Arts. 1071–1076

---

1. "Article 1191. Abortion

"If any person shall designedly administer to a pregnant woman or knowingly procure to be administered with her consent any drug or medicine, or shall use towards her any violence or means whatever externally or internally applied, and thereby procure an abortion, he shall be confined in the penitentiary not less than two nor more than five years; if it be done without her consent, the punishment shall be doubled. By 'abortion' is meant that the life of the fetus or embryo shall be destroyed in the woman's womb or that a premature birth thereof be caused.
"Art. 1192. Furnishing the means

"Whoever furnishes the means for procuring an abortion knowing the purpose intended is guilty as an accomplice.
"Art. 1193. Attempt at abortion

"If the means used shall fail to produce an abortion, the offender is nevertheless guilty of an attempt to produce abortion, provided it be shown that such means were calculated to produce that result, and shall be fined not less than one hundred nor more than one thousand dollars.
"Art. 1194. Murder in producing abortion

"If the death of the mother is occasioned by an abortion so produced or by an attempt to effect the same it is murder."
"Art. 1196. By medical advice

"Nothing in this chapter applies to an abortion procured or attempted by medical advice for the purpose of saving the life of the mother."

The foregoing Articles, together with Art. 1195, compose Chapter 9 of Title 15 of the Penal Code. Article 1195, not attacked here, reads:
"Art. 1195. Destroying unborn child

"Whoever shall during parturition of the mother destroy the vitality or life in a child in a state of being born and before actual birth, which child would otherwise have been born alive, shall be confined in the penitentiary for life or for not less than five years."

(1911). The final article in each of these compilations provided the same exception, as does the present Article 1196, for an abortion by "medical advice for the purpose of saving the life of the mother." . . .

II

Jane Roe,[4] a single woman who was residing in Dallas County, Texas, instituted this federal action in March 1970 against the District Attorney of the county. She sought a declaratory judgment that the Texas criminal abortion statutes were unconstitutional on their face, and an injunction restraining the defendant from enforcing the statutes.

Roe alleged that she was unmarried and pregnant; that she wished to terminate her pregnancy by an abortion "performed by a competent, licensed physician, under safe, clinical conditions"; that she was unable to get a "legal" abortion in Texas because her life did not appear to be threatened by the continuation of her pregnancy; and that she could not afford to travel to another jurisdiction in order to secure a legal abortion under safe conditions. She claimed that the Texas statutes were unconstitutionally vague and that they abridged her right of personal privacy, protected by the First, Fourth, Fifth, Ninth, and Fourteenth Amendments. By an amendment to her complaint Roe purported to sue "on behalf of herself and all other women" similarly situated . . . and the licensed practicing physician, all joining in the attack on the Texas criminal abortion statutes. . . .

V

The principal thrust of appellant's attack on the Texas statutes is that they improperly invade a right, said to be possessed by the pregnant woman, to choose to terminate her pregnancy. Appellant would discover this right in the concept of personal "liberty" embodied in the Fourteenth Amendment's Due Process Clause; or in personal, marital, familial, and sexual privacy said to be protected by the Bill of Rights or its penumbras, see *Griswold* v. *Connecticut*, 381 U.S. 479 (1965); *Eisenstadt* v. *Baird*, 405 U.S. 438 (1972); *id.*, at 460 (WHITE, J., concurring in result); or among those rights reserved to the people by the Ninth Amendment, *Griswold* v. *Connecticut*, 381 U.S., at 486 (Goldberg, J., concurring). Before addressing this claim, we feel it desirable briefly to survey, in several aspects, the history of abortion, for such insight as that history may afford us, and then to examine the state purposes and interests behind the criminal abortion laws.

---

4. The name is a pseudonym.

VI

It perhaps is not generally appreciated that the restrictive criminal abortion laws in effect in a majority of States today are of relatively recent vintage. Those laws, generally proscribing abortion or its attempt at any time during pregnancy except when necessary to preserve the pregnant woman's life, are not of ancient or even of common-law origin. Instead, they derive from statutory changes effected, for the most part, in the latter half of the 19th century.

1. *Ancient attitudes.* These are not capable of precise determination. We are told that at the time of the Persian Empire abortifacients were known and that criminal abortions were severely punished.[8] We are also told, however, that abortion was practiced in Greek times as well as in the Roman Era,[9] and that "it was resorted to without scruple."[10] The Ephesian, Soranos, often described as the greatest of the ancient gynecologists, appears to have been generally opposed to Rome's prevailing free-abortion practices. He found it necessary to think first of the life of the mother, and he resorted to abortion when, upon this standard, he felt the procedure advisable.[11] Greek and Roman law afforded little protection to the unborn. If abortion was prosecuted in some places, it seems to have been based on a concept of a violation of the father's right to his offspring. Ancient religion did not bar abortion.[12]

2. *The Hippocratic Oath.* What then of the famous Oath that has stood so long as the ethical guide of the medical profession and that bears the name of the great Greek (460(?)–377(?) B.C.), who has been described as the Father of Medicine, the "wisest and the greatest practitioner of his art," and the "most important and most complete medical personality of antiquity," who dominated the medical schools of his time, and who typified the sum of the medical knowledge of the past?[13] The Oath varies somewhat according to the particular translation, but in any translation the content is clear: "I will give no deadly medicine to anyone if asked, nor suggest any such counsel; and in like manner I

---

8. A. Castiglioni, A History of Medicine 84 (2d ed. 1947), E. Krumbhaar, translator and editor (hereinafter Castiglioni).

9. J. Ricci, The Genealogy of Gynaecology 52, 84, 113, 149 (2d ed. 1950) (hereinafter Ricci); L. Lader, Abortion 75–77 (1966) (hereinafter Lader); K. Niswander, Medical Abortion Practices in the United States, in Abortion and the Law 37, 38–40 (D. Smith ed. 1967); G. Williams, The Sanctity of Life and the Criminal Law 148 (1957) (hereinafter Williams); J. Noonan, An Almost Absolute Value in History, in The Morality of Abortion 1, 3–7 (J. Noonan ed. 1970) (hereinafter Noonan); Quay, Justifiable Abortion—Medical and Legal Foundations (pt. 2), 49 Geo. L. J. 395, 406–422 (1961) (hereinafter Quay).

10. L. Edelstein, The Hippocratic Oath 10 (1943) (hereinafter Edelstein). But see Castiglioni 227.

11. Edelstein 12; Ricci 113–114, 118–119; Noonan 5.

12. Edelstein 13–14.

13. Castiglioni 148.

will not give to a woman a pessary to produce abortion,"[14] or "I will neither give a deadly drug to anyone if asked for it, nor will I make a suggestion to this effect. Similarly, I will not give to a woman an abortive remedy."[15]

Although the Oath is not mentioned in any of the principal briefs in this case or in *Doe v. Bolton*, . . . it represents the apex of the development of strict ethical concepts in medicine, and its influence endures to this day. Why did not the authority of Hippocrates dissuade abortion practice in his time and that of Rome? The late Dr. Edelstein provides us with a theory:[16] The Oath was not uncontested even in Hippocrates' day; only the Pythagorean school of philosophers frowned upon the related act of suicide. Most Greek thinkers, on the other hand, commended abortion, at least prior to viability. See Plato, Republic, V, 461; Aristotle, Politics, VII, 1335b 25. For the Pythagoreans, however, it was a matter of dogma. For them the embryo was animate from the moment of conception, and abortion meant destruction of a living being. The abortion clause of the Oath, therefore, "echoes Pythagorean doctrines," and "[i]n no other stratum of Greek opinion were such views held or proposed in the same spirit of uncompromising austerity."[17]

Dr. Edelstein then concludes that the Oath originated in a group representing only a small segment of Greek opinion and that it certainly was not accepted by all ancient physicians. He points out that medical writings down to Galen (A.D. 130–200) "give evidence of the violation of almost every one of its injunctions."[18] But with the end of antiquity a decided change took place. Resistance against suicide and against abortion became common. The Oath came to be popular. The emerging teachings of Christianity were in agreement with the Pythagorean ethic. The Oath "became the nucleus of all medical ethics" and "was applauded as the embodiment of truth." Thus, suggests Dr. Edelstein, it is "a Pythagorean manifesto and not the expression of an absolute standard of medical conduct."[19]

This, it seems to us, is a satisfactory and acceptable explanation of the Hippocratic Oath's apparent rigidity. It enables us to understand, in historical context, a long-accepted and revered statement of medical ethics.

3. *The common law.* It is undisputed that at common law, abortion performed *before* "quickening"—the first recognizable movement of the fetus *in utero*, appearing usually from the 16th to the 18th week of pregnancy[20]—was not an indictable

---

14. *Id.,* at 154.
15. Edelstein 3.
16. *Id.,* at 12, 15–18.
17. *Id.,* at 18; Lader 76.
18. Edelstein 63.
19. *Id.,* at 64.
20. Dorland's Illustrated Medical Dictionary 1261 (24th ed. 1965).

offense.[21] The absence of a common-law crime for pre-quickening abortion appears to have developed from a confluence of earlier philosophical, theological, and civil and canon law concepts of when life begins. These disciplines variously approached the question in terms of the point at which the embryo or fetus became "formed" or recognizably human, or in terms of when a "person" came into being, that is, infused with a "soul" or "animated." A loose consensus evolved in early English law that these events occurred at some point between conception and live birth.[22] This was "mediate animation." Although Christian theology and the canon law came to fix the point of animation at 40 days for a male and 80 days for a female, a view that persisted until the 19th century, there was otherwise little agreement about the precise time of formation or animation. There was agreement, however, that prior to this point the fetus was to be regarded as part of the mother, and its destruction, therefore, was not homicide. Due to continued uncertainty about the precise time when animation occurred, to

---

21. E. Coke, Institutes III *50; 1 W. Hawkins, Pleas of the Crown, c. 31, § 16 (4th ed. 1762); 1 W. Blackstone, Commentaries *129–130; M. Hale, Pleas of the Crown 433 (1st Amer. ed. 1847). For discussions of the role of the quickening concept in English common law, see Lader 78; Noonan 223–226; Means, The Law of New York Concerning Abortion and the Status of the Foetus, 1664–1968: A Case of Cessation of Constitutionality (pt. 1), 14 N. Y. L. F. 411, 418–428 (1968) (hereinafter Means I); Stern, Abortion: Reform and the Law, 59 J. Crim. L. C. & P. S. 84 (1968) (hereinafter Stern); Quay 430–432; Williams 152.

22. Early philosophers believed that the embryo or fetus did not become formed and begin to live until at least 40 days after conception for a male, and 80 to 90 days for a female. See, for example, Aristotle, Hist. Anim. 7.3.583b; Gen. Anim. 2.3.736, 2.5.741; Hippocrates, Lib. de Nat. Puer., No. 10. Aristotle's thinking derived from his three-stage theory of life: vegetable, animal, rational. The vegetable stage was reached at conception, the animal at "animation," and the rational soon after live birth. This theory, together with the 40/80 day view, came to be accepted by early Christian thinkers.

The theological debate was reflected in the writings of St. Augustine, who made a distinction between *embryo inanimatus*, not yet endowed with a soul, and *embryo animatus*. He may have drawn upon Exodus 21:22. At one point, however, he expressed the view that human powers cannot determine the point during fetal development at which the critical change occurs. See Augustine, De Origine Animae 4.4 (Pub. Law 44.527). See also W. Reany, The Creation of the Human Soul, c. 2 and 83–86 (1932); Huser, The Crime of Abortion in Canon Law 15 (Catholic Univ. of America, Canon Law Studies No. 162, Washington, D. C., 1942).

Galen, in three treatises related to embryology, accepted the thinking of Aristotle and his followers. Quay 426–427. Later, Augustine on abortion was incorporated by Gratian into the Decretum, published about 1140. Decretum Magistri Gratiani 2.32.2.7 to 2.32.2.10, in 1 Corpus Juris Canonici 1122, 1123 (A. Friedburg, 2d ed. 1879). This Decretal and the Decretals that followed were recognized as the definitive body of canon law until the new Code of 1917.

For discussions of the canon-law treatment, see Means I, pp. 411–412; Noonan 20–26; Quay 426–430; see also J. Noonan, Contraception: A History of Its Treatment by the Catholic Theologians and Canonists 18–29 (1965).

the lack of any empirical basis for the 40–80-day view, and perhaps to Aquinas' definition of movement as one of the two first principles of life, Bracton focused upon quickening as the critical point. The significance of quickening was echoed by later common-law scholars and found its way into the received common law in this country.

Whether abortion of a *quick* fetus was a felony at common law, or even a lesser crime, is still disputed. Bracton, writing early in the 13th century, thought it homicide.[23] But the later and predominant view, following the great common-law scholars, has been that it was, at most, a Lesser offense. In a frequently cited passage, Coke took the position that abortion of a woman "quick with childe" is "a great misprision, and no murder."[24] Blackstone followed, saying that while abortion after quickening had once been considered manslaughter (though not murder), "modern law" took a less severe view.[25] A recent review of the common-law precedents argues, however, that those precedents contradict Coke and that even post-quickening abortion was never established as a common-law crime.[26] This is of some importance because while most American courts ruled, in holding or dictum, that abortion of an unquickened fetus was not criminal under their received common-law,[27] others followed Coke in stating that abortion of a quick fetus

---

23. Bracton took the position that abortion by blow or poison was homicide "if the foetus be already formed and animated, and particularly if it be animated." 2 H. Bracton, De Legibus et Consuetudinibus Angliae 279 (T. Twiss ed. 1879), or, as a later translation puts it, "if the foetus is already formed or quickened, especially if it is quickened," 2 H. Bracton, On the Laws and Customs of England 341 (S. Thorne ed. 1968). See Quay 431; see also 2 Fleta 60–61 (Book 1, c. 23) (Selden Society ed. 1955).

24. E. Coke, Institutes III *50.

25. 1 W. Blackstone, Commentaries *129–130.

26. Means, The Phoenix of Abortional Freedom: Is a Penumbral or Ninth-Amendment Right About to Arise from the Nineteenth-Century Legislative Ashes of a Fourteenth-Century Common-Law Liberty?, 17 N. Y. L. F. 335 (1971) (hereinafter Means II). The author examines the two principal precedents cited marginally by Coke, both contrary to his dictum, and traces the treatment of these and other cases by earlier commentators. He concludes that Coke, who himself participated as an advocate in an abortion case in 1601, may have intentionally misstated the law. The author even suggests a reason: Coke's strong feelings against abortion, coupled with his determination to assert common-law (secular) jurisdiction to assess penalties for an offense that traditionally had been an exclusively ecclesiastical or canon-law crime. See also Lader 78–79, who notes that some scholars doubt that the common law ever was applied to abortion; that the English ecclesiastical courts seem to have lost interest in the problem after 1527; and that the preamble to the English legislation of 1803, 43 Geo. 3, c. 58, § 1, referred to in the text, *infra*, at 136, states that "no adequate means have been hitherto provided for the prevention and punishment of such offenses."

27. *Commonwealth* v. *Bangs*, 9 Mass. 387, 388 (1812); *Commonwealth* v. *Parker*, 50 Mass. (9 Metc.) 263, 265–266 (1845); *State* v. *Cooper*, 22 N. J. L. 52, 58 (1849); *Abrams* v. *Foshee*, 3 Iowa 274, 278–280 (1856); *Smith* v. *Gaffard*, 31 Ala. 45, 51 (1857); *Mitchell* v. *Commonwealth*, 78 Ky. 204, 210 (1879); *Eggart* v. *State*, 40 Fla. 527, 532, 25 So. 144, 145 (1898); *State* v. *Alcorn*, 7 Idaho 599,

was a "misprision," a term they translated to mean "misdemeanor."[28] That their reliance on Coke on this aspect of the law was uncritical and, apparently in all the reported cases, dictum (due probably to the paucity of common-law prosecutions for post-quickening abortion), makes it now appear doubtful that abortion was ever firmly established as a common-law crime even with respect to the destruction of a quick fetus.

4. *The English statutory law.* England's first criminal abortion statute, Lord Ellenborough's Act, 43 Geo. 3, c. 58, came in 1803. It made abortion of a quick fetus, § 1, a capital crime, but in § 2 it provided lesser penalties for the felony of abortion before quickening, and thus preserved the "quickening" distinction. This contrast was continued in the general revision of 1828, 9 Geo. 4, c. 31, § 13. It disappeared, however, together with the death penalty, in 1837, 7 Will. 4 & 1 Vict., c. 85, § 6, and did not reappear in the Offenses Against the Person Act of 1861, 24 & 25 Vict., c. 100, § 59, that formed the core of English anti-abortion law until the liberalizing reforms of 1967. In 1929, the Infant Life (Preservation) Act, 19 & 20 Geo. 5, c. 34, came into being. Its emphasis was upon the destruction of "the life of a child capable of being born alive." It made a willful act performed with the necessary intent a felony. It contained a proviso that one was not to be found guilty of the offense "unless it is proved that the act which caused the death of the child was not done in good faith for the purpose only of preserving the life of the mother."

A seemingly notable development in the English law was the case of *Rex* v. *Bourne*, [1939] 1 K. B. 687. This case apparently answered in the affirmative the question whether an abortion necessary to preserve the life of the pregnant woman was excepted from the criminal penalties of the 1861 Act. In his instructions to the jury, Judge Macnaghten referred to the 1929 Act, and observed that the Act related to "the case where a child is killed by a wilful act at the time when it is being delivered in the ordinary course of nature." *Id.*, at 691. He concluded that the 1861 Act's use of the word "unlawfully," imported the same meaning expressed by the specific proviso in the 1929 Act, even though there was no mention of preserving the mother's life in the 1861 Act. He then construed the phrase "preserving the life of the mother" broadly, that is, "in a reasonable sense," to include a serious and permanent threat to the mother's *health*, and instructed the jury to acquit Dr. Bourne if it found he had acted in a good-faith belief that the abortion was necessary for this purpose. *Id.*, at 693–694. The jury did acquit.

Recently, Parliament enacted a new abortion law. This is the Abortion Act of 1967, 15 & 16 Eliz. 2, c. 87. The Act permits a licensed physician to perform an abortion where two other licensed physicians agree (a) "that the continuance of the pregnancy would

---

606, 64 P. 1014, 1016 (1901); *Edwards* v. *State*, 79 Neb. 251, 252, 112 N. W. 611, 612 (1907); *Gray* v. *State*, 77 Tex. Cr. R. 221, 224, 178 S. W. 337, 338 (1915); *Miller* v. *Bennett*, 190 Va. 162, 169, 56 S. E. 2d 217, 221 (1949). Contra, *Mills* v. *Commonwealth*, 13 Pa. 631, 633 (1850); *State* v. *Slagle*, 83 N. C. 630, 632 (1880).

28. See *Smith* v. *State*, 33 Me. 48, 55 (1851); *Evans* v. *People*, 49 N. Y. 86, 88 (1872); *Lamb* v. *State*, 67 Md. 524, 533, 10 A. 208 (1887).

involve risk to the life of the pregnant woman, or of injury to the physical or mental health of the pregnant woman or any existing children of her family, greater than if the pregnancy were terminated," or (b) "that there is a substantial risk that if the child were born it would suffer from such physical or mental abnormalities as to be seriously handicapped." The Act also provides that, in making this determination, "account may be taken of the pregnant woman's actual or reasonably foreseeable environment." It also permits a physician, without the concurrence of others, to terminate a pregnancy where he is of the good-faith opinion that the abortion "is immediately necessary to save the life or to prevent grave permanent injury to the physical or mental health of the pregnant woman."

5. *The American law.* In this country, the law in effect in all but a few States until mid-19th century was the pre-existing English common law. Connecticut, the first State to enact abortion legislation, adopted in 1821 that part of Lord Ellenborough's Act that related to a woman "quick with child."[29] The death penalty was not imposed. Abortion before quickening was made a crime in that State only in 1860.[30] In 1828, New York enacted legislation[31] that, in two respects, was to serve as a model for early antiabortion statutes. First, while barring destruction of an unquickened fetus as well as a quick fetus, it made the former only a misdemeanor, but the latter second-degree manslaughter. Second, it incorporated a concept of therapeutic abortion by providing that an abortion was excused if it "shall have been necessary to preserve the life of such mother, or shall have been advised by two physicians to be necessary for such purpose." By 1840, when Texas had received the common law,[32] only eight American States had statutes dealing with abortion.[33] It was not until after the War Between the States that legislation began generally to replace the common law. Most of these initial statutes dealt severely with abortion after quickening but were lenient with it before quickening. Most punished attempts equally with completed abortions. While many statutes included the exception for an abortion thought by one or more physicians to be necessary to save the mother's life, that provision soon disappeared and the typical law required that the procedure actually be necessary for that purpose.

Gradually, in the middle and late 19th century the quickening distinction disappeared from the statutory law of most States and the degree of the offense and the penalties were increased. By the end of the 1950's, a large majority of the jurisdictions banned abortion, however and whenever performed, unless done to save or preserve the life of the

---

29. Conn. Stat., Tit. 20, § 14 (1821).

30. Conn. Pub. Acts, c. 71, § 1 (1860).

31. N. Y. Rev. Stat., pt. 4, c. 1, Tit. 2, Art. 1, § 9, p. 661, and Tit. 6, § 21, p. 694 (1829).

32. Act of Jan. 20, 1840, § 1, set forth in 2 H. Gammel, Laws of Texas 177–178 (1898); see *Grigsby v. Reib*, 105 Tex. 597, 600, 153 S. W. 1124, 1125 (1913).

33. The early statutes are discussed in Quay 435–438. See also Lader 85–88; Stern 85–86; and Means II 375–376.

mother.[34] The exceptions, Alabama and the District of Columbia, permitted abortion to preserve the mother's health.[35] Three States permitted abortions that were not "unlawfully" performed or that were not "without lawful justification," leaving interpretation of those standards to the courts.[36] In the past several years, however, a trend toward liberalization of abortion statutes has resulted in adoption, by about one-third of the States, of less stringent laws, most of them patterned after the ALI Model Penal Code, § 230.3,[37] set forth as Appendix B to the opinion in *Doe* v. *Bolton*.

It is thus apparent that at common law, at the time of the adoption of our Constitution, and throughout the major portion of the 19th century, abortion was viewed with less disfavor than under most American statutes currently in effect. Phrasing it another way, a woman enjoyed a substantially broader right to terminate a pregnancy than she does in most States today. At least with respect to the early stage of pregnancy, and very possibly without such a limitation, the opportunity to make this choice was present in this country well into the 19th century. Even later, the law continued for some time to treat less punitively an abortion procured in early pregnancy. . . .

VII

Three reasons have been advanced to explain historically the enactment of criminal abortion laws in the 19th century and to justify their continued existence.

---

34. Criminal abortion statutes in effect in the States as of 1961, together with historical statutory development and important judicial interpretations of the state statutes, are cited and quoted in Quay 447–520. See Comment, A Survey of the Present Statutory and Case Law on Abortion: The Contradictions and the Problems, 1972 U. Ill. L. F. 177, 179, classifying the abortion statutes and listing 25 States as permitting abortion only if necessary to save or preserve the mother's life.

35. Ala. Code, Tit. 14, § 9 (1958); D. C. Code Ann. § 22–201 (1967).

36. Mass. Gen. Laws Ann., c. 272, § 19 (1970); N. J. Stat. Ann. § 2A:87–1 (1969); Pa. Stat. Ann., Tit. 18, §§ 4718, 4719 (1963).

37. Fourteen States have adopted some form of the ALI statute. See Ark. Stat. Ann. §§ 41–303 to 41–310 (Supp. 1971); Calif. Health & Safety Code §§ 25950–25955.5 (Supp. 1972); Colo. Rev. Stat. Ann. §§ 40–2–50 to 40–2–53 (Cum. Supp. 1967); Del. Code Ann., Tit. 24, §§ 1790–1793 (Supp. 1972); Florida Law of Apr. 13, 1972, c. 72–196, 1972 Fla. Sess. Law Serv., pp. 380–382; Ga. Code §§ 26–1201 to 26–1203 (1972); Kan. Stat. Ann § 21–3407 (Supp. 1971); Md. Ann. Code, Art. 43, §§ 137–139 (1971); Miss. Code Ann. § 2223 (Supp. 1972); N. M. Stat. Ann. §§ 40A–5–1 to 40A–5–3 (1972); N. C. Gen. Stat. § 14–45.1 (Supp. 1971); Ore. Rev. Stat. §§ 435.405 to 435.495 (1971); S C. Code Ann. §§ 16–82 to 16–89 (1962 and Supp. 1971); Va. Code Ann. §§ 18.1–62 to 18.1–62.3 (Supp. 1972). Mr. Justice Clark described some of these States as having "led the way." Religion, Morality, and Abortion: A Constitutional Appraisal, 2 Loyola U. (L. A.) L. Rev. 1, 11 (1969).

It has been argued occasionally that these laws were the product of a Victorian social concern to discourage illicit sexual conduct. Texas, however, does not advance this justification in the present case, and it appears that no court or commentator has taken the argument seriously.[42] The appellants and *amici* contend, moreover, that this is not a proper state purpose at all and suggest that, if it were, the Texas statutes are overbroad in protecting it since the law fails to distinguish between married and unwed mothers.

A second reason is concerned with abortion as a medical procedure. When most criminal abortion laws were first enacted, the procedure was a hazardous one for the woman.[43] This was particularly true prior to the development of antisepsis. Antiseptic techniques, of course, were based on discoveries by Lister, Pasteur, and others first announced in 1867, but were not generally accepted and employed until about the turn of the century. Abortion mortality was high. Even after 1900, and perhaps until as late as the development of antibiotics in the 1940's, standard modern techniques such as dilation and curettage were not nearly so safe as they are today. Thus, it has been argued that a State's real concern in enacting a criminal abortion law was to protect the pregnant woman, that is, to restrain her from submitting to a procedure that placed her life in serious jeopardy.

Modern medical techniques have altered this situation. Appellants and various *amici* refer to medical data indicating that abortion in early pregnancy, that is, prior to the end of the first trimester, although not without its risk, is now relatively safe. Mortality rates for women undergoing early abortions, where the procedure is legal, appear to be as low as or lower than the rates for normal childbirth.[44] Consequently, any interest of the State in protecting the woman from an inherently hazardous procedure, except when it would be equally dangerous for her to forgo it, has largely disappeared. Of course, important state interests in the areas of health and medical standards do remain. The State has a legitimate interest in seeing to it that abortion, like any other medical procedure, is performed under circumstances that insure maximum safety for the patient. This interest obviously extends at least to the performing physician and his staff, to the facilities involved, to the availability of after-care, and to adequate provision for any complication or emergency that might

---

42. See, for example, *YWCA* v. *Kugler*, 342 F. Supp. 1048, 1074 (N. J. 1972); *Abele* v. *Markle*, 342 F. Supp. 800, 805–806 (Conn. 1972) (Newman, J., concurring in result), appeal docketed, No. 72-56; *Walsingham* v. *State*, 250 So. 2d 857, 863 (Ervin, J., concurring) (Fla. 1971); *State* v. *Gedicke*, 43 N. J. L. 86, 90 (1881); Means II 381–382.

43. See C. Haagensen & W. Lloyd, A Hundred Years of Medicine 19 (1943).

44. Potts, Postconceptive Control of Fertility, 8 Int'l J. of G. & O. 957, 967 (1970) (England and Wales); Abortion Mortality, 20 Morbidity and Mortality 208, 209 (June 12, 1971) (U.S. Dept. of HEW, Public Health Service) (New York City); Tietze, United States: Therapeutic Abortions, 1963–1968, 59 Studies in Family Planning 5, 7 (1970); Tietze, Mortality with Contraception and Induced Abortion, 45 Studies in Family Planning 6 (1969) (Japan, Czechoslovakia, Hungary); Tietze & Lehfeldt, Legal Abortion in Eastern Europe, 175 J. A. M. A. 1149, 1152 (April 1961). Other sources are discussed in Lader 17–23.

arise. The prevalence of high mortality rates at illegal "abortion mills" strengthens, rather than weakens, the State's interest in regulating the conditions under which abortions are performed. Moreover, the risk to the woman increases as her pregnancy continues. Thus, the State retains a definite interest in protecting the woman's own health and safety when an abortion is proposed at a late stage of pregnancy.

The third reason is the State's interest—some phrase it in terms of duty—in protecting prenatal life. Some of the argument for this justification rests on the theory that a new human life is present from the moment of conception.[45] The State's interest and general obligation to protect life then extends, it is argued, to prenatal life. Only when the life of the pregnant mother herself is at stake, balanced against the life she carries within her, should the interest of the embryo or fetus not prevail. Logically, of course, a legitimate state interest in this area need not stand or fall on acceptance of the belief that life begins at conception or at some other point prior to live birth. In assessing the State's interest, recognition may be given to the less rigid claim that as long as at least *potential* life is involved, the State may assert interests beyond the protection of the pregnant woman alone.

Parties challenging state abortion laws have sharply disputed in some courts the contention that a purpose of these laws, when enacted, was to protect prenatal life.[46] Pointing to the absence of legislative history to support the contention, they claim that most state laws were designed solely to protect the woman. Because medical advances have lessened this concern, at least with respect to abortions in early pregnancy, they argue that with respect to such abortions the laws can no longer be justified by any state interest. There is some scholarly support for this view of original purpose.[47] The few state courts called upon to interpret their laws in the late 19th and early 20th centuries did focus on the State's interest in protecting the woman's health rather than in preserving the embryo and fetus.[48] Proponents of this view point out that in many States, including Texas,[49] by statute or judicial interpretation, the pregnant woman herself could not be prosecuted for

---

45. See Brief of *Amicus* National Right to Life Committee; R. Drinan, The Inviolability of the Right to Be Born, in Abortion and the Law 107 (D. Smith ed. 1967); Louisell, Abortion, The Practice of Medicine and the Due Process of Law, 16 U. C. L. A. L. Rev. 233 (1969); Noonan 1.

46. See, *e.g.*, *Abele* v. *Markle*, 342 F. Supp. 800 (Conn. 1972), appeal docketed, No. 72–56.

47. See discussions in Means I and Means II.

48. See, *e.g.*, *State* v. *Murphy*, 27 N. J. L. 112, 114 (1858).

49. *Watson* v. *State*, 9 Tex. App. 237, 244–245 (1880); *Moore* v. *State*, 37 Tex. Cr. R. 552, 561, 40 S. W. 287, 290 (1897); *Shaw* v. *State*, 73 Tex. Cr. R. 337, 339, 165 S. W. 930, 931 (1914); *Fondren* v. *State*, 74 Tex. Cr. R 552, 557, 169 S. W. 411, 414 (1914); *Gray* v. *State*, 77 Tex. Cr. R 221, 229, 178 S. W. 337, 341 (1915). There is no immunity in Texas for the father who is not married to the mother. *Hammett* v. *State*, 84 Tex. Cr. R. 635, 209 S. W. 661 (1919); *Thompson* v. *State* (Ct. Crim. App. Tex. 1971), appeal docketed, No. 71–1200.

self-abortion or for cooperating in an abortion performed upon her by another.[50] They claim that adoption of the "quickening" distinction through received common law and state statutes tacitly recognizes the greater health hazards inherent in late abortion and impliedly repudiates the theory that life begins at conception.

It is with these interests, and the weight to be attached to them, that this case is concerned.

VIII

The Constitution does not explicitly mention any right of privacy. In a line of decisions, however, going back perhaps as far as *Union Pacific R. Co.* v. *Botsford*, 141 U.S. 250, 251 (1891), the Court has recognized that a right of personal privacy, or a guarantee of certain areas or zones of privacy, does exist under the Constitution. In varying contexts, the Court or individual Justices have, indeed, found at least the roots of that right in the First Amendment, *Stanley* v. *Georgia*, 394 U.S. 557, 564 (1969); in the Fourth and Fifth Amendments, *Terry* v. *Ohio*, 392 U.S. 1, 8–9 (1968), *Katz* v. *United States*, 389 U.S. 347, 350 (1967), *Boyd* v. *United States*, 116 U.S. 616 (1886), see *Olmstead* v. *United States*, 277 U.S. 438, 478 (1928) (Brandeis, J., dissenting); in the penumbras of the Bill of Rights, *Griswold* v. *Connecticut*, 381 U.S., at 484–485; in the Ninth Amendment, *id.*, at 486 (Goldberg, J., concurring); or in the concept of liberty guaranteed by the first section of the Fourteenth Amendment, see *Meyer* v. *Nebraska*, 262 U.S. 390, 399 (1923). These decisions make it clear that only personal rights that can be deemed "fundamental" or "implicit in the concept of ordered liberty," *Palko* v. *Connecticut*, 302 U.S. 319, 325 (1937), are included in this guarantee of personal privacy. They also make it clear that the right has some extension to activities relating to marriage, *Loving* v. *Virginia*, 388 U.S. 1, 12 (1967); procreation, *Skinner* v. *Oklahoma*, 316 U.S. 535, 541–542 (1942); contraception, *Eisenstadt* v. *Baird*, 405 U.S., at 453–454; *id.*, at 460, 463–465 (WHITE, J., concurring in result); family relationships, *Prince* v. *Massachusetts*, 321 U.S. 158, 166 (1944); and child rearing and education, *Pierce* v. *Society of Sisters*, 268 U.S. 510, 535 (1925), *Meyer* v. *Nebraska, supra*.

This right of privacy, whether it be founded in the Fourteenth Amendment's concept of personal liberty and restrictions upon state action, as we feel it is, or, as the District Court determined, in the Ninth Amendment's reservation of rights to the people, is broad enough to encompass a woman's decision whether or not to terminate her pregnancy. The detriment that the State would impose upon the pregnant woman by denying this choice altogether is apparent. Specific and direct harm medically diagnosable even in

---

50. See *Smith* v. *State*, 33 Me., at 55; *In re Vince*, 2 N. J. 443, 450, 67 A. 2d 141, 144 (1949). A short discussion of the modern law on this issue is contained in the Comment to the ALI's Model Penal Code § 207.11, at 158 and nn. 35–37 (Tent. Draft No. 9, 1959).

early pregnancy may be involved. Maternity, or additional offspring, may force upon the woman a distressful life and future. Psychological harm may be imminent. Mental and physical health may be taxed by child care. There is also the distress, for all concerned, associated with the unwanted child, and there is the problem of bringing a child into a family already unable, psychologically and otherwise, to care for it. In other cases, as in this one, the additional difficulties and continuing stigma of unwed motherhood may be involved. All these are factors the woman and her responsible physician necessarily will consider in consultation.

On the basis of elements such as these, appellant and some *amici* argue that the woman's right is absolute and that she is entitled to terminate her pregnancy at whatever time, in whatever way, and for whatever reason she alone chooses. With this we do not agree. Appellant's arguments that Texas either has no valid interest at all in regulating the abortion decision, or no interest strong enough to support any limitation upon the woman's sole determination, are unpersuasive. The Court's decisions recognizing a right of privacy also acknowledge that some state regulation in areas protected by that right is appropriate. As noted above, a State may properly assert important interests in safeguarding health, in maintaining medical standards, and in protecting potential life. At some point in pregnancy, these respective interests become sufficiently compelling to sustain regulation of the factors that govern the abortion decision. The privacy right involved, therefore, cannot be said to be absolute. In fact, it is not clear to us that the claim asserted by some *amici* that one has an unlimited right to do with one's body as one pleases bears a close relationship to the right of privacy previously articulated in the Court's decisions. The Court has refused to recognize an unlimited right of this kind in the past. *Jacobson* v. *Massachusetts*, 197 U.S. 11 (1905) (vaccination); *Buck* v. *Bell*, 274 U.S. 200 (1927) (sterilization).

We, therefore, conclude that the right of personal privacy includes the abortion decision, but that this right is not unqualified and must be considered against important state interests in regulation.

We note that those federal and state courts that have recently considered abortion law challenges have reached the same conclusion. A majority, in addition to the District Court in the present case, have held state laws unconstitutional, at least in part, because of vagueness or because of overbreadth and abridgment of rights. *Abele* v. *Markle*, 342 F. Supp. 800 (Conn. 1972), appeal docketed, No. 72–56; *Abele* v. *Markle*, 351 F. Supp. 224 (Conn. 1972), appeal docketed, No. 72–730; *Doe* v. *Bolton*, 319 F. Supp. 1048 (ND Ga. 1970), appeal decided today, *post*, p. 179; *Doe* v. *Scott*, 321 F. Supp. 1385 (ND Ill. 1971), appeal docketed, No. 70–105; *Poe* v. *Menghini*, 339 F. Supp. 986 (Kan. 1972); *YWCA* v. *Kugler*, 342 F. Supp. 1048 (NJ 1972); *Babbitz* v. *McCann*, 310 F. Supp. 293 (ED Wis. 1970), appeal dismissed, 400 U.S. 1 (1970); *People* v. *Belous*, 71 Cal. 2d 954, 458 P. 2d 194 (1969), cert. denied, 397 U.S. 915 (1970); *State* v. *Barquet*, 262 So. 2d 431 (Fla. 1972).

Others have sustained state statutes. *Crossen* v. *Attorney General*, 344 F. Supp. 587 (ED Ky. 1972), appeal docketed, No. 72–256; *Rosen* v. *Louisiana State Board of Medical Examiners*, 318 F. Supp. 1217 (ED La. 1970), appeal docketed, No. 70–42; *Corkey* v.

Edwards, 322 F. Supp. 1248 (WDNC 1971), appeal docketed, No. 71–92; *Steinberg* v. *Brown*, 321 F. Supp. 741 (ND Ohio 1970); *Doe* v. *Rampton* (Utah 1971), appeal docketed, No. 71–5666; *Cheaney* v. *State*, Ind., 285 N. E. 2d 265 (1972); *Spears* v. *State*, 257 So. 2d 876 (Miss. 1972); *State* v. *Munson*, 86 S. D. 663, 201 N. W. 2d 123 (1972), appeal docketed, No. 72–631.

Although the results are divided, most of these courts have agreed that the right of privacy, however based, is broad enough to cover the abortion decision; that the right, nonetheless, is not absolute and is subject to some limitations; and that at some point the state interests as to protection of health, medical standards, and prenatal life, become dominant. We agree with this approach.

Where certain "fundamental rights" are involved, the Court has held that regulation limiting these rights may be justified only by a "compelling state interest," *Kramer* v. *Union Free School District*, 395 U.S. 621, 627 (1969); *Shapiro* v. *Thompson*, 394 U.S. 618, 634 (1969); *Sherbert* v. *Verner*, 374 U.S. 398, 406 (1963), and that legislative enactments must be narrowly drawn to express only the legitimate state interests at stake. *Griswold* v. *Connecticut*, 381 U.S., at 485; *Aptheker* v. *Secretary of State*, 378 U.S. 500, 508 (1964); *Cantwell* v. *Connecticut*, 310 U.S. 296, 307–308 (1940); see *Eisenstadt* v. *Baird*, 405 U.S., at 460, 463–464 (WHITE, J., concurring in result).

In the recent abortion cases, cited above, courts have recognized these principles. Those striking down state laws have generally scrutinized the State's interests in protecting health and potential life, and have concluded that neither interest justified broad limitations on the reasons for which a physician and his pregnant patient might decide that she should have an abortion in the early stages of pregnancy. Courts sustaining state laws have held that the State's determinations to protect health or prenatal life are dominant and constitutionally justifiable.

IX

The District Court held that the appellee failed to meet his burden of demonstrating that the Texas statute's infringement upon Roe's rights was necessary to support a compelling state interest, and that, although the appellee presented "several compelling justifications for state presence in the area of abortions," the statutes outstripped these justifications and swept "far beyond any areas of compelling state interest." 314 F. Supp., at 1222–1223. Appellant and appellee both contest that holding. Appellant, as has been indicated, claims an absolute right that bars any state imposition of criminal penalties in the area. Appellee argues that the State's determination to recognize and protect prenatal life from and after conception constitutes a compelling state interest. As noted above, we do not agree fully with either formulation.

A. The appellee and certain *amici* argue that the fetus is a "person" within the language and meaning of the Fourteenth Amendment. In support of this, they outline at length and in detail the well-known facts of fetal development. If this suggestion of personhood is established, the appellant's case, of course, collapses, for the fetus' right to life would then be guaranteed specifically by the Amendment. The appellant conceded as much on reargument.[51] On the other hand, the appellee conceded on reargument[52] that no case could be cited that holds that a fetus is a person within the meaning of the Fourteenth Amendment.

The Constitution does not define "person" in so many words. Section 1 of the Fourteenth Amendment contains three references to "person." The first, in defining "citizens," speaks of "persons born or naturalized in the United States." The word also appears both in the Due Process Clause and in the Equal Protection Clause. "Person" is used in other places in the Constitution: in the listing of qualifications for Representatives and Senators, Art. I, § 2, cl. 2, and § 3, cl. 3; in the Apportionment Clause, Art. I, § 2, cl. 3;[53] in the Migration and Importation provision, Art. I, § 9, cl. 1; in the Emolument Clause, Art. I, § 9, cl. 8; in the Electors provisions, Art. II, § 1, cl. 2, and the superseded cl. 3; in the provision outlining qualifications for the office of President, Art. II, § 1, cl. 5; in the Extradition provisions, Art. IV, § 2, cl. 2, and the superseded Fugitive Slave Clause 3; and in the Fifth, Twelfth, and Twenty-second Amendments, as well as in §§ 2 and 3 of the Fourteenth Amendment. But in nearly all these instances, the use of the word is such that it has application only postnatally. None indicates, with any assurance, that it has any possible prenatal application.[54]

All this, together with our observation, *supra*, that throughout the major portion of the 19th century prevailing legal abortion practices were far freer than they are today, persuades us that the word "person," as used in the Fourteenth Amendment, does not

---

51. Tr. of Oral Rearg. 20–21.

52. Tr. of Oral Rearg. 24.

53. We are not aware that in the taking of any census under this clause, a fetus has ever been counted.

54. When Texas urges that a fetus is entitled to Fourteenth Amendment protection as a person, it faces a dilemma. Neither in Texas nor in any other State are all abortions prohibited. Despite broad proscription, an exception always exists. The exception contained in Art. 1196, for an abortion procured or attempted by medical advice for the purpose of saving the life of the mother, is typical. But if the fetus is a person who is not to be deprived of life without due process of law, and if the mother's condition is the sole determinant, does not the Texas exception appear to be out of line with the Amendment's command?

There are other inconsistencies between Fourteenth Amendment status and the typical abortion statute. It has already been pointed out, n. 49, *supra*, that in Texas the woman is not a principal or an accomplice with respect to an abortion upon her. If the fetus is a person, why is the woman not a principal or an accomplice? Further, the penalty for criminal abortion specified by Art. 1195 is significantly less than the maximum penalty for murder prescribed by Art. 1257 of the Texas Penal Code. If the fetus is a person, may the penalties be different?

include the unborn.[55] This is in accord with the results reached in those few cases where the issue has been squarely presented. *McGarvey* v. *Magee-Womens Hospital*, 340 F. Supp. 751 (WD Pa. 1972); *Byrn* v. *New York City Health & Hospitals Corp.*, 31 N. Y. 2d 194, 286 N. E. 2d 887 (1972), appeal docketed, No. 72-434; *Abele* v. *Markle*, 351 F. Supp. 224 (Conn. 1972), appeal docketed, No. 72–730. Cf. *Cheaney* v. *State*, Ind., 285 N. E. 2d, at 270; *Montana* v. *Rogers*, 278 F. 2d 68, 72 (CA7 1960), aff'd *sub nom. Montana* v. *Kennedy*, 366 U.S. 308 (1961); *Keeler* v. *Superior Court*, 2 Cal. 3d 619, 470 P. 2d 617 (1970); *State* v. *Dickinson*, 28 Ohio St. 2d 65, 275 N. E. 2d 599 (1971). Indeed, our decision in *United States* v. *Vuitch*, 402 U.S. 62 (1971), inferentially is to the same effect, for we there would not have indulged in statutory interpretation favorable to abortion in specified circumstances if the necessary consequence was the termination of life entitled to Fourteenth Amendment protection.

This conclusion, however, does not of itself fully answer the contentions raised by Texas, and we pass on to other considerations.

B. The pregnant woman cannot be isolated in her privacy. She carries an embryo and, later, a fetus, if one accepts the medical definitions of the developing young in the human uterus. See Dorland's Illustrated Medical Dictionary 478–479, 547 (24th ed. 1965). The situation therefore is inherently different from marital intimacy, or bedroom possession of obscene material, or marriage, or procreation, or education, with which *Eisenstadt* and *Griswold*, *Stanley*, *Loving*, *Skinner*, and *Pierce* and *Meyer* were respectively concerned. As we have intimated above, it is reasonable and appropriate for a State to decide that at some point in time another interest, that of health of the mother or that of potential human life, becomes significantly involved. The woman's privacy is no longer sole and any right of privacy she possesses must be measured accordingly.

Texas urges that, apart from the Fourteenth Amendment, life begins at conception and is present throughout pregnancy, and that, therefore, the State has a compelling interest in protecting that life from and after conception. We need not resolve the difficult question of when life begins. When those trained in the respective disciplines of medicine, philosophy, and theology are unable to arrive at any consensus, the judiciary, at this point in the development of man's knowledge, is not in a position to speculate as to the answer.

It should be sufficient to note briefly the wide divergence of thinking on this most sensitive and difficult question. There has always been strong support for the view that life does not begin until live birth. This was the belief of the Stoics.[56] It appears to be the

---

55. Cf. the Wisconsin abortion statute, defining "unborn child" to mean "a human being from the time of conception until it is born alive," Wis. Stat. § 940.04 (6)(1969), and the new Connecticut statute, Pub. Act No. 1 (May 1972 special session), declaring it to be the public policy of the State and the legislative intent "to protect and preserve human life from the moment of conception."

56. Edelstein 16.

predominant, though not the unanimous, attitude of the Jewish faith.[57] It may be taken to represent also the position of a large segment of the Protestant community, insofar as that can be ascertained; organized groups that have taken a formal position on the abortion issue have generally regarded abortion as a matter for the conscience of the individual and her family.[58] As we have noted, the common law found greater significance in quickening. Physicians and their scientific colleagues have regarded that event with less interest and have tended to focus either upon conception, upon live birth, or upon the interim point at which the fetus becomes "viable," that is, potentially able to live outside the mother's womb, albeit with artificial aid.[59] Viability is usually placed at about seven months (28 weeks) but may occur earlier, even at 24 weeks.[60] The Aristotelian theory of "mediate animation," that held sway throughout the Middle Ages and the Renaissance in Europe, continued to be official Roman Catholic dogma until the 19th century, despite opposition to this "ensoulment" theory from those in the Church who would recognize the existence of life from the moment of conception.[61] The latter is now, of course, the official belief of the Catholic Church. As one brief *amicus* discloses, this is a view strongly held by many non-Catholics as well, and by many physicians. Substantial problems for precise definition of this view are posed, however, by new embryological data that purport to indicate that conception is a "process" over time, rather than an event, and by new medical techniques such as menstrual extraction, the "morning-after" pill, implantation of embryos, artificial insemination, and even artificial wombs.[62]

In areas other than criminal abortion, the law has been reluctant to endorse any theory that life, as we recognize it, begins before live birth or to accord legal rights to the unborn except in narrowly defined situations and except when the rights are contingent upon live birth. For example, the traditional rule of tort law denied recovery for prenatal

---

57. Lader 97–99; D. Feldman, Birth Control in Jewish Law 251–294 (1968). For a stricter view, see I. Jakobovits, Jewish Views on Abortion, in Abortion and the Law 124 (D. Smithed. 1967).

58. *Amicus* Brief for the American Ethical Union et al. For the position of the National Council of Churches and of other denominations, see Lader 99–101.

59. L. Hellman & J. Pritchard, Williams Obstetrics 493 (14th ed. 1971); Dorland's Illustrated Medical Dictionary 1689 (24th ed. 1965).

60. Hellman & Pritchard, *supra*, n. 59, at 493.

61. For discussions of the development of the Roman Catholic position, see D. Callahan, Abortion: Law, Choice, and Morality 409–447 (1970); Noonan 1.

62. See Brodie, The New Biology and the Prenatal Child, 9 J. Family L. 391, 397 (1970); Gorney, The New Biology and the Future of Man, 15 U. C. L. A. L. Rev. 273 (1968); Note, Criminal Law— Abortion—The "Morning-After Pill" and Other Pre-Implantation Birth-Control Methods and the Law, 46 Ore. L. Rev. 211 (1967); G. Taylor, The Biological Time Bomb 32 (1968); A. Rosenfeld, The Second Genesis 138–139 (1969); Smith, Through a Test Tube Darkly: Artificial Insemination and the Law, 67 Mich. L. Rev. 127 (1968); Note, Artificial Insemination and the Law, 1968 U. Ill. L. F. 203.

injuries even though the child was born alive.[63] That rule has been changed in almost every jurisdiction. In most States, recovery is said to be permitted only if the fetus was viable, or at least quick, when the injuries were sustained, though few courts have squarely so held.[64] In a recent development, generally opposed by the commentators, some States permit the parents of a stillborn child to maintain an action for wrongful death because of prenatal injuries.[65] Such an action, however, would appear to be one to vindicate the parents' interest and is thus consistent with the view that the fetus, at most, represents only the potentiality of life. Similarly, unborn children have been recognized as acquiring the rights or interests by way of inheritance or other devolution of property, and have been represented by guardians *ad litem*.[66] Perfection of the interests involved, again, has generally been contingent upon live birth. In short, the unborn have never been recognized in the law as persons in the whole sense.

X

In view of all this, we do not agree that, by adopting one theory of life, Texas may override the rights of the pregnant woman that are at stake. We repeat, however, that the State does have an important and legitimate interest in preserving and protecting the health of the pregnant woman, whether she be a resident of the State or a nonresident who seeks medical consultation and treatment there, and that it has still *another* important and legitimate interest in protecting the potentiality of human life. These interests are separate and distinct. Each grows in substantiality as the woman approaches term and, at a point during pregnancy, each becomes "compelling."

With respect to the State's important and legitimate interest in the health of the mother, the "compelling" point, in the light of present medical knowledge, is at approximately the end of the first trimester. This is so because of the now-established medical fact, referred to above at 149, that until the end of the first trimester mortality in abortion may be less than mortality in normal childbirth. It follows that, from and after this point, a State may regulate the abortion procedure to the extent that the regulation reasonably relates to the preservation and protection of maternal health. Examples of permissible

---

63. W. Prosser, The Law of Torts 335–338 (4th ed. 1971); 2 F. Harper & F. James, The Law of Torts 1028–1031 (1956); Note, 63 Harv. L. Rev. 173 (1949).

64. See cases cited in Prosser, *supra*, n. 63, at 336–338; Annotation, Action for Death of Unborn Child, 15 A. L. R 3d 992 (1967).

65. Prosser, *supra*, n. 63, at 338; Note, The Law and the Unborn Child: The Legal and Logical Inconsistencies, 46 Notre Dame Law. 349, 354–360 (1971).

66. Louisell, Abortion, The Practice of Medicine and the Due Process of Law, 16 U. C. L. A. L. Rev. 233, 235–238 (1969); Note, 56 Iowa L. Rev. 994, 999–1000 (1971); Note, The Law and the Unborn Child, 46 Notre Dame Law. 349, 351–354 (1971).

state regulation in this area are requirements as to the qualifications of the person who is to perform the abortion; as to the licensure of that person; as to the facility in which the procedure is to be performed, that is, whether it must be a hospital or may be a clinic or some other place of less-than-hospital status; as to the licensing of the facility; and the like.

This means, on the other hand, that, for the period of pregnancy prior to this "compelling" point, the attending physician, in consultation with his patient, is free to determine, without regulation by the State, that, in his medical judgment, the patient's pregnancy should be terminated. If that decision is reached, the judgment may be effectuated by an abortion free of interference by the State.

With respect to the State's important and legitimate interest in potential life, the "compelling" point is at viability. This is so because the fetus then presumably has the capability of meaningful life outside the mother's womb. State regulation protective of fetal life after viability thus has both logical and biological justifications. If the State is interested in protecting fetal life after viability, it may go so far as to proscribe abortion during that period, except when it is necessary to preserve the life or health of the mother.

Measured against these standards, Art. 1196 of the Texas Penal Code, in restricting legal abortions to those "procured or attempted by medical advice for the purpose of saving the life of the mother," sweeps too broadly. The statute makes no distinction between abortions performed early in pregnancy and those performed later, and it limits to a single reason, "saving" the mother's life, the legal justification for the procedure. The statute, therefore, cannot survive the constitutional attack made upon it here.

This conclusion makes it unnecessary for us to consider the additional challenge to the Texas statute asserted on grounds of vagueness. See *United States* v. *Vuitch*, 402 U.S., at 67–72.

XI

To summarize and to repeat:

1. A state criminal abortion statute of the current Texas type, that excepts from criminality only a *life-saving* procedure on behalf of the mother, without regard to pregnancy stage and without recognition of the other interests involved, is violative of the Due Process Clause of the Fourteenth Amendment.

(a) For the stage prior to approximately the end of the first trimester, the abortion decision and its effectuation must be left to the medical judgment of the pregnant woman's attending physician.

(b) For the stage subsequent to approximately the end of the first trimester, the State, in promoting its interest in the health of the mother, may, if it chooses, regulate the abortion procedure in ways that are reasonably related to maternal health.

(c) For the stage subsequent to viability, the State in promoting its interest in the potentiality of human life may, if it chooses, regulate, and even proscribe, abortion except where it is necessary, in appropriate medical judgment, for the preservation of the life or health of the mother. . . .

This holding, we feel, is consistent with the relative weights of the respective interests involved, with the lessons and examples of medical and legal history, with the lenity of the common law, and with the demands of the profound problems of the present day. The decision leaves the State free to place increasing restrictions on abortion as the period of pregnancy lengthens, so long as those restrictions are tailored to the recognized state interests. The decision vindicates the right of the physician to administer medical treatment according to his professional judgment up to the points where important state interests provide compelling justifications for intervention. Up to those points, the abortion decision in all its aspects is inherently, and primarily, a medical decision, and basic responsibility for it must rest with the physician. If an individual practitioner abuses the privilege of exercising proper medical judgment, the usual remedies, judicial and intraprofessional, are available. . . .

Mr. Justice Rehnquist, dissenting.

The Court's opinion brings to the decision of this troubling question both extensive historical fact and a wealth of legal scholarship. While the opinion thus commands my respect, I find myself nonetheless in fundamental disagreement with those parts of it that invalidate the Texas statute in question, and therefore dissent.

I

The Court's opinion decides that a State may impose virtually no restriction on the performance of abortions during the first trimester of pregnancy. Our previous decisions indicate that a necessary predicate for such an opinion is a plaintiff who was in her first trimester of pregnancy at some time during the pendency of her lawsuit. While a party may vindicate his own constitutional rights, he may not seek vindication for the rights of others. *Moose Lodge* v. *Irvis*, 407 U.S. 163 (1973); *Sierra Club* v. *Morton*, 405 U.S. 727 (1972). The Court's statement of facts in this case makes clear, however, that the record in no way indicates the presence of such a plaintiff. We know only that plaintiff Roe at the time of filing her complaint was a pregnant woman; for aught that appears in this record, she may have been in her *last* trimester of pregnancy as of the date the complaint was filed.

Nothing in the Court's opinion indicates that Texas might not constitutionally apply its proscription of abortion as written to a woman in that stage of pregnancy. Nonetheless, the Court uses her complaint against the Texas statute as a fulcrum for deciding that States may impose virtually no restrictions on medical abortions performed during the *first* trimester of pregnancy. In deciding such a hypothetical lawsuit, the Court departs from the longstanding admonition that it should never "formulate a rule of constitutional law broader than is required by the precise facts to which it is to be applied." *Liverpool New York & Philadelphia S. S. Co.* v. *Commissioners of Emigration*, 113 U.S. 33, 39 (1885). See also *Ashwander* v. *TVA*, 297 U.S. 288, 345 (1936) (Brandeis, J., concurring).

II

Even if there were a plaintiff in this case capable of litigating the issue which the Court decides, I would reach a conclusion opposite to that reached by the Court. I have difficulty in concluding, as the Court does, that the right of "privacy" is involved in this case. Texas, by the statute here challenged, bars the performance of a medical abortion by a licensed physician on a plaintiff such as Roe. A transaction resulting in an operation such as this is not "private" in the ordinary usage of that word. Nor is the "privacy" that the Court finds here even a distant relative of the freedom from searches and seizures protected by the Fourth Amendment to the Constitution, which the Court has referred to as embodying a right to privacy. *Katz* v. *United States*, 389 U.S. 347 (1967).

If the Court means by the term "privacy" no more than that the claim of a person to be free from unwanted state regulation of consensual transactions may be a form of "liberty" protected by the Fourteenth Amendment, there is no doubt that similar claims have been upheld in our earlier decisions on the basis of that liberty. I agree with the statement of Mr. Justice Stewart in his concurring opinion that the "liberty," against deprivation of which without due process the Fourteenth Amendment protects, embraces more than the rights found in the Bill of Rights. But that liberty is not guaranteed absolutely against deprivation, only against deprivation without due process of law. The test traditionally applied in the area of social and economic legislation is whether or not a law such as that challenged has a rational relation to a valid state objective. *Williamson* v. *Lee Optical Co.*, 348 U.S. 483, 491 (1955). The Due Process Clause of the Fourteenth Amendment undoubtedly does place a limit, albeit a broad one, on legislative power to enact laws such as this. If the Texas statute were to prohibit an abortion even where the mother's life is in jeopardy, I have little doubt that such a statute would lack a rational relation to a valid state objective under the test stated in *Williamson, supra*. But the Court's sweeping invalidation of any restrictions on abortion during the first trimester is impossible to justify under that standard, and the conscious weighing of competing factors that the Court's opinion apparently substitutes for the established test is far more appropriate to a legislative judgment than to a judicial one.

The Court eschews the history of the Fourteenth Amendment in its reliance on the "compelling state interest" test. See *Weber* v. *Aetna Casualty & Surety Co.*, 406 U.S. 164, 179 (1972) (dissenting opinion). But the Court adds a new wrinkle to this test by transposing it from the legal considerations associated with the Equal Protection Clause of the Fourteenth Amendment to this case arising under the Due Process Clause of the Fourteenth Amendment. Unless I misapprehend the consequences of this transplanting of the "compelling state interest test," the Court's opinion will accomplish the seemingly impossible feat of leaving this area of the law more confused than it found it.

While the Court's opinion quotes from the dissent of Mr. Justice Holmes in *Lochner v. New York*, 198 U.S. 45, 74 (1905), the result it reaches is more closely attuned to the majority opinion of Mr. Justice Peckham in that case. As in *Lochner* and similar cases applying substantive due process standards to economic and social welfare legislation, the adoption of the compelling state interest standard will inevitably require this Court to examine the legislative policies and pass on the wisdom of these policies in the very process of deciding whether a particular state interest put forward may or may not be "compelling." The decision here to break pregnancy into three distinct terms and to outline the permissible restrictions the State may impose in each one, for example, partakes more of judicial legislation than it does of a determination of the intent of the drafters of the Fourteenth Amendment.

The fact that a majority of the States reflecting, after all, the majority sentiment in those States, have had restrictions on abortions for at least a century is a strong indication, it seems to me, that the asserted right to an abortion is not "so rooted in the traditions and conscience of our people as to be ranked as fundamental," *Snyder* v. *Massachusetts*, 291 U.S. 97, 105 (1934). Even today, when society's views on abortion are changing, the very existence of the debate is evidence that the "right" to an abortion is not so universally accepted as the appellant would have us believe. . . .

DOE ET AL. *v.* BOLTON, ATTORNEY GENERAL OF GEORGIA, ET AL.

APPEAL FROM THE UNITED STATES DISTRICT COURT FOR THE NORTHERN DISTRICT OF GEORGIA

No. 70–40. Argued December 13, 1971—Reargued October 11, 1972—Decided January 22, 1973

BLACKMUN, J., delivered the opinion of the Court, in which BURGER, C. J., and DOUGLAS, BRENNAN, STEWART, MARSHALL, and POWELL, JJ., joined. BURGER, C. J., and DOUGLAS, J., filed concurring opinions. WHITE, J., filed a dissenting opinion, in which REHNQUIST, J., joined. REHNQUIST, J., filed a dissenting opinion.

MR. JUSTICE BLACKMUN delivered the opinion of the Court.

In this appeal, the criminal abortion statutes recently enacted in Georgia are challenged on constitutional grounds. The statutes are §§ 26–1201 through 26–1203 of the State's Criminal Code, formulated by Georgia Laws, 1968 Session, pp. 1249, 1277–1280. In *Roe* v. *Wade, ante,* p. 113, we today have struck down, as constitutionally defective, the Texas criminal abortion statutes that are representative of provisions long in effect in a majority of our States. The Georgia legislation, however, is different and merits separate consideration. . . .

Section 26–1201, with a referenced exception, makes abortion a crime, and § 26–1203 provides that a person convicted of that crime shall be punished by imprisonment for not less than one nor more than 10 years. Section 26–1202 (a) states the exception and removes from § 1201's definition of criminal abortion, and thus makes noncriminal, an abortion "performed by a physician duly licensed" in Georgia when, "based upon his best clinical judgment . . . an abortion is necessary because:

"(1) A continuation of the pregnancy would endanger the life of the pregnant woman or would seriously and permanently injure her health; or

"(2) The fetus would very likely be born with a grave, permanent, and irremediable mental or physical defect; or

"(3) The pregnancy resulted from forcible or statutory rape."[5]

---

5. In contrast with the ALI model, the Georgia statute makes no specific reference to pregnancy resulting from incest. We were assured by the State at reargument that this was because the statute's reference to "rape" was intended to include incest. Tr. of Oral Rearg. 32.

Section 26–1202 also requires, by numbered subdivisions of its subsection (b), that, for an abortion to be authorized or performed as a noncriminal procedure, additional conditions must be fulfilled. These are (1) and (2) residence of the woman in Georgia; (3) reduction to writing of the performing physician's medical judgment that an abortion is justified for one or more of the reasons specified by § 26–1202 (a), with written concurrence in that judgment by at least two other Georgia-licensed physicians, based upon their separate personal medical examinations of the woman; (4) performance of the abortion in a hospital licensed by the State Board of Health and also accredited by the Joint Commission on Accreditation of Hospitals; (5) advance approval by an abortion committee of not less than three members of the hospital's staff; (6) certifications in a rape situation; and (7), (8), and (9) maintenance and confidentiality of records. There is a provision (subsection (c)) for judicial determination of the legality of a proposed abortion on petition of the judicial circuit law officer or of a close relative, as therein defined, of the unborn child, and for expeditious hearing of that petition. There is also a provision (subsection (e)) giving a hospital the right not to admit an abortion patient and giving any physician and any hospital employee or staff member the right, on moral or religious grounds, not to participate in the procedure.

II

On April 16, 1970, Mary Doe,[6] 23 other individuals (nine described as Georgia-licensed physicians, seven as nurses registered in the State, five as clergymen, and two as social workers), and two nonprofit Georgia corporations that advocate abortion reform instituted this federal action in the Northern District of Georgia against the State's attorney general, the district attorney of Fulton County, and the chief of police of the city of Atlanta. The plaintiffs sought a declaratory judgment that the Georgia abortion statutes were unconstitutional in their entirety. They also sought injunctive relief restraining the defendants and their successors from enforcing the statutes.

Mary Doe alleged:

(1) She was a 22-year-old Georgia citizen, married, and nine weeks pregnant. She had three living children. The two older ones had been placed in a foster home because of Doe's poverty and inability to care for them. The youngest, born July 19, 1969, had been placed for adoption. Her husband had recently abandoned her and she was forced to live with her indigent parents and their eight children. She and her husband, however, had become reconciled. He was a construction worker employed only sporadically. She had been a mental patient at the State Hospital. She had been advised that an abortion could be performed on her with less danger to her health than if she gave birth to the child she was carrying. She would be unable to care for or support the new child.

---

6. Appellants by their complaint, App. 7, allege that the name is a pseudonym.

(2) On March 25, 1970, she applied to the Abortion Committee of Grady Memorial Hospital, Atlanta, for a therapeutic abortion under § 26–1202. Her application was denied 16 days later, on April 10, when she was eight weeks pregnant, on the ground that her situation was not one described in § 26–1202 (a).[7]

(3) Because her application was denied, she was forced either to relinquish "her right to decide when and how many children she will bear" or to seek an abortion that was illegal under the Georgia statutes. This invaded her rights of privacy and liberty in matters related to family, marriage, and sex, and deprived her of the right to choose whether to bear children. This was a violation of rights guaranteed her by the First, Fourth, Fifth, Ninth, and Fourteenth Amendments. The statutes also denied her equal protection and procedural due process and, because they were unconstitutionally vague, deterred hospitals and doctors from performing abortions. She sued "on her own behalf and on behalf of all others similarly situated."

The other plaintiffs alleged that the Georgia statutes "chilled and deterred" them from practicing their respective professions and deprived them of rights guaranteed by the First, Fourth, and Fourteenth Amendments. These plaintiffs also purported to sue on their own behalf and on behalf of others similarly situated. . . .

IV

The appellants attack on several grounds those portions of the Georgia abortion statutes that remain after the District Court decision: undue restriction of a right to personal and marital privacy; vagueness; deprivation of substantive and procedural due process; improper restriction to Georgia residents; and denial of equal protection.

A. *Roe* v. *Wade, supra,* sets forth our conclusion that a pregnant woman does not have an absolute constitutional right to an abortion on her demand. What is said there is applicable here and need not be repeated.

B. The appellants go on to argue, however, that the present Georgia statutes must be viewed historically, that is, from the fact that prior to the 1968 Act an abortion in Georgia was not criminal if performed to "preserve the life" of the mother. It is suggested that the present statute, as well, has this emphasis on the mother's rights, not on those of the fetus. Appellants contend that it is thus clear that Georgia has given little, and certainly not first, consideration to the unborn child. Yet, it is the unborn child's rights that Georgia asserts in justification of the statute. Appellants assert that this justification cannot be advanced at this late date.

---

7. In answers to interrogatories, Doe stated that her application for an abortion was approved at Georgia Baptist Hospital on May 5, 1970, but that she was not approved as a charity patient there and had no money to pay for an abortion. App. 64.

Appellants then argue that the statutes do not adequately protect the woman's right. This is so because it would be physically and emotionally damaging to Doe to bring a child into her poor, "fatherless"[10] family, and because advances in medicine and medical techniques have made it safer for a woman to have a medically induced abortion than for her to bear a child. Thus, "a statute that requires a woman to carry an unwanted pregnancy to term infringes not only on a fundamental right of privacy but on the right to life itself." Brief 27.

The appellants recognize that a century ago medical knowledge was not so advanced as it is today, that the techniques of antisepsis were not known, and that any abortion procedure was dangerous for the woman. To restrict the legality of the abortion to the situation where it was deemed necessary, in medical judgment, for the preservation of the woman's life was only a natural conclusion in the exercise of the legislative judgment of that time. A State is not to be reproached, however, for a past judgmental determination made in the light of then-existing medical knowledge. It is perhaps unfair to argue, as the appellants do, that because the early focus was on the preservation of the woman's life, the State's present professed interest in the protection of embryonic and fetal life is to be downgraded. That argument denies the State the right to readjust its views and emphases in the light of the advanced knowledge and techniques of the day. . . .

D. The appellants next argue that the District Court should have declared unconstitutional three procedural demands of the Georgia statute: (1) that the abortion be performed in a hospital accredited by the Joint Commission on Accreditation of Hospitals;[11] (2) that the procedure be approved by the hospital staff abortion committee; and (3) that the performing physician's judgment be confirmed by the independent examinations of the patient by two other licensed physicians. The appellants attack these provisions not only on the ground that they unduly restrict the woman's right of privacy, but also on procedural due process and equal protection grounds. The physician-appellants also argue that, by subjecting a doctor's individual medical judgment to committee approval and to confirming consultations, the statute impermissibly restricts the physician's right to practice his profession and deprives him of due process.

1. *JCAH accreditation.* The Joint Commission on Accreditation of Hospitals is an organization without governmental sponsorship or overtones. No question whatever is raised concerning the integrity of the organization or the high purpose of the accreditation process. . . . That process, however, has to do with hospital standards generally and has no present particularized concern with abortion as a medical or surgical procedure. . . . In Georgia, there is no restriction on the performance of nonabortion surgery in a hospital not yet accredited by the JCAH so long as other requirements imposed by the State, such as licensing of the hospital and of the operating surgeon, are met. See Georgia Code §§

---

10. Brief for Appellants 25.

11. We were advised at reargument, Tr. of Oral Rearg. 10, that only 54 of Georgia's 159 counties have a JCAH-accredited hospital.

88–1901 (a) and 88–1905 (1971) and 84–907 (Supp. 1971). Furthermore, accreditation by the Commission is not granted until a hospital has been in operation at least one year. The Model Penal Code, § 230.3, Appendix B hereto, contains no requirement for JCAH accreditation. And the Uniform Abortion Act (Final Draft, Aug. 1971) . . . approved by the American Bar Association in February 1972, contains no JCAH-accredited hospital specification. . . . Some courts have held that a JCAH-accreditation requirement is an overbroad infringement of fundamental rights because it does not relate to the particular medical problems and dangers of the abortion operation. *E.g., Poe* v. *Menghini*, 339 F. Supp., at 993–994.

We hold that the JCAH-accreditation requirement does not withstand constitutional scrutiny in the present context. It is a requirement that simply is not "based on differences that are reasonably related to the purposes of the Act in which it is found." *Morey* v. *Doud*, 354 U.S. 457, 465 (1957).

This is not to say that Georgia may not or should not, from and after the end of the first trimester, adopt standards for licensing all facilities where abortions may be performed so long as those standards are legitimately related to the objective the State seeks to accomplish. The appellants contend that such a relationship would be lacking even in a lesser requirement that an abortion be performed in a licensed hospital, as opposed to a facility, such as a clinic, that may be required by the State to possess all the staffing and services necessary to perform an abortion safely (including those adequate to handle serious complications or other emergency, or arrangements with a nearby hospital to provide such services). Appellants and various *amici* have presented us with a mass of data purporting to demonstrate that some facilities other than hospitals are entirely adequate to perform abortions if they possess these qualifications. The State, on the other hand, has not presented persuasive data to show that only hospitals meet its acknowledged interest in insuring the quality of the operation and the full protection of the patient.

We feel compelled to agree with appellants that the State must show more than it has in order to prove that only the full resources of a licensed hospital, rather than those of some other appropriately licensed institution, satisfy these health interests. We hold that the hospital requirement of the Georgia law, because it fails to exclude the first trimester of pregnancy, see *Roe* v. *Wade*, is also invalid. In so holding we naturally express no opinion on the medical judgment involved in any particular case, that is, whether the patient's situation is such that an abortion should be performed in a hospital, rather than in some other facility.

2. *Committee approval.* The second aspect of the appellants' procedural attack relates to the hospital abortion committee and to the pregnant woman's asserted lack of access to that committee. Relying primarily on *Goldberg* v. *Kelly*, 397 U.S. 254 (1970), concerning the termination of welfare benefits, and *Wisconsin* v. *Constantineau*, 400 U.S. 433 (1971), concerning the posting of an alcoholic's name, Doe first argues that she was denied due process because she could not make a presentation to the committee. It is not clear from the record, however, whether Doe's own consulting physician was or was not a member

of the committee or did or did not present her case, or, indeed, whether she herself was or was not there. We see nothing in the Georgia statute that explicitly denies access to the committee by or on behalf of the woman. If the access point alone were involved, we would not be persuaded to strike down the committee provision on the unsupported assumption that access is not provided.

Appellants attack the discretion the statute leaves to the committee. The most concrete argument they advance is their suggestion that it is still a badge of infamy "in many minds" to bear an illegitimate child, and that the Georgia system enables the committee members' personal views as to extramarital sex relations, and punishment therefor, to govern their decisions. This approach obviously is one founded on suspicion and one that discloses a lack of confidence in the integrity of physicians. To say that physicians will be guided in their hospital committee decisions by their predilections on extramarital sex unduly narrows the issue to pregnancy outside marriage. (Doe's own situation did not involve extramarital sex and its product.) The appellants' suggestion is necessarily somewhat degrading to the conscientious physician, particularly the obstetrician, whose professional activity is concerned with the physical and mental welfare, the woes, the emotions, and the concern of his female patients. He, perhaps more than anyone else, is knowledgeable in this area of patient care, and he is aware of human frailty, so-called "error," and needs. The good physician—despite the presence of rascals in the medical profession, as in all others, we trust that most physicians are "good"—will have sympathy and understanding for the pregnant patient that probably are not exceeded by those who participate in other areas of professional counseling. . . .

Saying all this, however, does not settle the issue of the constitutional propriety of the committee requirement. Viewing the Georgia statute as a whole, we see no constitutionally justifiable pertinence in the structure for the advance approval by the abortion committee. With regard to the protection of potential life, the medical judgment is already completed prior to the committee stage, and review by a committee once removed from diagnosis is basically redundant. We are not cited to any other surgical procedure made subject to committee approval as a matter of state criminal law. The woman's right to receive medical care in accordance with her licensed physician's best judgment and the physician's right to administer it are substantially limited by this statutorily imposed overview. And the hospital itself is otherwise fully protected. Under § 26–1202 (e), the hospital is free not to admit a patient for an abortion. It is even free not to have an abortion committee. Further, a physician or any other employee has the right to refrain, for moral or religious reasons, from participating in the abortion procedure. These provisions obviously are in the statute in order to afford appropriate protection to the individual and to the denominational hospital. Section 26–1202 (e) affords adequate protection to the hospital, and little more is provided by the committee prescribed by § 26–1202 (b)(5).

We conclude that the interposition of the hospital abortion committee is unduly restrictive of the patient's rights and needs that, at this point, have already been medically delineated and substantiated by her personal physician. To ask more serves neither the hospital nor the State.

3. *Two-doctor concurrence.* The third aspect of the appellants' attack centers on the "time and availability of adequate medical facilities and personnel." It is said that the system imposes substantial and irrational roadblocks and "is patently unsuited" to prompt determination of the abortion decision. Time, of course, is critical in abortion. Risks during the first trimester of pregnancy are admittedly lower than during later months. . . .

The statute's emphasis, as has been repetitively noted, is on the attending physician's "best clinical judgment that an abortion is necessary." That should be sufficient. The reasons for the presence of the confirmation step in the statute are perhaps apparent, but they are insufficient to withstand constitutional challenge. Again, no other voluntary medical or surgical procedure for which Georgia requires confirmation by two other physicians has been cited to us. If a physician is licensed by the State, he is recognized by the State as capable of exercising acceptable clinical judgment. If he fails in this, professional censure and deprivation of his license are available remedies. Required acquiescence by co-practitioners has no rational connection with a patient's needs and unduly infringes on the physician's right to practice. . . .

F. The last argument on this phase of the case is one that often is made, namely, that the Georgia system is violative of equal protection because it discriminates against the poor. The appellants do not urge that abortions should be performed by persons other than licensed physicians, so we have no argument that because the wealthy can better afford physicians, the poor should have non-physicians made available to them. The appellants acknowledged that the procedures are "nondiscriminatory in . . . express terms" but they suggest that they have produced invidious discriminations. The District Court rejected this approach out of hand. 319 F. Supp., at 1056. It rests primarily on the accreditation and approval and confirmation requirements, discussed above, and on the assertion that most of Georgia's counties have no accredited hospital. We have set aside the accreditation, approval, and confirmation requirements, however, and with that, the discrimination argument collapses in all significant aspects. . . .

Mr. Justice White, with whom Mr. Justice Rehnquist joins, dissenting.*

At the heart of the controversy in these cases are those recurring pregnancies that pose no danger whatsoever to the life or health of the mother but are, nevertheless, unwanted for any one or more of a variety of reasons—convenience, family planning, economics, dislike of children, the embarrassment of illegitimacy, etc. The common claim before us is that for any one of such reasons, or for no reason at all, and without asserting or claiming any threat to life or health, any woman is entitled to an abortion at her request if she is able to find a medical advisor willing to undertake the procedure.

---

*[This opinion applies also to No. 70–18, *Roe* v. *Wade*.]

The Court for the most part sustains this position: During the period prior to the time the fetus becomes viable, the Constitution of the United States values the convenience, whim, or caprice of the putative mother more than the life or potential life of the fetus; the Constitution, therefore, guarantees the right to an abortion as against any state law or policy seeking to protect the fetus from an abortion not prompted by more compelling reasons of the mother.

With all due respect, I dissent. I find nothing in the language or history of the Constitution to support the Court's judgment. The Court simply fashions and announces a new constitutional right for pregnant mothers and, with scarcely any reason or authority for its action, invests that right with sufficient substance to override most existing state abortion statutes. The upshot is that the people and the legislatures of the 50 States are constitutionally disentitled to weigh the relative importance of the continued existence and development of the fetus, on the one hand, against a spectrum of possible impacts on the mother, on the other hand. As an exercise of raw judicial power, the Court perhaps has authority to do what it does today; but in my view its judgment is an improvident and extravagant exercise of the power of judicial review that the Constitution extends to this Court.

The Court apparently values the convenience of the pregnant mother more than the continued existence and development of the life or potential life that she carries. Whether or not I might agree with that marshaling of values, I can in no event join the Court's judgment because I find no constitutional warrant for imposing such an order of priorities on the people and legislatures of the States. In a sensitive area such as this, involving as it does issues over which reasonable men may easily and heatedly differ, I cannot accept the Court's exercise of its clear power of choice by interposing a constitutional barrier to state efforts to protect human life and by investing mothers and doctors with the constitutionally protected right to exterminate it. This issue, for the most part, should be left with the people and to the political processes the people have devised to govern their affairs.

It is my view, therefore, that the Texas statute is not constitutionally infirm because it denies abortions to those who seek to serve only their convenience rather than to protect their life or health. Nor is this plaintiff, who claims no threat to her mental or physical health, entitled to assert the possible rights of those women whose pregnancy assertedly implicates their health. This, together with *United States* v. *Vuitch*, 402 U.S. 62 (1971), dictates reversal of the judgment of the District Court.

Likewise, because Georgia may constitutionally forbid abortions to putative mothers who, like the plaintiff in this case, do not fall within the reach of § 26–1202 (a) of its criminal code, I have no occasion, and the District Court had none, to consider the constitutionality of the procedural requirements of the Georgia statute as applied to those pregnancies posing substantial hazards to either life or health. I would reverse the judgment of the District Court in the Georgia case. . . .

PLANNED PARENTHOOD OF CENTRAL MISSOURI ET AL. v. DANFORTH, ATTORNEY GENERAL OF MISSOURI, ET AL.

APPEAL FROM THE UNITED STATES DISTRICT COURT FOR THE EASTERN DISTRICT OF MISSOURI

No. 74–1151. Argued March 23, 1976—Decided July 1, 1976

BLACKMUN, J., delivered the opinion of the Court, in which BRENNAN, STEWART, MARSHALL, and POWELL, JJ., joined, in all but Parts IV–D and IV–E of which STEVENS, J., joined, and in all but Parts IV–C, IV–D, IV–E, and IV–G of which BURGER, C. J., and WHITE and REHNQUIST, JJ., joined. STEWART, J., filed a concurring opinion, in which POWELL, J., joined. WHITE, J., filed an opinion concurring in part and dissenting in part, in which BURGER, C. J., and REHNQUIST, J., joined. STEVENS, J., filed an opinion concurring in part and dissenting in part.

MR. JUSTICE BLACKMUN delivered the opinion of the Court.

This case is a logical and anticipated corollary to *Roe* v. *Wade*, 410 U.S. 113 (1973), and *Doe* v. *Bolton*, 410 U.S. 179 (1973), for it raises issues secondary to those that were then before the Court. Indeed, some of the questions now presented were forecast and reserved in *Roe* and *Doe*. 410 U.S., at 165 n. 67.

I

After the decisions in *Roe* and *Doe*, this Court remanded for reconsideration a pending Missouri federal case in which the State's then-existing abortion legislation, Mo. Rev. Stat. §§ 559.100, 542.380, and 563.300 (1969), was under constitutional challenge. *Rodgers* v. *Danforth*, 410 U.S. 949 (1973). A three-judge federal court for the Western District of Missouri, in an unreported decision, thereafter declared the challenged Missouri statutes unconstitutional and granted injunctive relief. On appeal here, that judgment was summarily affirmed. *Danforth* v. *Rodgers*, 414 U.S. 1035 (1973).

In June 1974, somewhat more than a year after *Roe* and *Doe* had been decided, Missouri's 77th General Assembly, in its Second Regular Session, enacted House Committee Substitute for House Bill No. 1211 (hereinafter Act). The legislation was approved by the Governor on June 14, 1974, and became effective immediately by reason of an emergency clause contained in § A of the statute. The Act is set forth in full as the Appendix to this opinion. It imposes a structure for the control and regulation of abortions in Missouri during all stages of pregnancy.

II

Three days after the Act became effective, the present litigation was instituted in the United States District Court for the Eastern District of Missouri. The plaintiffs are Planned Parenthood of Central Missouri, a not-for-profit Missouri corporation which maintains a facility in Columbia, Mo., for the performance of abortions; David Hall, M. D.; and Michael Freiman, M. D. Doctor Hall is a resident of Columbia, is licensed as a physician in Missouri, is chairman of the Department and Professor of Obstetrics and Gynecology at the University of Missouri Medical School at Columbia, and supervises abortions at the Planned Parenthood facility. He was described by the three-judge court in the 1973 case as one of four plaintiffs who were "eminent, Missouri-licensed obstetricians and gynecologists." Jurisdictional Statement, App. 47, in *Danforth* v. *Rodgers*, No. 73–426, O. T. 1973. Doctor Freiman is a resident of St. Louis, is licensed as a physician in Missouri, is an instructor of Clinical Obstetrics and Gynecology at Washington University Medical School, and performs abortions at two St. Louis hospitals and at a clinic in that city.

The named defendants are the Attorney General of Missouri and the Circuit Attorney of the city of St. Louis "in his representative capacity" and "as the representative of the class of all similar Prosecuting Attorneys of the various counties of the State of Missouri." Complaint 10. . . .

IV

With the exception specified in n. 2, *infra*, we agree with the District Court that the physician-appellants clearly have standing. This was established in *Doe* v. *Bolton*, 410 U.S., at 188. Like the Georgia statutes challenged in that case, "[t]he physician is the one against whom [the Missouri Act] directly operate[s] in the event he procures an abortion that does not meet the statutory exceptions and conditions. The physician-appellants, therefore, assert a sufficiently direct threat of personal detriment. They should not be required to await and undergo a criminal prosecution as the sole means of seeking relief." . . . *Ibid.*

Our primary task, then, is to consider each of the challenged provisions of the new Missouri abortion statute in the particular light of the opinions and decisions in *Roe* and in *Doe*. To this we now turn, with the assistance of helpful briefs from both sides and from some of the *amici*.

A

The definition of viability. Section 2 (2) of the Act defines "viability" as "that stage of fetal development when the life of the unborn child may be continued indefinitely outside the womb by natural or artificial life-supportive systems." Appellants claim that this definition violates and conflicts with the discussion of viability in our opinion in *Roe*. 410 U.S., at 160, 163. In particular, appellants object to the failure of the definition to contain any reference to a gestational time period, to its failure to incorporate and reflect the three stages of pregnancy, to the presence of the word "indefinitely," and to the extra burden of regulation imposed. It is suggested that the definition expands the Court's definition of viability, as expressed in *Roe*, and amounts to a legislative determination of what is properly a matter for medical judgment. It is said that the "mere possibility of momentary survival is not the medical standard of viability." Brief for Appellants 67.

In *Roe*, we used the term "viable," properly we thought, to signify the point at which the fetus is "potentially able to live outside the mother's womb, albeit with artificial aid," and presumably capable of "meaningful life outside the mother's womb," 410 U.S., at 160, 163. We noted that this point "is usually placed" at about seven months or 28 weeks, but may occur earlier. *Id.*, at 160.

We agree with the District Court and conclude that the definition of viability in the Act does not conflict with what was said and held in *Roe*. In fact, we believe that § 2 (2), even when read in conjunction with § 5 (proscribing an abortion "not necessary to preserve the life or health of the mother . . . unless the attending physician first certifies with reasonable medical certainty that the fetus is not viable"), the constitutionality of which is not explicitly challenged here, reflects an attempt on the part of the Missouri General Assembly to comply with our observations and discussion in *Roe* relating to viability. Appellant Hall, in his deposition, had no particular difficulty with the statutory definition.[3] As noted above, we recognized in *Roe* that viability was a matter of medical judgment, skill, and technical ability, and we preserved the flexibility of the term. Section 2 (2) does the same. Indeed, one might argue, as the appellees do, that the presence of the statute's words "continued indefinitely" favor, rather than disfavor, the appellants, for, arguably, the point when life can be "continued indefinitely outside the womb" may well occur later in pregnancy than the point where the fetus is "potentially able to live outside the mother's womb." *Roe v. Wade*, 410 U.S., at 160.

In any event, we agree with the District Court that it is not the proper function of the legislature or the courts to place viability, which essentially is a medical concept, at a specific point in the gestation period. The time when viability is achieved may vary with each pregnancy, and the determination of whether a particular fetus is viable is, and must be, a matter for the judgment of the responsible attending physician. The definition of viability in § 2 (2) merely reflects this fact. The appellees do not contend otherwise, for they insist that the determination of viability rests with the physician in the exercise of his professional judgment. . . .

---

3. "[A]lthough I agree with the definition of 'viability,' I think that it must be understood that viability is a very difficult state to assess." Tr. 369.

B

The woman's consent. Under § 3 (2) of the Act, a woman, prior to submitting to an abortion during the first 12 weeks of pregnancy, must certify in writing her consent to the procedure and "that her consent is informed and freely given and is not the result of coercion." Appellants argue that this requirement is violative of *Roe* v. *Wade*, 410 U.S., at 164–165, by imposing an extra layer and burden of regulation on the abortion decision. See *Doe* v. *Bolton*, 410 U.S., at 195–200. Appellants also claim that the provision is overbroad and vague. . . .

. . . It is true that *Doe* and *Roe* clearly establish that the State may not restrict the decision of the patient and her physician regarding abortion during the first stage of pregnancy. Despite the fact that apparently no other Missouri statute, with the exceptions referred to in n. 6, *supra*, requires a patient's prior written consent to a surgical procedure,[7] the imposition by § 3 (2) of such a requirement for termination of pregnancy even during the first stage, in our view, is not in itself an unconstitutional requirement. The decision to abort, indeed, is an important, and often a stressful one, and it is desirable and imperative that it be made with full knowledge of its nature and consequences. The woman is the one primarily concerned, and her awareness of the decision and its significance may be assured, constitutionally, by the State to the extent of requiring her prior written consent. . . .

The spouse's consent. Section 3 (3) requires the prior written consent of the spouse of the woman seeking an abortion during the first 12 weeks of pregnancy, unless "the abortion is certified by a licensed physician to be necessary in order to preserve the life of the mother."[9]

The appellees defend § 3 (3) on the ground that it was enacted in the light of the General Assembly's "perception of marriage as an institution," Brief for Appellee Danforth 34, and that any major change in family status is a decision to be made jointly by the marriage partners. Reference is made to an abortion's possible effect on the woman's childbearing potential. It is said that marriage always has entailed some legislatively imposed limitations: Reference is made to adultery and bigamy as criminal offenses; to Missouri's general requirement, Mo. Rev. Stat. § 453.030.3 (1969), that for an adoption of a child born in wedlock the consent of both parents is necessary; to similar joint-consent requirements imposed by a number of States with respect to artificial insemination and the legitimacy of children so conceived; to the laws of two States requiring spousal consent for voluntary sterilization; and to the long-established requirement of spousal consent for the effective

---

7. There is some testimony in the record to the effect that taking from the patient a prior written consent to surgery is the custom. That may be so in some areas of Missouri, but we definitely refrain from characterizing it extremely as "the universal practice of the medical profession," as the appellees do. Brief for Appellee Danforth 32.

9. It is of some interest to note that the condition does not relate, as most statutory conditions in this area do, to the preservation of the life or *health* of the mother.

disposition of an interest in real property. It is argued that "[r]ecognizing that the consent of both parties is generally necessary . . . to begin a family, the legislature has determined that a change in the family structure set in motion by mutual consent should be terminated only by mutual consent," Brief for Appellee Danforth 38, and that what the legislature did was to exercise its inherent policy-making power "for what was believed to be in the best interests of all the people of Missouri." *Id.*, at 40.

The appellants, on the other hand, contend that § 3 (3) obviously is designed to afford the husband the right unilaterally to prevent or veto an abortion, whether or not he is the father of the fetus, and that this not only violates *Roe* and *Doe* but is also in conflict with other decided cases. See, *e.g.*, *Poe* v. *Gerstein*, 517 F. 2d 787, 794–796 (CA5 1975), appeal docketed, No. 75–713; *Wolfe* v. *Schroering*, 388 F. Supp., at 636–637; *Doe* v. *Rampton*, 366 F. Supp. 189, 193 (Utah 1973). They also refer to the situation where the husband's consent cannot be obtained because he cannot be located. And they assert that § 3 (3) is vague and overbroad.

In *Roe* and *Doe* we specifically reserved decision on the question whether a requirement for consent by the father of the fetus, by the spouse, or by the parents, or a parent, of an unmarried minor, may be constitutionally imposed. 410 U.S., at 165 n. 67. We now hold that the State may not constitutionally require the consent of the spouse, as is specified under § 3 (3) of the Missouri Act, as a condition for abortion during the first 12 weeks of pregnancy. We thus agree with the dissenting judge in the present case, and with the courts whose decisions are cited above, that the State cannot "delegate to a spouse a veto power which the state itself is absolutely and totally prohibited from exercising during the first trimester of pregnancy." 392 F. Supp., at 1375. Clearly, since the State cannot regulate or proscribe abortion during the first stage, when the physician and his patient make that decision, the State cannot delegate authority to any particular person, even the spouse, to prevent abortion during that same period.

We are not unaware of the deep and proper concern and interest that a devoted and protective husband has in his wife's pregnancy and in the growth and development of the fetus she is carrying. Neither has this Court failed to appreciate the importance of the marital relationship in our society. See, *e.g.*, *Griswold* v. *Connecticut*, 381 U.S. 479, 486 (1965); *Maynard* v. *Hill*, 125 U.S. 190, 211 (1888). . . . Moreover, we recognize that the decision whether to undergo or to forgo an abortion may have profound effects on the future of any marriage, effects that are both physical and mental, and possibly deleterious. Notwithstanding these factors, we cannot hold that the State has the constitutional authority to give the spouse unilaterally the ability to prohibit the wife from terminating her pregnancy, when the State itself lacks that right. See *Eisenstadt* v. *Baird*, 405 U.S. 438, 453 (1972).[11]

---

11. As the Court recognized in *Eisenstadt* v. *Baird*, "the marital couple is not an independent entity with a mind and heart of its own, but an association of two individuals each with a separate intellectual and emotional makeup. If the right of privacy means anything, it is the right of the *individual*, married or single, to be free from unwarranted governmental intrusion into matters so fundamentally affecting a person as the decision whether to bear or beget a child." 405 U.S., at 453 (emphasis in original). . . .

It seems manifest that, ideally, the decision to terminate a pregnancy should be one concurred in by both the wife and her husband. No marriage may be viewed as harmonious or successful if the marriage partners are fundamentally divided on so important and vital an issue. But it is difficult to believe that the goal of fostering mutuality and trust in a marriage, and of strengthening the marital relationship and the marriage institution, will be achieved by giving the husband a veto power exercisable for any reason whatsoever or for no reason at all. Even if the State had the ability to delegate to the husband a power it itself could not exercise, it is not at all likely that such action would further, as the District Court majority phrased it, the "interest of the state in protecting the mutuality of decisions vital to the marriage relationship." 392 F. Supp., at 1370.

We recognize, of course, that when a woman, with the approval of her physician but without the approval of her husband, decides to terminate her pregnancy, it could be said that she is acting unilaterally. The obvious fact is that when the wife and the husband disagree on this decision, the view of only one of the two marriage partners can prevail. Inasmuch as it is the woman who physically bears the child and who is the more directly and immediately affected by the pregnancy, as between the two, the balance weighs in her favor. Cf. *Roe* v. *Wade*, 410 U.S., at 153. . . .

D

Parental Consent. Section 3 (4) requires, with respect to the first 12 weeks of pregnancy, where the woman is unmarried and under the age of 18 years, the written consent of a parent or person *in loco parentis* unless, again, "the abortion is certified by a licensed physician as necessary in order to preserve the life of the mother." . . .

We agree with appellants . . . that the State may not impose a blanket provision, such as § 3 (4), requiring the consent of a parent or person *in loco parentis* as a condition for abortion of an unmarried minor during the first 12 weeks of her pregnancy. Just as with the requirement of consent from the spouse, so here, the State does not have the constitutional authority to give a third party an absolute, and possibly arbitrary, veto over the decision of the physician and his patient to terminate the patient's pregnancy, regardless of the reason for withholding the consent.

Constitutional rights do not mature and come into being magically only when one attains the state-defined age of majority. Minors, as well as adults, are protected by the Constitution and possess constitutional rights. See, *e.g.*, *Breed* v. *Jones*, 421 U.S. 519 (1975); *Goss* v. *Lopez*, 419 U.S. 565 (1975); *Tinker* v. *Des Moines School Dist.*, 393 U.S. 503 (1969); *In re Gault*, 387 U.S. 1 (1967). The Court indeed, however, long has recognized that the State has somewhat broader authority to regulate the activities of children than of adults. *Prince* v. *Massachusetts*, 321 U.S., at 170; *Ginsberg* v. *New York*, 390 U.S. 629 (1968). It remains, then, to examine whether there is any significant state interest in conditioning an abortion on the consent of a parent or person *in loco parentis* that is not present in the case of an adult.

One suggested interest is the safeguarding of the family unit and of parental authority. 392 F. Supp., at 1370. It is difficult, however, to conclude that providing a parent with absolute power to overrule a determination, made by the physician and his minor patient, to terminate the patient's pregnancy will serve to strengthen the family unit. Neither is it likely that such veto power will enhance parental authority or control where the minor and the nonconsenting parent are so fundamentally in conflict and the very existence of the pregnancy already has fractured the family structure. Any independent interest the parent may have in the termination of the minor daughter's pregnancy is no more weighty than the right of privacy of the competent minor mature enough to have become pregnant.

We emphasize that our holding that § 3 (4) is invalid does not suggest that every minor, regardless of age or maturity, may give effective consent for termination of her pregnancy. See *Bellotti* v. *Baird*. The fault with § 3 (4) is that it imposes a special-consent provision, exercisable by a person other than the woman and her physician, as a prerequisite to a minor's termination of her pregnancy and does so without a sufficient justification for the restriction. It violates the strictures of *Roe* and *Doe*.

E

Saline amniocentesis. Section 9 of the statute prohibits the use of saline amniocentesis, as a method or technique of abortion, after the first 12 weeks of pregnancy. It describes the method as one whereby the amniotic fluid is withdrawn and "a saline or other fluid" is inserted into the amniotic sac. The statute imposes this proscription on the ground that the technique "is deleterious to maternal health," and places it in the form of a legislative finding. . . .

We held in *Roe* that after the first stage, "the State, in promoting its interest in the health of the mother, may, if it chooses, regulate the abortion procedure in ways that are reasonably related to maternal health." 410 U.S., at 164. The question with respect to § 9 therefore is whether the flat prohibition of saline amniocentesis is a restriction which "reasonably relates to the preservation and protection of maternal health." . . .

. . . The State, through § 9, would prohibit the use of a method which the record shows is the one most commonly used nationally by physicians after the first trimester and which is safer, with respect to maternal mortality, than even continuation of the pregnancy until normal childbirth. Moreover, as a practical matter, it forces a woman and her physician to terminate her pregnancy by methods more dangerous to her health than the method outlawed.

As so viewed, particularly in the light of the present unavailability—as demonstrated by the record—of the prostaglandin technique, the outright legislative proscription of saline fails as a reasonable regulation for the protection of maternal health. It comes into focus, instead, as an unreasonable or arbitrary regulation designed to inhibit, and having the effect of inhibiting, the vast majority of abortions after the first 12 weeks. As such, it does not withstand constitutional challenge. See *Wolfe* v. *Schroering*, 388 F. Supp., at 637.

MR. JUSTICE WHITE, with whom THE CHIEF JUSTICE and MR. JUSTICE REHNQUIST join, concurring in part and dissenting in part.

In *Roe* v. *Wade*, 410 U.S. 113 (1973), this Court recognized a right to an abortion free from state prohibition. The task of policing this limitation on state police power is and will be a difficult and continuing venture in substantive due process. However, even accepting *Roe* v. *Wade*, there is nothing in the opinion in that case and nothing articulated in the Court's opinion in this case which justifies the invalidation of four provisions of House Committee Substitute for House Bill No. 1211 (hereafter Act) enacted by the Missouri 77th General Assembly in 1974 in response to *Roe* v. *Wade*. Accordingly, I dissent, in part.

I

Roe v. *Wade* holds that until a fetus becomes viable, the interest of the State in the life or potential life it represents is outweighed by the interest of the mother in choosing "whether or not to terminate her pregnancy." 410 U.S., at 153. Section 3 (3) of the Act provides that a married woman may not obtain an abortion without her husband's consent. The Court strikes down this statute in one sentence. It says that "since the State cannot . . . proscribe abortion . . . the State cannot delegate authority to any particular person, even the spouse, to prevent abortion. . . ." *Ante*, at 69. But the State is not—under § 3 (3)—delegating to the husband the power to vindicate the *State's* interest in the future life of the fetus. It is instead recognizing that the husband has an interest of his own in the life of the fetus which should not be extinguished by the unilateral decision of the wife.[1] It by no means follows, from the fact that the mother's interest in deciding "whether or not to terminate her pregnancy" outweighs the *State's* interest in the potential life of the fetus, that the husband's interest is also outweighed and may not be protected by the State.

---

1. There are countless situations in which the State prohibits conduct only when it is objected to by a private person most closely affected by it. Thus a State cannot forbid anyone to enter on private property with the owner's consent, but it may enact and enforce trespass laws against unauthorized entrances. It cannot forbid transfer of property held in tenancy by the entireties but it may require consent by both husband and wife to such a transfer. These situations plainly do not involve delegations of legislative power to private parties; and neither does the requirement in §3 (3) that a woman not deprive her husband of his future child without his consent.

A father's interest in having a child—perhaps his only child—may be unmatched by any other interest in his life. See *Stanley* v. *Illinois*, 405 U.S. 645, 651 (1972), and cases there cited. It is truly surprising that the majority finds in the United States Constitution, as it must in order to justify the result it reaches, a rule that the State must assign a greater value to a mother's decision to cut off a potential human life by abortion than to a father's decision to let it mature into a live child. Such a rule cannot be found there, nor can it be found in *Roe* v. *Wade, supra*. These are matters which a State should be able to decide free from the suffocating power of the federal judge, purporting to act in the name of the Constitution.

In describing the nature of a mother's interest in terminating a pregnancy, the Court in *Roe* v. *Wade* mentioned only the post-birth burdens of rearing a child, 410 U.S., at 153, and rejected a rule based on her interest in controlling her own body during pregnancy. *Id.*, at 154. Missouri has a law which prevents a woman from putting a child up for adoption over her husband's objection, Mo. Rev. Stat. § 453.030 (1969). This law represents a judgment by the State that the mother's interest in avoiding the burdens of child rearing do not outweigh or snuff out the father's interest in participating in bringing up his own child. That law is plainly valid, but no more so than § 3 (3) of the Act now before us, resting as it does on precisely the same judgment.

II

Section 3 (4) requires that an unmarried woman under 18 years of age obtain the consent of a parent or a person *in loco parentis* as a condition to an abortion. Once again the Court strikes the provision down in a sentence. It states: "Just as with the requirement of consent from the spouse, so here, the State does not have the constitutional authority to give a third party an absolute, and possibly arbitrary, veto over the decision of the physician and his patient to terminate the patient's pregnancy. . . ." The Court rejects the notions that the *State* has an interest in strengthening the family unit, or that the *parent* has an "independent interest" in the abortion decision, sufficient to justify § 3 (4) and apparently concludes that the provision is therefore unconstitutional. But the purpose of the parental-consent requirement is not merely to vindicate any interest of the parent or of the State. The purpose of the requirement is to vindicate the very right created in *Roe* v. *Wade, supra*—the right of the pregnant woman to decide "whether or *not* to terminate her pregnancy." 410 U.S., at 153 (emphasis added). The abortion decision is unquestionably important and has irrevocable consequences whichever way it is made. Missouri is entitled to protect the minor unmarried woman from making the decision in a way which is not in her own best interests, and it seeks to achieve this goal by requiring parental consultation and consent. This is the traditional way by which States have sought to protect children from their own immature and improvident decisions; . . . and there is absolutely no reason expressed by the majority why the State may not utilize that method here.

III

Section 9 of the Act prohibits abortion by the method known as saline amniocentesis—a method used at the time the Act was passed for 70% of abortions performed after the first trimester. Legislative history reveals that the Missouri Legislature viewed saline amniocentesis as far less safe a method of abortion than the so-called prostaglandin method. The court below took evidence on the question and summarized it as follows:

> "The record of trial discloses that use of the saline method exposes a woman to the danger of severe complications, regardless of the skill of the physician or the precaution taken. Saline may cause one or more of the following conditions: Disseminated intravascular coagulation or 'consumptive coagulapathy' (disruption of the blood clotting mechanism [Dr. Warren, Tr. 57–58; Dr. Klaus, Tr. 269–270; Dr. Anderson, Tr. 307; Defts' Exs. H & M]), which may result in severe bleeding and possibly death (Dr. Warren, Tr. 58); hypernatremia (increase in blood sodium level), which may lead to convulsions and death (Dr. Klaus, Tr. 268); and water intoxication (accumulated water in the body tissue which may occur when oxytoxin [*sic*] is used in conjunction with the injection of saline), resulting in damage to the central nervous system or death (Dr. Warren, Tr. 76; Dr. Klaus, Tr. 270–271; Dr. Anderson, Tr. 310; Defts' Ex. L). There is also evidence that saline amniocentesis causes massive tissue destruction to the inside of the uterus (Dr. Anderson, Tr. 308)." 392 F. Supp. 1362, 1372–1373 (1975).

The District Court also cited considerable evidence establishing that the prostaglandin method is safer. In fact, the Chief of Obstetrics at Yale University, Dr. Anderson, suggested that "physicians should be liable for malpractice if they chose saline over prostaglandin after having been given all the facts on both methods." *Id.*, at 1373. The Court nevertheless reverses the decision of the District Court sustaining § 9 against constitutional challenge. It does so apparently because saline amniocentesis was widely used before the Act was passed; because the prostaglandin method was seldom used and was not generally available; and because other abortion techniques more dangerous than saline amniocentesis were not banned. At bottom the majority's holding—as well as the concurrence—rests on its *factual* finding that the prostaglandin method is unavailable to the women of Missouri. It therefore concludes that the ban on the saline method is "an unreasonable or arbitrary regulation designed to inhibit, and having the effect of inhibiting, the vast majority of abortions after the first 12 weeks," *ante*, at 79. This factual finding was not made either by the majority or by the dissenting judge below. Appellants have not argued that the record below supports such a finding. In fact the record below does not support such a finding. There is *no* evidence in the record that women in Missouri will be unable to obtain abortions by the prostaglandin method. What evidence there is in the record on this question supports the contrary conclusion.[3] The record discloses that the prostaglandin method of abortion was the country's second most common method of abortion during the second trimester, Tr. 42, 89–90; that although the prostaglandin method had previously been available only on an experimental basis, it was, at the time of trial available in "small hospitals all over the country," *id.*, at 342; that in another year or so the prostaglandin method would become—even in the absence of legislation on the subject—the most prevalent method. Anderson deposition, at 69. Moreover, one doctor quite sensibly testified that if the saline method were banned, hospitals would quickly switch to the prostaglandin method.

The majority relies on the testimony of one doctor that—as already noted—prostaglandin had been available on an experimental basis only until January 1, 1974; and that its manufacturer, the Upjohn Co., restricted its sales to large medical centers for the following six months, after which sales were to be unrestricted. Tr. 334–335. In what manner this evidence supports the proposition that prostaglandin is unavailable to the women of Missouri escapes me. . . .

The only other basis for its factual finding which the majority offers is a citation to *another* case—*Wolfe* v. *Schroering*, 388 F. Supp. 631, 637 (WD Ky. 1974)—in which a different court concluded that the record in its case showed the prostaglandin method to be unavailable in another State—Kentucky—at another time—two years ago. This case must be decided on its own record. I am not yet prepared to accept the notion that normal rules of law, procedure, and constitutional adjudication suddenly become irrelevant solely because a case touches on the subject of abortion. The majority's finding of fact that women in Missouri will be unable to obtain abortions after the first trimester if the saline method is banned is wholly unjustifiable. . . .

IV

In my opinion, . . . the parental-consent requirement is consistent with the holding in *Roe*. The State's interest in the welfare of its young citizens justifies a variety of protective measures. Because he may not foresee the consequences of his decision, a minor may not make an enforceable bargain. He may not lawfully work or travel where he pleases, or even attend exhibitions of constitutionally protected adult motion pictures. Persons below a certain age may not marry without parental consent. Indeed, such consent is essential even when the young woman is already pregnant. The State's interest in protecting a young

---

3. The absence of more evidence on the subject in the record seems to be a result of the fact that the claim that the prostaglandin method is unavailable was not part of plaintiffs' litigating strategy below.

person from harm justifies the imposition of restraints on his or her freedom even though comparable restraints on adults would be constitutionally impermissible. Therefore, the holding in *Roe* v. *Wade* that the abortion decision is entitled to constitutional protection merely emphasizes the importance of the decision; it does not lead to the conclusion that the state legislature has no power to enact legislation for the purpose of protecting a young pregnant woman from the consequences of an incorrect decision.

The abortion decision is, of course, more important than the decision to attend or to avoid an adult motion picture, or the decision to work long hours in a factory. It is not necessarily any more important than the decision to run away from home or the decision to marry. But even if it is the most important kind of a decision a young person may ever make, that assumption merely enhances the quality of the State's interest in maximizing the probability that the decision be made correctly and with full understanding of the consequences of either alternative. . . .

SINGLETON, CHIEF, BUREAU OF MEDICAL SERVICES, DEPARTMENT OF HEALTH AND WELFARE OF MISSOURI *v.* WULFF ET AL.

CERTIORARI TO THE UNITED STATES COURT OF APPEALS FOR THE EIGHTH CIRCUIT

No. 74–1393. Argued March 23, 1976—Decided July 1, 1976

[This litigation concerned the constitutionality of a Missouri statute that denied Medicaid funding for abortions that are not "medically indicated." At issue was not only the constitutionality of the statute, but whether or not physicians had standing to bring suits of this kind. The Court did not decide the substantive question, on the grounds that it had not been properly presented in the courts below, but it did deal with the issue of physicians' standing in abortion litigation.]

BLACKMUN, J., announced the judgment of the Court and delivered an opinion of the Court with respect to Parts I, II–A, and III, in which all Members joined, and in which, as to Part II–B, BRENNAN, WHITE, and MARSHALL, JJ., joined. STEVENS, J., filed an opinion concurring in part, *post*, p 121. POWELL, J., filed an opinion concurring in part and dissenting in part, in which BURGER, C. J., and STEWART and REHNQUIST, JJ., joined, *post*, p. 122.

MR. JUSTICE BLACKMUN delivered the opinion of the Court (Parts I, II–A, and III) together with an opinion (Part II–B), in which MR. JUSTICE BRENNAN, MR. JUSTICE WHITE, and MR. JUSTICE MARSHALL joined.

I

. . . The closeness of the relationship is patent, as it was in *Griswold* and in *Doe*. A woman cannot safely secure an abortion without the aid of a physician, and an impecunious woman cannot easily secure an abortion without the physician's being paid by the State. The woman's exercise of her right to an abortion, whatever its dimension, is therefore necessarily at stake here. Moreover, the constitutionally protected abortion decision is one in which the physician is intimately involved. See *Roe* v. *Wade*, 410 U.S., at 153–156. Aside from the woman herself, therefore, the physician is uniquely qualified to litigate the constitutionality of the State's interference with, or discrimination against, that decision.

As to the woman's assertion of her own rights, there are several obstacles. For one thing, she may be chilled from such assertion by a desire to protect the very privacy of her decision from the publicity of a court suit. A second obstacle is the imminent mootness, at least in the technical sense, of any individual woman's claim. Only a few months, at the most, after the maturing of the decision to undergo an abortion, her right thereto will have been irrevocably lost, assuming, as it seems fair to assume, that unless the impecunious woman can establish Medicaid eligibility she must forgo abortion. It is true that these obstacles are not insurmountable. Suit may be brought under a pseudonym, as so frequently has been done. A woman who is no longer pregnant may nonetheless retain the right to litigate the point because it is "'capable of repetition yet evading review.'" *Roe* v. *Wade*, 410 U.S., at 124–125. And it may be that a class could be assembled, whose fluid membership always included some women with live claims. But if the assertion of the right is to be "representative" to such an extent anyway, there seems little loss in terms of effective advocacy from allowing its assertion by a physician.

For these reasons, we conclude that it generally is appropriate to allow a physician to assert the rights of women patients as against governmental interference with the abortion decision, and we decline to restrict our holding to that effect in *Doe* to its purely criminal context. . . .

MR. JUSTICE POWELL, with whom THE CHIEF JUSTICE, MR. JUSTICE STEWART, and MR. JUSTICE REHNQUIST join, concurring in part and dissenting in part.

The Court holds that the respondents have standing to bring this suit and to assert their own constitutional rights, if any, in an attack on Mo. Rev. Stat. § 208.152 (12) (Supp. 1975). The Court also holds that the Court of Appeals erred in proceeding to the merits of respondents' challenge. I agree with both of these holdings and therefore concur in Parts I, II–A, and III of JUSTICE BLACKMUN's opinion, as well as in the first four sentences of Part II–B.

The Court further holds that after remand to the District Court the respondents may assert, in addition to their own rights, the constitutional rights of their patients who would be eligible for Medicaid assistance in obtaining elective abortions but for the exclusion of such abortions in §208.152(12). I dissent from this holding. . . .

. . . The usual—and wise—stance of the federal courts when policing their own exercise of power . . . is one of cautious reserve. See generally *Ashwander* v. *TVA*, 297 U.S. 288, 346–348 (1936) (Brandeis, J., concurring). This caution has given rise to the general rule that a party may not defend against or attack governmental action on the ground that it infringes the rights of some third party, and to the corollary that any exception must rest on specific factors outweighing the policies behind the rule itself. . . . See *Barrows* v. *Jackson*, 346 U.S. 249, 257 (1953); cf. generally *United States* v. *Richardson*, 418 U.S. 166, 188–197 (1974) (POWELL, J., concurring).

The plurality acknowledges this general rule, but identifies "two factual elements"—thought to be derived from prior cases—that justify the adjudication of the asserted third-party rights: (i) obstacles to the assertion by the third party of her own rights, and (ii) the existence of some "relationship" such as the one between physician and patient. In my view these factors do not justify allowing these physicians to assert their patients' rights.

A

Our prior decisions are enlightening. In *Barrows* v. *Jackson, supra*, a covenantor who breached a racially restrictive covenant by selling to Negroes was permitted to set up the buyers' rights to equal protection in defense against a damages action by the covenantees. See *Shelley* v. *Kracmer*, 334 U.S. 1 (1948). The Court considered the general rule outweighed by "the need to protect [these] fundamental rights" in a situation "in which it would be difficult if not impossible for the persons whose rights are asserted to present their grievance before any court." 346 U.S., at 257. It would indeed have been difficult if not impossible for the rightholders to assert their own rights: the operation of the restrictive covenant and the threat of damages actions for its breach tended to insure they would not come into possession of the land, and there was at the time little chance of a successful suit based on a covenantor's failure to sell to them. In a second case, *NAACP* v. *Alabama*, 357 U.S. 449 (1958), an organization was allowed to resist an order to produce its membership list by asserting the associational rights of its members to anonymity because, as the plurality notes, *ante*, at 116, the members themselves would have had to forgo the rights in order to assert them. And in *Eisenstadt* v. *Baird*, 405 U.S. 438 (1972), the Court considered it necessary to relax the rule and permit a distributor of contraceptives to assert the constitutional rights of the recipients because the statutory scheme operating to deny the contraceptives to the recipients appeared to offer them no means of challenge. *Id.*, at 446.

The plurality purports to derive from these cases the principle that a party may assert another's rights if there is "some genuine obstacle" to the third party's own litigation. But this understates the teaching of those cases: On their facts they indicate that such an assertion is proper, not when there is merely some "obstacle" to the rightholder's own litigation, but when such litigation is in all practicable terms impossible. Thus, in its framing of this principle, the plurality has gone far beyond our major precedents. . . .

B

The plurality places primary reliance on a second element, the existence of a "confidential relationship" between the rightholder and the party seeking to assert her rights.[5]

---

[5]. The plurality's primary emphasis upon this relationship is in marked contrast to the Court's previous position that the relationship between litigant and rightholder was subordinate in importance to "the impact of the litigation on the third-party interests." *Eisenstadt* v. *Baird*, 405 U.S. 438, 445 (1972). I suspect the plurality's inversion of the previous order results from the weakness of the argument that this litigation is necessary to protect third-party interests. I would keep the emphasis where it has been before, and would consider the closeness of any "relationship" only as a factor imparting confidence that third-party interests will be represented adequately in a case in which allowing their assertion is justified on other grounds. Cf. n. 2, *supra*.

Focusing on the professional relationships present in *Griswold*, *Doe* and *Planned Parenthood of Missouri* v. *Danforth, ante*, p. 52, the plurality suggests that allowing the physicians in this case to assert their patients' rights flows naturally from those three. Indeed, its conclusion is couched in terms of the general appropriateness of allowing physicians to assert the privacy interests of their patients in attacks on "governmental interference with the abortion decision."

With all respect, I do not read these cases as merging the physician and his patient for constitutional purposes. The principle they support turns not upon the confidential nature of a physician-patient relationship but upon the nature of the State's impact upon that relationship. In each instance the State directly interdicted the normal functioning of the physician-patient relationship by criminalizing certain procedures. In the circumstances of direct interference, I agree that one party to the relationship should be permitted to assert the constitutional rights of the other, for a judicial rule of self-restraint should not preclude an attack on a State's proscription of constitutionally protected activity. See also *Meyer* v. *Nebraska*, 262 U.S. 390 (1923). But Missouri has not directly interfered with the abortion decision—neither the physicians nor their patients are forbidden to engage in the procedure.... The only impact of § 208.152 (12) is that, because of the way Missouri chose to structure its Medicaid payments, it causes these doctors financial detriment. This affords them Art. III standing because they aver injury in fact, but it does not justify abandonment of the salutary rule against assertion of third-party rights....

BEAL, SECRETARY, DEPARTMENT OF PUBLIC WELFARE OF PENNSYLVANIA, ET AL. *v.* DOE ET AL.

CERTIORARI TO THE UNITED STATES COURT OF APPEALS FOR THE THIRD CIRCUIT

No. 75–554. Argued January 11, 1977—Decided June 20, 1977

POWELL, J., delivered the opinion of the Court, in which BURGER, C. J., and STEWART, WHITE, REHNQUIST, and STEVENS, JJ., joined. BRENNAN, J., filed a dissenting opinion, in which MARSHALL and BLACKMUN, JJ., joined. MARSHALL, J., filed a dissenting opinion. BLACKMUN, J., filed a dissenting opinion, in which BRENNAN and MARSHALL, JJ., joined.

MR. JUSTICE POWELL delivered the opinion of the Court.

The issue in this case is whether Title XIX of the Social Security Act, as added, 79 Stat. 343, and amended, 42 U.S. C. § 1396 *et seq.* (1970 ed. and Supp. V), requires States that participate in the Medical Assistance (Medicaid) program to fund the cost of non-therapeutic abortions. . . .

The only question before us is one of statutory construction: whether Title XIX requires Pennsylvania to fund under its Medicaid program the cost of *all* abortions that are permissible under state law. "The starting point in every case involving construction of a statute is the language itself." *Blue Chip Stamps* v. *Manor Drug Stores,* 421 U.S. 723, 756 (1975) (POWELL, J., concurring). Title XIX makes no reference to abortions, or, for that matter, to any other particular medical procedure. Instead, the statute is cast in terms that require participating States to provide financial assistance with respect to five broad categories of medical treatment. See n. 2, *supra.* But nothing in the statute suggests that participating States are required to fund every medical procedure that falls within the delineated categories of medical care. Indeed, the statute expressly provides:

"A State plan for medical assistance must . . . include reasonable standards . . . for determining eligibility for and the extent of medical assistance under the plan which . . . are consistent with the objectives of this [Title]. . . ." 42 U.S. C. § 1396a (a) (17) (1970 ed., Supp. V).

This language confers broad discretion on the States to adopt standards for determining the extent of medical assistance, requiring only that such standards be "reasonable" and "consistent with the objectives" of the Act. . . .

Pennsylvania's regulation comports fully with Title XIX's broadly stated primary objective to enable each State, as far as practicable, to furnish medical assistance to individuals whose income and resources are insufficient to meet the costs of necessary medical services. See 42 U. S. C. §§ 1396, 1396a (10) (C) (1970 ed., Supp. V). Although serious statutory questions might be presented if a state Medicaid plan excluded necessary medical treatment from its coverage, it is hardly inconsistent with the objectives of the Act for a State to refuse to fund *unnecessary*—though perhaps desirable—medical services. . . .

Our interpretation of the statute is reinforced by two other relevant considerations. First, when Congress passed Title XIX in 1965, nontherapeutic abortions were unlawful in most States. . . . In view of the then-prevailing state law, the contention that Congress intended to require—rather than permit—participating States to fund nontherapeutic abortions requires far more convincing proof than respondents have offered. Second, the Department of Health, Education, and Welfare, the agency charged with the administration of this complicated statute, . . . takes the position that Title XIX allows—but does not mandate—funding for such abortions. "[W]e must be mindful that 'the construction of a statute by those charged with its execution should be followed unless there are compelling indications that it is wrong. . . .'" *New York Dept. of Soc. Services* v. *Dublino*, 413 U.S. 405, 421 (1973), quoting *Red Lion Broadcasting Co.* v. *FCC*, 395 U.S. 367, 381 (1969). Here, such indications are completely absent.

We therefore hold that Pennsylvania's refusal to extend Medicaid coverage to nontherapeutic abortions is not inconsistent with Title XIX. . . . We make clear, however, that the federal statute leaves a State free to provide such coverage if it so desires. . . .

Mr. Justice Brennan, with whom Mr. Justice Marshall and Mr. Justice Blackmun join, dissenting.

The Court holds that the "necessary medical services" which Pennsylvania must fund for individuals eligible for Medicaid do not include services connected with elective abortions. I dissent.

Though the question presented by this case is one of statutory interpretation, a difficult constitutional question would be raised where Title XIX of the Social Security Act, as amended, 42 U. S. C. § 1396 *et seq.* (1970 ed. and Supp. V), is read not to require funding of elective abortions. *Maher* v. *Roe, post,* p. 464; *Doe* v. *Bolton*, 410 U.S. 179 (1973); *Roe* v. *Wade*, 410 U.S. 113 (1973). Since the Court should "first ascertain whether a construction of the statute is fairly possible by which the [constitutional] question may be avoided," *Ashwander* v. *TVA*, 297 U.S. 288, 341, 348 (1936) (Brandeis, J., concurring); see *Westby* v. *Doe*, 420 U.S. 968 (1975), Title XIX, in my view, read fairly in light of the principle of avoidance of unnecessary constitutional decisions, requires agreement with the Court of Appeals that the legislative history of Title XIX and our abortion cases compel the conclusion that elective abortions constitute medically necessary treatment for the condition of pregnancy. I would therefore find that Title XIX requires that Pennsylvania pay the costs of elective abortions for women who are eligible participants in the Medicaid program.

Pregnancy is unquestionably a condition requiring medical services. See *Roe* v. *Norton*, 380 F. Supp. 726, 729 (Conn. 1974); *Klein* v. *Nassau County Medical Center*, 347 F. Supp. 496, 500 (EDNY 1972), vacated for further consideration (in light of *Roe* v. *Wade* and *Doe* v. *Bolton*), 412 U.S. 925 (1973). Treatment for the condition may involve medical procedures for its termination, or medical procedures to bring the pregnancy to term, resulting in a live birth. "[A]bortion and childbirth, when stripped of the sensitive moral arguments surrounding the abortion controversy, are simply two alternative medical methods of dealing with pregnancy. . . ." *Roe* v. *Norton*, 408 F. Supp. 660, 663 n. 3 (Conn. 175). The Medicaid statutes leave the decision as to choice among pregnancy procedures exclusively with the doctor and his patient, and make no provision whatever for intervention by the State in that decision. Section 1396a (a) (19) expressly imposes the obligation upon participating States to incorporate safeguards in their programs that assure medical "care and services will be provided, in a manner consistent with . . . the best interests of the recipients." And, significantly, the Senate Finance Committee Report on the Medicaid bill expressly stated that the "physician is to be the key figure in determining utilization of health services." S. Rep. No. 404, 89th Cong., 1st Sess., 46 (1965). Thus the very heart of the congressional scheme is that the physician and patient should have complete freedom to choose those medical procedures for a given condition which are best suited to the needs of the patient. . . .

If Pennsylvania is not obligated to fund medical services rendered in performing elective abortions because they are not "necessary" within the meaning of 42 U. S. C. § 1396 (1970 ed., Supp. V), it must follow that Pennsylvania also would not violate the statute if it refused to fund medical services for "therapeutic" abortions or live births. For if the availability of therapeutic abortions and live births makes elective abortions "unnecessary," the converse must also be true. This highlights the violence done the congressional mandate by today's decision. If the State must pay the costs of therapeutic abortions and of live birth as constituting medically necessary responses to the condition of pregnancy, it must, under the command of § 1396, also pay the costs of elective abortions; the procedures in each case constitute necessary medical treatment for the condition of pregnancy.

The 1972 family-planning amendment to the Act, 42 U. S. C. § 1396d (a) (4) (c) (1970 ed., Supp. V), buttresses my conclusion that the Court's construction frustrates the objectives of the Medicaid program. Section 1396 (2) states that an explicit purpose of Medicaid is to assist eligible indigent recipients to "attain or retain capability for independence or self-care." The 1972 amendment furthered this objective by assisting those who "desire to control family size in order to enhance their capacity and ability to seek employment and better meet family needs." S. Rep. No. 92–1230, p. 297 (1972). Though far less than an ideal family-planning mechanism, elective abortions are one method for limiting family size and avoiding the financial and emotional problems that are the daily lot of the impoverished. See Special Subcommittee on Human Resources of the Senate Committee on Labor and Public Welfare, 92d Cong., 1st Sess., Report of the Secretary of

Health, Education, and Welfare Submitting Five-Year Plan for Family Planning Services and Population Research Programs 319 (Comm. Print 1971).

Mr. Justice Blackmun, with whom Mr. Justice Brennan and Mr. Justice Marshall join, dissenting.*

The Court today, by its decisions in these cases, allows the States, and such municipalities as choose to do so, to accomplish indirectly what the Court in *Roe* v. *Wade*, 410 U.S. 113 (1973), and *Doe* v. *Bolton*, 410 U.S. 179 (1973)—by a substantial majority and with some emphasis, I had thought—said they could not do directly. The Court concedes the existence of a constitutional right but denies the realization and enjoyment of that right on the ground that existence and realization are separate and distinct. For the individual woman concerned, indigent and financially helpless, as the Court's opinions in the three cases concede her to be, the result is punitive and tragic. Implicit in the Court's holdings is the condescension that she may go elsewhere for her abortion. I find that disingenuous and alarming, almost reminiscent of: "Let them eat cake."

The result the Court reaches is particularly distressing in *Poelker* v. *Doe*, where a presumed majority, in electing as mayor one whom the record shows campaigned on the issue of closing public hospitals to nontherapeutic abortions, punitively impresses upon a needy minority its own concepts of the socially desirable, the publicly acceptable, and the morally sound, with a touch of the devil-take-the-hindmost. This is not the kind of thing for which our Constitution stands.

The Court's financial argument, of course, is specious. To be sure, welfare funds are limited and welfare must be spread perhaps as best meets the community's concept of its needs. But the cost of a nontherapeutic abortion is far less than the cost of maternity care and delivery, and holds no comparison whatsoever with the welfare costs that will burden the State for the new indigents and their support in the long, long years ahead.

Neither is it an acceptable answer, as the Court well knows, to say that the Congress and the States are free to authorize the use of funds for nontherapeutic abortions. Why should any politician incur the demonstrated wrath and noise of the abortion opponents when mere silence and non-activity accomplish the results the opponents want?

There is another world "out there," the existence of which the Court, I suspect, either chooses to ignore or fears to recognize. And so the cancer of poverty will continue to grow. This is a sad day for those who regard the Constitution as a force that would serve justice to all evenhandedly and, in so doing, would better the lot of the poorest among us.

---

*[This opinion applies also to No. 75–1440, *Maher, Commissioner of Social Services of Connecticut* v. *Roe et al.*, *post*, p. 464, and No. 75–442, *Poelker, Mayor of St. Louis, et al.* v. *Doe*, *post*, p. 519.]

MAHER, COMMISSIONER OF SOCIAL SERVICES OF CONNECTICUT *v.* ROE ET AL.

APPEAL FROM THE UNITED STATES DISTRICT COURT FOR THE DISTRICT OF CONNECTICUT

No. 75–1140. Argued January 11, 1977—Decided June 20, 1977

Powell, J., delivered the opinion of the Court, in which Burger, C. J., and Stewart, White, Rehnquist, and Stevens, JJ., joined. Burger, C. J., filed a concurring statement. Brennan, J., filed a dissenting opinion, in which Marshall and Blackmun, JJ., joined. Marshall, J., filed a dissenting opinion. Blackmun, J., filed a dissenting opinion, in which Brennan and Marshall, JJ., joined.

I

A regulation of the Connecticut Welfare Department limits state Medicaid benefits for first trimester abortions[1] to those that are "medically necessary," a term defined to include psychiatric necessity. Connecticut Welfare Department, Public Assistance Program Manual, Vol. 3, c. III, § 275 (1975).[2] Connecticut enforces this limitation through a system of prior authorization from its Department of Social Services. In order to obtain authorization for a first trimester abortion, the hospital or clinic where the abortion is to be performed must submit, among other things, a certificate from the patient's attending physician stating that the abortion is medically necessary.

---

1. The procedures governing abortions beyond the first trimester are not challenged here.

2. Section 275 provides in relevant part:
"The Department makes payment for abortion services under the Medical Assistance (Title XIX) Program when the following conditions are met:
"1. In the opinion of the attending physician the abortion is medically necessary. The term 'Medically Necessary' includes psychiatric necessity
"2. The abortion is to be performed in an accredited hospital or licensed clinic when the patient is in the first trimester of pregnancy. . . .
"3. The written request for the abortion is submitted by the patient, and in the case of a minor, from the parent or guardian.

. . . . .

"4. Prior authorization for the abortion is secured from the Chief of Medical Services, Division of Health Services, Department of Social Services."
See n. 4, *infra*.

This attack on the validity of the Connecticut regulation was brought against appellant Maher, the Commissioner of Social Services, by appellees Poe and Roe, two indigent women who were unable to obtain a physician's certificate of medical necessity.[3] In a complaint filed in the United States District Court for the District of Connecticut, they challenged the regulation both as inconsistent with the requirements of Title XIX of the Social Security Act, as added, 79 Stat. 343, as amended, 42 U.S. C. § 1396 *et seq.* (1970 ed. Supp. V), and as violative of their constitutional rights, including the Fourteenth Amendment's guarantees of due process and equal protection. . . .

II

The Constitution imposes no obligation on the States to pay the pregnancy-related medical expenses of indigent women, or indeed to pay any of the medical expenses of indigents. . . . But when a State decides to alleviate some of the hardships of poverty by providing medical care, the manner in which it dispenses benefits is subject to constitutional limitations. Appellees' claim is that Connecticut must accord equal treatment to both abortion and childbirth, and may not evidence a policy preference by funding only the medical expenses incident to childbirth. This challenge to the classifications established by the Connecticut regulation presents a question arising under the Equal Protection Clause of the Fourteenth Amendment. The basic framework of analysis of such a claim is well settled:

> "We must decide, first, whether [state legislation] operates to the disadvantage of some suspect class or impinges upon a fundamental right explicitly or implicitly protected by the Constitution, thereby requiring strict judicial scrutiny. . . . If not, the [legislative] scheme must still be examined to determine whether it rationally furthers some legitimate, articulated state purpose and therefore does not constitute an invidious discrimination. . . ." *San Antonio School Dist.* v. *Rodriguez*, 411 U.S. 1, 17 (1973).

Accord, *Massachusetts Bd. of Retirement* v. *Murgia*, 427 U.S. 307, 312, 314 (1976). Applying this analysis here, we think the District Court erred in holding that the Connecticut regulation violated the Equal Protection Clause of the Fourteenth Amendment.

---

3. At the time this action was filed, Mary Poe, a 16-year-old high school junior, had already obtained an abortion at a Connecticut hospital. Apparently because of Poe's inability to obtain a certificate of medical necessity, the hospital was denied reimbursement by the Department of Social Services. As a result, Poe was being pressed to pay the hospital bill of $244. Susan Roe, an unwed mother of three children, was unable to obtain an abortion because of her physician's refusal to certify that the procedure was medically necessary. By consent, a temporary restraining order was entered by the District Court enjoining the Connecticut officials from refusing to pay for Roe's abortion. After the remand from the Court of Appeals, the District Court issued temporary restraining orders covering three additional women. *Roe* v. *Norton*, 408 F. Supp. 660, 663 (1975).

A

This case involves no discrimination against a suspect class. An indigent woman desiring an abortion does not come within the limited category of disadvantaged classes so recognized by our cases. Nor does the fact that the impact of the regulation falls upon those who cannot pay lead to a different conclusion. In a sense, every denial of welfare to an indigent creates a wealth classification as compared to nonindigents who are able to pay for the desired goods or services. But this Court has never held that financial need alone identifies a suspect class for purposes of equal protection analysis. See *Rodriguez, supra*, at 29; *Dandridge* v. *Williams*, 397 U.S. 471 (1970).[6] Accordingly, the central question in this case is whether the regulation "impinges upon a fundamental right explicitly or implicitly protected by the Constitution." The District Court read our decisions in *Roe* v. *Wade*, 410 U.S. 113 (1973), and the subsequent cases applying it, as establishing a fundamental right to abortion and therefore concluded that nothing less than a compelling state interest would justify Connecticut's different treatment of abortion and childbirth. We think the District Court misconceived the nature and scope of the fundamental right recognized in *Roe*. . . .

B

These cases recognize a constitutionally protected interest "in making certain kinds of important decisions" free from governmental compulsion. *Whalen* v. *Roe*, 429 U.S. 589, 599–600, and nn. 24 and 26 (1977). As *Whalen* makes clear, the right in *Roe* v. *Wade* can be understood only by considering both the woman's interest and the nature of the State's interference with it. *Roe* did not declare an unqualified "constitutional right to an abortion," as the District Court seemed to think. Rather, the right protects the woman from unduly burdensome interference with her freedom to decide whether to terminate her pregnancy. It implies no limitation on the authority of a State to make a value judgment favoring childbirth over abortion, and to implement that judgment by the allocation of public funds.

The Connecticut regulation before us is different in kind from the laws invalidated in our previous abortion decisions. The Connecticut regulation places no obstacles—absolute or otherwise—in the pregnant woman's path to an abortion. An indigent woman

---

6. In cases such as *Griffin* v. *Illinois*, 351 U.S. 12 (1956) and *Douglas* v. *California*, 372 U.S. 353 (1963), the Court held that the Equal Protection Clause requires States that allow appellate review of criminal convictions to provide indigent defendants with trial transcripts and appellate counsel. These cases are grounded in the criminal justice system, a governmental monopoly in which participation is compelled. Cf. n. 5, *supra*. Our subsequent decisions have made it clear that the principles underlying *Griffin* and *Douglas* do not extend to legislative classifications generally.

who desires an abortion suffers no disadvantage as a consequence of Connecticut's decision to fund childbirth; she continues as before to be dependent on private sources for the service she desires. The State may have made childbirth a more attractive alternative, thereby influencing the woman's decision, but it has imposed no restriction on access to abortions that was not already there. The indigency that may make it difficult—and in some cases, perhaps, impossible—for some women to have abortions is neither created nor in any way affected by the Connecticut regulation. We conclude that the Connecticut regulation does not impinge upon the fundamental right recognized in *Roe*. . . .

In conclusion, we emphasize that our decision today does not proscribe government funding of nontherapeutic abortions. It is open to Congress to require provision of Medicaid benefits for such abortions as a condition of state participation in the Medicaid program. Also, under Title XIX as construed in *Beal* v. *Doe*, Connecticut is free—through normal democratic processes—to decide that such benefits should be provided. We hold only that the Constitution does not require a judicially imposed resolution of these difficult issues. . . .

Mr. Justice Brennan, with whom Mr. Justice Marshall and Mr. Justice Blackmun join, dissenting.

The District Court held:

"When Connecticut refuses to fund elective abortions while funding therapeutic abortions and prenatal and postnatal care, it weights the choice of the pregnant mother against choosing to exercise her constitutionally protected right to an elective abortion. . . . Her choice is affected not simply by the absence of payment for the abortion, but by the availability of public funds for childbirth if she chooses not to have the abortion. When the state thus infringes upon a fundamental interest, it must assert a compelling state interest." *Roe* v. *Norton*, 408 F. Supp. 660, 663–664 (1975).

This Court reverses on the ground that "the District Court misconceived the nature and scope of the fundamental right recognized in *Roe* [v. *Wade*, 410 U.S. 113 (1973)]," and therefore that Connecticut was not required to meet the "compelling interest" test to justify its discrimination against elective abortion but only "the less demanding test of rationality that applies in the absence of . . . the impingement of a fundamental right." This holding, the Court insists, "places no obstacles—absolute or otherwise—in the pregnant woman's path to an abortion"; she is still at liberty to finance the abortion from "private sources." True, "the State may [by funding childbirth] have made childbirth a more attractive alternative, thereby influencing the woman's decision, but it has imposed no restriction on access to abortions that was not already there." *Ibid.* True, also, indigency "may make it difficult—and in some cases, perhaps impossible—for some women to have abortions," but that regrettable consequence "is neither created nor in any way affected by the Connecticut regulation." *Ibid.*

But a distressing insensitivity to the plight of impoverished pregnant women is inherent in the Court's analysis. The stark reality for too many, not just "some," indigent pregnant women is that indigency makes access to competent licensed physicians not merely "difficult" but "impossible." As a practical matter, many indigent women will feel they have no choice but to carry their pregnancies to term because the State will pay for the associated medical services, even though they would have chosen to have abortions if the State had also provided funds for that procedure, or indeed if the State had provided funds for neither procedure. This disparity in funding by the State clearly operates to coerce indigent pregnant women to bear children they would not otherwise choose to have, and just as clearly, this coercion can only operate upon the poor, who are uniquely the victims of this form of financial pressure. Mr. Justice Frankfurter's words are apt:

> "To sanction such a ruthless consequence, inevitably resulting from a money hurdle erected by the State, would justify a latter-day Anatole France to add one more item to his ironic comments on the 'majestic equality' of the law. 'The law, in its majestic equality, forbids the rich as well as the poor to sleep under bridges, to beg in the streets, and to steal bread'. . . ." *Griffin* v. *Illinois*, 351 U.S. 12, 23 (1956) (concurring opinion).

None can take seriously the Court's assurance that its "conclusion signals no retreat from *Roe* [v. *Wade*] or the cases applying it." . . . That statement must occasion great surprise among the Courts of Appeals and District Courts that, relying upon *Roe* v. *Wade* and *Doe* v. *Bolton*, 410 U.S. 179 (1973), have held that States are constitutionally required to fund elective abortions if they fund pregnancies carried to term. See *Doe* v. *Rose*, 499 F. 2d 1112 (CA10 1974); *Wulff* v. *Singleton*, 508 F. 2d 1211 (CA8 1974), rev'd and remanded on other grounds, 428 U.S. 106 (1976); *Doe* v. *Westby*, 383 F. Supp. 1143 (WDSD 1974), vacated and remanded (in light of *Hagans* v. *Lavine*, 415 U.S. 528 (1974)), 420 U.S. 968, on remand, 402 F. Supp. 140 (1975); *Doe* v. *Wohlgemuth*, 376 F. Supp. 173 (WD Pa. 1974), aff'd on statutory grounds *sub nom. Doe* v. *Beal*, 523 F. 2d 611 (CA3 1975), rev'd and remanded, *ante*, p. 438; *Doe* v. *Rampton*, 366 F. Supp. 189 (Utah 1973); *Klein* v. *Nassau County Medical Center*, 347 F. Supp. 496 (EDNY 1972), vacated and remanded (in light of *Roe* v. *Wade* and *Doe* v. *Bolton*, 412 U.S. 925 (1973)), on remand, 409 F. Supp. 731 (1976). Indeed, it cannot be gainsaid that today's decision seriously erodes the principles that *Roe* and *Doe* announced to guide the determination of what constitutes an unconstitutional infringement of the fundamental right of pregnant women to be free to decide whether to have an abortion.

The Court's premise is that only an equal protection claim is presented here. Claims of interference with enjoyment of fundamental rights have, however, occupied a rather protean position in our constitutional jurisprudence. Whether or not the Court's analysis may reasonably proceed under the Equal Protection Clause, the Court plainly errs in ignoring, as it does, the unanswerable argument of appellees, and the holding of the District Court, that the regulation unconstitutionally impinges upon their claim of privacy derived from the Due Process Clause.

Roe v. *Wade* and cases following it hold that an area of privacy invulnerable to the State's intrusion surrounds the decision of a pregnant woman whether or not to carry her pregnancy to term. The Connecticut scheme clearly impinges upon that area of privacy by bringing financial pressures on indigent women that force them to bear children they would not otherwise have. That is an obvious impairment of the fundamental right established by *Roe* v. *Wade*. Yet the Court concludes that "the Connecticut regulation does not impinge upon [that] fundamental right." . . . This conclusion is based on a perceived distinction, on the one hand, between the imposition of criminal penalties for the procurement of an abortion present in *Roe* v. *Wade* and *Doe* v. *Bolton* and the absolute prohibition present in *Planned Parenthood of Central Missouri* v. *Danforth*, 428 U.S. 52 (1976), and, on the other, the assertedly lesser inhibition imposed by the Connecticut scheme. . . .

The last time our Brother POWELL espoused the concept in an abortion case that "[t]here is a basic difference between direct state interference with a protected activity and state encouragement of an alternative activity consonant with legislative policy," *ante*, at 475, the Court refused to adopt it. *Singleton* v. *Wulff*, 428 U.S. 106, 122 (1976). This was made explicit in Part II of our Brother BLACKMUN's opinion for four of us and is implicit in our Brother STEVENS' essential agreement with the analysis of Part II-B. *Id.*, at 121–122 (concurring in part). Part II-B stated:

> "MR. JUSTICE POWELL would so limit *Doe* and the other cases cited, explaining them as cases in which the State 'directly interfered with the abortion decision' and 'directly interdicted the normal functioning of the physician-patient relationship by criminalizing certain procedures,' [428 U.S.,] at 128. There is no support in the language of the cited cases for this distinction. . . . Moreover, a 'direct interference' or 'interdiction' test does not appear to be supported by precedent. . . . For a doctor who cannot afford to work for nothing, and a woman who cannot afford to pay him, the State's refusal to fund an abortion is as effective an 'interdiction' of it as would ever be necessary. Furthermore, since the right . . . is not simply the right to have an abortion, but the right to have abortions nondiscriminatorily funded, the denial of such funding is as complete an 'interdiction' of the exercise of the right as could ever exist." *Id.*, at 118 n. 7.

We have also rejected this approach in other abortion cases. *Doe* v. *Bolton*, the companion to *Roe* v. *Wade*, in addition to striking down the Georgia criminal prohibition against elective abortions, struck down the procedural requirements of certification of hospitals, of approval by a hospital committee, and of concurrence in the abortion decision by two doctors other than the woman's own doctor. None of these requirements operated as an absolute bar to elective abortions in the manner of the criminal prohibitions present in the other aspect of the case or in *Roe*, but this was not sufficient to save them from unconstitutionality. In *Planned Parenthood, supra*, we struck down a requirement for spousal consent to an elective abortion which the Court characterizes today simply as an "absolute obstacle" to a woman's obtaining an abortion. But the obstacle was "absolute" only in the limited sense that a woman who was unable to persuade her spouse to agree to an elective abortion was prevented from obtaining one. Any woman whose husband agreed, or could be persuaded to agree, was free to obtain an abortion, and the State never imposed directly any prohibition of its own. This requirement was qualitatively different from the criminal statutes that the Court today says are comparable, but we nevertheless found it unconstitutional. . . .

Until today, I had not thought the nature of the fundamental right established in *Roe* was open to question, let alone susceptible of the interpretation advanced, by the Court. The fact that the Connecticut scheme may not operate as an absolute bar preventing all indigent women from having abortions is not critical. What is critical is that the State has inhibited their fundamental right to make that choice free from state interference. . . .

POELKER, MAYOR OF ST. LOUIS, ET AL. v. DOE

CERTIORARI TO THE UNITED STATES COURT OF APPEALS FOR THE EIGHTH CIRCUIT

No. 75–442. Argued January 11, 1977—Decided June 20, 1977

PER CURIAM.

Respondent Jane Doe, an indigent, sought unsuccessfully to obtain a nontherapeutic abortion at Starkloff Hospital, one of two city-owned public hospitals in St. Louis, Mo. She subsequently brought this class action under 42 U.S. C. § 1983 against the Mayor of St. Louis and the Director of Health and Hospitals, alleging that the refusal by Starkloff Hospital to provide the desired abortion violated her constitutional rights. Although the District Court ruled against Doe following a trial, the Court of Appeals for the Eighth Circuit reversed in an opinion that accepted both her factual and legal arguments. 515 F. 2d 541 (1975). . . .

The Court of Appeals concluded that Doe's inability to obtain an abortion resulted from a combination of a policy directive by the Mayor and a longstanding staffing practice at Starkloff Hospital. The directive, communicated to the Director of Health and Hospitals by the Mayor, prohibited the performance of abortions in the city hospitals except when there was a threat of grave physiological injury or death to the mother. Under the staffing practice, the doctors and medical students at the obstetrics-gynecology clinic at the hospital are drawn from the faculty and students at the St. Louis University School of Medicine, a Jesuit-operated institution opposed to abortion. Relying on our decisions in *Roe* v. *Wade*, 410 U.S. 113 (1973), and *Doe* v. *Bolton*, 410 U.S. 179 (1973), the Court of Appeals held that the city's policy and the hospital's staffing practice denied the "constitutional rights of indigent pregnant women . . . long after those rights had been clearly enunciated" in *Roe* and *Doe*. 515 F. 2d, at 547. The court cast the issue in an equal protection mold, finding that the provision of publicly financed hospital services for childbirth but not for elective abortions constituted invidious discrimination. In support of its equal protection analysis, the court also emphasized the contrast between nonindigent women who can afford to obtain abortions in private hospitals and indigent women who cannot. Particular reliance was placed upon the previous decision in *Wulff* v. *Singleton*, 508 F. 2d 1211 (CA8 1974), reversed on other grounds, 428 U.S. 106 (1976), in which the Court of Appeals had held unconstitutional a state Medicaid statute that provided benefits for women who carried their pregnancies to term but denied them for women who sought elective abortions. The court stated that "[t]here is no practical distinction between that case and this one." 515 F. 2d, at 545.

We agree that the constitutional question presented here is identical in principle with that presented by a State's refusal to provide Medicaid benefits for abortions while providing them for childbirth. This was the issue before us in *Maher* v. *Roe*. For the reasons set forth in our opinion in that case, we find no constitutional violation by the city of St. Louis in electing, as a policy choice, to provide publicly financed hospital services for childbirth without providing corresponding services for nontherapeutic abortions. . . .

Mr. Justice Brennan, with whom Mr. Justice Marshall and Mr. Justice Blackmun join, dissenting.

The Court holds that St. Louis may constitutionally refuse to permit the performance of elective abortions in its city-owned hospitals while providing hospital services to women who carry their pregnancies to term. As stated by the Court of Appeals:

> "Stripped of all rhetoric, the city here, through its policy and staffing procedure, is simply telling indigent women, like Doe, that if they choose to carry their pregnancies to term, the city will provide physicians and medical facilities for full maternity care; but if they choose to exercise their constitutionally protected right to determine that they wish to terminate the pregnancy, the city will not provide physicians and facilities for the abortion procedure, even though it is probably safer than going through a full pregnancy and childbirth." 515 F. 2d 541, 544 (1975).

The Court of Appeals held that St. Louis could not in this way "interfer[e] in her decision of whether to bear a child or have an abortion simply because she is indigent and unable to afford private treatment," *ibid.*, because it was constitutionally impermissible that indigent women be "'subjected to State coercion to bear children which they do not wish to bear [while] no other women similarly situated are so coerced,'" *id.*, at 545.

For the reasons set forth in my dissent in *Maher* v. *Roe*, I would affirm the Court of Appeals. Here the fundamental right of a woman freely to choose to terminate her pregnancy has been infringed by the city of St. Louis through a deliberate policy based on opposition to elective abortions on moral grounds by city officials. While it may still be possible for some indigent women to obtain abortions in clinics or private hospitals, it is clear that the city policy is a significant, and in some cases insurmountable, obstacle to indigent pregnant women who cannot pay for abortions in those private facilities. Nor is the closing of St. Louis' public hospitals an isolated instance with little practical significance. The importance of today's decision is greatly magnified by the fact that during 1975 and the first quarter of 1976 only about 18% of all public hospitals in the country provided abortion services, and in 10 States there were no public hospitals providing such services.[1]

---

1. Sullivan, Tietze, & Dryfoos, Legal Abortion in the United States, 1975–1976, 9 Family Planning Perspectives 116, 121, 128 (1977).

A number of difficulties lie beneath the surface of the Court's holding. Public hospitals that do not permit the performance of elective abortions will frequently have physicians on their staffs who would willingly perform them. This may operate in some communities significantly to reduce the number of physicians who are both willing and able to perform abortions in a hospital setting. It is not a complete answer that many abortions may safely be performed in clinics, for some physicians will not be affiliated with those clinics, and some abortions may pose unacceptable risks if performed outside a hospital. Indeed, such an answer would be ironic, for if the result is to force some abortions to be performed in a clinic that properly should be performed in a hospital, the city policy will have operated to increase rather than reduce health risks associated with abortions; and in *Roe* v. *Wade*, 410 U.S. 113, 163 (1973), the Court permitted regulation by the State solely to *protect* maternal health.

The Court's holding will also pose difficulties in small communities where the public hospital is the only nearby health care facility. If such a public hospital is closed to abortions, any woman—rich or poor—will be seriously inconvenienced; and for some women—particularly poor women—the unavailability of abortions in the public hospital will be an insuperable obstacle. Indeed, a recent survey suggests that the decision in this case will be felt most strongly in rural areas, where the public hospital will in all likelihood be closed to elective abortions, and where there will not be sufficient demand to support a separate abortion clinic. . . .

COLAUTTI, SECRETARY OF WELFARE OF PENNSYLVANIA, ET AL. v. FRANKLIN ET AL.

APPEAL FROM THE UNITED STATES DISTRICT COURT FOR THE EASTERN DISTRICT OF PENNSYLVANIA

No. 77–891. Argued October 3, 1978—Decided January 9, 1979

BLACKMUN, J., delivered the opinion of the Court, in which BRENNAN, STEWART, MARSHALL, POWELL, and STEVENS, JJ., joined. WHITE, J., filed a dissenting opinion, in which BURGER, C. J., and REHNQUIST, J., joined.

MR. JUSTICE BLACKMUN delivered the opinion of the Court.

At issue here is the constitutionality of subsection (a) of § 5[1] of the Pennsylvania Abortion Control Act, 1974 Pa. Laws, Act No. 209, Pa. Stat. Ann., Tit. 35, § 6605 (a) (Purdon 1977). This statute subjects a physician who performs an abortion to potential criminal liability if he fails to utilize a statutorily prescribed technique when the fetus "is viable" or when there is "sufficient reason to believe that the fetus may be viable." . . . .

III

The attack mounted by the plaintiffs-appellees upon § 5 (a) centers on both the viability-determination requirement and the stated standard of care. The former provision,

---

1. Section 5 reads in pertinent part:

"(a) Every person who performs or induces an abortion shall prior thereto have made a determination based on his experience, judgment or professional competence that the fetus is not viable, and if the determination is that the fetus is viable or if there is sufficient reason to believe that the fetus may be viable, shall exercise that degree of professional skill, care and diligence to preserve the life and health of the fetus which such person would be required to exercise in order to preserve the life and health of any fetus intended to be born and not aborted and the abortion technique employed shall be that which would provide the best opportunity for the fetus to be aborted alive so long as a different technique would not be necessary in order to preserve the life or health of the mother.

. . . .

"(d) Any person who fails to make the determination provided for in subsection (a) of this section, or who fails to exercise the degree of professional skill, care and diligence or to provide the abortion technique as provided for in subsection (a) of this section . . . shall be subject to such civil or criminal liability as would pertain to him had the fetus been a child who was intended to be born and not aborted."

requiring the physician to observe the care standard when he determines that the fetus is viable, or when "there is sufficient reason to believe that the fetus may be viable," is asserted to be unconstitutionally vague because it fails to inform the physician when his duty to the fetus arises, and because it does not make the physician's good-faith determination of viability conclusive. This provision is also said to be unconstitutionally overbroad, because it carves out a new time period prior to the stage of viability, and could have a restrictive effect on a couple who wants to abort a fetus determined by genetic testing to be defective.[8] The standard of care, and in particular the requirement that the physician employ the abortion technique "which would provide the best opportunity for the fetus to be aborted alive so long as a different technique would not be necessary in order to preserve the life or health of the mother," is said to be void for vagueness and to be unconstitutionally restrictive in failing to afford the physician sufficient professional discretion in determining which abortion technique is appropriate. . . .

IV

We agree with plaintiffs-appellees that the viability-determination requirement of § 5 (a) is ambiguous, and that its uncertainty is aggravated by the absence of a scienter requirement with respect to the finding of viability. Because we conclude that this portion of the statute is void for vagueness, we find it unnecessary to consider appellees' alternative arguments based on the alleged overbreadth of § 5 (a).

A

It is settled that, as a matter of due process, a criminal statute that "fails to give a person of ordinary intelligence fair notice that his contemplated conduct is forbidden by the statute," *United States* v. *Harriss*, 347 U.S. 612, 617 (1954), or is so indefinite that "it encourages arbitrary and erratic arrests and convictions," *Papachristou* v. *Jacksonville*, 405 U.S. 156, 162 (1972), is void for vagueness. See generally *Grayned* v. *City of Rockford*, 408 U.S. 104, 108–109 (1972). This appears to be especially true where the uncertainty induced by the statute threatens to inhibit the exercise of constitutionally protected rights. *Id.*, at 109; *Smith* v. *Goguen*, 415 U.S. 566, 573 (1974); *Keyishian* v. *Board of Regents*, 385 U.S. 589, 603–604 (1967).

Section 5 (a) requires every person who performs or induces an abortion to make a determination, "based on his experience, judgment or professional competence," that

---

8. The plaintiffs-appellees introduced evidence that modern medical technology makes it possible to detect whether a fetus is afflicted with such disorders as Tay-Sachs disease and Down's syndrome (mongolism). Such testing, however, often cannot be completed until after 18–20 weeks' gestation. App. 53a–56a (testimony of Hope Punnett, Ph. D.).

the fetus is not viable. If such person determines that the fetus is viable, or if "there is sufficient reason to believe that the fetus may be viable," then he must adhere to the prescribed standard of care. This requirement contains a double ambiguity. First, it is unclear whether the statute imports a purely subjective standard, or whether it imposes a mixed subjective and objective standard. Second, it is uncertain whether the phrase "may be viable" simply refers to viability, as that term has been defined in *Roe* and in *Planned Parenthood*, or whether it refers to an undefined penumbral or "gray" area prior to the stage of viability.

The statute requires the physician to conform to the prescribed standard of care if one of two conditions is satisfied: if he determines that the fetus "is viable," or "if there is sufficient reason to believe that the fetus may be viable." Apparently, the determination of whether the fetus "is viable" is to be based on the attending physician's "experience, judgment or professional competence," a subjective point of reference. But it is unclear whether the same phrase applies to the second triggering condition, that is, to "sufficient reason to believe that the fetus may be viable." In other words, it is ambiguous whether there must be "sufficient reason" from the perspective of the judgment, skill, and training of the attending physician, or "sufficient reason" from the perspective of a cross section of the medical community or a panel of experts. The latter, obviously, portends not an inconsequential hazard for the typical private practitioner who may not have the skills and technology that are readily available at a teaching hospital or large medical center.

The intended distinction between the phrases "is viable" and "may be viable" is even more elusive. Appellants argue that no difference is intended, and that the use of the "may be viable" words "simply incorporates the acknowledged medical fact that a fetus is 'viable' if it has that statistical 'chance' of survival recognized by the medical community." Brief for Appellants 28. The statute, however, does not support the contention that "may be viable" is synonymous with, or merely intended to explicate the meaning of, "viable." . . .

Since we must reject appellants' theory that "may be viable" means "viable," a second serious ambiguity appears in the statute. On the one hand, as appellees urge and as the District Court found, see 401 F. Supp., at 572, it may be that "may be viable" carves out a new time period during pregnancy when there is a remote possibility of fetal survival outside the womb, but the fetus has not yet attained the reasonable likelihood of survival that physicians associate with viability. On the other hand, although appellants do not argue this, it may be that "may be viable" refers to viability as physicians understand it, and "viable" refers to some undetermined stage later in pregnancy. We need not resolve this question. The crucial point is that "viable" and "may be viable" apparently refer to distinct conditions, and that one of these conditions differs in some indeterminate way from the definition of viability as set forth in *Roe* and in *Planned Parenthood*. . . .

B

The vagueness of the viability-determination requirement of § 5 (a) is compounded by the fact that the Act subjects the physician to potential criminal liability without regard to fault. Under § 5 (d), see n. 1, *supra*, a physician who fails to abide by the standard of care when there is sufficient reason to believe that the fetus "may be viable" is subject "to such civil or criminal liability as would pertain to him had the fetus been a child who was intended to be born and not aborted." To be sure, the Pennsylvania law of criminal homicide, made applicable to the physician by § 5 (d), conditions guilt upon a finding of scienter. See Pa. Stat. Ann., Tit. 18, §§ 2501–2504 (Purdon 1973 and Supp. 1978). The required mental state, however, is that of "intentionally, knowingly, recklessly or negligently caus[ing] the death of another human being." § 2501 (1973). Thus, the Pennsylvania law of criminal homicide requires scienter with respect to whether the physician's actions will result in the death of the fetus. But neither the Pennsylvania law of criminal homicide, nor the Abortion Control Act, requires that the physician be culpable in failing to find sufficient reason to believe that the fetus may be viable. . . .

The perils of strict criminal liability are particularly acute here because of the uncertainty of the viability determination itself. As the record in this case indicates, a physician determines whether or not a fetus is viable after considering a number of variables: the gestational age of the fetus, derived from the reported menstrual history of the woman; fetal weight, based on an inexact estimate of the size and condition of the uterus; the woman's general health and nutrition; the quality of the available medical facilities; and other factors.[14] Because of the number and the imprecision of these variables, the probability of any particular fetus' obtaining meaningful life outside the womb can be determined only with difficulty. Moreover, the record indicates that even if agreement may be reached on the probability of survival, different physicians equate viability with different probabilities of survival, and some physicians refuse to equate viability with any numerical probability at all.[15] In the face of these uncertainties, it is not unlikely that experts will disagree over whether a particular fetus in the second trimester has advanced to the stage of viability. The prospect of such disagreement, in conjunction with a statute imposing strict civil and criminal liability for an erroneous determination of viability, could have a profound

---

14. See App. 5a–6a, 10a, 17a (testimony of Louis Gerstley III, M. D.); *id.*, at 77a–78a, 81a (testimony of Thomas W. Hilgers, M. D.); *id.*, at 93a–101a, 109a, 112a (testimony of William J. Keenan, M. D.).

15. See *id.*, at 8a (testimony of Dr. Gerstley) (viability means 5% chance of survival, "certainly at least two to three percent"); *id.*, at 104a (testimony of Dr. Keenan) (10% chance of survival would be viable); *id.*, at 144a (deposition of John Franklin, M. D.) (viability means "ten percent or better" probability of survival); *id.*, at 132a (testimony of Arturo Hervada, M. D.) (it is misleading to be obsessed with a particular percentage figure).

chilling effect on the willingness of physicians to perform abortions near the point of viability in the manner indicated by their best medical judgment.

Because we hold that the viability-determination provision of § 5 (a) is void on its face, we need not now decide whether, under a properly drafted statute, a finding of bad faith or some other type of scienter would be required before a physician could be held criminally responsible for an erroneous determination of viability. We reaffirm, however, that "the determination of whether a particular fetus is viable is, and must be, a matter for the judgment of the responsible attending physician." *Planned Parenthood of Central Missouri* v. *Danforth*, 428 U.S., at 64. State regulation that impinges upon this determination, if it is to be constitutional, must allow the attending physician "the room he needs to make his best medical judgment." *Doe* v. *Bolton*, 410 U.S., at 192. . . .

Mr. Justice White, with whom The Chief Justice and Mr. Justice Rehnquist join, dissenting.

Because the Court now withdraws from the States a substantial measure of the power to protect fetal life that was reserved to them in *Roe* v. *Wade*, 410 U.S. 113 (1973), and reaffirmed in *Planned Parenthood of Central Missouri* v. *Danforth*, 428 U.S. 52 (1976), I file this dissent.

I

In *Roe* v. *Wade*, the Court defined the term "viability" to signify the stage at which a fetus is "potentially able to live outside the mother's womb, albeit with artificial aid." This is the point at which the State's interest in protecting fetal life becomes sufficiently strong to permit it to "go so far as to proscribe abortion during that period, except when it is necessary to preserve the life or health of the mother." 410 U.S., at 163–164.

The Court obviously crafted its definition of viability with some care, and it chose to define that term not as that stage of development at which the fetus actually *is* able or actually *has* the ability to survive outside the mother's womb, with or without artificial aid, but as that point at which the fetus is *potentially* able to survive. In the ordinary usage of these words, being *able* and being *potentially able* do not mean the same thing. Potential ability is not actual ability. It is ability "[e]xisting in possibility, not in actuality." Webster's New International Dictionary (2d ed. 1958). The Court's definition of viability in *Roe* v. *Wade* reaches an earlier point in the development of the fetus than that stage at which a doctor could say with assurance that the fetus *would* survive outside the womb.

It was against this background that the Pennsylvania statute at issue here was adopted and the District Court's judgment was entered. Insofar as *Roe* v. *Wade* was concerned, Pennsylvania could have defined viability in the language of that case—"potentially able to live outside the mother's womb"—and could have forbidden all abortions after this stage of any pregnancy. The Pennsylvania Act, however, did not go so far. It forbade entirely only those abortions where the fetus had attained viability as defined in § 2 of the Act, that is, where the fetus had "the *capability* . . . to live outside the mother's womb albeit with artificial aid." Pa. Stat. Ann., Tit. 35, § 6602 (Purdon 1977) (emphasis added). But the State, understanding that it also had the power under *Roe* v. *Wade* to regulate where the fetus was only "potentially able" to exist outside the womb, also sought to regulate, but not forbid, abortions where there was sufficient reason to believe that the fetus "may be viable"; this language was reasonably believed by the State to be equivalent to what the Court meant in 1973 by the term "potentially able to live outside the mother's womb." Under § 5 (a), abortionists must not only determine whether the fetus is viable but also whether there is sufficient reason to believe that the fetus may be viable. If either condition exists, the method of abortion is regulated and a standard of care imposed. Under § 5 (d), breach of these regulations exposes the abortionist to the civil and criminal penalties that would be applicable if a live birth rather than an abortion had been intended. . . .

Affirmance of the District Court's judgment is untenable. The District Court originally thought § 5 (a) was vague because the term "viability" was itself vague. The Court scotched that notion in *Danforth*, and the District Court then sustained the Pennsylvania definition of viability. In doing so, it necessarily nullified the major reason for its prior invalidation of § 5 (a), which was that it incorporated the supposedly vague standard of § 2. But the District Court had also said that the "may be viable" standard was invalid as an impermissible effort to regulate a period of "potential" viability. This was the sole remaining articulated ground for invalidating § 5 (a). But this is the very ground that was urged and rejected in *Danforth*, where this Court sustained the Missouri provision defining viability as the stage at which the fetus "may" have the ability to survive outside the womb and reaffirmed the flexible concept of viability announced in *Roe*.

In affirming the District Court, the Court does not in so many words agree with the District Court but argues that it is too difficult to know whether the Pennsylvania Act simply intended, as the State urges, to go no further than *Roe* permitted in protecting a fetus that is potentially able to survive or whether it intended to carve out a protected period prior to viability as defined in *Roe*. The District Court, although otherwise seriously in error, had no such trouble with the Act. It understood the "may be viable" provision as an attempt to protect a period of potential life, precisely the kind of interest that *Roe* protected but which the District Court erroneously thought the State was not entitled to protect. . . . *Danforth*, as I have said, reaffirmed *Roe* in this respect. Only those with unalterable determination to invalidate the Pennsylvania Act can draw any measurable difference insofar as vagueness is concerned between "viability" defined as the ability to survive and "viability" defined as that stage at which the fetus may have the ability to survive. It seems to me that, in affirming, the Court is tacitly disowning the "may be" standard of the Missouri law as well as the "potential ability" component of viability as that concept was described in *Roe*. This is a further constitutionally unwarranted intrusion upon the police powers of the States.

II

Apparently uneasy with its work, the Court has searched for and seized upon two additional reasons to support affirmance, neither of which was relied upon by the District Court. The Court first notes that under § 5 (d), failure to make the determinations required by § 5 (a), or otherwise to comply with its provisions, subjects the abortionist to criminal prosecution under those laws that "would pertain to him had the fetus been a child who was intended to be born and not aborted." Although concededly the Pennsylvania law of criminal homicide conditions guilt upon a finding that the defendant intentionally, knowingly, recklessly, or negligently caused the death of another human being, the Court nevertheless goes on to declare that the abortionist could be successfully prosecuted for criminal homicide without any such fault or omission in determining whether or not the fetus is viable or may be viable. This alleged lack of a scienter requirement, the Court says, fortifies its holding that § 5 (a) is void for vagueness.

This seems to me an incredible construction of the Pennsylvania statutes.

The District Court suggested nothing of the sort, and appellees focus entirely on § 5 (a), ignoring the homicide statutes. The latter not only define the specified degrees of scienter that are required for the various homicides, but also provide that ignorance or mistake as to a matter of fact, for which there is a reasonable explanation, is a defense to a homicide charge if it negatives the mental state necessary for conviction. Pa. Stat. Ann., Tit. 18, § 304 (Purdon 1973). Given this background, I do not see how it can be seriously argued that a doctor who makes a good-faith mistake about whether a fetus is or is not viable could be successfully prosecuted for criminal homicide. This is the State's submission in this Court; the court below did not address the matter; and at the very least this is something the Court should not decide without hearing from the Pennsylvania courts. . . .

BELLOTTI, ATTORNEY GENERAL OF MASSACHUSETTS, ET AL. *v.* BAIRD ET AL.

APPEAL FROM THE UNITED STATES DISTRICT COURT FOR THE DISTRICT OF MASSACHUSETTS

No. 78–329. Argued February 27, 1979—Decided July 2, 1979

[A Massachusetts statute requires parental consent before an abortion can be performed on an unmarried woman under the age of 18. If one or both parents refuse such consent, however, the abortion may be obtained by order of a judge of the superior court "for good cause shown." In appellees' class action challenging the constitutionality of the statute, a three-judge District Court held it unconstitutional. Subsequently, this Court vacated the District Court's judgment, *Bellotti* v. *Baird*, 428 U.S. 132, holding that the District Court should have abstained and certified to the Massachusetts Supreme Judicial Court appropriate questions concerning the meaning of the statute. On remand, the District Court certified several questions to the Supreme Judicial Court. Among the questions certified was whether the statute permits any minors—mature or immature—to obtain judicial consent to an abortion without any parental consultation whatsoever. The Supreme Judicial Court answered that, in general, it does not; that consent must be obtained for every nonemergency abortion unless no parent is available; and that an available parent must be given notice of any judicial proceedings brought by a minor to obtain consent for an abortion. Another question certified was whether, if the superior court finds that the minor is capable of making, and has, in fact, made and adhered to, an informed and reasonable decision to have an abortion, the court may refuse its consent on a finding that a parent's, or its own, contrary decision is a better one. The Supreme Judicial Court answered in the affirmative. Following the Supreme Judicial Court's judgment, the District Court again declared the statute unconstitutional and enjoined its enforcement, and the United States Supreme Court took it on appeal.]

POWELL, J., announced the judgment of the Court and delivered an opinion, in which BURGER, C. J., and STEWART and REHNQUIST, JJ., joined. REHNQUIST, J., filed a concurring opinion. STEVENS, J., filed an opinion concurring in the judgment, in which BRENNAN, MARSHALL, and BLACKMUN, JJ., joined. WHITE, J., filed a dissenting opinion.

MR. JUSTICE POWELL announced the judgment of the Court and delivered an opinion, in which THE CHIEF JUSTICE, MR. JUSTICE STEWART, and MR. JUSTICE REHNQUIST joined.

II

... A child, merely on account of his minority, is not beyond the protection of the Constitution. As the Court said in *In re Gault*, 387 U.S. 1, 13 (1967), "whatever may be their precise impact, neither the Fourteenth Amendment nor the Bill of Rights is for adults alone." ... This observation, of course, is but the beginning of the analysis. The Court long has recognized that the status of minors under the law is unique in many respects. As Mr. Justice Frankfurter aptly put it: "Children have a very special place in life which law should reflect. Legal theories and their phrasing in other cases readily lead to fallacious reasoning if uncritically transferred to determination of a State's duty towards children." *May* v. *Anderson*, 345 U.S. 528, 536 (1953) (concurring opinion). The unique role in our society of the family, the institution by which "we inculcate and pass down many of our most cherished values, moral and cultural," *Moore* v. *East Cleveland*, 431 U.S. 494, 503–504 (1977) (plurality opinion), requires that constitutional principles be applied with sensitivity and flexibility to the special needs of parents and children. We have recognized three reasons justifying the conclusion that the constitutional rights of children cannot be equated with those of adults: the peculiar vulnerability of children; their inability to make critical decisions in an informed, mature manner; and the importance of the parental role in child rearing.

A

The Court's concern for the vulnerability of children is demonstrated in its decisions dealing with minors' claims to constitutional protection against deprivations of liberty or property interests by the State. With respect to many of these claims, we have concluded that the child's right is virtually coextensive with that of an adult. For example, the Court has held that the Fourteenth Amendment's guarantee against the deprivation of liberty without due process of law is applicable to children in juvenile delinquency proceedings. *In re Gault, supra*. In particular, minors involved in such proceedings are entitled to adequate notice, the assistance of counsel, and the opportunity to confront their accusers. They can be found guilty only upon proof beyond a reasonable doubt, and they may assert the privilege against compulsory self-incrimination. *In re Winship*, 397 U.S. 358 (1970); *In re Gault, supra*. See also *Ingraham* v. *Wright*, 430 U.S. 651, 674 (1977) (corporal punishment of schoolchildren implicates constitutionally protected liberty interest); cf. *Breed* v. *Jones*, 421 U.S. 519 (1975) (Double Jeopardy Clause prohibits prosecuting juvenile as an adult after an adjudicatory finding in juvenile court that he had violated a criminal statute). Similarly, in *Goss* v. *Lopez*, 419 U.S. 565 (1975), the Court held that children may not be deprived of certain property interests without due process.

These rulings have not been made on the uncritical assumption that the constitutional rights of children are indistinguishable from those of adults. Indeed, our acceptance of juvenile courts distinct from the adult criminal justice system assumes that juvenile offenders constitutionally may be treated differently from adults. In order to preserve this separate avenue for dealing with minors, the Court has said that hearings in juvenile delinquency cases need not necessarily "'conform with all of the requirements of a criminal trial or even of the usual administrative hearing.'" *In re Gault, supra*, at 30, quoting *Kent* v. *United States*, 383 U.S. 541, 562 (1966). Thus, juveniles are not constitutionally entitled to trial by jury in delinquency adjudications. *McKeiver* v. *Pennsylvania*, 403 U.S. 528 (1971). Viewed together, our cases show that although children generally are protected by the same constitutional guarantees against governmental deprivations as are adults, the State is entitled to adjust its legal system to account for children's vulnerability and their needs for "concern, . . . sympathy, and . . . paternal attention." *Id.*, at 550 (plurality opinion).

B

Second, the Court has held that the States validly may limit the freedom of children to choose for themselves in the making of important, affirmative choices with potentially serious consequences. These rulings have been grounded in the recognition that, during the formative years of childhood and adolescence, minors often lack the experience, perspective, and judgment to recognize and avoid choices that could be detrimental to them. . . .

Ginsberg v. *New York*, 390 U.S. 629 (1968), illustrates well the Court's concern over the inability of children to make mature choices, as the First Amendment rights involved are clear examples of constitutionally protected freedoms of choice. At issue was a criminal conviction for selling sexually oriented magazines to a minor under the age of 17 in violation of a New York state law. It was conceded that the conviction could not have stood under the First Amendment if based upon a sale of the same material to an adult. *Id.*, at 634. Notwithstanding the importance the Court always has attached to First Amendment rights, it concluded that "even where there is an invasion of protected freedoms 'the power of the state to control the conduct of children reaches beyond the scope of its authority over adults . . . ,'" *id.*, at 638, quoting *Prince* v. *Massachusetts*, 321 U.S. 158, 170 (1944). . . .

C

Third, the guiding role of parents in the upbringing of their children justifies limitations on the freedoms of minors. The State commonly protects its youth from adverse governmental action and from their own immaturity by requiring parental consent to or involvement in important decisions by minors.[16] But an additional and more important

---

16. See, *e.g.*, Mass. Gen. Laws Ann., ch. 207, §§ 7, 24, 25, 33, 33A (West 1958 and Supp. 1979) (parental consent required for marriage of person under 18); Mass. Gen. Laws Ann., ch. 119, § 55A (West Supp. 1979) (waiver of counsel by minor in juvenile delinquency proceedings must be made through parent or guardian).

justification for state deference to parental control over children is that "[t]he child is not the mere creature of the State; those who nurture him and direct his destiny have the right, coupled with the high duty, to recognize and prepare him for additional obligations." *Pierce* v. *Society of Sisters*, 268 U.S. 510, 535 (1925). "The duty to prepare the child for 'additional obligations' . . . must be read to include the inculcation of moral standards, religious beliefs, and elements of good citizenship." *Wisconsin* v. *Yoder*, 406 U.S. 205, 233 (1972). This affirmative process of teaching, guiding, and inspiring by precept and example is essential to the growth of young people into mature, socially responsible citizens. . . .

III

With these principles in mind, we consider the specific constitutional questions presented by these appeals. In § 12S, Massachusetts has attempted to reconcile the constitutional right of a woman, in consultation with her physician, to choose to terminate her pregnancy as established by *Roe* v. *Wade*, 410 U.S. 113 (1973), and *Doe* v. *Bolton*, 410 U.S. 179 (1973), with the special interest of the State in encouraging an unmarried pregnant minor to seek the advice of her parents in making the important decision whether or not to bear a child. As noted above, § 12S was before us in *Bellotti I*, 428 U.S. 132 (1976), where we remanded the case for interpretation of its provisions by the Supreme Judicial Court of Massachusetts. We previously had held in *Planned Parenthood of Central Missouri* v. *Danforth*, 428 U.S. 52 (1976), that a State could not lawfully authorize an absolute parental veto over the decision of a minor to terminate her pregnancy. *Id.*, at 74. In *Bellotti I*, *supra*, we recognized that § 12S could be read as "fundamentally different from a statute that creates a 'parental veto,'" 428 U.S., at 145, thus "avoid[ing] or substantially modify[ing] the federal constitutional challenge to the statute." *Id.*, at 148. The question before us—in light of what we have said in the prior cases—is whether § 12S, as authoritatively interpreted by the Supreme Judicial Court, provides for parental notice and consent in a manner that does not unduly burden the right to seek an abortion. See *id.*, at 147. . . .

The pregnant minor's options are much different from those facing a minor in other situations, such as deciding whether to marry. A minor not permitted to marry before the age of majority is required simply to postpone her decision. She and her intended spouse may preserve the opportunity for later marriage should they continue to desire it. A pregnant adolescent, however, cannot preserve for long the possibility of aborting, which effectively expires in a matter of weeks from the onset of pregnancy.

Moreover, the potentially severe detriment facing a pregnant woman, see *Roe* v. *Wade*, 410 U.S., at 153, is not mitigated by her minority. Indeed, considering her probable education, employment skills, financial resources, and emotional maturity, unwanted motherhood may be exceptionally burdensome for a minor. In addition, the fact of having a child brings with it adult legal responsibility, for parenthood, like attainment of the age of majority, is one of the traditional criteria for the termination of the legal disabilities of minority. In sum, there are few situations in which denying a minor the right to make an important decision will have consequences so grave and indelible.

Yet, an abortion may not be the best choice for the minor. The circumstances in which this issue arises will vary widely. In a given case, alternatives to abortion, such as marriage to the father of the child, arranging for its adoption, or assuming the responsibilities of motherhood with the assured support of family, may be feasible and relevant to the minor's best interests. Nonetheless, the abortion decision is one that simply cannot be postponed, or it will be made by default with far-reaching consequences.

For these reasons, as we held in *Planned Parenthood of Central Missouri* v. *Danforth*, 428 U.S., at 74, "the State may not impose a blanket provision . . . requiring the consent of a parent or person *in loco parentis* as a condition for abortion of an unmarried minor during the first 12 weeks of her pregnancy." Although, as stated in Part II, *supra*, such deference to parents may be permissible with respect to other choices facing a minor, the unique nature and consequences of the abortion decision make it inappropriate "to give a third party an absolute, and possibly arbitrary, veto over the decision of the physician and his patient to terminate the patient's pregnancy, regardless of the reason for withholding the consent." 428 U.S., at 74. We therefore conclude that if the State decides to require a pregnant minor to obtain one or both parents' consent to an abortion, it also must provide an alternative procedure . . . whereby authorization for the abortion can be obtained.

A pregnant minor is entitled in such a proceeding to show either: (1) that she is mature enough and well enough informed to make her abortion decision, in consultation with her physician, independently of her parents' wishes; . . . or (2) that even if she is not able to make this decision independently, the desired abortion would be in her best interests. The proceeding in which this showing is made must assure that a resolution of the issue, and any appeals that may follow, will be completed with anonymity and sufficient expedition to provide an effective opportunity for an abortion to be obtained. In sum, the procedure must ensure that the provision requiring parental consent does not in fact amount to the "absolute, and possibly arbitrary, veto" that was found impermissible in *Danforth*. *Ibid.* . . .

Among the questions certified to the Supreme Judicial Court was whether § 12S permits any minors—mature or immature—to obtain judicial consent to an abortion without any parental consultation whatsoever. See n. 9, *supra*. The state court answered that, in general, it does not. "[T]he consent required by [§ 12S must] be obtained for every nonemergency abortion where the mother is less than eighteen years of age and unmarried." *Attorney General, supra*, at 750, 360 N. E. 2d, at 294. The text of § 12S itself states an exception to this rule, making consent unnecessary from any parent who has "died or has deserted his or her family."[26] The Supreme Judicial Court construed the statute as

---

26. The statute also provides that "[i]f both parents have died or have deserted their family, consent of the mother's guardian or other person having duties similar to a guardian, or any person who had assumed the care and custody of the mother is sufficient."

containing an additional exception: Consent need not be obtained "where no parent (or statutory substitute) is available." 371 Mass., at 750, 360 N. E. 2d, at 294. The court also ruled that an available parent must be given notice of any judicial proceedings brought by a minor to obtain consent for an abortion. . . . *Id.*, at 755–756, 360 N. E. 2d, at 297.

We think that, construed in this manner, § 12S would impose an undue burden upon the exercise by minors of the right to seek an abortion. As the District Court recognized, "there are parents who would obstruct, and perhaps altogether prevent, the minor's right to go to court." *Baird III*, 450 F. Supp., at 1001. There is no reason to believe that this would be so in the majority of cases where consent is withheld. But many parents hold strong views on the subject of abortion, and young pregnant minors, especially those living at home, are particularly vulnerable to their parents' efforts to obstruct both an abortion and their access to court. It would be unrealistic, therefore, to assume that the mere existence of a legal right to seek relief in superior court provides an effective avenue of relief for some of those who need it the most.

We conclude, therefore, that under state regulation such as that undertaken by Massachusetts, every minor must have the opportunity—if she so desires—to go directly to a court without first consulting or notifying her parents. If she satisfies the court that she is mature and well enough informed to make intelligently the abortion decision on her own, the court must authorize her to act without parental consultation or consent. If she fails to satisfy the court that she is competent to make this decision independently, she must be permitted to show that an abortion nevertheless would be in her best interests. If the court is persuaded that it is, the court must authorize the abortion. If, however, the court is not persuaded by the minor that she is mature or that the abortion would be in her best interests, it may decline to sanction the operation.

There is, however, an important state interest in encouraging a family rather than a judicial resolution of a minor's abortion decision. Also, as we have observed above, parents naturally take an interest in the welfare of their children—an interest that is particularly strong where a normal family relationship exists and where the child is living with one or both parents. These factors properly may be taken into account by a court called upon to determine whether an abortion in fact is in a minor's best interests. If, all things considered, the court determines that an abortion is in the minor's best interests, she is entitled to court authorization without any parental involvement. On the other hand, the court may deny the abortion request of an immature minor in the absence of parental consultation if it concludes that her best interests would be served thereby, or the court may in such a case defer decision until there is parental consultation in which the court may participate. But this is the full extent to which parental involvement may be required.[28] For the reasons stated above, the constitutional right to seek an abortion may not be unduly burdened by state-imposed conditions upon initial access to court.

---

28. Of course, if the minor consults with her parents voluntarily and they withhold consent, she is free to seek judicial authorization for the abortion immediately.

(2)

Section 12S requires that both parents consent to a minor's abortion. The District Court found it to be "custom" to perform other medical and surgical procedures on minors with the consent of only one parent, and it concluded that "nothing about abortions . . . requires the minor's interest to be treated differently." *Baird I.* See *Baird III.*

We are not persuaded that, as a general rule, the requirement of obtaining both parents' consent unconstitutionally burdens a minor's right to seek an abortion. The abortion decision has implications far broader than those associated with most other kinds of medical treatment. At least when the parents are together and the pregnant minor is living at home, both the father and mother have an interest—one normally supportive—in helping to determine the course that is in the best interests of a daughter. Consent and involvement by parents in important decisions by minors long have been recognized as protective of their immaturity. In the case of the abortion decision, for reasons we have stated, the focus of the parents' inquiry should be the best interests of their daughter. As every pregnant minor is entitled in the first instance to go directly to the court for a judicial determination without prior parental notice, consultation, or consent, the general rule with respect to parental consent does not unduly burden the constitutional right. Moreover, where the pregnant minor goes to her parents and consent is denied, she still must have recourse to a prompt judicial determination of her maturity or best interests.

(3)

Another of the questions certified by the District Court to the Supreme Judicial Court was the following: "If the superior court finds that the minor is capable [of making], and has, in fact, made and adhered to, an informed and reasonable decision to have an abortion, may the court refuse its consent based on a finding that a parent's, or its own, contrary decision is a better one?" *Attorney General*, 371 Mass., at 747 n. 5 360 N. E. 2d, at 293 n. 5. To this the state court answered:

> "[W]e do not view the judge's role as limited to a determination that the minor is capable of making, and has made, an informed and reasonable decision to have an abortion. Certainly the judge must make a determination of those circumstances, but, if the statutory role of the judge to determine the best interests of the minor is to be carried out, he must make a finding on the basis of all relevant views presented to him. We suspect that the judge will give great weight to the minor's determination, if informed and reasonable, but in circumstances where he determines that the best interests of the minor will not be served by an abortion, the judge's determination should prevail, assuming that his conclusion is supported by the evidence and adequate findings of fact." *Id.*, at 748, 360 N.E.2d, at 293.

The Supreme Judicial Court's statement reflects the general rule that a State may require a minor to wait until the age of majority before being permitted to exercise legal rights independently. See n. 23, *supra*. But we are concerned here with the exercise of a constitutional right of unique character. See *supra*, at 642–643. As stated above, if the minor satisfies a court that she has attained sufficient maturity to make a fully informed decision, she then is entitled to make her abortion decision independently. We therefore agree with the District Court that § 12S cannot constitutionally permit judicial disregard of the abortion decision of a minor who has been determined to be mature and fully competent to assess the implications of the choice she has made. . . .

HARRIS, SECRETARY OF HEALTH AND HUMAN SERVICES *v.* McRAE ET AL.

APPEAL FROM THE UNITED STATES DISTRICT COURT FOR THE EASTERN DISTRICT OF NEW YORK

No. 79–1268. Argued April 21, 1980—Decided June 30, 1980

STEWART, J., delivered the opinion of the Court, in which BURGER, C. J., and WHITE, POWELL, and REHNQUIST, JJ., joined. WHITE, J., filed a concurring opinion. BRENNAN, J., filed a dissenting opinion, in which MARSHALL and BLACKMUN, JJ., joined. MARSHALL, J., BLACKMUN, J., and STEVENS, J., filed dissenting opinions.

MR. JUSTICE STEWART delivered the opinion of the Court.

Since September 1976, Congress has prohibited—either by an amendment to the annual appropriations bill for the Department of Health, Education, and Welfare . . . or by a joint resolution—the use of any federal funds to reimburse the cost of abortions under the Medicaid program except under certain specified circumstances. This funding restriction is commonly known as the "Hyde Amendment," after its original congressional sponsor, Representative Hyde. The current version of the Hyde Amendment, applicable for fiscal year 1980, provides:

> "[N]one of the funds provided by this joint resolution shall be used to perform abortions except where the life of the mother would be endangered if the fetus were carried to term; or except for such medical procedures necessary for the victims of rape or incest when such rape or incest has been reported promptly to a law enforcement agency or public health service." Pub. L. 96–123, § 109, 93 Stat. 926.

See also Pub. L. 96–86, § 118, 93 Stat. 662. This version of the Hyde Amendment is broader than that applicable for fiscal year 1977, which did not include the "rape or incest" exception, Pub. L. 94–439, § 209, 90 Stat. 1434, but narrower than that applicable for most of fiscal year 1978, . . . and all of fiscal year 1979, which had an additional exception for "instances where severe and long-lasting physical health damage to the mother would result if the pregnancy were carried to term when so determined by two physicians," Pub. L. 95–205, § 101, 91 Stat. 1460; Pub. L. 95–480, § 210, 92 Stat. 1586. . . .

On September 30, 1976, the day on which Congress enacted the initial version of the Hyde Amendment, these consolidated cases were filed in the District Court for the Eastern District of New York. The plaintiffs—Cora McRae, a New York Medicaid recipient then in the first trimester of a pregnancy that she wished to terminate; the New York

City Health and Hospitals Corp., a public benefit corporation that operates 16 hospitals, 12 of which provide abortion services; and others—sought to enjoin the enforcement of the funding restriction on abortions. They alleged that the Hyde Amendment violated the First, Fourth, Fifth, and Ninth Amendments of the Constitution insofar as it limited the funding of abortions to those necessary to save the life of the mother, while permitting the funding of costs associated with childbirth. . . .

After a lengthy trial, which inquired into the medical reasons for abortions and the diverse religious views on the subject,[6] the District Court filed an opinion and entered a judgment invalidating all versions of the Hyde Amendment on constitutional grounds. . . . The District Court rejected the plaintiffs' statutory argument, concluding that even though Title XIX would otherwise have required a participating State to fund medically necessary abortions, the Hyde Amendment had substantively amended Title XIX to relieve a State of that funding obligation. Turning then to the constitutional issues, the District Court concluded that the Hyde Amendment, though valid under the Establishment Clause, violates the equal protection component of the Fifth Amendment's Due Process Clause and the Free Exercise Clause of the First Amendment. With regard to the Fifth Amendment, the District Court noted that when an abortion is "medically necessary to safeguard the pregnant woman's health, . . . the disentitlement to [M]edicaid assistance impinges directly on the woman's right to decide, in consultation with her physician and in reliance on his judgment, to terminate her pregnancy in order to preserve her health." . . . *McRae v. Califano*, 491 F. Supp. 630, 737. The court concluded that the Hyde Amendment violates the equal protection guarantee because, in its view, the decision of Congress to fund medically necessary services generally but only certain medically necessary abortions serves no legitimate governmental interest. As to the Free Exercise Clause of the First Amendment, the court held that insofar as a woman's decision to seek a medically necessary abortion may be a product of her religious beliefs under certain Protestant and Jewish tenets, the funding restrictions of the Hyde Amendment violate that constitutional guarantee as well. . . .

We address first the appellees' argument that the Hyde Amendment, by restricting the availability of certain medically necessary abortions under Medicaid, impinges on the "liberty" protected by the Due Process Clause as recognized in *Roe v. Wade*, 410 U.S. 113, and its progeny. . . .

In *Maher v. Roe*, 432 U.S. 464, the Court was presented with the question whether the scope of personal constitutional freedom recognized in *Roe v. Wade* included an entitlement to Medicaid payments for abortions that are not medically necessary. At issue in *Maher* was a Connecticut welfare regulation under which Medicaid recipients received payments for medical services incident to childbirth, but not for medical services incident

---

6. The trial, which was conducted between August 1977 and September 1978, produced a record containing more than 400 documentary and film exhibits and a transcript exceeding 5,000 pages.

to nontherapeutic abortions. The District Court held that the regulation violated the Equal Protection Clause of the Fourteenth Amendment because the unequal subsidization of childbirth and abortion impinged on the "fundamental right to abortion" recognized in *Wade* and its progeny. . . .

The Hyde Amendment, like the Connecticut welfare regulation at issue in *Maher*, places no governmental obstacle in the path of a woman who chooses to terminate her pregnancy, but rather, by means of unequal subsidization of abortion and other medical services, encourages alternative activity deemed in the public interest. The present case does differ factually from *Maher* insofar as that case involved a failure to fund nontherapeutic abortions, whereas the Hyde Amendment withholds funding of certain medically necessary abortions. . . .

. . . [R]egardless of whether the freedom of a woman to choose to terminate her pregnancy for health reasons lies at the core or the periphery of the due process liberty recognized in *Wade*, it simply does not follow that a woman's freedom of choice carries with it a constitutional entitlement to the financial resources to avail herself of the full range of protected choices. The reason why was explained in *Maher*: although government may not place obstacles in the path of a woman's exercise of her freedom of choice, it need not remove those not of its own creation. Indigency falls in the latter category. The financial constraints that restrict an indigent woman's ability to enjoy the full range of constitutionally protected freedom of choice are the product not of governmental restrictions on access to abortions, but rather of her indigency. Although Congress has opted to subsidize medically necessary services generally, but not certain medically necessary abortions, the fact remains that the Hyde Amendment leaves an indigent woman with at least the same range of choice in deciding whether to obtain a medically necessary abortion as she would have had if Congress had chosen to subsidize no health care costs at all. We are thus not persuaded that the Hyde Amendment impinges on the constitutionally protected freedom of choice recognized in *Wade*. . . .

Although the liberty protected by the Due Process Clause affords protection against unwarranted government interference with freedom of choice in the context of certain personal decisions, it does not confer an entitlement to such funds as may be necessary to realize all the advantages of that freedom. To hold otherwise would mark a drastic change in our understanding of the Constitution. It cannot be that because government may not prohibit the use of contraceptives, *Griswold* v. *Connecticut*, 381 U.S. 479, or prevent parents from sending their child to a private school, *Pierce* v. *Society of Sisters*, 268 U.S. 510, government, therefore, has an affirmative constitutional obligation to ensure that all persons have the financial resources to obtain contraceptives or send their children to private schools. To translate the limitation on governmental power implicit in the Due Process Clause into an affirmative funding obligation would require Congress to subsidize the medically necessary abortion of an indigent woman even if Congress had not enacted a Medicaid program to subsidize other medically necessary services. . . .

The appellees also argue that the Hyde Amendment contravenes rights secured by the Religion Clauses of the First Amendment. It is the appellees' view that the Hyde Amendment violates the Establishment Clause because it incorporates into law the doctrines of the Roman Catholic Church concerning the sinfulness of abortion and the time at which life commences. Moreover, insofar as a woman's decision to seek a medically necessary abortion may be a product of her religious beliefs under certain Protestant and Jewish tenets, the appellees assert that the funding limitations of the Hyde Amendment impinge on the freedom of religion guaranteed by the Free Exercise Clause.

1

It is well settled that "a legislative enactment does not contravene the Establishment Clause if it has a secular legislative purpose, if its principal or primary effect neither advances nor inhibits religion, and if it does not foster an excessive governmental entanglement with religion." *Committee for Public Education* v. *Regan*, 444 U.S. 646, 653. Applying this standard, the District Court properly concluded that the Hyde Amendment does not run afoul of the Establishment Clause. Although neither a State nor the Federal Government can constitutionally "pass laws which aid one religion, aid all religions, or prefer one religion over another," *Everson* v. *Board of Education*, 330 U.S. 1, 15, it does not follow that a statute violates the Establishment Clause because it "happens to coincide or harmonize with the tenets of some or all religions." *McGowan* v. *Maryland*, 366 U.S. 420, 442. That the Judaeo-Christian religions oppose stealing does not mean that a State or the Federal Government may not, consistent with the Establishment Clause, enact laws prohibiting larceny. . . .

It remains to be determined whether the Hyde Amendment violates the equal protection component of the Fifth Amendment. This challenge is premised on the fact that, although federal reimbursement is available under Medicaid for medically necessary services generally, the Hyde Amendment does not permit federal reimbursement of all medically necessary abortions. The District Court held, and the appellees argue here, that this selective subsidization violates the constitutional guarantee of equal protection.

The guarantee of equal protection under the Fifth Amendment is not a source of substantive rights or liberties,[25] but rather a right to be free from invidious discrimination in statutory classifications and other governmental activity. It is well settled that

---

25. An exception to this statement is to be found in *Reynolds* v. *Sims*, 377 U.S. 533, and its progeny. Although the Constitution of the United States does not confer the right to vote in state elections, see *Minor* v. *Happersett*, 21 Wall. 162, 178, *Reynolds* held that if a State adopts an electoral system, the Equal Protection Clause of the Fourteenth Amendment confers upon a qualified voter a substantive right to participate in the electoral process equally with other qualified voters. See, *e.g.*, *Dunn* v. *Blumstein*, 405 U.S. 330, 336.

where a statutory classification does not itself impinge on a right or liberty protected by the Constitution, the validity of classification must be sustained unless "the classification rests on grounds wholly irrelevant to the achievement of [any legitimate governmental] objective." *McGowan* v. *Maryland*, 366 U.S., at 425. This presumption of constitutional validity, however, disappears if a statutory classification is predicated on criteria that are, in a constitutional sense, "suspect," the principal example of which is a classification based on race, *e.g.*, *Brown* v. *Board of Education*, 347 U.S. 483.

1

For the reasons stated above, we have already concluded that the Hyde Amendment violates no constitutionally protected substantive rights. We now conclude as well that it is not predicated on a constitutionally suspect classification....

Here, as in *Maher*, the principal impact of the Hyde Amendment falls on the indigent. But that fact does not itself render the funding restriction constitutionally invalid, for this Court has held repeatedly that poverty, standing alone, is not a suspect classification. See, *e.g.*, *James* v. *Valtierra*, 402 U.S. 137. That *Maher* involved the refusal to fund nontherapeutic abortions, whereas the present case involves the refusal to fund medically necessary abortions, has no bearing on the factors that render a classification "suspect" within the meaning of the constitutional guarantee of equal protection....

Mr. Justice Brennan, with whom Mr. Justice Marshall and Mr. Justice Blackmun join, dissenting.

I agree entirely with my Brother Stevens that the State's interest in protecting the potential life of the fetus cannot justify the exclusion of financially and medically needy women from the benefits to which they would otherwise be entitled solely because the treatment that a doctor has concluded is medically necessary involves an abortion. I write separately to express my continuing disagreement... with the Court's mischaracterization of the nature of the fundamental right recognized in *Roe* v. *Wade*, 410 U.S. 113 (1973), and its misconception of the manner in which that right is infringed by federal and state legislation withdrawing all funding for medically necessary abortions.

Roe v. *Wade* held that the constitutional right to personal privacy encompasses a woman's decision whether or not to terminate her pregnancy. *Roe* and its progeny... established that the pregnant woman has a right to be free from state interference with her choice to have an abortion—a right which, at least prior to the end of the first trimester, absolutely prohibits any governmental regulation of that highly personal decision.... The proposition for which these cases stand thus is not that the State is under an affirmative obligation to ensure access to abortions for all who may desire them; it is that the State must refrain from wielding its enormous power and influence in a manner that might burden the pregnant woman's freedom to choose whether to have an abortion. The Hyde Amendment's denial of public funds for medically necessary abortions plainly intrudes upon this constitutionally protected decision, for both by design and in effect it serves to coerce indigent pregnant women to bear children that they would otherwise elect not to have. . . .

When viewed in the context of the Medicaid program to which it is appended, it is obvious that the Hyde Amendment is nothing less than an attempt by Congress to circumvent the dictates of the Constitution and achieve indirectly what *Roe* v. *Wade* said it could not do directly. . . . Under Title XIX of the Social Security Act, the Federal Government reimburses participating States for virtually all medically necessary services it provides to the categorically needy. The sole limitation of any significance is the Hyde Amendment's prohibition against the use of any federal funds to pay for the costs of abortions (except where the life of the mother would be endangered if the fetus were carried to term). As my Brother STEVENS persuasively demonstrates, exclusion of medically necessary abortions from Medicaid coverage cannot be justified as a cost-saving device. Rather, the Hyde Amendment is a transparent attempt by the Legislative Branch to impose the political majority's judgment of the morally acceptable and socially desirable preference on a sensitive and intimate decision that the Constitution entrusts to the individual. Worse yet, the Hyde Amendment does not foist that majoritarian viewpoint with equal measure upon everyone in our Nation, rich and poor alike; rather, it imposes that viewpoint only upon that segment of our society which, because of its position of political powerless-ness, is least able to defend its privacy rights from the encroachments of state-mandated morality. The instant legislation thus calls for more exacting judicial review than in most other cases. "When elected leaders cower before public pressure, this Court, more than ever, must not shirk its duty to enforce the Constitution for the benefit of the poor and powerless." *Beal* v. *Doe*, 432 U.S. 438, 462 (1977) (MARSHALL, J., dissenting). Though it may not be this Court's mission "to decide whether the balance of competing interests reflected in the Hyde Amendment is wise social policy," it most assuredly is our responsibility to vindicate the pregnant woman's constitutional right to decide whether to bear children free from governmental intrusion. . . .

A poor woman in the early stages of pregnancy confronts two alternatives: she may elect either to carry the fetus to term or to have an abortion. In the abstract, of course, this choice is hers alone, and the Court rightly observes that the Hyde Amendment "places no governmental obstacle in the path of a woman who chooses to terminate her pregnancy." But the reality of the situation is that the Hyde Amendment has effectively removed this choice from the indigent woman's hands. By funding all of the expenses associated with childbirth and none of the expenses incurred in terminating pregnancy, the Government literally makes an offer that the indigent woman cannot afford to refuse. It matters not that in this instance the Government has used the carrot rather than the stick. What is critical is the realization that as a practical matter, many poverty-stricken women will choose to carry their pregnancy to term simply because the Government provides funds for the associated medical services, even though these same women would have chosen to have an abortion if the Government had also paid for that option, or indeed if the Government had stayed out of the picture altogether and had defrayed the costs of neither procedure.

The fundamental flaw in the Court's due process analysis, then, is its failure to acknowledge that the discriminatory distribution of the benefits of governmental largesse can discourage the exercise of fundamental liberties just as effectively as can an outright denial of those rights through criminal and regulatory sanctions. Implicit in the Court's reasoning is the notion that as long as the Government is not obligated to provide its citizens with certain benefits or privileges, it may condition the grant of such benefits on the recipient's relinquishment of his constitutional rights.

Mr. Justice Stevens, dissenting.

"The federal sovereign, like the States, must govern impartially. The concept of equal justice under law is served by the Fifth Amendment's guarantee of due process, as well as by the Equal Protection Clause of the Fourteenth Amendment." *Hampton* v. *Mow Sun Wong*, 426 U.S. 88, 100. When the sovereign provides a special benefit or a special protection for a class of persons, it must define the membership in the class by neutral criteria; it may not make special exceptions for reasons that are constitutionally insufficient. . . .

A fundamentally different question was decided in *Maher* v. *Roe*, 432 U.S. 464. Unlike these plaintiffs, the plaintiffs in *Maher* did not satisfy the neutral criterion of medical need; they sought a subsidy for nontherapeutic abortions—medical procedures which by definition they did not need. In rejecting that claim, the Court held that their constitutional right to choose that procedure did not impose a duty on the State to subsidize the exercise of that right. Nor did the fact that the State had undertaken to pay for the necessary medical care associated with childbirth require the State also to pay for abortions that were not necessary; for only necessary medical procedures satisfied the neutral statutory criteria. Nontherapeutic abortions were simply outside the ambit of the medical benefits program. Thus, in *Maher*, the plaintiffs' desire to exercise a constitutional right gave rise to neither special access nor special exclusion from the pool of benefits created by Title XIX.

These cases involve a special exclusion of women who, by definition, are confronted with a choice between two serious harms: serious health damage to themselves on the one hand and abortion on the other. The competing interests are the interest in maternal health and the interest in protecting potential human life. It is now part of our law that the pregnant woman's decision as to which of these conflicting interests shall prevail is entitled to constitutional protection.

If a woman has a constitutional right to place a higher value on avoiding either serious harm to her own health or perhaps an abnormal childbirth . . . than on protecting potential life, the exercise of that right cannot provide the basis for the denial of a benefit to which she would otherwise be entitled. The Court's sterile equal protection analysis evades this critical though simple point. The Court focuses exclusively on the "legitimate interest in protecting the potential life of the fetus." . . . It concludes that since the Hyde Amendments further that interest, the exclusion they create is rational and therefore constitutional. But it is misleading to speak of the Government's legitimate interest in the fetus without reference to the context in which that interest was held to be legitimate. For *Roe* v. *Wade* squarely held that the States may not protect that interest when a conflict with the interest in a pregnant woman's health exists. . . .

Nor can it be argued that the exclusion of this type of medically necessary treatment of the indigent can be justified on fiscal grounds. There are some especially costly forms of treatment that may reasonably be excluded from the program in order to preserve the assets in the pool and extend its benefits to the maximum number of needy persons. Fiscal considerations may compel certain difficult choices in order to improve the protection afforded to the entire benefited class. . . . But, ironically, the exclusion of medically necessary abortions harms the entire class as well as its specific victims. For the records in both *McRae* and *Zbaraz* demonstrate that the cost of an abortion is only a small fraction of the costs associated with childbirth. . . . Thus, the decision to tolerate harm to indigent persons who need an abortion in order to avoid "serious and long-lasting health damage" is one that is financed by draining money out of the pool that is used to fund all other necessary medical procedures. Unlike most invidious classifications, this discrimination harms not only its direct victims but also the remainder of the class of needy persons that the pool was designed to benefit. . . .

H. L. v. MATHESON, GOVERNOR OF UTAH, ET AL.

APPEAL FROM THE SUPREME COURT OF UTAH

No. 79–5903. Argued October 6, 1980—Decided March 23, 1981

BURGER, C. J., delivered the opinion of the Court, in which STEWART, WHITE, POWELL, and REHNQUIST, JJ., joined. POWELL, J., filed a concurring opinion, in which STEWART, J., joined. STEVENS, J., filed an opinion concurring in the judgment. MARSHALL, J., filed a dissenting opinion, in which BRENNAN and BLACKMUN, JJ., joined.

CHIEF JUSTICE BURGER delivered the opinion of the Court.

The question presented in this case is whether a state statute which requires a physician to "[n]otify, if possible," the parents of a dependent, unmarried minor girl prior to performing an abortion on the girl violates federal constitutional guarantees.

I

In the spring of 1978, appellant was an unmarried 15-year-old girl living with her parents in Utah and dependent on them for her support. She discovered she was pregnant. She consulted with a social worker and a physician. The physician advised appellant that an abortion would be in her best medical interest. However, because of Utah Code Ann. § 76–7–304 (1978), he refused to perform the abortion without first notifying appellant's parents.

Section 76–7–304, enacted in 1974, provides:

"To enable the physician to exercise his best medical judgment [in considering a possible abortion], he shall:

"(1) Consider all factors relevant to the well-being of the woman upon whom the abortion is to be performed including, but not limited to,

"(a) Her physical, emotional and psychological health and safety,

"(b) Her age,

"(c) Her familial situation.

"(2) *Notify, if possible, the parents or guardian of the woman upon whom the abortion is to be performed, if she is a minor* or the husband of the woman, if she is married." (Emphasis supplied.) . . .

Violation of this section is a misdemeanor punishable by imprisonment for not more than one year or a fine of not more than $1,000. . . .

Appellant believed "for [her] own reasons" that she should proceed with the abortion without notifying her parents. According to appellant, the social worker concurred in this decision.[3] While still in the first trimester of her pregnancy, appellant instituted this action in the Third Judicial District Court of Utah. . . . She sought a declaration that § 76–7–304 (2) is unconstitutional and an injunction prohibiting appellees, the Governor and the Attorney General of Utah, from enforcing the statute. Appellant sought to represent a class consisting of unmarried "minor women who are suffering unwanted pregnancies and desire to terminate the pregnancies but may not do so" because of their physicians' insistence on complying with § 76–7–304 (2). The trial judge declined to grant a temporary restraining order or a preliminary injunction.[5]

The trial judge held a hearing at which appellant was the only witness. Appellant affirmed the allegations of the complaint by giving monosyllabic answers to her attorney's leading questions.[6] However, when the State attempted to cross-examine appellant

---

3. Appellant's counsel stated in his jurisdictional statement and again in his brief that the physician concluded not only that an abortion would be in appellant's best interests, but also that parental notification would not be in appellant's best interests. However, at oral argument, counsel corrected this statement and conceded that there is no evidence to support this assertion. Tr. of Oral Arg. 8, 17.

5. The trial judge allowed appellant to proceed without appointment of a guardian *ad litem*. He noted that a guardian would be required to notify the parents.

6. The testimony was as follows:
"BY MR. DOLOWITZ [appellant's counsel]:
"Q At the time that the Complaint in this matter was signed, you were pregnant?
"A Yes.
"Q You had consulted with a counselor about that pregnancy?
"A Yeah.
"Q You had determined after talking to the counselor that you felt you should get an abortion?
"A Yes.
"Q You felt that you did not want to notify your parents—
"A Right.
"Q—of that decision? You did not feel for your own reasons that you could discuss it with them?
"A Right.
"Q After discussing the matter with a counselor, you still believed that you should not discuss it with your parents?
"A Right.
"Q And they shouldn't be notified?
"A Right.
"Q After talking the matter over with a counselor, the counselor concurred in your decision that your parents should not be notified?

about her reasons for not wishing to notify her parents, appellant's counsel vigorously objected,[7] insisting that "the specifics of the reasons are really irrelevant to the Constitutional issue."[8] The only constitutionally permissible prerequisites for performance of an

---

"A Right.
"Q You were advised that an abortion couldn't be performed without notifying them?
"A Yes.
"Q You then came to me to see about filing a suit?
"A Right.
"Q You and I discussed it as to whether or not you had a right to do what you wanted to do?
"A Yes.
"Q You decided that, after our discussion, you should still proceed with the action to try to obtain an abortion without notifying your parents?
"A Right.
"Q Now, at the time that you signed the Complaint and spoke with the counselor and spoke with me, you were in the first trimester of pregnancy, within your first twelve weeks of pregnancy?
"A Yes.
"Q You feel that, from talking to the counselor and thinking the situation over and discussing it with me, that you could make the decision on your own that you wished to abort the pregnancy?
"A Yes.
"Q You are living at home?
"A Yes.
"Q You still felt, even though you were living at home with your parents, that you couldn't discuss the matter with them?
"A Right."
Tr. 5–7.

7. "BY MR. McCARTHY [counsel for the State]:
"Q . . . Are you still living at home?
"A Yes.
"Q Are you dependent on your parents?
"A Yes.
"Q All your money comes from them?
"A Yes.
"Q How old are you now?
"A Fifteen.
"Q Aside from the issue of abortion, do you have any reason to feel that you can't talk to your parents about other problems?
"A Yes.
"Q What are those reasons?
"MR. DOLOWITZ: Now you are moving into the problem area that I indicated. . . ."
Id., at 8.

8. *Id.*, at 10. Appellant repeatedly pressed this point despite the trial court's statements that it could "conceive of a situation where a child probably wouldn't have to tell the parents" and that the statute

abortion, he insisted, were the desire of the girl and the medical approval of a physician. . . . The trial judge sustained the objection, tentatively construing the statute to require appellant's physician to notify her parents "if he is able to physically contact them."

Thereafter, the trial judge entered findings of fact and conclusions of law. He concluded that appellant "is an appropriate representative to represent the class she purports to represent." . . . He construed the statute to require notice to appellant's parents "if it is physically possible." He concluded that § 76-7-304 (2) "do[es] not unconstitutionally restrict the right of privacy of a minor to obtain an abortion or to enter into a doctor-patient relationship." . . . Accordingly, he dismissed the complaint.

On appeal, the Supreme Court of Utah unanimously upheld the statute. . . .

The Utah Supreme Court held that notifying the parents of a minor seeking an abortion is "substantially and logically related" to the *Doe* factors set out in § 76-7-304 (1) because parents ordinarily possess information essential to a physician's exercise of his best medical judgment concerning the child. 604 P. 2d, at 909-910. The court also concluded that encouraging an unmarried pregnant minor to seek the advice of her parents in making the decision of whether to carry her child to term promotes a significant state interest in supporting the important role of parents in child-rearing. *Id.*, at 912. The court reasoned that since the statute allows no veto power over the minor's decision, it does not unduly intrude upon a minor's rights. . . .

Although we have held that a state may not constitutionally legislate a blanket, unreviewable power of parents to veto their daughter's abortion,[15] a statute setting out a "mere requirement of parental notice" does not violate the constitutional rights of an immature, dependent minor.[16] Four Justices in *Bellotti II* joined in stating:

> "[Plaintiffs] suggest . . . that the mere requirement of parental notice [unduly burdens the right to seek an abortion]. As stated in Part II above, however, parental notice and consent are qualifications that typically may be imposed by the State on a minor's right to make important decisions. As immature minors often lack the ability to make fully informed choices that take account of both immediate and long-range consequences, a State reasonably may determine that parental consultation often is desirable and in the best interest of the minor. It may further determine, as a general proposition, that such consultation is particularly desirable with respect to the abortion decision—one that for some people raises profound moral and religious concerns. . . .

"might be [u]nconstitutional as it relates to a particular fact situation but [c]onstitutional as it relates to another fact situation." *Id.*, at 10, 17. . . .

15. *Bellotti II*, 443 U.S., at 642–643, 653–656; *Danforth*, 428 U.S., at 74.

16. *Bellotti II*, *supra*, at 640, 649; *id.*, at 657 (dissenting opinion); *Danforth*, *supra*, at 90–91 (concurring opinion); see *Bellotti* v. *Baird*, 428 U.S. 132, 145, 147 (1976) (*Bellotti I*); cf. *Carey* v. *Population Services International*, 431 U.S. 678, 709–710 (1977).

"'There can be little doubt that the State furthers a constitutionally permissible end by encouraging an unmarried pregnant minor to seek the help and advice of her parents in making the very important decision whether or not to bear a child. That is a grave decision, and a girl of tender years, under emotional stress, may be ill-equipped to make it without mature advice and emotional support. It seems unlikely that she will obtain adequate counsel and support from the attending physician at an abortion clinic, where abortions for pregnant minors frequently take place.'" *Id.*, at 640–641 (footnotes omitted), quoting *Danforth*, 428 U.S., at 91 (concurring opinion). . . .

The Utah statute gives neither parents nor judges a veto power over the minor's abortion decision.[17] As in *Bellotti I*, "we are concerned with a statute directed toward minors, as to whom there are unquestionably greater risks of inability to give an informed consent." 428 U.S., at 147. As applied to immature and dependent minors, the statute plainly serves the important considerations of family integrity[18] and protecting adolescents[19] which we identified in *Bellotti II*. In addition, as applied to that class, the statute serves a significant state interest by providing an opportunity for parents to supply essential medical and other information to a physician. The medical, emotional, and psychological consequences of an abortion are serious and can be lasting; this is particularly so when the patient is immature.[20] An adequate medical and psychological case history is important to the physician. Parents can provide medical and psychological data, refer the physician to other sources of medical history, such as family physicians, and authorize family physicians to give relevant data. . . .

As applied to the class properly before us, the statute plainly serves important state interests, is narrowly drawn to protect only those interests, and does not violate any guarantees of the Constitution. . . . The judgment of the Supreme Court of Utah is

Affirmed.

---

17. The main premise of the dissent seems to be that a requirement of notice to the parents is the functional equivalent of a requirement of parental consent. In *Bellotti II*, however, we expressly declined to equate notice requirements with consent requirements. 443 U.S., at 640, 657.

18. *Bellotti II*. The short shrift given by the dissent to "parental authority and family integrity," *post*, at 447, runs contrary to a long line of constitutional cases in this Court. See cases cited *supra*, at 410.

19. *Bellotti II*, at 634–637.

20. Abortion is associated with an increased risk of complication in subsequent pregnancies. Maine, Does Abortion Affect Later Pregnancies?, 11 Family Planning Perspectives 98 (1979). The emotional and psychological effects of the pregnancy and abortion experience are markedly more severe in girls under 18 than in adults. Wallerstein, Kurtz, & Bar-Din, Psychosocial Sequelae of Therapeutic Abortion in Young Unmarried Women, 27 Arch. Gen. Psychiatry 828 (1972); see also Babikian & Goldman, A Study in Teen-Age Pregnancy, 128 Am. J. Psychiatry 755 (1971).

JUSTICE MARSHALL, with whom JUSTICE BRENNAN and JUSTICE BLACKMUN join, dissenting.

In upholding the statute, the Utah Supreme Court concluded that the notification provision might encourage parental transmission of "additional information, which might prove invaluable to the physician in exercising his 'best medical judgment.'" . . . Yet neither the Utah courts nor the statute itself specifies the kind of information contemplated for this purpose, nor why it is available to the parents but not to the minor woman herself. Most parents lack the medical expertise necessary to supplement the physician's medical judgment, and at best could provide facts about the patient's medical history. It seems doubtful that a minor mature enough to become pregnant and to seek medical advice on her own initiative would be unable or unwilling to provide her physician with information crucial to the abortion decision. In addition, by law the physician already is obligated to obtain all information necessary to form his best medical judgment, . . . and nothing bars consultation with the parents should the physician find it necessary.

Even if mandatory parental notice serves a substantial state purpose in this regard, the Utah statute fails to implement it. Simply put, the statute on its face does not require or even encourage the transfer of information; it does not even call for a conversation between the physician and the parents. A letter from the physician to the parents would satisfy the statute, as would a brief telephone call made moments before the abortion. . . . Moreover, the statute is patently underinclusive if its aim is the transfer of information known to the parents but unavailable from the minor woman herself. The statute specifically excludes married minors from the parental notice requirement; only her husband need be told of the planned abortion, Utah Code Ann. § 76–7–304 (2) (1978), and Utah makes no claim that he possesses any information valuable to the physician's judgment but unavailable from the pregnant woman. Furthermore, no notice is required for other pregnancy-related care sought by the minor. See Utah Code Ann. § 78–14–5 (4) (f) (1977) (authorizing women of any age to consent to pregnancy-related medical care). The minor woman may consent to surgical removal and analysis of amniotic fluid, caesarian delivery, and other medical care related to pregnancy. The physician's decisions concerning such procedures would be enhanced by parental information as much as would the abortion decision, yet only the abortion decision triggers the parental notice requirement. This result is especially anomalous given the comparatively lesser health risks associated with abortion as contrasted with other pregnancy-related medical care.[38] Thus, the statute not only fails to promote the transfer of

---

38. I am baffled by the majority's statement today that "[i]f the pregnant girl elects to carry her child to term, the *medical* decisions to be made entail few—perhaps none—of the potentially grave and emotional and psychological consequences of the decision to abort," *ante*, at 412–413. Choosing to participate in diagnostic tests involves risks to both mother and child, and also may burden the pregnant woman with knowledge that the child will be handicapped. See 3 National Institutes of Health, Prevention of Embryonic, Fetal, and Perinatal Disease 347–352 (R. Brent & M. Harris eds.

information as is claimed, it does not apply to other closely related contexts in which such exchange of information would be no less important. The goal of promoting consultation between the physician and the parents of the pregnant minor cannot sustain a statute that is so ill-fitted to serve it. . . .

B

Appellees also claim the statute serves the legitimate purpose of improving the minor's decision by encouraging consultation between the minor woman and her parents. Appellees do not dispute that the State cannot legally or practically require such consultation. . . . Nor do appellees contest the fact that the decision is ultimately the minor's to make. . . . Nonetheless, the State seeks through the notice requirement to give parents the opportunity to contribute to the minor woman's abortion decision.

Ideally, facilitation of supportive conversation would assist the pregnant minor during an undoubtedly difficult experience. Again, however, when measured against the rationality of the means employed, the Utah statute simply fails to advance this asserted goal. The statute imposes no requirement that the notice be sufficiently timely to permit any discussion between the pregnant minor and the parents. Moreover, appellant's claims require us to examine the statute's purpose in relation to the parents who the minor believes are likely to respond with hostility or opposition. In this light, the statute is plainly overbroad. Parental consultation hardly seems a legitimate state purpose where the minor's pregnancy resulted from incest, where a hostile or abusive parental response is assured, or where the minor's fears of such a response deter her from the abortion she desires. The absolute nature of the statutory requirement, with exception permitted only if the parents are physically unavailable, violates the requirement that regulations in this fundamentally personal area be carefully tailored to serve a significant state interest.[42] "The need to preserve the constitutional right

---

1976); Risks in the Practice of Modern Obstetrics 59–81, 369–370 (S. Aladjem ed. 1975). The decision to undergo surgery to save the child's life certainly carries as serious "emotional and psychological consequences" for the pregnant adolescent as does the decision to abort; in both instances, the minor confronts the task of calculating not only medical risks, but also all the issues involved in giving birth to a child. See *id.*, at 59–81. For an unwed adolescent, these issues include her future educational and job opportunities, as well as the more immediate problems of finding financial and emotional support for offspring dependent entirely on her. *Michael M.* v. *Sonoma County Superior Court, post,* at 470, and nn. 3 and 4 (REHNQUIST, J.) (plurality opinion). When surgery to save the child's life poses greater risks to the mother's life, the emotional and ethical dimensions of the medical care decision assume crisis proportion. Of course, for minors, the mere fact of pregnancy and the experience of childbirth can produce psychological upheaval.

42. State-sponsored counseling services, in contrast, could promote family dialogue and also improve the minor's decision-making process. Appellant H. L., for example, consulted with a counselor who supported her decision. The role of counselors can be significant in facilitating the

and the unique nature of the abortion decision, especially when made by a minor, require a State to act with particular sensitivity when it legislates to foster parental involvement in this matter." *Bellotti II*, 443 U.S., at 642 (POWELL, J.). Because Utah's absolute notice requirement demonstrates no such sensitivity, I cannot approve its interference with the minor's private consultation with the physician during the first trimester of her pregnancy.

C

Finally, appellees assert a state interest in protecting parental authority and family integrity. . . . This Court, of course, has recognized that the "primary role of the parents in the upbringing of their children is now established beyond debate as an enduring American tradition." *Wisconsin* v. *Yoder*, 406 U.S. 205, 232 (1972). See *Prince* v. *Massachusetts*, 321 U.S. 158 (1944); *Meyer* v. *Nebraska*, 262 U.S. 390 (1923). Indeed, "those who nurture [the child] and direct his destiny have the right, coupled with the high duty, to recognize and prepare him for additional obligations." *Pierce* v. *Society of Sisters*, 268 U.S., at 535. Similarly, our decisions "have respected the private realm of family life which the state cannot enter." *Prince* v. *Massachusetts, supra*, at 166. See also *Moore* v. *East Cleveland*, 431 U.S., at 505.

The critical thrust of these decisions has been to protect the privacy of individual families from unwarranted state intrusion.[44] Ironically, appellees invoke these decisions in seeking to justify state interference in the normal functioning of the family. Through its notice requirement, the State in fact enters the private realm of the family rather than leaving unaltered the pattern of interactions chosen by the family. Whatever its motive, state intervention is hardly likely to resurrect parental authority that the parents themselves are unable to preserve.[45] . . .

---

pregnant woman's adjustment to decisions related to her pregnancy. See Smith, A Follow-Up Study of Women Who Request Abortion, 43 Am. J. Orthopsychiatry 574, 583–585 (1973).

44. *Wynn* v. *Carey*, 582 F. 2d, at 1385–1386; Note, The Minor's Right of Privacy: Limitations on State Action after *Danforth* and *Carey*, 77 Colum. L. Rev. 1216, 1224 (1977).

45. "The fact that the minor became pregnant and sought an abortion contrary to the parents' wishes indicates that whatever control the parent once had over the minor has diminished, if not evaporated entirely. And we believe that enforcing a single, albeit important, parental decision—at a time when the minor is near to majority status—by an instrument as blunt as a state statute is extremely unlikely to restore parental control." *Poe* v. *Gerstein*, 517 F. 2d 787, 793–794 (CA5 1975), summarily aff'd, 428 U.S. 901 (1976).

CITY OF AKRON v. AKRON CENTER FOR REPRODUCTIVE HEALTH, INC., ET AL.

CERTIORARI TO THE UNITED STATES COURT OF APPEALS FOR THE SIXTH CIRCUIT

No. 81-746. Argued November 30, 1982—Decided June 15, 1983

POWELL, J., delivered the opinion of the Court, in which BURGER, C. J., and BRENNAN, MARSHALL, BLACKMUN, and STEVENS, JJ., joined. O'CONNOR, J., filed a dissenting opinion, in which WHITE and REHNQUIST, JJ., joined.

JUSTICE POWELL delivered the opinion of the Court.

In this litigation we must decide the constitutionality of several provisions of an ordinance enacted by the city of Akron, Ohio, to regulate the performance of abortions. Today we also review abortion regulations enacted by the State of Missouri, see *Planned Parenthood Assn. of Kansas City, Mo., Inc.* v. *Ashcroft*, and by the State of Virginia, see *Simopoulos* v. *Virginia*.

These cases come to us a decade after we held in *Roe* v. *Wade*, 410 U.S. 113 (1973), that the right of privacy, grounded in the concept of personal liberty guaranteed by the Constitution, encompasses a woman's right to decide whether to terminate her pregnancy. Legislative responses to the Court's decision have required us on several occasions, and again today, to define the limits of a State's authority to regulate the performance of abortions. And arguments continue to be made, in these cases as well, that we erred in interpreting the Constitution. Nonetheless, the doctrine of *stare decisis*, while perhaps never entirely persuasive on a constitutional question, is a doctrine that demands respect in a society governed by the rule of law.[1] We respect it today, and reaffirm *Roe* v. *Wade*.

I

In February 1978 the City Council of Akron enacted Ordinance No. 160–1978, entitled "Regulation of Abortions." . . . The ordinance sets forth 17 provisions that regulate

---

1. There are especially compelling reasons for adhering to *stare decisis* in applying the principles of *Roe* v. *Wade*. That case was considered with special care. It was first argued during the 1971 Term, and reargued—with extensive briefing—the following Term. The decision was joined by THE CHIEF JUSTICE and six other Justices. Since *Roe* was decided in January 1973, the Court repeatedly and consistently has accepted and applied the basic principle that a woman has a fundamental right to make the highly personal choice whether or not to terminate her pregnancy. . . .

the performance of abortions, see Akron Codified Ordinances, ch. 1870, 5 of which are at issue in this case:

(i) Section 1870.03 requires that all abortions performed after the first trimester of pregnancy be performed in a hospital. . . .

(ii) Section 1870.05 sets forth requirements for notification of and consent by parents before abortions may be performed on unmarried minors. . . .

(iii) Section 1870.06 requires that the attending physician make certain specified statements to the patient "to insure that the consent for an abortion is truly informed consent." . . .

(iv) Section 1870.07 requires a 24-hour waiting period between the time the woman signs a consent form and the time the abortion is performed. . . .

(v) Section 1870.16 requires that fetal remains be "disposed of in a humane and sanitary manner." . . .

A violation of any section of the ordinance is punishable as a criminal misdemeanor. § 1870.18. If any provision is invalidated, it is to be severed from the remainder of the ordinance. . . . The ordinance became effective on May 1, 1978. . . .

In *Roe* v. *Wade*, the Court held that the "right of privacy, . . . founded in the Fourteenth Amendment's concept of personal liberty and restrictions upon state action, . . . is broad enough to encompass a woman's decision whether or not to terminate her pregnancy." 410 U.S., at 153. Although the Constitution does not specifically identify this right, the history of this Court's constitutional adjudication leaves no doubt that "the full scope of the liberty guaranteed by the Due Process Clause cannot be found in or limited by the precise terms of the specific guarantees elsewhere provided in the Constitution." *Poe* v. *Ullman*, 367 U.S. 497, 543 (1961) (Harlan, J., dissenting from dismissal of appeal). Central among these protected liberties is an individual's "freedom of personal choice in matters of marriage and family life." *Roe*, 410 U.S., at 169 (Stewart, J., concurring). . . .

At the same time, the Court in *Roe* acknowledged that the woman's fundamental right "is not unqualified and must be considered against important state interests in abortion." *Roe*, 410 U.S., at 154. But restrictive state regulation of the right to choose abortion, as with other fundamental rights subject to searching judicial examination, must be supported by a compelling state interest. *Id.*, at 155. We have recognized two such interests that may justify state regulation of abortions. . . .

First, a State has an "important and legitimate interest in protecting the potentiality of human life." *Id.*, at 162. Although this interest exists "throughout the course of the woman's pregnancy," *Beal* v. *Doe*, 432 U.S. 438, 446 (1977), it becomes compelling only at viability, the point at which the fetus "has the capability of meaningful life outside the mother's womb," *Roe*, *supra*, at 163. See *Planned Parenthood of Central Missouri* v. *Danforth*, 428 U.S. 52, 63–65 (1976). At viability this interest in protecting the potential life of the unborn child is so important that the State may proscribe abortions altogether, "except when it is necessary to preserve the life or health of the mother." *Roe*, 410 U.S., at 164.

Second, because a State has a legitimate concern with the health of women who undergo abortions, "a State may properly assert important interests in safeguarding health [and] in maintaining medical standards." We held in *Roe*, however, that this health interest does not become compelling until "approximately the end of the first trimester" of pregnancy. . . . Until that time, a pregnant woman must be permitted, in consultation with her physician, to decide to have an abortion and to effectuate that decision "free of interference by the State." . . .

This does not mean that a State never may enact a regulation touching on the woman's abortion right during the first weeks of pregnancy. Certain regulations that have no significant impact on the woman's exercise of her right may be permissible where justified by important state health objectives. In *Danforth, supra,* we unanimously upheld two Missouri statutory provisions, applicable to the first trimester, requiring the woman to provide her informed written consent to the abortion and the physician to keep certain records, even though comparable requirements were not imposed on most other medical procedures. See 428 U.S., at 65–67, 79–81. The decisive factor was that the State met its burden of demonstrating that these regulations furthered important health-related state concerns. . . . But even these minor regulations on the abortion procedure during the first trimester may not interfere with physician-patient consultation or with the woman's choice between abortion and childbirth.

From approximately the end of the first trimester of pregnancy, the State "may regulate the abortion procedure to the extent that the regulation reasonably relates to the preservation and protection of maternal health." . . . *Roe*, 410 U.S., at 163. The State's discretion to regulate on this basis does not, however, permit it to adopt abortion regulations that depart from accepted medical practice. We have rejected a State's attempt to ban a particular second-trimester abortion procedure, where the ban would have increased the costs and limited the availability of abortions without promoting important health benefits. See *Danforth*, 428 U.S., at 77–78. If a State requires licensing or undertakes to regulate the performance of abortions during this period, the health standards adopted must be "legitimately related to the objective the State seeks to accomplish." *Doe*, 410 U.S., at 195. . . .

There can be no doubt that § 1870.03's second-trimester hospitalization requirement places a significant obstacle in the path of women seeking an abortion. A primary burden created by the requirement is additional cost to the woman. The Court of Appeals noted that there was testimony that a second-trimester abortion costs more than twice as much in a hospital as in a clinic. See 651 F. 2d, at 1209 (in-hospital abortion costs $850–$900, whereas a dilatation-and-evacuation (D&E) abortion performed in a clinic costs $350–$400). . . . Moreover, the court indicated that second-trimester abortions were rarely performed in Akron hospitals. *Ibid.* (only nine second-trimester abortions [were] performed in Akron hospitals in the year before trial). . . . Thus, a second-trimester hospitalization requirement may force women to travel to find available facilities, resulting in both financial expense and additional health risk. . . .

Akron does not contend that § 1870.03 imposes only an insignificant burden on women's access to abortion, but rather defends it as a reasonable health regulation. This position had strong support at the time of *Roe* v. *Wade*, as hospitalization for second-trimester abortions was recommended by the American Public Health Association (APHA), see *Roe*, 410 U.S., at 143–146, and the American College of Obstetricians and Gynecologists (ACOG), see Standards for Obstetric-Gynecologic Services 65 (4th ed. 1974). Since then, however, the safety of second-trimester abortions has increased dramatically.[22] The principal reason is that the D&E procedure is now widely and successfully used for second-trimester abortions.[23] The Court of Appeals found that there was "an abundance of evidence that D&E is the safest method of performing post-first trimester abortions today." 651 F. 2d, at 1209. The availability of the D&E procedure during the interval between approximately 12 and 16 weeks of pregnancy, a period during which other second-trimester abortion techniques generally cannot be used,[24] has meant that women desiring an early second-trimester abortion no longer are forced to incur the health risks of waiting until at least the 16th week of pregnancy.

For our purposes, an even more significant factor is that experience indicates that D&E may be performed safely on an outpatient basis in appropriate nonhospital facilities. The evidence is strong enough to have convinced the APHA to abandon its prior recommendation of hospitalization for all second-trimester abortions. . . .

These developments, and the professional commentary supporting them, constitute impressive evidence that—at least during the early weeks of the second trimester—D&E abortions may be performed as safely in an outpatient clinic as in a full-service hospital. . . . We conclude, therefore, that "present medical knowledge," *Roe*, *supra*, at 163, convincingly undercuts Akron's justification for requiring that *all* second-trimester abortions be performed in a hospital. . . .

We turn next to § 1870.05(B), the provision prohibiting a physician from performing an abortion on a minor pregnant woman under the age of 15 unless he obtains "the informed written consent of one of her parents or her legal guardian" or unless the minor obtains "an order from a court having jurisdiction over her that the abortion be performed or induced." The District Court invalidated this provision because "[i]t does not establish

---

22. The death-to-case ratio for all second-trimester abortions in this country fell from 14.4 deaths per 100,000 abortions in 1972 to 7.6 per 100,000 in 1977. See Tyler, Cates, Schulz, Selik, & Smith, Second-Trimester Induced Abortion in the United States, published in Second-Trimester Abortion 17–20.

23. At the time *Roe* was decided, the D&E procedure was used only to perform first-trimester abortions.

24. Instillation procedures, the primary means of performing a second-trimester abortion before the development of D&E, generally cannot be performed until approximately the 16th week of pregnancy because until that time the amniotic sac is too small. See Grimes & Cates, Dilatation and Evacuation, published in Second-Trimester Abortion 121.

a procedure by which a minor can avoid a parental veto of her abortion decision by demonstrating that her decision is, in fact, informed. Rather, it requires, in all cases, both the minor's informed consent and either parental consent or a court order." 479 F. Supp., at 1201. The Court of Appeals affirmed on the same basis. . . .

The relevant legal standards are not in dispute. The Court has held that "the State may not impose a blanket provision . . . requiring the consent of a parent or person *in loco parentis* as a condition for abortion of an unmarried minor." *Danforth, supra*, at 74. In *Bellotti* v. *Baird*, 443 U.S. 622 (1979) (*Bellotti II*), a majority of the Court indicated that a State's interest in protecting immature minors will sustain a requirement of a consent substitute, either parental or judicial. See *id.*, at 640–642 (plurality opinion for four Justices); *id.*, at 656–657 (WHITE, J., dissenting) (expressing approval of absolute parental or judicial consent requirement). . . . The *Bellotti II* plurality cautioned, however, that the State must provide an alternative procedure whereby a pregnant minor may demonstrate that she is sufficiently mature to make the abortion decision herself or that, despite her immaturity, an abortion would be in her best interests. 443 U.S., at 643–644. Under these decisions, it is clear that Akron may not make a blanket determination that *all* minors under the age of 15 are too immature to make this decision or that an abortion never may be in the minor's best interests without parental approval.

Akron's ordinance does not create expressly the alternative procedure required by *Bellotti II*. But Akron contends that the Ohio Juvenile Court will qualify as a "court having jurisdiction" within the meaning of § 1870.05(B), and that "it is not to be assumed that during the course of the juvenile proceedings the Court will not construe the ordinance in a manner consistent with the constitutional requirement of a determination of the minor's ability to make an informed consent." Brief for Petitioner in No. 81–746, p. 28. Akron concludes that the courts below should not have invalidated § 1870.05(B) on its face. The city relies on *Bellotti* v. *Baird*, 428 U.S. 132 (1976) (*Bellotti I*), in which the Court did not decide whether a State's parental consent provisions were unconstitutional as applied to mature minors, holding instead that "abstention is appropriate where an unconstrued state statute is susceptible of a construction by the state judiciary 'which might avoid in whole or in part the necessity for federal constitutional adjudication, or at least materially change the nature of the problem.'" *Id.*, at 146–147 (quoting *Harrison* v. *NAACP*, 360 U.S. 167, 177 (1959)). See also *H. L.* v. *Matheson*, 450 U.S. 398 (1981) (refusing to decide whether parental notice statute would be constitutional as applied to mature minors). . . .

We do not think that the abstention principle should have been applied here. It is reasonable to assume, as we did in *Bellotti I* and *Matheson*, that a state court presented with a state statute specifically governing abortion consent procedures for pregnant minors will attempt to construe the statute consistently with constitutional requirements. This suit, however, concerns a municipal ordinance that creates no procedures for making the necessary determinations. Akron seeks to invoke the Ohio statute governing juvenile proceedings, but that statute neither mentions minors' abortions nor suggests that the

Ohio Juvenile Court has authority to inquire into a minor's maturity or emancipation.... In these circumstances, we do not think that the Akron ordinance, as applied in Ohio juvenile proceedings, is reasonably susceptible of being construed to create an "opportunity for case-by-case evaluations of the maturity of pregnant minors." *Bellotti II* (plurality opinion). We therefore affirm the Court of Appeals' judgment that § 1870.05(B) is unconstitutional.

V

The Akron ordinance provides that no abortion shall be performed except "with the informed written consent of the pregnant woman, . . . given freely and without coercion." § 1870.06(A). Furthermore, "in order to insure that the consent for an abortion is truly informed consent," the woman must be "orally informed by her attending physician" of the status of her pregnancy, the development of her fetus, the date of possible viability, the physical and emotional complications that may result from an abortion, and the availability of agencies to provide her with assistance and information with respect to birth control, adoption, and childbirth. § 1870.06(B). In addition, the attending physician must inform her "of the particular risks associated with her own pregnancy and the abortion technique to be employed . . . [and] other information which in his own medical judgment is relevant to her decision as to whether to have an abortion or carry her pregnancy to term." § 1870.06(C)....

The validity of an informed consent requirement . . . rests on the State's interest in protecting the health of the pregnant woman. The decision to have an abortion has "implications far broader than those associated with most other kinds of medical treatment," *Bellotti II*, 443 U.S., at 649 (plurality opinion), and thus the State legitimately may seek to ensure that it has been made "in the light of all attendant circumstances—psychological and emotional as well as physical—that might be relevant to the well-being of the patient." *Colautti v. Franklin*, 439 U.S., at 394.... This does not mean, however, that a State has unreviewable authority to decide what information a woman must be given before she chooses to have an abortion. It remains primarily the responsibility of the physician to ensure that appropriate information is conveyed to his patient, depending on her particular circumstances. *Danforth*'s recognition of the State's interest in ensuring that this information be given will not justify abortion regulations designed to influence the woman's informed choice between abortion or childbirth....

B

Viewing the city's regulations in this light, we believe that § 1870.06(B) attempts to extend the State's interest in ensuring "informed consent" beyond permissible limits. First, it is fair to say that much of the information required is designed not to inform the woman's consent but rather to persuade her to withhold it altogether. Subsection (3) requires the physician to inform his patient that "the unborn child is a human life from the moment of conception," a requirement inconsistent with the Court's holding in *Roe* v. *Wade* that a State may not adopt one theory of when life begins to justify its regulation of abortions. See 410 U.S., at 159–162. Moreover, much of the detailed description of "the anatomical and physiological characteristics of the particular unborn child" required by subsection (3) would involve at best speculation by the physician. . . . And subsection (5), that begins with the dubious statement that "abortion is a major surgical procedure" . . . and proceeds to describe numerous possible physical and psychological complications of abortion, . . . is a "parade of horribles" intended to suggest that abortion is a particularly dangerous procedure.

An additional, and equally decisive, objection to § 1870.06(B) is its intrusion upon the discretion of the pregnant woman's physician. This provision specifies a litany of information that the physician must recite to each woman regardless of whether in his judgment the information is relevant to her personal decision. For example, even if the physician believes that some of the risks outlined in subsection (5) are nonexistent for a particular patient, he remains obligated to describe them to her. In *Danforth* the Court warned against placing the physician in just such an "undesired and uncomfortable straitjacket." 428 U.S., at 67, n. 8. Consistent with its interest in ensuring informed consent, a State may require that a physician make certain that his patient understands the physical and emotional implications of having an abortion. But Akron has gone far beyond merely describing the general subject matter relevant to informed consent. By insisting upon recitation of a lengthy and inflexible list of information, Akron unreasonably has placed "obstacles in the path of the doctor upon whom [the woman is] entitled to rely for advice in connection with her decision." *Whalen* v. *Roe*, 429 U.S., at 604, n. 33. . . .

C

Section 1870.06(C) presents a different question. Under this provision, the "attending physician" must inform the woman

> "of the particular risks associated with her own pregnancy and the abortion technique to be employed including providing her with at least a general description of the medical instructions to be followed subsequent to the abortion in order to insure her safe recovery, and shall in addition provide her with such other information which in his own medical judgment is relevant to her decision as to whether to have an abortion or carry her pregnancy to term."

The information required clearly is related to maternal health and to the State's legitimate purpose in requiring informed consent. Nonetheless, the Court of Appeals determined that it interfered with the physician's medical judgment "in exactly the same way as section 1870.06(B). It requires the doctor to make certain disclosures in all cases, regardless of his own professional judgment as to the desirability of doing so." 651 F. 2d, at 1207. This was a misapplication of *Danforth.* There we construed "informed consent" to mean "the giving of information to the patient as to just what would be done and as to its consequences." 428 U.S., at 67, n. 8. We see no significant difference in Akron's requirement that the woman be told of the particular risks of her pregnancy and the abortion technique to be used, and be given general instructions on proper postabortion care. Moreover, in contrast to subsection (B), § 1870.06(C) merely describes in general terms the information to be disclosed. It properly leaves the precise nature and amount of this disclosure to the physician's discretion and "medical judgment."

The Court of Appeals also held, however, that § 1870.06(C) was invalid because it required that the disclosure be made by the "attending physician." The court found that "the practice of all three plaintiff clinics has been for the counseling to be conducted by persons other than the doctor who performs the abortion," 651 F. 2d, at 1207, and determined that Akron had not justified requiring the physician personally to describe the health risks. Akron challenges this holding as contrary to our cases that emphasize the importance of the physician-patient relationship. In Akron's view, as in the view of the dissenting judge below, the "attending physician" requirement "does no more than seek to ensure that there is in fact a true physician-patient relationship even for the woman who goes to an abortion clinic." *Id.*, at 1217 (Kennedy, J., concurring in part and dissenting in part). . . .

We are not convinced, however, that there is as vital a state need for insisting that the physician performing the abortion, or for that matter any physician, personally counsel the patient in the absence of a request. The State's interest is in ensuring that the woman's consent is informed and unpressured; the critical factor is whether she obtains the necessary information and counseling from a qualified person, not the identity of the person from whom she obtains it. . . . Akron and intervenors strongly urge that the non-physician counselors at the plaintiff abortion clinics are not trained or qualified to perform this important function. The courts below made no such findings, however, and on the record before us we cannot say that the woman's consent to the abortion will not be informed if a physician delegates the counseling task to another qualified individual. . . .

The Akron ordinance prohibits a physician from performing an abortion until 24 hours after the pregnant woman signs a consent form. § 1870.07.[42] The District Court upheld this provision on the ground that it furthered Akron's interest in ensuring "that a woman's abortion decision is made after careful consideration of all the facts applicable to her particular situation." 479 F. Supp., at 1204. The Court of Appeals reversed, finding

---

42. This provision does not apply if the physician certifies in writing that "there is an emergency need for an abortion to be performed or induced such that continuation of the pregnancy poses an immediate threat and grave risk to the life or physical health of the pregnant woman." § 1870.12.

that the inflexible waiting period had "no medical basis," and that careful consideration of the abortion decision by the woman "is beyond the state's power to require." 651 F. 2d, at 1208. We affirm the Court of Appeals' judgment. . . .

We find that Akron has failed to demonstrate that any legitimate state interest is furthered by an arbitrary and inflexible waiting period. There is no evidence suggesting that the abortion procedure will be performed more safely. Nor are we convinced that the State's legitimate concern that the woman's decision be informed is reasonably served by requiring a 24-hour delay as a matter of course. The decision whether to proceed with an abortion is one as to which it is important to "affor[d] the physician adequate discretion in the exercise of his medical judgment." *Colautti* v. *Franklin*, 439 U.S., at 387. In accordance with the ethical standards of the profession, a physician will advise the patient to defer the abortion when he thinks this will be beneficial to her. . . . But if a woman, after appropriate counseling, is prepared to give her written informed consent and proceed with the abortion, a State may not demand that she delay the effectuation of that decision.

VII

Section § 1870.16 of the Akron ordinance requires physicians performing abortions to "insure that the remains of the unborn child are disposed of in a humane and sanitary manner." The Court of Appeals found that the word "humane" was impermissibly vague as a definition of conduct subject to criminal prosecution. The court invalidated the entire provision, declining to sever the word "humane" in order to uphold the requirement that disposal be "sanitary." See 651 F. 2d, at 1211. We affirm this judgment.

Akron contends that the purpose of § 1870.16 is simply "'to preclude the mindless dumping of aborted fetuses onto garbage piles.'" *Planned Parenthood Assn.* v. *Fitzpatrick*, 401 F. Supp. 554, 573 (ED Pa. 1975) (three-judge court) (quoting State's characterization of legislative purpose), summarily aff'd *sub nom. Franklin* v. *Fitzpatrick*, 428 U.S. 901 (1976). . . . It is far from clear, however, that this provision has such a limited intent. The phrase "humane and sanitary" does, as the Court of Appeals noted, suggest a possible intent to "mandate some sort of 'decent burial' of an embryo at the earliest stages of formation." 651 F. 2d, at 1211. This level of uncertainty is fatal where criminal liability is imposed. See *Colautti* v. *Franklin, supra,* at 396. Because § 1870.16 fails to give a physician "fair notice that his contemplated conduct is forbidden," *United States* v. *Harriss*, 347 U.S. 612, 617(1954), we agree that it violates the Due Process Clause. . . .

JUSTICE O'CONNOR, with whom JUSTICE WHITE and JUSTICE REHNQUIST join, dissenting.

In *Roe* v. *Wade*, 410 U.S. 113 (1973), the Court held that the "right of privacy . . . founded in the Fourteenth Amendment's concept of personal liberty and restrictions upon state action . . . is broad enough to encompass a woman's decision whether or not to terminate her pregnancy." *Id.*, at 153. The parties in these cases have not asked the Court to re-examine the validity of that holding and the court below did not address it. Accordingly, the Court does not re-examine its previous holding. Nonetheless, it is apparent from the Court's opinion that neither sound constitutional theory nor our need to decide cases based on the application of neutral principles can accommodate an analytical framework that varies according to the "stages" of pregnancy, where those stages, and their concomitant standards of review, differ according to the level of medical technology available when a particular challenge to state regulation occurs. The Court's analysis of the Akron regulations is inconsistent both with the methods of analysis employed in previous cases dealing with abortion, and with the Court's approach to fundamental rights in other areas.

Our recent cases indicate that a regulation imposed on "a lawful abortion 'is not unconstitutional unless it unduly burdens the right to seek an abortion.'" *Maher* v. *Roe*, 432 U.S. 464, 473 (1977) (quoting *Bellotti* v. *Baird*, 428 U.S. 132, 147 (1977) (*Bellotti I*)). See also *Harris* v. *McRae*, 448 U.S. 297, 314 (1980). In my view, this "unduly burdensome" standard should be applied to the challenged regulations throughout the entire pregnancy without reference to the particular "stage" of pregnancy involved. If the particular regulation does not "unduly burde[n]" the fundamental right, *Maher, supra*, at 473, then our evaluation of that regulation is limited to our determination that the regulation rationally relates to a legitimate state purpose. Irrespective of what we may believe is wise or prudent policy in this difficult area, "the Constitution does not constitute us as 'Platonic Guardians' nor does it vest in this Court the authority to strike down laws because they do not meet our standards of desirable social policy, 'wisdom,' or 'common sense.'" *Plyler* v. *Doe*, 457 U.S. 202, 242 (1982) (BURGER, C. J., dissenting).

I

The trimester or "three-stage" approach adopted by the Court in *Roe*, . . . and, in a modified form, employed by the Court to analyze the regulations in these cases, cannot be supported as a legitimate or useful framework for accommodating the woman's right and the State's interests. The decision of the Court today graphically illustrates why the trimester approach is a completely unworkable method of accommodating the conflicting personal rights and compelling state interests that are involved in the abortion context.

As the Court indicates today, the State's compelling interest in maternal health changes as medical technology changes, and any health regulation must not "depart from accepted medical practice." . . . In applying this standard, the Court holds that "the safety of second-trimester abortions has increased dramatically" since 1973, when *Roe* was decided. . . . Although a regulation such as one requiring that all second-trimester abortions be performed in hospitals "had strong support" in 1973 "as a reasonable health regulation," *ante*, at 435, this regulation can no longer stand because, according to the

Court's diligent research into medical and scientific literature, the dilation and evacuation (D&E) procedure, used in 1973 only for first-trimester abortions, "is now widely and successfully used for second-trimester abortions." . . . Further, the medical literature relied on by the Court indicates that the D&E procedure may be performed in an appropriate nonhospital setting for "at least . . . the early weeks of the second trimester. . . ." *Ante*, at 437. The Court then chooses the period of 16 weeks of gestation as that point at which D&E procedures may be performed safely in a nonhospital setting, and thereby invalidates the Akron hospitalization regulation.

It is not difficult to see that despite the Court's purported adherence to the trimester approach adopted in *Roe*, the lines drawn in that decision have now been "blurred" because of what the Court accepts as technological advancement in the safety of abortion procedure. The State may no longer rely on a "bright line" that separates permissible from impermissible regulation, and it is no longer free to consider the second trimester as a unit and weigh the risks posed by all abortion procedures throughout that trimester. . . . Rather, the State must continuously and conscientiously study contemporary medical and scientific literature in order to determine whether the effect of a particular regulation is to "depart from accepted medical practice" insofar as particular procedures and particular periods within the trimester are concerned. Assuming that legislative bodies are able to engage in this exacting task . . . it is difficult to believe that our Constitution *requires* that they do it as a prelude to protecting the health of their citizens. It is even more difficult to believe that this Court, without the resources available to those bodies entrusted with making legislative choices, believes itself competent to make these inquiries and to revise these standards every time the American College of Obstetricians and Gynecologists (ACOG) or similar group revises its views about what is and what is not appropriate medical procedure in this area. Indeed, the ACOG Standards on which the Court relies were changed in 1982 after trial in the present cases. Before ACOG changed its Standards in 1982, it recommended that all mid-trimester abortions be performed in a hospital. See 651 F. 2d 1198, 1209 (CA6 1981). As today's decision indicates, medical technology is changing, and this change will necessitate our continued functioning as the Nation's "*ex officio* medical board with powers to approve or disapprove medical and operative practices and standards throughout the United States." *Planned Parenthood of Central Missouri* v. *Danforth*, 428 U.S. 52, 99 (1976) (WHITE, J., concurring in part and dissenting in part).

Just as improvements in medical technology inevitably will move *forward* the point at which the State may regulate for reasons of maternal health, different technological improvements will move *backward* the point of viability at which the State may proscribe abortions except when necessary to preserve the life and health of the mother.

In 1973, viability before 28 weeks was considered unusual. The 14th edition of L. Hellman & J. Pritchard, Williams Obstetrics (1971), on which the Court relied in *Roe* for its understanding of viability, stated, at 493, that "[a]ttainment of a [fetal] weight of 1,000 g [or a fetal age of approximately 28 weeks' gestation] is . . . widely used as the criterion of viability." However, recent studies have demonstrated increasingly earlier fetal viability.[5] It is certainly reasonable to believe that fetal viability in the first trimester of pregnancy may be possible in the not too distant future. Indeed, the Court has explicitly acknowledged that *Roe* left the point of viability "flexible for anticipated advancements in medical skill." *Colautti v. Franklin*, 439 U.S. 379, 387 (1979). "[W]e recognized in *Roe* that viability was a matter of medical judgment, skill, and technical ability, and we preserved the flexibility of the term." *Danforth, supra*, at 64.

The *Roe* framework, then, is clearly on a collision course with itself. As the medical risks of various abortion procedures decrease, the point at which the State may regulate for reasons of maternal health is moved further forward to actual childbirth. As medical science becomes better able to provide for the separate existence of the fetus, the point of viability is moved further back toward conception. Moreover, it is clear that the trimester approach violates the fundamental aspiration of judicial decision making through the application of neutral principles "sufficiently absolute to give them roots throughout the community and continuity over significant periods of time. . . ." A. Cox, The Role of the Supreme Court in American Government 114 (1976). The *Roe* framework is inherently tied to the state of medical technology that exists whenever particular litigation ensues. Although legislatures are better suited to make the necessary factual judgments in this area, the Court's framework forces legislatures, as a matter of constitutional law, to speculate about what constitutes "accepted medical practice" at any given time. Without the necessary expertise or ability, courts must then pretend to act as science review boards and examine those legislative judgments.

The Court adheres to the *Roe* framework because the doctrine of *stare decisis* "demands respect in a society governed by the rule of law." Although respect for *stare decisis* cannot

---

5. One study shows that infants born alive with a gestational age of less than 25 weeks and weight between 500 and 1,249 grams have a 20% chance of survival. See Phillip, Little, Polivy, & Lucey, Neonatal Mortality Risk for the Eighties: The Importance of Birth Weight/Gestational Age Groups, 68 Pediatrics 122 (1981). Another recent comparative study shows that preterm infants with a weight of 1,000 grams or less born in one hospital had a 42% rate of survival. Kopelman, The Smallest Preterm Infants: Reasons for Optimism and New Dilemmas, 132 Am. J. Diseases of Children 461 (1978). An infant weighing 484 grams and having a gestational age of 22 weeks at birth is now thriving in a Los Angeles hospital, and the attending physician has stated that the infant has a "95% chance of survival." Washington Post, Mar. 31, 1983, p. A2, col. 2. The aborted fetus in *Simopoulos v. Virginia, post*, p. 506, weighed 495 grams and had a gestational age of approximately 22 weeks.

Recent developments promise even greater success in overcoming the various respiratory and immunological neonatal complications that stand in the way of increased fetal viability. See, *e.g.*, Beddis, Collins, Levy, Godfrey, & Silverman, New Technique for Servo-Control of Arterial Oxygen Tension in Preterm Infants, 54 Archives of Disease in Childhood 278 (1979). "There is absolutely no question that in the current era there has been a sustained and progressive improvement in the outlook for survival of small premature infants." Stern, Intensive Care of the Pre-Term Infant, 26 Danish Med. Bull. 144 (1979).

be challenged, "this Court's considered practice [is] not to apply *stare decisis* as rigidly in constitutional as in non-constitutional cases." *Glidden Co.* v. *Zdanok*, 370 U.S. 530, 543 (1962). Although we must be mindful of the "desirability of continuity of decision in constitutional questions . . . when convinced of former error, this Court has never felt constrained to follow precedent. In constitutional questions, where correction depends upon amendment and not upon legislative action this Court throughout its history has freely exercised its power to reexamine the basis of its constitutional decisions." *Smith* v. *Allwright*, 321 U.S. 649, 665 (1944) (footnote omitted).

Even assuming that there is a fundamental right to terminate pregnancy in some situations, there is no justification in law or logic for the trimester framework adopted in *Roe* and employed by the Court today on the basis of *stare decisis*. For the reasons stated above, that framework is clearly an unworkable means of balancing the fundamental right and the compelling state interests that are indisputably implicated. . . .

The fallacy inherent in the *Roe* framework is apparent: just because the State has a compelling interest in ensuring maternal safety once an abortion may be more dangerous than childbirth, it simply does not follow that the State has *no* interest before that point that justifies state regulation to ensure that first-trimester abortions are performed as safely as possible. . . .

The state interest in potential human life is likewise extant throughout pregnancy. In *Roe*, the Court held that although the State had an important and legitimate interest in protecting potential life, that interest could not become compelling until the point at which the fetus was viable. The difficulty with this analysis is clear: *potential* life is no less potential in the first weeks of pregnancy than it is at viability or afterward. At any stage in pregnancy, there is the *potential* for human life. Although the Court refused to "resolve the difficult question of when life begins," *id.*, at 159, the Court chose the point of viability—when the fetus is *capable* of life independent of its mother—to permit the complete proscription of abortion. The choice of viability as the point at which the state interest in *potential* life becomes compelling is no less arbitrary than choosing any point before viability or any point afterward. Accordingly, I believe that the State's interest in protecting potential human life exists throughout the pregnancy.

III

Although the State possesses compelling interests in the protection of potential human life and in maternal health throughout pregnancy, not every regulation that the State imposes must be measured against the State's compelling interests and examined with strict scrutiny. This Court has acknowledged that "the right in *Roe* v. *Wade* can be understood only by considering both the woman's interest and the nature of the State's interference with it. *Roe* did not declare an unqualified 'constitutional right to an abortion.' . . . Rather, the right protects the woman from unduly burdensome interference with her freedom to decide whether to terminate her pregnancy." *Maher*, 432 U.S., at

473–474. The Court and its individual Justices have repeatedly utilized the "unduly burdensome" standard in abortion cases.[8]

The requirement that state interference "infringe[s] substantially" or "heavily burden[s]" a right before heightened scrutiny is applied is not novel in our fundamental-rights jurisprudence, or restricted to the abortion context. In *San Antonio Independent School District v. Rodriguez*, 411 U.S. 1, 37–38 (1973), we observed that we apply "strict judicial scrutiny" only when legislation may be said to have "'deprived,' 'infringed,' or 'interfered' with the free exercise of some such fundamental personal right or liberty." If the impact of the regulation does not rise to the level appropriate for our strict scrutiny, then our inquiry is limited to whether the state law bears "some rational relationship to legitimate state purposes." *Id.*, at 40. Even in the First Amendment context, we have required in some circumstances that state laws "infringe substantially" on protected conduct, *Gibson* v. *Florida Legislative Investigation Committee*, 372 U.S. 539, 545 (1963), or that there be "a significant encroachment upon personal liberty," *Bates* v. *City of Little Rock*, 361 U.S. 516, 524 (1960). . . .

The "unduly burdensome" standard is particularly appropriate in the abortion context because of the *nature* and *scope* of the right that is involved. The privacy right involved in the abortion context "cannot be said to be absolute." *Roe*, 410 U.S., at 154. "*Roe* did not declare an unqualified 'constitutional right to an abortion.'" *Maher*, 432 U.S., at 473. Rather, the *Roe* right is intended to protect against state action "drastically limiting the availability and safety of the desired service," *id.*, at 472, against the imposition of an "absolute obstacle" on the abortion decision, *Danforth*, 428 U.S., at 70–71, n. 11, or

---

8. See *Bellotti* v. *Baird*, 428 U.S. 132, 147 (1976) (*Bellotti I*) (State may not "impose undue burdens upon a minor capable of giving an informed consent." In *Bellotti I*, the Court left open the question whether a judicial hearing would unduly burden the *Roe* right of an adult woman. See 428 U.S., at 147); *Bellotti* v. *Baird*, 443 U.S. 622, 640 (1979) (*Bellotti II*) (opinion of POWELL, J.) (State may not "unduly burden the right to seek an abortion"); *Harris* v. *McRae*, 448 U.S. 297, 314 (1980) ("The doctrine of *Roe* v. *Wade*, the Court held in *Maher*, 'protects the woman from unduly burdensome interference with her freedom to decide whether to terminate her pregnancy,' [432 U.S.], at 473–474, such as the severe criminal sanctions at issue in *Roe* v. *Wade, supra*, or the absolute requirement of spousal consent for an abortion challenged in *Planned Parenthood of Central Missouri* v. *Danforth*, 428 U.S. 52"); *Beal* v. *Doe*, 432 U.S. 438, 446 (1977) (The state interest in protecting potential human life "does not, at least until approximately the third trimester, become sufficiently compelling to justify unduly burdensome state interference . . ."); *Carey* v. *Population Services International*, 431 U.S. 678, 705 (1977) (POWELL, J., concurring in part and concurring in judgment) ("In my view, [*Roe* and *Griswold* v. *Connecticut*, 381 U.S. 479 (1965),] make clear that the [compelling state interest] standard has been invoked only when the state regulation entirely frustrates or heavily burdens the exercise of constitutional rights in this area. See *Bellotti* v. *Baird*, 428 U.S. 132, 147 (1976)"). Even though the Court did not explicitly use the "unduly burdensome" standard in evaluating the informed-consent requirement in *Planned Parenthood of Central Missouri* v. *Danforth, supra*, the informed-consent requirement for first-trimester abortions in *Danforth* was upheld because it did not "unduly burde[n] the right to seek an abortion." *Bellotti I, supra*, at 147.

against "official interference" and "coercive restraint" imposed on the abortion decision, *Harris*, 448 U.S., at 328 (WHITE, J., concurring). That a state regulation may "inhibit" abortions to some degree does not require that we find that the regulation is invalid. See *H. L.* v. *Matheson*, 450 U.S. 398, 413 (1981).

The abortion cases demonstrate that an "undue burden" has been found for the most part in situations involving absolute obstacles or severe limitations on the abortion decision. In *Roe*, the Court invalidated a Texas statute that criminalized *all* abortions except those necessary to save the life of the mother. In *Danforth*, the Court invalidated a state prohibition of abortion by saline amniocentesis because the ban had "the effect of inhibiting . . . the vast majority of abortions after the first 12 weeks." 428 U.S., at 79. The Court today acknowledges that the regulation in *Danforth* effectively represented "a *complete* prohibition on abortions in certain circumstances" (emphasis added). In *Danforth*, the Court also invalidated state regulations requiring parental or spousal consent as a prerequisite to a first-trimester abortion because the consent requirements effectively and impermissibly delegated a "veto power" to parents and spouses during the first trimester of pregnancy. In both *Bellotti I*, 428 U.S. 132 (1977), and *Bellotti* v. *Baird*, 443 U.S. 622 (1979) (*Bellotti II*), the Court was concerned with effective parental veto over the abortion decision. . . .

Section 1870.03 of the Akron ordinance requires that second-trimester abortions be performed in hospitals. . . .

The hospitalization requirement does not impose an undue burden, and it is not necessary to apply an exacting standard of review. Further, the regulation has a "rational relation" to a valid state objective of ensuring the health and welfare of its citizens. See *Williamson* v. *Lee Optical Co.*, 348 U.S. 483, 491 (1955). . . .

Section 1870.05(B)(2) of the Akron ordinance provides that no physician shall perform an abortion on a minor under 15 years of age unless the minor gives written consent, and the physician first obtains the informed written consent of a parent or guardian, or unless the minor first obtains "an order from a court having jurisdiction over her that the abortion be performed or induced." . . .

Assuming, *arguendo*, that the Court is correct in holding that a parental notification requirement would be unconstitutional as applied to mature minors,[12] I see no reason to

---

[12]. In my view, no decision of this Court has yet held that parental notification in the case of mature minors is unconstitutional. Although the plurality opinion of JUSTICE POWELL in *Bellotti II* suggested that the state statute in that case was unconstitutional because, *inter alia*, it failed to provide *all* minors with an opportunity "to go directly to a court without first consulting or notifying her parents," 443 U.S., at 647, the Court in *H. L.* v. *Matheson* held that *unemancipated and immature minors* had "no constitutional right to notify a court in lieu of notifying their parents." 450 U.S., at 412, n. 22. Furthermore, the Court in *H. L.* v. *Matheson* expressly did *not* decide that a parental notification requirement would be unconstitutional if the State otherwise permitted *mature* minors to make abortion decisions free of parental or judicial "veto." See *id.*, at 406–407.

assume that the Akron ordinance and the State Juvenile Court statute compel state judges to notify the parents of a mature minor if such notification was contrary to the minor's best interests. Further, there is no reason to believe that the state courts would construe the consent requirement to impose any type of parental or judicial veto on the abortion decisions of mature minors. In light of the Court's complete lack of knowledge about how the Akron ordinance will operate, and how the Akron ordinance and the State Juvenile Court statute interact, our "'scrupulous regard for the rightful independence of state governments'" counsels against "unnecessary interference by the federal courts with proper and validly administered state concerns, a course so essential to the balanced working of our federal system." *Harrison* v. *NAACP* (quoting *Matthews* v. *Rodgers*, 284 U.S. 521, 525 (1932)).

The Court invalidates the informed-consent provisions of § 1870.06(B) and § 1870.06(C) of the Akron ordinance.... Although it finds that subsections (1), (2), (6), and (7) of § 1870.06(B) are "certainly ... not objectionable," it refuses to sever those provisions from subsections (3), (4), and (5) because the city requires that the "acceptable" information be provided by the attending physician when "much, if not all of it, could be given by a qualified person assisting the physician," *ibid*. Despite the fact that the Court finds that § 1870.06(C) "properly leaves the precise nature and amount of ... disclosure to the physician's discretion and 'medical judgment,'" the Court also finds § 1870.06(C) unconstitutional because it requires that the disclosure be made by the attending physician, rather than by other "qualified persons" who work at abortion clinics....

The validity of subsections (3), (4), and (5) is not before the Court because it appears that the city of Akron conceded their unconstitutionality before the court below. See Brief for City of Akron in No. 79–3757 (CA6), p. 35; Reply Brief for City of Akron in No. 79–3757 (CA6), pp. 5–9. In my view, the remaining subsections of § 1870.06(B) are separable from the subsections conceded to be unconstitutional. Section 1870.19 contains a separability clause which creates a "'presumption of divisibility'" and places "the burden ... on the litigant who would escape its operation." *Carter* v. *Carter Coal Co.*, 298 U.S. 238, 335 (1936) (opinion of Cardozo, J.). Akron Center has failed to show that severance of subsections (3), (4), and (5) would "create a program quite different from the one the legislature actually adopted." *Sloan* v. *Lemon*, 413 U.S. 825, 834 (1973).

The remainder of § 1870.06(B), and § 1870.06 (C), impose no undue burden or drastic limitation on the abortion decision. The city of Akron is merely attempting to ensure that the decision to abort is made in light of that knowledge that the city deems relevant to informed choice. As such, these regulations do not impermissibly affect any privacy right under the Fourteenth Amendment.

Section 1870.07 of the Akron ordinance requires a 24-hour waiting period between the signing of a consent form and the actual performance of the abortion, except in cases of emergency....

The waiting period does not apply in cases of medical emergency. Therefore, should the physician determine that the waiting period would increase risks significantly, he or she need not require the woman to wait. The Court's concern in this respect is simply misplaced. Although the waiting period may impose an additional cost on the abortion decision, this increased cost does not unduly burden the availability of abortions or impose an absolute obstacle to access to abortions. Further, the State is not required to "fine-tune" its abortion statutes so as to minimize the costs of abortions. *H. L. v. Matheson*, 450 U.S., at 413.

Assuming, *arguendo*, that any additional costs are such as to impose an undue burden on the abortion decision, the State's compelling interests in maternal physical and mental health and protection of fetal life clearly justify the waiting period. As we acknowledged in *Danforth*, 428 U.S., at 67, the decision to abort is "a stressful one," and the waiting period reasonably relates to the State's interest in ensuring that a woman does not make this serious decision in undue haste. The decision also has grave consequences for the fetus, whose life the State has a compelling interest to protect and preserve. "[N]o other [medical] procedure involves the purposeful termination of a potential life." *Harris*, 448 U.S., at 325. The waiting period is surely a small cost to impose to ensure that the woman's decision is well considered in light of its certain and irreparable consequences on fetal life, and the possible effects on her own. . . .

Finally, § 1870.16 of the Akron ordinance requires that "[a]ny physician who shall perform or induce an abortion upon a pregnant woman shall insure that the remains of the unborn child are disposed of in a humane and sanitary manner." The Court finds this provision void for vagueness. I disagree.

In *Planned Parenthood Assn. v. Fitzpatrick*, 401 F. Supp. 554 (ED Pa. 1975) (three-judge court), summarily aff'd *sub nom. Franklin v. Fitzpatrick*, 428 U.S. 901 (1976), the District Court upheld a "humane disposal" provision against a vagueness attack in light of the State's representation that the intent of the Act "'is to preclude the mindless dumping of aborted fetuses onto garbage piles.'" 401 F. Supp., at 573. The District Court held that different concerns would be implicated if the statute were, at some point, determined to require "expensive burial." *Ibid.* In the present cases, the city of Akron has informed this Court that the intent of the "humane" portion of its statute, as distinguished from the "sanitary" portion, is merely to ensure that fetuses will not be "'dump[ed] . . . on garbage piles.'" Brief for Petitioner in No. 81–746, p. 48. In light of the fact that the city of Akron indicates no intent to require that physicians provide "decent burials" for fetuses, and that "humane" is no more vague than the term "sanitary," the vagueness of which Akron Center does not question, I cannot conclude that the statute is void for vagueness. . . .

PLANNED PARENTHOOD ASSOCIATION OF KANSAS CITY, MISSOURI, INC., ET AL. *v.* ASHCROFT, ATTORNEY GENERAL OF MISSOURI, ET AL.

CERTIORARI TO THE UNITED STATES COURT OF APPEALS FOR THE EIGHTH CIRCUIT

No. 81–1255. Argued November 30, 1982—Decided June 15, 1983

Powell, J., announced the judgment of the Court in Part VI and delivered the opinion of the Court with respect to Parts I and II, in which Burger, C. J., and Brennan, Marshall, Blackmun, and Stevens, JJ., joined, and an opinion with respect to Parts III, IV, and V, in which Burger, C. J., joined. Blackmun, J., filed an opinion concurring in part and dissenting in part, in which Brennan, Marshall, and Stevens, JJ., joined. O'Connor, J., filed an opinion concurring in the judgment in part and dissenting in part, in which White and Rehnquist, JJ., joined.

Justice Powell announced the judgment of the Court in Part VI and delivered the opinion of the Court with respect to Parts I and II and an opinion with respect to Parts III, IV, and V, in which The Chief Justice joins.

. . . The statutory provision at issue in this case requires the attendance of a second physician at the abortion of a viable fetus. § 188.030.3. This section requires that the second physician "take all reasonable steps in keeping with good medical practice . . . to preserve the life and health of the viable unborn child; provided that it does not pose an increased risk to the life or health of the woman." See n. 3, *supra*. It also provides that the second physician "shall take control of and provide immediate medical care for a child born as a result of the abortion."

The lower courts invalidated § 188.030.3. . . . The plaintiffs, respondents here on this issue, urge affirmance on the grounds that the second-physician requirement distorts the traditional doctor-patient relationship, and is both impractical and costly. They note that Missouri does not require two physicians in attendance for any other medical or surgical procedure, including childbirth or delivery of a premature infant.

The first physician's primary concern will be the life and health of the woman. Many third-trimester abortions in Missouri will be emergency operations, . . . as the State permits these late abortions only when they are necessary to preserve the life or the health of the woman. It is not unreasonable for the State to assume that during the operation the first physician's attention and skills will be directed to preserving the woman's health, and not to protecting the actual life of those fetuses who survive the abortion procedure.

Viable fetuses will be in immediate and grave danger because of their premature birth. A second physician, in situations where Missouri permits third-trimester abortions, may be of assistance to the woman's physician in preserving the health and life of the child.

By giving immediate medical attention to a fetus that is delivered alive, the second physician will assure that the State's interests are protected more fully than the first physician alone would be able to do. And given the compelling interest that the State has in preserving life, we cannot say that the Missouri requirement of a second physician in those unusual circumstances where Missouri permits a third-trimester abortion is unconstitutional. Preserving the life of a viable fetus that is aborted may not often be possible, . . . but the State legitimately may choose to provide safeguards for the comparatively few instances of live birth that occur. We believe the second-physician requirement reasonably furthers the State's compelling interest in protecting the lives of viable fetuses, and we reverse the judgment of the Court of Appeals holding that § 188.030.3 is unconstitutional. . . .

SIMOPOULOS v. VIRGINIA

APPEAL FROM THE SUPREME COURT OF VIRGINIA

No. 81–185. Argued November 30, 1982—Decided June 15, 1983

Powell, J., delivered the opinion of the Court, in which Burger, C. J., and Brennan, Marshall, and Blackmun, JJ., joined, and in Parts I and II of which White, Rehnquist, and O'Connor, JJ., joined. O'Connor, J., filed an opinion concurring in part and concurring in the judgment, in which White and Rehnquist, JJ., joined. Stevens, J., filed a dissenting opinion.

Justice Powell delivered the opinion of the Court.

. . . In furtherance of its compelling interest in maternal health, Virginia has enacted a hospitalization requirement for abortions performed during the second trimester. As a general proposition, physicians' offices are not regulated under Virginia law. . . . Virginia law does not, however, permit a physician licensed in the practice of medicine and surgery to perform an abortion during the second trimester of pregnancy unless "such procedure is performed in a hospital licensed by the State Department of Health." . . .

It is readily apparent that Virginia's second-trimester hospitalization requirement differs from those at issue in *City of Akron, ante,* at 431–432, and *Planned Parenthood Assn. of Kansas City, Mo., Inc. v. Ashcroft.* In those cases, we recognized the medical fact that, "at least during the early weeks of the second trimester[,] D&E abortions may be performed as safely in an outpatient clinic as in a full-service hospital." *City of Akron.* The requirements at issue, however, mandated that "all second-trimester abortions must be performed in general, acute-care facilities." *Ashcroft, ante,* at 481. In contrast, the Virginia statutes and regulations do not require that second-trimester abortions be performed exclusively in full-service hospitals. Under Virginia's hospitalization requirement, outpatient surgical hospitals may qualify for licensing as "hospitals" in which second-trimester abortions lawfully may be performed. Thus, our decisions in *City of Akron* and *Ashcroft* are not controlling here.

In view of its interest in protecting the health of its citizens, the State necessarily has considerable discretion in determining standards for the licensing of medical facilities. Although its discretion does not permit it to adopt abortion regulations that depart from accepted medical practice, it does have a legitimate interest in regulating second-trimester abortions and setting forth the standards for facilities in which such abortions are performed.

On their face, the Virginia regulations appear to be generally compatible with accepted medical standards governing outpatient second-trimester abortions. The American Public

Health Association (APHA) (Resolution No. 7907), although recognizing "that greater use of the Dilatation and Evacuation procedure makes it possible to perform the vast majority of second trimester abortions during or prior to the 16th week after the last menstrual period," still "[u]rges endorsement of the provision of second trimester abortion in free-standing qualified clinics that meet the state standards required for certification." APHA, The Right to Second Trimester Abortion 1, 2 (1979). The medical profession has not thought that a State's standards need be relaxed merely because the facility performs abortions: "Ambulatory care facilities providing abortion services should meet the same standards of care as those recommended for other surgical procedures performed in the physician's office and outpatient clinic or the free-standing and hospital-based ambulatory setting." American College of Obstetricians and Gynecologists (ACOG), Standards for Obstetric-Gynecologic Services 54 (5th ed. 1982). . . . ("Free-standing or hospital-based ambulatory surgical facilities should be licensed to conform to requirements of state or federal legislation"). Indeed, the medical profession's standards for outpatient surgical facilities are stringent: "Such facilities should maintain the same surgical, anesthetic, and personnel standards as recommended for hospitals." . . .

Given the plain language of the Virginia regulations and the history of their adoption, we see no reason to doubt that an adequately equipped clinic could, upon proper application, obtain an outpatient hospital license permitting the performance of second-trimester abortions. We conclude that Virginia's requirement that second-trimester abortions be performed in licensed clinics is not an unreasonable means of furthering the State's compelling interest in "protecting the woman's own health and safety." *Roe*, 410 U.S., at 150. . . .

THORNBURGH, GOVERNOR OF PENNSYLVANIA, ET AL. *v.* AMERICAN COLLEGE OF OBSTETRICIANS AND GYNECOLOGISTS ET AL.

APPEAL FROM THE UNITED STATES COURT OF APPEALS FOR THE THIRD CIRCUIT

No. 84–495. Argued November 5, 1985—Decided June 11, 1986

BLACKMUN, J., delivered the opinion of the Court, in which BRENNAN, MARSHALL, POWELL, and STEVENS, JJ., joined. STEVENS, J., filed a concurring opinion. BURGER, C. J., filed a dissenting opinion. WHITE, J., filed a dissenting opinion, in which REHNQUIST, J., joined. O'CONNOR, J., filed a dissenting opinion, in which REHNQUIST, J., joined.

JUSTICE BLACKMUN delivered the opinion of the Court.

IV

. . . This case, as it comes to us, concerns the constitutionality of six provisions of the Pennsylvania Act that the Court of Appeals struck down as facially invalid: § 3205 ("informed consent"); § 3208 ("printed information"); §§ 3214(a) and (h) (reporting requirements); § 3211(a) (determination of viability); § 3210(b) (degree of care required in postviability abortions); and § 3210(c) (second-physician requirement). We have no reason to address the validity of the other sections of the Act challenged in the District Court. . . .

We turn to the challenged statutes:
1. Section 3205 ("informed consent") and § 3208 ("printed information"). Section 3205(a) requires that the woman give her "voluntary and informed consent" to an abortion. Failure to observe the provisions of § 3205 subjects the physician to suspension or revocation of his license, and subjects any other person obligated to provide information relating to informed consent to criminal penalties. § 3205(c). A requirement that the woman give what is truly a voluntary and informed consent, as a general proposition, is, of course, proper and is surely not unconstitutional. See *Planned Parenthood of Central Missouri* v. *Danforth*, 428 U.S. 52, 67 (1976). But the State may not require the delivery of information designed "to influence the woman's informed choice between abortion or childbirth." *Akron*, 462 U.S., at 443–444.

Appellants refer to the Akron ordinance, Brief for Appellants 67, as did this Court in *Akron* itself, 462 U.S., at 445, as "a litany of information" and as "'a parade of horribles'" of dubious validity plainly designed to influence the woman's choice. They would distinguish the Akron situation, however, from the Pennsylvania one. Appellants assert that statutes "describing the general subject matter relevant to informed consent," *ibid.*, and stating "in general terms the information to be disclosed," *id.*, at 447, are permissible, and they further assert that the Pennsylvania statutes do no more than that.

We do not agree. We conclude that, like Akron's ordinance, §§ 3205 and 3208 fail the *Akron* measurement. The two sections prescribe in detail the method for securing "informed consent." Seven explicit kinds of information must be delivered to the woman at least 24 hours before her consent is given, and five of these must be presented by the woman's physician. The five are: (a) the name of the physician who will perform the abortion, (b) the "fact that there may be detrimental physical and psychological effects which are not accurately foreseeable," (c) the "particular medical risks associated with the particular abortion procedure to be employed," (d) the probable gestational age, and (e) the "medical risks associated with carrying her child to term." The remaining two categories are (f) the "fact that medical assistance benefits may be available for prenatal care, childbirth and neonatal care," and (g) the "fact that the father is liable to assist" in the child's support, "even in instances where the father has offered to pay for the abortion." §§ 3205(a)(1) and (2). The woman also must be informed that materials printed and supplied by the Commonwealth that describe the fetus and that list agencies offering alternatives to abortion are available for her review. If she chooses to review the materials but is unable to read, the materials "shall be read to her," and any answer she seeks must be "provided her in her own language." § 3205(a)(2)(iii). She must certify in writing, prior to the abortion, that all this has been done. § 3205(a)(3). The printed materials "shall include the following statement":

> "'There are many public and private agencies willing and able to help you to carry your child to term, and to assist you and your child after your child is born, whether you choose to keep your child or place her or him for adoption. The Commonwealth of Pennsylvania strongly urges you to contact them before making a final decision about abortion. The law requires that your physician or his agent give you the opportunity to call agencies like these before you undergo an abortion.'" § 3208(a)(1).

The materials must describe the "probable anatomical and physiological characteristics of the unborn child at two-week gestational increments from fertilization to full term, including any relevant information on the possibility of the unborn child's survival." § 3208(a)(2). . . .

The requirements of §§ 3205(a)(2)(i) and (ii) that the woman be advised that medical assistance benefits may be available, and that the father is responsible for financial assistance in the support of the child similarly are poorly disguised elements of discouragement for the abortion decision. Much of this would be nonmedical information beyond the physician's area of expertise and, for many patients, would be irrelevant and inappropriate. For a patient with a life-threatening pregnancy, the "information" in its very rendition may be cruel as well as destructive of the physician-patient relationship. As any experienced social worker or other counselor knows, theoretical financial responsibility often does not equate with fulfillment. And a victim of rape should not have to hear gratuitous advice that an unidentified perpetrator is liable for support if she continues the pregnancy to term. Under the guise of informed consent, the Act requires the dissemination of information that is not relevant to such consent, and, thus, it advances no legitimate state interest.

The requirements of §§ 3205(a)(1)(ii) and (iii) that the woman be informed by the physician of "detrimental physical and psychological effects" and of all "particular medical risks" compound the problem of medical attendance, increase the patient's anxiety, and intrude upon the physician's exercise of proper professional judgment. This type of compelled information is the antithesis of informed consent. That the Commonwealth does not, and surely would not, compel similar disclosure of every possible peril of necessary surgery or of simple vaccination, reveals the anti-abortion character of the statute and its real purpose. Pennsylvania, like Akron, "has gone far beyond merely describing the general subject matter relevant to informed consent." *Akron*, 462 U.S., at 445. In addition, the Commonwealth would require the physician to recite its litany "regardless of whether in his judgment the information is relevant to [the patient's] personal decision." *Ibid.* These statutory defects cannot be saved by any facts that might be forthcoming at a subsequent hearing. Section 3205's informational requirements therefore are facially unconstitutional. . . .

JUSTICE WHITE, with whom JUSTICE REHNQUIST joins, dissenting. . . .

II

As it has evolved in the decisions of this Court, the freedom recognized by the Court in *Roe* v. *Wade* and its progeny is essentially a negative one, based not on the notion that abortion is a good in itself, but only on the view that the legitimate goals that may be served by state coercion of private choices regarding abortion are, at least under some circumstances, outweighed by the damage to individual autonomy and privacy that such coercion entails. In other words, the evil of abortion does not justify the evil of forbidding it. Cf. *Stanley* v. *Georgia*, 394 U.S. 557 (1969). But precisely because *Roe* v. *Wade* is not premised on the notion that abortion is itself desirable (either as a matter of constitutional entitlement or of social policy), the decision does not command the States to fund or encourage abortion, or even to approve of it. Rather, we have recognized that the States may legitimately adopt a policy of encouraging normal childbirth rather than abortion so long as the measures through which that policy is implemented do not amount to direct compulsion of the woman's choice regarding abortion. *Harris* v. *McRae*, 448 U.S.

297 (1980); *Maher* v. *Roe*, 432 U.S. 464 (1977); *Beal* v. *Doe*, 432 U.S. 438 (1977). The provisions before the Court today quite obviously represent the State's effort to implement such a policy.

The majority's opinion evinces no deference toward the State's legitimate policy. Rather, the majority makes it clear from the outset that it simply disapproves of any attempt by Pennsylvania to legislate in this area. The history of the state legislature's decade-long effort to pass a constitutional abortion statute is recounted as if it were evidence of some sinister conspiracy. In fact, of course, the legislature's past failure to predict the evolution of the right first recognized in *Roe* v. *Wade* is understandable and is in itself no ground for condemnation. Moreover, the legislature's willingness to pursue permissible policies through means that go to the limits allowed by existing precedents is no sign of *mens rea*. The majority, however, seems to find it necessary to respond by changing the rules to invalidate what before would have seemed permissible. The result is a decision that finds no justification in the Court's previous holdings, departs from sound principles of constitutional and statutory interpretation, and unduly limits the State's power to implement the legitimate (and in some circumstances compelling) policy of encouraging normal childbirth in preference to abortion. . . .

One searches the majority's opinion in vain for a convincing reason why the apparently laudable policy of promoting informed consent becomes unconstitutional when the subject is abortion. The majority purports to find support in *Akron* v. *Akron Center for Reproductive Health, Inc.*, 462 U.S. 416 (1983). But *Akron* is not controlling. The informed-consent provisions struck down in that case, as characterized by the majority, required the physician to advance tendentious statements concerning the unanswerable question of when human life begins, to offer merely speculative descriptions of the anatomical features of the fetus carried by the woman seeking the abortion, and to recite a "parade of horribles" suggesting that abortion is "a particularly dangerous procedure." I have no quarrel with the general proposition, for which I read *Akron* to stand, that a campaign of state-promulgated disinformation cannot be justified in the name of "informed consent" or "freedom of choice." But the Pennsylvania statute before us cannot be accused of sharing the flaws of the ordinance at issue in *Akron*. As the majority concedes, the statute does not, on its face, require that the patient be given any information that is false or unverifiable. Moreover, it is unquestionable that all of the information required would be relevant in many cases to a woman's decision whether or not to obtain an abortion.

Why, then, is the statute unconstitutional? The majority's argument, while primarily rhetorical, appears to offer three answers. First, the information that must be provided will in some cases be irrelevant to the woman's decision. This is true. Its pertinence to the question of the statute's constitutionality, however, is beyond me. Legislators are ordinarily entitled to proceed on the basis of rational generalizations about the subject matter of legislation, and the existence of particular cases in which a feature of a statute performs no function (or is even counterproductive) ordinarily does not render the statute unconstitutional or even constitutionally suspect. Only where the statute is subject to heightened scrutiny by virtue of its impingement on some fundamental right or its employment of a suspect classification does the imprecision of the "fit" between the statute's ends and means become potentially damning. Here, there is nothing to trigger such scrutiny, for the statute does not directly infringe the allegedly fundamental right at issue—the woman's right to choose an abortion. Indeed, I fail to see how providing a woman with accurate information—whether relevant or irrelevant—could ever be deemed to impair *any* constitutionally protected interest (even if, as the majority hypothesizes, the information may upset her). Thus, the majority's observation that the statute may require the provision of irrelevant information in some cases is itself an irrelevancy.

Second, the majority appears to reason that the informed-consent provisions are invalid because the information they require may increase the woman's "anxiety" about the procedure and even "influence" her in her choice. Again, both observations are undoubtedly true; but they by no means cast the constitutionality of the provisions into question. It is in the very nature of informed-consent provisions that they may produce some anxiety in the patient and influence her in her choice. This is in fact their reason for existence, and—provided that the information required is accurate and nonmisleading—it is an entirely salutary reason. If information may reasonably affect the patient's choice, the patient should have that information; and, as one authority has observed, "the greater the likelihood that particular information will influence [the patient's] decision, the more essential the information arguably becomes for securing her informed consent." Appleton, Doctors, Patients and the Constitution, 63 Wash. U. L. Q. 183, 211 (1985). That the result of the provision of information may be that some women will forgo abortions by no means suggests that providing the information is unconstitutional, for the ostensible objective of *Roe* v. *Wade* is not maximizing the number of abortions, but maximizing choice. Moreover, our decisions in *Maher*, *Beal*, and *Harris* v. *McRae* all indicate that the State may encourage women to make their choice in favor of childbirth rather than abortion, and the provision of accurate information regarding abortion and its alternatives is a reasonable and fair means of achieving that objective.

Third, the majority concludes that the informed-consent provisions are invalid because they "intrud[e] upon the discretion of the pregnant woman's physician," violate "the privacy of the informed-consent dialogue between the woman and her physician," *ibid.*, and "officially structur[e]" that dialogue, *ante*, at 763. The provisions thus constitute "state medicine" that "infringes upon [the physician's] professional responsibilities." *Ibid.* This is nonsensical. I can concede that the Constitution extends its protection to certain zones of personal autonomy and privacy, see *Griswold* v. *Connecticut*, 381 U.S., at 502 (WHITE, J., concurring in judgment), and I can understand, if not share, the notion that that protection may extend to a woman's decision regarding abortion. But I cannot concede the possibility that the Constitution provides more than minimal protection for the manner in which a physician practices his or her profession or for the "dialogues" in which he or she chooses to participate in the course of treating patients. I had thought it clear that regulation of the practice of medicine, like regulation of other professions and of economic affairs generally, was a matter peculiarly within the competence of legislatures, and that such regulation was subject to review only for rationality. See, *e.g.*, *Williamson* v. *Lee Optical of Oklahoma, Inc.*, 348 U.S. 483 (1955). . . .

WEBSTER, ATTORNEY GENERAL OF MISSOURI, ET AL. *v.* REPRODUCTIVE HEALTH SERVICES ET AL.

APPEAL FROM THE UNITED STATES COURT OF APPEALS FOR THE EIGHTH CIRCUIT

No. 88–605. Argued April 26, 1989—Decided July 3, 1989

REHNQUIST, C. J., announced the judgment of the Court and delivered the opinion for a unanimous Court with respect to Part II–C, the opinion of the Court with respect to Parts I, II–A, and II–B, in which WHITE, O'CONNOR, SCALIA, and KENNEDY, JJ., joined, and an opinion with respect to Parts II–D and III, in which WHITE and KENNEDY, JJ., joined. O'CONNOR, J., and SCALIA, J., filed opinions concurring in part and concurring in the judgment. BLACKMUN, J., filed an opinion concurring in part and dissenting in part, in which BRENNAN and MARSHALL, JJ., joined. STEVENS, J., filed an opinion concurring in part and dissenting in part.

CHIEF JUSTICE REHNQUIST announced the judgment of the Court and delivered the opinion of the Court with respect to Parts I, II–A, II–B, and II–C, and an opinion with respect to Parts II–D and III, in which JUSTICE WHITE and JUSTICE KENNEDY join.

Decision of this case requires us to address four sections of the Missouri Act: (a) the preamble; (b) the prohibition on the use of public facilities or employees to perform abortions; (c) the prohibition on public funding of abortion counseling; and (d) the requirement that physicians conduct viability tests prior to performing abortions. We address these *seriatim*.

A

The Act's preamble, as noted, sets forth "findings" by the Missouri legislature that "[t]he life of each human being begins at conception," and that "[u]nborn children have protectable interests in life, health, and well-being." Mo. Rev. Stat. §§ 1.205.1(1), (2) (1986). The Act then mandates that state laws be interpreted to provide unborn children with "all the rights, privileges, and immunities available to other persons, citizens, and residents of this state," subject to the Constitution and this Court's precedents. § 1.205.2. . . . In invalidating the preamble, the Court of Appeals relied on this Court's dictum that "'a State may not adopt one theory of when life begins to justify its regulation of abortions.'" 851 F. 2d, at 1075–1076, quoting *Akron* v. *Akron Center for Reproductive Health, Inc.*, 462 U.S. 416, 444 (1983), in turn citing *Roe* v. *Wade*, 410 U.S., at 159–162. It rejected Missouri's claim that the preamble was "abortion-neutral," and "merely determine[d] when life begins in a nonabortion context, a traditional state prerogative." 851 F. 2d, at 1076. The court thought that "[t]he only plausible inference" from the fact that "every remaining section of the bill save one regulates the performance of abortions" was that "the state intended its abortion regulations to be understood against the backdrop of its theory of life." . . .

The State contends that the preamble itself is precatory and imposes no substantive restrictions on abortions, and that appellees therefore do not have standing to challenge it. Brief for Appellants 21–24. Appellees, on the other hand, insist that the preamble is an operative part of the Act intended to guide the interpretation of other provisions of the Act. Brief for Appellees 19–23. They maintain, for example, that the preamble's definition of life may prevent physicians in public hospitals from dispensing certain forms of contraceptives, such as the intrauterine device.

In our view, the Court of Appeals misconceived the meaning of the *Akron* dictum, which was only that a State could not "justify" an abortion regulation otherwise invalid under *Roe* v. *Wade* on the ground that it embodied the State's view about when life begins. Certainly the preamble does not by its terms regulate abortion or any other aspect of appellees' medical practice. The Court has emphasized that *Roe* v. *Wade* "implies no limitation on the authority of a State to make a value judgment favoring childbirth over abortion." *Maher* v. *Roe*, 432 U.S., at 474. The preamble can be read simply to express that sort of value judgment. . . .

Section 188.210 provides that "[i]t shall be unlawful for any public employee within the scope of his employment to perform or assist an abortion, not necessary to save the life of the mother," while § 188.215 makes it "unlawful for any public facility to be used for the purpose of performing or assisting an abortion not necessary to save the life of the mother." . . . The Court of Appeals held that these provisions contravened this Court's abortion decisions. 851 F. 2d, at 1082–1083. We take the contrary view. . . .

. . . Relying on *Maher*, the Court in *Poelker* v. *Doe*, 432 U.S. 519, 521 (1977), held that the city of St. Louis committed "no constitutional violation . . . in electing, as a policy choice, to provide publicly financed hospital services for childbirth without providing corresponding services for nontherapeutic abortions."

More recently, in *Harris* v. *McRae*, 448 U.S. 297 (1980), the Court upheld "the most restrictive version of the Hyde Amendment," which withheld from States federal funds under the Medicaid program to reimburse the costs of abortions, "'except where the life of the mother would be endangered if the fetus were carried to term.'" *Ibid.* (quoting Pub. L. 94–439, § 209, 90 Stat. 1434). As in *Maher* and *Poelker*, the Court required only a showing that Congress' authorization of "reimbursement for medically necessary services generally, but not for certain medically necessary abortions" was rationally related to the legitimate governmental goal of encouraging childbirth. 448 U.S., at 325.

The Court of Appeals distinguished these cases on the ground that "[t]o prevent access to a public facility does more than demonstrate a political choice in favor of childbirth; it clearly narrows and in some cases forecloses the availability of abortion to women." 851 F. 2d, at 1081. The court reasoned that the ban on the use of public facilities "could prevent a woman's chosen doctor from performing an abortion because of his unprivileged status at other hospitals or because a private hospital adopted a similar anti-abortion stance." *Ibid.* It also thought that "[s]uch a rule could increase the cost of obtaining an abortion and delay the timing of it as well." *Ibid.*

We think that this analysis is much like that which we rejected in *Maher, Poelker,* and *McRae.* As in those cases, the State's decision here to use public facilities and staff to encourage childbirth over abortion "places no governmental obstacle in the path of a woman who chooses to terminate her pregnancy." *McRae,* 448 U.S., at 315. Just as Congress' refusal to fund abortions in *McRae* left "an indigent woman with at least the same range of choice in deciding whether to obtain a medically necessary abortion as she would have had if Congress had chosen to subsidize no health care costs at all," *id.,* at 317, Missouri's refusal to allow public employees to perform abortions in public hospitals leaves a pregnant woman with the same choices as if the State had chosen not to operate any public hospitals at all. The challenged provisions only restrict a woman's ability to obtain an abortion to the extent that she chooses to use a physician affiliated with a public hospital. This circumstance is more easily remedied, and thus considerably less burdensome, than indigency, which "may make it difficult—and in some cases, perhaps, impossible—for some women to have abortions" without public funding. *Maher,* 432 U.S., at 474. Having held that the State's refusal to fund abortions does not violate *Roe* v. *Wade,* it strains logic to reach a contrary result for the use of public facilities and employees. If the State may "make a value judgment favoring childbirth over abortion and . . . implement that judgment by the allocation of public funds," *Maher, supra,* at 474, surely it may do so through the allocation of other public resources, such as hospitals and medical staff. . . .

D

Section 188.029 of the Missouri Act provides:

"Before a physician performs an abortion on a woman he has reason to believe is carrying an unborn child of twenty or more weeks gestational age, the physician shall first determine if the unborn child is viable by using and exercising that degree of care, skill, and proficiency commonly exercised by the ordinarily skillful, careful, and prudent physician engaged in similar practice under the same or similar conditions. In making this determination of viability, the physician shall perform or cause to be performed such medical examinations and tests as are necessary to make a finding of the gestational age, weight, and lung maturity of the unborn child and shall enter such findings and determination of viability in the medical record of the mother." . . .

The viability-testing provision of the Missouri Act is concerned with promoting the State's interest in potential human life rather than in maternal health. Section 188.029

creates what is essentially a presumption of viability at 20 weeks, which the physician must rebut with tests indicating that the fetus is not viable prior to performing an abortion. It also directs the physician's determination as to viability by specifying consideration, if feasible, of gestational age, fetal weight, and lung capacity. The District Court found that "the medical evidence is uncontradicted that a 20-week fetus is *not* viable," and that "23½ to 24 weeks gestation is the earliest point in pregnancy where a reasonable possibility of viability exists." 662 F. Supp., at 420. But it also found that there may be a 4-week error in estimating gestational age, *id.*, at 421, which supports testing at 20 weeks.

In *Roe* v. *Wade*, the Court recognized that the State has "important and legitimate" interests in protecting maternal health and in the potentiality of human life. 410 U.S., at 162. During the second trimester, the State "may, if it chooses, regulate the abortion procedure in ways that are reasonably related to maternal health." *Id.*, at 164. After viability, when the State's interest in potential human life was held to become compelling, the State "may, if it chooses, regulate, and even proscribe, abortion except where it is necessary, in appropriate medical judgment, for the preservation of the life or health of the mother." *Id.*, at 165. . . .

In *Colautti* v. *Franklin*, 439 U.S. 379 (1979), upon which appellees rely, the Court held that a Pennsylvania statute regulating the standard of care to be used by a physician performing an abortion of a possibly viable fetus was void for vagueness. *Id.*, at 390–401. But in the course of reaching that conclusion, the Court reaffirmed its earlier statement in *Planned Parenthood of Central Mo.* v. *Danforth*, 428 U.S. 52, 64 (1976), that "'the determination of whether a particular fetus is viable is, and must be, a matter for the judgment of the responsible attending physician.'" 439 U.S., at 396. JUSTICE BLACKMUN, *post*, at 545, n. 6, ignores the statement in *Colautti* that "neither the legislature nor the courts may proclaim one of the elements entering into the ascertainment of viability—be it weeks of gestation or fetal weight or any other single factor—as the determinant of when the State has a compelling interest in the life or health of the fetus." 439 U.S., at 388–389. To the extent that § 188.029 regulates the method for determining viability, it undoubtedly does superimpose state regulation on the medical determination whether a particular fetus is viable. The Court of Appeals and the District Court thought it unconstitutional for this reason. 851 F. 2d, at 1074–1075; 662 F. Supp., at 423. To the extent that the viability tests increase the cost of what are in fact second-trimester abortions, their validity may also be questioned under *Akron*, 462 U.S., at 434–435, where the Court held that a requirement that second-trimester abortions must be performed in hospitals was invalid because it substantially increased the expense of those procedures.

We think that the doubt cast upon the Missouri statute by these cases is not so much a flaw in the statute as it is a reflection of the fact that the rigid trimester analysis of the course of a pregnancy enunciated in *Roe* has resulted in subsequent cases like *Colautti* and *Akron* making constitutional law in this area a virtual Procrustean bed. Statutes specifying elements of informed consent to be provided abortion patients, for example, were invalidated if they were thought to "structur[e] . . . the dialogue between the woman and her physician." *Thornburgh v. American College of Obstetricians and Gynecologists*, 476 U.S. 747, 763 (1986). As the dissenters in *Thornburgh* pointed out, such a statute would have been sustained under any traditional standard of judicial review, *id.*, at 802 (WHITE, J., dissenting), or for any other surgical procedure except abortion. *Id.*, at 783 (Burger, C. J., dissenting). . . .

In the first place, the rigid *Roe* framework is hardly consistent with the notion of a Constitution cast in general terms, as ours is, and usually speaking in general principles, as ours does. The key elements of the *Roe* framework—trimesters and viability—are not found in the text of the Constitution or in any place else one would expect to find a constitutional principle. Since the bounds of the inquiry are essentially indeterminate, the result has been a web of legal rules that have become increasingly intricate, resembling a code of regulations rather than a body of constitutional doctrine. . . . As JUSTICE WHITE has put it, the trimester framework has left this Court to serve as the country's "*ex officio* medical board with powers to approve or disapprove medical and operative practices and standards throughout the United States." *Planned Parenthood of Central Mo. v. Danforth*, 428 U.S., at 99 (opinion concurring in part and dissenting in part).

In the second place, we do not see why the State's interest in protecting potential human life should come into existence only at the point of viability, and that there should therefore be a rigid line allowing state regulation after viability but prohibiting it before viability. The dissenters in *Thornburgh*, writing in the context of the *Roe* trimester analysis, would have recognized this fact by positing against the "fundamental right" recognized in *Roe* the State's "compelling interest" in protecting potential human life throughout pregnancy. "[T]he State's interest, if compelling after viability, is equally compelling before viability." *Thornburgh*, 476 U.S., at 795 (WHITE, J., dissenting); see *id.*, at 828 (O'CONNOR, J., dissenting) ("State has compelling interests in ensuring maternal health and in protecting potential human life, and these interests exist 'throughout pregnancy'") (citation omitted).

The tests that § 188.029 requires the physician to perform are designed to determine viability. The State here has chosen viability as the point at which its interest in potential human life must be safeguarded. See Mo. Rev. Stat. § 188.030 (1986) ("No abortion of a viable unborn child shall be performed unless necessary to preserve the life or health of the woman"). It is true that the tests in question increase the expense of abortion, and regulate the discretion of the physician in determining the viability of the fetus. Since the tests will undoubtedly show in many cases that the fetus is not viable, the tests will have been performed for what were in fact second-trimester abortions. But we are satisfied that the requirement of these tests permissibly furthers the State's interest in protecting potential human life, and we therefore believe § 188.029 to be constitutional.

JUSTICE BLACKMUN takes us to task for our failure to join in a "great issues" debate as to whether the Constitution includes an "unenumerated" general right to privacy as recognized in cases such as *Griswold* v. *Connecticut*, 381 U.S. 479 (1965), and *Roe*. But *Griswold* v. *Connecticut*, unlike *Roe*, did not purport to adopt a whole framework, complete with detailed rules and distinctions, to govern the cases in which the asserted liberty interest would apply. As such, it was far different from the opinion, if not the holding, of *Roe* v. *Wade*, which sought to establish a constitutional framework for judging state regulation of abortion during the entire term of pregnancy. That framework sought to deal with areas of medical practice traditionally subject to state regulation, and it sought to balance once and for all by reference only to the calendar the claims of the State to protect the fetus as a form of human life against the claims of a woman to decide for herself whether or not to abort a fetus she was carrying. The experience of the Court in applying *Roe* v. *Wade* in later cases, see *supra*, at 518, n. 15, suggests to us that there is wisdom in not unnecessarily attempting to elaborate the abstract differences between a "fundamental right" to abortion, as the Court described it in *Akron*, 462 U.S. at 420, n. 1, a "limited fundamental constitutional right," which JUSTICE BLACKMUN today treats *Roe* as having established, *post*, at 555, or a liberty interest protected by the Due Process Clause, which we believe it to be. The Missouri testing requirement here is reasonably designed to ensure that abortions are not performed where the fetus is viable—an end which all concede is legitimate—and that is sufficient to sustain its constitutionality.

JUSTICE BLACKMUN also accuses us, *inter alia*, of cowardice and illegitimacy in dealing with "the most politically divisive domestic legal issue of our time." There is no doubt that our holding today will allow some governmental regulation of abortion that would have been prohibited under the language of cases such as *Colautti* v. *Franklin*, 439 U.S. 379 (1979), and *Akron* v. *Akron Center for Reproductive Health, Inc., supra*. But the goal of constitutional adjudication is surely not to remove inexorably "politically divisive" issues from the ambit of the legislative process, whereby the people through their elected representatives deal with matters of concern to them. The goal of constitutional adjudication is to hold true the balance between that which the Constitution puts beyond the reach of the democratic process and that which it does not. We think we have done that today. JUSTICE BLACKMUN's suggestion that legislative bodies, in a Nation where more than half of our population is women, will treat our decision today as an invitation to enact abortion regulation reminiscent of the dark ages not only misreads our views but does scant justice to those who serve in such bodies and the people who elect them.

III

Both appellants and the United States as *Amicus Curiae* have urged that we overrule our decision in *Roe* v. *Wade*. Brief for Appellants 12–18; Brief for United States as *Amicus Curiae* 8–24. The facts of the present case, however, differ from those at issue in *Roe*. Here, Missouri has determined that viability is the point at which its interest in potential human life must be safeguarded. In *Roe*, on the other hand, the Texas statute criminalized the performance of *all* abortions, except when the mother's life was at stake. 410 U.S., at 117–118. This case therefore affords us no occasion to revisit the holding of *Roe*, which was that the Texas statute unconstitutionally infringed the right to an abortion derived from the Due Process Clause, *id.*, at 164, and we leave it undisturbed. To the extent indicated in our opinion, we would modify and narrow *Roe* and succeeding cases. . . .

JUSTICE SCALIA, concurring in part and concurring in the judgment.

I join Parts I, II–A, II–B, and II–C of the opinion of the Court. As to Part II–D, I share JUSTICE BLACKMUN's view that it effectively would overrule *Roe* v. *Wade*, 410 U.S. 113 (1973). I think that should be done, but would do it more explicitly. Since today we contrive to avoid doing it, and indeed to avoid almost any decision of national import, I need not set forth my reasons, some of which have been well recited in dissents of my colleagues in other cases.

The outcome of today's case will doubtless be heralded as a triumph of judicial statesmanship. It is not that, unless it is statesmanlike needlessly to prolong this Court's self-awarded sovereignty over a field where it has little proper business since the answers to most of the cruel questions posed are political and not juridical—a sovereignty which therefore quite properly, but to the great damage of the Court, makes it the object of the sort of organized public pressure that political institutions in a democracy ought to receive.

JUSTICE O'CONNOR's assertion, that a "'fundamental rule of judicial restraint'" requires us to avoid reconsidering *Roe*, cannot be taken seriously. By finessing *Roe* we do not, as she suggests, adhere to the strict and venerable rule that we should avoid "'decid[ing] questions of a constitutional nature.'" We have not disposed of this case on some statutory or procedural ground, but have decided, and could not avoid deciding, whether the Missouri statute meets the requirements of the United States Constitution. The only choice available is whether, in deciding that constitutional question, we should use *Roe* v. *Wade* as the benchmark, or something else. What is involved, therefore, is not the rule of avoiding constitutional issues where possible, but the quite separate principle that we will not "'formulate a rule of constitutional law broader than is required by the precise facts to which it is to be applied.'" The latter is a sound general principle, but one often departed from when good reason exists. Just this Term, for example, in an opinion authored by JUSTICE O'CONNOR, despite the fact that we had already held a racially based set-aside unconstitutional because unsupported by evidence of identified discrimination, which was all that was needed to decide the case, we went on to outline the criteria for properly tailoring race-based remedies in cases where such evidence is present. *Richmond* v. *J. A. Croson Co.*, 488 U.S. 469, 506–508 (1989). Also this Term, in an opinion joined by JUSTICE O'CONNOR's, we announced the constitutional rule that deprivation of the right to confer with counsel during trial violates the Sixth Amendment even if no prejudice can be shown, despite our finding that there had been no such deprivation on the facts before us—which was all that was needed to decide that case. *Perry* v. *Leeke*, 488 U.S. 272, 278–280 (1989); see *id.*, at 285 (KENNEDY, J., concurring in part). I have not identified with certainty the first instance of our deciding a case on broader constitutional grounds than absolutely necessary, but it is assuredly no later than *Marbury* v. *Madison*, 1 Cranch 137 (1803), where we held that mandamus could constitutionally issue against the Secretary of State, although that was unnecessary given our holding that the law authorizing issuance of the mandamus by this Court was unconstitutional. . . .

The real question, then, is whether there are valid reasons to go beyond the most stingy possible holding today. It seems to me there are not only valid but compelling ones. Ordinarily, speaking no more broadly than is absolutely required avoids throwing settled law into confusion; doing so today preserves a chaos that is evident to anyone who can read and count. Alone sufficient to justify a broad holding is the fact that our retaining control, through *Roe*, of what I believe to be, and many of our citizens recognize to be, a political issue, continuously distorts the public perception of the role of this Court. We can now look forward to at least another Term with carts full of mail from the public, and streets full of demonstrators, urging us—their unelected and life-tenured judges who have been awarded those extraordinary, undemocratic characteristics precisely in order that we might follow the law despite the popular will—to follow the popular will. Indeed, I expect we can look forward to even more of that than before, given our indecisive decision today. And if these reasons for taking the unexceptional course of reaching a broader holding are not enough, then consider the nature of the constitutional question we avoid: In most cases, we do no harm by not speaking more broadly than the decision requires. Anyone affected by the conduct that the avoided holding would have prohibited will be able to challenge it himself and have his day in court to make the argument. Not so with respect to the harm that many States believed, pre-*Roe*, and many may continue to believe, is caused by largely unrestricted abortion. That will continue to occur if the States have the constitutional power to prohibit it, and would do so, but we skillfully avoid telling them so. Perhaps those abortions cannot constitutionally be proscribed. That is surely an arguable question, the question that reconsideration of *Roe* v. *Wade* entails. But what is not at all arguable, it seems to me, is that we should decide now and not insist that we be run into a corner before we grudgingly yield up our judgment. The only sound reason for the latter course is to prevent a change in the law—but to think that desirable begs the question to be decided. . . .

JUSTICE BLACKMUN, with whom JUSTICE BRENNAN and JUSTICE MARSHALL join, concurring in part and dissenting in part.

Today, *Roe* v. *Wade*, 410 U.S. 113 (1973), and the fundamental constitutional right of women to decide whether to terminate a pregnancy, survive but are not secure. Although the Court extricates itself from this case without making a single, even incremental, change in the law of abortion, the plurality and JUSTICE SCALIA would overrule *Roe* (the first silently, the other explicitly) and would return to the States virtually unfettered authority to control the quintessentially intimate, personal, and life-directing decision whether to carry a fetus to term. Although today, no less than yesterday, the Constitution and the decisions of this Court prohibit a State from enacting laws that inhibit women from the meaningful exercise of that right, a plurality of this Court implicitly invites every state legislature to enact more and more restrictive abortion regulations in order to provoke more and more test cases, in the hope that sometime down the line the Court will return the law of procreative freedom to the severe limitations that generally prevailed in this country before January 22, 1973. Never in my memory has a plurality announced a judgment of this Court that so foments disregard for the law and for our standing decisions.

Nor in my memory has a plurality gone about its business in such a deceptive fashion. At every level of its review, from its effort to read the real meaning out of the Missouri statute, to its intended evisceration of precedents and its deafening silence about the constitutional protections that it would jettison, the plurality obscures the portent of its analysis. With feigned restraint, the plurality announces that its analysis leaves *Roe* "undisturbed," albeit "modif[ied] and narrow[ed]." But this disclaimer is totally meaningless. The plurality opinion is filled with winks, and nods, and knowing glances to those who would do away with *Roe* explicitly, but turns a stone face to anyone in search of what the plurality conceives as the scope of a woman's right under the Due Process Clause to terminate a pregnancy free from the coercive and brooding influence of the State. The simple truth is that *Roe* would not survive the plurality's analysis, and that the plurality provides no substitute for *Roe*'s protective umbrella.

I fear for the future. I fear for the liberty and equality of the millions of women who have lived and come of age in the 16 years since *Roe* was decided. I fear for the integrity of, and public esteem for, this Court. . . .

. . . In the plurality's view, the viability-testing provision imposes a burden on second-trimester abortions as a way of furthering the State's interest in protecting the potential life of the fetus. Since under the *Roe* framework, the State may not fully regulate abortion in the interest of potential life (as opposed to maternal health) until the third trimester, the plurality finds it necessary, in order to save the Missouri testing provision, to throw out *Roe*'s trimester framework. In flat contradiction to *Roe*, 410 U.S., at 163, the plurality concludes that the State's interest in potential life is compelling before viability, and upholds the testing provision because it "permissibly furthers" that state interest. . . .

Had the plurality read the statute as written, it would have had no cause to reconsider the *Roe* framework. As properly construed, the viability-testing provision does not pass constitutional muster under even a rational-basis standard, the least restrictive level of review applied by this Court. See *Williamson* v. *Lee Optical Co.*, 348 U.S. 483 (1955). By mandating tests to determine fetal weight and lung maturity for every fetus thought to be more than 20 weeks gestational age, the statute requires physicians to undertake procedures, such as amniocentesis, that, in the situation presented, have no medical justification, impose significant additional health risks on both the pregnant woman and the fetus, and bear no rational relation to the State's interest in protecting fetal life. . . . As written, § 188.029 is an arbitrary imposition of discomfort, risk, and expense, furthering no discernible interest except to make the procurement of an abortion as arduous and difficult as possible. Thus, were it not for the plurality's tortured effort to avoid the plain import of § 188.029, it could have struck down the testing provision as patently irrational irrespective of the *Roe* framework....

The plurality eschews this straightforward resolution, in the hope of precipitating a constitutional crisis. Far from avoiding constitutional difficulty, the plurality attempts to engineer a dramatic retrenchment in our jurisprudence by exaggerating the conflict between its untenable construction of § 188.029 and the *Roe* trimester framework.

No one contests that under the *Roe* framework the State, in order to promote its interest in potential human life, may regulate and even proscribe nontherapeutic abortions once the fetus becomes viable. *Roe*, 410 U.S., at 164–165. If, as the plurality appears to hold, the testing provision simply requires a physician to use appropriate and medically sound tests to determine whether the fetus is actually viable when the estimated gestational age is greater than 20 weeks (and therefore within what the District Court found to be the margin of error for viability . . .), then I see little or no conflict with *Roe*. . . . Nothing in *Roe*, or any of its progeny, holds that a State may not effectuate its compelling interest in the potential life of a viable fetus by seeking to ensure that no viable fetus is mistakenly aborted because of the inherent lack of precision in estimates of gestational age. A requirement that a physician make a finding of viability, one way or the other, for every fetus that falls within the range of possible viability does no more than preserve the State's recognized authority. Although, as the plurality correctly points out, such a testing requirement would have the effect of imposing additional costs on second-trimester abortions where the tests indicated that the fetus was not viable, these costs would be merely incidental to, and a necessary accommodation of, the State's unquestioned right to prohibit nontherapeutic abortions after the point of viability. In short, the testing provision, as construed by the plurality, is consistent with the *Roe* framework and could be upheld effortlessly under current doctrine. . . .

How ironic it is, then, and disingenuous, that the plurality scolds the Court of Appeals for adopting a construction of the statute that fails to avoid constitutional difficulties. . . . By distorting the statute, the plurality manages to avoid invalidating the testing provision on what should have been noncontroversial constitutional grounds; having done so, however, the plurality rushes headlong into a much deeper constitutional thicket, brushing past an obvious basis for upholding § 188.029 in search of a pretext for scuttling the trimester framework. Evidently, from the plurality's perspective, the real problem with the Court of Appeals' construction of § 188.029 is not that it raised a constitutional difficulty, but that it raised the wrong constitutional difficulty—one not implicating *Roe*. The plurality has remedied that, traditional canons of construction and judicial forbearance notwithstanding.

B

Having set up the conflict between § 188.029 and the *Roe* trimester framework, the plurality summarily discards *Roe*'s analytic core as "'unsound in principle and unworkable in practice.'" . . . quoting *Garcia* v. *San Antonio Metropolitan Transit Authority*, 469 U.S. 528, 546 (1985). This is so, the plurality claims, because the key elements of the framework do not appear in the text of the Constitution, because the framework more closely resembles a regulatory code than a body of constitutional doctrine, and because under the framework the State's interest in potential human life is considered compelling only after viability, when, in fact, that interest is equally compelling throughout pregnancy. . . . The plurality does not bother to explain these alleged flaws in *Roe*. Bald assertion masquerades as reasoning. The object, quite clearly, is not to persuade, but to prevail.

1

The plurality opinion is far more remarkable for the arguments that it does not advance than for those that it does. The plurality does not even mention, much less join, the true jurisprudential debate underlying this case: whether the Constitution includes an "unenumerated" general right to privacy as recognized in many of our decisions, most notably *Griswold* v. *Connecticut*, 381 U.S. 479 (1965), and *Roe*, and, more specifically, whether, and to what extent, such a right to privacy extends to matters of childbearing and family life, including abortion. See, *e.g.*, *Eisenstadt* v. *Baird*, 405 U.S. 438 (1972) (contraception); *Loving* v. *Virginia*, 388 U.S. 1 (1967) (marriage); *Skinner* v. *Oklahoma ex rel. Williamson*, 316 U.S. 535 (1942) (procreation); *Pierce* v. *Society of Sisters*, 268 U.S. 510 (1925) (childrearing). . . . These are questions of unsurpassed significance in this Court's interpretation of the Constitution, and mark the battleground upon which this case was fought, by the parties, by the Solicitor General as *amicus* on behalf of petitioners, and by an unprecedented number of *amici*. On these grounds, abandoned by the plurality, the Court should decide this case.

But rather than arguing that the text of the Constitution makes no mention of the right to privacy, the plurality complains that the critical elements of the *Roe* framework—trimesters and viability—do not appear in the Constitution and are, therefore, somehow inconsistent with a Constitution cast in general terms. Were this a true concern, we would have to abandon most of our constitutional jurisprudence. As the plurality well knows, or should know, the "critical elements" of countless constitutional doctrines nowhere appear in the Constitution's text. The Constitution makes no mention, for example, of the First Amendment's "actual malice" standard for proving certain libels, see *New York Times Co.* v. *Sullivan*, 376 U.S. 254 (1964), or of the standard for determining when speech is obscene. See *Miller* v. *California*, 413 U.S. 15 (1973). Similarly, the Constitution makes no mention of the rational-basis test, or the specific verbal formulations of intermediate and strict scrutiny by which this Court evaluates claims under the Equal Protection Clause. The reason is simple. Like the *Roe* framework, these tests or standards are not, and do not purport to be, rights protected by the Constitution. Rather, they are judge-made methods for evaluating and measuring the strength and scope of constitutional rights or for balancing the constitutional rights of individuals against the competing interests of government. . . .

2

The plurality next alleges that the result of the trimester framework has "been a web of legal rules that have become increasingly intricate, resembling a code of regulations rather than a body of constitutional doctrine." Again, if this were a true and genuine concern, we would have to abandon vast areas of our constitutional jurisprudence. The plurality complains that under the trimester framework the Court has distinguished between a city ordinance requiring that second-trimester abortions be performed in clinics and a state law requiring that these abortions be performed in hospitals, or between laws requiring that certain information be furnished to a woman by a physician or his assistant and those requiring that such information be furnished by the physician exclusively. *Ante*, at 518, n. 15, citing *Simopoulos* v. *Virginia*, 462 U.S. 506 (1983), and *Akron* v. *Akron Center for Reproductive Health, Inc.*, 462 U.S. 416 (1983). Are these distinctions any finer, or more "regulatory," than the distinctions we have often drawn in our First Amendment jurisprudence, where, for example, we have held that a "release time" program permitting public-school students to leave school grounds during school hours to receive religious instruction does not violate the Establishment Clause, even though a release-time program permitting religious instruction on school grounds does violate the Clause? Compare *Zorach* v. *Clauson*, 343 U.S. 306 (1952), with *Illinois ex rel. McCollum* v. *Board of Education of School Dist. No. 71, Champaign County*, 333 U.S. 203 (1948). Our Fourth Amendment jurisprudence recognizes factual distinctions no less intricate. Just this Term, for example, we held that while an aerial observation from a helicopter hovering at 400 feet does not violate any reasonable expectation of privacy, such an expectation of privacy would be violated by a helicopter observation from an unusually low altitude. *Florida* v. *Riley*, 488 U.S. 445, 451 (1989) (O'CONNOR, J., concurring in judgment). Similarly, in a Sixth Amendment case, the Court held that although an overnight ban on attorney-client communication violated the constitutionally guaranteed right to counsel, *Geders* v. *United States*, 425 U.S. 80 (1976), that right was not violated when a trial judge separated a defendant from his lawyer during a 15-minute recess after the defendant's direct testimony. *Perry* v. *Leeke*, 488 U.S. 272 (1989).

That numerous constitutional doctrines result in narrow differentiations between similar circumstances does not mean that this Court has abandoned adjudication in favor of regulation. Rather, these careful distinctions reflect the process of constitutional adjudication itself, which is often highly fact specific, requiring such determinations as whether state laws are "unduly burdensome" or "reasonable" or bear a "rational" or "necessary" relation to asserted state interests. In a recent due process case, THE CHIEF JUSTICE wrote for the Court: "[M]any branches of the law abound in nice distinctions that may be troublesome but have been thought nonetheless necessary: 'I do not think we need trouble ourselves with the thought that my view depends upon differences of degree. The whole law does so as soon as it is civilized.'" *Daniels* v. *Williams*, 474 U.S. 327, 334 (1986), quoting *LeRoy Fibre Co.* v. *Chicago, M. & St. P. R. Co.*, 232 U.S. 340, 354 (1914) (Holmes, J., partially concurring).

These "differences of degree" fully account for our holdings in *Simopoulos, supra*, and *Akron, supra*. Those decisions rest on this Court's reasoned and accurate judgment that hospitalization and doctor-counseling requirements unduly burdened the right of women to terminate a pregnancy and were not rationally related to the State's asserted interest in the health of pregnant women, while Virginia's *substantially less restrictive* regulations were not unduly burdensome and did rationally serve the State's interest. . . . That the Court exercised its best judgment in evaluating these markedly different statutory schemes no more established the Court as an "'*ex officio* medical board,'" quoting *Planned Parenthood of Central Mo.* v. *Danforth*, 428 U.S. 52, 99 (1976) (opinion of WHITE, J., concurring in part and dissenting in part), than our decisions involving religion in the public schools establish the Court as a national school board, or our decisions concerning prison regulations establish the Court as a bureau of prisons. See *Thornburgh* v. *Abbott*, 490 U.S. 401 (1989) (adopting different standard of First Amendment review for incoming as opposed to outgoing prison mail). If, in delicate and complicated areas of constitutional law, our legal judgments "have become increasingly intricate," it is not, as the plurality contends, because we have overstepped our judicial role. Quite the opposite: the rules are intricate because we have remained conscientious in our duty to do justice carefully, especially when fundamental rights rise or fall with our decisions.

3

Finally, the plurality asserts that the trimester framework cannot stand because the State's interest in potential life is compelling throughout pregnancy, not merely after viability. The opinion contains not one word of rationale for its view of the State's interest. This "it-is-so-because-we-say-so" jurisprudence constitutes nothing other than an attempted exercise of brute force; reason, much less persuasion, has no place.

In answering the plurality's claim that the State's interest in the fetus is uniform and compelling throughout pregnancy, I cannot improve upon what JUSTICE STEVENS has written:

"I should think it obvious that the State's interest in the protection of an embryo—even if that interest is defined as 'protecting those who will be citizens' . . . —increases progressively and dramatically as the organism's capacity to feel pain, to experience pleasure, to survive, and to react to its surroundings increases day by day. The development of a fetus—and pregnancy itself—are not static conditions, and the assertion that the government's interest is static simply ignores this reality. . . . [U]nless the religious view that a fetus is a 'person' is adopted . . . there is a fundamental and well-recognized difference between a fetus and a human being; indeed, if there is not such a difference, the permissibility of terminating the life of a fetus could scarcely be left to the will of the state legislatures. And if distinctions may be drawn between a fetus and a human being in terms of the state interest in their protection—even though the fetus represents one of 'those who will be citizens'—it seems to me quite odd to argue that distinctions may not also be drawn between the state interest in protecting the freshly fertilized egg and the state interest in protecting the 9-month-gestated, fully sentient fetus on the eve of birth. Recognition of this distinction is supported not only by logic, but also by history and by our shared experiences." *Thornburgh*, 476 U.S., at 778–779 (footnote omitted).

See also *Roe*, 410 U.S., at 129–147.

For my own part, I remain convinced, as six other Members of this Court 16 years ago were convinced, that the *Roe* framework, and the viability standard in particular, fairly, sensibly, and effectively functions to safeguard the constitutional liberties of pregnant women while recognizing and accommodating the State's interest in potential human life. The viability line reflects the biological facts and truths of fetal development; it marks that threshold moment prior to which a fetus cannot survive separate from the woman and cannot reasonably and objectively be regarded as a subject of rights or interests distinct from, or paramount to, those of the pregnant woman. At the same time, the viability standard takes account of the undeniable fact that as the fetus evolves into its postnatal form, and as it loses its dependence on the uterine environment, the State's interest in the fetus' potential human life, and in fostering a regard for human life in general, becomes compelling. As a practical matter, because viability follows "quickening"—the point at which a woman feels movement in her womb—and because viability occurs no earlier than 23 weeks gestational age, it establishes an easily applicable standard for regulating abortion while providing a pregnant woman ample time to exercise her fundamental right with her responsible physician to terminate her pregnancy. . . . Although I have stated previously for a majority of this Court that "[c]onstitutional rights do not always have easily ascertainable boundaries," to seek and establish those boundaries remains the special responsibility of this Court. *Thornburgh*, 476 U.S., at 771. In *Roe*, we discharged that responsibility as logic and science compelled. The plurality today advances not one reasonable argument as to why our judgment in that case was wrong and should be abandoned. . . .

The plurality pretends that *Roe* survives, explaining that the facts of this case differ from those in *Roe*: here, Missouri has chosen to assert its interest in potential life only at the point of viability, whereas, in *Roe*, Texas had asserted that interest from the point of conception, criminalizing all abortions, except where the life of the mother was at stake. This, of course, is a distinction without a difference. The plurality repudiates every principle for which *Roe* stands; in good conscience, it cannot possibly believe that *Roe* lies "undisturbed" merely because this case does not call upon the Court to reconsider the Texas statute, or one like it. If the Constitution permits a State to enact any statute that reasonably furthers its interest in potential life, and if that interest arises as of conception, why would the Texas statute fail to pass muster? One suspects that the plurality agrees. It is impossible to read the plurality opinion and especially its final paragraph, without recognizing its implicit invitation to every State to enact more and more restrictive abortion laws, and to assert their interest in potential life as of the moment of conception. All these laws will satisfy the plurality's nonscrutiny, until sometime, a new regime of old dissenters and new appointees will declare what the plurality intends: that *Roe* is no longer good law. . . .

Thus, "not with a bang, but a whimper," the plurality discards a landmark case of the last generation, and casts into darkness the hopes and visions of every woman in this country who had come to believe that the Constitution guaranteed her right to exercise some control over her unique ability to bear children. The plurality does so either oblivious or insensitive to the fact that millions of women, and their families, have ordered their lives around the right to reproductive choice, and that this right has become vital to the full participation of women in the economic and political walks of American life. The plurality would clear the way once again for government to force upon women the physical labor and specific and direct medical and psychological harms that may accompany carrying a fetus to term. The plurality would clear the way again for the State to conscript a woman's body and to force upon her a "distressful life and future." *Roe*, 410 U.S., at 153.

The result, as we know from experience, see Cates & Rochat, Illegal Abortions in the United States: 1972–1974, 8 Family Planning Perspectives 86, 92 (1976), would be that every year hundreds of thousands of women, in desperation, would defy the law, and place their health and safety in the unclean and unsympathetic hands of back-alley abortionists, or they would attempt to perform abortions upon themselves, with disastrous results. Every year, many women, especially poor and minority women, would die or suffer debilitating physical trauma, all in the name of enforced morality or religious dictates or lack of compassion, as it may be.

Of the aspirations and settled understandings of American women, of the inevitable and brutal consequences of what it is doing, the tough-approach plurality utters not a word. This silence is callous. It is also profoundly destructive of this Court as an institution. To overturn a constitutional decision is a rare and grave undertaking. To overturn a constitutional decision that secured a fundamental personal liberty to millions of persons would be unprecedented in our 200 years of constitutional history. Although the doctrine of *stare decisis* applies with somewhat diminished force in constitutional cases generally, even in ordinary constitutional cases "any departure from . . . *stare decisis* demands special justification." *Arizona* v. *Rumsey*, 467 U.S. 203, 212 (1984). See also *Vasquez* v. *Hillery*, 474 U.S. 254, 266 (1986) ("[T]he careful observer will discern that any detours from the straight path of *stare decisis* in our past have occurred for articulable reasons, and only when the Court has felt obliged 'to bring its opinions into agreement with experience and with facts newly ascertained,'" quoting *Burnet* v. *Coronado Oil & Gas Co.*, 285 U.S. 393, 412 (1932) (Brandeis, J., dissenting)). This requirement of justification applies with unique force where, as here, the Court's abrogation of precedent would destroy people's firm belief, based on past decisions of this Court, that they possess an unabridgeable right to undertake certain conduct. . . .

OHIO v. AKRON CENTER FOR REPRODUCTIVE HEALTH ET AL.

APPEAL FROM THE UNITED STATES COURT OF APPEALS FOR THE SIXTH CIRCUIT

No. 88–805. Argued November 29, 1989—Decided June 25, 1990

KENNEDY, J., announced the judgment of the Court, and delivered the opinion of the Court with respect to Parts I, II, III, and IV, in which REHNQUIST, C J., and WHITE, STEVENS, O'CONNOR, and SCALIA, JJ., joined, and an opinion with respect to Part V, in which REHNQUIST, C. J., and WHITE and SCALIA, JJ., joined. SCALIA, J., filed a concurring opinion. STEVENS, J., filed an opinion concurring in part and concurring in the judgment. BLACKMUN, J., filed a dissenting opinion, in which BRENNAN and MARSHALL, JJ., joined.

JUSTICE KENNEDY announced the judgment of the Court and delivered the opinion of the Court with respect to Parts I, II, III, and IV,* and an opinion with respect to Part V, in which THE CHIEF JUSTICE, JUSTICE WHITE, and JUSTICE SCALIA join.

The Court of Appeals held invalid an Ohio statute that, with certain exceptions, prohibits any person from performing an abortion on an unmarried, unemancipated, minor woman absent notice to one of the woman's parents or a court order of approval. We reverse, for we determine that the statute accords with our precedents on parental notice and consent in the abortion context and does not violate the Fourteenth Amendment.

. . . We have decided five cases addressing the constitutionality of parental notice or parental consent statutes in the abortion context. See *Planned Parenthood of Central Mo.* v. *Danforth*, 428 U.S. 52 (1976); *Bellotti* v. *Baird*, 443 U.S. 622 (1979); *H. L.* v. *Matheson*, 450 U.S. 398 (1981); *Planned Parenthood Assn. of Kansas City, Mo., Inc.* v. *Ashcroft*, 462 U.S. 476 (1983); *Akron* v. *Akron Center for Reproductive Health, Inc.*, 462 U.S. 416 (1983). We do not need to determine whether a statute that does not accord with these cases would violate the Constitution, for we conclude that H. B. 319 is consistent with them.

A

This dispute turns, to a large extent, on the adequacy of H. B. 319's judicial bypass procedure. In analyzing this aspect of the dispute, we note that, although our cases have required bypass procedures for parental consent statutes, we have not decided whether parental notice statutes must contain such procedures. See *Matheson*, and n. 25 (upholding

---

*JUSTICE STEVENS and JUSTICE O'CONNOR join only Parts I, II, III, and IV of the opinion.

a notice statute without a bypass procedure as applied to immature, dependent minors). We leave the question open, because, whether or not the Fourteenth Amendment requires notice statutes to contain bypass procedures, H. B. 319's bypass procedure meets the requirements identified for parental consent statutes in *Danforth*, *Bellotti*, *Ashcroft*, and *Akron*. *Danforth* established that, in order to prevent another person from having an absolute veto power over a minor's decision to have an abortion, a State must provide some sort of bypass procedure if it elects to require parental consent. See 428 U.S., at 74. As we hold today in *Hodgson* v. *Minnesota*, it is a corollary to the greater intrusiveness of consent statutes that a bypass procedure that will suffice for a consent statute will suffice also for a notice statute. See also *Matheson* (notice statutes are not equivalent to consent statutes because they do not give anyone a veto power over a minor's abortion decision).

The principal opinion in *Bellotti* stated four criteria that a bypass procedure in a consent statute must satisfy. Appellees contend that the bypass procedure does not satisfy these criteria. We disagree. First, the *Bellotti* principal opinion indicated that the procedure must allow the minor to show that she possesses the maturity and information to make her abortion decision, in consultation with her physician, without regard to her parents' wishes. See 443 U.S., at 643 (opinion of Powell, J.). The Court reaffirmed this requirement in *Akron* by holding that a State cannot presume the immaturity of girls under the age of 15. 462 U.S., at 440. In the case now before us, we have no difficulty concluding that H. B. 319 allows a minor to show maturity in conformity with the principal opinion in *Bellotti*. The statute permits the minor to show that she "is sufficiently mature and well enough informed to decide intelligently whether to have an abortion." Ohio. Rev. Code Ann. § 2151.85(C)(1) (Supp. 1988).

Second, the *Bellotti* principal opinion indicated that the procedure must allow the minor to show that, even if she cannot make the abortion decision by herself, "the desired abortion would be in her best interests." 443 U.S., at 644. We believe that H. B. 319 satisfies the *Bellotti* language as quoted. The statute requires the juvenile court to authorize the minor's consent where the court determines that the abortion is in the minor's best interest and in cases where the minor has shown a pattern of physical, sexual, or emotional abuse. See § 2151.85(C)(2).

Third, the *Bellotti* principal opinion indicated that the procedure must insure the minor's anonymity. See 443 U.S., at 644. H. B. 319 satisfies this standard. Section 2151.85 (D) provides that "[t]he [juvenile] court shall not notify the parents, guardian, or custodian of the complainant that she is pregnant or that she wants to have an abortion." Section 2151.85(F) further states:

> "Each hearing under this section shall be conducted in a manner that will preserve the anonymity of the complainant. The complaint and all other papers and records that pertain to an action commenced under this section shall be kept confidential and are not public records."

Section 2505.073(B), in a similar fashion, requires the court of appeals to preserve the minor's anonymity and confidentiality of all papers on appeal. The State, in addition, makes it a criminal offense for an employee to disclose documents not designated as public records. See §§ 102.03(B), 102.99(B).

Appellees argue that the complaint forms prescribed by the Ohio Supreme Court will require the minor to disclose her identity. Unless the minor has counsel, she must sign a complaint form to initiate the bypass procedure and, even if she has counsel, she must supply the name of one of her parents at four different places. See App. 6–14 (pleading forms). Appellees would prefer protections similar to those included in the statutes that we reviewed in *Bellotti* and *Ashcroft*. The statute in *Bellotti* protected anonymity by permitting use of a pseudonym, see *Planned Parenthood League of Massachusetts v. Bellotti*, 641 F. 2d 1006, 1025 (CA1 1981), and the statute in *Ashcroft* allowed the minor to sign the petition with her initials, see 462 U.S., at 491, n. 16. Appellees also maintain that the Ohio laws requiring court employees not to disclose public documents are irrelevant because the right to anonymity is broader than the right not to have officials reveal one's identity to the public at large.

Confidentiality differs from anonymity, but we do not believe that the distinction has constitutional significance in the present context. The distinction has not played a part in our previous decisions, and, even if the *Bellotti* principal opinion is taken as setting the standard, we do not find complete anonymity critical. H. B. 319, like the statutes in *Bellotti* and *Ashcroft*, takes reasonable steps to prevent the public from learning of the minor's identity. We refuse to base a decision on the facial validity of a statute on the mere possibility of unauthorized, illegal disclosure by state employees. H. B. 319, like many sophisticated judicial procedures, requires participants to provide identifying information for administrative purposes, not for public disclosure.

Fourth, the *Bellotti* principal opinion indicated that courts must conduct a bypass procedure with expedition to allow the minor an effective opportunity to obtain the abortion. See 443 U.S., at 644. H. B. 319, as noted above, requires the trial court to make its decision within five "business day[s]" after the minor files her complaint, § 2151.85(B)(1); requires the court of appeals to docket an appeal within four "days" after the minor files a notice of appeal, § 2505.073(A); and requires the court of appeals to render a decision within five "days" after docketing the appeal, *ibid.*

The District Court and the Court of Appeals assumed that all of the references to days in §§ 2151.85(B)(1) and 2505.073(A) meant business days as opposed to calendar days. Cf. Ohio Rule App. Proc. 14(A) (excluding nonbusiness days from computations of less than seven days). They calculated, as a result, that the procedure could take up to 22 calendar days because the minor could file at a time during the year in which the 14 business days needed for the bypass procedure would encompass 3 Saturdays, 3 Sundays, and 2 legal holidays. Appellees maintain, on the basis of an affidavit included in the record, that a 3-week delay could increase by a substantial measure both the costs and the medical risks of an abortion. See App. 18. They conclude, as did those courts, that H. B. 319 does not satisfy the *Bellotti* principal opinion's expedition requirement.

As a preliminary matter, the 22-day calculation conflicts with two well-known rules of construction discussed in our abortion cases and elsewhere. "Where fairly possible, courts should construe a statute to avoid a danger of unconstitutionality." . . . (opinion of POWELL, J.). Although we recognize that the other federal courts "'are better schooled in and more able to interpret the laws of their respective States'" than are we, *Frisby* v. *Schultz,* 487 U.S. 474, 482 (1988), the Court of Appeals' decision strikes us as dubious. Interpreting the term "days" in § 2505.073(A) to mean business days instead of calendar days seems inappropriate and unnecessary because of the express and contrasting use of "business day[s]" in § 2151.85(B)(1). In addition, because appellees are making a facial challenge to a statute, they must show that "no set of circumstances exists under which the Act would be valid." *Webster* v. *Reproductive Health Services,* 492 U.S. 490, 524 (1989) (O'CONNOR, J., concurring). The Court of Appeals should not have invalidated the Ohio statute on a facial challenge based upon a worst-case analysis that may never occur. Cf. Ohio Rev. Code § 2505.073(A) (Supp. 1988) (allowing the court of appeals, upon the minor's motion, to shorten or extend the time periods). Moreover, under our precedents, the mere possibility that the procedure may require up to 22 days in a rare case is plainly insufficient to invalidate the statute on its face. *Ashcroft,* for example, upheld a Missouri statute that contained a bypass procedure that could require 17 calendar days plus a sufficient time for deliberation and decisionmaking at both the trial and appellate levels. See 462 U.S., at 477, n. 4, 491, n. 16.

B

Appellees ask us, in effect, to extend the criteria used by some Members of the Court in *Bellotti* and the cases following it by imposing three additional requirements on bypass procedures. First, they challenge the constructive authorization provisions in H. B. 319, which enable a minor to obtain an abortion without notifying one of her parents if either the juvenile court or the court of appeals fails to act within the prescribed time limits. See Ohio Rev. Code Ann. §§ 2151.85(B)(1), 2505.073(A), and § 2919.12(B)(1)(a)(iv) (1987 and Supp. 1988). They speculate that the absence of an affirmative order when a court fails to process the minor's complaint will deter the physician from acting.

We discern no constitutional defect in the statute. Absent a demonstrated pattern of abuse or defiance, a State may expect that its judges will follow mandated procedural requirements. There is no showing that the time limitations imposed by H. B. 319 will be ignored. With an abundance of caution, and concern for the minor's interests, Ohio added the constructive authorization provisions in H. B. 319 to ensure expedition of the bypass procedures even if these time limits are not met. The State represents that a physician can obtain certified documentation from the juvenile or appellate court that constructive authorization has occurred. Brief for Appellant 36. We did not require a similar safety net in the bypass procedures in n. 4, and find no defect in the procedures that Ohio has provided.

Second, appellees ask us to rule that a bypass procedure cannot require a minor to prove maturity or best interests by a standard of clear and convincing evidence. They maintain that, when a State seeks to deprive an individual of liberty interests, it must take upon itself the risk of error. See *Santosky* v. *Kramer*, 455 U.S. 745, 755 (1982). House Bill 319 violates this standard, in their opinion, not only by placing the burden of proof upon the minor, but also by imposing a heightened standard of proof.

This contention lacks merit. A State does not have to bear the burden of proof on the issues of maturity or best interests. The principal opinion in *Bellotti* indicates that a State may require the minor to prove these facts in a bypass procedure. See 443 U.S., at 643 (opinion of Powell, J.). A State, moreover, may require a heightened standard of proof when, as here, the bypass procedure contemplates an *ex parte* proceeding at which no one opposes the minor's testimony. We find the clear and convincing standard used in H. B. 319 acceptable. The Ohio Supreme Court has stated:

"Clear and convincing evidence is that measure or degree of proof which will produce in the mind of the trier of facts a firm belief or conviction as to the allegations sought to be established. It is intermediate, being more than a mere preponderance, but not to the extent of such certainty as is required beyond a reasonable doubt as in criminal cases. It does not mean clear and unequivocal." *Cross* v. *Ledford*, 161 Ohio St. 469, 477, 120 N. E. 2d 118, 123 (1954) (emphasis deleted).

Our precedents do not require the State to set a lower standard. Given that the minor is assisted in the courtroom by an attorney as well as a guardian *ad litem*, this aspect of H. B. 319 is not infirm under the Constitution.

Third, appellees contend that the pleading requirements in H. B. 319 create a trap for the unwary. The minor, under the statutory scheme and the requirements prescribed by the Ohio Supreme Court, must choose among three pleading forms. See Ohio Rev. Code § 2151.85(C) (Supp. 1988); App. 6–14. The first alleges only maturity and the second alleges only best interests. She may not attempt to prove both maturity and best interests unless she chooses the third form, which alleges both of these facts. Appellees contend that the complications imposed by this scheme deny a minor the opportunity, required by the principal opinion in *Bellotti*, to prove either maturity or best interests or both. See 443 U.S., at 643–644.

Even on the assumption that the pleading scheme could produce some initial confusion because few minors would have counsel when pleading, the simple and straightforward procedure does not deprive the minor of an opportunity to prove her case. It seems unlikely that the Ohio courts will treat a minor's choice of complaint form without due care and understanding for her unrepresented status. In addition, we note that the minor does not make a binding election by the initial choice of pleading form. The minor, under H. B. 319, receives appointed counsel after filing the complaint and may move for leave to amend the pleadings. See 2151.85(B) (2); Ohio Rule Juvenile Proc. 22(B); see also *Hambleton* v. *R. G. Barry Corp.*, 12 Ohio St. 3d 179, 183–184, 465 N. E. 2d 1298, 1302 (1984) (finding a liberal amendment policy in the state civil rules). Regardless of whether Ohio could have written a simpler statute, H. B. 319 survives a facial challenge. . . .

HODGSON ET AL. v. MINNESOTA ET AL.

CERTIORARI TO THE UNITED STATES COURT OF APPEALS FOR THE EIGHTH CIRCUIT

No. 88-1125. Argued November 29, 1989—Decided June 25, 1990

STEVENS, J., announced the judgment of the Court and delivered the opinion of the Court with respect to Parts I, II, IV, and VII, in which BRENNAN, MARSHALL, BLACKMUN, and O'CONNOR, JJ., joined, an opinion with respect to Part III, in which BRENNAN, J., joined, an opinion with respect to Parts V and VI, in which O'CONNOR, J., joined, and a dissenting opinion with respect to Part VIII. O'CONNOR, J., filed an opinion concurring in part and concurring in the judgment. MARSHALL, J., filed an opinion concurring in part, concurring in the judgment in part, and dissenting in part, in which BRENNAN and BLACKMUN, JJ., joined. SCALIA, J., filed an opinion concurring in the judgment in part and dissenting in part. KENNEDY, J., filed an opinion concurring in the judgment in part and dissenting in part, in which REHNQUIST, C. J., and WHITE and SCALIA, JJ., joined.

JUSTICE STEVENS announced the judgment of the Court and delivered the opinion of the Court with respect to Parts I, II, IV, and VII, an opinion with respect to Part III in which JUSTICE BRENNAN joins, an opinion with respect to Parts V and VI in which JUSTICE O'CONNOR joins, and a dissenting opinion with respect to Part VIII.

A Minnesota statute, Minn. Stat. §§ 144.343(2)–(7) (1988), provides, with certain exceptions, that no abortion shall be performed on a woman under 18 years of age until at least 48 hours after both of her parents have been notified. In subdivisions 2–4 of the statute the notice is mandatory unless (1) the attending physician certifies that an immediate abortion is necessary to prevent the woman's death and there is insufficient time to provide the required notice; (2) both of her parents have consented in writing; or (3) the woman declares that she is a victim of parental abuse or neglect, in which event notice of her declaration must be given to the proper authorities. The United States Court of Appeals for the Eighth Circuit, sitting en banc, unanimously held this provision unconstitutional. In No. 88-1309, we granted the State's petition to review that holding. Subdivision 6 of the same statute provides that if a court enjoins the enforcement of subdivision 2, the same notice requirement shall be effective unless the pregnant woman obtains a court order permitting the abortion to proceed. By a vote of 7 to 3, the Court of Appeals upheld the constitutionality of subdivision 6. In No. 88-1125, we granted the plaintiffs' petition to review that holding.

For reasons that follow, we now conclude that the requirement of notice to both of the pregnant minor's parents is not reasonably related to legitimate state interests and that subdivision 2 is unconstitutional. A different majority of the Court, for reasons stated in separate opinions, concludes that subdivision 6 is constitutional. Accordingly, the judgment of the Court of Appeals in its entirety is affirmed.

I

The parental notice statute was enacted in 1981 as an amendment to the Minors' Consent to Health Services Act. The earlier statute, which remains in effect as subdivision 1 of § 144.343 and as § 144.346, had modified the common-law requirement of parental consent for any medical procedure performed on minors. It authorized "[a]ny minor" to give effective consent without any parental involvement for the treatment of "pregnancy and conditions associated therewith, venereal disease, alcohol and other drug abuse." . . . The statute, unlike others of its age, . . . applied to abortion services.

The 1981 amendment qualified the authority of an "unemancipated minor" . . . to give effective consent to an abortion by requiring that either her physician or an agent notify "the parent" personally or by certified mail at least 48 hours before the procedure is performed. . . . The term "parent" is defined in subdivision 3 to mean "both parents of the pregnant woman if they are both living." No exception is made for a divorced parent, a noncustodial parent, or a biological parent who never married or lived with the pregnant woman's mother. . . . The statute does provide, however, that if only one parent is living, or "if the second one cannot be located through reasonably diligent effort," notice to one parent is sufficient. . . .

Subdivision 6 authorizes a judicial bypass of the two-parent notice requirement if subdivision 2 is ever "temporarily or permanently" enjoined by judicial order. If the pregnant minor can convince "any judge of a court of competent jurisdiction" that she is "mature and capable of giving informed consent to the proposed abortion," or that an abortion without notice to both parents would be in her best interest, the court can authorize the physician to proceed without notice. The statute provides that the bypass procedure shall be confidential, that it shall be expedited, that the minor has a right to court-appointed counsel, and that she shall be afforded free access to the court "24 hours a day, seven days a week." An order denying an abortion can be appealed on an expedited basis, but an order authorizing an abortion without notification is not subject to appeal. . . .

Three separate but related interests—the interest in the welfare of the pregnant minor, the interest of the parents, and the interest of the family unit—are relevant to our consideration of the constitutionality of the 48-hour waiting period and the two-parent notification requirement.

The State has a strong and legitimate interest in the welfare of its young citizens, whose immaturity, inexperience, and lack of judgment may sometimes impair their ability to exercise their rights wisely. See *Bellotti II*, 443 U.S., at 634–639 (opinion of Powell,

J.); *Prince* v. *Massachusetts*, 321 U.S. 158, 166–167 (1944).[31] That interest, which justifies state-imposed requirements that a minor obtain his or her parent's consent before undergoing an operation, marrying, or entering military service, see *Parham* v. *J. R.*, 442 U.S. 584, 603–604 (1979); *Planned Parenthood of Central Mo.* v. *Danforth*, 428 U.S., at 95 (WHITE, J., concurring in part and dissenting in part); *id.*, at 102–103 (STEVENS, J., concurring in part and dissenting in part), extends also to the minor's decision to terminate her pregnancy. Although the Court has held that parents may not exercise "an absolute, and possibly arbitrary, veto" over that decision, *Danforth*, 428 U.S., at 74, it has never challenged a State's reasonable judgment that the decision should be made after notification to and consultation with a parent. See *Ohio* v. *Akron Center for Reproductive Health*, *post*, at 510–511; *Akron* v. *Akron Center for Reproductive Health, Inc.*, 462 U.S. 416, 428, n. 10, 439 (1983); *H. L.* v. *Matheson*, 450 U.S., at 409–410; *Bellotti II*, 443 U.S., at 640–641 (opinion of Powell, J.); *Danforth*, 428 U.S., at 75. As Justice Stewart, joined by Justice Powell, pointed out in his concurrence in *Danforth*:

> "There can be little doubt that the State furthers a constitutionally permissible end by encouraging an unmarried pregnant minor to seek the help and advice of her parents in making the very important decision whether or not to bear a child." *Id.*, at 91.

Parents have an interest in controlling the education and upbringing of their children but that interest is "a counterpart of the responsibilities they have assumed." *Lehr* v. *Robertson*, 463 U.S. 248, 257 (1983); see also *Parham*, 442 U.S., at 602 (citing 1 W. Blackstone, Commentaries *447; 2 J. Kent, Commentaries on American Law *190); *Pierce* v. *Society of Sisters*, 268 U.S. 510, 535 (1925). The fact of biological parentage generally offers a person only "an opportunity . . . to develop a relationship with his offspring." *Lehr*, 463 U.S., at 262; see also *Caban* v. *Mohammed*, 441 U.S. 380, 397 (1979) (Stewart, J., dissenting). But the demonstration of commitment to the child through the assumption of personal, financial, or custodial responsibility may give the natural parent a stake in the relationship with the child rising to the level of a liberty interest. See *Stanley* v. *Illinois*, 405 U.S. 645, 651 (1972); *Lehr*, 463 U.S., at 261; *Michael H.* v. *Gerald D.*, 491 U.S. 110, 157–160 (1989) (WHITE, J., dissenting); cf. *Caban*, 441 U.S., at 393, n. 14. But see *Michael H.*, 491 U.S., at 123–127 (plurality opinion).

While the State has a legitimate interest in the creation and dissolution of the marriage contract, see *Sosna* v. *Iowa*, 419 U.S. 393, 404 (1975); *Maynard* v. *Hill*, 125 U.S. 190, 205 (1888), the family has a privacy interest in the upbringing and education of

---

31. "Properly understood . . . the tradition of parental authority is not inconsistent with our tradition of individual liberty; rather, the former is one of the basic presuppositions of the latter. Legal restrictions on minors, especially those supportive of the parental role, may be important to the child's chances for the full growth and maturity that make eventual participation in a free society meaningful and rewarding." *Bellotti II*, 443 U.S., at 638–639 (opinion of Powell, J.). . . .

children and the intimacies of the marital relationship which is protected by the Constitution against undue state interference. See *Wisconsin* v. *Yoder*, 406 U.S. 205, 233–234 (1972); *Griswold* v. *Connecticut*, 381 U.S., at 495–496 (Goldberg, J., concurring); *Poe* v. *Ullman*, 367 U.S. 497, 551–552 (1961) (Harlan, J., dissenting); *Gilbert* v. *Minnesota*, 254 U.S. 325, 335–336 (1920) (Brandeis, J., dissenting); see also *Michael H.*, 491 U.S., at 132 (O'Connor, J., concurring in part); *Roberts* v. *United States Jaycees*, 468 U.S. 609, 618–620 (1984); *Cleveland Bd. of Education* v. *LaFleur*, 414 U.S., at 639–640. The family may assign one parent to guide the children's education and the other to look after their health.[32] "The statist notion that governmental power should supersede parental authority in *all* cases because *some* parents abuse and neglect children is repugnant to American tradition." *Parham*, 442 U.S., at 603. We have long held that there exists a "private realm of family life which the state cannot enter." *Prince* v. *Massachusetts*, 321 U.S., at 166. Thus, when the government intrudes on choices concerning the arrangement of the household, this Court has carefully examined the "governmental interests advanced and the extent to which they are served by the challenged regulation." *Moore* v. *East Cleveland*, 431 U.S. 494, 499 (1977) (plurality opinion); *id.*, at 507, 510–511 (Brennan, J., concurring); see also *Meyer* v. *Nebraska*, 262 U.S. 390, 399–400 (1923). . . .

We think it is clear that a requirement that a minor wait 48 hours after notifying a single parent of her intention to get an abortion would reasonably further the legitimate state interest in ensuring that the minor's decision is knowing and intelligent. We have held that when a parent or another person has assumed "primary responsibility" for a minor's well-being, the State may properly enact "laws designed to aid discharge of that responsibility." *Ginsberg* v. *New York*, 390 U.S. 629, 639 (1968). To the extent that subdivision 2 of the Minnesota statute requires notification of only one parent, it does just that. The brief waiting period provides the parent the opportunity to consult with his or her spouse and a family physician, and it permits the parent to inquire into the competency of the doctor performing the abortion, discuss the religious or moral implications of the abortion decision, and provide the daughter needed guidance and counsel in evaluating the impact of the decision on her future. See *Zbaraz* v. *Hartigan*, 763 F. 2d 1532, 1552 (CA7 1985) (Coffey, J., dissenting), aff'd by an equally divided Court, 484 U.S. 171 (1987).

The 48-hour delay imposes only a minimal burden on the right of the minor to decide whether or not to terminate her pregnancy. Although the District Court found that scheduling factors, weather, and the minor's school and work commitments may combine, in many cases, to create a delay of a week or longer between the initiation of notification and the abortion, 648 F. Supp., at 765, there is no evidence that the 48-hour period itself is unreasonable or longer than appropriate for adequate consultation between

---

32. Under common-law principles, one parent has authority to act as agent for the other in matters of their child's upbringing and education. See E. Spencer, Law of Domestic Relations 432 (1911); T. Reeve, Law of Baron and Femme 295 (1816).

parent and child. The statute does not impose any period of delay once a court, acting *in loco parentis*, or the parents express their agreement that the minor is mature or that the procedure would be in her best interest. . . .

It is equally clear that the requirement that *both* parents be notified, whether or not both wish to be notified or have assumed responsibility for the upbringing of the child, does not reasonably further any legitimate state interest. The usual justification for a parental consent or notification provision is that it supports the authority of a parent who is presumed to act in the minor's best interest and thereby assures that the minor's decision to terminate her pregnancy is knowing, intelligent, and deliberate. To the extent that such an interest is legitimate, it would be fully served by a requirement that the minor notify one parent who can then seek the counsel of his or her mate or any other party, when such advice and support is deemed necessary to help the child make a difficult decision. In the ideal family setting, of course, notice to either parent would normally constitute notice to both. A statute requiring two-parent notification would not further any state interest in those instances. In many families, however, the parent notified by the child would not notify the other parent. In those cases the State has no legitimate interest in questioning one parent's judgment that notice to the other parent would not assist the minor or in presuming that the parent who has assumed parental duties is incompetent to make decisions regarding the health and welfare of the child.

Not only does two-parent notification fail to serve any state interest with respect to functioning families, it disserves the state interest in protecting and assisting the minor with respect to dysfunctional families. The record reveals that in the thousands of dysfunctional families affected by this statute, the two-parent notice requirement proved positively harmful to the minor and her family. The testimony at trial established that this requirement, ostensibly designed for the benefit of the minor, resulted in major trauma to the child, and often to a parent as well. In some cases, the parents were divorced and the second parent did not have custody or otherwise participate in the child's upbringing. App. 244–245; *id.*, at 466; *id.*, at 115. In these circumstances, the privacy of the parent and child was violated, even when they suffered no other physical or psychological harm. In other instances, however, the second parent had either deserted or abused the child, *id.*, at 462, 464, had died under tragic circumstances, *id.*, at 120–121, or was not notified because of the considered judgment that notification would inflict unnecessary stress on a parent who was ill. *Id.*, at 204, 465. . . . In these circumstances, the statute was not merely ineffectual in achieving the State's goals but actually counterproductive. The focus on notifying the second parent distracted both the parent and minor from the minor's imminent abortion decision. . . .

The Court holds that the constitutional objection to the two-parent notice requirement is removed by the judicial bypass option provided in subdivision 6 of the Minnesota statute. I respectfully dissent from that holding.

A majority of the Court has previously held that a statute requiring one parent's consent to a minor's abortion will be upheld if the State provides an "'alternative procedure whereby a pregnant minor may demonstrate that she is sufficiently mature to make the abortion decision herself or that, despite her immaturity, an abortion would be in her best interests.'" *Planned Parenthood Assn. of Kansas City, Mo., Inc.* v. *Ashcroft*, 462 U.S. 476, 491 (1983) (opinion of Powell, J.); *id.*, at 505 (opinion of O'CONNOR, J.). Indeed, in *Bellotti II*, four Members of the Court expressed the same opinion about a statute requiring the consent of both parents. See 443 U.S., at 643–644 (opinion of Powell, J.). Neither of those precedents should control our decision today.

In *Bellotti II*, eight Members of the Court joined the judgment holding the Massachusetts statute unconstitutional. Thus, the Court did not *hold* that the judicial bypass set forth in that statute was valid; it held just the opposite. Moreover, the discussion of the minimum requirements for a valid judicial bypass in Justice Powell's opinion was joined by only three other Members of the Court. Indeed, neither the arguments of the parties, nor any of the opinions in the case, considered the significant difference between a statute requiring the involvement of *both* parents in the abortion decision and a statute that merely requires the involvement of one. Thus, the doctrine of *stare decisis* does not require that the standards articulated in Justice Powell's opinion be applied to a statute that mandates the involvement of both parents.

Unlike *Bellotti II*, the judgment in *Ashcroft* sustained the constitutionality of the statute containing a judicial bypass as an alternative to the requirement of *one* parent's consent to a minor's abortion. The distinctions between notice and consent and between notification of both parents rather than just one arguably constitute a sufficient response to an argument resting on *stare decisis*. Further analysis is necessary, however, because, at least on the surface, the consent requirement would appear to be more onerous than a requirement of mere notice. . . .

A judicial bypass that is designed to handle exceptions from a reasonable general rule, and thereby preserve the constitutionality of that rule, is quite different from a requirement that a minor—or a minor and one of her parents—must apply to a court for permission to avoid the application of a rule that is not reasonably related to legitimate state goals. A requirement that a minor acting with the consent of *both* parents apply to a court for permission to effectuate her decision clearly would constitute an unjustified official interference with the privacy of the minor and her family. The requirement that the bypass procedure must be invoked when the minor and one parent agree that the other parent should not be notified represents an equally unjustified governmental intrusion into the family's decisional process. When the parents are living together and have joint custody over the child, the State has no legitimate interest in the communication between father and mother about the child. "[W]here the parents are divorced, the minor and/or custodial parent, and not a court, is in the best position to determine whether notifying the non-custodial parent would be in the child's best interests." App. to Pet. for Cert. in No. 88–1125, p. 69a. As the Court of Appeals panel originally concluded, the "minor and custodial parent, . . . by virtue of their major interest and superior position, should alone have the opportunity to decide to whom, if anyone, notice of the minor's abortion decision should be given." *Ibid.* (citation omitted). I agree with that conclusion. . . .

PLANNED PARENTHOOD OF SOUTHEASTERN PENNSYLVANIA ET AL. *v.* ROBERT P. CASEY ET AL.

Nos. 91–744, 91–902. Argued April 22, 1992.—Decided June 29, 1992.

O'CONNOR, KENNEDY, and SOUTER, JJ., announced the judgment of the Court and delivered the opinion of the Court with respect to Parts I, II, III, V–A, V–C, and VI, in which BLACKMUN and STEVENS, JJ., joined, an opinion with respect to Part V–E, in which STEVENS, J., joined, and an opinion with respect to Parts IV, V–B, and V–D. STEVENS, J., filed an opinion concurring in part and dissenting in part. BLACKMUN, J., filed an opinion concurring in part, concurring in the judgment in part, and dissenting in part. REHNQUIST, C. J., filed an opinion concurring in the judgment in part and dissenting in part, in which WHITE, SCALIA, and THOMAS, JJ., joined. SCALIA, J., filed an opinion concurring in the judgment in part and dissenting in part, in which REHNQUIST, C. J., and WHITE and THOMAS, JJ., joined.

JUSTICE O'CONNOR, JUSTICE KENNEDY, and JUSTICE SOUTER announced the judgment of the Court and delivered the opinion of the Court with respect to Parts I, II, III, V–A, V–C, and VI, an opinion with respect to Part V–E, in which JUSTICE STEVENS joins, and an opinion with respect to Parts IV, V–B, and V–D.

I

Liberty finds no refuge in a jurisprudence of doubt. Yet 19 years after our holding that the Constitution protects a woman's right to terminate her pregnancy in its early stages, *Roe v. Wade*, 410 U.S. 113, 93 S.Ct. 705, 35 L. Ed. 2d 147 (1973), that definition of liberty is still questioned. Joining the respondents as *amicus curiae*, the United States, as it has done in five other cases in the last decade, again asks us to overrule *Roe*. See Brief for Respondents 104–117; Brief for United States as *Amicus Curiae* 8.

At issue in these cases are five provisions of the Pennsylvania Abortion Control Act of 1982 as amended in 1988 and 1989. 18 Pa. Cons. Stat. §§ 3203–3220 (1990). Relevant portions of the Act are set forth in the appendix. The Act requires that a woman seeking an abortion give her informed consent prior to the abortion procedure, and specifies that she be provided with certain information at least 24 hours before the abortion is performed. § 3205. For a minor to obtain an abortion, the Act requires the informed consent of one of her parents, but provides for a judicial bypass option if the minor does not wish to or cannot obtain a parent's consent. § 3206. Another provision of the Act requires that, unless certain exceptions apply, a married woman seeking an abortion must sign a statement indicating that she has notified her husband of her intended abortion. §

3209. The Act exempts compliance with these three requirements in the event of a "medical emergency," which is defined in § 3203 of the Act. See §§ 3203, 3205(a), 3206(a), 3209(c). In addition to the above provisions regulating the performance of abortions, the Act imposes certain reporting requirements on facilities that provide abortion services. §§ 3207(b), 3214(a), 3214(f).

Before any of these provisions took effect, the petitioners, who are five abortion clinics and one physician representing himself as well as a class of physicians who provide abortion services, brought this suit seeking declaratory and injunctive relief. Each provision was challenged as unconstitutional on its face. The District Court entered a preliminary injunction against the enforcement of the regulations, and, after a 3-day bench trial, held all the provisions at issue here unconstitutional, entering a permanent injunction against Pennsylvania's enforcement of them. 744 F. Supp. 1323 (ED Pa. 1990). The Court of Appeals for the Third Circuit affirmed in part and reversed in part, upholding all of the regulations except for the husband notification requirement. 947 F. 2d 682 (1991). We granted certiorari. 502 U.S. 112 S.Ct. 631, 632, 117 L. Ed. 2d 104 (1992).

The Court of Appeals found it necessary to follow an elaborate course of reasoning even to identify the first premise to use to determine whether the statute enacted by Pennsylvania meets constitutional standards. See 947 F. 2d, at 687–698. And at oral argument in this Court, the attorney for the parties challenging the statute took the position that none of the enactments can be upheld without overruling *Roe* v. *Wade*. Tr. of Oral Arg. 5–6. We disagree with that analysis; but we acknowledge that our decisions after *Roe* cast doubt upon the meaning and reach of its holding. Further, THE CHIEF JUSTICE admits that he would overrule the central holding of *Roe* and adopt the rational relationship test as the sole criterion of constitutionality. State and federal courts as well as legislatures throughout the Union must have guidance as they seek to address this subject in conformance with the Constitution. Given these premises, we find it imperative to review once more the principles that define the rights of the woman and the legitimate authority of the State respecting the termination of pregnancies by abortion procedures.

After considering the fundamental constitutional questions resolved by *Roe*, principles of institutional integrity, and the rule of *stare decisis*, we are led to conclude this: the essential holding of *Roe* v. *Wade* should be retained and once again reaffirmed.

It must be stated at the outset and with clarity that *Roe*'s essential holding, the holding we reaffirm, has three parts. First is a recognition of the right of the woman to choose to have an abortion before viability and to obtain it without undue interference from the State. Before viability, the State's interests are not strong enough to support a prohibition of abortion or the imposition of a substantial obstacle to the woman's effective right to elect the procedure. Second is a confirmation of the State's power to restrict abortions after fetal viability, if the law contains exceptions for pregnancies which endanger a woman's life or health. And third is the principle that the State has legitimate interests from the outset of the pregnancy in protecting the health of the woman and the life of the fetus that may become a child. These principles do not contradict one another; and we adhere to each.

II

Constitutional protection of the woman's decision to terminate her pregnancy derives from the Due Process Clause of the Fourteenth Amendment. It declares that no State shall "deprive any person of life, liberty, or property, without due process of law." The controlling word in the case before us is "liberty." Although a literal reading of the Clause might suggest that it governs only the procedures by which a State may deprive persons of liberty, for at least 105 years, at least since *Mugler* v. *Kansas*, 123 U.S. 623, 660–661, 8 S.Ct. 273, 291, 31 L. Ed. 205 (1887), the Clause has been understood to contain a substantive component as well, one "barring certain government actions regardless of the fairness of the procedures used to implement them." *Daniels* v. *Williams*, 474 U.S. 327, 331, 106 S.Ct. 662, 665, 88 L. Ed. 2d 662 (1986). As Justice Brandeis (joined by Justice Holmes) observed, "[d]espite arguments to the contrary which had seemed to me persuasive, it is settled that the due process clause of the Fourteenth Amendment applies to matters of substantive law as well as to matters of procedure. Thus all fundamental rights comprised within the term 'liberty' are protected by the Federal Constitution from invasion by the States." *Whitney* v. *California*, 274 U.S. 357, 373, 47 S.Ct. 641, 647, 71 L. Ed. 1095 (1927) (Brandeis, J., concurring). "[T]he guaranties of due process, though having their roots in Magna Carta's '*per legem terrae*' and considered as procedural safeguards 'against executive usurpation and tyranny,' have in this country 'become bulwarks also against arbitrary legislation.'" *Poe* v. *Ullman*, 367 U.S. 497, 541, 81 S.Ct. 1752, 1776, 6 L. Ed. 2d 989 (1961) (Harlan, J., dissenting from dismissal on jurisdictional grounds) (quoting *Hurtado* v. *California*, 110 U.S. 516, 532, 4 S.Ct. 111, 119, 28 L. Ed. 232 (1884)).

The most familiar of the substantive liberties protected by the Fourteenth Amendment are those recognized by the Bill of Rights. We have held that the Due Process Clause of the Fourteenth Amendment incorporates most of the Bill of Rights against the States. See, *e.g.*, *Duncan* v. *Louisiana*, 391 U.S. 145, 147–148, 88 S.Ct. 1444, 1446, 20 L. Ed. 2d 491 (1968). It is tempting, as a means of curbing the discretion of federal judges, to suppose that liberty encompasses no more than those rights already guaranteed to the individual against federal interference by the express provisions of the first eight amendments to the Constitution. See *Adamson* v. *California*, 332 U.S. 46, 68–92, 67 S.Ct. 1672, 1683–1697, 91 L. Ed. 1903 (1947) (Black, J., dissenting). But of course this Court has never accepted that view.

It is also tempting, for the same reason, to suppose that the Due Process Clause protects only those practices, defined at the most specific level, that were protected against government interference by other rules of law when the Fourteenth Amendment was ratified. See *Michael H.* v. *Gerald D.*, 491 U.S. 110, 127–128, n. 6, 109 S.Ct. 2333, 2344, n. 6, 105 L. Ed. 2d 91 (1989) (opinion of SCALIA, J.). But such a view would be inconsistent with our law. It is a promise of the Constitution that there is a realm of personal liberty which the government may not enter. We have vindicated this principle before.

Marriage is mentioned nowhere in the Bill of Rights and interracial marriage was illegal in most States in the 19th century, but the Court was no doubt correct in finding it to be an aspect of liberty protected against state interference by the substantive component of the Due Process Clause in *Loving* v. *Virginia*, 388 U.S. 1, 12, 87 S.Ct. 1817, 1824, 18 L. Ed. 2d 1010 (1967) (relying, in an opinion for eight Justices, on the Due Process Clause). Similar examples may be found in *Turner* v. *Safley*, 482 U.S. 78, 94–99, 107 S.Ct. 2254, 2265–2267, 96 L. Ed. 2d 64 (1987); in *Carey* v. *Population Services International*, 431 U.S. 678, 684–686, 97 S.Ct. 2010, 2015–2017, 52 L. Ed. 2d 675 (1977); in *Griswold* v. *Connecticut*, 381 U.S. 479, 481–482, 85 S.Ct. 1678, 1680–1681, 14 L. Ed. 2d 510 (1965), as well as in the separate opinions of a majority of the Members of the Court in that case, *id.*, at 486–488, 85 S.Ct., at 1682–1683 (Goldberg, J., joined by Warren, C. J., and Brennan, J., concurring) (expressly relying on due process), *id.*, at 500–502, 85 S.Ct., at 1690–1691 (Harlan, J., concurring in judgment) (same), *id.*, at 502–507, 85 S.Ct., at 1691–1694 (WHITE, J., concurring in judgment) (same); in *Pierce* v. *Society of Sisters*, 268 U.S. 510, 534–535, 45 S.Ct. 571, 573, 69 L. Ed. 1070 (1925); and in *Meyer* v. *Nebraska*, 262 U.S. 390, 399–403, 43 S.Ct. 625, 627, 67 L. Ed. 1042 (1923).

Neither the Bill of Rights nor the specific practices of States at the time of the adoption of the Fourteenth Amendment marks the outer limits of the substantive sphere of liberty which the Fourteenth Amendment protects. See U.S. Const., Amend. 9. As the second Justice Harlan recognized:

> "[T]he full scope of the liberty guaranteed by the Due Process Clause cannot be found in or limited by the precise terms of the specific guarantees elsewhere provided in the Constitution. This 'liberty' is not a series of isolated points pricked out in terms of the taking of property; the freedom of speech, press, and religion; the right to keep and bear arms; the freedom from unreasonable searches and seizures; and so on. It is a rational continuum which, broadly speaking, includes a freedom from all substantial arbitrary impositions and purposeless restraints, . . . and which also recognizes, what a reasonable and sensitive judgment must, that certain interests require particularly careful scrutiny of the state needs asserted to justify their abridgment." *Poe* v. *Ullman*, *supra*, 367 U.S., at 543, 81 S.Ct., at 1777 (Harlan, J., dissenting from dismissal on jurisdictional grounds).

Justice Harlan wrote these words in addressing an issue the full Court did not reach in *Poe* v. *Ullman*, but the Court adopted his position four Terms later in *Griswold* v. *Connecticut*, *supra*. In *Griswold*, we held that the Constitution does not permit a State to forbid a married couple to use contraceptives. That same freedom was later guaranteed, under the Equal Protection Clause, for unmarried couples. See *Eisenstadt* v. *Baird*, 405 U.S. 438, 92 S.Ct. 1029, 31 L. Ed. 2d 349 (1972). Constitutional protection was extended to the sale and distribution of contraceptives in *Carey* v. *Population Services International*, *supra*. It is settled now, as it was when the Court heard arguments in *Roe* v. *Wade*, that the

Constitution places limits on a State's right to interfere with a person's most basic decisions about family and parenthood, see *Carey* v. *Population Services International, supra*; *Moore* v. *East Cleveland*, 431 U.S. 494, 97 S.Ct. 1932, 52 L. Ed. 2d 531 (1977); *Eisenstadt* v. *Baird, supra*; *Loving* v. *Virginia, supra*; *Griswold* v. *Connecticut, supra*; *Skinner* v. *Oklahoma ex rel. Williamson*, 316 U.S. 535, 62 S.Ct. 1110, 86 L. Ed. 1655 (1942); *Pierce* v. *Society of Sisters, supra; Meyer* v. *Nebraska, supra*, as well as bodily integrity. See, *e.g., Washington* v. *Harper*, 494 U.S. 210, 221–222, 110 S.Ct. 1028, 1036–1037, 108 L. Ed. 2d 178 (1990); *Winston* v. *Lee*, 470 U.S. 753, 105 S.Ct. 1611, 84 L. Ed. 2d 662 (1985); *Rochin* v. *California*, 342 U.S. 165, 72 S.Ct. 205, 96 L. Ed. 183 (1952).

The inescapable fact is that adjudication of substantive due process claims may call upon the Court in interpreting the Constitution to exercise that same capacity which by tradition courts always have exercised: reasoned judgment. Its boundaries are not susceptible of expression as a simple rule. That does not mean we are free to invalidate state policy choices with which we disagree; yet neither does it permit us to shrink from the duties of our office. As Justice Harlan observed:

> "Due process has not been reduced to any formula; its content cannot be determined by reference to any code. The best that can be said is that through the course of this Court's decisions it has represented the balance which our Nation, built upon postulates of respect for the liberty of the individual, has struck between that liberty and the demands of organized society. If the supplying of content to this Constitutional concept has of necessity been a rational process, it certainly has not been one where judges have felt free to roam where unguided speculation might take them. The balance of which I speak is the balance struck by this country, having regard to what history teaches are the traditions from which it developed as well as the traditions from which it broke. That tradition is a living thing. A decision of this Court which radically departs from it could not long survive, while a decision which builds on what has survived is likely to be sound. No formula could serve as a substitute, in this area, for judgment and restraint." *Poe* v. *Ullman*, 367 U.S., at 542, 81 S.Ct., at 1776 (Harlan, J., dissenting from dismissal on jurisdictional grounds).

See also *Rochin* v. *California, supra*, 342 U.S., at 171–172, 72 S.Ct., at 209 (Frankfurter, J., writing for the Court) ("To believe that this judicial exercise of judgment could be avoided by freezing 'due process of law' at some fixed stage of time or thought is to suggest that the most important aspect of constitutional adjudication is a function for inanimate machines and not for judges").

Men and women of good conscience can disagree, and we suppose some always shall disagree, about the profound moral and spiritual implications of terminating a pregnancy, even in its earliest stage. Some of us as individuals find abortion offensive to our most basic principles of morality, but that cannot control our decision. Our obligation is to define the liberty of all, not to mandate our own moral code. The underlying constitutional issue is whether the State can resolve these philosophic questions in such a definitive way that a woman lacks all choice in the matter, except perhaps in those rare circumstances in which the pregnancy is itself a danger to her own life or health, or is the result of rape or incest.

It is conventional constitutional doctrine that where reasonable people disagree the government can adopt one position or the other. See, *e.g., Ferguson* v. *Skrupa*, 372 U.S. 726, 83 S.Ct. 1028, 10 L. Ed. 2d 93 (1963); *Williamson* v. *Lee Optical of Oklahoma, Inc.*, 348 U.S. 483, 75 S.Ct. 461, 99 L. Ed. 563 (1955). That theorem, however, assumes a state of affairs in which the choice does not intrude upon a protected liberty. Thus, while some people might disagree about whether or not the flag should be saluted, or disagree about the proposition that it may not be defiled, we have ruled that a State may not compel or enforce one view or the other. See *West Virginia State Bd. of Education* v. *Barnette*, 319 U.S. 624, 63 S.Ct. 1178, 87 L. Ed. 1628 (1943); *Texas* v. *Johnson*, 491 U.S. 397, 109 S.Ct. 2533, 105 L. Ed. 2d 342 (1989).

Our law affords constitutional protection to personal decisions relating to marriage, procreation, contraception, family relationships, child rearing, and education. *Carey* v. *Population Services International*, 431 U.S., at 685, 97 S.Ct., at 2016. Our cases recognize "the right of the *individual*, married or single, to be free from unwarranted governmental intrusion into matters so fundamentally affecting a person as the decision whether to bear or beget a child." *Eisenstadt* v. *Baird*, *supra*, 405 U.S., at 453, 92 S.Ct., at 1038 (emphasis in original). Our precedents "have respected the private realm of family life which the state cannot enter." *Prince* v. *Massachusetts*, 321 U.S. 158, 166, 64 S.Ct. 438, 442, 88 L. Ed. 645 (1944). These matters, involving the most intimate and personal choices a person may make in a lifetime, choices central to personal dignity and autonomy, are central to the liberty protected by the Fourteenth Amendment. At the heart of liberty is the right to define one's own concept of existence, of meaning, of the universe, and of the mystery of human life. Beliefs about these matters could not define the attributes of personhood were they formed under compulsion of the State.

These considerations begin our analysis of the woman's interest in terminating her pregnancy but cannot end it, for this reason: though the abortion decision may originate within the zone of conscience and belief, it is more than a philosophic exercise. Abortion is a unique act. It is an act fraught with consequences for others: for the woman who must live with the implications of her decision; for the persons who perform and assist in the procedure; for the spouse, family, and society which must confront the knowledge that these procedures exist, procedures some deem nothing short of an act of violence against innocent human life; and, depending on one's beliefs, for the life or potential life that is aborted. Though abortion is conduct, it does not follow that the State is entitled to proscribe it in all instances. That is because the liberty of the woman is at stake in a sense unique to the human condition and so unique to the law. The mother who carries a child to full term is subject to anxieties, to physical constraints, to pain that only she must bear. That these sacrifices have from the beginning of the human race been endured by woman with a pride that ennobles her in the eyes of others and gives to the infant a bond of love cannot alone be grounds for the State to insist she make the sacrifice. Her suffering is too intimate and personal for the State to insist, without more, upon its own vision of the woman's role, however dominant that vision has been in the course of our history and our culture. The destiny of the woman must be shaped to a large extent on her own conception of her spiritual imperatives and her place in society.

It should be recognized, moreover, that in some critical respects the abortion decision is of the same character as the decision to use contraception, to which *Griswold* v. *Connecticut*, *Eisenstadt* v. *Baird*, and *Carey* v. *Population Services International* afford constitutional protection. We have no doubt as to the correctness of those decisions. They support the reasoning in *Roe* relating to the woman's liberty because they involve personal decisions concerning not only the meaning of procreation but also human responsibility and respect for it. As with abortion, reasonable people will have differences of opinion about these matters. One view is based on such reverence for the wonder of creation that any pregnancy ought to be welcomed and carried to full term no matter how difficult it will be to provide for the child and ensure its well-being. Another is that the inability to provide for the nurture and care of that infant is a cruelty to the child and an anguish to the parent. These are intimate views with infinite variations, and their deep, personal character underlay our decisions in *Griswold*, *Eisenstadt*, and *Carey*. The same concerns are present when the woman confronts the reality that, perhaps despite her attempts to avoid it, she has become pregnant.

It was this dimension of personal liberty that *Roe* sought to protect, and its holding invoked the reasoning and the tradition of the precedents we have discussed, granting protection to substantive liberties of the person. *Roe* was, of course, an extension of those cases and, as the decision itself indicated, the separate States could act in some degree to further their own legitimate interests in protecting pre-natal life. The extent to which the legislatures of the States might act to outweigh the interests of the woman in choosing to terminate her pregnancy was a subject of debate both in *Roe* itself and in decisions following it.

While we appreciate the weight of the arguments made on behalf of the State in the case before us, arguments which in their ultimate formulation conclude that *Roe* should be overruled, the reservations any of us may have in reaffirming the central holding of *Roe* are outweighed by the explication of individual liberty we have given combined with the force of *stare decisis*. We turn now to that doctrine.

III

A

The obligation to follow precedent begins with necessity, and a contrary necessity marks its outer limit. With Cardozo, we recognize that no judicial system could do society's work if it eyed each issue afresh in every case that raised it. See B. Cardozo, The

Nature of the Judicial Process 149 (1921). Indeed, the very concept of the rule of law underlying our own Constitution requires such continuity over time that a respect for precedent is, by definition, indispensable. See Powell, Stare Decisis and Judicial Restraint, 1991 Journal of Supreme Court History 13, 16. At the other extreme, a different necessity would make itself felt if a prior judicial ruling should come to be seen so clearly as error that its enforcement was for that very reason doomed.

Even when the decision to overrule a prior case is not, as in the rare, latter instance, virtually foreordained, it is common wisdom that the rule of *stare decisis* is not an "inexorable command," and certainly it is not such in every constitutional case, see *Burnet* v. *Coronado Oil Gas Co.*, 285 U.S. 393, 405–411, 52 S.Ct. 443, 446–449, 76 L. Ed. 815 (1932) (Brandeis, J., dissenting). See also *Payne* v. *Tennessee*, 501 U.S. 111 S.Ct. 2597, 115 L. Ed. 2d 720 (1991) (SOUTER, J., joined by KENNEDY, J., concurring); *Arizona* v. *Rumsey*, 467 U.S. 203, 212, 104 S.Ct. 2305, 2310, 81 L. Ed. 2d 164 (1984). Rather, when this Court reexamines a prior holding, its judgment is customarily informed by a series of prudential and pragmatic considerations designed to test the consistency of overruling a prior decision with the ideal of the rule of law, and to gauge the respective costs of reaffirming and overruling a prior case. Thus, for example, we may ask whether the rule has proved to be intolerable simply in defying practical workability, *Swift & Co.* v. *Wickham*, 382 U.S. 111, 116, 86 S.Ct. 258, 261, 15 L. Ed. 2d 194 (1965); whether the rule is subject to a kind of reliance that would lend a special hardship to the consequences of overruling and add inequity to the cost of repudiation, *e.g., United States* v. *Title Ins. & Trust Co.*, 265 U.S. 472, 486, 44 S.Ct. 621, 623, 68 L. Ed. 1110 (1924); whether related principles of law have so far developed as to have left the old rule no more than a remnant of abandoned doctrine, see *Patterson* v. *McLean Credit Union*, 491 U.S. 164, 173–174, 109 S.Ct. 2363, 2371, 105 L. Ed. 2d 132 (1989); or whether facts have so changed or come to be seen so differently, as to have robbed the old rule of significant application or justification, *e.g., Burnet, supra*, 285 U.S., at 412, 52 S.Ct., at 449 (Brandeis, J., dissenting).

So in this case we may inquire whether *Roe*'s central rule has been found unworkable; whether the rule's limitation on state power could be removed without serious inequity to those who have relied upon it or significant damage to the stability of the society governed by the rule in question; whether the law's growth in the intervening years has left *Roe*'s central rule a doctrinal anachronism discounted by society; and whether *Roe*'s premises of fact have so far changed in the ensuing two decades as to render its central holding somehow irrelevant or unjustifiable in dealing with the issue it addressed.

1

Although *Roe* has engendered opposition, it has in no sense proven "unworkable," see *Garcia* v. *San Antonio Metropolitan Transit Authority*, 469 U.S. 528, 546, 105 S.Ct. 1005, 1015, 83 L. Ed. 2d 1016 (1985), representing as it does a simple limitation beyond which a state law is unenforceable. While *Roe* has, of course, required judicial assessment of state laws affecting the exercise of the choice guaranteed against government infringement, and although the need for such review will remain as a consequence of today's decision, the required determinations fall within judicial competence.

2

The inquiry into reliance counts the cost of a rule's repudiation as it would fall on those who have relied reasonably on the rule's continued application. Since the classic case for weighing reliance heavily in favor of following the earlier rule occurs in the commercial context, see *Payne* v. *Tennessee*, where advance planning of great precision is most obviously a necessity, it is no cause for surprise that some would find no reliance worthy of consideration in support of *Roe*. . . .

To eliminate the issue of reliance that easily, however, one would need to limit cognizable reliance to specific instances of sexual activity. But to do this would be simply to refuse to face the fact that for two decades of economic and social developments, people have organized intimate relationships and made choices that define their views of themselves and their places in society, in reliance on the availability of abortion in the event that contraception should fail. The ability of women to participate equally in the economic and social life of the Nation has been facilitated by their ability to control their reproductive lives. See, *e.g.*, R. Petchesky, Abortion and Woman's Choice 109, 133, n. 7 (rev. ed. 1990). The Constitution serves human values, and while the effect of reliance on *Roe* cannot be exactly measured, neither can the certain cost of overruling *Roe* for people who have ordered their thinking and living around that case be dismissed.

3

No evolution of legal principle has left *Roe*'s doctrinal footings weaker than they were in 1973. No development of constitutional law since the case was decided has implicitly or explicitly left *Roe* behind as a mere survivor of obsolete constitutional thinking.

It will be recognized, of course, that *Roe* stands at an intersection of two lines of decisions, but in whichever doctrinal category one reads the case, the result for present purposes will be the same. The *Roe* Court itself placed its holding in the succession of cases most prominently exemplified by *Griswold* v. *Connecticut*, 381 U.S. 479, 85 S.Ct. 1678, 14 L. Ed. 2d 510 (1965), see *Roe*, 410 U.S., at 152–153, 93 S.Ct., at 726. When it is so seen, *Roe* is clearly in no jeopardy, since subsequent constitutional developments have neither disturbed, nor do they threaten to diminish, the scope of recognized protection accorded to the liberty relating to intimate relationships, the family, and decisions about whether or not to beget or bear a child. See, *e.g.*, *Carey* v. *Population Services International*,

431 U.S. 678, 97 S.Ct. 2010, 52 L. Ed. 2d 675 (1977); *Moore* v. *East Cleveland*, 431 U.S. 494, 97 S.Ct. 1932, 52 L. Ed. 2d 531 (1977). . . .

From what we have said so far it follows that it is a constitutional liberty of the woman to have some freedom to terminate her pregnancy. We conclude that the basic decision in *Roe* was based on a constitutional analysis which we cannot now repudiate. The woman's liberty is not so unlimited, however, that from the outset the State cannot show its concern for the life of the unborn, and at a later point in fetal development the State's interest in life has sufficient force so that the right of the woman to terminate the pregnancy can be restricted.

That brings us, of course, to the point where much criticism has been directed at *Roe*, a criticism that always inheres when the Court draws a specific rule from what in the Constitution is but a general standard. We conclude, however, that the urgent claims of the woman to retain the ultimate control over her destiny and her body, claims implicit in the meaning of liberty, require us to perform that function. Liberty must not be extinguished for want of a line that is clear. And it falls to us to give some real substance to the woman's liberty to determine whether to carry her pregnancy to full term.

We conclude the line should be drawn at viability, so that before that time the woman has a right to choose to terminate her pregnancy. We adhere to this principle for two reasons. First, as we have said, is the doctrine of *stare decisis*. Any judicial act of line-drawing may seem somewhat arbitrary, but *Roe* was a reasoned statement, elaborated with great care. We have twice reaffirmed it in the face of great opposition. See *Thornburgh* v. *American College of Obstetricians & Gynecologists*, 476 U.S., at 759, 106 S.Ct., at 2178; *Akron I*, 462 U.S., at 419–420, 103 S.Ct., at 2487–2488. Although we must overrule those parts of *Thornburgh* and *Akron I* which, in our view, are inconsistent with *Roe*'s statement that the State has a legitimate interest in promoting the life or potential life of the unborn, the central premise of those cases represents an unbroken commitment by this Court to the essential holding of *Roe*. It is that premise which we reaffirm today.

The second reason is that the concept of viability, as we noted in *Roe*, is the time at which there is a realistic possibility of maintaining and nourishing a life outside the womb, so that the independent existence of the second life can in reason and all fairness be the object of state protection that now overrides the rights of the woman. See *Roe* v. *Wade*, 410 U.S., at 163, 93 S.Ct., at 731. Consistent with other constitutional norms, legislatures may draw lines which appear arbitrary without the necessity of offering a justification. But courts may not. We must justify the lines we draw. And there is no line other than viability which is more workable. To be sure, as we have said, there may be some medical developments that affect the precise point of viability, but this is an imprecision within tolerable limits given that the medical community and all those who must apply its discoveries will continue to explore the matter. The viability line also has, as a practical matter, an element of fairness. In some broad sense it might be said that a woman who fails to act before viability has consented to the State's intervention on behalf of the developing child.

The woman's right to terminate her pregnancy before viability is the most central principle of *Roe* v. *Wade*. It is a rule of law and a component of liberty we cannot renounce.

On the other side of the equation is the interest of the State in the protection of potential life. The *Roe* Court recognized the State's "important and legitimate interest in protecting the potentiality of human life." *Roe*. The weight to be given this state interest, not the strength of the woman's interest, was the difficult question faced in *Roe*. We do not need to say whether each of us, had we been Members of the Court when the valuation of the State interest came before it as an original matter, would have concluded, as the *Roe* Court did, that its weight is insufficient to justify a ban on abortions prior to viability even when it is subject to certain exceptions. The matter is not before us in the first instance, and coming as it does after nearly 20 years of litigation in *Roe*'s wake we are satisfied that the immediate question is not the soundness of *Roe*'s resolution of the issue, but the precedential force that must be accorded to its holding. And we have concluded that the essential holding of *Roe* should be reaffirmed.

Yet it must be remembered that *Roe* v. *Wade* speaks with clarity in establishing not only the woman's liberty but also the State's "important and legitimate interest in potential life." *Roe, supra*, at 163, 93 S.Ct., at 731. That portion of the decision in *Roe* has been given too little acknowledgment and implementation by the Court in its subsequent cases. Those cases decided that any regulation touching upon the abortion decision must survive strict scrutiny, to be sustained only if drawn in narrow terms to further a compelling state interest. See *e.g., Akron I*, 462 U.S., at 427. Not all of the cases decided under that formulation can be reconciled with the holding in *Roe* itself that the State has legitimate interests in the health of the woman and in protecting the potential life within her. In resolving this tension, we choose to rely upon *Roe*, as against the later cases.

Roe established a trimester framework to govern abortion regulations. Under this elaborate but rigid construct, almost no regulation at all is permitted during the first trimester of pregnancy; regulations designed to protect the woman's health, but not to further the State's interest in potential life, are permitted during the second trimester; and during the third trimester, when the fetus is viable, prohibitions are permitted provided the life or health of the mother is not at stake. *Roe* v. *Wade*, 410 U.S., at 163–166, 93 S.Ct., at 731–733. Most of our cases since *Roe* have involved the application of rules derived from the trimester framework. See, *e.g., Thornburgh* v. *American College of Obstetricians and Gynecologists, supra; Akron I, supra*.

The trimester framework no doubt was erected to ensure that the woman's right to choose not become so subordinate to the State's interest in promoting fetal life that her choice exists in theory but not in fact. We do not agree, however, that the trimester approach is necessary to accomplish this objective. A framework of this rigidity was unnecessary and in its later interpretation sometimes contradicted the State's permissible exercise of its powers.

Though the woman has a right to choose to terminate or continue her pregnancy before viability, it does not at all follow that the State is prohibited from taking steps to ensure that this choice is thoughtful and informed. Even in the earliest stages of pregnancy, the State may enact rules and regulations designed to encourage her to know that there are philosophic and social arguments of great weight that can be brought to bear in favor of continuing the pregnancy to full term and that there are procedures and institutions to allow adoption of unwanted children as well as a certain degree of state assistance if the mother chooses to raise the child herself. "'[T]he Constitution does not forbid a State or city, pursuant to democratic processes, from expressing a preference for normal childbirth.'" *Webster* v. *Reproductive Health Services*, 492 U.S., at 511, 109 S.Ct., at 3053 (opinion of the Court) (quoting *Poelker* v. *Doe*, 432 U.S. 519, 521, 97 S.Ct. 2391, 2392, 53 L. Ed. 2d 528 (1977). It follows that States are free to enact laws to provide a reasonable framework for a woman to make a decision that has such profound and lasting meaning. This, too, we find consistent with *Roe*'s central premises, and indeed the inevitable consequence of our holding that the State has an interest in protecting the life of the unborn.

We reject the trimester framework, which we do not consider to be part of the essential holding of *Roe*. See *Webster* v. *Reproductive Health Services, supra*, 492 U.S., at 518, 109 S.Ct., at 3056 (opinion of REHNQUIST, C. J.); *id.*, at 529, 109 S.Ct., at 3062 (O'CONNOR, J., concurring in part and concurring in judgment) (describing the trimester framework as "problematic"). Measures aimed at ensuring that a woman's choice contemplates the consequences for the fetus do not necessarily interfere with the right recognized in *Roe*, although those measures have been found to be inconsistent with the rigid trimester framework announced in that case. A logical reading of the central holding in *Roe* itself, and a necessary reconciliation of the liberty of the woman and the interest of the State in promoting prenatal life, require, in our view, that we abandon the trimester framework as a rigid prohibition on all previability regulation aimed at the protection of fetal life. The trimester framework suffers from these basic flaws: in its formulation it misconceives the nature of the pregnant woman's interest; and in practice it undervalues the State's interest in potential life, as recognized in *Roe*. . . .

The very notion that the State has a substantial interest in potential life leads to the conclusion that not all regulations must be deemed unwarranted. Not all burdens on the right to decide whether to terminate a pregnancy will be undue. In our view, the undue burden standard is the appropriate means of reconciling the State's interest with the woman's constitutionally protected liberty.

The concept of an undue burden has been utilized by the Court as well as individual Members of the Court, including two of us, in ways that could be considered inconsistent. See *e.g.*, *Hodgson* v. *Minnesota*, 497 U.S., at 417 (O'CONNOR, J., concurring in part and concurring in judgment); *Akron II*, 497 U.S., at 502 (opinion of KENNEDY, J.); *Thornburgh* v. *American College of Obstetricians and Gynecologists*, 476 U.S., at 828–829, 106 S.Ct., at 2214 (O'CONNOR, J., dissenting); *Akron I, supra*, 462 U.S., at 461–466, 103 S.Ct., at 2509–2511 (O'CONNOR, J., dissenting); *Harris* v. *McRae, supra*, 448 U.S., at 314, 100 S.Ct., at 2686; *Maher* v. *Roe, supra*, 432 U.S., at 473, 97 S.Ct., at 2382; *Beal* v.

Doe, 432 U.S. 438, 446, 97 S.Ct. 2366, 2371, 53 L. Ed. 2d 464 (1977); *Bellotti I, supra,* 428 U.S., at 147, 96 S.Ct., at 2866. Because we set forth a standard of general application to which we intend to adhere, it is important to clarify what is meant by an undue burden.

A finding of an undue burden is a shorthand for the conclusion that a state regulation has the purpose or effect of placing a substantial obstacle in the path of a woman seeking an abortion of a nonviable fetus. A statute with this purpose is invalid because the means chosen by the State to further the interest in potential life must be calculated to inform the woman's free choice, not hinder it. And a statute which, while furthering the interest in potential life or some other valid state interest, has the effect of placing a substantial obstacle in the path of a woman's choice cannot be considered a permissible means of serving its legitimate ends. To the extent that the opinions of the Court or of individual Justices use the undue burden standard in a manner that is inconsistent with this analysis, we set out what in our view should be the controlling standard . . . (attempting to "define the doctrine of abuse of the writ with more precision" after acknowledging tension among earlier cases). In our considered judgment, an undue burden is an unconstitutional burden. See *Akron II, supra,* 497 U.S., at 502 (opinion of KENNEDY, J.). Understood another way, we answer the question, left open in previous opinions discussing the undue burden formulation, whether a law designed to further the State's interest in fetal life which imposes an undue burden on the woman's decision before fetal viability could be constitutional. See, *e.g., Akron I,* 462 U.S., at 462–463 (O'CONNOR, J., dissenting). The answer is no.

Some guiding principles should emerge. What is at stake is the woman's right to make the ultimate decision, not a right to be insulated from all others in doing so. Regulations which do no more than create a structural mechanism by which the State, or the parent or guardian of a minor, may express profound respect for the life of the unborn are permitted, if they are not a substantial obstacle to the woman's exercise of the right to choose. See *infra* (addressing Pennsylvania's parental consent requirement). Unless it has that effect on her right of choice, a state measure designed to persuade her to choose childbirth over abortion will be upheld if reasonably related to that goal. Regulations designed to foster the health of a woman seeking an abortion are valid if they do not constitute an undue burden.

Even when jurists reason from shared premises, some disagreement is inevitable. Compare *Hodgson,* 497 U.S., at 417 (opinion of KENNEDY, J.) with *id.,* 110 S.Ct. (O'CONNOR, J., concurring in part and concurring in judgment in part). That is to be expected in the application of any legal standard which must accommodate life's complexity. We do not expect it to be otherwise with respect to the undue burden standard. We give this summary:

(a) To protect the central right recognized by *Roe* v. *Wade* while at the same time accommodating the State's profound interest in potential life, we will employ the undue burden analysis as explained in this opinion. An undue burden exists, and therefore a provision of law is invalid, if its purpose or effect is to place a substantial obstacle in the path of a woman seeking an abortion before the fetus attains viability.

(b) We reject the rigid trimester framework of *Roe* v. *Wade*. To promote the State's profound interest in potential life, throughout pregnancy the State may take measures to ensure that the woman's choice is informed, and measures designed to advance this interest will not be invalidated as long as their purpose is to persuade the woman to choose childbirth over abortion. These measures must not be an undue burden on the right.

(c) As with any medical procedure, the State may enact regulations to further the health or safety of a woman seeking an abortion. Unnecessary health regulations that have the purpose or effect of presenting a substantial obstacle to a woman seeking an abortion impose an undue burden on the right.

(d) Our adoption of the undue burden analysis does not disturb the central holding of *Roe* v. *Wade*, and we reaffirm that holding. Regardless of whether exceptions are made for particular circumstances, a State may not prohibit any woman from making the ultimate decision to terminate her pregnancy before viability.

(e) We also reaffirm *Roe*'s holding that "subsequent to viability, the State in promoting its interest in the potentiality of human life may, if it chooses, regulate, and even proscribe, abortion except where it is necessary, in appropriate medical judgment, for the preservation of the life or health of the mother." *Roe* v. *Wade*, 410 U.S., at 164–165, 93 S.Ct., at 732.

These principles control our assessment of the Pennsylvania statute, and we now turn to the issue of the validity of its challenged provisions.

V

The Court of Appeals applied what it believed to be the undue burden standard and upheld each of the provisions except for the husband notification requirement. We agree generally with this conclusion, but refine the undue burden analysis in accordance with the principles articulated above. We now consider the separate statutory sections at issue.

A

Because it is central to the operation of various other requirements, we begin with the statute's definition of medical emergency. Under the statute, a medical emergency is

> "[t]hat condition which, on the basis of the physician's good faith clinical judgment, so complicates the medical condition of a pregnant woman as to necessitate the immediate abortion of her pregnancy to avert her death or for which a delay will create serious risk of substantial and irreversible impairment of a major bodily function." 18 Pa. Cons. Stat. (1990). § 3203. . . .

The District Court found that there were three serious conditions which would not be covered by the statute: preeclampsia, inevitable abortion, and premature ruptured membrane. 744 F.Supp., at 1378. Yet, as the Court of Appeals observed, 947 F. 2d, at 700–701, it is undisputed that under some circumstances each of these conditions could lead to an illness with substantial and irreversible consequences. While the definition could be interpreted in an unconstitutional manner, the Court of Appeals construed the phrase "serious risk" to include those circumstances. *Id.*, at 701. It stated: "we read the medical emergency exception as intended by the Pennsylvania legislature to assure that compliance with its abortion regulations would not in any way pose a significant threat to the life or health of a woman." *Ibid.* As we said in *Brockett* v. *Spokane Arcades, Inc.*, 472 U.S. 491, 499–500, 105 S.Ct. 2794, 2799–2800, 86 L. Ed. 2d 394 (1985): "Normally, . . . we defer to the construction of a state statute given it by the lower federal courts." Indeed, we have said that we will defer to lower court interpretations of state law unless they amount to "plain" error. *Palmer* v. *Hoffman*, 318 U.S. 109, 118, 63 S.Ct. 477, 482, 87 L. Ed. 645 (1943). This "'reflect[s] our belief that district courts and courts of appeals are better schooled in and more able to interpret the laws of their respective States.'" *Frisby* v. *Schultz*, 487 U.S. 474, 482, 108 S.Ct. 2495, 2501, 101 L. Ed. 2d 420 (1988) (citation omitted). We adhere to that course today, and conclude that, as construed by the Court of Appeals, the medical emergency definition imposes no undue burden on a woman's abortion right.

B

We next consider the informed consent requirement. 18 Pa. Cons. Stat. Ann. § 3205. Except in a medical emergency, the statute requires that at least 24 hours before performing an abortion a physician inform the woman of the nature of the procedure, the health risks of the abortion and of childbirth, and the "probable gestational age of the unborn child." The physician or a qualified nonphysician must inform the woman of the availability of printed materials published by the State describing the fetus and providing information about medical assistance for childbirth, information about child support from the father, and a list of agencies which provide adoption and other services as alternatives to abortion. An abortion may not be performed unless the woman certifies in writing that she has been informed of the availability of these printed materials and has been provided them if she chooses to view them.

Our prior decisions establish that as with any medical procedure, the State may require a woman to give her written informed consent to an abortion. See *Planned Parenthood of Central Mo.* v. *Danforth*, 428 U.S., at 67, 96 S.Ct., at 2840. In this respect, the statute is unexceptional. Petitioners challenge the statute's definition of informed consent because it includes the provision of specific information by the doctor and the mandatory 24-hour waiting period. The conclusions reached by a majority of the Justices in the separate opinions filed today and the undue burden standard adopted in this opinion require us to overrule in part some of the Court's past decisions, decisions driven by the trimester framework's prohibition of all previability regulations designed to further the State's interest in fetal life. . . .

To the extent *Akron I* and *Thornburgh* find a constitutional violation when the government requires, as it does here, the giving of truthful, nonmisleading information about the nature of the procedure, the attendant health risks and those of childbirth, and the "probable gestational age" of the fetus, those cases go too far, are inconsistent with *Roe*'s acknowledgment of an important interest in potential life, and are overruled. This is clear even on the very terms of *Akron I* and *Thornburgh*. Those decisions, along with *Danforth*, recognize a substantial government interest justifying a requirement that a woman be apprised of the health risks of abortion and childbirth. *E.g., Danforth, supra*, 428 U.S., at 66–67, 96 S.Ct., at 2840. It cannot be questioned that psychological well-being is a facet of health. Nor can it be doubted that most women considering an abortion would deem the impact on the fetus relevant, if not dispositive, to the decision. In attempting to ensure that a woman apprehend the full consequences of her decision, the State furthers the legitimate purpose of reducing the risk that a woman may elect an abortion, only to discover later, with devastating psychological consequences, that her decision was not fully informed. If the information the State requires to be made available to the woman is truthful and not misleading, the requirement may be permissible.

We also see no reason why the State may not require doctors to inform a woman seeking an abortion of the availability of materials relating to the consequences to the fetus, even when those consequences have no direct relation to her health. An example illustrates the point. We would think it constitutional for the State to require that in order for there to be informed consent to a kidney transplant operation the recipient must be supplied with information about risks to the donor as well as risks to himself or herself. A requirement that the physician make available information similar to that mandated by the statute here was described in *Thornburgh* as "an outright attempt to wedge the Commonwealth's message discouraging abortion into the privacy of the informed-consent dialogue between the woman and her physician." 476 U.S., at 762, 106 S.Ct., at 2179. We conclude, however, that informed choice need not be defined in such narrow terms that all considerations of the effect on the fetus are made irrelevant. As we have made clear, we depart from the holdings of *Akron I* and *Thornburgh* to the extent that we permit a State to further its legitimate goal of protecting the life of the unborn by enacting legislation aimed at ensuring a decision that is mature and informed, even when in so doing the State expresses a preference for childbirth over abortion. In short, requiring that the woman be informed of the availability of information relating to fetal development and the assistance available should she decide to carry the pregnancy to full term is a reasonable measure to insure an informed choice, one which might cause the woman to choose childbirth over abortion. This requirement cannot be considered a substantial obstacle to obtaining an abortion, and, it follows, there is no undue burden. . . .

Our analysis of Pennsylvania's 24-hour waiting period between the provision of the information deemed necessary to informed consent and the performance of an abortion under the undue burden standard requires us to reconsider the premise behind the decision in *Akron I* invalidating a parallel requirement. In *Akron I* we said: "Nor are we convinced that the State's legitimate concern that the woman's decision be informed is reasonably served by requiring a 24-hour delay as a matter of course." 462 U.S., at 450, 103 S.Ct., at 2503. We consider that conclusion to be wrong. The idea that important decisions will be more informed and deliberate if they follow some period of reflection does not strike us as unreasonable, particularly where the statute directs that important information become part of the background of the decision. The statute, as construed by the Court of Appeals, permits avoidance of the waiting period in the event of a medical emergency and the record evidence shows that in the vast majority of cases, a 24-hour delay does not create any appreciable health risk. In theory, at least, the waiting period is a reasonable measure to implement the State's interest in protecting the life of the unborn, a measure that does not amount to an undue burden.

Whether the mandatory 24-hour waiting period is nonetheless invalid because in practice it is a substantial obstacle to a woman's choice to terminate her pregnancy is a closer question. The findings of fact by the District Court indicate that because of the distances many women must travel to reach an abortion provider, the practical effect will often be a delay of much more than a day because the waiting period requires that a woman seeking an abortion make at least two visits to the doctor. The District Court also found that in many instances this will increase the exposure of women seeking abortions to "the harassment and hostility of anti-abortion protestors demonstrating outside a clinic." 744 F. Supp., at 1351. As a result, the District Court found that for those women who have the fewest financial resources, those who must travel long distances, and those who have difficulty explaining their whereabouts to husbands, employers, or others, the 24-hour waiting period will be "particularly burdensome." *Id.*, at 1352.

These findings are troubling in some respects, but they do not demonstrate that the waiting period constitutes an undue burden. We do not doubt that, as the District Court held, the waiting period has the effect of "increasing the cost and risk of delay of abortions," *id.*, at 1378, but the District Court did not conclude that the increased costs and potential delays amount to substantial obstacles. Rather, applying the trimester framework's strict prohibition of all regulation designed to promote the State's interest in potential life before viability, see *id.*, at 1374, the District Court concluded that the waiting period does not further the state "interest in maternal health" and "infringes the physician's discretion to exercise sound medical judgment." *Id.*, at 1378. Yet, as we have stated, under the undue burden standard a State is permitted to enact persuasive measures which favor childbirth over abortion, even if those measures do not further a health interest. And while the waiting period does limit a physician's discretion, that is not, standing alone, a reason to invalidate it. In light of the construction given the statute's definition of medical emergency by the Court of Appeals, and the District Court's findings, we cannot say that the waiting period imposes a real health risk.

We also disagree with the District Court's conclusion that the "particularly burdensome" effects of the waiting period on some women require its invalidation. A particular burden is not of necessity a substantial obstacle. Whether a burden falls on a particular group is a distinct inquiry from whether it is a substantial obstacle even as to the women in that group. And the District Court did not conclude that the waiting period is such an obstacle even for the women who are most burdened by it. Hence, on the record before us, and in the context of this facial challenge, we are not convinced that the 24-hour waiting period constitutes an undue burden. . . .

C

Section 3209 of Pennsylvania's abortion law provides, except in cases of medical emergency, that no physician shall perform an abortion on a married woman without receiving a signed statement from the woman that she has notified her spouse that she is about to undergo an abortion. The woman has the option of providing an alternative signed statement certifying that her husband is not the man who impregnated her; that her husband could not be located; that the pregnancy is the result of spousal sexual assault which she has reported; or that the woman believes that notifying her husband will cause him or someone else to inflict bodily injury upon her. A physician who performs an abortion on a married woman without receiving the appropriate signed statement will have his or her license revoked, and is liable to the husband for damages.

The District Court heard the testimony of numerous expert witnesses, and made detailed findings of fact regarding the effect of this statute. These included:

"273. The vast majority of women consult their husbands prior to deciding to terminate their pregnancy. . .

. . . .

"279. The 'bodily injury' exception could not be invoked by a married woman whose husband, if notified, would, in her reasonable belief, threaten to (a) publicize her intent to have an abortion to family, friends or acquaintances; (b) retaliate against her in future child custody or divorce proceedings; (c) inflict psychological intimidation or emotional harm upon her, her children or other persons; (d) inflict bodily harm on other persons such as children, family members or other loved ones; or (e) use his control over finances to deprive of necessary monies for herself or her children. . . .

. . .

"281. Studies reveal that family violence occurs in two million families in the United States. This figure, however, is a conservative one that substantially understates (because battering is usually not reported until it reaches life-threatening proportions) the actual number of families affected by domestic violence. In fact, researchers estimate that one of every two women will be battered at some time in their life. . . .

"282. A wife may not elect to notify her husband of her intention to have an abortion for a variety of reasons, including the husband's illness, concern about her own health, the imminent failure of the marriage, or the husband's absolute opposition to the abortion. . . .

"283. The required filing of the spousal consent form would require plaintiff-clinics to change their counseling procedures and force women to reveal their most intimate decision-making on pain of criminal sanctions. The confidentiality of these revelations could not be guaranteed, since the woman's records are not immune from subpoena. . . .

"284. Women of all class levels, educational backgrounds, and racial, ethnic and religious groups are battered. . . .

"285. Wife-battering or abuse can take on many physical and psychological forms. The nature and scope of the battering can cover a broad range of actions and be gruesome and torturous. . . .

"286. Married women, victims of battering, have been killed in Pennsylvania and throughout the United States. . . .

"287. Battering can often involve a substantial amount of sexual abuse, including marital rape and sexual mutilation. . . .

"288. In a domestic abuse situation, it is common for the battering husband to also abuse the children in an attempt to coerce the wife. . . .

"289. Mere notification of pregnancy is frequently a flashpoint for battering and violence within the family. The number of battering incidents is high during the pregnancy and often the worst abuse can be associated with pregnancy. . . . The battering husband may deny parentage and use the pregnancy as an excuse for abuse. . . .

"290. Secrecy typically shrouds abusive families. Family members are instructed not to tell anyone, especially police or doctors, about the abuse and violence. Battering husbands often threaten their wives or her children with further abuse if she tells an outsider of the violence and tells her that nobody will believe her. A battered woman, therefore, is highly unlikely to disclose the violence against her for fear of retaliation by the abuser. . . .

"291. Even when confronted directly by medical personnel or other helping professionals, battered women often will not admit to the battering because they have not admitted to themselves that they are battered. . . .

. . . .

"294. A woman in a shelter or a safe house unknown to her husband is not 'reasonably likely' to have bodily harm inflicted upon her by her batterer, however her attempt to notify her husband pursuant to section 3209 could accidentally disclose her whereabouts to her husband. Her fear of future ramifications would be realistic under the circumstances.

"295. Marital rape is rarely discussed with others or reported to law enforcement authorities, and of those reported only few are prosecuted. . . .

"296. It is common for battered women to have sexual intercourse with their husbands to avoid being battered. While this type of coercive sexual activity would be spousal sexual assault as defined by the Act, many women may not consider it to be so and others would fear disbelief. . . .

"297. The marital rape exception to section 3209 cannot be claimed by women who are victims of coercive sexual behavior other than penetration. The 90-day reporting requirement of the spousal sexual assault statute, 18 Pa. Con. Stat. Ann. § 3218(c), further narrows the class of sexually abused wives who can claim the exception, since many of these women may be psychologically unable to discuss or report the rape for several years after the incident. . . .

"298. Because of the nature of the battering relationship, battered women are unlikely to avail themselves of the exceptions to section 3209 of the Act, regardless of whether the section applies to them." 744 F. Supp., at 1360–1362.

These findings are supported by studies of domestic violence. The American Medical Association (AMA) has published a summary of the recent research in this field, which indicates that in an average 12-month period in this country, approximately two million women are the victims of severe assaults by their male partners. In a 1985 survey, women reported that nearly one of every eight husbands had assaulted their wives during the past year. The AMA views these figures as "marked underestimates," because the nature of these incidents discourages women from reporting them, and because surveys typically exclude the very poor, those who do not speak English well, and women who are homeless or in institutions or hospitals when the survey is conducted. According to the AMA, "[r]esearchers on family violence agree that the true incidence of partner violence is probably *double* the above estimates; or four million severely assaulted women per year. Studies suggest that from one-fifth to one-third of all women will be physically assaulted by a partner or ex-partner during their lifetime." AMA Council on Scientific Affairs, Violence Against Women 7 (1991) (emphasis in original). Thus on an average day in the United States, nearly 11,000 women are severely assaulted by their male partners. Many of these incidents involve sexual assault. *Id.*, at 3–4; Shields & Hanneke, Battered Wives' Reactions to Marital Rape, in The Dark Side of Families: Current Family Violence Research 131, 144 (D. Finkelhor, R. Gelles, G. Hataling, & M. Straus eds. 1983). In families where wife-beating takes place, moreover, child abuse is often present as well. Violence Against Women, at 12.

Other studies fill in the rest of this troubling picture. Physical violence is only the most visible form of abuse. Psychological abuse, particularly forced social and economic isolation of women, is also common. L. Walker, The Battered Woman Syndrome 27–28 (1984). Many victims of domestic violence remain with their abusers, perhaps because they perceive no superior alternative. Herbert, Silver, & Ellard, Coping with an Abusive Relationship: I. How and Why do Women Stay?, 53 J. Marriage & the Family 311 (1991).

Many abused women who find temporary refuge in shelters return to their husbands, in large part because they have no other source of income. Aguirre, Why Do They Return? Abused Wives in Shelters, 30 J.Nat.Assn. of Social Workers 350, 352 (1985). Returning to one's abuser can be dangerous. Recent Federal Bureau of Investigation statistics disclose that 8.8% of all homicide victims in the United States are killed by their spouse. Mercy & Saltzman, Fatal Violence Among Spouses in the United States, 1976–85, 79 Am.J.Public Health 595 (1989). Thirty percent of female homicide victims are killed by their male partners. Domestic Violence: Terrorism in the Home, Hearing before the Subcommittee on Children, Family, Drugs and Alcoholism of the Senate Committee on Labor and Human Resources, 101st Cong., 2d Sess., 3 (1990).

The limited research that has been conducted with respect to notifying one's husband about an abortion, although involving samples too small to be representative, also supports the District Court's findings of fact. The vast majority of women notify their male partners of their decision to obtain an abortion. In many cases in which married women do not notify their husbands, the pregnancy is the result of an extramarital affair. Where the husband is the father, the primary reason women do not notify their husbands is that the husband and wife are experiencing marital difficulties, often accompanied by incidents of violence. Ryan & Plutzer, When Married Women Have Abortions: Spousal Notification and Marital Interaction, 51 J. Marriage & the Family 41, 44 (1989).

This information and the District Court's findings reinforce what common sense would suggest. In well-functioning marriages, spouses discuss important intimate decisions such as whether to bear a child. But there are millions of women in this country who are the victims of regular physical and psychological abuse at the hands of their husbands. Should these women become pregnant, they may have very good reasons for not wishing to inform their husbands of their decision to obtain an abortion. Many may have justifiable fears of physical abuse, but may be no less fearful of the consequences of reporting prior abuse to the Commonwealth of Pennsylvania. Many may have a reasonable fear that notifying their husbands will provoke further instances of child abuse; these women are not exempt from § 3209's notification requirement. Many may fear devastating forms of psychological abuse from their husbands, including verbal harassment, threats of future violence, the destruction of possessions, physical confinement to the home, the withdrawal of financial support, or the disclosure of the abortion to family and friends. These methods of psychological abuse may act as even more of a deterrent to notification than the possibility of physical violence, but women who are the victims of the abuse are not exempt from § 3209's notification requirement. And many women who are pregnant as a result of sexual assaults by their husbands will be unable to avail themselves of the exception for spousal sexual assault, § 3209(b)(3), because the exception requires that the woman have notified law enforcement authorities within 90 days of the assault, and her husband will be notified of her report once an investigation begins. § 3128(c). If anything in this field is certain, it is that victims of spousal sexual assault are extremely reluctant to report the abuse to the government; hence, a great many spousal rape victims will not be exempt from the notification requirement imposed by § 3209.

The spousal notification requirement is thus likely to prevent a significant number of women from obtaining an abortion. It does not merely make abortions a little more difficult or expensive to obtain; for many women, it will impose a substantial obstacle. We must not blind ourselves to the fact that the significant number of women who fear for their safety and the safety of their children are likely to be deterred from procuring an abortion as surely as if the Commonwealth had outlawed abortion in all cases. . . .

We recognize that a husband has a "deep and proper concern and interest . . . in his wife's pregnancy and in the growth and development of the fetus she is carrying." With regard to the children he has fathered and raised, the Court has recognized his "cognizable and substantial" interest in their custody. *Stanley* v. *Illinois*, 405 U.S. 645, 651–652, 92 S.Ct. 1208, 1213, 31 L. Ed. 2d 551 (1972); see also *Quilloin* v. *Walcott*, 434 U.S. 246, 98 S.Ct. 549, 54 L. Ed. 2d 511 (1978); *Caban* v. *Mohammed*, 441 U.S. 380, 99 S.Ct. 1760, 60 L. Ed. 2d 297 (1979); *Lehr* v. *Robertson*, 463 U.S. 248, 103 S.Ct. 2985, 77 L. Ed. 2d 614 (1983). If this case concerned a State's ability to require the mother to notify the father before taking some action with respect to a living child raised by both, therefore, it would be reasonable to conclude as a general matter that the father's interest in the welfare of the child and the mother's interest are equal.

Before birth, however, the issue takes on a very different cast. It is an inescapable biological fact that state regulation with respect to the child a woman is carrying will have a far greater impact on the mother's liberty than on the father's. The effect of state regulation on a woman's protected liberty is doubly deserving of scrutiny in such a case, as the State has touched not only upon the private sphere of the family but upon the very bodily integrity of the pregnant woman. Cf. *Cruzan* v. *Director, Missouri Dept. of Health*, 497 U.S. The Court has held that "when the wife and the husband disagree on this decision, the view of only one of the two marriage partners can prevail. Inasmuch as it is the woman who physically bears the child and who is the more directly and immediately affected by the pregnancy, as between the two, the balance weighs in her favor." This conclusion rests upon the basic nature of marriage and the nature of our Constitution: "[T]he marital couple is not an independent entity with a mind and heart of its own, but an association of two individuals each with a separate intellectual and emotional makeup. If the right of privacy means anything, it is the right of the *individual*, married or single, to be free from unwarranted governmental intrusion into matters so fundamentally affecting a person as the decision whether to bear or beget a child." *Eisenstadt* v. *Baird*, 405 U.S., at 453, 92 S.Ct., at 1038 (emphasis in original). The Constitution protects individuals, men and women alike, from unjustified state interference, even when that interference is enacted into law for the benefit of their spouses.

There was a time, not so long ago, when a different understanding of the family and of the Constitution prevailed. In *Bradwell* v. *Illinois*, 16 Wall. 130, 21 L. Ed. 442 (1873), three Members of this Court reaffirmed the common-law principle that "a woman had no legal existence separate from her husband, who was regarded as her head and representative in the social state; and, notwithstanding some recent modifications of this civil status, many of the special rules of law flowing from and dependent upon this cardinal principle still exist in full force in most States." *Id.*, at 141 (Bradley J., joined by Swayne and Field, JJ., concurring in judgment). Only one generation has passed since this Court observed that "woman is still regarded as the center of home and family life," with attendant "special responsibilities" that precluded full and independent legal status under the Constitution. *Hoyt* v. *Florida*, 368 U.S. 57, 62, 82 S.Ct. 159, 162, 7 L. Ed. 2d 118 (1961). These views, of course, are no longer consistent with our understanding of the family, the individual, or the Constitution.

In keeping with our rejection of the common-law understanding of a woman's role within the family, the Court held in *Danforth* that the Constitution does not permit a State to require a married woman to obtain her husband's consent before undergoing an abortion. 428 U.S., at 69, 96 S.Ct., at 2841. The principles that guided the Court in *Danforth* should be our guides today. For the great many women who are victims of abuse inflicted by their husbands, or whose children are the victims of such abuse, a spousal notice requirement enables the husband to wield an effective veto over his wife's decision. Whether the prospect of notification itself deters such women from seeking abortions, or whether the husband, through physical force or psychological pressure or economic coercion, prevents his wife from obtaining an abortion until it is too late, the notice requirement will often be tantamount to the veto found unconstitutional in *Danforth*. . . .

D

We next consider the parental consent provision. Except in a medical emergency, an unemancipated young woman under 18 may not obtain an abortion unless she and one of her parents (or guardian) provides informed consent as defined above. If neither a parent nor a guardian provides consent, a court may authorize the performance of an abortion upon a determination that the young woman is mature and capable of giving informed consent and has in fact given her informed consent, or that an abortion would be in her best interests.

We have been over most of this ground before. Our cases establish, and we reaffirm today, that a State may require a minor seeking an abortion to obtain the consent of a parent or guardian, provided that there is an adequate judicial bypass procedure. See, *e.g.*, *Akron II*, 497 U.S., at 502, *Hodgson*, 497 U.S., at 417, *Akron I*, *supra*, 462 U.S., at 440, 103 S.Ct., at 2497; *Bellotti II*, *supra*, 443 U.S., at 643–644 (plurality opinion). Under these precedents, in our view, the one-parent consent requirement and judicial bypass procedure are constitutional.

The only argument made by petitioners respecting this provision and to which our prior decisions do not speak is the contention that the parental consent requirement is invalid because it requires informed parental consent. For the most part, petitioners' argument is a reprise of their argument with respect to the informed consent requirement in general, and we reject it for the reasons given above. Indeed, some of the provisions regarding informed consent have particular force with respect to minors: the waiting period, for example, may provide the parent or parents of a pregnant young woman the opportunity to consult with her in private, and to discuss the consequences of her decision in the context of the values and moral or religious principles of their family. See *Hodgson, supra,* 497 U.S., at 417.

E

Under the recordkeeping and reporting requirements of the statute, every facility which performs abortions is required to file a report stating its name and address as well as the name and address of any related entity, such as a controlling or subsidiary organization. In the case of state-funded institutions, the information becomes public.

For each abortion performed, a report must be filed identifying: the physician (and the second physician where required); the facility; the referring physician or agency; the woman's age; the number of prior pregnancies and prior abortions she has had; gestational age; the type of abortion procedure; the date of the abortion; whether there were any pre-existing medical conditions which would complicate pregnancy; medical complications with the abortion; where applicable, the basis for the determination that the abortion was medically necessary; the weight of the aborted fetus; and whether the woman was married, and if so, whether notice was provided or the basis for the failure to give notice. Every abortion facility must also file quarterly reports showing the number of abortions performed broken down by trimester. See 18 Pa. Cons. Stat. §§ 3207, 3214 (1990). In all events, the identity of each woman who has had an abortion remains confidential.

In *Danforth,* 428 U.S., at 80, we held that recordkeeping and reporting provisions "that are reasonably directed to the preservation of maternal health and that properly respect a patient's confidentiality and privacy are permissible." We think that under this standard, all the provisions at issue here except that relating to spousal notice are constitutional. Although they do not relate to the State's interest in informing the woman's choice, they do relate to health. The collection of information with respect to actual patients is a vital element of medical research, and so it cannot be said that the requirements serve no purpose other than to make abortions more difficult. Nor do we find that the requirements impose a substantial obstacle to a woman's choice. At most they might increase the cost of some abortions by a slight amount. While at some point increased cost could become a substantial obstacle, there is no such showing on the record before us. . . .

JUSTICE BLACKMUN, concurring in part, concurring in the judgment in part, and dissenting in part.

Three years ago, in *Webster* v. *Reproductive Health Serv.*, 492 U.S. 490, 109 S.Ct. 3040, 106 L. Ed. 2d 410 (1989), four Members of this Court appeared poised to "cas[t] into darkness the hopes and visions of every woman in this country" who had come to believe that the Constitution guaranteed her the right to reproductive choice. *Id.*, at 557, 109 S.Ct., at 3077 (BLACKMUN, J., dissenting). See *id.*, at 499, 109 S.Ct., at 3046 (opinion of REHNQUIST, C. J.); *id.*, at 532, 109 S.Ct., at 3064 (opinion of SCALIA, J.). All that remained between the promise of *Roe* and the darkness of the plurality was a single, flickering flame. Decisions since *Webster* gave little reason to hope that this flame would cast much light. See, *e.g.*, *Ohio* v. *Akron Center for Reproductive Health*, 497 U.S. 502, 524 (1990) (opinion of BLACKMUN, J.). But now, just when so many expected the darkness to fall, the flame has grown bright.

I do not underestimate the significance of today's joint opinion. Yet I remain steadfast in my belief that the right to reproductive choice is entitled to the full protection afforded by this Court before *Webster*. And I fear for the darkness as four Justices anxiously await the single vote necessary to extinguish the light.

I

Make no mistake, the joint opinion of Justices O'CONNOR, KENNEDY, and SOUTER is an act of personal courage and constitutional principle. In contrast to previous decisions in which Justices O'CONNOR and KENNEDY postponed reconsideration of *Roe* v. *Wade*, 410 U.S. 113, 93 S.Ct. 705, 35 L. Ed. 2d 147 (1973), the authors of the joint opinion today join JUSTICE STEVENS and me in concluding that "the essential holding of *Roe* should be retained and once again reaffirmed." In brief, five Members of this Court today recognize that "the Constitution protects a woman's right to terminate her pregnancy in its early stages."

A fervent view of individual liberty and the force of *stare decisis* have led the Court to this conclusion. Today a majority reaffirms that the Due Process Clause of the Fourteenth Amendment establishes "a realm of personal liberty which the government may not enter,"—a realm whose outer limits cannot be determined by interpretations of the Constitution that focus only on the specific practices of States at the time the Fourteenth Amendment was adopted. Included within this realm of liberty is "'the right of the *individual*, married or single, to be free from unwarranted governmental intrusion into matters so fundamentally affecting a person as the decision whether to bear or beget a child.'" *Eisenstadt* v. *Baird*, 405 U.S. 438, 453, 92 S.Ct. 1029, 1038, 31 L. Ed. 2d 349 (1972) (emphasis in original). "These matters, involving the most intimate and personal choices a person may make in a lifetime, choices central to personal dignity and autonomy, are *central* to the liberty protected by the Fourteenth Amendment." (Emphasis added.) Finally, the Court today recognizes that in the case of abortion, "the liberty of the woman is at stake in a sense unique to the human condition and so unique to the law. The mother who carries a child to full term is subject to anxieties, to physical constraints, to pain that only she must bear."

The Court's reaffirmation of *Roe*'s central holding is also based on the force of *stare decisis*. "[N]o erosion of principle going to liberty or personal autonomy has left *Roe*'s central holding a doctrinal remnant; *Roe* portends no developments at odds with other precedent for the analysis of personal liberty; and no changes of fact have rendered viability more or less appropriate as the point at which the balance of interests tips." Indeed, the Court acknowledges that *Roe*'s limitation on state power could not be removed "without serious inequity to those who have relied upon it or significant damage to the stability of the society governed by the rule in question." In the 19 years since *Roe* was decided, that case has shaped more than reproductive planning—"an entire generation has come of age free to assume *Roe*'s concept of liberty in defining the capacity of women to act in society and to make reproductive decisions." The Court understands that, having "call[ed] the contending sides . . . to end their national division by accepting a common mandate rooted in the Constitution," a decision to overrule *Roe* "would seriously weaken the Court's capacity to exercise the judicial power and to function as the Supreme Court of a Nation dedicated to the rule of law." What has happened today should serve as a model for future Justices and a warning to all who have tried to turn this Court into yet another political branch.

In striking down the Pennsylvania statute's spousal notification requirement, the Court has established a framework for evaluating abortion regulations that responds to the social context of women facing issues of reproductive choice. . . . In determining the burden imposed by the challenged regulation, the Court inquires whether the regulation's "*purpose or effect* is to place a substantial obstacle in the path of a woman seeking an abortion before the fetus attains viability." (emphasis added). The Court reaffirms: "The proper focus of constitutional inquiry is the group for whom the law is a restriction, not the group for whom the law is irrelevant." Looking at this group, the Court inquires, based on expert testimony, empirical studies, and common sense, whether "in a large fraction of the cases in which [the restriction] is relevant, it will operate as a substantial obstacle to a woman's choice to undergo an abortion." "A statute with this purpose is invalid because the means chosen by the State to further the interest in potential life must be calculated to inform the woman's free choice, not hinder it." And in applying its test, the Court remains sensitive to the unique role of women in the decision-making process. Whatever may have been the practice when the Fourteenth Amendment was adopted, the Court observes, "[w]omen do not lose their constitutionally protected liberty when they marry. The Constitution protects all individuals, male or female, married or unmarried, from the abuse of governmental power, even when that power is employed for the supposed benefit of a member of the individual's family." . . .

Lastly, while I believe that the joint opinion errs in failing to invalidate the other regulations, I am pleased that the joint opinion has not ruled out the possibility that these regulations may be shown to impose an unconstitutional burden. The joint opinion makes clear that its specific holdings are based on the insufficiency of the record before it. I am confident that in the future evidence will be produced to show that "in a large fraction of the cases in which [these regulations are] relevant, [they] will operate as a substantial obstacle to a woman's choice to undergo an abortion."

II

Today, no less than yesterday, the Constitution and decisions of this Court require that a State's abortion restrictions be subjected to the strictest of judicial scrutiny. Our precedents and the joint opinion's principles require us to subject all non–*de minimis* abortion regulations to strict scrutiny. Under this standard, the Pennsylvania statute's provisions requiring content-based counseling, a 24-hour delay, informed parental consent, and reporting of abortion-related information must be invalidated.

A

The Court today reaffirms the long recognized rights of privacy and bodily integrity. As early as 1891, the Court held, "[n]o right is held more sacred, or is more carefully guarded by the common law, than the right of every individual to the possession and control of his own person, free from all restraint or interference of others. . . ." *Union Pacific R. Co. v. Botsford*, 141 U.S. 250, 251, 11 S.Ct. 1000, 1001, 35 L. Ed. 734 (1891). Throughout this century, this Court also has held that the fundamental right of privacy protects citizens against governmental intrusion in such intimate family matters as procreation, child rearing, marriage, and contraceptive choice. See *ante*, at 2804–2805. These cases embody the principle that personal decisions that profoundly affect bodily integrity, identity, and destiny should be largely beyond the reach of government. *Eisenstadt*, 405 U.S., at 453, 92 S.Ct., at 1038. In *Roe v. Wade*, this Court correctly applied these principles to a woman's right to choose abortion.

State restrictions on abortion violate a woman's right of privacy in two ways. First, compelled continuation of a pregnancy infringes upon a woman's right to bodily integrity by imposing substantial physical intrusions and significant risks of physical harm. During pregnancy, women experience dramatic physical changes and a wide range of health consequences. Labor and delivery pose additional health risks and physical demands. In short, restrictive abortion laws force women to endure physical invasions far more substantial than those this Court has held to violate the constitutional principle of bodily integrity in other contexts. See, *e.g.*, *Winston v. Lee*, 470 U.S. 753, 105 S.Ct. 1611, 84 L. Ed. 2d 662 (1985) (invalidating surgical removal of bullet from murder suspect); *Rochin v. California*, 342 U.S. 165, 72 S.Ct. 205, 96 L. Ed. 183 (1952) (invalidating stomach-pumping). . . .

Further, when the State restricts a woman's right to terminate her pregnancy, it deprives a woman of the right to make her own decision about reproduction and family planning—critical life choices that this Court long has deemed central to the right to privacy. The decision to terminate or continue a pregnancy has no less an impact on a woman's life than decisions about contraception or marriage. 410 U.S., at 153, 93 S.Ct., at 727. Because motherhood has a dramatic impact on a woman's educational prospects, employment opportunities, and self-determination, restrictive abortion laws deprive her of basic control over her life. For these reasons, "the decision whether or not to beget or bear a child" lies at "the very heart of this cluster of constitutionally protected choices." *Carey* v. *Population Services, Int'l*, 431 U.S. 678, 97 S.Ct. 2010, 52 L. Ed. 2d 675 (1977).

A State's restrictions on a woman's right to terminate her pregnancy also implicate constitutional guarantees of gender equality. State restrictions on abortion compel women to continue pregnancies they otherwise might terminate. By restricting the right to terminate pregnancies, the State conscripts women's bodies into its service, forcing women to continue their pregnancies, suffer the pains of childbirth, and in most instances, provide years of maternal care. The State does not compensate women for their services; instead, it assumes that they owe this duty as a matter of course. This assumption—that women can simply be forced to accept the "natural" status and incidents of motherhood—appears to rest upon a conception of women's role that has triggered the protection of the Equal Protection Clause. See, *e.g.*, *Mississippi Univ. for Women* v. *Hogan*, 458 U.S. 718, 724–726, 102 S.Ct. 3331, 3336–3337, 73 L. Ed. 2d 1090 (1982); *Craig* v. *Boren*, 429 U.S. 190, 198–199, 97 S.Ct. 451, 457–458, 50 L. Ed. 2d 397 (1976). . . . The joint opinion recognizes that these assumptions about women's place in society "are no longer consistent with our understanding of the family, the individual, or the Constitution."

B

The Court has held that limitations on the right of privacy are permissible only if they survive "strict" constitutional scrutiny—that is, only if the governmental entity imposing the restriction can demonstrate that the limitation is both necessary and narrowly tailored to serve a compelling governmental interest. *Griswold* v. *Connecticut*, 381 U.S. 479, 485, 85 S.Ct. 1678, 1682, 14 L. Ed. 2d 510 (1965). We have applied this principle specifically in the context of abortion regulations. *Roe* v. *Wade*, 410 U.S., at 155, 93 S.Ct., at 728. . . .

Roe implemented these principles through a framework that was designed "to insure that the woman's right to choose not become so subordinate to the State's interest in promoting fetal life that her choice exists in theory but not in fact." *Roe* identified two relevant State interests: "an interest in preserving and protecting the health of the pregnant woman" and an interest in "protecting the potentiality of human life." 410 U.S., at 162, 93 S.Ct., at 731. With respect to the State's interest in the health of the mother, "the 'compelling' point . . . is at approximately the end of the first trimester," because it is at that point that the mortality rate in abortion approaches that in childbirth. *Roe*, 410 U.S., at 163, 93 S.Ct., at 731. With respect to the State's interest in potential life, "the 'compelling' point is at viability," because it is at that point that the fetus "presumably has the capability of meaningful life outside the mother's womb." *Ibid.* In order to fulfill the requirement of narrow tailoring, "the State is obligated to make a reasonable effort to limit the effect of its regulations to the period in the trimester during which its health interest will be furthered." *Akron,* 462 U.S., at 434, 103 S.Ct., at 2495.

In my view, application of this analytical framework is no less warranted than when it was approved by seven Members of this Court in *Roe.* Strict scrutiny of state limitations on reproductive choice still offers the most secure protection of the woman's right to make her own reproductive decisions, free from state coercion. No majority of this Court has ever agreed upon an alternative approach. The factual premises of the trimester framework have not been undermined, see *Webster,* 492 U.S., at 553, 109 S.Ct., at 3075 (BLACKMUN, J, dissenting), and the *Roe* framework is far more administrable, and far less manipulable, than the "undue burden" standard adopted by the joint opinion. . . .

CHIEF JUSTICE REHNQUIST, with whom JUSTICE WHITE, JUSTICE SCALIA, and JUSTICE THOMAS join, concurring in the judgment in part and dissenting in part.

The joint opinion, following its newly minted variation on *stare decisis,* retains the outer shell of *Roe v. Wade,* 410 U.S. 113, 93 S.Ct. 705, 35 L. Ed. 2d 147 (1973), but beats a wholesale retreat from the substance of that case. We believe that *Roe* was wrongly decided, and that it can and should be overruled consistently with our traditional approach to *stare decisis* in constitutional cases. We would adopt the approach of the plurality in *Webster* v. *Reproductive Health Services,* 492 U.S. 490, 109 S.Ct. 3040, 106 L. Ed. 2d 410 (1989), and uphold the challenged provisions of the Pennsylvania statute in their entirety.

I

In ruling on this case below, the Court of Appeals for the Third Circuit first observed that "this appeal does not directly implicate *Roe;* this case involves the regulation of abortions rather than their outright prohibition." 947 F. 2d 682, 687 (1991). Accordingly, the court directed its attention to the question of the standard of review for abortion regulations. In attempting to settle on the correct standard, however, the court confronted the confused state of this Court's abortion jurisprudence. After considering the several opinions in *Webster* v. *Reproductive Health Services, supra,* and *Hodgson* v. *Minnesota,* 497 U.S. 417, 110 S.Ct. 2926, 111 L. Ed. 2d 344 (1990), the Court of Appeals concluded that JUSTICE O'CONNOR's "undue burden" test was controlling, as that was the narrowest ground on which we had upheld recent abortion regulations. 947 F. 2d, at 693–697 ("'When a fragmented court decides a case and no single rationale explaining the result enjoys the assent of five Justices, the holding of the Court may be viewed as that position taken by those Members who concurred in the judgments on the narrowest grounds'" (quoting *Marks* v. *United States*, 430 U.S. 188, 193, 97 S.Ct. 990, 993, 51 L. Ed. 2d 260 (1977) (internal quotation marks omitted)). Applying this standard, the Court of Appeals upheld all of the challenged regulations except the one requiring a woman to notify her spouse of an intended abortion.

In arguing that this Court should invalidate each of the provisions at issue, petitioners insist that we reaffirm our decision in *Roe* v. *Wade, supra,* in which we held unconstitutional a Texas statute making it a crime to procure an abortion except to save the life of the mother. . . . We agree with the Court of Appeals that our decision in *Roe* is not directly implicated by the Pennsylvania statute, which does not prohibit, but simply regulates, abortion. But, as the Court of Appeals found, the state of our post-*Roe* decisional law dealing with the regulation of abortion is confusing and uncertain, indicating that a reexamination of that line of cases is in order. Unfortunately for those who must apply this Court's decisions, the reexamination undertaken today leaves the Court no less divided than beforehand. Although they reject the trimester framework that formed the underpinning of *Roe*, Justices O'CONNOR, KENNEDY, and SOUTER adopt a revised undue burden standard to analyze the challenged regulations. We conclude, however, that such an outcome is an unjustified constitutional compromise, one which leaves the Court in a position to closely scrutinize all types of abortion regulations despite the fact that it lacks the power to do so under the Constitution. . . .

We have held that a liberty interest protected under the Due Process Clause of the Fourteenth Amendment will be deemed fundamental if it is "implicit in the concept of ordered liberty." *Palko* v. *Connecticut,* 302 U.S. 319, 325, 58 S.Ct. 149, 152, 82 L. Ed. 288 (1937). Three years earlier, in *Snyder* v. *Massachusetts,* 291 U.S. 97, 54 S.Ct. 330, 78 L. Ed. 674 (1934), we referred to a "principle of justice so rooted in the traditions and conscience of our people as to be ranked as fundamental." *Id.*, at 105, 54 S.Ct., at 332; see also *Michael H.* v. *Gerald D.*, 491 U.S. 110, 122, 109 S.Ct. 2333, 2341, 105 L. Ed. 2d 91 (1989) (plurality opinion) (citing the language from *Snyder*). These expressions are admittedly not precise, but our decisions implementing this notion of "fundamental" rights do not afford any more elaborate basis on which to base such a classification.

In construing the phrase "liberty" incorporated in the Due Process Clause of the Fourteenth Amendment, we have recognized that its meaning extends beyond freedom from physical restraint. In *Pierce* v. *Society of Sisters,* 268 U.S. 510, 45 S.Ct. 571, 69 L. Ed. 1070 (1925), we held that it included a parent's right to send a child to private school; in *Meyer* v. *Nebraska,* 262 U.S. 390, 43 S.Ct. 625, 67 L. Ed. 1042 (1923), we held that it included a right to teach a foreign language in a parochial school. Building on these cases, we have held that the term "liberty" includes a right to marry, *Loving* v. *Virginia,* 388 U.S. 1, 87 S.Ct. 1817, 18 L. Ed. 2d 1010 (1967); a right to procreate, *Skinner* v. *Oklahoma ex rel. Williamson,* 316 U.S. 535, 62 S.Ct. 1110, 86 L. Ed. 1655 (1942); and a right to use contraceptives, *Griswold* v. *Connecticut,* 381 U.S. 479, 85 S.Ct. 1678, 14 L. Ed. 2d 510

(1965); *Eisenstadt* v. *Baird*, 405 U.S. 438, 92 S.Ct. 1029, 31 L. Ed. 2d 349 (1972). But a reading of these opinions makes clear that they do not endorse any all-encompassing "right to privacy."

In *Roe* v. *Wade*, the Court recognized a "guarantee of personal privacy" which "is broad enough to encompass a woman's decision whether or not to terminate her pregnancy." 410 U.S., at 152–153, 93 S.Ct., at 727. We are now of the view that, in terming this right fundamental, the Court in *Roe* read the earlier opinions upon which it based its decision much too broadly. Unlike marriage, procreation and contraception, abortion "involves the purposeful termination of potential life." *Harris* v. *McRae*, 448 U.S. 297, 325, 100 S.Ct. 2671, 2692, 65 L. Ed. 2d 784 (1980). The abortion decision must therefore "be recognized as *sui generis*, different in kind from the others that the Court has protected under the rubric of personal or family privacy and autonomy." *Thornburgh* v. *American College of Obstetricians and Gynecologists, supra*, 476 U S., at 792, 106 S.Ct., at 2195 (WHITE, J., dissenting). One cannot ignore the fact that a woman is not isolated in her pregnancy, and that the decision to abort necessarily involves the destruction of a fetus. See *Michael H.* v. *Gerald D., supra*, 491 U.S., at 124, n. 4, 109 S.Ct., at 2342, n. 4 (To look "at the act which is assertedly the subject of a liberty interest in isolation from its effect upon other people [is] like inquiring whether there is a liberty interest in firing a gun where the case at hand happens to involve its discharge into another person's body").

Nor do the historical traditions of the American people support the view that the right to terminate one's pregnancy is "fundamental." The common law which we inherited from England made abortion after "quickening" an offense. At the time of the adoption of the Fourteenth Amendment, statutory prohibitions or restrictions on abortion were commonplace; in 1868, at least 28 of the then 37 States and 8 Territories had statutes banning or limiting abortion. J. Mohr, Abortion in America 200 (1978). By the turn of the century virtually every State had a law prohibiting or restricting abortion on its books. By the middle of the present century, a liberalization trend had set in. But 21 of the restrictive abortion laws in effect in 1868 were still in effect in 1973 when *Roe* was decided, and an overwhelming majority of the States prohibited abortion unless necessary to preserve the life or health of the mother. *Roe* v. *Wade*, 410 U.S., at 139–140, 93 S.Ct., at 720; *id.*, at 176–177, n. 2, 93 S.Ct., at 738–739, n. 2 (REHNQUIST, J., dissenting). On this record, it can scarcely be said that any deeply rooted tradition of relatively unrestricted abortion in our history supported the classification of the right to abortion as "fundamental" under the Due Process Clause of the Fourteenth Amendment. . . .

The joint opinion of Justices O'CONNOR, KENNEDY, and SOUTER cannot bring itself to say that *Roe* was correct as an original matter, but the authors are of the view that "the immediate question is not the soundness of *Roe*'s resolution of the issue, but the precedential force that must be accorded to its holding." Instead of claiming that *Roe* was correct as a matter of original constitutional interpretation, the opinion therefore contains an elaborate discussion of *stare decisis*. This discussion of the principle of *stare decisis* appears to be almost entirely dicta, because the joint opinion does not apply that principle in dealing with *Roe*. *Roe* decided that a woman had a fundamental right to an abortion. The joint opinion rejects that view. *Roe* decided that abortion regulations were to be subjected to "strict scrutiny" and could be justified only in the light of "compelling state interests." The joint opinion rejects that view. See *Roe* v. *Wade, supra,* 410 U.S., at 162–164, 93 S.Ct., at 731–732. *Roe* analyzed abortion regulation under a rigid trimester framework, a framework which has guided this Court's decisionmaking for 19 years. The joint opinion rejects that framework.

Stare decisis is defined in Black's Law Dictionary as meaning "to abide by, or adhere to, decided cases." Black's Law Dictionary 1406 (6th ed. 1990). Whatever the "central holding" of *Roe* that is left after the joint opinion finishes dissecting it is surely not the result of that principle. While purporting to adhere to precedent, the joint opinion instead revises it. *Roe* continues to exist, but only in the way a storefront on a western movie set exists: a mere facade to give the illusion of reality. Decisions following *Roe*, such as *Akron* v. *Akron Center for Reproductive Health, Inc.*, 462 U.S. 416, 103 S.Ct. 2481, 76 L. Ed. 2d 687 (1983), and *Thornburgh* v. *American College of Obstetricians and Gynecologists*, 476 U.S. 747, 106 S.Ct. 2169, 90 L. Ed. 2d 779 (1986), are frankly overruled in part under the "undue burden" standard expounded in the joint opinion.

In our view, authentic principles of *stare decisis* do not require that any portion of the reasoning in *Roe* be kept intact. "*Stare decisis* is not . . . a universal, inexorable command," especially in cases involving the interpretation of the Federal Constitution. *Burnet* v. *Coronado Oil & Gas Co.*, 285 U.S. 393, 405, 52 S.Ct. 443, 446, 76 L. Ed. 815 (1932) (Brandeis, J., dissenting). Erroneous decisions in such constitutional cases are uniquely durable, because correction through legislative action, save for constitutional amendment, is impossible. It is therefore our duty to reconsider constitutional interpretations that "depar[t] from a proper understanding" of the Constitution. *Garcia* v. *San Antonio Metropolitan Transit Authority*, 469 U.S., at 557, 105 S.Ct., at 1020; see *United States* v. *Scott*, 437 U.S. 82, 101, 98 S.Ct. 2187, 2199, 57 L. Ed. 2d 65 (1978) ("'[I]n cases involving the Federal Constitution, . . . [t]he Court bows to the lessons of experience and the force of better reasoning, recognizing that the process of trial and error, so fruitful in the physical sciences, is appropriate also in the judicial function.'" (quoting *Burnet* v. *Coronado Oil & Gas Co., supra*, 285 U.S., at 406–408, 52 S.Ct., at 447–448 (Brandeis, J., dissenting))); *Smith* v. *Allwright*, 321 U.S. 649, 665, 64 S.Ct. 757, 765, 88 L. Ed. 987 (1944). Our constitutional watch does not cease merely because we have spoken before on an issue; when it becomes clear that a prior constitutional interpretation is unsound we are obliged to reexamine the question. See, *e.g., West Virginia State Bd. of Education* v. *Barnette*, 319 U.S. 624, 642, 63 S.Ct. 1178, 1187, 87 L. Ed. 1628 (1943); *Erie R. Co.* v. *Tompkins*, 304 U.S. 64, 74–78, 58 S.Ct. 817, 820–822, 82 L. Ed. 1188 (1938).

The joint opinion discusses several *stare decisis* factors which, it asserts, point toward retaining a portion of *Roe*. Two of these factors are that the main "factual underpinning" of *Roe* has remained the same, and that its doctrinal foundation is no weaker now than it was in 1973. Of course, what might be called the basic facts which gave rise to *Roe* have remained the same—women become pregnant, there is a point somewhere, depending on medical technology, where a fetus becomes viable, and women give birth to children. But this is only to say that the same facts which gave rise to *Roe* will continue to give rise to similar cases. It is not a reason, in and of itself, why those cases must be decided in the same incorrect manner as was the first case to deal with the question. And surely there is no requirement, in considering whether to depart from *stare decisis* in a constitutional case, that a decision be more wrong now than it was at the time it was rendered. If that were true, the most outlandish constitutional decision could survive forever, based simply on the fact that it was no more outlandish later than it was when originally rendered.

Nor does the joint opinion faithfully follow this alleged requirement. The opinion frankly concludes that *Roe* and its progeny were wrong in failing to recognize that the State's interests in maternal health and in the protection of unborn human life exist throughout pregnancy. But there is no indication that these components of *Roe* are any more incorrect at this juncture than they were at its inception.

The joint opinion also points to the reliance interests involved in this context in its effort to explain why precedent must be followed for precedent's sake. Certainly it is true that where reliance is truly at issue, as in the case of judicial decisions that have formed the basis for private decisions, "[c]onsiderations in favor of *stare decisis* are at their acme." *Payne* v. *Tennessee*, 501 U.S., 111 S.Ct., at 2610. But, as the joint opinion apparently agrees, *ante*, at 2809, any traditional notion of reliance is not applicable here. The Court today cuts back on the protection afforded by *Roe*, and no one claims that this action defeats any reliance interest in the disavowed trimester framework. Similarly, reliance interests would not be diminished were the Court to go further and acknowledge the full error of *Roe*, as "reproductive planning could take virtually immediate account of" this action.

The joint opinion thus turns to what can only be described as an unconventional—and unconvincing—notion of reliance, a view based on the surmise that the availability of abortion since *Roe* has led to "two decades of economic and social developments" that would be undercut if the error of *Roe* were recognized. *Ibid.* The joint opinion's assertion of this fact is undeveloped and totally conclusory. In fact, one can not be sure to what economic and social developments the opinion is referring. Surely it is dubious to suggest that women have reached their "places in society" in reliance upon *Roe*, rather than as a result of their determination to obtain higher education and compete with men in the job market, and of society's increasing recognition of their ability to fill positions that were previously thought to be reserved only for men. *Ibid.* . . .

Taking the joint opinion on its own terms, we doubt that its distinction between *Roe*, on the one hand, and *Plessy* and *Lochner*, on the other, withstands analysis. The joint opinion acknowledges that the Court improved its stature by overruling *Plessy* in *Brown* on a deeply divisive issue. And our decision in *West Coast Hotel*, which overruled *Adkins* v. *Children's Hospital*, *supra*, and *Lochner*, was rendered at a time when Congress was considering President Franklin Roosevelt's proposal to "reorganize" this Court and enable him to name six additional Justices in the event that any member of the Court over the age of 70 did not elect to retire. It is difficult to imagine a situation in which the Court would face more intense opposition to a prior ruling than it did at that time, and, under the general principle proclaimed in the joint opinion, the Court seemingly should have responded to this opposition by stubbornly refusing to reexamine the *Lochner* rationale, lest it lose legitimacy by appearing to "overrule under fire."

The joint opinion agrees that the Court's stature would have been seriously damaged if in *Brown* and *West Coast Hotel* it had dug in its heels and refused to apply normal principles of *stare decisis* to the earlier decisions. But the opinion contends that the Court was entitled to overrule *Plessy* and *Lochner* in those cases, despite the existence of opposition to the original decisions, only because both the Nation and the Court had learned new lessons in the interim. This is at best a feebly supported, *post hoc* rationalization for those decisions.

For example, the opinion asserts that the Court could justifiably overrule its decision in *Lochner* only because the Depression had convinced "most people" that constitutional protection of contractual freedom contributed to an economy that failed to protect the welfare of all. Surely the joint opinion does not mean to suggest that people saw this Court's failure to uphold minimum wage statutes as the cause of the Great Depression! In any event, the *Lochner* Court did not base its rule upon the policy judgment that an unregulated market was fundamental to a stable economy; it simply believed, erroneously, that "liberty" under the Due Process Clause protected the "right to make a contract." *Lochner* v. *New York*, 198 U.S., at 53, 25 S.Ct., at 541. Nor is it the case that the people of this Nation only discovered the dangers of extreme laissez faire economics because of the Depression. State laws regulating maximum hours and minimum wages were in existence well before that time. A Utah statute of that sort enacted in 1896 was involved in our decision in *Holden* v. *Hardy*, 169 U.S. 366, 18 S.Ct. 383, 42 L. Ed. 780 (1898), and other states followed suit shortly afterwards. See, *e.g.*, *Muller* v. *Oregon*, 208 U.S. 412, 28 S.Ct. 324, 52 L. Ed. 551 (1908); *Bunting* v. *Oregon*, 243 U.S. 426, 37 S.Ct. 435, 61 L.Ed. 830 (1917). These statutes were indeed enacted because of a belief on the part of their sponsors that "freedom of contract" did not protect the welfare of workers, demonstrating that that belief manifested itself more than a generation before the Great Depression. Whether "most people" had come to share it in the hard times of the 1930's is, insofar as anything the joint opinion advances, entirely speculative. The crucial failing at that time was not that workers were not paid a fair wage, but that there was no work available at *any* wage.

When the Court finally recognized its error in *West Coast Hotel*, it did not engage in the *post hoc* rationalization that the joint opinion attributes to it today; it did not state that *Lochner* had been based on an economic view that had fallen into disfavor, and that it therefore should be overruled. Chief Justice Hughes in his opinion for the Court simply recognized what Justice Holmes had previously recognized in his *Lochner* dissent, that "[t]he Constitution does not speak of freedom of contract." *West Coast Hotel Co.* v. *Parrish*, 300 U.S., at 391, 57 S.Ct., at 581; *Lochner* v. *New York*, *supra*, 198 U.S., at 75, 25 S.Ct., at 546 (Holmes, J., dissenting) ("[A] Constitution is not intended to embody a particular economic theory, whether of paternalism and the organic relation of the citizen to the State or of *laissez faire*"). Although the Court did acknowledge in the last paragraph of its opinion the state of affairs during the then-current Depression, the theme of the opinion is that the Court had been mistaken as a matter of constitutional law when it embraced "freedom of contract" 32 years previously. . . .

Section 3209 of the Act contains the spousal notification provision. It requires that, before a physician may perform an abortion on a married woman, the woman must sign a statement indicating that she has notified her husband of her planned abortion. A woman is not required to notify her husband if (1) her husband is not the father, (2) her husband, after diligent effort, cannot be located, (3) the pregnancy is the result of a spousal sexual assault that has been reported to the authorities, or (4) the woman has reason to believe that notifying her husband is likely to result in the infliction of bodily injury upon her by him or by another individual. In addition, a woman is exempted from the notification requirement in the case of a medical emergency. 18 Pa. Cons. Stat. § 3209 (1990).

We first emphasize that Pennsylvania has not imposed a spousal *consent* requirement of the type the Court struck down in *Planned Parenthood of Central Mo.* v. *Danforth*, 428 U.S., at 67–72, 96 S.Ct., at 2840–2842. Missouri's spousal consent provision was invalidated in that case because of the Court's view that it unconstitutionally granted to the husband "a veto power exercisable for any reason whatsoever or for no reason at all." *Id.*, at 71, 96 S.Ct., at 2842. But this case involves a much less intrusive requirement of spousal *notification*, not consent. Such a law requiring only notice to the husband "does not give any third party the legal right to make the [woman's] decision for her, or to prevent her from obtaining an abortion should she choose to have one performed." *Hodgson* v. *Minnesota, supra*, 497 U.S., at 496 (KENNEDY, J., concurring in judgment in part and dissenting in part); see *H. L.* v. *Matheson*, 450 U.S., at 411, n. 17, 101 S.Ct., at 1172, n. 17. *Danforth* thus does not control our analysis. Petitioners contend that it should, however; they argue that the real effect of such a notice requirement is to give the power to husbands to veto a woman's abortion choice. The District Court indeed found that the notification provision created a risk that some woman who would otherwise have an abortion will be prevented from having one. 947 F. 2d, at 712. For example, petitioners argue, many notified husbands will prevent abortions through physical force, psychological coercion, and other types of threats. But Pennsylvania has incorporated exceptions in the notice provision in an attempt to deal with these problems. For instance, a woman need not notify her husband if the pregnancy is result of a reported sexual assault, or if she has reason to believe that she would suffer bodily injury as a result of the notification. 18 Pa. Cons. Stat. § 3209(b) (1990). Furthermore, because this is a facial challenge to the Act, it is insufficient for petitioners to show that the notification provision "might operate unconstitutionally under some conceivable set of circumstances." *United States* v. *Salerno*, 481 U.S. 739, 745, 107 S.Ct. 2095, 2100, 95 L. Ed. 2d 697 (1987). Thus, it is not enough for petitioners to show that, in some "worst-case" circumstances, the notice provision will operate as a grant of veto power to husbands. *Ohio* v. *Akron Center for Reproductive Health*, 497 U.S., at 514, 110 S.Ct. Because they are making a facial challenge to the provision, they must "show that no set of circumstances exists under which the [provision] would be valid." *Ibid.* (internal quotation marks omitted). This they have failed to do. . . .

The question before us is therefore whether the spousal notification requirement rationally furthers any legitimate state interests. We conclude that it does. First, a husband's interests in procreation within marriage and in the potential life of his unborn child are certainly substantial ones. See *Planned Parenthood of Central Mo.* v. *Danforth*, 428 U.S., at 69, 96 S.Ct., at 2841 ("We are not unaware of the deep and proper concern and interest that a devoted and protective husband has in his wife's pregnancy and in the growth and development of the fetus she is carrying"), *id.*, at 93, 96 S.Ct., at 2852 (WHITE, J., concurring in part and dissenting in part); *Skinner* v. *Oklahoma ex rel. Williamson*, 316 U.S., at 541, 62 S.Ct., at 1113. The State itself has legitimate interests both in protecting these interests of the father and in protecting the potential life of the fetus, and the spousal notification requirement is reasonably related to advancing those state interests. By providing that a husband will usually know of his spouse's intent to have an abortion, the provision makes it more likely that the husband will participate in deciding the fate of his unborn child, a possibility that might otherwise have been denied him. This participation might in some cases result in a decision to proceed with the pregnancy. As Judge Alito observed in his dissent below, "[t]he Pennsylvania legislature could have rationally believed that some married women are initially inclined to obtain an abortion without their husbands' knowledge because of perceived problems—such as economic constraints, future plans, or the husbands' previously expressed opposition—that may be obviated by discussion prior to the abortion." 947 F. 2d, at 726 (Alito, J., concurring in part and dissenting in part).

The State also has a legitimate interest in promoting "the integrity of the marital relationship." 18 Pa. Cons. Stat. § 3209(a) (1990). This Court has previously recognized "the importance of the marital relationship in our society." *Planned Parenthood of Central Mo.* v. *Danforth*, *supra*, 428 U.S., at 69, 96 S.Ct., at 2841. In our view, the spousal notice requirement is a rational attempt by the State to improve truthful communication between spouses and encourage collaborative decisionmaking, and thereby fosters marital integrity. See *Labine* v. *Vincent*, 401 U.S. 532, 538, 91 S.Ct. 1017, 1020, 28 L. Ed. 2d 288 (1971) ("[T]he power to make rules to establish, protect, and strengthen family life" is committed to the state legislatures). Petitioners argue that the notification requirement does not further any such interest; they assert that the majority of wives already notify their husbands of their abortion decisions, and the remainder have excellent reasons for keeping their decisions a secret. In the first case, they argue, the law is unnecessary, and in the second case it will only serve to foster marital discord and threats of harm. Thus, petitioners see the law as a totally irrational means of furthering whatever legitimate interest the State might have. But, in our view, it is unrealistic to assume that every husband-wife relationship is either (1) so perfect that this type of truthful and important communication will take place as a matter of course, or (2) so imperfect that, upon notice, the husband will react selfishly, violently, or contrary to the best interests of his wife. See *Planned Parenthood of Central Mo. v. Danforth, supra,* 428 U.S., at 103–104, 96 S.Ct., at 2857 (STEVENS, J., concurring in part and dissenting in part) (making a similar point in the context of a parental consent statute). The spousal notice provision will admittedly be unnecessary in some circumstances, and possibly harmful in others, but "the existence of particular cases in which a feature of a statute performs no function (or is even counterproductive) ordinarily does not render the statute unconstitutional or even constitutionally suspect." *Thornburgh v. American College of Obstetricians and Gynecologists,* 476 U.S., at 800, 106 S.Ct., at 2199 (WHITE, J., dissenting). The Pennsylvania Legislature was in a position to weigh the likely benefits of the provision against its likely adverse effects, and presumably concluded, on balance, that the provision would be beneficial. Whether this was a wise decision or not, we cannot say that it was irrational. We therefore conclude that the spousal notice provision comports with the Constitution. See *Harris v. McRae,* 448 U.S., at 325–326, 100 S.Ct., at 2692–2693 ("It is not the mission of this Court or any other to decide whether the balance of competing interests . . . is wise social policy"). . . .

JUSTICE SCALIA, with whom THE CHIEF JUSTICE, JUSTICE WHITE, and JUSTICE THOMAS join, concurring in the judgment in part and dissenting in part.

. . . I will not swell the United States Reports with repetition of what I have said before; and applying the rational basis test, I would uphold the Pennsylvania statute in its entirety. I must, however, respond to a few of the more outrageous arguments in today's opinion, which it is beyond human nature to leave unanswered. I shall discuss each of them under a quotation from the Court's opinion to which they pertain.

"The inescapable fact is that adjudication of substantive due process claims may call upon the Court in interpreting the Constitution to exercise that same capacity which by tradition courts always have exercised: reasoned judgment." . . .

The authors of the joint opinion, of course, do not squarely contend that *Roe v. Wade* was a *correct* application of "reasoned judgment"; merely that it must be followed, because of *stare decisis.* But in their exhaustive discussion of all the factors that go into the determination of when *stare decisis* should be observed and when disregarded, they never mention "how wrong was the decision on its face?" Surely, if "[t]he Court's power lies . . . in its legitimacy, a product of substance and perception," the "substance" part of the equation demands that plain error be acknowledged and eliminated. *Roe* was plainly wrong—even on the Court's methodology of "reasoned judgment," and even more so (of course) if the proper criteria of text and tradition are applied.

The emptiness of the "reasoned judgment" that produced *Roe* is displayed in plain view by the fact that, after more than 19 years of effort by some of the brightest (and most determined) legal minds in the country, after more than 10 cases upholding abortion rights in this Court, and after dozens upon dozens of *amicus* briefs submitted in this and other cases, the best the Court can do to explain how it is that the word "liberty" *must* be thought to include the right to destroy human fetuses is to rattle off a collection of adjectives that simply decorate a value judgment and conceal a political choice. The right to abort, we are told, inheres in "liberty" because it is among "a person's most basic decisions"; it involves a "most intimate and personal choic[e]"; it is "central to personal dignity and autonomy," *ibid.*; it "originate[s] within the zone of conscience and belief," *ibid.*; it is "too intimate and personal" for state interference; it reflects "intimate views" of a "deep, personal character"; it involves "intimate relationships," and notions of "personal autonomy and bodily integrity"; and it concerns a particularly "'important decisio[n]'" (citation omitted). . . . But it is obvious to anyone applying "reasoned judgment" that the same adjectives can be applied to many forms of conduct that this Court (including one of the Justices in today's majority, see *Bowers* v. *Hardwick*, 478 U.S. 186, 106 S.Ct. 2841, 92 L. Ed. 2d 140 (1986)) has held are *not* entitled to constitutional protection—because, like abortion, they are forms of conduct that have long been criminalized in American society. Those adjectives might be applied, for example, to homosexual sodomy, polygamy, adult incest, and suicide, all of which are equally "intimate" and "deep[ly] personal" decisions involving "personal autonomy and bodily integrity," and all of which can constitutionally be proscribed because it is our unquestionable constitutional tradition that they are proscribable. It is not reasoned judgment that supports the Court's decision; only personal predilection. . . .

"Liberty finds no refuge in a jurisprudence of doubt."
One might have feared to encounter this august and sonorous phrase in an opinion defending the real *Roe* v. *Wade*, rather than the revised version fabricated today by the authors of the joint opinion. The shortcomings of *Roe* did not include lack of clarity: Virtually all regulation of abortion before the third trimester was invalid. But to come across this phrase in the joint opinion—which calls upon federal district judges to apply an "undue burden" standard as doubtful in application as it is unprincipled in origin—is really more than one should have to bear.

The joint opinion frankly concedes that the amorphous concept of "undue burden" has been inconsistently applied by the Members of this Court in the few brief years since that "test" was first explicitly propounded by JUSTICE O'CONNOR in her dissent in *Akron I, supra.* . . . Because the three Justices now wish to "set forth a standard of general application," the joint opinion announces that "it is important to clarify what is meant by an undue burden," *ibid.* I certainly agree with that, but I do not agree that the joint opinion succeeds in the announced endeavor. To the contrary, its efforts at clarification make clear only that the standard is inherently manipulable and will prove hopelessly unworkable in practice.

The joint opinion explains that a state regulation imposes an "undue burden" if it "has the purpose or effect of placing a substantial obstacle in the path of a woman seeking an abortion of a nonviable fetus." An obstacle is "substantial," we are told, if it is "calculated[,] [not] to inform the woman's free choice, [but to] hinder it." . . . This latter statement cannot possibly mean what it says. *Any* regulation of abortion that is intended to advance what the joint opinion concedes is the State's "substantial" interest in protecting unborn life will be "calculated [to] hinder" a decision to have an abortion. It thus seems more accurate to say that the joint opinion would uphold abortion regulations only if they do not *unduly* hinder the woman's decision. That, of course, brings us right back to square one: Defining an "undue burden" as an "undue hindrance" (or a "substantial obstacle") hardly "clarifies" the test. Consciously or not, the joint opinion's verbal shell game will conceal raw judicial policy choices concerning what is "appropriate" abortion legislation. . . .

The rootless nature of the "undue burden" standard, a phrase plucked out of context from our earlier abortion decisions, is further reflected in the fact that the joint opinion finds it necessary expressly to repudiate the more narrow formulations used in JUSTICE O'CONNOR's earlier opinions. Those opinions stated that a statute imposes an "undue burden" if it imposes "*absolute* obstacles or *severe* limitations on the abortion decision," *Akron I*, 462 U.S., at 464, 103 S.Ct., at 2510 (O'CONNOR, J., dissenting) (emphasis added); see also *Thornburgh* v. *American College of Obstetricians and Gynecologists*, 476 U.S. 747, 828, 106 S.Ct. 2169, 2214, 90 L. Ed. 2d 779 (1986) (O'CONNOR, J., dissenting). Those strong adjectives are conspicuously missing from the joint opinion, whose authors have for some unexplained reason now determined that a burden is "undue" if it merely imposes a "substantial" obstacle to abortion decisions. JUSTICE O'CONNOR has also abandoned (again without explanation) the view she expressed in *Planned Parenthood Assn. of Kansas City, Mo., Inc.* v. *Ashcroft*, 462 U.S. 476, 103 S.Ct. 2517, 76 L. Ed. 2d 733 (1983) (dissenting opinion), that a medical regulation which imposes an "undue burden" could nevertheless be upheld if it "reasonably relate[s] to the preservation and protection of maternal health," *id.*, at 505, 103 S.Ct., at 2532 (citation and internal quotation marks omitted). In today's version, even health measures will be upheld only "*if they do not constitute an undue burden*" (emphasis added). Gone too is JUSTICE O'CONNOR's statement that "the State possesses *compelling* interests in the protection of potential human life . . . throughout pregnancy," *Akron I, supra*, 462 U.S., at 461, 103 S.Ct., at 2509 (emphasis added); see also *Ashcroft, supra*, 462 U.S., at 505, 103 S.Ct., at 2532 (O'CONNOR, J., concurring in judgment in part and dissenting in part); *Thornburgh, supra*, 476 U.S., at 828, 106 S.Ct., at 2214 (O'CONNOR, J., dissenting); instead, the State's interest in unborn human life is stealthily downgraded to a merely "substantial" or "profound" interest. (That had to be done, of course, since designating the interest as "compelling" throughout pregnancy would have been, shall we say, a "substantial obstacle" to the joint opinion's determined effort to reaffirm what it views as the "central holding" of *Roe*. See *Akron I*, 462 U.S., at 420, n. 1, 103 S.Ct., at 2487, n. 1.) And "viability" is no longer the "arbitrary" dividing line previously decried by JUSTICE O'CONNOR in *Akron I, id.*, at 461, 103 S.Ct., at 2509; the Court now announces that "the attainment of viability may continue to serve as the critical fact." . . . It is difficult to maintain the illusion that we are interpreting a Constitution rather than inventing one, when we amend its provisions so breezily.

Because the portion of the joint opinion adopting and describing the undue-burden test provides no more useful guidance than the empty phrases discussed above, one must turn to pages . . . applying that standard to the present facts for further guidance. In evaluating Pennsylvania's abortion law, the joint opinion relies extensively on the factual findings of the District Court, and repeatedly qualifies its conclusions by noting that they are contingent upon the record developed in this case. Thus, the joint opinion would uphold the 24-hour waiting period contained in the Pennsylvania statute's informed consent provision, 18 Pa. Cons. Stat. § 3205 (1990), because "the record evidence shows that in the vast majority of cases, a 24-hour delay does not create any appreciable health risk." The three Justices therefore conclude that "on the record before us, . . . we are not convinced that the 24-hour waiting period constitutes an undue burden." The requirement that a doctor provide the information pertinent to informed consent would also be upheld because "there is no evidence on this record that [this requirement] would amount in practical terms to a substantial obstacle to a woman seeking an abortion." . . . Similarly, the joint opinion would uphold the reporting requirements of the Act, §§ 3207, 3214, because "there is no . . . showing on the record before us" that these requirements constitute a "substantial obstacle" to abortion decisions. But at the same time the opinion pointedly observes that these reporting requirements may increase the costs of abortions and that "at some point [that fact] could become a substantial obstacle," *ibid.* Most significantly, the joint opinion's conclusion that the spousal notice requirement of the Act, see § 3209, imposes an "undue burden" is based in large measure on the District Court's "detailed findings of fact," which the joint opinion sets out at great length.

I do not, of course, have any objection to the notion that, in applying legal principles, one should rely only upon the facts that are contained in the record or that are properly subject to judicial notice. . . . But what is remarkable about the joint opinion's fact-intensive analysis is that it does not result in any measurable clarification of the "undue burden" standard. Rather, the approach of the joint opinion is, for the most part, simply to highlight certain facts in the record that apparently strike the three Justices as particularly significant in establishing (or refuting) the existence of an undue burden; after describing these facts, the opinion then simply announces that the provision either does or does not impose a "substantial obstacle" or an "undue burden." . . . We do not know whether the same conclusions could have been reached on a different record, or in what respects the record would have had to differ before an opposite conclusion would have been appropriate. The inherently standardless nature of this inquiry invites the district judge to give effect to his personal preferences about abortion. By finding and relying upon the right facts, he can invalidate, it would seem, almost any abortion restriction that strikes him as "undue"—subject, of course, to the possibility of being reversed by a Circuit Court or Supreme Court that is as unconstrained in reviewing his decision as he was in making it.

To the extent I can discern *any* meaningful content in the "undue burden" standard as applied in the joint opinion, it appears to be that a State may not regulate abortion in such a way as to reduce significantly its incidence. The joint opinion repeatedly emphasizes that an important factor in the "undue burden" analysis is whether the regulation "prevents[s] a significant number of women from obtaining an abortion," *ante*, at 2829; whether a "significant number of women . . . are likely to be deterred from procuring an abortion," *ibid.*; and whether the regulation often "deters" women from seeking abortions, *ante*, at 2830–2831. We are not told, however, what forms of "deterrence" are impermissible or what degree of success in deterrence is too much to be tolerated. If, for example, a State required a woman to read a pamphlet describing, with illustrations, the facts of fetal development before she could obtain an abortion, the effect of such legislation might be to "deter" a "significant number of women" from procuring abortions, thereby seemingly allowing a district judge to invalidate it as an undue burden. Thus, despite flowery rhetoric about the State's "substantial" and "profound" interest in "potential human life," and criticism of *Roe* for undervaluing that interest, the joint opinion permits the State to pursue that interest only so long as it is not too successful. As JUSTICE BLACKMUN recognizes (with evident hope), . . . the "undue burden" standard may ultimately require the invalidation of each provision upheld today if it can be shown, on a better record, that the State is too effectively "express[ing] a preference for childbirth over abortion." . . . Reason finds no refuge in this jurisprudence of confusion.

"While we appreciate the weight of the arguments . . . that *Roe* should be overruled, the reservations any of us may have in reaffirming the central holding of *Roe* are outweighed by the explication of individual liberty we have given combined with the force of *stare decisis*."

The Court's reliance upon *stare decisis* can best be described as contrived. It insists upon the necessity of adhering not to all of *Roe*, but only to what it calls the "central holding." It seems to me that *stare decisis* ought to be applied even to the doctrine of *stare decisis*, and I confess never to have heard of this new, keep-what-you-want-and-throw-away-the-rest version. I wonder whether, as applied to *Marbury* v. *Madison*, 1 Cranch 137, 2 L. Ed. 60 (1803), for example, the new version of *stare decisis* would be satisfied if we allowed courts to review the constitutionality of only those statutes that (like the one in *Marbury*) pertain to the jurisdiction of the courts.

I am certainly not in a good position to dispute that the Court *has saved* the "central holding" of *Roe*, since to do that effectively I would have to know what the Court has saved, which in turn would require me to understand (as I do not) what the "undue burden" test means. I must confess, however, that I have always thought, and I think a lot of other people have always thought, that the arbitrary trimester framework, which the Court today discards, was quite as central to *Roe* as the arbitrary viability test, which the Court today retains. It seems particularly ungrateful to carve the trimester framework out of the core of *Roe*, since its very rigidity (in sharp contrast to the utter indeterminability of the "undue burden" test) is probably the only reason the Court is able to say, in urging *stare decisis*, that *Roe* "has in no sense proven 'unworkable.'" . . . I suppose the Court is entitled to call a "central holding" whatever it wants to call a "central holding"—which is, come to think of it, perhaps one of the difficulties with this modified version of *stare decisis*. I thought I might note, however, that the following portions of *Roe* have not been saved:

- Under *Roe*, requiring that a woman seeking an abortion be provided truthful information about abortion before giving informed written consent is unconstitutional, if the information is designed to influence her choice, *Thornburgh*, 476 U.S., at 759–765, 106 S.Ct., at 2178–2181; *Akron I*, 462 U.S., 442–445, 103 S.Ct., at 2499–2500. Under the joint opinion's "undue burden" regime (as applied today, at least) such a requirement is constitutional.
- Under *Roe*, requiring that information be provided by a doctor, rather than by nonphysician counselors, is unconstitutional, *Akron I, supra*, at 446–449, 103 S.Ct., at 2501–2502. Under the "undue burden" regime (as applied today, at least) it is not.
- Under *Roe*, requiring a 24-hour waiting period between the time the woman gives her informed consent and the time of the abortion is unconstitutional, *Akron I, supra*, at 449–451, 103 S.Ct., at 2502–2503. Under the "undue burden" regime (as applied today, at least) it is not.
- Under *Roe*, requiring detailed reports that include demographic data about each woman who seeks an abortion and various information about each abortion is unconstitutional, *Thornburgh, supra*, 476 U.S., at 765–768, 106 S.Ct., at 2181–2183. Under the "undue burden" regime (as applied today, at least) it generally is not.

"Where, in the performance of its judicial duties, the Court decides a case in such a way as to resolve the sort of intensely divisive controversy reflected in *Roe* . . . , its decision has a dimension that the resolution of the normal case does not carry. It is the dimension present whenever the Court's interpretation of the Constitution calls the contending sides of a national controversy to end their national division by accepting a common mandate rooted in the Constitution."

The Court's description of the place of *Roe* in the social history of the United States is unrecognizable. Not only did *Roe* not, as the Court suggests, *resolve* the deeply divisive issue of abortion; it did more than anything else to nourish it, by elevating it to the national level where it is infinitely more difficult to resolve. National politics were not plagued by abortion protests, national abortion lobbying, or abortion marches on Congress, before *Roe* v. *Wade* was decided. Profound disagreement existed among our citizens over the issue—as it does over other issues, such as the death penalty—but that disagreement was being worked out at the state level. As with many other issues, the division of sentiment within each State was not as closely balanced as it was among the population of the Nation as a whole, meaning not only that more people would be satisfied with the results of state-by-state resolution, but also that those results would be more stable. Pre-*Roe*, moreover, political compromise was possible. . . .

"[T]o overrule under fire . . . would subvert the Court's legitimacy. . . .

"To all those who will be . . . tested by following, the Court implicitly undertakes to remain steadfast. . . . The promise of constancy, once given, binds its maker for as long as the power to stand by the decision survives and . . . the commitment [is not] obsolete. . . .

"[The American people's] belief in themselves as . . . a people [who aspire to live according to the rule of law] is not readily separable from their understanding of the Court invested with the authority to decide their constitutional cases and speak before all others for their constitutional ideals. If the Court's legitimacy should be undermined, then, so would the country be in its very ability to see itself through its constitutional ideals."

The Imperial Judiciary lives. It is instructive to compare this Nietzschean vision of us unelected, life-tenured judges—leading a Volk who will be "tested by following," and whose very "belief in themselves" is mystically bound up in their "understanding" of a Court that "speak[s] before all others for their constitutional ideals"—with the somewhat more modest role envisioned for these lawyers by the Founders.

"The judiciary . . . has . . . no direction either of the strength or of the wealth of the society, and can take no active resolution whatever. It may truly be said to have neither FORCE nor WILL but merely judgment. . . ." The Federalist No. 78, pp. 393–394 (G. Wills ed. 1982).

Or, again, to compare this ecstasy of a Supreme Court in which there is, especially on controversial matters, no shadow of change or hint of alteration ("There is a limit to the amount of error that can plausibly be imputed to prior courts," . . .) with the more democratic views of a more humble man:

"[T]he candid citizen must confess that if the policy of the Government upon vital questions affecting the whole people is to be irrevocably fixed by decisions of the Supreme Court, . . . the people will have ceased to be their own rulers, having to that extent practically resigned their Government into the hands of that eminent tribunal." A. Lincoln, First Inaugural Address (Mar. 4, 1861), reprinted in Inaugural Addresses of the Presidents of the United States, S. Doc. No. 101–10, p. 139 (1989).

It is particularly difficult, in the circumstances of the present decision, to sit still for the Court's lengthy lecture upon the virtues of "constancy," of "remain[ing] steadfast," of adhering to "principle." Among the five Justices who purportedly adhere to *Roe*, at most three agree upon the *principle* that constitutes adherence (the joint opinion's "undue burden" standard)—and that principle is inconsistent with *Roe*, see 410 U.S., at 154–156, 93 S.Ct., at 727–728. . . . To make matters worse, two of the three, in order thus to remain steadfast, had to abandon previously stated positions. It is beyond me how the Court expects these accommodations to be accepted "as grounded truly in principle, not as compromises with social and political pressures having, as such, no bearing on the principled choices that the Court is obliged to make." The only principle the Court "adheres" to, it seems to me, is the principle that the Court must be seen as standing by *Roe*. That is not a principle of law (which is what I thought the Court was talking about), but a principle of *Realpolitik*—and a wrong one at that.

I cannot agree with, indeed I am appalled by, the Court's suggestion that the decision whether to stand by an erroneous constitutional decision must be strongly influenced—*against* overruling, no less—by the substantial and continuing public opposition the decision has generated. The Court's judgment that any other course would "subvert the Court's legitimacy" must be another consequence of reading the error-filled history book that described the deeply divided country brought together by *Roe*. In my history book, the Court was covered with dishonor and deprived of legitimacy by *Dred Scott* v. *Sandford*, 19 How. 393, 15 L. Ed. 691 (1857), an erroneous (and widely opposed) opinion that it did not abandon, rather than by *West Coast Hotel Co.* v. *Parrish*, 300 U.S. 379, 57 S.Ct. 578, 81 L. Ed. 703 (1937), which produced the famous "switch in time" from the Court's erroneous (and widely opposed) constitutional opposition to the social measures of the New Deal. (Both *Dred Scott* and one line of the cases resisting the New Deal rested upon the concept of "substantive due process" that the Court praises and employs today. Indeed, *Dred Scott* was "very possibly the first application of substantive due process in the Supreme Court, the original precedent for *Lochner* v. *New York* and *Roe* v. *Wade*." D. Currie, The Constitution in the Supreme Court 271 (1985) (footnotes omitted).)

But whether it would "subvert the Court's legitimacy" or not, the notion that we would decide a case differently from the way we otherwise would have in order to show that we can stand firm against public disapproval is frightening. It is a bad enough idea, even in the head of someone like me, who believes that the text of the Constitution, and our traditions, say what they say and there is no fiddling with them. But when it is in the mind of a Court that believes the Constitution has an evolving meaning; that the Ninth Amendment's reference to "othe[r]" rights is not a disclaimer, but a charter for action, *ibid.*; and that the function of this Court is to "speak before all others for [the people's] constitutional ideals" unrestrained by meaningful text or tradition—then the notion that the Court must adhere to a decision for as long as the decision faces "great opposition" and the Court is "under fire" acquires a character of almost czarist arrogance. We are offended by these marchers who descend upon us, every year on the anniversary of *Roe*, to protest our saying that the Constitution requires what our society has never thought the Constitution requires. These people who refuse to be "tested by following" must be taught a lesson. We have no Cossacks, but at least we can stubbornly refuse to abandon an erroneous opinion that we might otherwise change—to show how little they intimidate us.

Of course, as THE CHIEF JUSTICE points out, we have been subjected to what the Court calls "political pressure" by *both* sides of this issue. Maybe today's decision *not* to overrule *Roe* will be seen as buckling to pressure from *that* direction. Instead of engaging in the hopeless task of predicting public perception—a job not for lawyers but for political campaign managers—the Justices should do what is *legally* right by asking two questions: (1) Was *Roe* correctly decided? (2) Has *Roe* succeeded in producing a settled body of law? If the answer to both questions is no, *Roe* should undoubtedly be overruled.

In truth, I am as distressed as the Court is—and expressed my distress several years ago, see *Webster*, 492 U.S., at 535, 109 S.Ct., at 3065—about the "political pressure" directed to the Court: the marches, the mail, the protests aimed at inducing us to change our opinions. How upsetting it is, that so many of our citizens (good people, not lawless ones, on both sides of this abortion issue, and on various sides of other issues as well) think that we Justices should properly take into account their views, as though we were engaged not in ascertaining an objective law but in determining some kind of social consensus. The Court would profit, I think, from giving less attention to the *fact* of this distressing phenomenon, and more attention to the *cause* of it. That cause permeates today's opinion: a new mode of constitutional adjudication that relies not upon text and traditional practice to determine the law, but upon what the Court calls "reasoned judgment," *ante*, at 2806, which turns out to be nothing but philosophical predilection and moral intuition. All manner of "liberties," the Court tells us, inhere in the Constitution and are enforceable by this Court—not just those mentioned in the text or established in the traditions of our society. Why even the Ninth Amendment—which says only that "[t]he enumeration in the Constitution of certain rights shall not be construed to deny or disparage others retained by the people"—is, despite our contrary understanding for almost 200 years, a literally boundless source of additional, unnamed, unhinted-at "rights," definable and enforceable by us, through "reasoned judgment."

What makes all this relevant to the bothersome application of "political pressure" against the Court are the twin facts that the American people love democracy and the American people are not fools. As long as this Court thought (and the people thought) that we Justices were doing essentially lawyers' work up here—reading text and discerning our society's traditional understanding of that text—the public pretty much left us alone. Texts and traditions are facts to study, not convictions to demonstrate about. But if in reality our process of constitutional adjudication consists primarily of making *value judgments*; if we can ignore a long and clear tradition clarifying an ambiguous text, as we did, for example, five days ago in declaring unconstitutional invocations and benedictions at public-high-school graduation ceremonies, *Lee* v. *Weisman*, 505 U.S., S.Ct., L. Ed. 2d (1992); if, as I say, our pronouncement of constitutional law rests primarily on value judgments, then a free and intelligent people's attitude towards us can be expected to be (*ought* to be) quite different. The people know that their value judgments are quite as good as those taught in any law school—maybe better. If, indeed, the "liberties" protected by the Constitution are, as the Court says, undefined and unbounded, then the people *should* demonstrate, to protest that we do not implement *their* values instead of *ours*. Not only that, but confirmation hearings for new Justices *should* deteriorate into question-and-answer sessions in which Senators go through a list of their constituents' most favored and most disfavored alleged constitutional rights, and seek the nominee's commitment to support or oppose them. Value judgments, after all, should be voted on, not dictated; and if our Constitution has somehow accidently committed them to the Supreme Court, at least we can have a sort of plebiscite each time a new nominee to that body is put forward. JUSTICE BLACKMUN not only regards this prospect with equanimity, he solicits it.

* * *

There is a poignant aspect to today's opinion. Its length, and what might be called its epic tone, suggest that its authors believe they are bringing to an end a troublesome era in the history of our Nation and of our Court. "It is the dimension" of authority, they say, to "cal[l] the contending sides of national controversy to end their national division by accepting a common mandate rooted in the Constitution."

There comes vividly to mind a portrait by Emanuel Leutze that hangs in the Harvard Law School: Roger Brooke Taney, painted in 1859, the 82nd year of his life, the 24th of his Chief Justiceship, the second after his opinion in *Dred Scott*. He is all in black, sitting in a shadowed red armchair, left hand resting upon a pad of paper in his lap, right hand hanging limply, almost lifelessly, beside the inner arm of the chair. He sits facing the viewer, and staring straight out. There seems to be on his face, and in his deep-set eyes, an expression of profound sadness and disillusionment. Perhaps he always looked that way, even when dwelling upon the happiest of thoughts. But those of us who know how the lustre of his great Chief Justiceship came to be eclipsed by *Dred Scott* cannot help believing that he had that case—its already apparent consequences for the Court, and its soon-to-be-played-out consequences for the Nation—burning on his mind. I expect that two years earlier he, too, had thought himself "call[ing] the contending sides of national controversy to end their national division by accepting a common mandate rooted in the Constitution."

It is no more realistic for us in this case, than it was for him in that, to think that an issue of the sort they both involved—an issue involving life and death, freedom and subjugation—can be "speedily and finally settled" by the Supreme Court, as President James Buchanan in his inaugural address said the issue of slavery in the territories would be. See Inaugural Addresses of the Presidents of the United States, S. Doc. No. 101–10, p. 126 (1989). Quite to the contrary, by foreclosing all democratic outlet for the deep passions this issue arouses, by banishing the issue from the political forum that gives all participants, even the losers, the satisfaction of a fair hearing and an honest fight, by continuing the imposition of a rigid national rule instead of allowing for regional differences, the Court merely prolongs and intensifies the anguish.

We should get out of this area, where we have no right to be, and where we do neither ourselves nor the country any good by remaining.

DON STENBERG, ATTORNEY GENERAL OF NEBRASKA, ET AL., PETITIONERS *v.* LEROY CARHART

ON WRIT OF CERTIORARI TO THE UNITED STATES COURT OF APPEALS FOR THE EIGHTH CIRCUIT

No. 99–830. Argued April 25, 2000—Decided June 28, 2000

Breyer, J., delivered the opinion of the Court, in which Stevens, O'Connor, Souter, and Ginsburg, JJ., joined. Stevens, J., filed a concurring opinion, in which Ginsburg, J., joined. O'Connor, J., filed a concurring opinion. Ginsburg, J., filed a concurring opinion, in which Stevens, J., joined. Rehnquist, C. J., and Scalia, J., filed dissenting opinions. Kennedy, J., filed a dissenting opinion, in which Rehnquist, C. J., joined. Thomas, J., filed a dissenting opinion, in which Rehnquist, C. J., and Scalia, J., joined. All footnotes to this opinion have been omitted.

Justice Breyer delivered the opinion of the Court.

We again consider the right to an abortion. We understand the controversial nature of the problem. Millions of Americans believe that life begins at conception and consequently that an abortion is akin to causing the death of an innocent child; they recoil at the thought of a law that would permit it. Other millions fear that a law that forbids abortion would condemn many American women to lives that lack dignity, depriving them of equal liberty and leading those with the least resources to undergo illegal abortions with the attendant risks of death and suffering. Taking account of these virtually irreconcilable points of view, aware that constitutional law must govern a society whose different members sincerely hold directly opposing views, and considering the matter in light of the Constitution's guarantees of fundamental individual liberty, this Court, in the course of a generation, has determined and then redetermined that the Constitution offers basic protection to the woman's right to choose. *Roe* v. *Wade*, 410 U.S. 113 (1973); *Planned Parenthood of Southeastern Pa.* v. *Casey*, 505 U.S. 833 (1992). We shall not revisit those legal principles. Rather, we apply them to the circumstances of this case. Three established principles determine the issue before us. We shall set them forth in the language of the joint opinion in *Casey*. First, before "viability . . . the woman has a right to choose to terminate her pregnancy." *Id.*, at 870 (joint opinion of O'Connor, Kennedy, and Souter, JJ.).

Second, "a law designed to further the State's interest in fetal life which imposes an undue burden on the woman's decision before fetal viability" is unconstitutional. *Id.*, at 877. An "undue burden is . . . shorthand for the conclusion that a state regulation has the purpose or effect of placing a substantial obstacle in the path of a woman seeking an abortion of a nonviable fetus." *Ibid.*

Third, "'subsequent to viability, the State in promoting its interest in the potentiality of human life may, if it chooses, regulate, and even proscribe, abortion except where it is necessary, in appropriate medical judgment, for the preservation of the life or health of the mother.'" *Id.*, at 879 (quoting *Roe* v. *Wade, supra,* at 164–165).

We apply these principles to a Nebraska law banning "partial birth abortion." The statute reads as follows:

"No partial birth abortion shall be performed in this state, unless such procedure is necessary to save the life of the mother whose life is endangered by a physical disorder, physical illness, or physical injury, including a life-endangering physical condition caused by or arising from the pregnancy itself." Neb. Rev. Stat. Ann. § 28–328 (1) (Supp. 1999).

The statute defines "partial birth abortion" as: "an abortion procedure in which the person performing the abortion partially delivers vaginally a living unborn child before killing the unborn child and completing the delivery." § 28–326 (9). It further defines "partially delivers vaginally a living unborn child before killing the unborn child" to mean "deliberately and intentionally delivering into the vagina a living unborn child, or a substantial portion thereof, for the purpose of performing a procedure that the person performing such procedure knows will kill the unborn child and does kill the unborn child." *Ibid.* The law classifies violation of the statute as a "Class III felony" carrying a prison term of up to 20 years, and a fine of up to $25,000. §§ 28–328 (2), 28–105. It also provides for the automatic revocation of a doctor's license to practice medicine in Nebraska. § 28–328(4).

We hold that this statute violates the Constitution. . . .

I

B

Because Nebraska law seeks to ban one method of aborting a pregnancy, we must describe and then discuss several different abortion procedures. Considering the fact that those procedures seek to terminate a potential human life, our discussion may seem clinically cold or callous to some, perhaps horrifying to others. There is no alternative way, however, to acquaint the reader with the technical distinctions among different abortion methods and related factual matters, upon which the outcome of this case depends. For that reason, drawing upon the findings of the trial court, underlying testimony, and related medical texts, we shall describe the relevant methods of performing abortions in technical detail.

The evidence before the trial court, as supported or supplemented in the literature, indicates the following:

1. About 90 percent of all abortions performed in the United States take place during the first trimester of pregnancy, before 12 weeks of gestational age. Centers for Disease

Control and Prevention, Abortion Surveillance—United States, 1996, p. 41 (July 30, 1999) (hereinafter Abortion Surveillance). During the first trimester, the predominant abortion method is "vacuum aspiration," which involves insertion of a vacuum tube (cannula) into the uterus to evacuate the contents. Such an abortion is typically performed on an out-patient basis under local anesthesia. 11 F. Supp. 2d, at 1102; Obstetrics: Normal & Problem Pregnancies 1253–1254 (S. Gabbe, J. Niebyl, & J. Simpson eds., 3d ed., 1996). Vacuum aspiration is considered particularly safe. The procedure's mortality rates for first trimester abortion are, for example, 5 to 10 times lower than those associated with carrying the fetus to term. Complication rates are also low. . . . As the fetus grows in size, however, the vacuum aspiration method becomes increasingly difficult to use. 11 F. Supp. 2d, at 1102–1103; Obstetrics: Normal & Problem Pregnancies, *supra*, at 1268.

2. Approximately 10 percent of all abortions are performed during the second trimester of pregnancy (12 to 24 weeks). Abortion Surveillance 41. In the early 1970s, inducing labor through the injection of saline into the uterus was the predominant method of second-trimester abortion. *Id.*, at 8; *Planned Parenthood of Central Mo. v. Danforth*, 428 U.S. 52, 76 (1976). Today, however, the medical profession has switched from medical induction of labor to surgical procedures for most second-trimester abortions. The most commonly used procedure is called "dilation and evacuation" (D&E). That procedure (together with a modified form of vacuum aspiration used in the early second trimester) accounts for about 95 percent of all abortions performed from 12 to 20 weeks of gestational age. Abortion Surveillance 41.

3. D&E "refers generically to transcervical procedures performed at 13 weeks gestation or later." American Medical Association, Report of Board of Trustees on Late-Term Abortion, App. 490 (hereinafter AMA Report). The AMA Report, adopted by the District Court, describes the process as follows.

Between 13 and 15 weeks of gestation:
"D&E is similar to vacuum aspiration except that the cervix must be dilated more widely because surgical instruments are used to remove larger pieces of tissue. Osmotic dilators are usually used. Intravenous fluids and an analgesic or sedative may be administered. A local anesthetic such as a paracervical block may be administered. Dilating agents, if used, are removed and instruments are inserted through the cervix into the uterus to remove fetal and placental tissue. Because fetal tissue is friable and easily broken, the fetus may not be removed intact. The walls of the uterus are scraped with a curette to ensure that no tissue remains." *Id.*, at 490–491.

After 15 weeks:
"Because the fetus is larger at this stage of gestation (particularly the head), and because bones are more rigid, dismemberment or other destructive procedures are more likely to be required than at earlier gestational ages to remove fetal and placental tissue." *Id.*, at 491.

After 20 weeks:

"Some physicians use intrafetal potassium chloride or digoxin to induce fetal demise prior to a late D&E (after 20 weeks), to facilitate evacuation." *Id.*, at 491–492. . . .

4. When instrumental disarticulation incident to D&E is necessary, it typically occurs as the doctor pulls a portion of the fetus through the cervix into the birth canal. . . .

5. The D&E procedure carries certain risks. The use of instruments within the uterus creates a danger of accidental perforation and damage to neighboring organs. Sharp fetal bone fragments create similar dangers. And fetal tissue accidentally left behind can cause infection and various other complications. . . . Nonetheless studies show that the risks of mortality and complication that accompany the D&E procedure between the 12th and 20th weeks of gestation are significantly lower than those accompanying induced labor procedures (the next safest mid-second-trimester procedures). . . .

6. At trial, Dr. Carhart and Dr. Stubblefield described a variation of the D&E procedure, which they referred to as an "intact D&E." See 11 F. Supp. 2d, at 1105, 1111. Like other versions of the D&E technique, it begins with induced dilation of the cervix. The procedure then involves removing the fetus from the uterus through the cervix "intact," *i.e.*, in one pass, rather than in several passes. *Ibid.* It is used after 16 weeks at the earliest, as vacuum aspiration becomes ineffective and the fetal skull becomes too large to pass through the cervix. *Id.*, at 1105. The intact D&E proceeds in one of two ways, depending on the presentation of the fetus. If the fetus presents head first (a vertex presentation), the doctor collapses the skull; and the doctor then extracts the entire fetus through the cervix. If the fetus presents feet first (a breech presentation), the doctor pulls the fetal body through the cervix, collapses the skull, and extracts the fetus through the cervix. *Ibid.* The breech extraction version of the intact D&E is also known commonly as "dilation and extraction," or D&X. *Id.*, at 1112. In the late second trimester, vertex, breech, and traverse/compound (sideways) presentations occur in roughly similar proportions. Medical and Surgical Abortion 135; 11 F. Supp. 2d, at 1108. . . .

9. Dr. Carhart testified that he attempts to use the intact D&E procedure during weeks 16 to 20 because (1) it reduces the dangers from sharp bone fragments passing through the cervix, (2) minimizes the number of instrument passes needed for extraction and lessens the likelihood of uterine perforations caused by those instruments, (3) reduces the likelihood of leaving infection-causing fetal and placental tissue in the uterus, and (4) could help to prevent potentially fatal absorption of fetal tissue into the maternal circulation. See 11 F. Supp. 2d, at 1107. The District Court made no findings about the D&X procedure's overall safety. *Id.*, at 1126, n. 39. The District Court concluded, however, that "the evidence is both clear and convincing that Carhart's D&X procedure is superior to, and safer than, the . . . other abortion procedures used during the relevant gestational period in the 10 to 20 cases a year that present to Dr. Carhart." *Id.*, at 1126.

10. The materials presented at trial referred to the potential benefits of the D&X procedure in circumstances involving nonviable fetuses, such as fetuses with abnormal fluid accumulation in the brain (hydrocephaly). See 11 F. Supp. 2d, at 1107 (quoting AMA Report, App. 492 ("'Intact D&X may be preferred by some physicians, particularly when the fetus has been diagnosed with hydrocephaly or other anomalies incompatible with life outside the womb'")); see also Grimes, The Continuing Need for Late Abortions, 280 JAMA 747, 748 (Aug. 26, 1998) (D&X "may be especially useful in the presence of fetal anomalies, such as hydrocephalus," because its reduction of the cranium allows "a smaller diameter to pass through the cervix, thus reducing risk of cervical injury"). Others have emphasized its potential for women with prior uterine scars, or for women for whom induction of labor would be particularly dangerous. . . .

11. There are no reliable data on the number of D&X abortions performed annually. Estimates have ranged between 640 and 5,000 per year. . . .

II

The question before us is whether Nebraska's statute, making criminal the performance of a "partial birth abortion," violates the Federal Constitution, as interpreted in *Planned Parenthood of Southeastern Pa.* v. *Casey*, 505 U.S. 833 (1992), and *Roe* v. *Wade*, 410 U.S. 113 (1973). We conclude that it does, for at least two independent reasons. First, the law lacks any exception "'for the preservation of the . . . health of the mother.'" *Casey*, 505 U.S., at 879 (joint opinion of O'CONNOR, KENNEDY, and SOUTER, JJ.). Second, it "imposes an undue burden on a woman's ability" to choose a D&E abortion, thereby unduly burdening the right to choose abortion itself. *Id.*, at 874. We shall discuss each of these reasons in turn.

A

The *Casey* joint opinion reiterated what the Court held in *Roe*; that "'subsequent to viability, the State in promoting its interest in the potentiality of human life may, if it chooses, regulate, and even proscribe, abortion except where it is necessary, in appropriate medical judgment, for the preservation of the life or health of the mother.'" 505 U.S., at 879 (quoting *Roe, supra*, at 164–165).

The fact that Nebraska's law applies both pre- and postviability aggravates the constitutional problem presented. The State's interest in regulating abortion previability is considerably weaker than postviability. See *Casey, supra*, at 870. Since the law requires a health exception in order to validate even a postviability abortion regulation, it at a minimum requires the same in respect to previability regulation. See *Casey, supra*, at 880 (majority opinion) (assuming need for health exception previability); see also *Harris* v. *McRae*, 448 U.S. 297, 316 (1980).

The quoted standard also depends on the state regulations "promoting [the State's] interest in the potentiality of human life." The Nebraska law, of course, does not directly further an interest "in the potentiality of human life" by saving the fetus in question from destruction, as it regulates only a method of performing abortion. Nebraska describes its interests differently. It says the law "'show[s] concern for the life of the unborn,'" "prevent[s] cruelty to partially born children," and "preserve[s] the integrity of the medical profession." Brief for Petitioners 48. But we cannot see how the interest-related differences could make any difference to the question at hand, namely, the application of the "health" requirement.

Consequently, the governing standard requires an exception "where it is necessary, in appropriate medical judgment for the preservation of the life or health of the mother," *Casey, supra,* at 879, for this Court has made clear that a State may promote but not endanger a woman's health when it regulates the methods of abortion. *Thornburgh* v. *American College of Obstetricians and Gynecologists,* 476 U.S. 747, 768–769 (1986); *Colautti* v. *Franklin,* 439 U.S. 379, 400 (1979); *Danforth,* 428 U.S., at 76–79; *Doe* v. *Bolton,* 410 U.S. 179, 197 (1973).

Justice Thomas says that the cases just cited limit this principle to situations where the pregnancy itself creates a threat to health. . . . He is wrong. The cited cases, reaffirmed in *Casey*, recognize that a State cannot subject women's health to significant risks both in that context, and also where state regulations force women to use riskier methods of abortion. Our cases have repeatedly invalidated statutes that in the process of regulating the methods of abortion, imposed significant health risks. They make clear that a risk to a woman's health is the same whether it happens to arise from regulating a particular method of abortion, or from barring abortion entirely. Our holding does not go beyond those cases, as ratified in *Casey*.

1

Nebraska responds that the law does not require a health exception unless there is a need for such an exception. And here there is no such need, it says. It argues that "safe alternatives remain available," and "a ban on partial-birth abortion/D&X would create no risk to the health of women." Brief for Petitioners 29, 40. The problem for Nebraska is that the parties strongly contested this factual question in the trial court below; and the findings and evidence support Dr. Carhart. The State fails to demonstrate that banning D&X without a health exception may not create significant health risks for women, because the record shows that significant medical authority supports the proposition that in some circumstances, D&X would be the safest procedure.

We shall reiterate in summary form the relevant findings and evidence. On the basis of medical testimony the District Court concluded that "Carhart's D&X procedure is . . . safer tha[n] the D&E and other abortion procedures used during the relevant gestational period in the 10 to 20 cases a year that present to Dr. Carhart." 11 F. Supp. 2d, at 1126. It found that the D&X procedure permits the fetus to pass through the cervix with a minimum of instrumentation. *Ibid.* It thereby "reduces operating time, blood loss and risk of infection; reduces complications from bony fragments; reduces instrument-inflicted damage to the uterus and cervix; prevents the most common causes of maternal mortality (DIC and amniotic fluid embolus); and eliminates the possibility of 'horrible complications' arising from retained fetal parts." *Ibid.* The District Court also noted that a select panel of the American College of Obstetricians and Gynecologists concluded that D&X "'may be the best or most appropriate procedure in a particular circumstance to save the life or preserve the health of a woman.'" . . . With one exception, the federal trial courts that have heard expert evidence on the matter have reached similar factual conclusions. . . .

2

Nebraska, along with supporting *amici*, replies that these findings are irrelevant, wrong, or applicable only in a tiny number of instances. It says (1) the D&X procedure is "little-used," (2) by only "a handful of doctors." Brief for Petitioners 32. It argues (3) D&E and labor induction are at all times "safe alternative procedures." *Id.*, at 36. It refers to the testimony of petitioners' medical expert, who testified (4) the ban would not increase a woman's risk of several rare abortion complications (disseminated intravascular coagulopathy and amniotic fluid embolus), *id.*, at 37; App. 642–644.

The Association of American Physicians and Surgeons et al., *amici* supporting Nebraska, argue (5) that elements of the D&X procedure may create special risks, including cervical incompetence caused by overdilatation, injury caused by conversion of the fetal presentation, and dangers arising from the "blind" use of instrumentation to pierce the fetal skull while lodged in the birth canal. . . .

Nebraska further emphasizes (6) there are no medical studies "establishing the safety of the partial-birth abortion/D&X procedure," Brief for Petitioners 39, and "no medical studies comparing the safety of partial-birth abortion/D&X to other abortion procedures," *ibid.* It points to, *id.*, at 35, (7) an American Medical Association policy statement that "'there does not appear to be any identified situation in which intact D&X is the only appropriate procedure to induce abortion,'" . . . And it points out (8) the American College of Obstetricians and Gynecologists qualified its statement that D&X "may be the best or most appropriate procedure," by adding that the panel "could identify no circumstances under which [the D&X] procedure . . . would be the only option to save the life or preserve the health of the woman." App. 600–601.

3

We find these eight arguments insufficient to demonstrate that Nebraska's law needs no health exception. For one thing, certain of the arguments are beside the point. The D&X procedure's relative rarity (argument (1)) is not highly relevant. The D&X is an infrequently used abortion procedure, but the health exception question is whether protecting women's health requires an exception for those infrequent occasions. A rarely used treatment might be necessary to treat a rarely occurring disease that could strike anyone; the State cannot prohibit a person from obtaining treatment simply by pointing out that most people do not need it. Nor can we know whether the fact that only a "handful" of doctors use the procedure (argument (2)) reflects the comparative rarity of late second-term abortions, the procedure's recent development, Gynecologic, Obstetric, and Related Surgery, at 1043, the controversy surrounding it, or, as Nebraska suggests, the procedure's lack of utility.

For another thing, the record responds to Nebraska's (and *amici*'s) medically based arguments. With respect to argument (3), for example, the District Court agreed that alternatives, such as D&E and induced labor, are "safe" but found that the D&X method was significantly safer in certain circumstances. 11 F. Supp. 2d, at 1125–1126. With respect to argument (4), the District Court simply relied on different expert testimony—testimony stating that "'[a]nother advantage of the Intact D&E is that it eliminates the risk of embolism of cerebral tissue into the woman's blood stream.'" . . .

In response to *amici*'s argument (5), the American College of Obstetricians and Gynecologists, in its own *amici* brief, denies that D&X generally poses risks greater than the alternatives. It says that the suggested alternative procedures involve similar or greater risks of cervical and uterine injury, for "D&E procedures involve similar amounts of dilatation" and "of course childbirth involves even greater cervical dilatation." Brief for American College of Obstetricians and Gynecologists et al. as *Amici Curiae* 23. The College points out that Dr. Carhart does not reposition the fetus, thereby avoiding any risks stemming from conversion to breech presentation, and that, as compared with D&X, D&E involves the same, if not greater, "blind" use of sharp instruments in the uterine cavity. *Id.*, at 23–24.

We do not quarrel with Nebraska's argument (6), for Nebraska is right. There are no general medical studies documenting comparative safety. Neither do we deny the import of the American Medical Association's statement (argument (7))—even though the State does omit the remainder of that statement: "The AMA recommends that the procedure not be used unless alternative procedures pose materially greater risk to the woman." Late Term Pregnancy Termination Techniques, AMA Policy H–5.982.

We cannot, however, read the American College of Obstetricians and Gynecologists panel's qualification (that it could not "identify" a circumstance where D&X was the "only" life- or health-preserving option) as if, according to Nebraska's argument (8), it denied the potential health-related need for D&X. That is because the College writes the following in its *amici* brief:

"Depending on the physician's skill and experience, the D&X procedure can be the most appropriate abortion procedure for some women in some circumstances. D&X presents a variety of potential safety advantages over other abortion procedures used during the same gestational period. Compared with D&Es involving dismemberment, D&X involves less risk of uterine perforation or cervical laceration because it requires the physician to make fewer passes into the uterus with sharp instruments and reduces the presence of sharp fetal bone fragments that can injure the uterus and cervix. There is also considerable evidence that D&X reduces the risk of retained fetal tissue, a serious abortion complication that can cause maternal death, and that D&X reduces the incidence of a 'free floating' fetal head that can be difficult for a physician to grasp and remove and can thus cause maternal injury. That D&X procedures usually take less time than other abortion methods used at a comparable stage of pregnancy can also have health advantages. The shorter the procedure, the less blood loss, trauma, and exposure to anesthesia. The intuitive safety advantages of intact D&E are supported by clinical experience. Especially for women with particular health conditions, there is medical evidence that D&X may be safer than available alternatives." Brief for American College of Obstetricians and Gynecologists et al. as *Amici Curiae* 21–22 (citation and footnotes omitted).

4

The upshot is a District Court finding that D&X significantly obviates health risks in certain circumstances, a highly plausible record-based explanation of why that might be so, a division of opinion among some medical experts over whether D&X is generally safer, and an absence of controlled medical studies that would help answer these medical questions. Given these medically related evidentiary circumstances, we believe the law requires a health exception.

The word "necessary" in *Casey*'s phrase "necessary, in appropriate medical judgment, for the preservation of the life or health of the mother," 505 U.S., at 879 (internal quotation marks omitted), cannot refer to an absolute necessity or to absolute proof. Medical treatments and procedures are often considered appropriate (or inappropriate) in light of estimated comparative health risks (and health benefits) in particular cases. Neither can that phrase require unanimity of medical opinion. Doctors often differ in their estimation of comparative health risks and appropriate treatment. And *Casey*'s words "appropriate medical judgment" must embody the judicial need to tolerate responsible differences of medical opinion—differences of a sort that the American Medical Association's and American College of Obstetricians and Gynecologists' statements together indicate are present here.

For another thing, the division of medical opinion about the matter at most means uncertainty, a factor that signals the presence of risk, not its absence. That division here involves highly qualified knowledgeable experts on both sides of the issue. Where a significant body of medical opinion believes a procedure may bring with it greater safety for some patients and explains the medical reasons supporting that view, we cannot say that the presence of a different view by itself proves the contrary. Rather, the uncertainty means a significant likelihood that those who believe that D&X is a safer abortion method in certain circumstances may turn out to be right. If so, then the absence of a health exception will place women at an unnecessary risk of tragic health consequences. If they are wrong, the exception will simply turn out to have been unnecessary.

In sum, Nebraska has not convinced us that a health exception is "never necessary to preserve the health of women." Reply Brief for Petitioners 4. Rather, a statute that altogether forbids D&X creates a significant health risk. The statute consequently must contain a health exception. This is not to say, as JUSTICE THOMAS and JUSTICE KENNEDY claim, that a State is prohibited from proscribing an abortion procedure whenever a particular physician deems the procedure preferable. By no means must a State grant physicians "unfettered discretion" in their selection of abortion methods. *Post*, at 14 (KENNEDY, J., dissenting). But where substantial medical authority supports the proposition that banning a particular abortion procedure could endanger women's health, *Casey* requires the statute to include a health exception when the procedure is "'necessary, in appropriate medical judgment, for the preservation of the life or health of the mother.'" 505 U.S., at 879. Requiring such an exception in this case is no departure from *Casey*, but simply a straightforward application of its holding.

B

The Eighth Circuit found the Nebraska statute unconstitutional because, in *Casey*'s words, it has the "effect of placing a substantial obstacle in the path of a woman seeking an abortion of a nonviable fetus." 505 U.S., at 877. It thereby places an "undue burden" upon a woman's right to terminate her pregnancy before viability. *Ibid.* Nebraska does not deny that the statute imposes an "undue burden" if it applies to the more commonly used D&E procedure as well as to D&X. And we agree with the Eighth Circuit that it does so apply. . . .

Even if the statute's basic aim is to ban D&X, its language makes clear that it also covers a much broader category of procedures. The language does not track the medical differences between D&E and D&X—though it would have been a simple matter, for example, to provide an exception for the performance of D&E and other abortion procedures. . . . Thus, the dissenters' argument that the law was generally intended to bar D&X can be both correct and irrelevant. The relevant question is not whether the legislature wanted to ban D&X; it is whether the law was intended to apply only to D&X. The plain language covers both procedures. . . .

The Attorney General also points to the Nebraska legislature's debates, where the term "partial birth abortion" appeared frequently. But those debates hurt his argument more than they help it. Nebraska's legislators focused directly upon the meaning of the word "substantial." One senator asked the bill's sponsor, "[Y]ou said that as small a portion of the fetus as a foot would constitute a substantial portion in your opinion. Is that correct?" The sponsoring senator replied, "Yes, I believe that's correct." App. 452–453; see also *id.*, at 442–443 (same senator explaining "substantial" would "indicate that more than a little bit has been delivered into the vagina," *i.e.*, "[e]nough that would allow for the procedure to end up with the killing of the unborn child"); *id.*, at 404 (rejecting amendment to limit law to D&X). The legislature seems to have wanted to avoid more limiting language lest it become too easy to evade the statute's strictures—a motive that JUSTICE THOMAS well explains. *Post*, at 24–25. That goal, however, exacerbates the problem.

The Attorney General, again echoed by the dissents, further argues that the statute "distinguishes between the overall 'abortion procedure' itself and the separate 'procedure' used to kill the unborn child." Brief for Petitioners 16–18; *post*, at 13–14 (opinion of THOMAS, J.), 21 (opinion of KENNEDY, J.). Even assuming that the distinction would help the Attorney General make the D&E/D&X distinction he seeks, however, we cannot find any language in the statute that supports it. He wants us to read "procedure" in the statute's last sentence to mean "separate procedure," i.e., the killing of the fetus, as opposed to a whole procedure, *i.e.*, a D&E or D&X abortion. But the critical word "separate" is missing. And the same word "procedure," in the same subsection and throughout the statute, is used to refer to an entire abortion procedure. Neb. Rev. Stat. Ann. §§ 28–326(9), 28–328(1)-(4) (Supp. 1999); cf. *Gustafson* v. *Alloyd Co.*, 513 U.S. 561, 570 (1995) ("[I]dentical words used in different parts of the same act are intended to have the same meaning" (internal quotation marks omitted)).

The dissenters add that the statutory words "partially delivers" can be read to exclude D&E. *Post*, at 12–13 (opinion of THOMAS, J.), 19–20 (opinion of KENNEDY, J.). They say that introduction of, say, a limb or both limbs into the vagina does not involve "delivery." But obstetric textbooks and even dictionaries routinely use that term to describe any facilitated removal of tissue from the uterus, not only the removal of an intact fetus. . . . In any event, the statute itself specifies that it applies both to delivering "an intact unborn child" or "a substantial portion thereof." The dissents cannot explain how introduction of a substantial portion of a fetus into the vagina pursuant to D&X is a "delivery," while introduction pursuant to D&E is not. . . .

In sum, using this law some present prosecutors and future Attorneys General may choose to pursue physicians who use D&E procedures, the most commonly used method for performing previability second-trimester abortions. All those who perform abortion procedures using that method must fear prosecution, conviction, and imprisonment. The result is an undue burden upon a woman's right to make an abortion decision. We must consequently find the statute unconstitutional.

The judgment of the Court of Appeals is *Affirmed.*

JUSTICE STEVENS, with whom JUSTICE GINSBURG joins, concurring.

Although much ink is spilled today describing the gruesome nature of late-term abortion procedures, that rhetoric does not provide me a reason to believe that the procedure Nebraska here claims it seeks to ban is more brutal, more gruesome, or less respectful of "potential life" than the equally gruesome procedure Nebraska claims it still allows. JUSTICE GINSBURG and Judge Posner have, I believe, correctly diagnosed the underlying reason for the enactment of this legislation—a reason that also explains much of the Court's rhetoric directed at an objective that extends well beyond the narrow issue that this case presents. The rhetoric is almost, but not quite, loud enough to obscure the quiet fact that during the past 27 years, the central holding of *Roe* v. *Wade*, 410 U.S. 113 (1973), has been endorsed by all but 4 of the 17 Justices who have addressed the issue. That holding—that the word "liberty" in the Fourteenth Amendment includes a woman's right to make this difficult and extremely personal decision—makes it impossible for me to understand how a State has any legitimate interest in requiring a doctor to follow any procedure other than the one that he or she reasonably believes will best protect the woman in her exercise of this constitutional liberty. But one need not even approach this view today to conclude that Nebraska's law must fall. For the notion that either of these two equally gruesome procedures performed at this late stage of gestation is more akin to infanticide than the other, or that the State furthers any legitimate interest by banning one but not the other, is simply irrational. See U.S. Const., Amdt. 14.

JUSTICE O'CONNOR, concurring.

... I write separately to emphasize the following points.

First, the Nebraska statute is inconsistent with *Casey* because it lacks an exception for those instances when the banned procedure is necessary to preserve the health of the mother. See *id.,* at 879 (joint opinion of O'CONNOR, KENNEDY, and SOUTER, JJ.). Importantly, Nebraska's own statutory scheme underscores this constitutional infirmity. As we held in *Casey,* prior to viability "the woman has a right to choose to terminate her pregnancy." *Id.,* at 870. After the fetus has become viable, States may substantially regulate and even proscribe abortion, but any such regulation or proscription must contain an exception for instances "'where it is necessary, in appropriate medical judgment, for the preservation of the life or health of the mother.'" *Id.,* at 879 (quoting *Roe* v. *Wade*, 410 U.S. 113, 165 (1973)). Nebraska has recognized this constitutional limitation in its separate statute generally proscribing postviability abortions. See Neb. Rev. Stat. Ann. § 28–329 (Supp. 1999). That statute provides that "[n]o abortion shall be performed after the time at which, in the sound medical judgment of the attending physician, the unborn child clearly appears to have reached viability, except when necessary to preserve the life or health of the mother." *Ibid.* Because even a postviability proscription of abortion would be invalid absent a health exception, Nebraska's ban on previability partial birth abortions, under the circumstances presented here, must include a health exception as well, since the State's interest in regulating abortions before viability is "considerably weaker" than after viability. . . . This lack of a health exception necessarily renders the statute unconstitutional.

Contrary to the assertions of JUSTICE KENNEDY and JUSTICE THOMAS, the need for a health exception does not arise from "the individual views of Dr. Carhart and his supporters." *Post*, at 14 (KENNEDY, J., dissenting); see also *post*, at 35–36 (THOMAS, J., dissenting). Rather, as the majority explains, where, as here, "a significant body of medical opinion believes a procedure may bring with it greater safety for some patients and explains the medical reasons supporting that view," *ante*, at 19, then Nebraska cannot say that the procedure will not, in some circumstances, be "necessary to preserve the life or health of the mother." Accordingly, our precedent requires that the statute include a health exception.

Second, Nebraska's statute is unconstitutional on the alternative and independent ground that it imposes an undue burden on a woman's right to choose to terminate her pregnancy before viability. Nebraska's ban covers not just the dilation-and-extraction (D&X) procedure, but also the dilation-and-evacuation (D&E) procedure, "the most commonly used method for performing previability second trimester abortions." *Ante*, at 27. The statute defines the banned procedure as "deliberately and intentionally delivering into the vagina a living unborn child, or a substantial portion thereof, for the purpose of performing a procedure that the person performing such procedure knows will kill the unborn child and does kill the unborn child." Neb. Rev. Stat. Ann. § 28–326(9) (Supp. 1999). As the Court explains, the medical evidence establishes that the D&E procedure is included in this definition. Thus, it is not possible to interpret the statute's language as applying only to the D&X procedure. . . .

It is important to note that, unlike Nebraska, some other States have enacted statutes more narrowly tailored to proscribing the D&X procedure alone. Some of those statutes have done so by specifically excluding from their coverage the most common methods of abortion, such as the D&E and vacuum aspiration procedures. . . . If Nebraska's statute limited its application to the D&X procedure and included an exception for the life and health of the mother, the question presented would be quite different than the one we face today. As we held in *Casey*, an abortion regulation constitutes an undue burden if it "has the purpose or effect of placing a substantial obstacle in the path of a woman seeking an abortion of a nonviable fetus." 505 U.S., at 877. If there were adequate alternative methods for a woman safely to obtain an abortion before viability, it is unlikely that prohibiting the D&X procedure alone would "amount in practical terms to a substantial obstacle to a woman seeking an abortion." *Id.*, at 884. Thus, a ban on partial birth abortion that only proscribed the D&X method of abortion and that included an exception to preserve the life and health of the mother would be constitutional in my view. . . .

JUSTICE GINSBURG, with whom JUSTICE STEVENS joins, concurring.

I write separately only to stress that amid all the emotional uproar caused by an abortion case, we should not lose sight of the character of Nebraska's "partial birth abortion" law. As the Court observes, this law does not save any fetus from destruction, for it targets only "a method of performing abortion." *Ante*, at 11–12. Nor does the statute seek to protect the lives or health of pregnant women. Moreover, as JUSTICE STEVENS points out, *ante*, at 1 (concurring opinion), the most common method of performing previability second-trimester abortions is no less distressing or susceptible to gruesome description. Seventh Circuit Chief Judge Posner correspondingly observed, regarding similar bans in Wisconsin and Illinois, that the law prohibits the D&X procedure "not because the procedure kills the fetus, not because it risks worse complications for the woman than alternative procedures would do, not because it is a crueler or more painful or more disgusting method of terminating a pregnancy." *Hope Clinic* v. *Ryan*, 195 F.3d 857, 881 (CA7 1999) (dissenting opinion). Rather, Chief Judge Posner commented, "[T]he law prohibits the procedure because the State legislators seek to chip away at the private choice shielded by *Roe* v. *Wade*, even as modified by *Casey*." *Id.*, at 880–882.

A state regulation that "has the purpose or effect of placing a substantial obstacle in the path of a woman seeking an abortion of a nonviable fetus" violates the Constitution. *Planned Parenthood of Southeastern Pa.* v. *Casey*, 505 U.S. 833, 877 (1992) (joint opinion of O'CONNOR, KENNEDY, and SOUTER, JJ.). Such an obstacle exists if the State stops a woman from choosing the procedure her doctor "reasonably believes will best protect the woman in [the] exercise of [her] constitutional liberty." *Ante*, at 1 (STEVENS, J., concurring); see *Casey*, 505 U.S., at 877 ("means chosen by the State to further the interest in potential life must be calculated to inform the woman's free choice, not hinder it"). Again as stated by Chief Judge Posner, "if a statute burdens constitutional rights and all that can be said on its behalf is that it is the vehicle that legislators have chosen for expressing their hostility to those rights, the burden is undue." *Hope Clinic*, 195 F.3d, at 881.

CHIEF JUSTICE REHNQUIST, dissenting.

I did not join the joint opinion in *Planned Parenthood of Southeastern Pa.* v. *Casey*, 505 U.S. 833 (1992), and continue to believe that case is wrongly decided. Despite my disagreement with the opinion, under the rule laid down in *Marks* v. *United States*, 430 U.S. 188, 193 (1977), the *Casey* joint opinion represents the holding of the Court in that case. I believe JUSTICE KENNEDY and JUSTICE THOMAS have correctly applied *Casey*'s principles and join their dissenting opinions.

JUSTICE KENNEDY, with whom THE CHIEF JUSTICE joins, dissenting.

. . . The Court's failure to accord any weight to Nebraska's interest in prohibiting partial birth abortion is erroneous and undermines its discussion and holding. The Court's approach in this regard is revealed by its description of the abortion methods at issue, which the Court is correct to describe as "clinically cold or callous." *Ante,* at 3–4. The majority views the procedures from the perspective of the abortionist, rather than from the perspective of a society shocked when confronted with a new method of ending human life. Words invoked by the majority, such as "transcervical procedures," "[o]smotic dilators," "instrumental disarticulation," and "paracervical block," may be accurate and are to some extent necessary, *ante,* at 5–6; but for citizens who seek to know why laws on this subject have been enacted across the nation, the words are insufficient. Repeated references to sources understandable only to a trained physician may obscure matters for persons not trained in medical terminology. Thus it seems necessary at the outset to set forth what may happen during an abortion.

. . . As described by Dr. Carhart, the D&E procedure requires the abortionist to use instruments to grasp a portion (such as a foot or hand) of a developed and living fetus and drag the grasped portion out of the uterus into the vagina. *Id.,* at 61. Dr. Carhart uses the traction created by the opening between the uterus and vagina to dismember the fetus, tearing the grasped portion away from the remainder of the body. *Ibid.* The traction between the uterus and vagina is essential to the procedure because attempting to abort a fetus without using that traction is described by Dr. Carhart as "pulling the cat's tail" or "drag[ging] a string across the floor, you'll just keep dragging it. It's not until something grabs the other end that you are going to develop traction." *Id.,* at 62. "The fetus, in many cases, dies just as a human adult or child would: it bleeds to death as it is torn from limb from limb." *Id.,* at 63. The fetus can be alive at the beginning of the dismemberment process and can survive for a time while its limbs are being torn off. Dr. Carhart agreed that "[w]hen you pull out a piece of the fetus, let's say, an arm or a leg and remove that, at the time just prior to removal of the portion of the fetus, . . . the fetus [is] alive." *Id.,* at 62. Dr. Carhart has observed fetal heartbeat via ultrasound with "extensive parts of the fetus removed," *id.,* at 64, and testified that mere dismemberment of a limb does not always cause death because he knows of a physician who removed the arm of a fetus only to have the fetus go on to be born "as a living child with one arm." *Id.,* at 63. At the conclusion of a D&E abortion no intact fetus remains. In Dr. Carhart's words, the abortionist is left with "a tray full of pieces." *Id.,* at 125.

The other procedure implicated today is called "partial birth abortion" or the D&X. The D&X can be used, as a general matter, after 19 weeks gestation because the fetus has become so developed that it may survive intact partial delivery from the uterus into the vagina. *Id.,* at 61. In the D&X, the abortionist initiates the woman's natural delivery process by causing the cervix of the woman to be dilated, sometimes over a sequence of days. *Id.,* at 492. The fetus' arms and legs are delivered outside the uterus while the fetus is alive; witnesses to the procedure report seeing the body of the fetus moving outside the woman's body. Brief for Petitioners 4. At this point, the abortion procedure has the appearance of a live birth. As stated by one group of physicians, "[a]s the physician manually performs breech extraction of the body of a live fetus, excepting the head, she continues in the apparent role of an obstetrician delivering a child." Brief for Association of American Physicians and Surgeons et al. as *Amici Curiae* 27. With only the head of the fetus remaining in utero, the abortionist tears open the skull. According to Dr. Martin Haskell, a leading proponent of the procedure, the appropriate instrument to be used at this stage of the abortion is a pair of scissors. M. Haskell, Dilation and Extraction for Late Second Trimester Abortion (1992), in 139 Cong. Rec. 8605 (1993). Witnesses report observing the portion of the fetus outside the woman react to the skull penetration. Brief for Petitioners 4. The abortionist then inserts a suction tube and vacuums out the developing brain and other matter found within the skull. The process of making the size of the fetus' head smaller is given the clinically neutral term "reduction procedure." 11 F. Supp. 2d 1099, 1106 (Neb. 1998). Brain death does not occur until after the skull invasion, and, according to Dr. Carhart, the heart of the fetus may continue to beat for minutes after the contents of the skull are vacuumed out. App. 58. The abortionist next completes the delivery of a dead fetus, intact except for the damage to the head and the missing contents of the skull. . . .

Casey is premised on the States having an important constitutional role in defining their interests in the abortion debate. It is only with this principle in mind that Nebraska's interests can be given proper weight. The State's brief describes its interests as including concern for the life of the unborn and "for the partially born," in preserving the integrity of the medical profession, and in "erecting a barrier to infanticide." Brief for Petitioners 48–49. A review of *Casey* demonstrates the legitimacy of these policies. The Court should say so. States may take sides in the abortion debate and come down on the side of life, even life in the unborn: "Even in the earliest stages of pregnancy, the State may enact rules and regulations designed to encourage [a woman] to know that there are philosophic and social arguments of great weight that can be brought to bear in favor of continuing the pregnancy to full term and that there are procedures and institutions to allow adoption of unwanted children as well as a certain degree of state assistance if the mother chooses to raise the child herself." 505 U.S., at 872 (joint opinion of O'CONNOR, KENNEDY, and SOUTER, JJ.).

States also have an interest in forbidding medical procedures which, in the State's reasonable determination, might cause the medical profession or society as a whole to become insensitive, even disdainful, to life, including life in the human fetus. Abortion, *Casey* held, has consequences beyond the woman and her fetus. The States' interests in regulating are of concomitant extension. *Casey* recognized that abortion is "fraught with consequences for . . . the persons who perform and assist in the procedure [and for] society which must confront the knowledge that these procedures exist, procedures some deem nothing short of an act of violence against innocent human life." *Id.*, at 852.

A State may take measures to ensure that the medical profession and its members are viewed as healers, sustained by a compassionate and rigorous ethic and cognizant of the dignity and value of human life, even life which cannot survive without the assistance of others. *Ibid.*; *Washington* v. *Glucksberg*, 521 U.S. 702, 730–734 (1997).

Casey demonstrates that the interests asserted by the State are legitimate and recognized by law. It is argued, however, that a ban on the D&X does not further these interests. This is because, the reasoning continues, the D&E method, which Nebraska claims to be beyond its intent to regulate, can still be used to abort a fetus and is no less dehumanizing than the D&X method. While not adopting the argument in express terms, the Court indicates tacit approval of it by refusing to reject it in a forthright manner. Rendering express what is only implicit in the majority opinion, JUSTICE STEVENS and JUSTICE GINSBURG are forthright in declaring that the two procedures are indistinguishable and that Nebraska has acted both irrationally and without a proper purpose in enacting the law. The issue is not whether members of the judiciary can see a difference between the two procedures. It is whether Nebraska can. . . .

Nebraska was entitled to find the existence of a consequential moral difference between the procedures. We are referred to substantial medical authority that D&X perverts the natural birth process to a greater degree than D&E, commandeering the live birth process until the skull is pierced. American Medical Association (AMA) publications describe the D&X abortion method as "ethically wrong." AMA Board of Trustees Factsheet on HR 1122 (June 1997), in App. to Brief for Association of American Physicians and Surgeons et al. as *Amici Curiae* 1 (AMA Factsheet). The D&X differs from the D&E because in the D&X the fetus is "killed outside of the womb" where the fetus has "an autonomy which separates it from the right of the woman to choose treatments for her own body." *Ibid.*; see also App. 639–640; Brief for Association of American Physicians and Surgeons et al. as *Amici Curiae* 27 ("Intact D&X is aberrant and troubling because the technique confuses the disparate role of a physician in childbirth and abortion in such a way as to blur the medical, legal, and ethical line between infanticide and abortion"). Witnesses to the procedure relate that the fingers and feet of the fetus are moving prior to the piercing of the skull; when the scissors are inserted in the back of the head, the fetus' body, wholly outside the woman's body and alive, reacts as though startled and goes limp. D&X's stronger resemblance to infanticide means Nebraska could conclude the procedure presents a greater risk of disrespect for life and a consequent greater risk to the profession and society, which depend for their sustenance upon reciprocal recognition of dignity and respect. The Court is without authority to second-guess this conclusion.

Those who oppose abortion would agree, indeed would insist, that both procedures are subject to the most severe moral condemnation, condemnation reserved for the most repulsive human conduct. This is not inconsistent, however, with the further proposition that as an ethical and moral matter D&X is distinct from D&E and is a more serious concern for medical ethics and the morality of the larger society the medical profession must serve. Nebraska must obey the legal regime which has declared the right of the woman to have an abortion before viability. Yet it retains its power to adopt regulations which do not impose an undue burden on the woman's right. By its regulation, Nebraska instructs all participants in the abortion process, including the mother, of its moral judgment that all life, including the life of the unborn, is to be respected. The participants, Nebraska has determined, cannot be indifferent to the procedure used and must refrain from using the natural delivery process to kill the fetus. The differentiation between the procedures is itself a moral statement, serving to promote respect for human life. . . .

Demonstrating a further and basic misunderstanding of *Casey*, the Court holds, the ban on the D&X procedure fails because it does not include an exception permitting an abortionist to perform a D&X whenever he believes it will best preserve the health of the woman. Casting aside the views of distinguished physicians and the statements of leading medical organizations, the Court awards each physician a veto power over the State's judgment that the procedures should not be performed. Dr. Carhart has made the medical judgment to use the D&X procedure in every case, regardless of indications, after 15 weeks gestation. 11 F. Supp. 2d, at 1105. Requiring Nebraska to defer to Dr. Carhart's judgment is no different than forbidding Nebraska from enacting a ban at all; for it is now Dr. Leroy Carhart who sets abortion policy for the State of Nebraska, not the legislature or the people. . . .

The holding of *Casey*, allowing a woman to elect abortion in defined circumstances, is not in question here. Nebraska, however, was entitled to conclude that its ban, while advancing important interests regarding the sanctity of life, deprived no woman of a safe abortion and therefore did not impose a substantial obstacle on the rights of any woman. The American College of Obstetricians and Gynecologists (ACOG) "could identify no circumstances under which [D&X] would be the only option to save the life or preserve the health of the woman." App. 600–601. The American Medical Association agrees, stating the "AMA's expert panel, which included an ACOG representative, could not find 'any' identified circumstance where it was 'the only appropriate alternative.'" AMA Factsheet 1. The Court's conclusion that the D&X is the safest method requires it to replace the words "may be" with the word "is" in the following sentence from ACOG's position statement: "An intact D&X, however, may be the best or most appropriate procedure in a particular circumstance." App. 600–601.

No studies support the contention that the D&X abortion method is safer than other abortion methods. Brief for Respondent 36, n. 41. Leading proponents of the procedure acknowledge that the D&X has "disadvantages" versus other methods because it requires a high degree of surgical skill to pierce the skull with a sharp instrument in a blind procedure. Haskell, 139 Cong. Rec. 8605 (1993). Other doctors point to complications that may arise from the D&X. Brief for American Physicians and Surgeons et al. as *Amici Curiae* 21–23; App. 186. A leading physician, Frank Boehm, M. D., who has performed and supervised abortions as director of the Fetal Intensive Care Unit and the Maternal/Fetal Medicine Division at Vanderbilt University Hospital, has refused to support use of the D&X, both because no medical need for the procedure exists and because of ethical concerns. *Id.*, at 636, 639–640, 656–657. Dr. Boehm, a fellow of ACOG, *id.*, at 565, supports abortion rights and has provided sworn testimony in opposition to previous state attempts to regulate abortion. *Id.*, at 608–614.

The Court cannot conclude the D&X is part of standard medical practice. It is telling that no expert called by Dr. Carhart, and no expert testifying in favor of the procedure, had in fact performed a partial birth abortion in his or her medical practice. *E.g., id.*, at 308 (testimony of Dr. Phillip Stubblefield). In this respect their opinions were courtroom conversions of uncertain reliability. Litigation in other jurisdictions establishes that physicians do not adopt the D&X procedure as part of standard medical practice. *E.g., Richmond Medical Center for Women* v. *Gilmore*, 144 F.3d 326, 328 (CA4 1998); *Hope Clinic* v. *Ryan*, 195 F.3d 857, 871 (CA7 1999); see also App. 603–604. It is quite wrong for the Court to conclude, as it seems to have done here, that Dr. Carhart conforms his practice to the proper standard of care because he has incorporated the procedure into his practice. Neither Dr. Boehm nor Dr. Carhart's lead expert, Dr. Stubblefield (the chairman of the Department of Obstetrics and Gynecology at Boston University School of Medicine and director of Obstetrics and Gynecology for the Boston Medical Center), has done so. . . .

Courts are ill-equipped to evaluate the relative worth of particular surgical procedures. The legislatures of the several States have superior factfinding capabilities in this regard. In an earlier case, JUSTICE O'CONNOR had explained that the general rule extends to abortion cases, writing that the Court is not suited to be "the Nation's *ex officio* medical board with powers to approve or disapprove medical and operative practices and standards throughout the United States." 462 U.S., at 456 (dissenting opinion) (internal quotation marks omitted). "Irrespective of the difficulty of the task, legislatures, with their superior factfinding capabilities, are certainly better able to make the necessary judgments than are courts." *Id.*, at 456, n. 4. Nebraska's judgment here must stand.

In deferring to the physician's judgment, the Court turns back to cases decided in the wake of *Roe*, cases which gave a physician's treatment decisions controlling weight. Before it was repudiated by *Casey*, the approach of deferring to physicians had reached its apex in *Akron, supra*, where the Court held that an informed consent requirement was unconstitutional. The law challenged in *Akron* required the abortionist to inform the woman of the status of her pregnancy, the development of her fetus, the date of possible viability, the physical and emotional complications that may result from an abortion, and the availability of agencies to provide assistance and information. *Id.*, at 442. The physician was also required to advise the woman of the risks associated with the abortion technique to be employed and other information. *Ibid.* The law was invalidated based on the physician's right to practice medicine in the way he or she saw fit; for, according to the *Akron* Court, "[i]t remains primarily the responsibility of the physician to ensure that appropriate information is conveyed to his patient, depending on her particular circumstances." *Id.*, at 443. Dispositive for the Court was that the law was an "intrusion upon the discretion of the pregnant woman's physician." *Id.*, at 445. The physician was placed in an "undesired and uncomfortable straitjacket." *Ibid.* (internal quotation marks omitted). The Court's decision today echoes the *Akron* Court's deference to a physician's right to practice medicine in the way he sees fit. . . . Instructive is *Jacobson* v. *Massachusetts,* 197 U.S. 11 (1905), where the defendant was convicted because he refused to undergo a smallpox vaccination. The defendant claimed the mandatory vaccination violated his liberty to "care for his own body and health in such way as to him seems best." *Id.,* at 26. He offered to prove that members of the medical profession took the position that the vaccination was of no value and, in fact, was harmful. *Id.,* at 30. The Court rejected the claim, establishing beyond doubt the right of the legislature to resolve matters upon which physicians disagreed: "Those offers [of proof by the defendant] in the main seem to have had no purpose except to state the general theory of those of the medical profession who attach little or no value to vaccination as a means of preventing the spread of smallpox, or who think that vaccination causes other diseases of the body. What everybody knows the court must know, and therefore the state court judicially knew, as this Court knows, that an opposite theory accords with the common belief, and is maintained by high medical authority. We must assume that, when the statute in question was passed, the legislature of Massachusetts was not unaware of these opposing theories, and was compelled, of necessity, to choose between them. It was not compelled to commit a matter involving the public health and safety to the final decision of a court or jury. It is no part of the function of a court or a jury to determine which one of two modes was likely to be the most effective for the protection of the public against disease. That was for the legislative department to determine in the light of all the information it had or could obtain. It could not properly abdicate its function to guard the public health and safety." *Ibid.*

The *Jacobson* Court quoted with approval a recent state-court decision which observed, in words having full application today: "The fact that the belief is not universal [in the medical community] is not controlling, for there is scarcely any belief that is accepted by everyone. The possibility that the belief may be wrong, and that science may yet show it to be wrong, is not conclusive; for the legislature has the right to pass laws which, according to common belief of the people, are adapted to [address medical matters]. In a free country, where government is by the people, through their chosen representatives, practical legislation admits of no other standard of action." *Id.,* at 35 (quoting *Viemester* v. *White,* 179 N. Y. 235, 241, 72 N.E. 97, 99 (1904)).

JUSTICE O'CONNOR assures the people of Nebraska they are free to redraft the law to include an exception permitting the D&X to be performed when "the procedure, in appropriate medical judgment, is necessary to preserve the health of the mother." *Ante,* at 5. The assurance is meaningless. She has joined an opinion which accepts that Dr. Carhart exercises "appropriate medical judgment" in using the D&X for every patient in every procedure, regardless of indications, after 15 weeks' gestation. *Ante,* at 18–19 (requiring any health exception to "tolerate responsible differences of medical opinion" which "are present here"). A ban which depends on the "appropriate medical judgment" of Dr. Carhart is no ban at all. He will be unaffected by any new legislation. This, of course, is the vice of a health exception resting in the physician's discretion. . . .

The term "partial birth abortion" means an abortion performed using the D&X method as described above. The Court of Appeals acknowledged the term "is commonly understood to refer to a particular procedure known as intact dilation and extraction (D&X)." *Little Rock Family Planning Servs.* v. *Jegley,* 192 F.3d 794, 795 (CA8 1999). Dr. Carhart's own lead expert, Dr. Phillip Stubblefield, prefaced his description of the D&X procedure by describing it as the procedure "which, in the lay press, has been called a partial birth abortion." App. 271–272. And the AMA has declared: "The 'partial birth abortion' legislation is by its very name aimed exclusively [at the D&X.] There is no other abortion procedure which could be confused with that description." AMA Factsheet 3. A commonsense understanding of the statute's reference to "partial-birth abortion" demonstrates its intended reach and provides all citizens the fair warning required by the law. *McBoyle* v. *United States,* 283 U.S. 25, 27 (1931).

The statute's intended scope is demonstrated by its requirement that the banned procedure include a partial "delivery" of the fetus into the vagina and the completion of a "delivery" at the end of the procedure. Only removal of an intact fetus can be described as a "delivery" of a fetus and only the D&X involves an intact fetus. In a D&E, portions of the fetus are pulled into the vagina with the intention of dismembering the fetus by using the traction at the opening between the uterus and vagina. This cannot be considered a delivery of a portion of a fetus. In Dr. Carhart's own words, the D&E leaves the abortionist with a "tray full of pieces," App. 125, at the end of the procedure. Even if it could be argued, as the majority does, *ante,* at 25–26, that dragging a portion of an intact fetus into the vagina as the first step of a D&E is a delivery of that portion of an intact fetus, the D&E still does not involve "completing the delivery" of an intact fetus. Whatever the statutory term "completing the delivery" of an unborn child means, it cannot mean, as the Court would have it, placing fetal remains on a tray. See *Planned Parenthood of Wis.* v. *Doyle,* 9 F. Supp. 2d 1033, 1041 (WD Wis. 1998) (the statute is "readily applied to the partial delivery of an intact child but hardly applicable to the delivery of dismembered body parts").

Medical descriptions of the abortion procedures confirm the point, for it is only the description of the D&X that invokes the word "delivery." App. 600. The United States, as *amicus,* cannot bring itself to describe the D&E as involving a "delivery," instead substituting the word "emerges" to describe how the fetus is brought into the vagina in a D&E. Brief for United States as *Amicus Curiae* 10. The Court, in a similar admission, uses the words "a physician pulling" a portion of a fetus, *ante,* at 20, rather than a "physician delivering" a portion of a fetus; yet only a procedure involving a delivery is banned by the law. Of all the definitions of "delivery" provided by the Court, *ante,* at 25–26, not one supports (or, more important for statutory construction purposes, requires) the conclusion that the statutory term "completing the delivery" refers to the placement of dismembered body parts on a tray rather than the removal of an intact fetus from the woman's body. . . .

In light of the statutory text, the commonsense understanding must be that the statute covers only the D&X. See *Broadrick* v. *Oklahoma,* 413 U.S. 601, 698 (1973). The AMA does not disagree. It writes: "The partial birth abortion legislation is by its very name aimed exclusively at a procedure by which a living fetus is intentionally and deliberately given partial birth and delivered for the purpose of killing it. There is no other abortion procedure which could be confused with that description." AMA Factsheet 3 (internal quotation marks omitted). *Casey* disavows strict scrutiny review; and Nebraska must be afforded leeway when attempting to regulate the medical profession. See *Kansas* v. *Hendricks*, 521 U.S., at 359 ("[W]e have traditionally left to legislators the task of defining terms of a medical nature that have legal significance"). To hold that the statute covers the D&E, the Court must disagree with the AMA and disregard the known intent of the legislature, adequately expressed in the statute. . . .

JUSTICE THOMAS, with whom THE CHIEF JUSTICE and JUSTICE SCALIA join, dissenting.

. . . My views on the merits of the *Casey* joint opinion have been fully articulated by others. *Id.*, at 944 (REHNQUIST, C. J., concurring in judgment in part and dissenting in part); *id.*, at 979 (SCALIA, J., concurring in judgment in part and dissenting in part). I will not restate those views here, except to note that the *Casey* joint opinion was constructed by its authors out of whole cloth. The standard set forth in the *Casey* joint opinion has no historical or doctrinal pedigree. The standard is a product of its authors' own philosophical views about abortion, and it should go without saying that it has no origins in or relationship to the Constitution and is, consequently, as illegitimate as the standard it purported to replace. Even assuming, however, as I will for the remainder of this dissent, that *Casey*'s fabricated undue burden standard merits adherence (which it does not), today's decision is extraordinary. Today, the Court inexplicably holds that the States cannot constitutionally prohibit a method of abortion that millions find hard to distinguish from infanticide and that the Court hesitates even to describe. *Ante*, at 4. This holding cannot be reconciled with *Casey*'s undue burden standard, as that standard was explained to us by the authors of the joint opinion, and the majority hardly pretends otherwise. In striking down this statute—which expresses a profound and legitimate respect for fetal life and which leaves unimpeded several other safe forms of abortion—the majority opinion gives the lie to the promise of *Casey* that regulations that do no more than "express profound respect for the life of the unborn are permitted, if they are not a substantial obstacle to the woman's exercise of the right to choose" whether or not to have an abortion. 505 U.S., at 877. Today's decision is so obviously irreconcilable with *Casey*'s explication of what its undue burden standard requires, let alone the Constitution, that it should be seen for what it is, a reinstitution of the pre-*Webster* abortion-on-demand era in which the mere invocation of "abortion rights" trumps any contrary societal interest. If this statute is unconstitutional under *Casey*, then *Casey* meant nothing at all, and the Court should candidly admit it. . . .

Nebraska, along with 29 other States, has attempted to ban the partial birth abortion procedure. Although the Nebraska statute purports to prohibit only "partial birth abortion," a phrase which is commonly used, as I mentioned, to refer to the breech extraction version of intact D&E, the majority concludes that this statute could also be read in some future case to prohibit ordinary D&E, the first procedure described above. According to the majority, such an application would pose a substantial obstacle to some women seeking abortions and, therefore, the statute is unconstitutional. . . .

Starting with the statutory definition of "partial birth abortion," I think it highly doubtful that the statute could be applied to ordinary D&E. First, the Nebraska statute applies only if the physician "partially delivers vaginally a living unborn child," which phrase is defined to mean "deliberately and intentionally delivering into the vagina a living unborn child, or a substantial portion thereof." § 28–326(9). When read in context, the term "partially delivers" cannot be fairly interpreted to include removing pieces of an unborn child from the uterus one at a time.

The word "deliver," particularly delivery of an "unborn child," refers to the process of "assist[ing] in giving birth," which suggests removing an intact unborn child from the womb, rather than pieces of a child. [Citations omitted.] The majority has pointed to no source in which "delivery" is used to refer to removal of first a fetal arm, then a leg, then the torso, etc. In fact, even the majority describes the D&E procedure without using the word "deliver" to refer to the removal of fetal tissue from the uterus. See *ante*, at 20 ("pulling a 'substantial portion' of a still living fetus"); *ibid.* ("portion of a living fetus has been pulled into the vagina"). No one, including the majority, understands the act of pulling off a part of a fetus to be a "delivery."

To make the statute's meaning even more clear, the statute applies only if the physician "partially delivers vaginally a living unborn child before killing the unborn child and completing the delivery." The statute defines this phrase to mean that the physician must complete the delivery "for the purpose of performing a procedure" that will kill the unborn child. It is clear from these phrases that the procedure that kills the fetus must be subsequent to, and therefore separate from, the "partia[l] deliver[y]" or the "deliver[y] into the vagina" of "a living unborn child or substantial portion thereof." In other words, even if one assumes, *arguendo*, that dismemberment—the act of grasping a fetal arm or leg and pulling until it comes off, leaving the remaining part of the fetal body still in the uterus—is a kind of "delivery," it does not take place "before" the death-causing procedure or "for the purpose of performing" the death-causing procedure; it is the death-causing procedure. Under the majority's view, D&E is covered by the statute because when the doctor pulls on a fetal foot until it tears off he has "delivered" a substantial portion of the unborn child and has performed a procedure known to cause death. But, significantly, the physician has not "delivered" the child before performing the death-causing procedure or "for the purpose of" performing the death-causing procedure; the dismemberment "delivery" is itself the act that causes the fetus' death.

Moreover, even if removal of a fetal foot or arm from the uterus incidental to severing it from the rest of the fetal body could amount to delivery before, or for the purpose of, performing a death-causing procedure, the delivery would not be of an "unborn child, or a substantial portion thereof." And even supposing that a fetal foot or arm could conceivably be a "substantial portion" of an unborn child, both the common understanding of "partial birth abortion" and the principle that statutes will be interpreted to avoid constitutional difficulties would require one to read "substantial" otherwise....

Were there any doubt remaining whether the statute could apply to a D&E procedure, that doubt is no ground for invalidating the statute. Rather, we are bound to first consider whether a construction of the statute is fairly possible that would avoid the constitutional question. *Erznoznik* v. *Jacksonville*, 422 U.S. 205, 216 (1975) ("[A] state statute should not be deemed facially invalid unless it is not readily subject to a narrowing construction by the state courts"); *Frisby* v. *Schultz*, 487 U.S. 474, 482 (1988) ("The precise scope of the ban is not further described within the text of the ordinance, but in our view the ordinance is readily subject to a narrowing construction that avoids constitutional difficulties"). This principle is, as JUSTICE O'CONNOR has said, so "well-established" that failure to apply is "plain error." *Id.*, at 483. Although our interpretation of a Nebraska law is of course not binding on Nebraska courts, it is clear, as *Erznoznik* and *Frisby* demonstrate, that, absent a conflicting interpretation by Nebraska (and there is none here), we should, if the text permits, adopt such a construction.

The majority contends that application of the Nebraska statute to D&E would pose constitutional difficulties because it would eliminate the most common form of second-trimester abortions. To the extent that the majority's contention is true, there is no doubt that the Nebraska statute is susceptible of a narrowing construction by Nebraska courts that would preserve a physicians' ability to perform D&E. See *State* v. *Carpenter*, 250 Neb. 427, 434, 551 N. W. 2d 518, 524 (1996) ("A penal statute must be construed so as to meet constitutional requirements if such can reasonably be done"). For example, the statute requires that the physician "deliberately and intentionally delive[r] into the vagina a living unborn child, or a substantial portion thereof" before performing a death-causing procedure. The term "substantial portion" is susceptible to a narrowing construction that would exclude the D&E procedure. One definition of the word "substantial" is "being largely but not wholly that which is specified." Webster's Ninth New Collegiate Dictionary, at 1176. See *Pierce* v. *Underwood*, 487 U.S. 552, 564 (1988) (describing different meanings of the term "substantial"). In other words, "substantial" can mean "almost all" of the thing denominated. If nothing else, a court could construe the statute to require that the fetus be "largely, but not wholly," delivered out of the uterus before the physician performs a procedure that he knows will kill the unborn child. Or, as I have discussed, a court could (and should) construe "for the purpose of performing a procedure" to mean "for the purpose of performing a separate procedure." . . .

Having resolved that Nebraska's partial birth abortion statute permits doctors to perform D&E abortions, the question remains whether a State can constitutionally prohibit the partial birth abortion procedure without a health exception. Although the majority and JUSTICE O'CONNOR purport to rely on the standard articulated in the *Casey* joint opinion in concluding that a State may not, they in fact disregard it entirely....

Though JUSTICES O'CONNOR, KENNEDY, and SOUTER declined in *Casey*, on the ground of *stare decisis*, to reconsider whether abortion enjoys any constitutional protection,

505 U.S., at 844–846, 854–869 (majority opinion); *id.*, at 871 (joint opinion), *Casey* professed to be, in part, a repudiation of *Roe* and its progeny. The *Casey* joint opinion expressly noted that prior case law had undervalued the State's interest in potential life, 505 U.S., at 875–876, and had invalidated regulations of abortion that "in no real sense deprived women of the ultimate decision," *id.*, at 875. See *id.*, at 871 ("*Roe* v. *Wade* speaks with clarity in establishing . . . the State's 'important and legitimate interest in potential life.' That portion of the decision in *Roe* has been given too little acknowledgment" (citation omitted)). The joint opinion repeatedly recognized the States' weighty interest in this area. See *id.*, at 877 ("State . . . may express profound respect for the life of the unborn"); *id.*, at 878 ("the State's profound interest in potential life"); *id.*, at 850 (majority opinion) ("profound moral and spiritual implications of terminating a pregnancy, even in its earliest stage"). And, the joint opinion expressed repeatedly the States' legitimate role in regulating abortion procedures. See *id.*, at 876 ("The very notion that the State has a substantial interest in potential life leads to the conclusion that not all regulations must be deemed unwarranted"); *id.*, at 875 ("Not all governmental intrusion [with abortion] is of necessity unwarranted"). According to the joint opinion, "The fact that a law which serves a valid purpose, one not designed to strike at the right itself, has the incidental effect of making it more difficult or more expensive to procure an abortion cannot be enough to invalidate it." *Id.*, at 874. . . .

There is no question that the State of Nebraska has a valid interest—one not designed to strike at the right itself—in prohibiting partial birth abortion. *Casey* itself noted that States may "express profound respect for the life of the unborn." *Ibid.* States may, without a doubt, express this profound respect by prohibiting a procedure that approaches infanticide, and thereby dehumanizes the fetus and trivializes human life. The AMA has recognized that this procedure is "ethically different from other destructive abortion techniques because the fetus, normally twenty weeks or longer in gestation, is killed outside the womb. The 'partial birth' gives the fetus an autonomy which separates it from the right of the woman to choose treatments for her own body." AMA Board of Trustees Factsheet on H. R. 1122 (June 1997), in App. to Brief for Association of American Physicians and Surgeons et al. as *Amici Curiae* 1. Thirty States have concurred with this view.

Although the description of this procedure set forth above should be sufficient to demonstrate the resemblance between the partial birth abortion procedure and infanticide, the testimony of one nurse who observed a partial birth abortion procedure makes the point even more vividly:

"The baby's little fingers were clasping and unclasping, and his little feet were kicking. Then the doctor stuck the scissors in the back of his head, and the baby's arms jerked out, like a startle reaction, like a flinch, like a baby does when he thinks he is going to fall.

"The doctor opened up the scissors, stuck a high-powered suction tube into the opening, and sucked the baby's brains out. Now the baby went completely limp." H. R. 1833 Hearing 18 (statement of Brenda Pratt Shafer).

The question whether States have a legitimate interest in banning the procedure does not require additional authority. See *ante*, at 6–9 (KENNEDY, J., dissenting). In a civilized society, the answer is too obvious, and the contrary arguments too offensive to merit further discussion. . . .

The *Casey* joint opinion makes clear that the Court should not strike down State regulations of abortion based on the fact that some women might face a marginally higher health risk from the regulation. In *Casey*, the Court upheld a 24-hour waiting period even though the Court credited evidence that for some women the delay would, in practice, be much longer than 24 hours, and even though it was undisputed that any delay in obtaining an abortion would impose additional health risks. *Id.*, at 887; *id.*, at 937 (Blackmun, J., concurring in part, concurring in judgment in part, and dissenting in part) ("The District Court found that the mandatory 24-hour delay could lead to delays in excess of 24 hours, thus increasing health risks"). Although some women would be able to avoid the waiting period because of a "medical emergency," the medical emergency exception in the statute was limited to those women for whom delay would create "serious risk of substantial and irreversible impairment of a major bodily function." *Id.*, at 902 (internal quotation marks omitted). Without question, there were women for whom the regulation would impose some additional health risk who would not fall within the medical emergency exception. The Court concluded, despite the certainty of this increased risk, that there was no showing that the burden on any of the women was substantial. *Id.*, at 887. . . .

Like the *Casey* 24-hour waiting period, and in contrast to the situation in *Danforth*, any increased health risk to women imposed by the partial birth abortion ban is minimal at most. Of the 5.5 percent of abortions that occur after 15 weeks (the time after which a partial birth abortion would be possible), the vast majority are performed with a D&E or induction procedure. And, for any woman with a vertex presentation fetus, the vertex presentation form of intact D&E, which presumably shares some of the health benefits of the partial birth abortion procedure but is not covered by the Nebraska statute, is available. Of the remaining women—that is, those women for whom a partial birth abortion procedure would be considered and who have a breech presentation fetus—there is no showing that any one faces a significant health risk from the partial birth abortion ban. A select committee of ACOG "could identify no circumstances under which this procedure . . . would be the only option to save the life or preserve the health of the woman." App. 600 (ACOG Executive Board, Statement on Intact Dilation and Extraction (Jan. 12, 1997)). See also *Hope Clinic* v. *Ryan*, 195 F.3d 857, 872 (CA7 1999) (en banc) ("'There does not appear to be any identified situation in which intact D&X is the only appropriate procedure to induce abortion'" (quoting Late Term Pregnancy Techniques, AMA Policy H–5.982 W. D. Wis. 1999)); *Planned Parenthood of Wis.* v. *Doyle*, 44 F. Supp. 2d, at 980 (citing testimony of Dr. Haskell that "the D&X procedure is never medically necessary to . . . preserve the health of a woman"), vacated, 195 F.3d 857 (CA7 1999). And, an ad hoc coalition of doctors, including former Surgeon General Koop, concluded that there are no medical conditions that require use of the partial birth abortion procedure to preserve the mother's health. See App. 719.

In fact, there was evidence before the Nebraska legislature that partial birth abortion increases health risks relative to other procedures. During floor debates, a proponent of the Nebraska legislation read from and cited several articles by physicians concluding that partial birth abortion procedures are risky. App. in Nos. 98–3245, 98–3300 (CA8), p. 812. One doctor testifying before a committee of the Nebraska legislature stated that partial birth abortion involves three "very risky procedures": dilation of the cervix, using instruments blindly, and conversion of the fetus. App. 721 (quoting testimony of Paul Hays, M. D.).

There was also evidence before Congress that partial birth abortion "does not meet medical standards set by ACOG nor has it been adequately proven to be safe nor efficacious." H. R. 1833 Hearing 112 (statement of Nancy G. Romer, M. D.); see *id.*, at 110–111.23. The AMA supported the congressional ban on partial birth abortion, concluding that the procedure is "not medically indicated" and "not good medicine." See 143 Cong. Rec. S4670 (May 19, 1997) (reprinting a letter from the AMA to Sen. Santorum). And there was evidence before Congress that there is "certainly no basis upon which to state the claim that [partial birth abortion] is a safer or even a preferred procedure." Partial Birth Abortion: The Truth, S. 6 and H. R. 929 Joint Hearing 123 (statement of Curtis Cook, M. D.). This same doctor testified that "partial-birth abortion is an unnecessary, unsteady, and potentially dangerous procedure," and that "safe alternatives are in existence." *Id.*, at 122.

The majority justifies its result by asserting that a "significant body of medical opinion" supports the view that partial birth abortion may be a safer abortion procedure. *Ante*, at 19. I find this assertion puzzling. If there is a "significant body of medical opinion" supporting this procedure, no one in the majority has identified it. In fact, it is uncontested that although this procedure has been used since at least 1992, no formal studies have compared partial birth abortion with other procedures. . . . The majority's conclusion makes sense only if the undue burden standard is not whether a "significant body of medical opinion," supports the result, but rather, as JUSTICE GINSBURG candidly admits, whether any doctor could reasonably believe that the partial birth abortion procedure would best protect the woman. *Ante*, at 2.

Moreover, even if I were to assume credible evidence on both sides of the debate, that fact should resolve the undue burden question in favor of allowing Nebraska to legislate. Where no one knows whether a regulation of abortion poses any burden at all, the burden surely does not amount to a "substantial obstacle." Under *Casey*, in such a case we should defer to the legislative judgment. We have said: "[I]t is precisely where such disagreement exists that legislatures have been afforded the widest latitude in drafting such statutes. . . . [W]hen a legislature undertakes to act in areas fraught with medical and scientific uncertainty, legislative options must be especially broad. . . ." *Kansas* v. *Hendricks*, 521 U.S., at 360, n. 3 (internal quotation marks omitted). In JUSTICE O'CONNOR's words: "It is . . . difficult to believe that this Court, without the resources available to those bodies entrusted with making legislative choices, believes itself competent to make these inquiries and to revise these standards every time the American College of Obstetricians and Gynecologists (ACOG) or similar group revises its views about what is and what is not appropriate medical procedure in this area." *Akron* v. *Akron Center for Reproductive Health, Inc.*, 462 U.S., at 456 (dissenting opinion). . . . We were reassured repeatedly in *Casey* that not all regulations of abortion are unwarranted and that the States may express profound respect for fetal life. Under *Casey*, the regulation before us today should easily pass constitutional muster. But the Court's abortion jurisprudence is a particularly virulent strain of constitutional exegesis. And so today we are told that 30 States are prohibited from banning one rarely used form of abortion that they believe to border on infanticide. It is clear that the Constitution does not compel this result.

I respectfully dissent.

JUSTICE SCALIA, dissenting.

I am optimistic enough to believe that, one day, *Stenberg* v. *Carhart* will be assigned its rightful place in the history of this Court's jurisprudence beside *Korematsu* and *Dred Scott*. The method of killing a human child—one cannot even accurately say an entirely unborn human child—proscribed by this statute is so horrible that the most clinical description of it evokes a shudder of revulsion. And the Court must know (as most state legislatures banning this procedure have concluded) that demanding a "health exception"—which requires the abortionist to assure himself that, in his expert medical judgment, this method is, in the case at hand, marginally safer than others (how can one prove the contrary beyond a reasonable doubt?)—is to give live-birth abortion free rein. The notion that the Constitution of the United States, designed, among other things, "to establish Justice, insure domestic Tranquility, . . . and secure the Blessings of Liberty to ourselves and our Posterity," prohibits the States from simply banning this visibly brutal means of eliminating our half-born posterity is quite simply absurd.

The two lengthy dissents in this case have, appropriately enough, set out to establish that today's result does not follow from this Court's most recent pronouncement on the matter of abortion, *Planned Parenthood of Southeastern Pa.* v. *Casey*, 505 U.S. 833 (1992). It would be unfortunate, however, if those who disagree with the result were induced to regard it as merely a regrettable misapplication of *Casey*. It is not that, but is *Casey*'s logical and entirely predictable consequence. To be sure, the Court's construction of this statute so as to make it include procedures other than live-birth abortion involves not only a disregard of fair meaning, but an abandonment of the principle that even ambiguous statutes should be interpreted in such fashion as to render them valid rather than void. *Casey* does not permit that jurisprudential novelty—which must be chalked up to the Court's inclination to bend the rules when any effort to limit abortion, or even to speak in opposition to abortion, is at issue. It is of a piece, in other words, with *Hill* v. *Colorado*, also decided today.

But the Court gives a second and independent reason for invalidating this humane (not to say anti-barbarian) law: That it fails to allow an exception for the situation in which the abortionist believes that this live-birth method of destroying the child might be safer for the woman. (As pointed out by JUSTICE THOMAS, and elaborated upon by JUSTICE KENNEDY, there is no good reason to believe this is ever the case, but—who knows?—it sometime might be.)

I have joined JUSTICE THOMAS's dissent because I agree that today's decision is an "unprecedented expansio[n]" of our prior cases, *post*, at 35, "is not mandated" by *Casey*'s "undue burden" test, *post*, at 33, and can even be called (though this pushes me to the limit of my belief) "obviously irreconcilable with *Casey*'s explication of what its undue-burden standard requires," *post*, at 4. But I never put much stock in *Casey*'s explication of the inexplicable. In the last analysis, my judgment that *Casey* does not support today's tragic result can be traced to the fact that what I consider to be an "undue burden" is different from what the majority considers to be an "undue burden"—a conclusion that cannot be demonstrated true or false by factual inquiry or legal reasoning. It is a value judgment, dependent upon how much one respects (or believes society ought to respect) the life of a partially delivered fetus, and how much one respects (or believes society ought to respect) the freedom of the woman who gave it life to kill it. Evidently, the five Justices in today's majority value the former less, or the latter more, (or both), than the four of us in dissent. Case closed. There is no cause for anyone who believes in *Casey* to feel betrayed by this outcome. It has been arrived at by precisely the process *Casey* promised—a democratic vote by nine lawyers, not on the question whether the text of the Constitution has anything to say about this subject (it obviously does not); nor even on the question (also appropriate for lawyers) whether the legal traditions of the American people would have sustained such a limitation upon abortion (they obviously would); but upon the pure policy question whether this limitation upon abortion is "undue"—*i.e.*, goes too far.

In my dissent in *Casey*, I wrote that the "undue burden" test made law by the joint opinion created a standard that was "as doubtful in application as it is unprincipled in origin," *Casey*, 505 U.S., at 985; "hopelessly unworkable in practice," *id.*, at 986; "ultimately standardless," *id.*, at 987. Today's decision is the proof. As long as we are debating this issue of necessity for a health-of-the-mother exception on the basis of *Casey*, it is really quite impossible for us dissenters to contend that the majority is wrong on the law—any more than it could be said that one is wrong in law to support or oppose the death penalty, or to support or oppose mandatory minimum sentences. The most that we can honestly say is that we disagree with the majority on their policy-judgment-couched-as-law. And those who believe that a 5-to-4 vote on a policy matter by unelected lawyers should not overcome the judgment of 30 state legislatures have a problem, not with the *application* of *Casey*, but with its *existence*. *Casey* must be overruled.

While I am in an I-told-you-so mood, I must recall my bemusement, in *Casey*, at the joint opinion's expressed belief that *Roe* v. *Wade* had "call[ed] the contending sides of a national controversy to end their national division by accepting a common mandate rooted in the Constitution," *Casey*, 505 U.S., at 867, and that the decision in *Casey* would ratify that happy truce. It seemed to me, quite to the contrary, that "*Roe* fanned into life an issue that has inflamed our national politics in general, and has obscured with its smoke the selection of Justices to this Court in particular, ever since"; and that, "by keeping us in the abortion-umpiring business, it is the perpetuation of that disruption, rather than of any *Pax Roeana*, that the Court's new majority decrees." *Id.*, at 995–996. Today's decision, that the Constitution of the United States prevents the prohibition of a horrible mode of abortion, will be greeted by a firestorm of criticism—as well it should. . . . [T]he Court should return this matter to the people—where the Constitution, by its silence on the subject, left it—and let them decide, State by State, whether this practice should be allowed. *Casey* must be overruled.

ALBERTO R. GONZALES, ATTORNEY GENERAL, PETITIONER *v.* LEROY CARHART ET AL.

ON WRIT OF CERTIORARI TO THE UNITED STATES COURT OF APPEALS FOR THE EIGHTH CIRCUIT

ALBERTO R. GONZALES, ATTORNEY GENERAL, PETITIONER *v.* PLANNED PARENTHOOD FEDERATION OF AMERICA, INC., ET AL.

ON WRIT OF CERTIORARI TO THE UNITED STATES COURT OF APPEALS FOR THE NINTH CIRCUIT

Nos. 05–380, 05–1382. Argued November 8, 2006—Decided April 18, 2007

KENNEDY, J., delivered the opinion of the Court, in which ROBERTS, C. J., and SCALIA, THOMAS, and ALITO, JJ., joined. THOMAS, J., filed a concurring opinion, in which SCALIA, J., joined. GINSBURG, J., filed a dissenting opinion, in which STEVENS, SOUTER, and BREYER, JJ., joined.

KENNEDY, J., delivered the opinion of the Court.

These cases require us to consider the validity of the Partial-Birth Abortion Ban Act of 2003 (Act), 18 U.S.C. §1531 (2000 ed., Supp. IV), a federal statute regulating abortion procedures. In recitations preceding its operative provisions the Act refers to the Court's opinion in *Stenberg* v. *Carhart*, 530 U.S. 914 (2000), which also addressed the subject of abortion procedures used in the later stages of pregnancy. Compared to the state statute at issue in *Stenberg*, the Act is more specific concerning the instances to which it applies and in this respect more precise in its coverage. We conclude the Act should be sustained against the objections lodged by the broad, facial attack brought against it. . . .

I

B

In 2003, after this Court's decision in *Stenberg*, Congress passed the Act at issue here. H. R. Rep. No. 108–58, at 12–14. On November 5, 2003, President Bush signed the Act into law. It was to take effect the following day. 18 U.S.C. §1531(a) (2000 ed., Supp. IV).

The Act responded to *Stenberg* in two ways. First, Congress made factual findings. Congress determined that this Court in *Stenberg* "was required to accept the very questionable findings issued by the district court judge," §2(7), 117 Stat. 1202, notes following 18 U.S.C. §1531 (2000 ed., Supp. IV), p. 768, ¶(7) (Congressional Findings), but that Congress was "not bound to accept the same factual findings," *ibid.*, ¶(8)....

Second, and more relevant here, the Act's language differs from that of the Nebraska statute struck down in *Stenberg*. See 530 U.S., at 921–922 (quoting Neb. Rev. Stat. Ann. §§28–328(1), 28–326(9) (Supp. 1999)). The operative provisions of the Act provide in relevant part:

"(a) Any physician who, in or affecting interstate or foreign commerce, knowingly performs a partial-birth abortion and thereby kills a human fetus shall be fined under this title or imprisoned not more than 2 years, or both. This subsection does not apply to a partial-birth abortion that is necessary to save the life of a mother whose life is endangered by a physical disorder, physical illness, or physical injury, including a life-endangering physical condition caused by or arising from the pregnancy itself. This sub-section takes effect 1 day after the enactment.
"(b) As used in this section—
"(1) the term 'partial-birth abortion' means an abortion in which the person performing the abortion—
"(A) deliberately and intentionally vaginally delivers a living fetus until, in the case of a head-first presentation, the entire fetal head is outside the body of the mother, or, in the case of breech presentation, any part of the fetal trunk past the navel is outside the body of the mother, for the purpose of performing an overt act that the person knows will kill the partially delivered living fetus; and
"(B) performs the overt act, other than completion of delivery, that kills the partially delivered living fetus; . . ."

C

The District Court in *Carhart* concluded the Act was unconstitutional for two reasons. First, it determined the Act was unconstitutional because it lacked an exception allowing the procedure where necessary for the health of the mother. 331 F. Supp. 2d, at 1004–1030. Second, the District Court found the Act deficient because it covered not merely intact D&E but also certain other D&Es. *Id.*, at 1030–1037.

The Court of Appeals for the Eighth Circuit addressed only the lack of a health exception. 413 F. 3d, at 803–804. The court began its analysis with what it saw as the appropriate question—"whether 'substantial medical authority' supports the medical necessity of the banned procedure." *Id.*, at 796 (quoting *Stenberg*, 530 U.S., at 938). This was the proper framework, according to the Court of Appeals, because "when a lack of consensus exists in the medical community, the Constitution requires legislatures to err on the side of protecting women's health by including a health exception." 413 F. 3d, at 796. The court rejected the Attorney General's attempt to demonstrate changed evidentiary circumstances since *Stenberg* and considered itself bound by *Stenberg*'s conclusion that a health exception was required. 413 F. 3d, at 803 (explaining "[t]he record in [the] case and the record in *Stenberg* [were] similar in all significant respects"). It invalidated the Act. *Ibid*. . . .

II

The principles set forth in the joint opinion in *Planned Parenthood of Southeastern Pa.* v. *Casey*, 505 U.S. 833 (1992), did not find support from all those who join the instant opinion. See *id.*, at 979–1002 (SCALIA, J., joined by THOMAS, J., *inter alios*, concurring in judgment in part and dissenting in part). Whatever one's views concerning the *Casey* joint opinion, it is evident a premise central to its conclusion—that the government has a legitimate and substantial interest in preserving and promoting fetal life—would be repudiated were the Court now to affirm the judgments of the Courts of Appeals. . . . We assume the following principles for the purposes of this opinion. Before viability, a State "may not prohibit any woman from making the ultimate decision to terminate her pregnancy." 505 U.S., at 879 (plurality opinion). It also may not impose upon this right an undue burden, which exists if a regulation's "purpose or effect is to place a substantial obstacle in the path of a woman seeking an abortion before the fetus attains viability." *Id.*, at 878. On the other hand, "[r]egulations which do no more than create a structural mechanism by which the State, or the parent or guardian of a minor, may express profound respect for the life of the unborn are permitted, if they are not a substantial obstacle to the woman's exercise of the right to choose." *Id.*, at 877. *Casey*, in short, struck a balance. The balance was central to its holding. We now apply its standard to the cases at bar. . . .

III

B

Respondents contend the language described above is indeterminate, and they thus argue the Act is unconstitutionally vague on its face. "As generally stated, the void-for-vagueness doctrine requires that a penal statute define the criminal offense with sufficient definiteness that ordinary people can understand what conduct is prohibited and in a manner that does not encourage arbitrary and discriminatory enforcement." *Kolender* v. *Lawson*, 461 U.S. 352, 357 (1983); *Posters 'N' Things, Ltd.* v. *United States*, 511 U.S. 513, 525 (1994). The Act satisfies both requirements.

The Act provides doctors "of ordinary intelligence a reasonable opportunity to know what is prohibited." *Grayned* v. *City of Rockford*, 408 U.S. 104, 108 (1972). Indeed, it sets forth "relatively clear guidelines as to prohibited conduct" and provides "objective criteria" to evaluate whether a doctor has performed a prohibited procedure. *Posters 'N' Things, supra*, at 525–526. Unlike the statutory language in *Stenberg* that prohibited the delivery of a "'substantial portion'" of the fetus—where a doctor might question how much of the fetus is a substantial portion—the Act defines the line between potentially criminal conduct on the one hand and lawful abortion on the other. *Stenberg*, 530 U.S., at 922 (quoting Neb. Rev. Stat. Ann. §28–326(9) (Supp. 1999)). Doctors performing D&E will know that if they do not deliver a living fetus to an anatomical landmark they will not face criminal liability.

This conclusion is buttressed by the intent that must be proved to impose liability. The Court has made clear that scienter requirements alleviate vagueness concerns. *Posters 'N' Things, supra*, at 526; see also *Colautti* v. *Franklin*, 439 U.S. 379, 395 (1979) ("This Court has long recognized that the constitutionality of a vague statutory standard is closely related to whether that standard incorporates a requirement of *mens rea*"). The Act requires the doctor deliberately to have delivered the fetus to an anatomical landmark. §1531(b)(1)(A) (2000 ed., Supp. IV). Because a doctor performing a D&E will not face criminal liability if he or she delivers a fetus beyond the prohibited point by mistake, the Act cannot be described as "a trap for those who act in good faith." *Colautti, supra*, at 395 (internal quotation marks omitted). . . .

C

We next determine whether the Act imposes an undue burden, as a facial matter, because its restrictions on second-trimester abortions are too broad. A review of the statutory text discloses the limits of its reach. The Act prohibits intact D&E; and, notwithstanding respondents' arguments, it does not prohibit the D&E procedure in which the fetus is removed in parts. . . .

1

The canon of constitutional avoidance, finally, extinguishes any lingering doubt as to whether the Act covers the prototypical D&E procedure. "'[T]he elementary rule is that every reasonable construction must be resorted to, in order to save a statute from unconstitutionality.'" *Edward J. DeBartolo Corp.* v. *Florida Gulf Coast Building & Constr. Trades Council*, 485 U.S. 568, 575 (1988) (quoting *Hooper* v. *California*, 155 U.S. 648, 657 (1895)). It is true this long-standing maxim of statutory interpretation has, in the past, fallen by the wayside when the Court confronted a statute regulating abortion. The Court at times employed an antagonistic "'canon of construction under which in cases involving abortion, a permissible reading of a statute [was] to be avoided at all costs.'" *Stenberg, supra*, at 977 (KENNEDY, J., dissenting) (quoting *Thornburgh*, 476 U.S., at 829 (O'CONNOR, J., dissenting)). *Casey* put this novel statutory approach to rest. *Stenberg, supra*, at 977 (KENNEDY, J., dissenting). *Stenberg* need not be interpreted to have revived it. We read that decision instead to stand for the uncontroversial proposition that the canon of constitutional avoidance does not apply if a statute is not "genuinely susceptible to two constructions." *Almendarez-Torres* v. *United States*, 523 U.S. 224, 238 (1998); see also *Clark* v. *Martinez*, 543 U.S. 371, 385 (2005). In *Stenberg* the Court found the statute covered D&E. 530 U.S., at 938–945. Here, by contrast, interpreting the Act so that it does not prohibit standard D&E is the most reasonable reading and understanding of its terms. . . .

IV

A

The Act's purposes are set forth in recitals preceding its operative provisions. A description of the prohibited abortion procedure demonstrates the rationale for the congressional enactment. The Act proscribes a method of abortion in which a fetus is killed just inches before completion of the birth process. Congress stated as follows: "Implicitly approving such a brutal and inhumane procedure by choosing not to prohibit it will further coarsen society to the humanity of not only newborns, but all vulnerable and innocent human life, making it increasingly difficult to protect such life." Congressional Findings (14)(N), in notes following 18 U.S.C. §1531 (2000 ed., Supp. IV), p. 769. The Act expresses respect for the dignity of human life.

Congress was concerned, furthermore, with the effects on the medical community and on its reputation caused by the practice of partial-birth abortion. The findings in the Act explain:

> "Partial-birth abortion . . . confuses the medical, legal, and ethical duties of physicians to preserve and promote life, as the physician acts directly against the physical life of a child, whom he or she had just delivered, all but the head, out of the womb, in order to end that life." Congressional Findings (14)(J), *ibid.*

There can be no doubt the government "has an interest in protecting the integrity and ethics of the medical profession." *Washington* v. *Glucksberg*, 521 U.S. 702, 731 (1997); see also *Barsky* v. *Board of Regents of Univ. of N. Y.*, 347 U.S. 442, 451 (1954) (indicating the State has "legitimate concern for maintaining high standards of professional conduct" in the practice of medicine). Under our precedents it is clear the State has a significant role to play in regulating the medical profession. . . .

The Act's ban on abortions that involve partial delivery of a living fetus furthers the Government's objectives. No one would dispute that, for many, D&E is a procedure itself laden with the power to devalue human life. Congress could nonetheless conclude that the type of abortion proscribed by the Act requires specific regulation because it implicates additional ethical and moral concerns that justify a special prohibition. Congress determined that the abortion methods it proscribed had a "disturbing similarity to the killing of a newborn infant," Congressional Findings (14)(L), in notes following 18 U.S.C. §1531 (2000 ed., Supp. IV), p. 769, and thus it was concerned with "draw[ing] a bright line that clearly distinguishes abortion and infanticide." Congressional Findings (14)(G), *ibid.* The Court has in the past confirmed the validity of drawing boundaries to prevent certain practices that extinguish life and are close to actions that are condemned. *Glucksberg* found reasonable the State's "fear that permitting assisted suicide will start it down the path to voluntary and perhaps even involuntary euthanasia." 521 U.S., at 732–735, and n. 23. . . .

It is objected that the standard D&E is in some respects as brutal, if not more, than the intact D&E, so that the legislation accomplishes little. What we have already said, however, shows ample justification for the regulation. Partial-birth abortion, as defined by the Act, differs from a standard D&E because the former occurs when the fetus is partially outside the mother to the point of one of the Act's anatomical landmarks. It was reasonable for Congress to think that partial-birth abortion, more than standard D&E, "undermines the public's perception of the appropriate role of a physician during the delivery process, and perverts a process during which life is brought into the world." Congressional Findings (14)(K), in notes following 18 U.S.C. §1531 (2000 ed., Supp. IV), p. 769. There would be a flaw in this Court's logic, and an irony in its jurisprudence, were we first to conclude a ban on both D&E and intact D&E was overbroad and then to say it is irrational to ban only intact D&E because that does not proscribe both procedures. In sum, we reject the contention that the congressional purpose of the Act was "to place a substantial obstacle in the path of a woman seeking an abortion." 505 U.S., at 878 (plurality opinion).

B

The Act's furtherance of legitimate government interests bears upon, but does not resolve, the next question: whether the Act has the effect of imposing an unconstitutional burden on the abortion right because it does not allow use of the barred procedure where "'necessary, in appropriate medical judgment, for [the] preservation of the . . . health of the mother.'" *Ayotte*, 546 U.S., at 327–328 (quoting *Casey, supra*, at 879 (plurality opinion)). The prohibition in the Act would be unconstitutional, under precedents we here assume to be controlling, if it "subject[ed] [women] to significant health risks." *Ayotte, supra*, at 328; see also *Casey, supra*, at 880 (opinion of the Court). In *Ayotte* the parties agreed a health exception to the challenged parental-involvement statute was necessary "to avert serious and often irreversible damage to [a pregnant minor's] health." 546 U.S., at 328. Here, by contrast, whether the Act creates significant health risks for women has been a contested factual question. The evidence presented in the trial courts and before Congress demonstrates both sides have medical support for their position. . . .

There is documented medical disagreement whether the Act's prohibition would ever impose significant health risks on women. . . .

The question becomes whether the Act can stand when this medical uncertainty persists. The Court's precedents instruct that the Act can survive this facial attack. The Court has given state and federal legislatures wide discretion to pass legislation in areas where there is medical and scientific uncertainty. See *Kansas* v. *Hendricks*, 521 U.S. 346, 360, n. 3 (1997); *Jones* v. *United States*, 463 U.S. 354, 370 (1983); *Lambert* v. *Yellowley*, 272 U.S. 581, 597 (1926); *Collins* v. *Texas*, 223 U.S. 288, 297–298 (1912); *Jacobson* v. *Massachusetts*, 197 U.S. 11, 30–31 (1905); see also *Stenberg, supra*, at 969–972 (KENNEDY, J., dissenting); *Marshall* v. *United States*, 414 U.S. 417, 427 (1974) ("When Congress undertakes to act in areas fraught with medical and scientific uncertainties, legislative options must be especially broad"). . . .

Medical uncertainty does not foreclose the exercise of legislative power in the abortion context any more than it does in other contexts. See *Hendricks, supra*, at 360, n. 3. The medical uncertainty over whether the Act's prohibition creates significant health risks provides a sufficient basis to conclude in this facial attack that the Act does not impose an undue burden. . . .

The instant cases, then, are different from *Planned Parenthood of Central Mo.* v. *Danforth*, 428 U.S. 52, 77–79 (1976), in which the Court invalidated a ban on saline amniocentesis, the then-dominant second-trimester abortion method. The Court found the ban in *Danforth* to be "an unreasonable or arbitrary regulation designed to inhibit, and having the effect of inhibiting, the vast majority of abortions after the first 12 weeks." *Id.*, at 79. Here the Act allows, among other means, a commonly used and generally accepted method, so it does not construct a substantial obstacle to the abortion right.

In reaching the conclusion the Act does not require a health exception we reject certain arguments made by the parties on both sides of these cases. On the one hand, the Attorney General urges us to uphold the Act on the basis of the congressional findings alone. Brief for Petitioner in No. 05–380, at 23. Although we review congressional factfinding under a deferential standard, we do not in the circumstances here place dispositive weight on Congress' findings. The Court retains an independent constitutional duty to review factual findings where constitutional rights are at stake. See *Crowell* v. *Benson*, 285 U.S. 22, 60 (1932) ("In cases brought to enforce constitutional rights, the judicial power of the United States necessarily extends to the independent determination of all questions, both of fact and law, necessary to the performance of that supreme function").

As respondents have noted, and the District Courts recognized, some recitations in the Act are factually incorrect. See *Nat. Abortion Federation*, 330 F. Supp. 2d, at 482, 488–491. Whether or not accurate at the time, some of the important findings have been superseded.

Two examples suffice. Congress determined no medical schools provide instruction on the prohibited procedure. Congressional Findings (14)(B), in notes following 18 U.S.C. §1531 (2000 ed., Supp. IV), p. 769. The testimony in the District Courts, however, demonstrated intact D&E is taught at medical schools. *Nat. Abortion Federation, supra*, at 490; *Planned Parenthood*, 320 F. Supp. 2d, at 1029. Congress also found there existed a medical consensus that the prohibited procedure is never medically necessary. Congressional Findings (1), in notes following 18 U.S.C. §1531 (2000 ed., Supp. IV), p. 767. The evidence presented in the District Courts contradicts that conclusion. See, *e.g., Carhart, supra*, at 1012–1015; *Nat. Abortion Federation, supra*, at 488–489; *Planned Parenthood, supra*, at 1025–1026. Uncritical deference to Congress' factual findings in these cases is inappropriate.

On the other hand, relying on the Court's opinion in *Stenberg*, respondents contend that an abortion regulation must contain a health exception "if 'substantial medical authority supports the proposition that banning a particular procedure could endanger women's health.'" Brief for Respondents in No. 05–380, p. 19 (quoting 530 U.S., at 938); see also Brief for Respondent Planned Parenthood et al. in No. 05–1382, at 12 (same). As illustrated by respondents' arguments and the decisions of the Courts of Appeals, *Stenberg* has been interpreted to leave no margin of error for legislatures to act in the face of medical uncertainty. *Carhart*, 413 F. 3d, at 796; *Planned Parenthood*, 435 F. 3d, at 1173; see also *Nat. Abortion Federation*, 437 F. 3d, at 296 (Walker, C. J., concurring) (explaining the standard under *Stenberg* "is a virtually insurmountable evidentiary hurdle").

A zero tolerance policy would strike down legitimate abortion regulations, like the present one, if some part of the medical community were disinclined to follow the proscription. This is too exacting a standard to impose on the legislative power, exercised in this instance under the Commerce Clause, to regulate the medical profession. Considerations of marginal safety, including the balance of risks, are within the legislative competence when the regulation is rational and in pursuit of legitimate ends. When standard medical options are available, mere convenience does not suffice to displace them; and if some procedures have different risks than others, it does not follow that the State is altogether barred from imposing reasonable regulations. The Act is not invalid on its face where there is uncertainty over whether the barred procedure is ever necessary to preserve a woman's health, given the availability of other abortion procedures that are considered to be safe alternatives. . . .

V

* * *

Respondents have not demonstrated that the Act, as a facial matter, is void for vagueness, or that it imposes an undue burden on a woman's right to abortion based on its overbreadth or lack of a health exception. For these reasons the judgments of the Courts of Appeals for the Eighth and Ninth Circuits are reversed.

It is so ordered.

JUSTICE THOMAS, with whom JUSTICE SCALIA joins, concurring.

I join the Court's opinion because it accurately applies current jurisprudence, including *Planned Parenthood of Southeastern Pa. v. Casey*, 505 U.S. 833 (1992). I write separately to reiterate my view that the Court's abortion jurisprudence, including *Casey* and *Roe* v. *Wade*, 410 U.S. 113 (1973), has no basis in the Constitution. See *Casey, supra*, at 979 (SCALIA, J., concurring in judgment in part and dissenting in part); *Stenberg* v. *Carhart*, 530 U.S. 914, 980–983 (2000) (THOMAS, J., dissenting). I also note that whether the Act constitutes a permissible exercise of Congress' power under the Commerce Clause is not before the Court. The parties did not raise or brief that issue; it is outside the question presented; and the lower courts did not address it. See *Cutter* v. *Wilkinson*, 544 U.S. 709, n. 2 (2005) (THOMAS, J., concurring).

JUSTICE GINSBURG, with whom JUSTICE STEVENS, JUSTICE SOUTER, and JUSTICE BREYER join, dissenting.

In *Planned Parenthood of Southeastern Pa. v. Casey*, 505 U.S. 833, 844 (1992), the Court declared that "[l]iberty finds no refuge in a jurisprudence of doubt." There was, the Court said, an "imperative" need to dispel doubt as to "the meaning and reach" of the Court's 7-to-2 judgment, rendered nearly two decades earlier in *Roe* v. *Wade*, 410 U.S. 113 (1973). 505 U.S., at 845. Responsive to that need, the Court endeavored to provide secure guidance to "[s]tate and federal courts as well as legislatures throughout the Union," by defining "the rights of the woman and the legitimate authority of the State respecting the termination of pregnancies by abortion procedures." *Ibid.*

Taking care to speak plainly, the *Casey* Court restated and reaffirmed *Roe*'s essential holding. 505 U.S., at 845–846. First, the Court addressed the type of abortion regulation permissible prior to fetal viability. It recognized "the right of the woman to choose to have an abortion before viability and to obtain it without undue interference from the State." *Id.*, at 846. Second, the Court acknowledged "the State's power to restrict abortions *after fetal viability*, if the law contains exceptions for pregnancies which endanger the woman's life or *health*." *Ibid.* (emphasis added). Third, the Court confirmed that "the State has legitimate interests from the outset of the pregnancy in protecting *the health of the woman* and the life of the fetus that may become a child." *Ibid.* (emphasis added).

In reaffirming *Roe*, the *Casey* Court described the centrality of "the decision whether to bear . . . a child," *Eisenstadt* v. *Baird*, 405 U.S. 438, 453 (1972), to a woman's "dignity and autonomy," her "personhood" and "destiny," her "conception of . . . her place in society." 505 U.S., at 851–852. Of signal importance here, the *Casey* Court stated with unmistakable clarity that state regulation of access to abortion procedures, even after viability, must protect "the health of the woman." *Id.*, at 846. . . .

Today's decision is alarming. It refuses to take *Casey* and *Stenberg* seriously. It tolerates, indeed applauds, federal intervention to ban nationwide a procedure found necessary and proper in certain cases by the American College of Obstetricians and Gynecologists (ACOG). It blurs the line, firmly drawn in *Casey*, between previability and postviability abortions. And, for the first time since *Roe*, the Court blesses a prohibition with no exception safeguarding a woman's health.

I dissent from the Court's disposition. Retreating from prior rulings that abortion restrictions cannot be imposed absent an exception safeguarding a woman's health, the Court upholds an Act that surely would not survive under the close scrutiny that previously attended state-decreed limitations on a woman's reproductive choices.

I

A

As *Casey* comprehended, at stake in cases challenging abortion restrictions is a woman's "control over her [own] destiny." 505 U.S., at 869 (plurality opinion). See also *id.*, at 852 (majority opinion).[2] "There was a time, not so long ago," when women were "regarded as the center of home and family life, with attendant special responsibilities that precluded full and independent legal status under the Constitution." *Id.*, at 896–897 (quoting *Hoyt* v. *Florida*, 368 U.S. 57, 62 (1961)). Those views, this Court made clear in *Casey*, "are no longer consistent with our understanding of the family, the individual, or the Constitution." 505 U.S., at 897. Women, it is now acknowledged, have the talent, capacity, and right "to participate equally in the economic and social life of the Nation." *Id.*, at 856. Their ability to realize their full potential, the Court recognized, is intimately connected to "their ability to control their reproductive lives." *Ibid.* Thus, legal challenges to undue restrictions on abortion procedures do not seek to vindicate some generalized notion of privacy; rather, they center on a woman's autonomy to determine her life's course, and thus to enjoy equal citizenship stature. See, *e.g.*, Siegel, Reasoning from the Body: A Historical Perspective on Abortion Regulation and Questions of Equal Protection, 44 Stan. L. Rev. 261 (1992); Law, Rethinking Sex and the Constitution,132 U. Pa. L. Rev. 955, 1002–1028 (1984).

In keeping with this comprehension of the right to reproductive choice, the Court has consistently required that laws regulating abortion, at any stage of pregnancy and in all cases, safeguard a woman's health. See, *e.g.*, *Ayotte*, 546 U.S., at 327–328 ("[O]ur precedents hold . . . that a State may not restrict access to abortions that are necessary,

---

2. *Planned Parenthood of Southeastern Pa.* v. *Casey*, 505 U.S. 833, 851–852 (1992), described more precisely than did *Roe* v. *Wade*, 410 U.S. 113 (1973), the impact of abortion restrictions on women's liberty. *Roe*'s focus was in considerable measure on "vindicat[ing] the right of the physician to administer medical treatment according to his professional judgment." *Id.*, at 165.

in appropriate medical judgment, for preservation of the life or health of the [woman]" (quoting *Casey*, 505 U.S., at 879 (plurality opinion))). . . .

We have thus ruled that a State must avoid subjecting women to health risks not only where the pregnancy itself creates danger, but also where state regulation forces women to resort to less safe methods of abortion. See *Planned Parenthood of Central Mo. v. Danforth*, 428 U.S. 52, 79 (1976). . . .

In *Stenberg*, we expressly held that a statute banning intact D&E was unconstitutional in part because it lacked a health exception. 530 U.S., at 930, 937. We noted that there existed a "division of medical opinion" about the relative safety of intact D&E, *id.*, at 937, but we made clear that as long as "substantial medical authority supports the proposition that banning a particular abortion procedure could endanger women's health," a health exception is required, *id.*, at 938. We explained:

> "The word 'necessary' in *Casey*'s phrase 'necessary, in appropriate medical judgment, for the preservation of the life or health of the [pregnant woman],' cannot refer to an absolute necessity or to absolute proof. Medical treatments and procedures are often considered appropriate (or inappropriate) in light of estimated comparative health risks (and health benefits) in particular cases. Neither can that phrase require unanimity of medical opinion. Doctors often differ in their estimation of comparative health risks and appropriate treatment. And *Casey*'s words 'appropriate medical judgment' must embody the judicial need to tolerate responsible differences of medical opinion. . . ." *Id.*, at 937 (citation omitted).

Thus, we reasoned, division in medical opinion "at most means uncertainty, a factor that signals the presence of risk, not its absence." *Ibid.* "[A] statute that altogether forbids [intact D&E] . . . consequently must contain a health exception." *Id.*, at 938. See also *id.*, at 948 (O'CONNOR, J., concurring) ("Th[e] lack of a health exception necessarily renders the statute unconstitutional.").

B

In 2003, a few years after our ruling in *Stenberg*, Congress passed the Partial-Birth Abortion Ban Act—without an exception for women's health. See 18 U.S.C. §1531(a) (2000 ed., Supp. IV).[4] The congressional findings on which the Partial-Birth Abortion

---

4. The Act's sponsors left no doubt that their intention was to nullify our ruling in *Stenberg*, 530 U.S. 914. See, *e.g.*, 149 Cong. Rec. 5731 (2003) (statement of Sen. Santorum) ("Why are we here? We are here because the Supreme Court defended the indefensible. . . . We have responded to the Supreme Court."). See also 148 Cong. Rec. 14273 (2002) (statement of Rep. Linder) (rejecting proposition that Congress has "no right to legislate a ban on this horrible practice because the Supreme Court says [it] cannot").

Ban Act rests do not withstand inspection, as the lower courts have determined and this Court is obliged to concede. . . . Many of the Act's recitations are incorrect. See *ante*, at 35–36. For example, Congress determined that no medical schools provide instruction on intact D&E. §2(14)(B), 117 Stat. 1204, notes following 18 U.S.C. §1531 (2000 ed., Supp. IV), p. 769, ¶(14)(B) (Congressional Findings). But in fact, numerous leading medical schools teach the procedure. . . .

More important, Congress claimed there was a medical consensus that the banned procedure is never necessary. Congressional Findings (1), in notes following 18 U.S.C. §1531 (2000 ed., Supp. IV), p. 767. But the evidence "very clearly demonstrate[d] the opposite." *Planned Parenthood*, 320 F. Supp. 2d, at 1025. See also *Carhart*, 331 F. Supp. 2d, at 1008–1009 ("[T]here was no evident consensus in the record that Congress compiled. There was, however, a substantial body of medical opinion presented to Congress in opposition. If anything . . . the congressional record establishes that there was a 'consensus' in favor of the banned procedure."); *National Abortion Federation*, 330 F. Supp. 2d, at 488 ("The congressional record itself undermines [Congress'] finding" that there is a medical consensus that intact D&E "is never medically necessary and should be prohibited." (internal quotation marks omitted)).

Similarly, Congress found that "[t]here is no credible medical evidence that partial-birth abortions are safe or are safer than other abortion procedures." Congressional Findings (14)(B), in notes following 18 U.S.C. §1531 (2000 ed., Supp. IV), p. 769. But the congressional record includes letters from numerous individual physicians stating that pregnant women's health would be jeopardized under the Act, as well as statements from nine professional associations, including ACOG, the American Public Health Association, and the California Medical Association, attesting that intact D&E carries meaningful safety advantages over other methods. . . .

C

In contrast to Congress, the District Courts made findings after full trials at which all parties had the opportunity to present their best evidence. The courts had the benefit of "much more extensive medical and scientific evidence . . . concerning the safety and necessity of intact D&Es." *Planned Parenthood*, 320 F. Supp. 2d, at 1014; cf. *National Abortion Federation*, 330 F. Supp. 2d, at 482 (District Court "heard more evidence during its trial than Congress heard over the span of eight years.").

During the District Court trials, "numerous" "extraordinarily accomplished" and "very experienced" medical experts explained that, in certain circumstances and for certain women, intact D&E is safer than alternative procedures and necessary to protect women's health. *Carhart*, 331 F. Supp. 2d, at 1024–1027; see *Planned Parenthood*, 320 F. Supp. 2d, at 1001 ("[A]ll of the doctors who actually perform intact D&Es concluded that in their opinion and clinical judgment, intact D&Es remain the safest option for certain individual women under certain individual health circumstances, and are significantly safer for these women than other abortion techniques, and are thus medically necessary."); cf. *ante*, at 31 ("Respondents presented evidence that intact D&E may be the safest method of abortion, for reasons similar to those adduced in *Stenberg*."). . . .

Based on thoroughgoing review of the trial evidence and the congressional record, each of the District Courts to consider the issue rejected Congress' findings as unreasonable and not supported by the evidence. See *Carhart*, 331 F. Supp. 2d, at 1008–1027; *National Abortion Federation*, 330 F. Supp. 2d, at 482, 488–491; *Planned Parenthood*, 320 F. Supp. 2d, at 1032. The trial courts concluded, in contrast to Congress' findings, that "significant medical authority supports the proposition that in some circumstances, [intact D&E] is the safest procedure." *Id.*, at 1033 (quoting *Stenberg*, 530 U.S., at 932); accord *Carhart*, 331 F. Supp. 2d, at 1008–1009, 1017–1018; *National Abortion Federation*, 330 F. Supp. 2d, at 480–482;[5] cf. *Stenberg*, 530 U.S., at 932 ("[T]he record shows that significant medical authority supports the proposition that in some circumstances, [intact D&E] would be the safest procedure.").

The District Courts' findings merit this Court's respect. See, *e.g.*, Fed. Rule Civ. Proc. 52(a); *Salve Regina College* v. *Russell*, 499 U.S. 225, 233 (1991). Today's opinion supplies no reason to reject those findings. Nevertheless, despite the District Courts' appraisal of the weight of the evidence, and in undisguised conflict with *Stenberg*, the Court asserts that the Partial-Birth Abortion Ban Act can survive "when . . . medical uncertainty persists." *Ante*, at 33. This assertion is bewildering. Not only does it defy the Court's longstanding precedent affirming the necessity of a health exception, with no carve-out for circumstances of medical uncertainty, see *supra*, at 4–5; it gives short shrift to the records before us, carefully canvassed by the District Courts. Those records indicate that "the majority of highly-qualified experts on the subject believe intact D&E to be the safest, most appropriate procedure under certain circumstances." *Planned Parenthood*, 320 F. Supp. 2d, at 1034. See *supra*, at 9–10.

The Court acknowledges some of this evidence, *ante*, at 31, but insists that, because some witnesses disagreed with the ACOG and other experts' assessment of risk, the Act can stand. *Ante*, at 32–33, 37. In this insistence, the Court brushes under the rug the District Courts' well-supported findings that the physicians who testified that intact D&E is never necessary to preserve the health of a woman had slim authority for their opinions.

---

5. Even the District Court for the Southern District of New York, which was more skeptical of the health benefits of intact D&E, see *ante*, at 32, recognized: "[T]he Government's own experts disagreed with almost all of Congress's factual findings"; a "significant body of medical opinion" holds that intact D&E has safety advantages over nonintact D&E; "[p]rofessional medical associations have also expressed their view that [intact D&E] may be the safest procedure for some women"; and "[t]he evidence indicates that the same disagreement among experts found by the Supreme Court in *Stenberg* existed throughout the time that Congress was considering the legislation, despite Congress's findings to the contrary." *National Abortion Federation*, 330 F. Supp. 2d, at 480–482.

They had no training for, or personal experience with, the intact D&E procedure, and many performed abortions only on rare occasions. See *Planned Parenthood*, 320 F. Supp. 2d, at 980; *Carhart*, 331 F. Supp. 2d, at 1025; cf. *National Abortion Federation*, 330 F. Supp. 2d, at 462–464. Even indulging the assumption that the Government witnesses were equally qualified to evaluate the relative risks of abortion procedures, their testimony could not erase the "significant medical authority support[ing] the proposition that in some circumstances, [intact D&E] would be the safest procedure." *Stenberg*, 530 U.S., at 932. . . .

II

A

The Court offers flimsy and transparent justifications for upholding a nationwide ban on intact D&E *sans* any exception to safeguard a woman's health. Today's ruling, the Court declares, advances "a premise central to [*Casey*'s] conclusion"—*i.e.*, the Government's "legitimate and substantial interest in preserving and promoting fetal life." *Ante*, at 14. See also *ante*, at 15 ("[W]e must determine whether the Act furthers the legitimate interest of the Government in protecting the life of the fetus that may become a child."). But the Act scarcely furthers that interest: The law saves not a single fetus from destruction, for it targets only a *method* of performing abortion. See *Stenberg*, 530 U.S., at 930. And surely the statute was not designed to protect the lives or health of pregnant women. . . .

As another reason for upholding the ban, the Court emphasizes that the Act does not proscribe the nonintact D&E procedure. See *ante*, at 34. But why not, one might ask. Nonintact D&E could equally be characterized as "brutal," *ante*, at 26, involving as it does "tear[ing] [a fetus] apart" and "ripp[ing] off" its limbs, *ante*, at 4, 6. "[T]he notion that either of these two equally gruesome procedures . . . is more akin to infanticide than the other, or that the State furthers any legitimate interest by banning one but not the other, is simply irrational." *Stenberg*, 530 U.S., at 946–947 (STEVENS, J., concurring).

Delivery of an intact, albeit nonviable, fetus warrants special condemnation, the Court maintains, because a fetus that is not dismembered resembles an infant. *Ante*, at 28. But so, too, does a fetus delivered intact after it is terminated by injection a day or two before the surgical evacuation, *ante*, at 5, 34–35, or a fetus delivered through medical induction or cesarean, *ante*, at 9. Yet, the availability of those procedures—along with D&E by dismemberment—the Court says, saves the ban on intact D&E from a declaration of unconstitutionality. *Ante*, at 34–35. Never mind that the procedures deemed acceptable might put a woman's health at greater risk. See *supra*, at 13, and n. 6; cf. *ante*, at 5, 31–32.

Ultimately, the Court admits that "moral concerns" are at work, concerns that could yield prohibitions on any abortion. See *ante*, at 28 ("Congress could . . . conclude that the type of abortion proscribed by the Act requires specific regulation because it implicates additional ethical and moral concerns that justify a special prohibition."). Notably, the concerns expressed are untethered to any ground genuinely serving the Government's interest in preserving life. By allowing such concerns to carry the day and case, overriding fundamental rights, the Court dishonors our precedent. See, *e.g.*, *Casey*, 505 U.S., at 850 ("Some of us as individuals find abortion offensive to our most basic principles of morality, but that cannot control our decision. Our obligation is to define the liberty of all, not to mandate our own moral code."); *Lawrence* v. *Texas*, 539 U.S. 558, 571 (2003) (Though "[f]or many persons [objections to homosexual conduct] are not trivial concerns but profound and deep convictions accepted as ethical and moral principles," the power of the State may not be used "to enforce these views on the whole society through operation of the criminal law." (citing *Casey*, 505 U.S., at 850)).

Revealing in this regard, the Court invokes an antiabortion shibboleth for which it concededly has no reliable evidence: Women who have abortions come to regret their choices, and consequently suffer from "[s]evere depression and loss of esteem." *Ante*, at 29. . . . Because of women's fragile emotional state and because of the "bond of love the mother has for her child," the Court worries, doctors may withhold information about the nature of the intact D&E procedure. *Ante*, at 28–29.[8] The solution the Court approves, then, is not to require doctors to inform women, accurately and adequately, of the different procedures and their attendant risks. Cf. *Casey*, 505 U.S., at 873 (plurality opinion) ("States are free to enact laws to provide a reasonable framework for a woman to make a decision that has such profound and lasting meaning."). Instead, the Court deprives women of the right to make an autonomous choice, even at the expense of their safety.[9]

This way of thinking reflects ancient notions about women's place in the family and under the Constitution—ideas that have long since been discredited. Compare, *e.g.*, *Muller* v. *Oregon*, 208 U.S. 412, 422–423 (1908) ("protective" legislation imposing hours-of-work limitations on women only held permissible in view of women's "physical structure and a proper discharge of her maternal funct[ion]"); *Bradwell* v. *State*, 16 Wall. 130, 141 (1873) (Bradley, J., concurring) ("Man is, or should be, woman's protector and defender. The natural and proper timidity and delicacy which belongs to the female sex evidently unfits it for many of the occupations of civil life. . . . The paramount destiny and mission of woman are to fulfil[l] the noble and benign offices of wife and mother."), with *United*

---

8. Notwithstanding the "bond of love" women often have with their children, see *ante*, at 28, not all pregnancies, this Court has recognized, are wanted, or even the product of consensual activity. See *Casey*, 505 U.S., at 891 ("[O]n an average day in the United States, nearly 11,000 women are severely assaulted by their male partners. Many of these incidents involve sexual assault."). [Citations omitted.]

9. Eliminating or reducing women's reproductive choices is manifestly not a means of protecting them. When safe abortion procedures cease to be an option, many women seek other means to end unwanted or coerced pregnancies. [Citations omitted.]

States v. *Virginia*, 518 U.S. 515, n. 12 (1996) (State may not rely on "overbroad generalizations" about the "talents, capacities, or preferences" of women; "[s]uch judgments have . . . impeded . . . women's progress toward full citizenship stature throughout our Nation's history"); *Califano* v. *Goldfarb*, 430 U.S. 199, 207 (1977) (gender-based Social Security classification rejected because it rested on "archaic and overbroad generalizations" "such as assumptions as to [women's] dependency" (internal quotation marks omitted)).

Though today's majority may regard women's feelings on the matter as "self-evident," *ante*, at 29, this Court has repeatedly confirmed that "[t]he destiny of the woman must be shaped . . . on her own conception of her spiritual imperatives and her place in society." *Casey*, 505 U.S., at 852. See also *id.*, at 877 (plurality opinion) ("[M]eans chosen by the State to further the interest in potential life must be calculated to inform the woman's free choice, not hinder it."); *supra*, at 3–4.

B

In cases on a "woman's liberty to determine whether to [continue] her pregnancy," this Court has identified viability as a critical consideration. See *Casey*, 505 U.S., at 869–870 (plurality opinion). . . .

Today, the Court blurs that line, maintaining that "[t]he Act [legitimately] appl[ies] both previability and postviability because . . . a fetus is a living organism while within the womb, whether or not it is viable outside the womb." *Ante*, at 17. Instead of drawing the line at viability, the Court refers to Congress' purpose to differentiate "abortion and infanticide" based not on whether a fetus can survive outside the womb, but on where a fetus is anatomically located when a particular medical procedure is performed. See *ante*, at 28 (quoting Congressional Findings (14)(G), in notes following 18 U.S.C. §1531 (2000 ed., Supp. IV), p. 769).

One wonders how long a line that saves no fetus from destruction will hold in face of the Court's "moral concerns." See *supra*, at 15; cf. *ante*, at 16 (noting that "[i]n this litigation" the Attorney General "does not dispute that the Act would impose an undue burden if it covered standard D&E"). The Court's hostility to the right *Roe* and *Casey* secured is not concealed. Throughout, the opinion refers to obstetrician-gynecologists and surgeons who perform abortions not by the titles of their medical specialties, but by the pejorative label "abortion doctor." *Ante*, at 14, 24, 25, 31, 33. A fetus is described as an "unborn child," and as a "baby," *ante*, at 3, 8; second-trimester, previability abortions are referred to as "late-term," *ante*, at 26; and the reasoned medical judgments of highly trained doctors are dismissed as "preferences" motivated by "mere convenience," *ante*, at 3, 37. Instead of the heightened scrutiny we have previously applied, the Court determines that a "rational" ground is enough to uphold the Act, *ante*, at 28, 37. And, most troubling, *Casey*'s principles, confirming the continuing vitality of "the essential holding of *Roe*," are merely "assume[d]" for the moment, *ante*, at 15, 31, rather than "retained" or "reaffirmed," *Casey*, 505 U.S., at 846.

III

A

The Court further confuses our jurisprudence when it declares that "facial attacks" are not permissible in "these circumstances," *i.e.*, where medical uncertainty exists. *Ante*, at 37; see *ibid.* ("In an as-applied challenge the nature of the medical risk can be better quantified and balanced than in a facial attack."). This holding is perplexing given that, in materially identical circumstances we held that a statute lacking a health exception was unconstitutional on its face. . . .

Without attempting to distinguish *Stenberg* and earlier decisions, the majority asserts that the Act survives review because respondents have not shown that the ban on intact D&E would be unconstitutional "in a large fraction of relevant cases." *Ante*, at 38 (citing *Casey*, 505 U.S., at 895). But *Casey* makes clear that, in determining whether any restriction poses an undue burden on a "large fraction" of women, the relevant class is *not* "all women," nor "all pregnant women," nor even all women "seeking abortions." 505 U.S., at 895. Rather, a provision restricting access to abortion, "must be judged by reference to those [women] for whom it is an actual rather than an irrelevant restriction," *ibid.* Thus the absence of a health exception burdens *all* women for whom it is relevant—women who, in the judgment of their doctors, require an intact D&E because other procedures would place their health at risk.[10] . . . It makes no sense to conclude that this facial challenge fails because respondents have not shown that a health exception is necessary for a large fraction of second-trimester abortions, including those for which a health exception is unnecessary: The very purpose of a health *exception* is to protect women in *exceptional* cases. . . .

B

The Court's allowance only of an "as-applied challenge in a discrete case," *ante*, at 38—jeopardizes women's health and places doctors in an untenable position. Even if courts were able to carve-out exceptions through piecemeal litigation for "discrete and well-defined instances," *ante*, at 37, women whose circumstances have not been anticipated by prior litigation could well be left unprotected. In treating those women, physicians would risk criminal prosecution, conviction, and imprisonment if they exercise their best judgment as to the safest medical procedure for their patients. The Court is thus gravely mistaken to conclude that narrow as-applied challenges are "the proper manner to protect the health of the woman." Cf. *ibid.*

---

10. There is, in short, no fraction because the numerator and denominator are the same: The health exception reaches only those cases where a woman's health is at risk. Perhaps for this reason, in mandating safeguards for women's health, we have never before invoked the "large fraction" test.

IV

As the Court wrote in *Casey*, "overruling *Roe*'s central holding would not only reach an unjustifiable result under principles of *stare decisis*, but would seriously weaken the Court's capacity to exercise the judicial power and to function as the Supreme Court of a Nation dedicated to the rule of law." 505 U.S., at 865. "[T]he very concept of the rule of law underlying our own Constitution requires such continuity over time that a respect for precedent is, by definition, indispensable." *Id.*, at 854. See also *id.*, at 867 ("[T]o overrule under fire in the absence of the most compelling reason to reexamine a watershed decision would subvert the Court's legitimacy beyond any serious question."). Though today's opinion does not go so far as to discard *Roe* or *Casey*, the Court, differently composed than it was when we last considered a restrictive abortion regulation, is hardly faithful to our earlier invocations of "the rule of law" and the "principles of *stare decisis*." Congress imposed a ban despite our clear prior holdings that the State cannot proscribe an abortion procedure when its use is necessary to protect a woman's health. See *supra*, at 7, n. 4. Although Congress' findings could not withstand the crucible of trial, the Court defers to the legislative override of our Constitution-based rulings. See *supra*, at 7–9. A decision so at odds with our jurisprudence should not have staying power.

In sum, the notion that the Partial-Birth Abortion Ban Act furthers any legitimate governmental interest is, quite simply, irrational. The Court's defense of the statute provides no saving explanation. In candor, the Act, and the Court's defense of it, cannot be understood as anything other than an effort to chip away at a right declared again and again by this Court—and with increasing comprehension of its centrality to women's lives. See *supra*, at 3, n. 2; *supra*, at 7, n. 4. When "a statute burdens constitutional rights and all that can be said on its behalf is that it is the vehicle that legislators have chosen for expressing their hostility to those rights, the burden is undue." *Stenberg*, 530 U.S., at 952 (GINSBURG, J., concurring) (quoting *Hope Clinic* v. *Ryan*, 195 F. 3d 857, 881 (CA7 1999) (POSNER, C. J., dissenting)).

* * *

For the reasons stated, I dissent from the Court's disposition and would affirm the judgments before us for review.

WHOLE WOMAN'S HEALTH ET AL. *v.* HELLERSTEDT, COMMISSSIONER, TEXAS DEPARTMENT OF STATE HEALTH SERVICES, ET AL.

CERTIORARI TO THE UNITED STATES COURT OF APPEALS FOR THE FIFTH CIRCUIT

No. 15–274. Argued March 2, 2016—Decided June 27, 2016

BREYER, J., delivered the opinion of the Court, in which KENNEDY, GINSBURG, SOTOMAYOR, and KAGAN, JJ., joined. GINSBURG, J., filed a concurring opinion. THOMAS, J., filed a dissenting opinion. ALITO, J., filed a dissenting opinion, in which ROBERTS, C. J., and THOMAS, J., joined.

JUSTICE BREYER delivered the opinion of the Court.

In *Planned Parenthood of Southeastern Pa.* v. *Casey*, 505 U.S. 833, 878 (1992), a plurality of the Court concluded that there "exists" an "undue burden" on a woman's right to decide to have an abortion, and consequently a provision of law is constitutionally invalid, if the "*purpose or effect*" of the provision "*is to place a substantial obstacle* in the path of a woman seeking an abortion before the fetus attains viability." (Emphasis added.) The plurality added that "[u]nnecessary health regulations that have the purpose or effect of presenting a substantial obstacle to a woman seeking an abortion impose an undue burden on the right." *Ibid.*

We must here decide whether two provisions of Texas' House Bill 2 violate the Federal Constitution as interpreted in *Casey*. The first provision, which we shall call the "*admitting-privileges requirement*," says that

"[a] physician performing or inducing an abortion . . . must, on the date the abortion is performed or induced, have active admitting privileges at a hospital that . . . is located not further than 30 miles from the location at which the abortion is performed or induced." Tex. Health & Safety Code Ann. §171.0031(a) (West Cum. Supp. 2015).

This provision amended Texas law that had previously required an abortion facility to maintain a written protocol "for managing medical emergencies and the transfer of patients requiring further emergency care to a hospital." 38 Tex. Reg. 6546 (2013).

The second provision, which we shall call the "*surgical-center requirement*," says that

"the minimum standards for an abortion facility must be equivalent to the minimum standards adopted under [the Texas Health and Safety Code section] for ambulatory surgical centers." Tex. Health & Safety Code Ann. §245.010(a).

We conclude that neither of these provisions confers medical benefits sufficient to justify the burdens upon access that each imposes. Each places a substantial obstacle in the path of women seeking a previability abortion, each constitutes an undue burden on abortion access, *Casey, supra,* at 878 (plurality opinion), and each violates the Federal Constitution. Amdt. 14, §1.

III

Undue Burden—Legal Standard

We begin with the standard, as described in *Casey.* We recognize that the "State has a legitimate interest in seeing to it that abortion, like any other medical procedure, is performed under circumstances that insure maximum safety for the patient." *Roe* v. *Wade,* 410 U.S. 113, 150 (1973). But, we added, "a statute which, while furthering [a] valid state interest, has the effect of placing a substantial obstacle in the path of a woman's choice cannot be considered a permissible means of serving its legitimate ends." *Casey,* 505 U.S., at 877 (plurality opinion). Moreover, "[u]nnecessary health regulations that have the purpose or effect of presenting a substantial obstacle to a woman seeking an abortion impose an undue burden on the right." *Id.,* at 878.

The Court of Appeals wrote that a state law is "constitutional if: (1) it does not have the purpose or effect of placing a substantial obstacle in the path of a woman seeking an abortion of a nonviable fetus; and (2) it is reasonably related to (or designed to further) a legitimate state interest." 790 F. 3d, at 572. The Court of Appeals went on to hold that "the district court erred by substituting its own judgment for that of the legislature" when it conducted its "undue burden inquiry," in part because "medical uncertainty underlying a statute is for resolution by legislatures, not the courts." *Id.,* at 587 (citing *Gonzales* v. *Carhart,* 550 U.S. 124, 163 (2007)).

The Court of Appeals' articulation of the relevant standard is incorrect. The first part of the Court of Appeals' test may be read to imply that a district court should not consider the existence or nonexistence of medical benefits when considering whether a regulation of abortion constitutes an undue burden. The rule announced in *Casey,* however, requires that courts consider the burdens a law imposes on abortion access together with the benefits those laws confer. See 505 U.S., at 887–898 (opinion of the Court) (performing this balancing with respect to a spousal notification provision); *id.,* at 899–901 (joint opinion of O'Connor, Kennedy, and Souter, JJ.) (same balancing with respect to a parental notification provision). And the second part of the test is wrong to equate the judicial review applicable to the regulation of a constitutionally protected personal liberty with the less strict review applicable where, for example, economic legislation is at issue. See, *e.g., Williamson* v. *Lee Optical of Okla., Inc.,* 348 U.S. 483, 491 (1955). The Court of Appeals' approach simply does not match the standard that this Court laid out in *Casey,* which asks courts to consider whether any burden imposed on abortion access is "undue."

The statement that legislatures, and not courts, must resolve questions of medical uncertainty is also inconsistent with this Court's case law. Instead, the Court, when determining the constitutionality of laws regulating abortion procedures, has placed considerable weight upon evidence and argument presented in judicial proceedings. In *Casey*, for example, we relied heavily on the District Court's factual findings and the research-based submissions of *amici* in declaring a portion of the law at issue unconstitutional. 505 U.S., at 888–894 (opinion of the Court) (discussing evidence related to the prevalence of spousal abuse in determining that a spousal notification provision erected an undue burden to abortion access). And, in *Gonzales* the Court, while pointing out that we must review legislative "factfinding under a deferential standard," added that we must not "place dispositive weight" on those "findings." 550 U.S., at 165. *Gonzales* went on to point out that the "*Court retains an independent constitutional duty to review factual findings where constitutional rights are at stake.*" *Ibid.* (emphasis added). Although there we upheld a statute regulating abortion, we did not do so solely on the basis of legislative findings explicitly set forth in the statute, noting that "evidence presented in the District Courts contradicts" some of the legislative findings. *Id.*, at 166. In these circumstances, we said, "[u]ncritical deference to Congress' factual findings . . . is inappropriate." *Ibid.*

Unlike in *Gonzales*, the relevant statute here does not set forth any legislative findings. Rather, one is left to infer that the legislature sought to further a constitutionally acceptable objective (namely, protecting women's health). *Id.*, at 149–150. For a district court to give significant weight to evidence in the judicial record in these circumstances is consistent with this Court's case law. As we shall describe, the District Court did so here. It did not simply substitute its own judgment for that of the legislature. It considered the evidence in the record—including expert evidence, presented in stipulations, depositions, and testimony. It then weighed the asserted benefits against the burdens. We hold that, in so doing, the District Court applied the correct legal standard.

IV

Undue Burden—Admitting-Privileges Requirement

Turning to the lower courts' evaluation of the evidence, we first consider the admitting-privileges requirement. Before the enactment of H. B. 2, doctors who provided abortions were required to "have admitting privileges *or* have a working arrangement with a physician(s) who has admitting privileges at a local hospital in order to ensure the necessary back up for medical complications." Tex. Admin. Code, tit. 25, §139.56 (2009) (emphasis added). The new law changed this requirement by requiring that a "physician performing or inducing an abortion . . . must, on the date the abortion is performed or induced, have active admitting privileges at a hospital that . . . is located not further than 30 miles from the location at which the abortion is performed or induced." Tex. Health & Safety Ann. §171.0031(a). The District Court held that the legislative change imposed an "undue burden" on a woman's right to have an abortion. We conclude that there is adequate legal and factual support for the District Court's conclusion.

The purpose of the admitting-privileges requirement is to help ensure that women have easy access to a hospital should complications arise during an abortion procedure. Brief for Respondents 32–37. But the District Court found that it brought about no such health-related benefit. The court found that "[t]he great weight of evidence demonstrates that, before the act's passage, abortion in Texas was extremely safe with particularly low rates of serious complications and virtually no deaths occurring on account of the procedure." 46 F. Supp. 3d, at 684. Thus, there was no significant health-related problem that the new law helped to cure. . . .

We have found nothing in Texas' record evidence that shows that, compared to prior law (which required a "working arrangement" with a doctor with admitting privileges), the new law advanced Texas' legitimate interest in protecting women's health. . . .

At the same time, the record evidence indicates that the admitting-privileges requirement places a "substantial obstacle in the path of a woman's choice." *Casey*, 505 U.S., at 877 (plurality opinion). The District Court found, as of the time the admitting-privileges requirement began to be enforced, the number of facilities providing abortions dropped in half, from about 40 to about 20. 46 F. Supp. 3d, at 681. Eight abortion clinics closed in the months leading up to the requirement's effective date. See App. 229–230; cf. Brief for Planned Parenthood Federation of America et al. as *Amici Curiae* 14 (noting that abortion facilities in Waco, San Angelo, and Midland no longer operate because Planned Parenthood is "unable to find local physicians in those communities with privileges who are willing to provide abortions due to the size of those communities and the hostility that abortion providers face"). Eleven more closed on the day the admitting-privileges requirement took effect. See App. 229–230; Tr. of Oral Arg. 58.

Other evidence helps to explain why the new requirement led to the closure of clinics. We read that other evidence in light of a brief filed in this Court by the Society of Hospital Medicine. That brief describes the undisputed general fact that "hospitals often condition admitting privileges on reaching a certain number of admissions per year." Brief for Society of Hospital Medicine et al. as *Amici Curiae* 11. Returning to the District Court record, we note that, in direct testimony, the president of Nova Health Systems, implicitly relying on this general fact, pointed out that it would be difficult for doctors regularly performing abortions at the El Paso clinic to obtain admitting privileges at nearby hospitals because "[d]uring the past 10 years, over 17,000 abortion procedures were performed at the El Paso clinic [and n]ot a single one of those patients had to be transferred to a hospital for emergency treatment, much less admitted to the hospital." App. 730. In a word, doctors would be unable to maintain admitting privileges or obtain those privileges for the future, because the fact that abortions are so safe meant that providers were unlikely to have any patients to admit. . . .

In our view, the record contains sufficient evidence that the admitting-privileges requirement led to the closure of half of Texas' clinics, or thereabouts. Those closures meant fewer doctors, longer waiting times, and increased crowding. Record evidence also supports the finding that after the admitting-privileges provision went into effect, the "number of women of reproductive age living in a county . . . more than 150 miles from a provider increased from approximately 86,000 to 400,000 . . . and the number of women living in a county more than 200 miles from a provider from approximately 10,000 to 290,000." 46 F. Supp. 3d, at 681. We recognize that increased driving distances do not always constitute an "undue burden." See *Casey*, 505 U.S., at 885–887 (joint opinion of O'Connor, KENNEDY, and Souter, JJ.). But here, those increases are but one additional burden, which, when taken together with others that the closings brought about, and when viewed in light of the virtual absence of any health benefit, lead us to conclude that the record adequately supports the District Court's "undue burden" conclusion. Cf. *id.*, at 895 (opinion of the Court) (finding burden "undue" when requirement places "substantial obstacle to a woman's choice" in "a large fraction of the cases in which" it "is relevant"). . . .

V

Undue Burden—Surgical-Center Requirement

The second challenged provision of Texas' new law sets forth the surgical-center requirement. Prior to enactment of the new requirement, Texas law required abortion facilities to meet a host of health and safety requirements. Under those pre-existing laws, facilities were subject to annual reporting and recordkeeping requirements, see Tex. Admin. Code, tit. 25, §§139.4, 139.5, 139.55, 139.58; a quality assurance program, see §139.8; personnel policies and staffing requirements, see §§139.43, 139.46; physical and environmental requirements, see §139.48; infection control standards, see §139.49; disclosure requirements, see §139.50; patient-rights standards, see §139.51; and medical- and clinical-services standards, see §139.53, including anesthesia standards, see §139.59. These requirements are policed by random and announced inspections, at least annually, see §§139.23, 139.31; Tex. Health & Safety Code Ann. §245.006(a) (West 2010), as well as administrative penalties, injunctions, civil penalties, and criminal penalties for certain violations, see Tex. Admin. Code, tit. 25, §139.33; Tex. Health & Safety Code Ann. §245.011 (criminal penalties for certain reporting violations).

H. B. 2 added the requirement that an "abortion facility" meet the "minimum standards . . . for ambulatory surgical centers" under Texas law. §245.010(a) (West Cum. Supp. 2015). The surgical-center regulations include, among other things, detailed specifications relating to the size of the nursing staff, building dimensions, and other building requirements. The nursing staff must comprise at least "an adequate number of [registered nurses] on duty to meet the following minimum staff requirements: director of the department (or designee), and supervisory and staff personnel for each service area to assure the immediate availability of [a registered nurse] for emergency care or for any patient when needed," Tex. Admin. Code, tit. 25, §135.15(a)(3) (2016), as well as "a second individual on duty on the premises who is trained and currently certified in basic cardiac life support until all patients have been discharged from the facility" for facilities that provide moderate sedation, such as most abortion facilities, §135.15(b)(2)(A). Facilities must include a full surgical suite with an operating room that has "a clear floor area of at least 240 square feet" in which "[t]he minimum clear dimension between built-in cabinets, counters, and shelves shall be 14 feet." §135.52(d)(15)(A). There must be a preoperative patient holding room and a postoperative recovery suite. The former "shall be provided and arranged in a one-way traffic pattern so that patients entering from outside the surgical suite can change, gown, and move directly into the restricted corridor of the surgical suite," §135.52(d)(10)(A), and the latter "shall be arranged to provide a one-way traffic pattern from the restricted surgical corridor to the postoperative recovery suite, and then to the extended observation rooms or discharge," §135.52(d)(9)(A). Surgical centers must meet numerous other spatial requirements, see generally §135.52, including specific corridor widths, §135.52(e)(1)(B)(iii). Surgical centers must also have an advanced heating, ventilation, and air conditioning system, §135.52(g)(5), and must satisfy particular piping system and plumbing requirements, §135.52(h). Dozens of other sections list additional requirements that apply to surgical centers. See generally §§135.1–135.56.

There is considerable evidence in the record supporting the District Court's findings indicating that the statutory provision requiring all abortion facilities to meet all surgical-center standards does not benefit patients and is not necessary. The District Court found that "risks are not appreciably lowered for patients who undergo abortions at ambulatory surgical centers as compared to nonsurgical-center facilities." 46 F. Supp. 3d, at 684. The court added that women "will not obtain better care or experience more frequent positive outcomes at an ambulatory surgical center as compared to a previously licensed facility." *Ibid.* And these findings are well supported. . . .

The upshot is that this record evidence, along with the absence of any evidence to the contrary, provides ample support for the District Court's conclusion that "[m]any of the building standards mandated by the act and its implementing rules have such a tangential relationship to patient safety in the context of abortion as to be nearly arbitrary." 46 F. Supp. 3d, at 684. That conclusion, along with the supporting evidence, provides sufficient support for the more general conclusion that the surgical-center requirement "will not [provide] better care or . . . more frequent positive outcomes." *Ibid.* The record evidence thus supports the ultimate legal conclusion that the surgical-center requirement is not necessary.

At the same time, the record provides adequate evidentiary support for the District Court's conclusion that the surgical-center requirement places a substantial obstacle in the path of women seeking an abortion. The parties stipulated that the requirement would further reduce the number of abortion facilities available to seven or eight facilities, located in Houston, Austin, San Antonio, and Dallas/Fort Worth. See App. 182–183. In the District Court's view, the proposition that these "seven or eight providers could meet the demand of the entire State stretches credulity." 46 F. Supp. 3d, at 682. We take this statement as a finding that these few facilities could not "meet" that "demand."

The Court of Appeals held that this finding was "clearly erroneous." 790 F. 3d, at 590. It wrote that the finding rested upon the "'*ipse dixit*'" of one expert, Dr. Grossman, and that there was no evidence that the current surgical centers (*i.e.*, the seven or eight) are operating at full capacity or could not increase capacity. *Ibid*. Unlike the Court of Appeals, however, we hold that the record provides adequate support for the District Court's finding. . . .

Texas suggests that the seven or eight remaining clinics could expand sufficiently to provide abortions for the 60,000 to 72,000 Texas women who sought them each year. Because petitioners had satisfied their burden, the obligation was on Texas, if it could, to present evidence rebutting that issue to the District Court. Texas admitted that it presented no such evidence. Tr. of Oral Arg. 46. Instead, Texas argued before this Court that one new clinic now serves 9,000 women annually. *Ibid*. In addition to being outside the record, that example is not representative. The clinic to which Texas referred apparently cost $26 million to construct—a fact that even more clearly demonstrates that requiring seven or eight clinics to serve five times their usual number of patients does indeed represent an undue burden on abortion access. See Planned Parenthood Debuts New Building: Its $26 Million Center in Houston is Largest of Its Kind in U.S., Houston Chronicle, May 21, 2010, p. B1. . . .

More fundamentally, in the face of no threat to women's health, Texas seeks to force women to travel long distances to get abortions in crammed-to-capacity superfacilities. Patients seeking these services are less likely to get the kind of individualized attention, serious conversation, and emotional support that doctors at less taxed facilities may have offered. Healthcare facilities and medical professionals are not fungible commodities. Surgical centers attempting to accommodate sudden, vastly increased demand, see 46 F. Supp. 3d, at 682, may find that quality of care declines. Another commonsense inference that the District Court made is that these effects would be harmful to, not supportive of, women's health. See *id.*, at 682–683.

Finally, the District Court found that the costs that a currently licensed abortion facility would have to incur to meet the surgical-center requirements were considerable, ranging from $1 million per facility (for facilities with adequate space) to $3 million per facility (where additional land must be purchased). *Id.*, at 682. This evidence supports the conclusion that more surgical centers will not soon fill the gap when licensed facilities are forced to close.

We agree with the District Court that the surgical-center requirement, like the admitting-privileges requirement, provides few, if any, health benefits for women, poses a substantial obstacle to women seeking abortions, and constitutes an "undue burden" on their constitutional right to do so. . . .

JUSTICE THOMAS, dissenting.

... I write separately to emphasize how today's decision perpetuates the Court's habit of applying different rules to different constitutional rights—especially the putative right to abortion.

To begin, the very existence of this suit is a jurisprudential oddity. Ordinarily, plaintiffs cannot file suits to vindicate the constitutional rights of others. But the Court employs a different approach to rights that it favors. So in this case and many others, the Court has erroneously allowed doctors and clinics to vicariously vindicate the putative constitutional right of women seeking abortions.

This case also underscores the Court's increasingly common practice of invoking a given level of scrutiny—here, the abortion-specific undue burden standard—while applying a different standard of review entirely. Whatever scrutiny the majority applies to Texas' law, it bears little resemblance to the undue-burden test the Court articulated in *Planned Parenthood of Southeastern Pa. v. Casey*, 505 U.S. 833 (1992), and its successors. Instead, the majority eviscerates important features of that test to return to a regime like the one that *Casey* repudiated.

Ultimately, this case shows why the Court never should have bent the rules for favored rights in the first place. Our law is now so riddled with special exceptions for special rights that our decisions deliver neither predictability nor the promise of a judiciary bound by the rule of law. . . .

II

Today's opinion also reimagines the undue-burden standard used to assess the constitutionality of abortion restrictions. Nearly 25 years ago, in *Planned Parenthood of Southeastern Pa. v. Casey*, 505 U.S. 833, a plurality of this Court invented the "undue burden" standard as a special test for gauging the permissibility of abortion restrictions. *Casey* held that a law is unconstitutional if it imposes an "undue burden" on a woman's ability to choose to have an abortion, meaning that it "has the purpose or effect of placing a substantial obstacle in the path of a woman seeking an abortion of a nonviable fetus." *Id.*, at 877. *Casey* thus instructed courts to look to whether a law substantially impedes women's access to abortion, and whether it is reasonably related to legitimate state interests. As the Court explained, "[w]here it has a rational basis to act, and it does not impose an undue burden, the State may use its regulatory power" to regulate aspects of abortion procedures, "all in furtherance of its legitimate interests in regulating the medical profession in order to promote respect for life, including life of the unborn." *Gonzales v. Carhart*, 550 U.S. 124, 158 (2007).

I remain fundamentally opposed to the Court's abortion jurisprudence. *E.g., id.*, at 168–169 (THOMAS, J., concurring); *Stenberg*, 530 U.S., at 980, 982 (THOMAS, J., dissenting). Even taking *Casey* as the baseline, however, the majority radically rewrites the undue-burden test in three ways. First, today's decision requires courts to "consider the burdens a law imposes on abortion access together with the benefits those laws confer." *Ante*, at 19. Second, today's opinion tells the courts that, when the law's justifications are medically uncertain, they need not defer to the legislature, and must instead assess medical justifications for abortion restrictions by scrutinizing the record themselves. *Ibid.* Finally, even if a law imposes no "substantial obstacle" to women's access to abortions, the law now must have more than a "reasonabl[e] relat[ion] to . . . a legitimate state interest." *Ibid.* (internal quotation marks omitted). These precepts are nowhere to be found in *Casey* or its successors, and transform the undue-burden test to something much more akin to strict scrutiny.

First, the majority's free-form balancing test is contrary to *Casey*. When assessing Pennsylvania's recordkeeping requirements for abortion providers, for instance, *Casey* did not weigh its benefits and burdens. Rather, *Casey* held that the law had a legitimate purpose because data collection advances medical research, "so it cannot be said that the requirements serve no purpose other than to make abortions more difficult." 505 U.S., at 901 (joint opinion of O'Connor, Kennedy, and Souter, JJ.). The opinion then asked whether the recordkeeping requirements imposed a "substantial obstacle," and found none. *Ibid.* Contrary to the majority's statements, see *ante*, at 19, *Casey* did not balance the benefits and burdens of Pennsylvania's spousal and parental notification provisions, either. Pennsylvania's spousal notification requirement, the plurality said, imposed an undue burden because findings established that the requirement would "likely . . . prevent a significant number of women from obtaining an abortion"—not because these burdens outweighed its benefits. 505 U.S., at 893 (majority opinion); see *id.*, at 887–894. And *Casey* summarily upheld parental notification provisions because even pre-*Casey* decisions had done so. *Id.*, at 899–900 (joint opinion).

Decisions in *Casey*'s wake further refute the majority's benefits-and-burdens balancing test. The Court in *Mazurek* v. *Armstrong*, 520 U.S. 968 (1997) (*per curiam*), had no difficulty upholding a Montana law authorizing only physicians to perform abortions—even though no legislative findings supported the law, and the challengers claimed that "all health evidence contradict[ed] the claim that there is any health basis for the law." *Id.*, at 973 (internal quotation marks omitted). *Mazurek* also deemed objections to the law's lack of benefits "squarely foreclosed by *Casey* itself." *Ibid.* Instead, the Court explained, "'the Constitution gives the States broad latitude to decide that particular functions may be performed only by licensed professionals, even if *an objective assessment might suggest that those same tasks could be performed by others.*'" *Ibid.* (quoting *Casey, supra*, at 885; emphasis in original); see *Gonzales, supra*, at 164 (relying on *Mazurek*).

Second, by rejecting the notion that "legislatures, and not courts, must resolve questions of medical uncertainty," *ante*, at 20, the majority discards another core element of the *Casey* framework. Before today, this Court had "given state and federal legislatures wide discretion to pass legislation in areas where there is medical and scientific uncertainty." *Gonzales*, 550 U.S., at 163. This Court emphasized that this "traditional rule" of deference "is consistent with *Casey*." *Ibid.* This Court underscored that legislatures should not be hamstrung "if some part of the medical community were disinclined to follow the proscription." *Id.*, at 166. And this Court concluded that "[c]onsiderations of marginal safety, including the balance of risks, are within the legislative competence when the regulation is rational and in pursuit of legitimate ends." *Ibid.*; see *Stenberg, supra,* at 971 (KENNEDY, J., dissenting) ("the right of the legislature to resolve matters on which physicians disagreed" is "establish[ed] beyond doubt"). This Court could not have been clearer: Whenever medical justifications for an abortion restriction are debatable, that "provides a sufficient basis to conclude in [a] facial attack that the [law] does not impose an undue burden." *Gonzales,* 550 U.S., at 164. Otherwise, legislatures would face "too exacting" a standard. *Id.*, at 166.

Today, however, the majority refuses to leave disputed medical science to the legislature because past cases "placed considerable weight upon the evidence and argument presented in judicial proceedings." *Ante,* at 20. But while *Casey* relied on record evidence to uphold Pennsylvania's spousal-notification requirement, that requirement had nothing to do with debated medical science. 505 U.S., at 888–894 (majority opinion). And while *Gonzales* observed that courts need not blindly accept all legislative findings, see *ante,* at 20, that does not help the majority. *Gonzales* refused to accept Congress' finding of "a medical consensus that the prohibited procedure is never medically necessary" because the procedure's necessity was debated within the medical community. 550 U.S., at 165–166. Having identified medical uncertainty, *Gonzales* explained how courts should resolve conflicting positions: by respecting the legislature's judgment. See *id.*, at 164.

Finally, the majority overrules another central aspect of *Casey* by requiring laws to have more than a rational basis even if they do not substantially impede access to abortion. *Ante,* at 19–20. "Where [the State] has a rational basis to act and it does not impose an undue burden," this Court previously held, "the State may use its regulatory power" to impose regulations "in furtherance of its legitimate interests in regulating the medical profession in order to promote respect for life, including life of the unborn." *Gonzales, supra,* at 158 (emphasis added); see *Casey, supra,* at 878 (plurality opinion) (similar). No longer. Though the majority declines to say how substantial a State's interest must be, *ante,* at 20, one thing is clear: The State's burden has been ratcheted to a level that has not applied for a quarter century.

Today's opinion does resemble *Casey* in one respect: After disregarding significant aspects of the Court's prior jurisprudence, the majority applies the undue-burden standard in a way that will surely mystify lower courts for years to come. As in *Casey,* today's opinion "simply . . . highlight[s] certain facts in the record that apparently strike the . . . Justices as particularly significant in establishing (or refuting) the existence of an undue burden." 505 U.S., at 991 (Scalia, J., concurring in judgment in part and dissenting in part); see *ante,* at 23–24, 31–34. As in *Casey,* "the opinion then simply announces that the provision either does or does not impose a 'substantial obstacle' or an 'undue burden.'" 505 U.S., at 991 (opinion of Scalia, J.); see *ante,* at 26, 36. And still "[w]e do not know whether the same conclusions could have been reached on a different record, or in what respects the record would have had to differ before an opposite conclusion would have been appropriate." 505 U.S., at 991 (opinion of Scalia, J.); cf. *ante*, at 26, 31–32. All we know is that an undue burden now has little to do with whether the law, in a "real sense, deprive[s] women of the ultimate decision," *Casey, supra*, at 875, and more to do with the loss of "individualized attention, serious conversation, and emotional support," *ante*, at 36.

The majority's undue-burden test looks far less like our post-*Casey* precedents and far more like the strict-scrutiny standard that *Casey* rejected, under which only the most compelling rationales justified restrictions on abortion. See *Casey, supra*, at 871, 874–875 (plurality opinion). One searches the majority opinion in vain for any acknowledgment of the "premise central" to *Casey*'s rejection of strict scrutiny: "that the government has a legitimate and substantial interest in preserving and promoting fetal life" from conception, not just in regulating medical procedures. *Gonzales, supra*, at 145 (internal quotation marks omitted); see *Casey, supra*, at 846 (majority opinion), 871 (plurality opinion). Meanwhile, the majority's undue-burden balancing approach risks ruling out even minor, previously valid infringements on access to abortion. Moreover, by second-guessing medical evidence and making its own assessments of "quality of care" issues, *ante*, at 23–24, 30–31, 36, the majority reappoints this Court as "the country's *ex officio* medical board with powers to disapprove medical and operative practices and standards throughout the United States." *Gonzales, supra*, at 164 (internal quotation marks omitted). And the majority seriously burdens States, which must guess at how much more compelling their interests must be to pass muster and what "commonsense inferences" of an undue burden this Court will identify next. . . .

KRISTINA BOX, COMMISSIONER, INDIANA DEPARTMENT OF HEALTH, ET AL. *v.* PLANNED PARENTHOOD OF INDIANA AND KENTUCKY, INC., ET AL.

ON PETITION FOR WRIT OF CERTIORARI TO THE UNITED STATES COURT OF APPEALS FOR THE SEVENTH CIRCUIT

No. 18–483. Decided May 28, 2019

PER CURIAM.

Indiana's petition for certiorari argues that the Court of Appeals for the Seventh Circuit incorrectly invalidated two new provisions of Indiana law: the first relating to the disposition of fetal remains by abortion providers; and the second barring the knowing provision of sex-, race-, or disability-selective abortions by abortion providers. See Ind. Code §§16-34-2-1.1(a)(1)(K), 16-34-3-4(a), 16-34-4-4, 16-34-4-5, 16-34-4-6, 16-34-4-7, 16-34-4-8, 16-41-16-4(d), 16-41-16-5 (2018). We reverse the judgment of the Seventh Circuit with respect to the first question presented, and we deny the petition with respect to the second question presented.

I

The first challenged provision altered the manner in which abortion providers may dispose of fetal remains. Among other changes, it excluded fetal remains from the definition of infectious and pathological waste, §§16-41-16-4(d), 16-41-16-5, thereby preventing incineration of fetal remains along with surgical byproducts. It also authorized simultaneous cremation of fetal remains, §16-34-3-4(a), which Indiana does not generally allow for human remains, §23-14-31-39(a). The law did not affect a woman's right under existing law "to determine the final disposition of the aborted fetus." §16-34-3-2(a).

Respondents have never argued that Indiana's law creates an undue burden on a woman's right to obtain an abortion. Cf. *Planned Parenthood of Southeastern Pa.* v. *Casey,* 505 U. S. 833, 874 (1992) (plurality opinion). Respondents have instead litigated this case on the assumption that the law does not implicate a fundamental right and is therefore subject only to ordinary rational basis review. See *Planned Parenthood of Indiana and Kentucky, Inc.* v. *Commissioner of Indiana State Dept. of Health,* 888 F. 3d 300, 307 (2018). To survive under that standard, a state law need only be "rationally related to legitimate government interests." *Washington* v. *Glucksberg,* 521 U. S. 702, 728 (1997).

The Seventh Circuit found Indiana's disposition law invalid even under this deferential test. It first held that Indiana's stated interest in "the 'humane and dignified disposal of human remains'" was "not . . . legitimate." 888 F. 3d, at 309. It went on to hold that even if Indiana's stated interest were legitimate, "it [could not] identify a rational relationship" between that interest and "the law as written," because the law preserves a woman's right to dispose of fetal remains however she wishes and allows for simultaneous cremation. *Ibid.*

We now reverse that determination. This Court has already acknowledged that a State has a "legitimate interest in proper disposal of fetal remains." *Akron* v. *Akron Center for Reproductive Health, Inc.*, 462 U.S. 416, 452, n. 45 (1983). The Seventh Circuit clearly erred in failing to recognize that interest as a permissible basis for Indiana's disposition law. See *Armour* v. *Indianapolis*, 566 U.S. 673, 685 (2012) (on rational basis review, "the burden is on the one attacking the legislative arrangement to negative [*sic*] every conceivable basis which might support it"). The only remaining question, then, is whether Indiana's law is rationally related to the State's interest in proper disposal of fetal remains. We conclude that it is, even if it is not perfectly tailored to that end. See *ibid.* (the State need not have drawn "the perfect line," as long as "the line actually drawn [is] a rational" one). We therefore uphold Indiana's law under rational basis review. . . .

II

Our opinion likewise expresses no view on the merits of the second question presented, *i.e.*, whether Indiana may prohibit the knowing provision of sex-, race-, and disability-selective abortions by abortion providers. Only the Seventh Circuit has thus far addressed this kind of law. We follow our ordinary practice of denying petitions insofar as they raise legal issues that have not been considered by additional Courts of Appeals. See this Court's Rule 10. . . .

JUSTICE SOTOMAYOR would deny the petition for a writ of certiorari as to both questions presented.

JUSTICE THOMAS, concurring.

. . . I write separately to address the other aspect of Indiana law at issue here—the "Sex Selective and Disability Abortion Ban." Ind. Code §16–34–4–1 et seq. This statute makes it illegal for an abortion provider to perform an abortion in Indiana when the provider knows that the mother is seeking the abortion solely because of the child's race, sex, diagnosis of Down syndrome, disability, or related characteristics. §§16–34–4–1 to 16–34–4–8; see §16–34–4–1(b) (excluding "lethal fetal anomal[ies]" from the definition of disability). The law requires that the mother be advised of this restriction and given information about financial assistance and adoption alternatives, but it imposes liability only on the provider. See §§16–34–2–1.1(a)(1)(K), (2)(A)–(C), 16–34–4–9. Each of the immutable characteristics protected by this law can be known relatively early in a pregnancy, and the law prevents them from becoming the sole criterion for deciding whether the child will live or die. Put differently, this law and other laws like it promote a State's compelling interest in preventing abortion from becoming a tool of modern-day eugenics.[2]

The use of abortion to achieve eugenic goals is not merely hypothetical. The foundations for legalizing abortion in America were laid during the early 20th-century birth-control movement. That movement developed alongside the American eugenics movement. And significantly, Planned Parenthood founder Margaret Sanger recognized the eugenic potential of her cause. She emphasized and embraced the notion that birth control "opens the way to the eugenist." Sanger, Birth Control and Racial Betterment, Birth Control Rev., Feb. 1919, p. 12 (Racial Betterment). As a means of reducing the "ever increasing, unceasingly spawning class of human beings who never should have been born at all," Sanger argued that "Birth Control . . . is really the greatest and most truly eugenic method" of "human generation." M. Sanger, Pivot of Civilization 187, 189 (1922) (Pivot of Civilization). In her view, birth control had been "accepted by the most clear thinking and far seeing of the Eugenists themselves as the most constructive and necessary of the means to racial health." Id., at 189.

It is true that Sanger was not referring to abortion when she made these statements, at least not directly. She recognized a moral difference between "contraceptives" and other, more "extreme" ways for "women to limit their families," such as "the horrors of abortion and infanticide." M. Sanger, Woman and the New Race 25, 5 (1920) (Woman and the New Race). But Sanger's arguments about the eugenic value of birth control in securing "the elimination of the unfit," Racial Betterment 11, apply with even greater force to abortion, making it significantly more effective as a tool of eugenics. Whereas Sanger believed that birth control could prevent "unfit" people from reproducing, abortion can prevent them from being born in the first place. Many eugenicists therefore supported legalizing abortion, and abortion advocates—including future Planned Parenthood President Alan Guttmacher—endorsed the use of abortion for eugenic reasons. Technological advances have only heightened the eugenic potential for abortion, as abortion can now be used to eliminate children with unwanted characteristics, such as a particular sex or disability.

---

2. See, e.g., Ariz. Rev. Stat. Ann. §13–3603.02 (2018) (sex and race); Ark. Code §20–16–1904 (2018) (sex); Kan. Stat. Ann. §65–6726 (2017) (sex); La. Rev. Stat. Ann. §40:1061.1.2 (2019) (genetic abnormality); N. C. Gen. Stat. §90–21.121 (2017) (sex); N. D. Cent. Code Ann. §14–02.1–04.1 (2017) (sex and genetic abnormality); Ohio Rev. Code Ann. §2919.10 (2018) (Down syndrome); Okla. Stat., Tit. 63, §1–731.2(B) (2016) (sex); 18 Pa. Cons. Stat. §3204(c) (2015) (sex); S. D. Codified Laws §34–23A–64 (2018) (sex). My focus on a State's compelling interest in prohibiting eugenics in abortion does not suggest that States lack other compelling interests in adopting these or other abortion-related laws.

Given the potential for abortion to become a tool of eugenic manipulation, the Court will soon need to confront the constitutionality of laws like Indiana's. But because further percolation may assist our review of this issue of first impression, I join the Court in declining to take up the issue now. . . .

JUSTICE GINSBURG, concurring in part and dissenting in part.

I agree with the Court's disposition of the second question presented. As to the first question, I would not summarily reverse a judgment when application of the proper standard would likely yield restoration of the judgment. In the District Court and on appeal to the Seventh Circuit, Planned Parenthood of Indiana and Kentucky urged that Indiana's law on the disposition of fetal remains should not pass even rational-basis review.[1] But as Chief Judge Wood observed, "rational basis" is not the proper review standard. *Planned Parenthood of Indiana and Kentucky, Inc. v. Commissioner of Indiana State Dept. of Health*, 917 F. 3d 532, 534 (CA7 2018) (opinion concurring in denial of rehearing en banc). This case implicates "the right of [a] woman to choose to have an abortion before viability and to obtain it without undue interference from the State," *Planned Parenthood of Southeastern Pa. v. Casey*, 505 U.S. 833, 846 (1992), so heightened review is in order, *Whole Woman's Health v. Hellerstedt*, 579 U.S. ___, ___ (2016) (slip op., at 20). . . .

---

1. One may "wonder how, if respect for the humanity of fetal remains after a miscarriage or abortion is the [S]tate's goal, [Indiana's] statute rationally achieves that goal when it simultaneously allows any form of disposal whatsoever if the [woman] elects to handle the remains herself," *Planned Parenthood of Indiana and Kentucky, Inc. v. Commissioner of Indiana State Dept. of Health*, 917 F. 3d 532, 534 (CA7 2018) (Wood, C. J., concurring in denial of rehearing en banc), "and continues to allow for mass cremation of fetuses," *Planned Parenthood of Indiana and Kentucky, Inc. v. Commissioner of Indiana State Dept. of Health*, 888 F. 3d 300, 309 (CA7 2018) (case below).

JUNE MEDICAL SERVICES L. L. C. ET AL. *v.* RUSSO, INTERIM SECRETARY, LOUISIANA DEPARTMENT OF HEALTH AND HOSPITALS

CERTIORARI TO THE UNITED STATES COURT OF APPEALS FOR THE FIFTH CIRCUIT NO. 18–1323.

No. 18–1323. Argued March 4, 2020—Decided June 29, 2020

JUSTICE BREYER announced the judgment of the Court and delivered an opinion, in which JUSTICE GINSBURG, JUSTICE SOTOMAYOR, and JUSTICE KAGAN join.

In *Whole Woman's Health* v. *Hellerstedt*, 579 U. S. ___ (2016), we held that "'[u]nnecessary health regulations that have the purpose or effect of presenting a substantial obstacle to a woman seeking an abortion impose an undue burden on the right'" and are therefore "constitutionally invalid." *Id.*, at ___ (slip op., at 1) (quoting *Planned Parenthood of Southeastern Pa.* v. *Casey*, 505 U. S. 833, 878 (1992) (plurality opinion); alteration in original). We explained that this standard requires courts independently to review the legislative findings upon which an abortion-related statute rests and to weigh the law's "asserted benefits against the burdens" it imposes on abortion access. 579 U. S., at ___ (slip op., at 21) (citing *Gonzales* v. *Carhart*, 550 U. S. 124, 165 (2007)).

The Texas statute at issue in *Whole Woman's Health* required abortion providers to hold "'active admitting privileges at a hospital'" within 30 miles of the place where they perform abortions. 579 U. S., at ___ (slip op., at 1) (quoting Tex. Health & Safety Ann. Code §171.0031(a) (West Cum. Supp. 2015)). Reviewing the record for ourselves, we found ample evidence to support the District Court's finding that the statute did not further the State's asserted interest in protecting women's health. The evidence showed, moreover, that conditions on admitting privileges that served no "relevant credentialing function," 579 U. S., at ___ (slip op., at 25), "help[ed] to explain" the closure of half of Texas' abortion clinics, *id.*, at ___ (slip op., at 24). Those closures placed a substantial obstacle in the path of Texas women seeking an abortion. *Ibid.* And that obstacle, "when viewed in light of the virtual absence of any health benefit," imposed an "undue burden" on abortion access in violation of the Federal Constitution. *Id.*, at ___ (slip op., at 26); see *Casey*, 505 U. S., at 878 (plurality opinion).

In this case, we consider the constitutionality of a Louisiana statute, Act 620, that is almost word-for-word identical to Texas' admitting-privileges law. See La. Rev. Stat. Ann. §40:1061.10(A)(2)(a) (West 2020). As in *Whole Woman's Health*, the District Court found that the statute offers no significant health benefit. It found that conditions on admitting privileges common to hospitals throughout the State have made and will continue to make it impossible for abortion providers to obtain conforming privileges for reasons that have nothing to do with the State's asserted interests in promoting women's health and safety. And it found that this inability places a substantial obstacle in the path of women seeking an abortion. As in *Whole Woman's Health*, the substantial obstacle the Act imposes, and the absence of any health-related benefit, led the District Court to conclude that the law imposes an undue burden and is therefore unconstitutional. See U.S. Const., Amdt. 14, §1.

The Court of Appeals agreed with the District Court's interpretation of the standards we have said apply to regulations on abortion. It thought, however, that the District Court was mistaken on the facts. We disagree. We have examined the extensive record carefully and conclude that it supports the District Court's findings of fact. Those findings mirror those made in *Whole Woman's Health* in every relevant respect and require the same result. We consequently hold that the Louisiana statute is unconstitutional. . . .

CHIEF JUSTICE ROBERTS, concurring in the judgment.

. . . I joined the dissent in *Whole Woman's Health* and continue to believe that the case was wrongly decided. The question today however is not whether *Whole Woman's Health* was right or wrong, but whether to adhere to it in deciding the present case. See *Moore* v. *Texas*, 586 U.S. ___, ___ (2019) (ROBERTS, C. J., concurring) (slip op., at 1). . . .

The legal doctrine of *stare decisis* requires us, absent special circumstances, to treat like cases alike. The Louisiana law imposes a burden on access to abortion just as severe as that imposed by the Texas law, for the same reasons. Therefore Louisiana's law cannot stand under our precedents.

II

A

Both Louisiana and the providers agree that the undue burden standard announced in Casey provides the appropriate framework to analyze Louisiana's law. Brief for Petitioners in No. 18–1323, pp. 45–47; Brief for Respondent in No. 18–1323, pp. 60–62. Neither party has asked us to reassess the constitutional validity of that standard. . . .

Under *Casey*, the State may not impose an undue burden on the woman's ability to obtain an abortion. "A finding of an undue burden is a shorthand for the conclusion that a state regulation has the purpose or effect of placing a substantial obstacle in the path of a woman seeking an abortion of a nonviable fetus." *Id.*, at 877. Laws that do not pose a substantial obstacle to abortion access are permissible, so long as they are "reasonably related" to a legitimate state interest. *Id.*, at 878.

After faithfully reciting this standard, the Court in *Whole Woman's Health* added the following observation: "The rule announced in *Casey* . . . requires that courts consider the burdens a law imposes on abortion access together with the benefits those laws confer."

579 U.S., at ___–___ (slip op., at 19–20). The plurality repeats today that the undue burden standard requires courts "to weigh the law's asserted benefits against the burdens it imposes on abortion access." *Ante*, at 2 (internal quotation marks omitted).

Read in isolation from *Casey*, such an inquiry could invite a grand "balancing test in which unweighted factors mysteriously are weighed." *Marrs v. Motorola, Inc.*, 577 F. 3d 783, 788 (CA7 2009). Under such tests, "equality of treatment is . . . impossible to achieve; predictability is destroyed; judicial arbitrariness is facilitated; judicial courage is impaired." Scalia, The Rule of Law as a Law of Rules, 56 U. Chi. L. Rev. 1175, 1182 (1989).

In this context, courts applying a balancing test would be asked in essence to weigh the State's interests in "protecting the potentiality of human life" and the health of the woman, on the one hand, against the woman's liberty interest in defining her "own concept of existence, of meaning, of the universe, and of the mystery of human life" on the other. *Casey*, 505 U.S., at 851 (opinion of the Court); *id.*, at 871 (plurality opinion) (internal quotation marks omitted). There is no plausible sense in which anyone, let alone this Court, could objectively assign weight to such imponderable values and no meaningful way to compare them if there were. Attempting to do so would be like "judging whether a particular line is longer than a particular rock is heavy," *Bendix Autolite Corp. v. Midwesco Enterprises, Inc.*, 486 U.S. 888, 897 (1988) (Scalia, J., concurring in judgment). Pretending that we could pull that off would require us to act as legislators, not judges, and would result in nothing other than an "unanalyzed exercise of judicial will" in the guise of a "neutral utilitarian calculus." *New Jersey v. T. L. O.*, 469 U.S. 325, 369 (1985) (Brennan, J., concurring in part and dissenting in part).

Nothing about *Casey* suggested that a weighing of costs and benefits of an abortion regulation was a job for the courts. On the contrary, we have explained that the "traditional rule" that "state and federal legislatures [have] wide discretion to pass legislation in areas where there is medical and scientific uncertainty" is "consistent with *Casey*." *Gonzales v. Carhart*, 550 U.S. 124, 163 (2007). *Casey* instead focuses on the existence of a substantial obstacle, the sort of inquiry familiar to judges across a variety of contexts. See, *e.g., Burwell v. Hobby Lobby Stores, Inc.*, 573 U.S. 682, 694–695 (2014) (asking whether the government "substantially burdens a person's exercise of religion" under the Religious Freedom Restoration Act); *Arizona Free Enterprise Club's Freedom Club PAC v. Bennett*, 564 U.S. 721, 748 (2011) (asking whether a law "imposes a substantial burden on the speech of privately financed candidates and independent expenditure groups"); *Murphy v. United Parcel Service, Inc.*, 527 U.S. 516, 521 (1999) (asking, in the context of the Americans with Disabilities Act, whether an individual's impairment "substantially limits one or more major life activities" (internal quotation marks omitted)). . . .

To be sure, the Court at times discussed the benefits of the regulations, including when it distinguished spousal notification from parental consent. See *Whole Woman's Health*, 579 U.S., at ___–___ (slip op., at 19–20) (citing *Casey*, 505 U.S., at 887–898 (opinion of the Court); *id.*, at 899–901 (joint opinion). But in the context of *Casey's* governing standard, these benefits were not placed on a scale opposite the law's burdens. Rather, *Casey* discussed benefits in considering the threshold requirement that the State have a "legitimate purpose" and that the law be "reasonably related to that goal." *Id.*, at 878 (plurality opinion); *id.*, at 882 (joint opinion).

So long as that showing is made, the only question for a court is whether a law has the "effect of placing a substantial obstacle in the path of a woman seeking an abortion of a nonviable fetus." *Id.*, at 877 (plurality opinion). *Casey* repeats that "substantial obstacle" standard nearly verbatim no less than 15 times. *Id.*, at 846, 894, 895 (opinion of the Court); *id.*, at 877, 878 (plurality opinion); *id.*, at 883, 884, 885, 886, 887, 901 (joint opinion).[2]

The only place a balancing test appears in *Casey* is in Justice Stevens's partial dissent. "Weighing the State's interest in potential life and the woman's liberty interest," Justice Stevens would have gone further than the plurality to strike down portions of the State's informed consent requirements and 24-hour waiting period. *Id.*, at 916–920 (opinion concurring in part and dissenting in part). But that approach did not win the day.

Mazurek v. *Armstrong* places this understanding of *Casey*'s undue burden standard beyond doubt. *Mazurek* involved a challenge to a Montana law restricting the performance of abortions to licensed physicians. 520 U.S., at 969. It was "uncontested that there was insufficient evidence of a 'substantial obstacle' to abortion." *Id.*, at 972. Therefore, once the Court found that the Montana Legislature had not acted with an "unlawful motive," the Court's work was complete. *Ibid.* In fact, the Court found the challengers' argument—that the law was invalid because "all health evidence contradicts the [State's] claim that there is any health basis for the law"—to be "*squarely foreclosed* by *Casey* itself." *Id.*, at 973 (internal quotation marks omitted; emphasis added).

We should respect the statement in *Whole Woman's Health* that it was applying the undue burden standard of *Casey*. The opinion in *Whole Woman's Health* began by saying, "We must here decide whether two provisions of [the Texas law] violate the Federal Constitution as interpreted in *Casey*." 579 U.S., at ___ (slip op., at 1). Nothing more. The Court explicitly stated that it was applying "the standard, as described in *Casey*," and reversed the Court of Appeals for applying an approach that did "not match the standard that this Court laid out in *Casey*." *Id.*, at ___, ___ (slip op., at 19, 20).

---

2. Justice Gorsuch correctly notes that *Casey* "expressly disavowed any test as strict as strict scrutiny." *Post*, at 20 (dissenting opinion). But he certainly is wrong to suggest that my position is in any way inconsistent with that disavowal. Applying strict scrutiny would require "*any* regulation touching upon the abortion decision" to be the least restrictive means to further a compelling state interest. *Casey*, 505 U.S., at 871 (plurality opinion) (emphasis added). *Casey* however recognized that such a test would give "too little acknowledgement and implementation" to the State's "legitimate interests in the health of the woman and in protecting the potential life within her." *Ibid.* Under *Casey*, abortion regulations are valid so long as they do not pose a substantial obstacle and meet the threshold requirement of being "reasonably related" to a "legitimate purpose." *Id.*, at 878; *id.*, at 882 (joint opinion).

Here the plurality expressly acknowledges that we are not considering how to analyze an abortion regulation that does not present a substantial obstacle. "That," the plurality explains, "is not this case." *Ante*, at 40. In this case, *Casey*'s requirement of finding a substantial obstacle before invalidating an abortion regulation is therefore a sufficient basis for the decision, as it was in *Whole Woman's Health*. In neither case, nor in *Casey* itself, was there call for consideration of a regulation's benefits, and nothing in *Casey* commands such consideration. Under principles of *stare decisis*, I agree with the plurality that the determination in *Whole Woman's Health* that Texas's law imposed a substantial obstacle requires the same determination about Louisiana's law. Under those same principles, I would adhere to the holding of *Casey*, requiring a substantial obstacle before striking down an abortion regulation. . . .

JUSTICE THOMAS, dissenting.

II

C

. . . THE CHIEF JUSTICE advocates for a Burkean approach to the law that favors adherence to "'the general bank and capital of nations and of ages.'" *Ante*, at 3 (quoting 3 E. Burke, Reflections on the Revolution in France 110 (1790)). But such adherence to precedent was conspicuously absent when the Court broke new ground with its decisions in *Griswold* and *Roe*. And no one could seriously claim that these revolutionary decisions—or *Whole Woman's Health*, decided just four Terms ago—are part of the "*inheritance from our forefathers*," fidelity to which demonstrates "reverence to antiquity." E. Burke, Reflections on the Revolution in France 27–28 (J. Pocock ed. 1987).

More importantly, we exceed our constitutional authority whenever we "appl[y] demonstrably erroneous precedent instead of the relevant law's text." *Gamble, supra*, at ___ (THOMAS, J., concurring) (slip op., at 2). Because we can reconcile neither Roe nor its progeny with the text of our Constitution, those decisions should be overruled. . . .

JUSTICE ALITO, with whom JUSTICE GORSUCH joins, with whom JUSTICE THOMAS joins except as to Parts III–C and IV–F, and with whom JUSTICE KAVANAUGH joins as to Parts I, II, and III, dissenting.

The majority bills today's decision as a facsimile of *Whole Woman's Health* v. *Hellerstedt*, 579 U.S. ___, ___ (2016), and it's true they have something in common. In both, the abortion right recognized in this Court's decisions is used like a bulldozer to flatten legal rules that stand in the way.

In *Whole Woman's Health*, res judicata and our standard approach to severability were laid low. Even *Planned Parenthood of Southeastern Pa. v. Casey*, 505 U.S. 833 (1992), was altered.

Today's decision claims new victims. The divided majority cannot agree on what the abortion right requires, but it nevertheless strikes down a Louisiana law, Act 620, that the legislature enacted for the asserted purpose of protecting women's health. To achieve this end, the majority misuses the doctrine of *stare decisis*, invokes an inapplicable standard of appellate review, and distorts the record. . . .

Both the plurality and THE CHIEF JUSTICE hold that abortion providers can invoke a woman's abortion right when they attack state laws that are enacted to protect a woman's health. Neither waiver nor *stare decisis* can justify this holding, which clashes with our general rule on third-party standing. And the idea that a regulated party can invoke the right of a third party for the purpose of attacking legislation enacted to protect the third party is stunning. Given the apparent conflict of interest, that concept would be rejected out of hand in a case not involving abortion. . . .

IV

B

This case features a blatant conflict of interest between an abortion provider and its patients. Like any other regulated entity, an abortion provider has a financial interest in avoiding burdensome regulations such as Act 620's admitting privileges requirement. Applying for privileges takes time and energy, and maintaining privileges may impose additional burdens. See App. 1335. Women seeking abortions, on the other hand, have an interest in the preservation of regulations that protect their health. The conflict inherent in such a situation is glaring.

Some may not see the conflict in this case because they are convinced that the admitting privileges requirement does nothing to promote safety and is really just a ploy. But an abortion provider's ability to assert the rights of women when it challenges ostensible safety regulations should not turn on the merits of its claim.

The problem with the rule that the majority embraces is highlighted if we consider challenges to other safety regulations. Suppose, for example, that a clinic in a State that allows certified non-physicians to perform abortions claims that the State's certification requirements are too onerous and that they imperil the clinic's continued operation. Should the clinic be able to assert the rights of women in attacking this regulation, which the state lawmakers thought was important to protect women's health?

When an abortion regulation is enacted for the asserted purpose of protecting the health of women, an abortion provider seeking to strike down that law should not be able to rely on the constitutional rights of women. Like any other party unhappy with burdensome regulation, the provider should be limited to its own rights. . . .

WHOLE WOMAN'S HEALTH ET AL. *v.* AUSTIN REEVE JACKSON, JUDGE, ET AL. ON APPLICATION FOR INJUNCTIVE RELIEF

No. 21A24 [September 1, 2021]

The application for injunctive relief or, in the alternative, to vacate stays of the district court proceedings presented to JUSTICE ALITO and by him referred to the Court is denied. To prevail in an application for a stay or an injunction, an applicant must carry the burden of making a "strong showing" that it is "likely to succeed on the merits," that it will be "irreparably injured absent a stay," that the balance of the equities favors it, and that a stay is consistent with the public interest. *Nken* v. *Holder*, 556 U.S. 418, 434 (2009); *Roman Catholic Diocese of Brooklyn* v. *Cuomo*, 141 S. Ct. 63, 66 (2020) (citing *Winter* v. *Natural Resources Defense Council, Inc.*, 555 U.S. 7, 20 (2008)). The applicants now before us have raised serious questions regarding the constitutionality of the Texas law at issue. But their application also presents complex and novel antecedent procedural questions on which they have not carried their burden. For example, federal courts enjoy the power to enjoin individuals tasked with enforcing laws, not the laws themselves. *California* v. *Texas*, 593 U.S. ___, ___ (2021) (slip op., at 8). And it is unclear whether the named defendants in this lawsuit can or will seek to enforce the Texas law against the applicants in a manner that might permit our intervention. *Clapper* v. *Amnesty Int'l USA*, 568 U.S. 398, 409 (2013) ("threatened injury must be *certainly impending*" (citation omitted)). The State has represented that neither it nor its executive employees possess the authority to enforce the Texas law either directly or indirectly. Nor is it clear whether, under existing precedent, this Court can issue an injunction against state judges asked to decide a lawsuit under Texas's law. See *Ex parte Young*, 209 U.S. 123, 163 (1908). Finally, the sole private-citizen respondent before us has filed an affidavit stating that he has no present intention to enforce the law. In light of such issues, we cannot say the applicants have met their burden to prevail in an injunction or stay application. In reaching this conclusion, we stress that we do not purport to resolve definitively any jurisdictional or substantive claim in the applicants' lawsuit. In particular, this order is not based on any conclusion about the constitutionality of Texas's law, and in no way limits other procedurally proper challenges to the Texas law, including in Texas state courts.

JUSTICE SOTOMAYOR, with whom JUSTICE BREYER and JUSTICE KAGAN join, dissenting.

The Court's order is stunning. Presented with an application to enjoin a flagrantly unconstitutional law engineered to prohibit women from exercising their constitutional rights and evade judicial scrutiny, a majority of Justices have opted to bury their heads in the sand. Last night, the Court silently acquiesced in a State's enactment of a law that flouts nearly 50 years of federal precedents. Today, the Court belatedly explains that it declined to grant relief because of procedural complexities of the State's own invention.

Ante, at 1. Because the Court's failure to act rewards tactics designed to avoid judicial review and inflicts significant harm on the applicants and on women seeking abortions in Texas, I dissent.

In May 2021, the Texas Legislature enacted S. B. 8 (the Act). The Act, which took effect statewide at midnight on September 1, makes it unlawful for physicians to perform abortions if they either detect cardiac activity in an embryo or fail to perform a test to detect such activity. §3 (to be codified at Tex. Health & Safety Code Ann. §§171.201(1), 171.204(a) (West 2021)). This equates to a near-categorical ban on abortions beginning six weeks after a woman's last menstrual period, before many women realize they are pregnant, and months before fetal viability. According to the applicants, who are abortion providers and advocates in Texas, the Act immediately prohibits care for at least 85% of Texas abortion patients and will force many abortion clinics to close.

The Act is clearly unconstitutional under existing precedents. See, *e.g.*, *June Medical Servs. L. L. C.* v. *Russo*, 591 U. S. ___, ___ (2020) (Roberts, C. J., concurring in judgment) (slip op., at 5) (explaining that "the State may not impose an undue burden on the woman's ability to obtain an abortion" of a "nonviable fetus" (citing *Roe* v. *Wade*, 410 U. S. 113 (1973), and *Planned Parenthood of Southeastern Pa.* v. *Casey*, 505 U. S. 833 (1992); internal quotation marks omitted)). The respondents do not even try to argue otherwise. Nor could they: No federal appellate court has upheld such a comprehensive prohibition on abortions before viability under current law.

The Texas Legislature was well aware of this binding precedent. To circumvent it, the Legislature took the extraordinary step of enlisting private citizens to do what the State could not. The Act authorizes any private citizen to file a lawsuit against any person who provides an abortion in violation of the Act, "aids or abets" such an abortion (including by paying for it) regardless of whether they know the abortion is prohibited under the Act, or even intends to engage in such conduct. §3 (to be codified at Tex. Health & Safety Code Ann. §171.208). Courts are required to enjoin the defendant from engaging in these actions in the future and to award the private-citizen plaintiff at least $10,000 in "statutory damages" for each forbidden abortion performed or aided by the defendant. *Ibid.* In effect, the Texas Legislature has deputized the State's citizens as bounty hunters, offering them cash prizes for civilly prosecuting their neighbors' medical procedures.

The Legislature fashioned this scheme because federal constitutional challenges to state laws ordinarily are brought against state officers who are in charge of enforcing the law. See, *e.g.*, *Virginia Office for Protection and Advocacy* v. *Stewart*, 563 U. S. 247, 254 (2011) (citing *Ex parte Young*, 209 U. S. 123 (1908)). By prohibiting state officers from enforcing the Act directly and relying instead on citizen bounty hunters, the Legislature sought to make it more complicated for federal courts to enjoin the Act on a statewide basis.

Taken together, the Act is a breathtaking act of defiance of the Constitution, of this Court's precedents, and of the rights of women seeking abortions throughout Texas. But over six weeks after the applicants filed suit to prevent the Act from taking effect, a Fifth

Circuit panel abruptly stayed all proceedings before the District Court and vacated a preliminary injunction hearing that was scheduled to begin on Monday. The applicants requested emergency relief from this Court, but the Court said nothing. The Act took effect at midnight last night.*

Today, the Court finally tells the Nation that it declined to act because, in short, the State's gambit worked. The structure of the State's scheme, the Court reasons, raises "complex and novel antecedent procedural questions" that counsel against granting the application, *ante*, at 1, just as the State intended. This is untenable. It cannot be the case that a State can evade federal judicial scrutiny by outsourcing the enforcement of unconstitutional laws to its citizenry. Moreover, the District Court held this case justiciable in a thorough and well-reasoned opinion after weeks of briefing and consideration. 2021 WL 3821062, *8–*26 (WD Tex., Aug. 25, 2021). At a minimum, this Court should have stayed implementation of the Act to allow the lower courts to evaluate these issues in the normal course. *Ante*, at 2 (ROBERTS, C. J., dissenting). Instead, the Court has rewarded the State's effort to delay federal review of a plainly unconstitutional statute, enacted in disregard of the Court's precedents, through procedural entanglements of the State's own creation. . . .

---

*The Court's inaction has had immediate impact. Two hours before the Act took effect, one applicant reported that its waiting rooms were "'filled with patients'" urgently seeking care while "'protesters [we]re outside, shining lights on the parking [lot].'" De Vogue, Texas 6-Week Abortion Ban Takes Effect after Supreme Court Inaction, CNN (Sept. 1, 2021), www.cnn.com/2021/09/01 /politics/texas-abortion-supreme-courtsb8-roe-wade/index.html. Then, at midnight, the Act became law, and many abortion providers, including applicants, ceased providing abortion care after more than six weeks from a woman's last menstrual period (LMP). See, *e.g.*, Alamo Women's Reproductive Care (Sept. 1, 2021), https://alamowomensclinic.com ("We cannot provide abortion services to anyone with detectable embryonic or fetal cardiac activity[,] which is typically found at 6 weeks or more from last menstrual period"); Southwestern Women's Surgery Center (Sept. 1, 2021), https:// southwesternwomens.com/southwestern-womens-surgery-center-dallas-texas/ ("In compliance with Texas Senate Bill 8 of 2021, starting on September 1st 2021, our facility cannot provide abortions to patients with detectible embryonic or fetal cardiac activity, which typically starts at 6 weeks LMP"). Since then, at least one applicant has stopped providing abortions entirely. Planned Parenthood South Texas (Sept. 1, 2021), https://www.plannedparenthood.org/planned-parenthood -south-texas ("Due to Texas' SB 8 law, we are unable to provide abortion procedures at this time").

UNITED STATES v. TEXAS, ET AL.

ON APPLICATION TO VACATE STAY AND PETITION FOR WRIT OF CERTIORARI BEFORE JUDGMENT

No. 21A85 (21-588) [October 22, 2021]

Consideration of the application (21A85) to vacate stay presented to JUSTICE ALITO and by him referred to the Court is deferred pending oral argument.

In addition, the application is treated as a petition for a writ of certiorari before judgment, and the petition is granted limited to the following question: May the United States bring suit in federal court and obtain injunctive or declaratory relief against the State, state court judges, state court clerks, other state officials, or all private parties to prohibit S.B. 8 from being enforced. . . .

JUSTICE SOTOMAYOR, concurring in part and dissenting in part.

II

Recognizing that Texas' scheme raises concerns of imperative public importance, the Court properly grants certiorari before judgment. See this Court's Rule 11. However, the Court's failure to issue an administrative stay of the Fifth Circuit's order pending its decision on this application will have profound and immediate consequences. By delaying any remedy, the Court enables continued and irreparable harm to women seeking abortion care and providers of such care in Texas—exactly as S. B. 8's architects intended, see *infra*, at 6–7. Whatever equities favor caution in staying a state law under normal circumstances cannot outweigh the total and intentional denial of a constitutional right to women while this Court considers the serious questions presented.

The District Court concluded that S. B. 8 "'has had an immediate and devastating effect on abortion care in Texas.'" 2021 WL 4593319, *36. That is because the Act's chilling effects "operate . . . as an effective deterrent to provision of pre-viability abortion services in Texas, precluding the vast majority of individuals from accessing this constitutional right" and causing a "dismantling of the provider network" across the State. *Id.*, at *38. Before the District Court, Texas identified only one abortion that had occurred in the State beyond S. B. 8's unlawful 6-week restriction since the law took effect. *Id.*, at *41. The court explained that most abortion patients in Texas first seek care more than six weeks after their last menstrual periods. *Id.*, at *2. The court thus found that S. B. 8 has prohibited as many as 95% of abortions previously provided in the State. *Id.*, at *40; see *Whole Woman's Health*, 594 U.S., at ___ (SOTOMAYOR, J., dissenting) (slip op., at 2) (warning that

S. B. 8 would "immediately prohibi[t] care for at least 85% of Texas abortion patients and . . . force many abortion clinics to close").

On a human level, the District Court relied on credible declarations that described the threat of liability under S. B. 8 as "nothing short of agonizing" for abortion care providers. 2021 WL 4593319, *38 (internal quotation marks omitted). Providers are "seriously concerned that even providing abortions in compliance with S. B. 8 will draw lawsuits from anti-abortion vigilantes or others seeking financial gain." *Ibid.* (internal quotation marks omitted). Patients are "devastated" to learn they cannot access care, and the "turmoil" caused by the Act leaves them "panicked, both for themselves and their loved ones." *Id.,* at *40 (internal quotation marks omitted).* Even among the few women who are able to receive abortion services in Texas, S. B. 8 pushes patients "to make a decision about their abortion before they are truly ready to do so." *Ibid.* (internal quotation marks omitted).

The District Court rejected the State's claim that Texas residents could travel to other States to access abortion care. *Id.,* at *41. To be sure, the court agreed, "[p]regnant people from Texas are scared and are frantically trying to get appointments" in other States. *Id.,* at *43 (internal quotation marks omitted). The court found, however, that many patients are unable to seek out-of-state care based on financial constraints, dangerous family situations, immigration status, or other reasons. *Id.,* at *42. These individuals "are being forced to carry their pregnancy to term against their will or to seek ways to end their pregnancies on their own." *Id.,* at *41 (internal quotation marks omitted).

The court also found that patients who are able to leave Texas have encountered restrictions and backlogs exacerbated by S. B. 8, citing evidence of the Act's "stunning" and "crushing" impacts on clinics in Oklahoma, Kansas, Colorado, New Mexico, and Nevada. *Id.,* at *43–*45. An Oklahoma provider, for example, reported a "staggering 646% increase of Texan patients per day," occupying between 50% and 75% of capacity. *Id.,* at *43 (internal quotation marks omitted). A Kansas clinic similarly reported that about half of its patients now come from Texas. *Id.,* at *44. The District Court found that this "constant stream of Texas patients has created backlogs that in some places prevent residents from accessing abortion services in their own communities." *Id.,* at *45.

I cannot capture the totality of this harm in these pages. But as these excerpts illustrate, the State (empowered by this Court's inaction) has so thoroughly chilled the exercise of the right recognized in *Roe* as to nearly suspend it within its borders and strain access to it in other States. The State's gambit has worked. The impact is catastrophic. . . .

---

*The harm to vulnerable populations is especially acute. For example, because Texas' judicial bypass process for minors seeking abortion care "cannot realistically happen" before six weeks after the last menstrual period, S. B. 8 forces pregnant minors who cannot confide in their families (and unaccompanied migrant teenagers who cannot reach their families) to choose between "carry[ing] to term" and "tak[ing] matters into their own hands." 2021 WL 4593319, *40, and n. 62 (internal quotation marks omitted).

WHOLE WOMAN'S HEALTH ET AL. *v.* JACKSON, JUDGE, DISTRICT COURT OF TEXAS, 114TH DISTRICT, ET AL.

CERTIORARI TO THE UNITED STATES COURT OF APPEALS FOR THE FIFTH CIRCUIT

No. 21–463. Argued November 1, 2021—Decided December 10, 2021

Gorsuch, J., announced the judgment of the Court, and delivered the opinion of the Court except as to Part II–C. Alito, Kavanaugh, and Barrett, JJ., joined that opinion in full, and Thomas, J., joined except for Part II–C. Thomas, J., filed an opinion concurring in part and dissenting in part. Roberts, C. J., filed an opinion concurring in the judgment in part and dissenting in part, in which Breyer, Sotomayor, and Kagan, JJ., joined.

Sotomayor, J., filed an opinion concurring in the judgment in part and dissenting in part, in which Breyer and Kagan, JJ., joined.

Justice Gorsuch delivered the opinion of the Court, except as to Part II–C.

The Court granted certiorari before judgment in this case to determine whether, under our precedents, certain abortion providers can pursue a pre-enforcement challenge to a recently enacted Texas statute. We conclude that such an action is permissible against some of the named defendants but not others. . . .

II

Because this Court granted certiorari before judgment, we effectively stand in the shoes of the Court of Appeals. See *United States* v. *Nixon*, 418 U.S. 683, 690–692 (1974); S. Shapiro, K. Geller, T. Bishop, E. Hartnett, D. Himmelfarb, Supreme Court Practice 2-11 (11th ed. 2019). In this case, that means we must review the defendants' appeals challenging the District Court's order denying their motions to dismiss. As with any interlocutory appeal, our review is limited to the particular orders under review and any other ruling "inextricably intertwined with" or "necessary to ensure meaningful review of" them. *Swint* v. *Chambers County Comm'n*, 514 U.S. 35, 51 (1995). In this preliminary posture, the ultimate merits question—whether S. B. 8 is consistent with the Federal Constitution—is not before the Court. Nor is the wisdom of S. B. 8 as a matter of public policy.

A

Turning to the matters that are properly put to us, we begin with the sovereign immunity appeal involving the state-court judge, Austin Jackson, and the state-court clerk, Penny Clarkston. While this lawsuit names only one state-court judge and one state-court clerk as defendants, the petitioners explain that they hope eventually to win certification of a class including all Texas state-court judges and clerks as defendants. In the end, the petitioners say, they intend to seek an order enjoining all state-court clerks from docketing S. B. 8 cases and all state-court judges from hearing them.

Almost immediately, however, the petitioners' theory confronts a difficulty. Generally, States are immune from suit under the terms of the Eleventh Amendment and the doctrine of sovereign immunity. See, *e.g.*, *Alden* v. *Maine*, 527 U.S. 706, 713 (1999). To be sure, in *Ex parte Young*, this Court recognized a narrow exception grounded in traditional equity practice—one that allows certain private parties to seek judicial orders in federal court preventing state executive officials from enforcing state laws that are contrary to federal law. 209 U.S. 123, 159–160 (1908). But as *Ex parte Young* explained, this traditional exception does not normally permit federal courts to issue injunctions against state-court judges or clerks. Usually, those individuals do not enforce state laws as executive officials might; instead, they work to resolve disputes between parties. If a state court errs in its rulings, too, the traditional remedy has been some form of appeal, including to this Court, not the entry of an *ex ante* injunction preventing the state court from hearing cases. As *Ex parte Young* put it, "an injunction against a state court" or its "machinery" "would be a violation of the whole scheme of our Government." *Id.*, at 163.

Nor is that the only problem confronting the petitioners' court-and-clerk theory. Article III of the Constitution affords federal courts the power to resolve only "actual controversies arising between adverse litigants." *Muskrat* v. *United States*, 219 U.S. 346, 361 (1911). Private parties who seek to bring S. B. 8 suits in state court may be litigants adverse to the petitioners. But the state-court clerks who docket those disputes and the state-court judges who decide them generally are not. Clerks serve to file cases as they arrive, not to participate as adversaries in those disputes. Judges exist to resolve controversies about a law's meaning or its conformance to the Federal and State Constitutions, not to wage battle as contestants in the parties' litigation. As this Court has explained, "no case or controversy" exists "between a judge who adjudicates claims under a statute and a litigant who attacks the constitutionality of the statute." *Pulliam* v. *Allen*, 466 U.S. 522, 538, n. 18 (1984). . . .

C

While this Court's precedents foreclose some of the petitioners' claims for relief, others survive. The petitioners also name as defendants Stephen Carlton, Katherine Thomas,

Allison Benz, and Cecile Young. On the briefing and argument before us, it appears that these particular defendants fall within the scope of *Ex parte Young*'s historic exception to state sovereign immunity. Each of these individuals is an executive licensing official who may or must take enforcement actions against the petitioners if they violate the terms of Texas's Health and Safety Code, including S. B. 8. See, *e.g.*, Tex. Occ. Code Ann. §164.055(a); Brief for Petitioners 33–34. Accordingly, we hold that sovereign immunity does not bar the petitioners' suit against these named defendants at the motion to dismiss stage. . . .[3]

IV

The petitioners' theories for relief face serious challenges but also present some opportunities. To summarize: (1) The Court unanimously rejects the petitioners' theory for relief against state-court judges and agrees Judge Jackson should be dismissed from this suit. (2) A majority reaches the same conclusion with respect to the petitioners' parallel theory for relief against state-court clerks. (3) With respect to the back-up theory of relief the petitioners present against Attorney General Paxton, a majority concludes that he must be dismissed. (4) At the same time, eight Justices hold this case may proceed past the motion to dismiss stage against Mr. Carlton, Ms. Thomas, Ms. Benz, and Ms. Young, defendants with specific disciplinary authority over medical licensees, including the petitioners. (5) Every Member of the Court accepts that the only named private-individual defendant, Mr. Dickson, should be dismissed. . . .

CHIEF JUSTICE ROBERTS, with whom JUSTICE BREYER, JUSTICE SOTOMAYOR, and JUSTICE KAGAN join, concurring in the judgment in part and dissenting in part.

. . . The clear purpose and actual effect of S. B. 8 has been to nullify this Court's rulings. It is, however, a basic principle that the Constitution is the "fundamental and paramount law of the nation," and "[i]t is emphatically the province and duty of the judicial department to say what the law is." *Marbury* v. *Madison*, 1 Cranch 137, 177 (1803). Indeed, "[i]f the legislatures of the several states may, at will, annul the judgments of the courts of the United States, and destroy the rights acquired under those judgments, the constitution itself becomes a solemn mockery." *United States* v. *Peters*, 5 Cranch 115, 136 (1809). The nature of the federal right infringed does not matter; it is the role of the Supreme Court in our constitutional system that is at stake.

---

3. The petitioners may proceed against Ms. Young solely based on her authority to supervise licensing of abortion facilities and ambulatory surgical centers, and not with respect to any other enforcement authority under Chapter 171 of the Texas Health and Safety Code.

JUSTICE SOTOMAYOR, with whom JUSTICE BREYER and JUSTICE KAGAN join, concurring in the judgment in part and dissenting in part.

. . . The Court should have put an end to this madness months ago, before S. B. 8 first went into effect. It failed to do so then, and it fails again today. I concur in the Court's judgment that the petitioners' suit may proceed against certain executive licensing officials who retain enforcement authority under Texas law, and I trust the District Court will act expeditiously to enter much-needed relief. I dissent, however, from the Court's dangerous departure from its precedents, which establish that federal courts can and should issue relief when a State enacts a law that chills the exercise of a constitutional right and aims to evade judicial review. By foreclosing suit against state-court officials and the state attorney general, the Court effectively invites other States to refine S. B. 8's model for nullifying federal rights. The Court thus betrays not only the citizens of Texas, but also our constitutional system of government. . . .

III

My disagreement with the Court runs far deeper than a quibble over how many defendants these petitioners may sue. The dispute is over whether States may nullify federal constitutional rights by employing schemes like the one at hand. The Court indicates that they can, so long as they write their laws to more thoroughly disclaim all enforcement by state officials, including licensing officials. This choice to shrink from Texas' challenge to federal supremacy will have far-reaching repercussions. I doubt the Court, let alone the country, is prepared for them.

The State's concessions at oral argument laid bare the sweeping consequences of its position. In response to questioning, counsel for the State conceded that pre-enforcement review would be unavailable even if a statute imposed a bounty of $1,000,000 or higher. Tr. of Oral Arg. 50–53. Counsel further admitted that no individual constitutional right was safe from attack under a similar scheme. Tr. of Oral Arg. in *United States* v. *Texas*, No. 21–588, pp. 59–61, 64–65. Counsel even asserted that a State could further rig procedures by abrogating a state supreme court's power to bind its own lower courts. *Id.*, at 78–79. Counsel maintained that even if a State neutered appellate courts' power in such an extreme manner, aggrieved parties' only path to a federal forum would be to violate the unconstitutional law, accede to infringement of their substantive and procedural rights all the way through the state supreme court, and then, at last, ask this Court to grant discretionary certiorari review. *Ibid.* All of these burdens would layer atop S. B. 8's existing manipulation of state-court procedures and defenses.

This is a brazen challenge to our federal structure. It echoes the philosophy of John C. Calhoun, a virulent defender of the slaveholding South who insisted that States had the right to "veto" or "nullif[y]" any federal law with which they disagreed. Address of J. Calhoun, Speeches of John C. Calhoun 17–43 (1843). Lest the parallel be lost on the Court, analogous sentiments were expressed in this case's companion: "The Supreme Court's *interpretations* of the Constitution are not the Constitution itself—they are, after all, called *opinions*." Reply Brief for Intervenors in No. 21–50949 (CA5), p. 4.

The Nation fought a Civil War over that proposition, but Calhoun's theories were not extinguished. They experienced a revival in the post-war South, and the violence that ensued led Congress to enact Rev. Stat. §1979, 42 U.S. C. §1983. "Proponents of the legislation noted that state courts were being used to harass and injure individuals, either because the state courts were powerless to stop deprivations or were in league with those who were bent upon abrogation of federally protected rights." *Mitchum*, 407 U.S., at 240. Thus, §1983's "very purpose," consonant with the values that motivated the *Young* Court some decades later, was "to protect the people from unconstitutional action under color of state law, 'whether that action be executive, legislative, or judicial.'" *Mitchum*, 407 U.S., at 242 (quoting *Ex parte Virginia*, 100 U.S. 339, 346 (1880)).

S. B. 8 raises another challenge to federal supremacy, and by blessing significant portions of the law's effort to evade review, the Court comes far short of meeting the moment. The Court's delay in allowing this case to proceed has had catastrophic consequences for women seeking to exercise their constitutional right to an abortion in Texas. These consequences have only rewarded the State's effort at nullification. Worse, by foreclosing suit against state-court officials and the state attorney general, the Court clears the way for States to reprise and perfect Texas' scheme in the future to target the exercise of any right recognized by this Court with which they disagree. . . .

* * *

In its finest moments, this Court has ensured that constitutional rights "can neither be nullified openly and directly by state legislators or state executive or judicial officers, nor nullified indirectly by them through evasive schemes . . . whether attempted 'ingeniously or ingenuously.'" *Cooper* v. *Aaron*, 358 U.S. 1, 17 (1958) (quoting *Smith* v. *Texas*, 311 U.S. 128, 132 (1940)). Today's fractured Court evinces no such courage. While the Court properly holds that this suit may proceed against the licensing officials, it errs gravely in foreclosing relief against state-court officials and the state attorney general. By so doing, the Court leaves all manner of constitutional rights more vulnerable than ever before, to the great detriment of our Constitution and our Republic.

DOBBS, STATE HEALTH OFFICER OF THE MISSISSIPPI DEPARTMENT OF HEALTH, ET AL. *v.* JACKSON WOMEN'S HEALTH ORGANIZATION ET AL.

CERTIORARI TO THE UNITED STATES COURT OF APPEALS FOR THE FIFTH CIRCUIT

No. 19–1392. Argued December 1, 2021—Decided June 24, 2022

ALITO, J., delivered the opinion of the Court, in which THOMAS, GORSUCH, KAVANAUGH, and BARRETT, JJ., joined. THOMAS, J., and KAVANAUGH, J., filed concurring opinions. ROBERTS, C. J., filed an opinion concurring in the judgment. BREYER, SOTOMAYOR, and KAGAN, JJ., filed a dissenting opinion.

JUSTICE ALITO delivered the opinion of the Court.

Abortion presents a profound moral issue on which Americans hold sharply conflicting views. Some believe fervently that a human person comes into being at conception and that abortion ends an innocent life. Others feel just as strongly that any regulation of abortion invades a woman's right to control her own body and prevents women from achieving full equality. Still others in a third group think that abortion should be allowed under some but not all circumstances, and those within this group hold a variety of views about the particular restrictions that should be imposed.

For the first 185 years after the adoption of the Constitution, each State was permitted to address this issue in accordance with the views of its citizens. Then, in 1973, this Court decided *Roe* v. *Wade*, 410 U.S. 113. Even though the Constitution makes no mention of abortion, the Court held that it confers a broad right to obtain one. It did not claim that American law or the common law had ever recognized such a right, and its survey of history ranged from the constitutionally irrelevant (*e.g.*, its discussion of abortion in antiquity) to the plainly incorrect (*e.g.*, its assertion that abortion was probably never a crime under the common law). After cataloging a wealth of other information having no bearing on the meaning of the Constitution, the opinion concluded with a numbered set of rules much like those that might be found in a statute enacted by a legislature.

Under this scheme, each trimester of pregnancy was regulated differently, but the most critical line was drawn at roughly the end of the second trimester, which, at the time, corresponded to the point at which a fetus was thought to achieve "viability," *i.e.*, the ability to survive outside the womb. Although the Court acknowledged that States had a legitimate interest in protecting "potential life,"[1] it found that this interest could

---

1. *Roe* v. *Wade*, 410 U.S. 113, 163 (1973).

not justify any restriction on pre-viability abortions. The Court did not explain the basis for this line, and even abortion supporters have found it hard to defend *Roe*'s reasoning. One prominent constitutional scholar wrote that he "would vote for a statute very much like the one the Court end[ed] up drafting" if he were "a legislator," but his assessment of *Roe* was memorable and brutal: *Roe* was "not constitutional law" at all and gave "almost no sense of an obligation to try to be."[2]

At the time of *Roe*, 30 States still prohibited abortion at all stages. In the years prior to that decision, about a third of the States had liberalized their laws, but *Roe* abruptly ended that political process. It imposed the same highly restrictive regime on the entire Nation, and it effectively struck down the abortion laws of every single State.[3] As Justice Byron White aptly put it in his dissent, the decision represented the "exercise of raw judicial power," 410 U.S., at 222, and it sparked a national controversy that has embittered our political culture for a half century.[4]

Eventually, in *Planned Parenthood of Southeastern Pa. v. Casey*, 505 U.S. 833 (1992), the Court revisited *Roe*, but the Members of the Court split three ways. Two Justices expressed no desire to change *Roe* in any way.[5] Four others wanted to overrule the decision in its entirety.[6] And the three remaining Justices, who jointly signed the controlling opinion, took a third position.[7] Their opinion did not endorse *Roe*'s reasoning, and it even hinted that one or more of its authors might have "reservations" about whether the Constitution protects a right to abortion.[8] But the opinion concluded that *stare decisis*, which calls for prior decisions to be followed in most instances, required adherence to what it called *Roe*'s "central holding"—that a State may not constitutionally protect fetal life before "viability"—even if that holding was wrong.[9] Anything less, the opinion claimed, would undermine respect for this Court and the rule of law.

---

2. J. Ely, The Wages of Crying Wolf: A Comment on *Roe* v. *Wade*, 82 Yale L. J. 920, 926, 947 (1973) (Ely) (emphasis deleted).

3. L. Tribe, Foreword: Toward a Model of Roles in the Due Process of Life and Law, 87 Harv. L. Rev. 1, 2 (1973) (Tribe).

4. See R. Ginsburg, Speaking in a Judicial Voice, 67 N. Y. U. L. Rev. 1185, 1208 (1992) ("*Roe* ... halted a political process that was moving in a reform direction and thereby, I believed, prolonged divisiveness and deferred stable settlement of the issue").

5. See 505 U.S., at 911 (Stevens, J., concurring in part and dissenting in part); *id.*, at 922 (Blackmun, J., concurring in part, concurring in judgment in part, and dissenting in part).

6. See *id.*, at 944 (Rehnquist, C. J., concurring in judgment in part and dissenting in part); *id.*, at 979 (Scalia, J., concurring in judgment in part and dissenting in part).

7. See *id.*, at 843 (joint opinion of O'Connor, Kennedy, and Souter, JJ.).

8. *Id.*, at 853.

9. *Id.*, at 860.

Paradoxically, the judgment in *Casey* did a fair amount of overruling. Several important abortion decisions were overruled *in toto*, and *Roe* itself was overruled in part.[10] *Casey* threw out *Roe*'s trimester scheme and substituted a new rule of uncertain origin under which States were forbidden to adopt any regulation that imposed an "undue burden" on a woman's right to have an abortion.[11] The decision provided no clear guidance about the difference between a "due" and an "undue" burden. But the three Justices who authored the controlling opinion "call[ed] the contending sides of a national controversy to end their national division" by treating the Court's decision as the final settlement of the question of the constitutional right to abortion.[12]

As has become increasingly apparent in the intervening years, *Casey* did not achieve that goal. Americans continue to hold passionate and widely divergent views on abortion, and state legislatures have acted accordingly. Some have recently enacted laws allowing abortion, with few restrictions, at all stages of pregnancy. Others have tightly restricted abortion beginning well before viability. And in this case, 26 States have expressly asked this Court to overrule *Roe* and *Casey* and allow the States to regulate or prohibit pre-viability abortions.

Before us now is one such state law. The State of Mississippi asks us to uphold the constitutionality of a law that generally prohibits an abortion after the 15th week of pregnancy—several weeks before the point at which a fetus is now regarded as "viable" outside the womb. In defending this law, the State's primary argument is that we should reconsider and overrule *Roe* and *Casey* and once again allow each State to regulate abortion as its citizens wish. On the other side, respondents and the Solicitor General ask us to reaffirm *Roe* and *Casey*, and they contend that the Mississippi law cannot stand if we do so. Allowing Mississippi to prohibit abortions after 15 weeks of pregnancy, they argue, "would be no different than overruling *Casey* and *Roe* entirely." Brief for Respondents 43. They contend that "no half-measures" are available and that we must either reaffirm or overrule *Roe* and *Casey*. Brief for Respondents 50.

We hold that *Roe* and *Casey* must be overruled. The Constitution makes no reference to abortion, and no such right is implicitly protected by any constitutional provision, including the one on which the defenders of *Roe* and *Casey* now chiefly rely—the Due Process Clause of the Fourteenth Amendment. That provision has been held to guarantee some rights that are not mentioned in the Constitution, but any such right must be "deeply rooted in this Nation's history and tradition" and "implicit in the concept of ordered liberty." *Washington* v. *Glucksberg*, 521 U.S. 702, 721 (1997) (internal quotation marks omitted).

---

10. *Id.*, at 861, 870, 873 (overruling *Akron* v. *Akron Center for Reproductive Health, Inc.*, 462 U.S. 416 (1983), and *Thornburgh* v. *American College of Obstetricians and Gynecologists*, 476 U.S. 747 (1986)).

11. 505 U.S., at 874.

12. *Id.*, at 867.

The right to abortion does not fall within this category. Until the latter part of the 20th century, such a right was entirely unknown in American law. Indeed, when the Fourteenth Amendment was adopted, three quarters of the States made abortion a crime at all stages of pregnancy. The abortion right is also critically different from any other right that this Court has held to fall within the Fourteenth Amendment's protection of "liberty." *Roe*'s defenders characterize the abortion right as similar to the rights recognized in past decisions involving matters such as intimate sexual relations, contraception, and marriage, but abortion is fundamentally different, as both *Roe* and *Casey* acknowledged, because it destroys what those decisions called "fetal life" and what the law now before us describes as an "unborn human being."[13]

Stare decisis, the doctrine on which *Casey*'s controlling opinion was based, does not compel unending adherence to *Roe*'s abuse of judicial authority. *Roe* was egregiously wrong from the start. Its reasoning was exceptionally weak, and the decision has had damaging consequences. And far from bringing about a national settlement of the abortion issue, *Roe* and *Casey* have enflamed debate and deepened division.

It is time to heed the Constitution and return the issue of abortion to the people's elected representatives. "The permissibility of abortion, and the limitations, upon it, are to be resolved like most important questions in our democracy: by citizens trying to persuade one another and then voting." *Casey*, 505 U.S., at 979 (Scalia, J., concurring in judgment in part and dissenting in part). That is what the Constitution and the rule of law demand.

I

The law at issue in this case, Mississippi's Gestational Age Act, see Miss. Code Ann. §41–41–191 (2018), contains this central provision: "Except in a medical emergency or in the case of a severe fetal abnormality, a person shall not intentionally or knowingly perform . . . or induce an abortion of an unborn human being if the probable gestational age of the unborn human being has been determined to be greater than fifteen (15) weeks." §4(b).[14]

To support this Act, the legislature made a series of factual findings. It began by noting that, at the time of enactment, only six countries besides the United States "permit[ted] nontherapeutic or elective abortion-on-demand after the twentieth week of gestation."[15]

---

13. Miss. Code Ann. §41–41–191(4)(b) (2018).

14. The Act defines "gestational age" to be "the age of an unborn human being as calculated from the first day of the last menstrual period of the pregnant woman." §3(f).

15. Those other six countries were Canada, China, the Netherlands, North Korea, Singapore, and Vietnam. See A. Baglini, Charlotte Lozier Institute, Gestational Limits on Abortion in the United States Compared to International Norms 6–7 (2014); M. Lee, Is the United States One of Seven

§2(a). The legislature then found that at 5 or 6 weeks' gestational age an "unborn human being's heart begins beating"; at 8 weeks the "unborn human being begins to move about in the womb"; at 9 weeks "all basic physiological functions are present"; at 10 weeks "vital organs begin to function," and "[h]air, fingernails, and toenails . . . begin to form"; at 11 weeks "an unborn human being's diaphragm is developing," and he or she may "move about freely in the womb"; and at 12 weeks the "unborn human being" has "taken on 'the human form' in all relevant respects." §2(b)(i) (quoting *Gonzales* v. *Carhart*, 550 U.S. 124, 160 (2007)). It found that most abortions after 15 weeks employ "dilation and evacuation procedures which involve the use of surgical instruments to crush and tear the unborn child," and it concluded that the "intentional commitment of such acts for nontherapeutic or elective reasons is a barbaric practice, dangerous for the maternal patient, and demeaning to the medical profession." §2(b)(i)(8).

Respondents are an abortion clinic, Jackson Women's Health Organization, and one of its doctors. On the day the Gestational Age Act was enacted, respondents filed suit in Federal District Court against various Mississippi officials, alleging that the Act violated this Court's precedents establishing a constitutional right to abortion. The District Court granted summary judgment in favor of respondents and permanently enjoined enforcement of the Act, reasoning that "viability marks the earliest point at which the State's interest in fetal life is constitutionally adequate to justify a legislative ban on nontherapeutic abortions" and that 15 weeks' gestational age is "prior to viability." *Jackson Women's Health Org.* v. *Currier*, 349 F. Supp. 3d 536, 539–540 (SD Miss. 2019) (internal quotation marks omitted). The Fifth Circuit affirmed. 945 F. 3d 265 (2019).

We granted certiorari, 593 U.S. ___ (2021), to resolve the question whether "all pre-viability prohibitions on elective abortions are unconstitutional," Pet. for Cert. i. Petitioners' primary defense of the Mississippi Gestational Age Act is that *Roe* and *Casey* were wrongly decided and that "the Act is constitutional because it satisfies rational-basis review." Brief for Petitioners 49. Respondents answer that allowing Mississippi to ban pre-viability abortions "would be no different than overruling *Casey* and *Roe* entirely." Brief for Respondents 43. They tell us that "no half-measures" are available: We must either reaffirm or overrule *Roe* and *Casey*. Brief for Respondents 50.

Countries That "Allow Elective Abortions After 20 Weeks of Pregnancy?" Wash. Post (Oct. 8, 2017), www.washingtonpost.com/news/fact-checker/wp/2017/10/09/is-the-united-states-one-of-seven-countries-that-allow-elective-abortions-after-20-weeks-of-pregnacy (stating that the claim made by the Mississippi Legislature and the Charlotte Lozier Institute was "backed by data"). A more recent compilation from the Center for Reproductive Rights indicates that Iceland and Guinea-Bissau are now also similarly permissive. See The World's Abortion Laws, Center for Reproductive Rights (Feb. 23, 2021), https://reproductiverights.org/maps/worlds-abortion-laws/.

II

We begin by considering the critical question whether the Constitution, properly understood, confers a right to obtain an abortion. Skipping over that question, the controlling opinion in *Casey* reaffirmed *Roe*'s "central holding" based solely on the doctrine of *stare decisis*, but as we will explain, proper application of *stare decisis* required an assessment of the strength of the grounds on which *Roe* was based. See *infra*, at 45–56.

We therefore turn to the question that the *Casey* plurality did not consider, and we address that question in three steps. First, we explain the standard that our cases have used in determining whether the Fourteenth Amendment's reference to "liberty" protects a particular right. Second, we examine whether the right at issue in this case is rooted in our Nation's history and tradition and whether it is an essential component of what we have described as "ordered liberty." Finally, we consider whether a right to obtain an abortion is part of a broader entrenched right that is supported by other precedents.

A

1

Constitutional analysis must begin with "the language of the instrument," *Gibbons v. Ogden*, 9 Wheat. 1, 186–189 (1824), which offers a "fixed standard" for ascertaining what our founding document means, 1 J. Story, Commentaries on the Constitution of the United States §399, p. 383 (1833). The Constitution makes no express reference to a right to obtain an abortion, and therefore those who claim that it protects such a right must show that the right is somehow implicit in the constitutional text.

Roe, however, was remarkably loose in its treatment of the constitutional text. It held that the abortion right, which is not mentioned in the Constitution, is part of a right to privacy, which is also not mentioned. See 410 U.S., at 152–153. And that privacy right, *Roe* observed, had been found to spring from no fewer than five different constitutional provisions—the First, Fourth, Fifth, Ninth, and Fourteenth Amendments. *Id.*, at 152.

The Court's discussion left open at least three ways in which some combination of these provisions could protect the abortion right. One possibility was that the right was "founded . . . in the Ninth Amendment's reservation of rights to the people." *Id.*, at 153. Another was that the right was rooted in the First, Fourth, or Fifth Amendment, or in some combination of those provisions, and that this right had been "incorporated" into the Due Process Clause of the Fourteenth Amendment just as many other Bill of Rights provisions had by then been incorporated. *Ibid.*; see also *McDonald v. Chicago*, 561 U.S. 742, 763–766 (2010) (majority opinion) (discussing incorporation). And a third path was that the First, Fourth, and Fifth Amendments played no role and that the right was simply a component of the "liberty" protected by the Fourteenth Amendment's Due Process

Clause. *Roe*, 410 U.S., at 153. *Roe* expressed the "feel[ing]" that the Fourteenth Amendment was the provision that did the work, but its message seemed to be that the abortion right could be found *somewhere* in the Constitution and that specifying its exact location was not of paramount importance.[16] The *Casey* Court did not defend this unfocused analysis and instead grounded its decision solely on the theory that the right to obtain an abortion is part of the "liberty" protected by the Fourteenth Amendment's Due Process Clause.

We discuss this theory in depth below, but before doing so, we briefly address one additional constitutional provision that some of respondents' *amici* have now offered as yet another potential home for the abortion right: the Fourteenth Amendment's Equal Protection Clause. See Brief for United States as *Amicus Curiae* 24 (Brief for United States); see also Brief for Equal Protection Constitutional Law Scholars as *Amici Curiae*. Neither *Roe* nor *Casey* saw fit to invoke this theory, and it is squarely foreclosed by our precedents, which establish that a State's regulation of abortion is not a sex-based classification and is thus not subject to the "heightened scrutiny" that applies to such classifications.[17] The regulation of a medical procedure that only one sex can undergo does not trigger heightened constitutional scrutiny unless the regulation is a "mere pretex[t] designed to effect an invidious discrimination against members of one sex or the other." *Geduldig* v. *Aiello*, 417 U.S. 484, 496, n. 20 (1974). And as the Court has stated, the "goal of preventing abortion" does not constitute "invidiously discriminatory animus" against women. *Bray* v. *Alexandria Women's Health Clinic*, 506 U.S. 263, 273–274 (1993) (internal quotation marks omitted). Accordingly, laws regulating or prohibiting abortion are not subject to heightened scrutiny. Rather, they are governed by the same standard of review as other health and safety measures.[18]

With this new theory addressed, we turn to *Casey*'s bold assertion that the abortion right is an aspect of the "liberty" protected by the Due Process Clause of the Fourteenth Amendment. 505 U.S., at 846; Brief for Respondents 17; Brief for United States 21–22.

2

The underlying theory on which this argument rests—that the Fourteenth Amendment's Due Process Clause provides substantive, as well as procedural, protection for

---

16. The Court's words were as follows: "This right of privacy, whether it be founded in the Fourteenth Amendment's concept of personal liberty and restrictions upon state action, as we feel it is, or, as the District Court determined, in the Ninth Amendment's reservation of rights to the people, is broad enough to encompass a woman's decision whether or not to terminate her pregnancy." 410 U.S., at 153.

17. See, *e.g.*, *Sessions* v. *Morales-Santana*, 582 U.S. 47, ___ (2017) (slip op., at 8).

18. We discuss this standard in Part VI of this opinion.

"liberty"—has long been controversial. But our decisions have held that the Due Process Clause protects two categories of substantive rights.

The first consists of rights guaranteed by the first eight Amendments. Those Amendments originally applied only to the Federal Government, *Barron ex rel. Tiernan* v. *Mayor of Baltimore*, 7 Pet. 243, 247–251 (1833) (opinion for the Court by Marshall, C. J.), but this Court has held that the Due Process Clause of the Fourteenth Amendment "incorporates" the great majority of those rights and thus makes them equally applicable to the States. See *McDonald*, 561 U.S., at 763–767, and nn. 12–13. The second category—which is the one in question here—comprises a select list of fundamental rights that are not mentioned anywhere in the Constitution.

In deciding whether a right falls into either of these categories, the Court has long asked whether the right is "deeply rooted in [our] history and tradition" and whether it is essential to our Nation's "scheme of ordered liberty." *Timbs* v. *Indiana*, 586 U.S. ___, ___ (2019) (slip op., at 3) (internal quotation marks omitted); *McDonald*, 561 U.S., at 764, 767 (internal quotation marks omitted); *Glucksberg*, 521 U.S., at 721 (internal quotation marks omitted).[19] And in conducting this inquiry, we have engaged in a careful analysis of the history of the right at issue.

Justice Ginsburg's opinion for the Court in *Timbs* is a recent example. In concluding that the Eighth Amendment's protection against excessive fines is "fundamental to our scheme of ordered liberty" and "deeply rooted in this Nation's history and tradition," 586 U.S., at ___ (slip op., at 7) (internal quotation marks omitted), her opinion traced the right back to Magna Carta, Blackstone's Commentaries, and 35 of the 37 state constitutions in effect at the ratification of the Fourteenth Amendment. 586 U.S., at ___–___ (slip op., at 3–7).

A similar inquiry was undertaken in *McDonald*, which held that the Fourteenth Amendment protects the right to keep and bear arms. The lead opinion surveyed the origins of the Second Amendment, the debates in Congress about the adoption of the Fourteenth Amendment, the state constitutions in effect when that Amendment was ratified (at least 22 of the 37 States protected the right to keep and bear arms), federal laws enacted during the same period, and other relevant historical evidence. 561 U.S., at 767–777. Only then did the opinion conclude that "the Framers and ratifiers of the Fourteenth Amendment counted the right to keep and bear arms among those fundamental rights necessary to our system of ordered liberty." *Id.*, at 778; see also *id.*, at 822–850 (THOMAS, J., concurring in part and concurring in judgment) (surveying history and reaching the same result under the Fourteenth Amendment's Privileges or Immunities Clause).

---

19. See also, *e.g., Duncan* v. *Louisiana*, 391 U.S. 145, 148 (1968) (asking whether "a right is among those 'fundamental principles of liberty and justice which lie at the base of our civil and political institutions'"); *Palko* v. *Connecticut*, 302 U.S. 319, 325 (1937) (requiring "a 'principle of justice so rooted in the traditions and conscience of our people as to be ranked as fundamental'" (quoting *Snyder* v. *Massachusetts*, 291 U.S. 97, 105 (1934))).

Timbs and *McDonald* concerned the question whether the Fourteenth Amendment protects rights that are expressly set out in the Bill of Rights, and it would be anomalous if similar historical support were not required when a putative right is not mentioned anywhere in the Constitution. Thus, in *Glucksberg*, which held that the Due Process Clause does not confer a right to assisted suicide, the Court surveyed more than 700 years of "Anglo-American common law tradition," 521 U.S., at 711, and made clear that a fundamental right must be "objectively, deeply rooted in this Nation's history and tradition," *id.*, at 720–721.

Historical inquiries of this nature are essential whenever we are asked to recognize a new component of the "liberty" protected by the Due Process Clause because the term "liberty" alone provides little guidance. "Liberty" is a capacious term. As Lincoln once said: "We all declare for Liberty; but in using the same word we do not all mean the same thing."[20] In a well-known essay, Isaiah Berlin reported that "[h]istorians of ideas" had cataloged more than 200 different senses in which the term had been used.[21]

In interpreting what is meant by the Fourteenth Amendment's reference to "liberty," we must guard against the natural human tendency to confuse what that Amendment protects with our own ardent views about the liberty that Americans should enjoy. That is why the Court has long been "reluctant" to recognize rights that are not mentioned in the Constitution. *Collins* v. *Harker Heights*, 503 U.S. 115, 125 (1992). "Substantive due process has at times been a treacherous field for this Court," *Moore* v. *East Cleveland*, 431 U.S. 494, 503 (1977) (plurality opinion), and it has sometimes led the Court to usurp authority that the Constitution entrusts to the people's elected representatives. See *Regents of Univ. of Mich.* v. *Ewing*, 474 U.S. 214, 225–226 (1985). As the Court cautioned in *Glucksberg*, "[w]e must . . . exercise the utmost care whenever we are asked to break new ground in this field, lest the liberty protected by the Due Process Clause be subtly transformed into the policy preferences of the Members of this Court." 521 U.S., at 720 (internal quotation marks and citation omitted).

On occasion, when the Court has ignored the "[a]ppropriate limits" imposed by "'respect for the teachings of history,'" *Moore*, 431 U.S., at 503 (plurality opinion), it has fallen into the freewheeling judicial policymaking that characterized discredited decisions such as *Lochner* v. *New York*, 198 U.S. 45 (1905). The Court must not fall prey to such an unprincipled approach. Instead, guided by the history and tradition that map the essential components of our Nation's concept of ordered liberty, we must ask what the *Fourteenth Amendment* means by the term "liberty." When we engage in that inquiry in the present

---

20. Address at Sanitary Fair at Baltimore, Md. (Apr. 18, 1864), reprinted in 7 The Collected Works of Abraham Lincoln 301 (R. Basler ed. 1953).

21. Four Essays on Liberty 121 (1969).

case, the clear answer is that the Fourteenth Amendment does not protect the right to an abortion.[22]

B

1

Until the latter part of the 20th century, there was no support in American law for a constitutional right to obtain an abortion. No state constitutional provision had recognized such a right. Until a few years before *Roe* was handed down, no federal or state court had recognized such a right. Nor had any scholarly treatise of which we are aware. And although law review articles are not reticent about advocating new rights, the earliest article proposing a constitutional right to abortion that has come to our attention was published only a few years before *Roe*.[23]

Not only was there no support for such a constitutional right until shortly before *Roe*, but abortion had long been a *crime* in every single State. At common law, abortion was criminal in at least some stages of pregnancy and was regarded as unlawful and could have very serious consequences at all stages. American law followed the common law until a wave of statutory restrictions in the 1800s expanded criminal liability for abortions. By the time of the adoption of the Fourteenth Amendment, three-quarters of the States had

---

22. That is true regardless of whether we look to the Amendment's Due Process Clause or its Privileges or Immunities Clause. Some scholars and Justices have maintained that the Privileges or Immunities Clause is the provision of the Fourteenth Amendment that guarantees substantive rights. See, *e.g.*, *McDonald* v. *Chicago*, 561 U.S. 742, 813–850 (2010) (THOMAS, J., concurring in part and concurring in judgment); *Duncan*, 391 U.S., at 165–166 (Black, J., concurring); A. Amar, Bill of Rights: Creation and Reconstruction 163–180 (1998) (Amar); J. Ely, Democracy and Distrust 22–30 (1980); 2 W. Crosskey, Politics and the Constitution in the History of the United States 1089–1095 (1953). But even on that view, such a right would need to be rooted in the Nation's history and tradition. See *Corfield* v. *Coryell*, 6 F. Cas. 546, 551–552 (No. 3,230) (CC ED Pa. 1823) (describing unenumerated rights under the Privileges and Immunities Clause, Art. IV, §2, as those "fundamental" rights "which have, at all times, been enjoyed by the citizens of the several states"); Amar 176 (relying on *Corfield* to interpret the Privileges or Immunities Clause); cf. *McDonald*, 561 U.S., at 819–820, 832, 854 (opinion of THOMAS, J.) (reserving the question whether the Privileges or Immunities Clause protects "any rights besides those enumerated in the Constitution").

23. See R. Lucas, Federal Constitutional Limitations on the Enforcement and Administration of State Abortion Statutes, 46 N. C. L. Rev. 730 (1968) (Lucas); see also D. Garrow, Liberty and Sexuality 334–335 (1994) (Garrow) (stating that Lucas was "undeniably the first person to fully articulate on paper" the argument that "a woman's right to choose abortion was a fundamental individual freedom protected by the U.S. Constitution's guarantee of personal liberty").

made abortion a crime at any stage of pregnancy, and the remaining States would soon follow.

Roe either ignored or misstated this history, and *Casey* declined to reconsider *Roe*'s faulty historical analysis. It is therefore important to set the record straight.

2

a

We begin with the common law, under which abortion was a crime at least after "quickening"—*i.e.*, the first felt movement of the fetus in the womb, which usually occurs between the 16th and 18th week of pregnancy.[24]

The "eminent common-law authorities (Blackstone, Coke, Hale, and the like)," *Kahler* v. *Kansas*, 589 U.S. ___, ___ (2020) (slip op., at 7), *all* describe abortion after quickening as criminal. Henry de Bracton's 13th-century treatise explained that if a person has "struck a pregnant woman, or has given her poison, whereby he has caused abortion, if the foetus be already formed and animated, and particularly if it be animated, he commits homicide." 2 De Legibus et Consuetudinibus Angliae 279 (T. Twiss ed. 1879); see also 1 Fleta, c. 23, reprinted in 72 Selden Soc. 60–61 (H. Richardson & G. Sayles eds. 1955) (13th-century treatise).[25]

Sir Edward Coke's 17th-century treatise likewise asserted that abortion of a quick child was "murder" if the "childe be born alive" and a "great misprision" if the "childe dieth in her body." 3 Institutes of the Laws of England 50–51 (1644). ("Misprision" referred to "some heynous offence under the degree of felony." *Id.*, at 139.) Two treatises by Sir Matthew Hale likewise described abortion of a quick child who died in the womb as a "great crime" and a "great misprision." Pleas of the Crown 53 (P. Glazebrook ed. 1972); 1 History of the Pleas of the Crown 433 (1736) (Hale). And writing near the

---

24. The exact meaning of "quickening" is subject to some debate. Compare Brief for Scholars of Jurisprudence as *Amici Curiae* 12–14, and n. 32 (emphasis deleted) ("'a quick child'" meant simply a "live" child, and under the era's outdated knowledge of embryology, a fetus was thought to become "quick" at around the sixth week of pregnancy), with Brief for American Historical Association et al. as *Amici Curiae* 6, n. 2 ("quick" and "quickening" consistently meant "the woman's perception of fetal movement"). We need not wade into this debate. First, it suffices for present purposes to show that abortion was criminal by *at least* the 16th or 18th week of pregnancy. Second, as we will show, during the relevant period—*i.e.*, the period surrounding the enactment of the Fourteenth Amendment—the quickening distinction was abandoned as States criminalized abortion at all stages of pregnancy. See *infra*, at 21–25.

25. Even before Bracton's time, English law imposed punishment for the killing of a fetus. See Leges Henrici Primi 222–223 (L. Downer ed. 1972) (imposing penalty for any abortion and treating a woman who aborted a "quick" child "as if she were a murderess").

time of the adoption of our Constitution, William Blackstone explained that abortion of a "quick" child was "by the ancient law homicide or manslaughter" (citing Bracton), and at least a very "heinous misdemeanor" (citing Coke). 1 Commentaries on the Laws of England 129–130 (7th ed. 1775) (Blackstone).

English cases dating all the way back to the 13th century corroborate the treatises' statements that abortion was a crime. See generally J. Dellapenna, Dispelling the Myths of Abortion History 126, and n. 16, 134–142, 188–194, and nn. 84–86 (2006) (Dellapenna); J. Keown, Abortion, Doctors and the Law 3–12 (1988) (Keown). In 1732, for example, Eleanor Beare was convicted of "destroying the Foetus in the Womb" of another woman and "thereby causing her to miscarry."[26] For that crime and another "misdemeanor," Beare was sentenced to two days in the pillory and three years' imprisonment.[27]

Although a pre-quickening abortion was not itself considered homicide, it does not follow that abortion was *permissible* at common law—much less that abortion was a legal *right*. Cf. *Glucksberg*, 521 U.S., at 713 (removal of "common law's harsh sanctions did not represent an acceptance of suicide"). Quite to the contrary, in the 1732 case mentioned above, the judge said of the charge of abortion (with no mention of quickening) that he had "never met with a case so barbarous and unnatural."[28] Similarly, an indictment from 1602, which did not distinguish between a pre-quickening and post-quickening abortion, described abortion as "pernicious" and "against the peace of our Lady the Queen, her crown and dignity." Keown 7 (discussing *R.* v. *Webb*, Calendar of Assize Records, Surrey Indictments 512 (1980)).

That the common law did not condone even pre-quickening abortions is confirmed by what one might call a proto-felony-murder rule. Hale and Blackstone explained a way in which a pre-quickening abortion could rise to the level of a homicide. Hale wrote that if a physician gave a woman "with child" a "potion" to cause an abortion, and the woman died, it was "murder" because the potion was given "*unlawfully* to destroy her child within her." 1 Hale 429–430 (emphasis added). As Blackstone explained, to be "murder" a killing had to be done with "malice aforethought, . . . either express or implied." 4 Blackstone 198 (emphasis deleted). In the case of an abortionist, Blackstone wrote, "the law will imply [malice]" for the same reason that it would imply malice if a person who intended to kill one person accidentally killed a different person:

"[I]f one shoots at A and misses *him*, but kills B, this is murder; because of the previous felonious intent, which the law transfers from one to the other. The same is the case, where one lays poison for A; and B, against whom the prisoner had no malicious intent, takes it, and it kills him; this is likewise murder. *So also*, if one gives *a woman*

---

26. 2 Gentleman's Magazine 931 (Aug. 1732).

27. *Id.*, at 932.

28. *Ibid.*

with child a medicine to procure abortion, and it operates so violently as to kill the woman, *this is murder* in the person who gave it." *Id.*, at 200–201 (emphasis added; footnote omitted).[29]

Notably, Blackstone, like Hale, did not state that this proto-felony-murder rule required that the woman be "with quick child"—only that she be "with child." *Id.*, at 201. And it is revealing that Hale and Blackstone treated abortionists differently from *other* physicians or surgeons who caused the death of a patient "without any intent of doing [the patient] any bodily hurt." Hale 429; see 4 Blackstone 197. These other physicians—even if "unlicensed"—would not be "guilty of murder or manslaughter." Hale 429. But a physician performing an abortion would, precisely because his aim was an "unlawful" one.

In sum, although common-law authorities differed on the severity of punishment for abortions committed at different points in pregnancy, none endorsed the practice. Moreover, we are aware of no common-law case or authority, and the parties have not pointed to any, that remotely suggests a positive *right* to procure an abortion at any stage of pregnancy.

b

In this country, the historical record is similar. The "most important early American edition of Blackstone's Commentaries," *District of Columbia v. Heller*, 554 U.S. 570, 594 (2008), reported Blackstone's statement that abortion of a quick child was at least "a heinous misdemeanor," 2 St. George Tucker, Blackstone's Commentaries 129–130 (1803), and that edition also included Blackstone's discussion of the proto-felony-murder rule, 5 *id.*, at 200–201. Manuals for justices of the peace printed in the Colonies in the 18th century typically restated the common-law rule on abortion, and some manuals repeated Hale's and Blackstone's statements that anyone who prescribed medication "unlawfully to destroy the child" would be guilty of murder if the woman died. See, *e.g.*, J. Parker, Conductor Generalis 220 (1788); 2 R. Burn, Justice of the Peace, and Parish Officer 221–222 (7th ed. 1762) (English manual stating the same).[30]

---

29. Other treatises restated the same rule. See 1 W. Russell & C. Greaves, Crimes and Misdemeanors 540 (5th ed. 1845) ("So where a person gave medicine to a woman to procure an abortion, and where a person put skewers into the woman for the same purpose, by which in both cases the women were killed, these acts were clearly held to be murder" (footnotes omitted)); 1 E. East, Pleas of the Crown 230 (1803) (similar).

30. For manuals restating one or both rules, see J. Davis, Criminal Law 96, 102–103, 339 (1838); Conductor Generalis 194–195 (1801) (printed in Philadelphia); Conductor Generalis 194–195 (1794) (printed in Albany); Conductor Generalis 220 (1788) (printed in New York); Conductor Generalis 198 (1749) (printed in New York); G. Webb, Office and Authority of a Justice of Peace

The few cases available from the early colonial period corroborate that abortion was a crime. See generally Dellapenna 215–228 (collecting cases). In Maryland in 1652, for example, an indictment charged that a man "Murtherously endeavoured to destroy or Murther the Child by him begotten in the Womb." *Proprietary* v. *Mitchell*, 10 Md. Archives 80, 183 (1652) (W. Browne ed. 1891). And by the 19th century, courts frequently explained that the common law made abortion of a quick child a crime. See, *e.g.*, *Smith* v. *Gaffard*, 31 Ala. 45, 51 (1857); *Smith* v. *State*, 33 Me. 48, 55 (1851); *State* v. *Cooper*, 22 N. J. L. 52, 52–55 (1849); *Commonwealth* v. *Parker*, 50 Mass. 263, 264–268 (1845).

c

. . . In this country during the 19th century, the vast majority of the States enacted statutes criminalizing abortion at all stages of pregnancy. See Appendix A, *infra* (listing state statutory provisions in chronological order).[33] By 1868, the year when the Fourteenth Amendment was ratified, three-quarters of the States, 28 out of 37, had enacted statutes making abortion a crime even if it was performed before quickening.[34] See *ibid.* Of the nine States that had not yet criminalized abortion at all stages, all but one did so by 1910. See *ibid.*

The trend in the Territories that would become the last 13 States was similar: All of them criminalized abortion at all stages of pregnancy between 1850 (the Kingdom of Hawaii) and 1919 (New Mexico). See Appendix B, *infra*; see also *Casey*, 505 U.S., at 952

---

232 (1736) (printed in Williamsburg); Conductor Generalis 161 (1722) (printed in Philadelphia); see also J. Conley, Doing It by the Book: Justice of the Peace Manuals and English Law in Eighteenth Century America, 6 J. Legal Hist. 257, 265, 267 (1985) (noting that these manuals were the justices' "primary source of legal reference" and of "practical value for a wider audience than the justices"). For cases stating the proto-felony-murder rule, see, *e.g.*, *Commonwealth* v. *Parker*, 50 Mass. 263, 265 (1845); *People* v. *Sessions*, 58 Mich. 594, 595–596, 26 N. W. 291, 292–293 (1886); *State* v. *Moore*, 25 Iowa 128, 131–132 (1868); *Smith* v. *State*, 33 Me. 48, 54–55 (1851).

33. See generally Dellapenna 315–319 (cataloging the development of the law in the States); E. Quay, Justifiable Abortion—Medical and Legal Foundations, 49 Geo. L. J. 395, 435–437, 447–520 (1961) (Quay) (same); J. Witherspoon, Reexamining *Roe*: Nineteenth-Century Abortion Statutes and The Fourteenth Amendment, 17 St. Mary's L. J. 29, 34–36 (1985) (Witherspoon) (same).

34. Some scholars assert that only 27 States prohibited abortion at all stages. See, *e.g.*, Dellapenna 315; Witherspoon 34–35, and n. 15. Those scholars appear to have overlooked Rhode Island, which criminalized abortion at all stages in 1861. See Acts and Resolves R. I. 1861, ch. 371, §1, p. 133 (criminalizing the attempt to "procure the miscarriage" of "any pregnant woman" or "any woman supposed by such person to be pregnant," without mention of quickening). The *amicus* brief for the American Historical Association asserts that only 26 States prohibited abortion at all stages, but that brief incorrectly excludes West Virginia and Nebraska from its count. Compare Brief for American Historical Association 27–28 (citing Quay), with Appendix A, *infra*.

(Rehnquist, C. J., concurring in judgment in part and dissenting in part); Dellapenna 317–319. By the end of the 1950s, according to the *Roe* Court's own count, statutes in all but four States and the District of Columbia prohibited abortion "however and whenever performed, unless done to save or preserve the life of the mother." 410 U.S., at 139.[35]

This overwhelming consensus endured until the day *Roe* was decided. At that time, also by the *Roe* Court's own count, a substantial majority—30 States—still prohibited abortion at all stages except to save the life of the mother. See *id.*, at 118, and n. 2 (listing States). And though *Roe* discerned a "trend toward liberalization" in about "one-third of the States," those States still criminalized some abortions and regulated them more stringently than *Roe* would allow. *Id.*, at 140, and n. 37; Tribe 2. In short, the "Court's opinion in *Roe* itself convincingly refutes the notion that the abortion liberty is deeply rooted in the history or tradition of our people." *Thornburgh* v. *American College of Obstetricians and Gynecologists*, 476 U.S. 747, 793 (1986) (White, J., dissenting).

d

The inescapable conclusion is that a right to abortion is not deeply rooted in the Nation's history and traditions. On the contrary, an unbroken tradition of prohibiting abortion on pain of criminal punishment persisted from the earliest days of the common law until 1973. The Court in *Roe* could have said of abortion exactly what *Glucksberg* said of assisted suicide: "Attitudes toward [abortion] have changed since Bracton, but our laws have consistently condemned, and continue to prohibit, [that practice]." 521 U.S., at 719.

3

Respondents and their *amici* have no persuasive answer to this historical evidence.

Neither respondents nor the Solicitor General disputes the fact that by 1868 the vast majority of States criminalized abortion at all stages of pregnancy. See Brief for Petitioners

---

35. The statutes of three States (Massachusetts, New Jersey, and Pennsylvania) prohibited abortions performed "unlawfully" or "without lawful justification." *Roe*, 410 U.S., at 139 (internal quotation marks omitted). In Massachusetts, case law held that abortion was allowed when, according to the judgment of physicians in the relevant community, the procedure was necessary to preserve the woman's life or her physical or emotional health. *Commonwealth* v. *Wheeler*, 315 Mass. 394, 395, 53 N. E. 2d 4, 5 (1944). In the other two States, however, there is no clear support in case law for the proposition that abortion was lawful where the mother's life was not at risk. See *State* v. *Brandenberg*, 137 N. J. L. 124, 58 A. 2d 709 (1948); *Commonwealth* v. *Trombetta*, 131 Pa. Super. 487, 200 A. 107 (1938).

Statutes in the two remaining jurisdictions (the District of Columbia and Alabama) permitted "abortion to preserve the mother's health." *Roe*, 410 U.S., at 139. Case law in those jurisdictions does not clarify the breadth of these exceptions.

12–13; see also Brief for American Historical Association et al. as *Amici Curiae* 27–28, and nn. 14–15 (conceding that 26 out of 37 States prohibited abortion before quickening); Tr. of Oral Arg. 74–75 (respondents' counsel conceding the same). Instead, respondents are forced to argue that it "does [not] matter that some States prohibited abortion at the time *Roe* was decided or when the Fourteenth Amendment was adopted." Brief for Respondents 21. But that argument flies in the face of the standard we have applied in determining whether an asserted right that is nowhere mentioned in the Constitution is nevertheless protected by the Fourteenth Amendment. . . .

Another *amicus* brief relied upon by respondents (see Brief for Respondents 21) tries to dismiss the significance of the state criminal statutes that were in effect when the Fourteenth Amendment was adopted by suggesting that they were enacted for illegitimate reasons. According to this account, which is based almost entirely on statements made by one prominent proponent of the statutes, important motives for the laws were the fear that Catholic immigrants were having more babies than Protestants and that the availability of abortion was leading White Protestant women to "shir[k their] maternal duties." Brief for American Historical Association et al. as *Amici Curiae* 20.

Resort to this argument is a testament to the lack of any real historical support for the right that *Roe* and *Casey* recognized. This Court has long disfavored arguments based on alleged legislative motives. See, *e.g., Erie* v. *Pap's A. M.*, 529 U.S. 277, 292 (2000) (plurality opinion); *Turner Broadcasting System, Inc.* v. *FCC*, 512 U.S. 622, 652 (1994); *United States* v. *O'Brien*, 391 U.S. 367, 383 (1968); *Arizona* v. *California*, 283 U.S. 423, 455 (1931) (collecting cases). The Court has recognized that inquiries into legislative motives "are a hazardous matter." *O'Brien*, 391 U.S., at 383. Even when an argument about legislative motive is backed by statements made by legislators who voted for a law, we have been reluctant to attribute those motives to the legislative body as a whole. "What motivates one legislator to make a speech about a statute is not necessarily what motivates scores of others to enact it." *Id.*, at 384.

Here, the argument about legislative motive is not even based on statements by legislators, but on statements made by a few supporters of the new 19th-century abortion laws, and it is quite a leap to attribute these motives to all the legislators whose votes were responsible for the enactment of those laws. Recall that at the time of the adoption of the Fourteenth Amendment, over three-quarters of the States had adopted statutes criminalizing abortion (usually at all stages of pregnancy), and that from the early 20th century until the day *Roe* was handed down, every single State had such a law on its books. Are we to believe that the hundreds of lawmakers whose votes were needed to enact these laws were motivated by hostility to Catholics and women?

There is ample evidence that the passage of these laws was instead spurred by a sincere belief that abortion kills a human being. Many judicial decisions from the late 19th and early 20th centuries made that point. See, *e.g., Nash* v. *Meyer*, 54 Idaho 283, 301, 31 P. 2d 273, 280 (1934); *State* v. *Ausplund*, 86 Ore. 121, 131–132, 167 P. 1019, 1022–1023 (1917); *Trent* v. *State*, 15 Ala. App. 485, 488, 73 S. 834, 836 (1916); *State* v. *Miller*, 90

Kan. 230, 233, 133 P. 878, 879 (1913); *State* v. *Tippie*, 89 Ohio St. 35, 39–40, 105 N. E. 75, 77 (1913); *State* v. *Gedicke*, 43 N.J.L. 86, 90 (1881); *Dougherty* v. *People*, 1 Colo. 514, 522–523 (1873); *State* v. *Moore*, 25 Iowa 128, 131–132 (1868); *Smith*, 33 Me., at 57; see also *Memphis Center for Reproductive Health* v. *Slatery*, 14 F. 4th 409, 446, and n. 11 (CA6 2021) (Thapar, J., concurring in judgment in part and dissenting in part) (citing cases).

One may disagree with this belief (and our decision is not based on any view about when a State should regard prenatal life as having rights or legally cognizable interests), but even *Roe* and *Casey* did not question the good faith of abortion opponents. See, *e.g.*, *Casey*, 505 U.S., at 850 ("Men and women of good conscience can disagree . . . about the profound moral and spiritual implications of terminating a pregnancy even in its earliest stage"). And we see no reason to discount the significance of the state laws in question based on these *amici*'s suggestions about legislative motive.[41]

C

1

Instead of seriously pressing the argument that the abortion right itself has deep roots, supporters of *Roe* and *Casey* contend that the abortion right is an integral part of a broader entrenched right. *Roe* termed this a right to privacy, 410 U.S., at 154, and *Casey* described it as the freedom to make "intimate and personal choices" that are "central to personal dignity and autonomy," 505 U.S., at 851. *Casey* elaborated: "At the heart of liberty is the right to define one's own concept of existence, of meaning, of the universe, and of the mystery of human life." *Ibid.*

The Court did not claim that this broadly framed right is absolute, and no such claim would be plausible. While individuals are certainly free *to think* and *to say* what they wish about "existence," "meaning," the "universe," and "the mystery of human life," they are not always free *to act* in accordance with those thoughts. License to act on the basis of such beliefs may correspond to one of the many understandings of "liberty," but it is certainly not "ordered liberty."

---

41. Other *amicus* briefs present arguments about the motives of proponents of liberal access to abortion. They note that some such supporters have been motivated by a desire to suppress the size of the African-American population. See Brief for African-American Organization et al. as *Amici Curiae* 14–21; see also *Box* v. *Planned Parenthood of Ind. and Ky., Inc.*, 587 U.S. ___, ___–___ (2019) (Thomas, J., concurring) (slip op., at 1–4). And it is beyond dispute that *Roe* has had that demographic effect. A highly disproportionate percentage of aborted fetuses are Black. See, *e.g.*, Dept. of Health and Human Servs., Centers for Disease Control and Prevention (CDC), K. Kortsmit et al., Abortion Surveillance—United States, 2019, 70 Morbidity and Mortality Report, Surveillance Summaries, p. 20 (Nov. 26, 2021) (Table 6). For our part, we do not question the motives of either those who have supported or those who have opposed laws restricting abortions.

Ordered liberty sets limits and defines the boundary between competing interests. *Roe* and *Casey* each struck a particular balance between the interests of a woman who wants an abortion and the interests of what they termed "potential life." *Roe*, 410 U.S., at 150 (emphasis deleted); *Casey*, 505 U.S., at 852. But the people of the various States may evaluate those interests differently. In some States, voters may believe that the abortion right should be even more extensive than the right that *Roe* and *Casey* recognized. Voters in other States may wish to impose tight restrictions based on their belief that abortion destroys an "unborn human being." Miss. Code Ann. §41–41–191(4)(b). Our Nation's historical understanding of ordered liberty does not prevent the people's elected representatives from deciding how abortion should be regulated.

Nor does the right to obtain an abortion have a sound basis in precedent. *Casey* relied on cases involving the right to marry a person of a different race, *Loving* v. *Virginia*, 388 U.S. 1 (1967); the right to marry while in prison, *Turner* v. *Safley*, 482 U.S. 78 (1987); the right to obtain contraceptives, *Griswold* v. *Connecticut*, 381 U.S. 479 (1965), *Eisenstadt* v. *Baird*, 405 U.S. 438 (1972), *Carey* v. *Population Services Int'l*, 431 U.S. 678 (1977); the right to reside with relatives, *Moore* v. *East Cleveland*, 431 U.S. 494 (1977); the right to make decisions about the education of one's children, *Pierce* v. *Society of Sisters*, 268 U.S. 510 (1925), *Meyer* v. *Nebraska*, 262 U.S. 390 (1923); the right not to be sterilized without consent, *Skinner* v. *Oklahoma ex rel. Williamson*, 316 U.S. 535 (1942); and the right in certain circumstances not to undergo involuntary surgery, forced administration of drugs, or other substantially similar procedures, *Winston* v. *Lee*, 470 U.S. 753 (1985), *Washington* v. *Harper*, 494 U.S. 210 (1990), *Rochin* v. *California*, 342 U.S. 165 (1952). Respondents and the Solicitor General also rely on post-*Casey* decisions like *Lawrence* v. *Texas*, 539 U.S. 558 (2003) (right to engage in private, consensual sexual acts), and *Obergefell* v. *Hodges*, 576 U.S. 644 (2015) (right to marry a person of the same sex). See Brief for Respondents 18; Brief for United States 23–24.

These attempts to justify abortion through appeals to a broader right to autonomy and to define one's "concept of existence" prove too much. *Casey*, 505 U.S., at 851. Those criteria, at a high level of generality, could license fundamental rights to illicit drug use, prostitution, and the like. See *Compassion in Dying* v. *Washington*, 85 F. 3d 1440, 1444 (CA9 1996) (O'Scannlain, J., dissenting from denial of rehearing en banc). None of these rights has any claim to being deeply rooted in history. *Id.*, at 1440, 1445.

What sharply distinguishes the abortion right from the rights recognized in the cases on which *Roe* and *Casey* rely is something that both those decisions acknowledged: Abortion destroys what those decisions call "potential life" and what the law at issue in this case regards as the life of an "unborn human being." See *Roe*, 410 U.S., at 159 (abortion is "inherently different"); *Casey*, 505 U.S., at 852 (abortion is "a unique act"). None of the other decisions cited by *Roe* and *Casey* involved the critical moral question posed by abortion. They are therefore inapposite. They do not support the right to obtain an abortion, and by the same token, our conclusion that the Constitution does not confer such a right does not undermine them in any way. . . .

D

1

The dissent is very candid that it cannot show that a constitutional right to abortion has any foundation, let alone a "'deeply rooted'" one, "'in this Nation's history and tradition.'" *Glucksberg*, 521 U.S., at 721; see *post*, at 12–14 (joint opinion of Breyer, Sotomayor, and Kagan, JJ.). The dissent does not identify *any* pre-*Roe* authority that supports such a right—no state constitutional provision or statute, no federal or state judicial precedent, not even a scholarly treatise. Compare *post*, at 12–14, n. 2, with *supra*, at 15–16, and n. 23. Nor does the dissent dispute the fact that abortion was illegal at common law at least after quickening; that the 19th century saw a trend toward criminalization of pre-quickening abortions; that by 1868, a supermajority of States (at least 26 of 37) had enacted statutes criminalizing abortion at all stages of pregnancy; that by the late 1950s at least 46 States prohibited abortion "however and whenever performed" except if necessary to save "the life of the mother," *Roe*, 410 U.S., at 139; and that when *Roe* was decided in 1973 similar statutes were still in effect in 30 States. Compare *post*, at 12–14, nn. 2–3, with *supra*, at 23–25, and nn. 33–34.[47]

The dissent's failure to engage with this long tradition is devastating to its position. We have held that the "established method of substantive-due-process analysis" requires that an unenumerated right be "'deeply rooted in this Nation's history and tradition'" before it can be recognized as a component of the "liberty" protected in the Due Process Clause. *Glucksberg*, 521 U.S., at 721; cf. *Timbs*, 586 U.S., at ___ (slip op., at 7). But despite the dissent's professed fidelity to *stare decisis*, it fails to seriously engage with that important precedent—which it cannot possibly satisfy.

The dissent attempts to obscure this failure by misrepresenting our application of *Glucksberg*. The dissent suggests that we have focused only on "the legal status of abortion in the 19th century," *post*, at 26, but our review of this Nation's tradition extends well past that period. As explained, for more than a century after 1868—including "another half-century" after women gained the constitutional right to vote in 1920, see *post*, at 15; Amdt. 19—it was firmly established that laws prohibiting abortion like the Texas law at issue in *Roe* were permissible exercises of state regulatory authority. And today, another half century later, more than half of the States have asked us to overrule *Roe* and *Casey*. The dissent cannot establish that a right to abortion has *ever* been part of this Nation's tradition.

---

47. By way of contrast, at the time *Griswold* v. *Connecticut*, 381 U.S. 479 (1965), was decided, the Connecticut statute at issue was an extreme outlier. See Brief for Planned Parenthood Federation of America, Inc. as *Amicus Curiae* in *Griswold* v. *Connecticut*, O. T. 1964, No. 496, p. 27.

2

Because the dissent cannot argue that the abortion right is rooted in this Nation's history and tradition, it contends that the "constitutional tradition" is "not captured whole at a single moment," and that its "meaning gains content from the long sweep of our history and from successive judicial precedents." *Post*, at 18 (internal quotation marks omitted). This vague formulation imposes no clear restraints on what Justice White called the "exercise of raw judicial power," *Roe*, 410 U.S., at 222 (dissenting opinion), and while the dissent claims that its standard "does not mean anything goes," *post*, at 17, any real restraints are hard to discern.

The largely limitless reach of the dissenters' standard is illustrated by the way they apply it here. First, if the "long sweep of history" imposes any restraint on the recognition of unenumerated rights, then *Roe* was surely wrong, since abortion was never allowed (except to save the life of the mother) in a majority of States for over 100 years before that decision was handed down. Second, it is impossible to defend *Roe* based on prior precedent because all of the precedents *Roe* cited, including *Griswold* and *Eisenstadt*, were critically different for a reason that we have explained: None of those cases involved the destruction of what *Roe* called "potential life." See *supra*, at 32.

So without support in history or relevant precedent, *Roe*'s reasoning cannot be defended even under the dissent's proposed test, and the dissent is forced to rely solely on the fact that a constitutional right to abortion was recognized in *Roe* and later decisions that accepted *Roe*'s interpretation. Under the doctrine of *stare decisis*, those precedents are entitled to careful and respectful consideration, and we engage in that analysis below. But as the Court has reiterated time and time again, adherence to precedent is not "'an inexorable command.'" *Kimble* v. *Marvel Entertainment, LLC*, 576 U.S. 446, 455 (2015). There are occasions when past decisions should be overruled, and as we will explain, this is one of them.

3

The most striking feature of the dissent is the absence of any serious discussion of the legitimacy of the States' interest in protecting fetal life. This is evident in the analogy that the dissent draws between the abortion right and the rights recognized in *Griswold* (contraception), *Eisenstadt* (same), *Lawrence* (sexual conduct with member of the same sex), and *Obergefell* (same-sex marriage). Perhaps this is designed to stoke unfounded fear that our decision will imperil those other rights, but the dissent's analogy is objectionable for a more important reason: what it reveals about the dissent's views on the protection of what *Roe* called "potential life." The exercise of the rights at issue in *Griswold, Eisenstadt, Lawrence*, and *Obergefell* does not destroy a "potential life," but an abortion has that effect. So if the rights at issue in those cases are fundamentally the same as the right recognized in *Roe* and *Casey*, the implication is clear: The Constitution does not permit the States to regard the destruction of a "potential life" as a matter of any significance.

That view is evident throughout the dissent. The dissent has much to say about the effects of pregnancy on women, the burdens of motherhood, and the difficulties faced by poor women. These are important concerns. However, the dissent evinces no similar regard for a State's interest in protecting prenatal life. The dissent repeatedly praises the "balance," *post*, at 2, 6, 8, 10, 12, that the viability line strikes between a woman's liberty interest and the State's interest in prenatal life. But for reasons we discuss later, see *infra*, at 50–54, 55–56, and given in the opinion of The Chief Justice, *post*, at 2–5 (opinion concurring in judgment), the viability line makes no sense. It was not adequately justified in *Roe*, and the dissent does not even try to defend it today. Nor does it identify any other point in a pregnancy after which a State is permitted to prohibit the destruction of a fetus.

Our opinion is not based on any view about if and when prenatal life is entitled to any of the rights enjoyed after birth. The dissent, by contrast, would impose on the people a particular theory about when the rights of personhood begin. According to the dissent, the Constitution *requires* the States to regard a fetus as lacking even the most basic human right—to live—at least until an arbitrary point in a pregnancy has passed. Nothing in the Constitution or in our Nation's legal traditions authorizes the Court to adopt that "'theory of life.'" *Post*, at 8.

III

. . . Some of our most important constitutional decisions have overruled prior precedents. We mention three. In *Brown* v. *Board of Education*, 347 U.S. 483 (1954), the Court repudiated the "separate but equal" doctrine, which had allowed States to maintain racially segregated schools and other facilities. *Id.*, at 488 (internal quotation marks omitted). In so doing, the Court overruled the infamous decision in *Plessy* v. *Ferguson*, 163 U.S. 537 (1896), along with six other Supreme Court precedents that had applied the separate-but-equal rule. See *Brown*, 347 U.S., at 491.

In *West Coast Hotel Co.* v. *Parrish*, 300 U.S. 379 (1937), the Court overruled *Adkins* v. *Children's Hospital of D. C.*, 261 U.S. 525 (1923), which had held that a law setting minimum wages for women violated the "liberty" protected by the Fifth Amendment's Due Process Clause. *Id.*, at 545. *West Coast Hotel* signaled the demise of an entire line of important precedents that had protected an individual liberty right against state and federal health and welfare legislation. See *Lochner* v. *New York*, 198 U.S. 45 (1905) (holding invalid a law setting maximum working hours); *Coppage* v. *Kansas*, 236 U.S. 1 (1915) (holding invalid a law banning contracts forbidding employees to join a union); *Jay Burns Baking Co.* v. *Bryan*, 264 U.S. 504 (1924) (holding invalid laws fixing the weight of loaves of bread).

Finally, in *West Virginia Bd. of Ed.* v. *Barnette*, 319 U.S. 624 (1943), after the lapse of only three years, the Court overruled *Minersville School Dist.* v. *Gobitis*, 310 U.S. 586 (1940), and held that public school students could not be compelled to salute the flag in violation of their sincere beliefs. *Barnette* stands out because nothing had changed during the intervening period other than the Court's belated recognition that its earlier decision had been seriously wrong. . . .

No Justice of this Court has ever argued that the Court should *never* overrule a constitutional decision, but overruling a precedent is a serious matter. It is not a step that should be taken lightly. Our cases have attempted to provide a framework for deciding when a precedent should be overruled, and they have identified factors that should be considered in making such a decision. *Janus* v. *State, County, and Municipal Employees*, 585 U.S. ___, ___–___ (2018) (slip op., at 34–35); *Ramos* v. *Louisiana*, 590 U.S. ___, ___–___ (2020) (KAVANAUGH, J., concurring in part) (slip op., at 7–9).

In this case, five factors weigh strongly in favor of overruling *Roe* and *Casey*: the nature of their error, the quality of their reasoning, the "workability" of the rules they imposed on the country, their disruptive effect on other areas of the law, and the absence of concrete reliance.

A

The nature of the Court's error. An erroneous interpretation of the Constitution is always important, but some are more damaging than others.

The infamous decision in *Plessy* v. *Ferguson*, was one such decision. It betrayed our commitment to "equality before the law." 163 U.S., at 562 (Harlan, J., dissenting). It was "egregiously wrong" on the day it was decided, see *Ramos*, 590 U.S., at ___ (opinion of KAVANAUGH, J.) (slip op., at 7), and as the Solicitor General agreed at oral argument, it should have been overruled at the earliest opportunity, see Tr. of Oral Arg. 92–93.

Roe was also egregiously wrong and deeply damaging. For reasons already explained, *Roe*'s constitutional analysis was far outside the bounds of any reasonable interpretation of the various constitutional provisions to which it vaguely pointed.

Roe was on a collision course with the Constitution from the day it was decided, *Casey* perpetuated its errors, and those errors do not concern some arcane corner of the law of little importance to the American people. Rather, wielding nothing but "raw judicial power," *Roe*, 410 U.S., at 222 (White, J., dissenting), the Court usurped the power to address a question of profound moral and social importance that the Constitution unequivocally leaves for the people. *Casey* described itself as calling both sides of the national controversy to resolve their debate, but in doing so, *Casey* necessarily declared a winning side. Those on the losing side—those who sought to advance the State's interest in fetal life—could no longer seek to persuade their elected representatives to adopt policies consistent with their views. The Court short-circuited the democratic process by closing it to the large number of Americans who dissented in any respect from *Roe*. "*Roe* fanned into life an issue that has inflamed our national politics in general, and has obscured with its smoke the selection of Justices to this Court in particular, ever since." *Casey*, 505 U.S., at 995–996 (opinion of Scalia, J.). Together, *Roe* and *Casey* represent an error that cannot be allowed to stand.

As the Court's landmark decision in *West Coast Hotel* illustrates, the Court has previously overruled decisions that wrongly removed an issue from the people and the democratic process. As Justice White later explained, "decisions that find in the Constitution principles or values that cannot fairly be read into that document usurp the people's authority, for such decisions represent choices that the people have never made and that they cannot disavow through corrective legislation. For this reason, it is essential that this Court maintain the power to restore authority to its proper possessors by correcting constitutional decisions that, on reconsideration, are found to be mistaken." *Thornburgh*, 476 U.S., at 787 (dissenting opinion).

B

The quality of the reasoning. Under our precedents, the quality of the reasoning in a prior case has an important bearing on whether it should be reconsidered. See *Janus*, 585 U.S., at ___ (slip op., at 38); *Ramos*, 590 U.S., at ___–___ (opinion of Kavanaugh, J.) (slip op., at 7–8). In Part II, *supra*, we explained why *Roe* was incorrectly decided, but that decision was more than just wrong. It stood on exceptionally weak grounds. . . .

1

a

The weaknesses in *Roe*'s reasoning are well-known. Without any grounding in the constitutional text, history, or precedent, it imposed on the entire country a detailed set of rules much like those that one might expect to find in a statute or regulation. See 410 U.S., at 163–164. Dividing pregnancy into three trimesters, the Court imposed special rules for each. During the first trimester, the Court announced, "the abortion decision and its effectuation must be left to the medical judgment of the pregnant woman's attending physician." *Id.*, at 164. After that point, a State's interest in regulating abortion for the sake of a woman's health became compelling, and accordingly, a State could "regulate the abortion procedure in ways that are reasonably related to maternal health." *Ibid.* Finally, in "the stage subsequent to viability," which in 1973 roughly coincided with the beginning of the third trimester, the State's interest in "the potentiality of human life" became compelling, and therefore a State could "regulate, and even proscribe, abortion except where it is necessary, in appropriate medical judgment, for the preservation of the life or health of the mother." *Id.*, at 164–165.

This elaborate scheme was the Court's own brainchild. Neither party advocated the trimester framework; nor did either party or any *amicus* argue that "viability" should mark the point at which the scope of the abortion right and a State's regulatory authority should be substantially transformed. See Brief for Appellant and Brief for Appellee in *Roe* v. *Wade*, O. T. 1972, No. 70–18; see also C. Forsythe, Abuse of Discretion: The Inside Story of *Roe* v. *Wade* 127, 141 (2012).

b

Not only did this scheme resemble the work of a legislature, but the Court made little effort to explain how these rules could be deduced from any of the sources on which constitutional decisions are usually based. We have already discussed *Roe*'s treatment of constitutional text, and the opinion failed to show that history, precedent, or any other cited source supported its scheme.

Roe featured a lengthy survey of history, but much of its discussion was irrelevant, and the Court made no effort to explain why it was included. For example, multiple paragraphs were devoted to an account of the views and practices of ancient civilizations where infanticide was widely accepted. See 410 U.S., at 130–132 (discussing ancient Greek and Roman practices).[49] When it came to the most important historical fact—how the States regulated abortion when the Fourteenth Amendment was adopted—the Court said almost nothing. It allowed that States had tightened their abortion laws "in the middle and late 19th century," *id.*, at 139, but it implied that these laws might have been enacted not to protect fetal life but to further "a Victorian social concern" about "illicit sexual conduct," *id.*, at 148.

Roe's failure even to note the overwhelming consensus of state laws in effect in 1868 is striking, and what it said about the common law was simply wrong. Relying on two discredited articles by an abortion advocate, the Court erroneously suggested—contrary to Bracton, Coke, Hale, Blackstone, and a wealth of other authority—that the common law had probably never really treated post-quickening abortion as a crime. See *id.*, at 136 ("[I]t now appear[s] doubtful that abortion was ever firmly established as a common-law crime even with respect to the destruction of a quick fetus"). This erroneous understanding appears to have played an important part in the Court's thinking because the opinion

---

49. See, *e.g.*, C. Patterson, "Not Worth the Rearing": The Causes of Infant Exposure in Ancient Greece, 115 Transactions Am. Philosophical Assn. 103, 111–123 (1985); A. Cameron, The Exposure of Children and Greek Ethics, 46 Classical Rev. 105–108 (1932); H. Bennett, The Exposure of Infants in Ancient Rome, 18 Classical J. 341–351 (1923); W. Harris, Child-Exposure in the Roman Empire, 84 J. Roman Studies 1 (1994).

cited "the lenity of the common law" as one of the four factors that informed its decision. *Id.*, at 165. . . .

When the Court summarized the basis for the scheme it imposed on the country, it asserted that its rules were "consistent with" the following: (1) "the relative weights of the respective interests involved," (2) "the lessons and examples of medical and legal history," (3) "the lenity of the common law," and (4) "the demands of the profound problems of the present day." *Roe*, 410 U.S., at 165. Put aside the second and third factors, which were based on the Court's flawed account of history, and what remains are precisely the sort of considerations that legislative bodies often take into account when they draw lines that accommodate competing interests. The scheme *Roe* produced *looked* like legislation, and the Court provided the sort of explanation that might be expected from a legislative body.

c

What *Roe* did not provide was any cogent justification for the lines it drew. Why, for example, does a State have no authority to regulate first trimester abortions for the purpose of protecting a woman's health? The Court's only explanation was that mortality rates for abortion at that stage were lower than the mortality rates for childbirth. *Id.*, at 163. But the Court did not explain why mortality rates were the only factor that a State could legitimately consider. Many health and safety regulations aim to avoid adverse health consequences short of death. And the Court did not explain why it departed from the normal rule that courts defer to the judgments of legislatures "in areas fraught with medical and scientific uncertainties." *Marshall* v. *United States*, 414 U.S. 417, 427 (1974).

An even more glaring deficiency was *Roe*'s failure to justify the critical distinction it drew between pre- and post-viability abortions. Here is the Court's entire explanation:

> "With respect to the State's important and legitimate interest in potential life, the 'compelling' point is at viability. This is so because the fetus then presumably has the capability of meaningful life outside the womb." 410 U.S., at 163.

As Professor Laurence Tribe has written, "[c]learly, this mistakes 'a definition for a syllogism.'" Tribe 4 (quoting Ely 924). The definition of a "viable" fetus is one that is capable of surviving outside the womb, but why is this the point at which the State's interest becomes compelling? If, as *Roe* held, a State's interest in protecting prenatal life is compelling "after viability," 410 U.S., at 163, why isn't that interest "equally compelling before viability"? *Webster* v. *Reproductive Health Services*, 492 U.S. 490, 519 (1989) (plurality opinion) (quoting *Thornburgh*, 476 U.S., at 795 (White, J., dissenting)). *Roe* did not say, and no explanation is apparent.

This arbitrary line has not found much support among philosophers and ethicists who have attempted to justify a right to abortion. Some have argued that a fetus should not be entitled to legal protection until it acquires the characteristics that they regard as defining what it means to be a "person." Among the characteristics that have been offered as essential attributes of "personhood" are sentience, self-awareness, the ability to reason, or some combination thereof.[50] By this logic, it would be an open question whether even born individuals, including young children or those afflicted with certain developmental or medical conditions, merit protection as "persons." But even if one takes the view that "personhood" begins when a certain attribute or combination of attributes is acquired, it is very hard to see why viability should mark the point where "personhood" begins.

The most obvious problem with any such argument is that viability is heavily dependent on factors that have nothing to do with the characteristics of a fetus. One is the state of neonatal care at a particular point in time. Due to the development of new equipment and improved practices, the viability line has changed over the years. In the 19th century, a fetus may not have been viable until the 32d or 33d week of pregnancy or even later.[51] When *Roe* was decided, viability was gauged at roughly 28 weeks. See 410 U.S., at 160. Today, respondents draw the line at 23 or 24 weeks. Brief for Respondents 8. So,

---

50. See, *e.g.*, P. Singer, Rethinking Life & Death 218 (1994) (defining a person as "a being with awareness of her or his own existence over time, and the capacity to have wants and plans for the future"); B. Steinbock, Life Before Birth: The Moral and Legal Status of Embryos and Fetuses 9–13 (1992) (arguing that "the possession of interests is both necessary and sufficient for moral status" and that the "capacity for conscious awareness is a necessary condition for the possession of interests" (emphasis deleted)); M. Warren, On the Moral and Legal Status of Abortion, 57 The Monist 1, 5 (1973) (arguing that, to qualify as a person, a being must have at least one of five traits that are "central to the concept of personhood": (1) "consciousness (of objects and events external and/or internal to the being), and in particular the capacity to feel pain"; (2) "reasoning (the developed capacity to solve new and relatively complex problems)"; (3) "self-motivated activity (activity which is relatively independent of either genetic or direct external control)"; (4) "the capacity to communicate, by whatever means, messages of an indefinite variety of types"; and (5) "the presence of self-concepts, and self-awareness, either individual or racial, or both" (emphasis deleted)); M. Tooley, Abortion & Infanticide, 2 Philosophy & Pub. Affairs 37, 49 (Autumn 1972) (arguing that "having a right to life presupposes that one is capable of desiring to continue existing as a subject of experiences and other mental states").

51. See W. Lusk, Science and the Art of Midwifery 74–75 (1882) (explaining that "[w]ith care, the life of a child born within [the eighth month of pregnancy] may be preserved"); *id.*, at 326 ("Where the choice lies with the physician, the provocation of labor is usually deferred until the thirty-third or thirty-fourth week"); J. Beck, Researches in Medicine and Medical Jurisprudence 68 (2d ed. 1835) ("Although children born before the completion of the seventh month have occasionally survived, and been reared, yet in a medico-legal point of view, no child ought to be considered as capable of sustaining an independent existence until the seventh month has been fully completed"); see also J. Baker, The Incubator and the Medical Discovery of the Premature Infant, J. Perinatology 322 (2000) (explaining that, in the 19th century, infants born at seven to eight months' gestation were unlikely to survive beyond "the first days of life").

according to *Roe*'s logic, States now have a compelling interest in protecting a fetus with a gestational age of, say, 26 weeks, but in 1973 States did not have an interest in protecting an identical fetus. How can that be?

Viability also depends on the "quality of the available medical facilities." *Colautti* v. *Franklin*, 439 U.S. 379, 396 (1979). Thus, a 24-week-old fetus may be viable if a woman gives birth in a city with hospitals that provide advanced care for very premature babies, but if the woman travels to a remote area far from any such hospital, the fetus may no longer be viable. On what ground could the constitutional status of a fetus depend on the pregnant woman's location? And if viability is meant to mark a line having universal moral significance, can it be that a fetus that is viable in a big city in the United States has a privileged moral status not enjoyed by an identical fetus in a remote area of a poor country?

In addition, as the Court once explained, viability is not really a hard-and-fast line. *Ibid.* A physician determining a particular fetus's odds of surviving outside the womb must consider "a number of variables," including "gestational age," "fetal weight," a woman's "general health and nutrition," the "quality of the available medical facilities," and other factors. *Id.*, at 395–396. It is thus "only with difficulty" that a physician can estimate the "probability" of a particular fetus's survival. *Id.*, at 396. And even if each fetus's probability of survival could be ascertained with certainty, settling on a "probabilit[y] of survival" that should count as "viability" is another matter. *Ibid.* Is a fetus viable with a 10 percent chance of survival? 25 percent? 50 percent? Can such a judgment be made by a State? And can a State specify a gestational age limit that applies in all cases? Or must these difficult questions be left entirely to the individual "attending physician on the particular facts of the case before him"? *Id.*, at 388. . . .

2

When *Casey* revisited *Roe* almost 20 years later, very little of *Roe*'s reasoning was defended or preserved. The Court abandoned any reliance on a privacy right and instead grounded the abortion right entirely on the Fourteenth Amendment's Due Process Clause. 505 U.S., at 846. The Court did not reaffirm *Roe*'s erroneous account of abortion history. In fact, none of the Justices in the majority said anything about the history of the abortion right. And as for precedent, the Court relied on essentially the same body of cases that *Roe* had cited. Thus, with respect to the standard grounds for constitutional decisionmaking— text, history, and precedent—*Casey* did not attempt to bolster *Roe*'s reasoning.

The Court also made no real effort to remedy one of the greatest weaknesses in *Roe*'s analysis: its much-criticized discussion of viability. The Court retained what it called *Roe*'s "central holding"—that a State may not regulate pre-viability abortions for the purpose of protecting fetal life—but it provided no principled defense of the viability line. 505 U.S., at 860, 870–871. Instead, it merely rephrased what *Roe* had said, stating that viability marked the point at which "the independent existence of a second life can in reason and fairness be the object of state protection that now overrides the rights of the woman." 505 U.S., at 870. Why "reason and fairness" demanded that the line be drawn at viability the Court did not explain. And the Justices who authored the controlling opinion conspicuously failed to say that they agreed with the viability rule; instead, they candidly acknowledged "the reservations [some] of us may have in reaffirming [that] holding of *Roe.*" *Id.*, at 853.

The controlling opinion criticized and rejected *Roe*'s trimester scheme, 505 U.S., at 872, and substituted a new "undue burden" test, but the basis for this test was obscure. And as we will explain, the test is full of ambiguities and is difficult to apply.

Casey, in short, either refused to reaffirm or rejected important aspects of *Roe*'s analysis, failed to remedy glaring deficiencies in *Roe*'s reasoning, endorsed what it termed *Roe*'s central holding while suggesting that a majority might not have thought it was correct, provided no new support for the abortion right other than *Roe*'s status as precedent, and imposed a new and problematic test with no firm grounding in constitutional text, history, or precedent. . . .

C

Workability. Our precedents counsel that another important consideration in deciding whether a precedent should be overruled is whether the rule it imposes is workable—that is, whether it can be understood and applied in a consistent and predictable manner. *Montejo* v. *Louisiana*, 556 U.S. 778, 792 (2009); *Patterson* v. *McLean Credit Union*, 491 U.S. 164, 173 (1989); *Gulfstream Aerospace Corp.* v. *Mayacamas Corp.*, 485 U.S. 271, 283–284 (1988). *Casey*'s "undue burden" test has scored poorly on the workability scale.

1

Problems begin with the very concept of an "undue burden." As Justice Scalia noted in his *Casey* partial dissent, determining whether a burden is "due" or "undue" is "inherently standardless." 505 U.S., at 992; see also *June Medical Services L. L. C.* v. *Russo*, 591 U.S. ___, ___ (2020) (GORSUCH, J., dissenting) (slip op., at 17) ("[W]hether a burden is deemed undue depends heavily on which factors the judge considers and how much weight he accords each of them" (internal quotation marks and alterations omitted)).

The *Casey* plurality tried to put meaning into the "undue burden" test by setting out three subsidiary rules, but these rules created their own problems. The first rule is that "a provision of law is invalid, if its purpose or effect is to place a *substantial obstacle* in the path of a woman seeking an abortion before the fetus attains viability." 505 U.S., at 878 (emphasis added); see also *id.*, at 877. But whether a particular obstacle qualifies as "substantial" is often open to reasonable debate. In the sense relevant here, "substantial" means "of ample or considerable amount, quantity, or size." Random House Webster's Unabridged Dictionary 1897 (2d ed. 2001). Huge burdens are plainly "substantial," and trivial ones are not, but in between these extremes, there is a wide gray area.

This ambiguity is a problem, and the second rule, which applies at all stages of a pregnancy, muddies things further. It states that measures designed "to ensure that the woman's choice is informed" are constitutional so long as they do not impose "an undue burden on the right." *Casey*, 505 U.S., at 878. To the extent that this rule applies to pre-viability abortions, it overlaps with the first rule and appears to impose a different standard. Consider a law that imposes an insubstantial obstacle but serves little purpose. As applied to a pre-viability abortion, would such a regulation be constitutional on the ground that it does not impose a "*substantial* obstacle"? Or would it be unconstitutional on the ground that it creates an "*undue* burden" because the burden it imposes, though slight, outweighs its negligible benefits? *Casey* does not say, and this ambiguity would lead to confusion down the line. Compare *June Medical*, 591 U.S., at ___–___ (plurality opinion) (slip op., at 1–2), with *id.*, at ___–___ (ROBERTS, C. J., concurring) (slip op., at 5–6).

The third rule complicates the picture even more. Under that rule, "[u]nnecessary health regulations that have the purpose or effect of presenting a *substantial obstacle* to a woman seeking an abortion impose an *undue burden* on the right." *Casey*, 505 U.S., at 878 (emphasis added). This rule contains no fewer than three vague terms. It includes the two already discussed—"undue burden" and "substantial obstacle"—even though they are inconsistent. And it adds a third ambiguous term when it refers to "*unnecessary* health regulations." The term "necessary" has a range of meanings—from "essential" to merely "useful." See Black's Law Dictionary 928 (5th ed. 1979); American Heritage Dictionary of the English Language 877 (1971). *Casey* did not explain the sense in which the term is used in this rule.

In addition to these problems, one more applies to all three rules. They all call on courts to examine a law's effect on women, but a regulation may have a very different impact on different women for a variety of reasons, including their places of residence, financial resources, family situations, work and personal obligations, knowledge about fetal development and abortion, psychological and emotional disposition and condition, and the firmness of their desire to obtain abortions. In order to determine whether a regulation presents a substantial obstacle to women, a court needs to know which set of women it should have in mind and how many of the women in this set must find that an obstacle is "substantial."

Casey provided no clear answer to these questions. It said that a regulation is unconstitutional if it imposes a substantial obstacle "in a large fraction of cases in which [it] is relevant," 505 U.S., at 895, but there is obviously no clear line between a fraction that is "large" and one that is not. Nor is it clear what the Court meant by "cases in which" a regulation is "relevant." These ambiguities have caused confusion and disagreement. Compare *Whole Woman's Health* v. *Hellerstedt*, 579 U.S. 582, 627–628 (2016), with *id.*, at 666–667, and n. 11 (ALITO, J., dissenting).

2

The difficulty of applying *Casey*'s new rules surfaced in that very case. The controlling opinion found that Pennsylvania's 24-hour waiting period requirement and its informed-consent provision did not impose "undue burden[s]," *Casey*, 505 U.S., at 881–887, but Justice Stevens, applying the same test, reached the opposite result, *id.*, at 920–922 (opinion concurring in part and dissenting in part). That did not bode well, and then-Chief Justice Rehnquist aptly observed that "the undue burden standard presents nothing more workable than the trimester framework." *Id.*, at 964–966 (dissenting opinion).

The ambiguity of the "undue burden" test also produced disagreement in later cases. In *Whole Woman's Health*, the Court adopted the cost-benefit interpretation of the test, stating that "[t]he rule announced in *Casey* . . . requires that courts consider the burdens a law imposes on abortion access *together with the benefits those laws confer*." 579 U.S., at 607 (emphasis added). But five years later, a majority of the Justices rejected that interpretation. See *June Medical*, 591 U.S. ___. Four Justices reaffirmed *Whole Woman's Health*'s instruction to "weigh" a law's "benefits" against "the burdens it imposes on abortion access." 591 U.S., at ___ (plurality opinion) (slip op., at 2) (internal quotation marks omitted). But THE CHIEF JUSTICE—who cast the deciding vote—argued that "[n]othing about *Casey* suggested that a weighing of costs and benefits of an abortion regulation was a job for the courts." *Id.*, at ___ (opinion concurring in judgment) (slip op., at 6). And the four Justices in dissent rejected the plurality's interpretation of *Casey*. See 591 U.S., at ___ (opinion of ALITO, J., joined in relevant part by THOMAS, GORSUCH, and KAVANAUGH, JJ.) (slip op., at 4); *id.*, at ___–___ (opinion of GORSUCH, J.) (slip op., at 15–18); *id.*, at ___–___ (opinion of KAVANAUGH, J.) (slip op., at 1–2) ("[F]ive Members of the Court reject the *Whole Woman's Health* cost-benefit standard").

This Court's experience applying *Casey* has confirmed Chief Justice Rehnquist's prescient diagnosis that the undue-burden standard was "not built to last." *Casey*, 505 U.S., at 965 (opinion concurring in judgment in part and dissenting in part). . . .

D

Effect on other areas of law. *Roe* and *Casey* have led to the distortion of many important but unrelated legal doctrines, and that effect provides further support for overruling those decisions. See *Ramos*, 590 U.S., at ___ (opinion of KAVANAUGH, J.) (slip op., at 8); *Janus*, 585 U.S., at ___ (slip op., at 34).

Members of this Court have repeatedly lamented that "no legal rule or doctrine is safe from ad hoc nullification by this Court when an occasion for its application arises in a case involving state regulation of abortion." *Thornburgh*, 476 U.S., at 814 (O'Connor, J., dissenting); see *Madsen* v. *Women's Health Center, Inc.*, 512 U.S. 753, 785 (1994) (Scalia, J., concurring in judgment in part and dissenting in part); *Whole Woman's Health*, 579 U.S., at 631–633 (THOMAS, J., dissenting); *id.*, at 645–666, 678–684 (ALITO, J., dissenting); *June Medical*, 591 U.S., at ___–___ (GORSUCH, J., dissenting) (slip op., at 1–15).

The Court's abortion cases have diluted the strict standard for facial constitutional challenges.[60] They have ignored the Court's third-party standing doctrine.[61] They have disregarded standard *res judicata* principles.[62] They have flouted the ordinary rules on the severability of unconstitutional provisions,[63] as well as the rule that statutes should be read where possible to avoid unconstitutionality.[64] And they have distorted First Amendment doctrines.[65]

When vindicating a doctrinal innovation requires courts to engineer exceptions to longstanding background rules, the doctrine "has failed to deliver the 'principled and intelligible' development of the law that *stare decisis* purports to secure." *Id.*, at ___ (THOMAS, J., dissenting) (slip op., at 19) (quoting *Vasquez* v. *Hillery*, 474 U.S. 254, 265 (1986)).

E

Reliance interests. We last consider whether overruling *Roe* and *Casey* will upend substantial reliance interests. See *Ramos*, 590 U.S., at ___ (opinion of KAVANAUGH, J.) (slip op., at 15); *Janus*, 585 U.S., at ___–___ (slip op., at 34–35).

1

Traditional reliance interests arise "where advance planning of great precision is most obviously a necessity." *Casey*, 505 U.S., at 856 (joint opinion); see also *Payne*, 501 U.S., at 828. In *Casey*, the controlling opinion conceded that those traditional reliance interests were not implicated because getting an abortion is generally "unplanned activity," and "reproductive planning could take virtually immediate account of any sudden restoration

---

60. Compare *United States* v. *Salerno*, 481 U.S. 739, 745 (1987), with *Casey*, 505 U.S., at 895; see also *supra*, at 56–59.

61. Compare *Warth* v. *Seldin*, 422 U.S. 490, 499 (1975), and *Elk Grove Unified School Dist.* v. *Newdow*, 542 U.S. 1, 15, 17–18 (2004), with *June Medical*, 591 U.S., at ___ (ALITO, J., dissenting) (slip op., at 28), *id.*, at ___–___ (GORSUCH, J., dissenting) (slip op., at 6–7) (collecting cases), and *Whole Woman's Health*, 579 U.S., at 632, n. 1 (THOMAS, J., dissenting).

62. Compare *id.*, at 598–606 (majority opinion), with *id.*, at 645–666 (ALITO, J., dissenting).

63. Compare *id.*, at 623–626 (majority opinion), with *id.*, at 644–645 (ALITO, J., dissenting).

64. See *Stenberg* v. *Carhart*, 530 U.S. 914, 977–978 (2000) (Kennedy, J., dissenting); *id.*, at 996–997 (THOMAS, J., dissenting).

65. See *Hill* v. *Colorado*, 530 U.S. 703, 741–742 (2000) (Scalia, J., dissenting); *id.*, at 765 (Kennedy, J., dissenting).

of state authority to ban abortions." 505 U.S., at 856. For these reasons, we agree with the *Casey* plurality that conventional, concrete reliance interests are not present here.

2

Unable to find reliance in the conventional sense, the controlling opinion in *Casey* perceived a more intangible form of reliance. It wrote that "people [had] organized intimate relationships and made choices that define their views of themselves and their places in society . . . in reliance on the availability of abortion in the event that contraception should fail" and that "[t]he ability of women to participate equally in the economic and social life of the Nation has been facilitated by their ability to control their reproductive lives." *Ibid.* But this Court is ill-equipped to assess "generalized assertions about the national psyche." *Id.*, at 957 (opinion of Rehnquist, C. J.). *Casey*'s notion of reliance thus finds little support in our cases, which instead emphasize very concrete reliance interests, like those that develop in "cases involving property and contract rights." *Payne*, 501 U.S., at 828.

When a concrete reliance interest is asserted, courts are equipped to evaluate the claim, but assessing the novel and intangible form of reliance endorsed by the *Casey* plurality is another matter. That form of reliance depends on an empirical question that is hard for anyone—and in particular, for a court—to assess, namely, the effect of the abortion right on society and in particular on the lives of women. The contending sides in this case make impassioned and conflicting arguments about the effects of the abortion right on the lives of women. Compare Brief for Petitioners 34–36; Brief for Women Scholars et al. as *Amici Curiae* 13–20, 29–41, with Brief for Respondents 36–41; Brief for National Women's Law Center et al. as *Amici Curiae* 15–32. The contending sides also make conflicting arguments about the status of the fetus. This Court has neither the authority nor the expertise to adjudicate those disputes, and the *Casey* plurality's speculations and weighing of the relative importance of the fetus and mother represent a departure from the "original constitutional proposition" that "courts do not substitute their social and economic beliefs for the judgment of legislative bodies." *Ferguson* v. *Skrupa*, 372 U.S. 726, 729–730 (1963).

Our decision returns the issue of abortion to those legislative bodies, and it allows women on both sides of the abortion issue to seek to affect the legislative process by influencing public opinion, lobbying legislators, voting, and running for office. Women are not without electoral or political power. It is noteworthy that the percentage of women who register to vote and cast ballots is consistently higher than the percentage of men who do so.[66] In the last election in November 2020, women, who make up around 51.5

---

66. See Dept. of Commerce, U.S. Census Bureau (Census Bureau), An Analysis of the 2018 Congressional Election 6 (Dec. 2021) (Fig. 5) (showing that women made up over 50 percent of the voting population in every congressional election between 1978 and 2018).

percent of the population of Mississippi,[67] constituted 55.5 percent of the voters who cast ballots.[68]

3

Unable to show concrete reliance on *Roe* and *Casey* themselves, the Solicitor General suggests that overruling those decisions would "threaten the Court's precedents holding that the Due Process Clause protects other rights." Brief for United States 26 (citing *Obergefell*, 576 U.S. 644; *Lawrence*, 539 U.S. 558; *Griswold*, 381 U.S. 479). That is not correct for reasons we have already discussed. As even the *Casey* plurality recognized, "[a] bortion is a unique act" because it terminates "life or potential life." 505 U.S., at 852; see also *Roe*, 410 U.S., at 159 (abortion is "inherently different from marital intimacy," "marriage," or "procreation"). And to ensure that our decision is not misunderstood or mischaracterized, we emphasize that our decision concerns the constitutional right to abortion and no other right. Nothing in this opinion should be understood to cast doubt on precedents that do not concern abortion

IV

Having shown that traditional *stare decisis* factors do not weigh in favor of retaining *Roe* or *Casey*, we must address one final argument that featured prominently in the *Casey* plurality opinion.

The argument was cast in different terms, but stated simply, it was essentially as follows. The American people's belief in the rule of law would be shaken if they lost respect for this Court as an institution that decides important cases based on principle, not "social and political pressures." 505 U.S., at 865. There is a special danger that the public will perceive a decision as having been made for unprincipled reasons when the Court overrules a controversial "watershed" decision, such as *Roe*. 505 U.S., at 866–867. A decision overruling *Roe* would be perceived as having been made "under fire" and as a "surrender to political pressure," 505 U.S., at 867, and therefore the preservation of public approval of the Court weighs heavily in favor of retaining *Roe*, see 505 U.S., at 869.

This analysis starts out on the right foot but ultimately veers off course. The *Casey* plurality was certainly right that it is important for the public to perceive that our decisions are based on principle, and we should make every effort to achieve that objective by

---

67. Census Bureau, QuickFacts, Mississippi (July 1, 2021), https://www.census.gov/quickfacts/MS.

68. Census Bureau, Voting and Registration in the Election of November 2020, Table 4b: Reported Voting and Registration, by Sex, Race and Hispanic Origin, for States: November 2020, https://www.census.gov/data/tables/time-series/demo/voting-and-registration/p20-585.html.

issuing opinions that carefully show how a proper understanding of the law leads to the results we reach. But we cannot exceed the scope of our authority under the Constitution, and we cannot allow our decisions to be affected by any extraneous influences such as concern about the public's reaction to our work. Cf. *Texas* v. *Johnson*, 491 U.S. 397 (1989); *Brown*, 347 U.S. 483. That is true both when we initially decide a constitutional issue *and* when we consider whether to overrule a prior decision. As Chief Justice Rehnquist explained, "The Judicial Branch derives its legitimacy, not from following public opinion, but from deciding by its best lights whether legislative enactments of the popular branches of Government comport with the Constitution. The doctrine of *stare decisis* is an adjunct of this duty, and should be no more subject to the vagaries of public opinion than is the basic judicial task." *Casey*, 505 U.S., at 963 (opinion concurring in judgment in part and dissenting in part). In suggesting otherwise, the *Casey* plurality went beyond this Court's role in our constitutional system.

The *Casey* plurality "call[ed] the contending sides of a national controversy to end their national division," and claimed the authority to impose a permanent settlement of the issue of a constitutional abortion right simply by saying that the matter was closed. *Id.*, at 867. That unprecedented claim exceeded the power vested in us by the Constitution. As Alexander Hamilton famously put it, the Constitution gives the judiciary "neither Force nor Will." The Federalist No. 78, p. 523 (J. Cooke ed. 1961). Our sole authority is to exercise "judgment"—which is to say, the authority to judge what the law means and how it should apply to the case at hand. *Ibid.* The Court has no authority to decree that an erroneous precedent is *permanently* exempt from evaluation under traditional *stare decisis* principles. A precedent of this Court is subject to the usual principles of *stare decisis* under which adherence to precedent is the norm but not an inexorable command. If the rule were otherwise, erroneous decisions like *Plessy* and *Lochner* would still be the law. That is not how *stare decisis* operates.

The *Casey* plurality also misjudged the practical limits of this Court's influence. *Roe* certainly did not succeed in ending division on the issue of abortion. On the contrary, *Roe* "inflamed" a national issue that has remained bitterly divisive for the past half century. *Casey*, 505 U.S., at 995 (opinion of Scalia, J.); see also R. Ginsburg, Speaking in a Judicial Voice, 67 N. Y. U. L. Rev. 1185, 1208 (1992) (*Roe* may have "halted a political process," "prolonged divisiveness," and "deferred stable settlement of the issue"). And for the past 30 years, *Casey* has done the same.

Neither decision has ended debate over the issue of a constitutional right to obtain an abortion. Indeed, in this case, 26 States expressly ask us to overrule *Roe* and *Casey* and to return the issue of abortion to the people and their elected representatives. This Court's inability to end debate on the issue should not have been surprising. This Court cannot bring about the permanent resolution of a rancorous national controversy simply by dictating a settlement and telling the people to move on. Whatever influence the Court may have on public attitudes must stem from the strength of our opinions, not an attempt to exercise "raw judicial power." *Roe*, 410 U.S., at 222 (White, J., dissenting).

We do not pretend to know how our political system or society will respond to today's decision overruling *Roe* and *Casey*. And even if we could foresee what will happen, we would have no authority to let that knowledge influence our decision. We can only do our job, which is to interpret the law, apply longstanding principles of *stare decisis*, and decide this case accordingly.

We therefore hold that the Constitution does not confer a right to abortion. *Roe* and *Casey* must be overruled, and the authority to regulate abortion must be returned to the people and their elected representatives. . . .

V

B

3

The concurrence would "leave for another day whether to reject any right to an abortion at all," *post*, at 7, but "another day" would not be long in coming. Some States have set deadlines for obtaining an abortion that are shorter than Mississippi's. See, *e.g.*, *Memphis Center for Reproductive Health* v. *Slatery*, 14 F. 4th, at 414 (considering law with bans "at cascading intervals of two to three weeks" beginning at six weeks), reh'g en banc granted, 14 F. 4th 550 (CA6 2021). If we held only that Mississippi's 15-week rule is constitutional, we would soon be called upon to pass on the constitutionality of a panoply of laws with shorter deadlines or no deadline at all. The "measured course" charted by the concurrence would be fraught with turmoil until the Court answered the question that the concurrence seeks to defer.

Even if the Court ultimately adopted the new rule suggested by the concurrence, we would be faced with the difficult problem of spelling out what it means. For example, if the period required to give women a "reasonable" opportunity to obtain an abortion were pegged, as the concurrence seems to suggest, at the point when a certain percentage of women make that choice, see *post*, at 1–2, 9–10, we would have to identify the relevant percentage. It would also be necessary to explain what the concurrence means when it refers to "rare circumstances" that might justify an exception. *Post*, at 10. And if this new right aims to give women a reasonable opportunity to get an abortion, it would be necessary to decide whether factors other than promptness in deciding might have a bearing on whether such an opportunity was available.

In sum, the concurrence's quest for a middle way would only put off the day when we would be forced to confront the question we now decide. The turmoil wrought by *Roe* and *Casey* would be prolonged. It is far better—for this Court and the country—to face up to the real issue without further delay.

VI

We must now decide what standard will govern if state abortion regulations undergo constitutional challenge and whether the law before us satisfies the appropriate standard.

A

Under our precedents, rational-basis review is the appropriate standard for such challenges. As we have explained, procuring an abortion is not a fundamental constitutional right because such a right has no basis in the Constitution's text or in our Nation's history. See *supra*, at 8–39.

It follows that the States may regulate abortion for legitimate reasons, and when such regulations are challenged under the Constitution, courts cannot "substitute their social and economic beliefs for the judgment of legislative bodies." *Ferguson*, 372 U.S., at 729–730; see also *Dandridge* v. *Williams*, 397 U.S. 471, 484–486 (1970); *United States* v. *Carolene Products Co.*, 304 U.S. 144, 152 (1938). That respect for a legislature's judgment applies even when the laws at issue concern matters of great social significance and moral substance. See, *e.g.*, *Board of Trustees of Univ. of Ala.* v. *Garrett*, 531 U.S. 356, 365–368 (2001) ("treatment of the disabled"); *Glucksberg*, 521 U.S., at 728 ("assisted suicide"); *San Antonio Independent School Dist.* v. *Rodriguez*, 411 U.S. 1, 32–35, 55 (1973) ("financing public education").

A law regulating abortion, like other health and welfare laws, is entitled to a "strong presumption of validity." *Heler* v. *Doe*, 509 U.S. 312, 319 (1993). It must be sustained if there is a rational basis on which the legislature could have thought that it would serve legitimate state interests. *Id.*, at 320; *FCC* v. *Beach Communications, Inc.*, 508 U.S. 307, 313 (1993); *New Orleans* v. *Dukes*, 427 U.S. 297, 303 (1976) (*per curiam*); *Williamson* v. *Lee Optical of Okla., Inc.*, 348 U.S. 483, 491 (1955). These legitimate interests include respect for and preservation of prenatal life at all stages of development, *Gonzales*, 550 U.S., at 157–158; the protection of maternal health and safety; the elimination of particularly gruesome or barbaric medical procedures; the preservation of the integrity of the medical profession; the mitigation of fetal pain; and the prevention of discrimination on the basis of race, sex, or disability. See *id.*, at 156–157; *Roe*, 410 U.S., at 150; cf. *Glucksberg*, 521 U.S., at 728–731 (identifying similar interests). . . .

JUSTICE THOMAS, concurring.

. . . I write separately to emphasize a second, more fundamental reason why there is no abortion guarantee lurking in the Due Process Clause. Considerable historical evidence indicates that "due process of law" merely required executive and judicial actors to comply with legislative enactments and the common law when depriving a person of life, liberty, or property. See, *e.g.*, *Johnson* v. *United States*, 576 U.S. 591, 623 (2015) (THOMAS, J., concurring in judgment). Other sources, by contrast, suggest that "due process of law" prohibited legislatures "from authorizing the deprivation of a person's life, liberty, or property without providing him the customary procedures to which freemen were entitled by the old law of England." *United States* v. *Vaello Madero*, 596 U.S. ___, ___ (2022) (THOMAS, J., concurring) (slip op., at 3) (internal quotation marks omitted). Either way, the Due Process Clause at most guarantees *process*. It does not, as the Court's substantive due process cases suppose, "forbi[d] the government to infringe certain 'fundamental' liberty interests *at all*, no matter what process is provided." *Reno* v. *Flores*, 507 U.S. 292, 302 (1993); see also, *e.g.*, *Collins* v. *Harker Heights*, 503 U.S. 115, 125 (1992).

As I have previously explained, "substantive due process" is an oxymoron that "lack[s] any basis in the Constitution." *Johnson*, 576 U.S., at 607–608 (opinion of THOMAS, J.); see also, *e.g.*, *Vaello Madero*, 596 U.S., at ___ (THOMAS, J., concurring) (slip op., at 3) ("[T]ext and history provide little support for modern substantive due process doctrine"). "The notion that a constitutional provision that guarantees only 'process' before a person is deprived of life, liberty, or property could define the substance of those rights strains credulity for even the most casual user of words." *McDonald* v. *Chicago*, 561 U.S. 742, 811 (2010) (THOMAS, J., concurring in part and concurring in judgment); see also *United States* v. *Carlton*, 512 U.S. 26, 40 (1994) (Scalia, J., concurring in judgment). The resolution of this case is thus straightforward. Because the Due Process Clause does not secure *any* substantive rights, it does not secure a right to abortion.

The Court today declines to disturb substantive due process jurisprudence generally or the doctrine's application in other, specific contexts. Cases like *Griswold* v. *Connecticut*, 381 U.S. 479 (1965) (right of married persons to obtain contraceptives)*; *Lawrence* v. *Texas*, 539 U.S. 558 (2003) (right to engage in private, consensual sexual acts); and *Obergefell* v. *Hodges*, 576 U.S. 644 (2015) (right to same-sex marriage), are not at issue. The Court's abortion cases are unique, see *ante*, at 31–32, 66, 71–72, and no party has asked us to decide "whether our entire Fourteenth Amendment jurisprudence must be preserved or revised," *McDonald*, 561 U.S., at 813 (opinion of THOMAS, J.). Thus, I agree that "[n]othing in [the Court's] opinion should be understood to cast doubt on precedents that do not concern abortion." *Ante*, at 66.

For that reason, in future cases, we should reconsider all of this Court's substantive due process precedents, including *Griswold*, *Lawrence*, and *Obergefell*. Because any

---

*Griswold v. *Connecticut* purported not to rely on the Due Process Clause, but rather reasoned "that specific guarantees in the Bill of Rights"—including rights enumerated in the First, Third, Fourth, Fifth, and Ninth Amendments—"have penumbras, formed by emanations," that create "zones of privacy." 381 U.S., at 484. Since *Griswold*, the Court, perhaps recognizing the facial absurdity of *Griswold*'s penumbral argument, has characterized the decision as one rooted in substantive due process. See, *e.g.*, *Obergefell* v. *Hodges*, 576 U.S. 644, 663 (2015); *Washington* v. *Glucksberg*, 521 U.S. 702, 720 (1997).

substantive due process decision is "demonstrably erroneous," *Ramos* v. *Louisiana*, 590 U.S. ___, ___ (2020) (THOMAS, J., concurring in judgment) (slip op., at 7), we have a duty to "correct the error" established in those precedents, *Gamble* v. *United States*, 587 U.S. ___, ___ (2019) (THOMAS, J., concurring) (slip op., at 9). After overruling these demonstrably erroneous decisions, the question would remain whether other constitutional provisions guarantee the myriad rights that our substantive due process cases have generated. For example, we could consider whether any of the rights announced in this Court's substantive due process cases are "privileges or immunities of citizens of the United States" protected by the Fourteenth Amendment. Amdt. 14, §1; see *McDonald*, 561 U.S., at 806 (opinion of THOMAS, J.). To answer that question, we would need to decide important antecedent questions, including whether the Privileges or Immunities Clause protects *any* rights that are not enumerated in the Constitution and, if so, how to identify those rights. See *id.*, at 854. That said, even if the Clause does protect unenumerated rights, the Court conclusively demonstrates that abortion is not one of them under any plausible interpretive approach. See *ante*, at 15, n. 22. . . .

CHIEF JUSTICE ROBERTS, concurring in the judgment.

. . . I would take a more measured course. I agree with the Court that the viability line established by *Roe* and *Casey* should be discarded under a straightforward *stare decisis* analysis. That line never made any sense. Our abortion precedents describe the right at issue as a woman's right to choose to terminate her pregnancy. That right should therefore extend far enough to ensure a reasonable opportunity to choose, but need not extend any further—certainly not all the way to viability. Mississippi's law allows a woman three months to obtain an abortion, well beyond the point at which it is considered "late" to discover a pregnancy. See A. Ayoola, Late Recognition of Unintended Pregnancies, 32 Pub. Health Nursing 462 (2015) (pregnancy is discoverable and ordinarily discovered by six weeks of gestation). I see no sound basis for questioning the adequacy of that opportunity.

But that is all I would say, out of adherence to a simple yet fundamental principle of judicial restraint: If it is not necessary to decide more to dispose of a case, then it is necessary *not* to decide more. Perhaps we are not always perfect in following that command, and certainly there are cases that warrant an exception. But this is not one of them. Surely we should adhere closely to principles of judicial restraint here, where the broader path the Court chooses entails repudiating a constitutional right we have not only previously recognized, but also expressly reaffirmed applying the doctrine of *stare decisis*. The Court's opinion is thoughtful and thorough, but those virtues cannot compensate for the fact that its dramatic and consequential ruling is unnecessary to decide the case before us. . . .

II

... When the State petitioned for our review, its basic request was straightforward: "clarify whether abortion prohibitions before viability are always unconstitutional." Pet. for Cert. 14. The State made a number of strong arguments that the answer is no, *id.*, at 15–26—arguments that, as discussed, I find persuasive. And it went out of its way to make clear that it was *not* asking the Court to repudiate entirely the right to choose whether to terminate a pregnancy: "To be clear, the questions presented in this petition do not require the Court to overturn *Roe* or *Casey*." *Id.*, at 5. Mississippi tempered that statement with an oblique one-sentence footnote intimating that, if the Court could not reconcile *Roe* and *Casey* with current facts or other cases, it "should not retain erroneous precedent." Pet. for Cert. 5–6, n. 1. But the State never argued that we should grant review for that purpose.

After we granted certiorari, however, Mississippi changed course. In its principal brief, the State bluntly announced that the Court should overrule *Roe* and *Casey*. The Constitution does not protect a right to an abortion, it argued, and a State should be able to prohibit elective abortions if a rational basis supports doing so. See Brief for Petitioners 12–13.

The Court now rewards that gambit, noting three times that the parties presented "no half-measures" and argued that "we must either reaffirm or overrule *Roe* and *Casey*." *Ante*, at 5, 8, 72. Given those two options, the majority picks the latter.

This framing is not accurate. In its brief on the merits, Mississippi in fact argued at length that a decision simply rejecting the viability rule would result in a judgment in its favor. See Brief for Petitioners 5, 38–48. But even if the State had not argued as much, it would not matter. There is no rule that parties can confine this Court to disposing of their case on a particular ground—let alone when review was sought and granted on a different one. Our established practice is instead not to "formulate a rule of constitutional law broader than is required by the precise facts to which it is to be applied." *Washington State Grange* v. *Washington State Republican Party*, 552 U.S. 442, 450 (2008) (quoting *Ashwander* v. *TVA*, 297 U.S. 288, 347 (1936) (Brandeis, J., concurring)); see also *United States* v. *Raines*, 362 U.S. 17, 21 (1960).

Following that "fundamental principle of judicial restraint," *Washington State Grange*, 552 U.S., at 450, we should begin with the narrowest basis for disposition, proceeding to consider a broader one only if necessary to resolve the case at hand. See, *e.g.*, *Office of Personnel Management* v. *Richmond*, 496 U.S. 414, 423 (1990). It is only where there is no valid narrower ground of decision that we should go on to address a broader issue, such as whether a constitutional decision should be overturned. See *Federal Election Comm'n* v. *Wisconsin Right to Life, Inc.*, 551 U.S. 449, 482 (2007) (declining to address the claim that a constitutional decision should be overruled when the appellant prevailed on its narrower constitutional argument).

Here, there is a clear path to deciding this case correctly without overruling *Roe* all the way down to the studs: recognize that the viability line must be discarded, as the majority rightly does, and leave for another day whether to reject any right to an abortion at all. See *Webster* v. *Reproductive Health Services*, 492 U.S. 490, 518, 521 (1989) (plurality opinion) (rejecting *Roe*'s viability line as "rigid" and "indeterminate," while also finding "no occasion to revisit the holding of *Roe*" that, under the Constitution, a State must provide an opportunity to choose to terminate a pregnancy). . . .

III

. . . The Court's decision to overrule *Roe* and *Casey* is a serious jolt to the legal system—regardless of how you view those cases. A narrower decision rejecting the misguided viability line would be markedly less unsettling, and nothing more is needed to decide this case.

Our cases say that the effect of overruling a precedent on reliance interests is a factor to consider in deciding whether to take such a step, and respondents argue that generations of women have relied on the right to an abortion in organizing their relationships and planning their futures. Brief for Respondents 36–41; see also *Casey*, 505 U.S., at 856 (making the same point). The Court questions whether these concerns are pertinent under our precedents, see *ante*, at 64–65, but the issue would not even arise with a decision rejecting only the viability line: It cannot reasonably be argued that women have shaped their lives in part on the assumption that they would be able to abort up to viability, as opposed to fifteen weeks.

In support of its holding, the Court cites three seminal constitutional decisions that involved overruling prior precedents: *Brown* v. *Board of Education*, 347 U.S. 483 (1954), *West Virginia Bd. of Ed.* v. *Barnette*, 319 U.S. 624 (1943), and *West Coast Hotel Co.* v. *Parrish*, 300 U.S. 379 (1937). See *ante*, at 40–41. The opinion in *Brown* was unanimous and eleven pages long; this one is neither. *Barnette* was decided only three years after the decision it overruled, three Justices having had second thoughts. And *West Coast Hotel* was issued against a backdrop of unprecedented economic despair that focused attention on the fundamental flaws of existing precedent. It also was part of a sea change in this Court's interpretation of the Constitution, "signal[ing] the demise of an entire line of important precedents," *ante*, at 40—a feature the Court expressly disclaims in today's decision, see *ante*, at 32, 66. None of these leading cases, in short, provides a template for what the Court does today.

The Court says we should consider whether to overrule *Roe* and *Casey* now, because if we delay we would be forced to consider the issue again in short order. See *ante*, at 76–77. There would be "turmoil" until we did so, according to the Court, because of existing state laws with "shorter deadlines or no deadline at all." *Ante*, at 76. But under the narrower approach proposed here, state laws outlawing abortion altogether would still violate binding precedent. And to the extent States have laws that set the cutoff date earlier than fifteen weeks, any litigation over that timeframe would proceed free of the distorting effect that the viability rule has had on our constitutional debate. The same could be true, for that matter, with respect to legislative consideration in the States. We would then be free to exercise our discretion in deciding whether and when to take up the issue, from a more informed perspective. . . .

JUSTICE BREYER, JUSTICE SOTOMAYOR, and JUSTICE KAGAN, dissenting.

. . . *Roe* and *Casey* well understood the difficulty and divisiveness of the abortion issue. The Court knew that Americans hold profoundly different views about the "moral[ity]" of "terminating a pregnancy, even in its earliest stage." *Casey*, 505 U.S., at 850. And the Court recognized that "the State has legitimate interests from the outset of the pregnancy in protecting" the "life of the fetus that may become a child." *Id.*, at 846. So the Court struck a balance, as it often does when values and goals compete. It held that the State could prohibit abortions after fetal viability, so long as the ban contained exceptions to safeguard a woman's life or health. It held that even before viability, the State could regulate the abortion procedure in multiple and meaningful ways. But until the viability line was crossed, the Court held, a State could not impose a "substantial obstacle" on a woman's "right to elect the procedure" as she (not the government) thought proper, in light of all the circumstances and complexities of her own life. *Ibid.*

Today, the Court discards that balance. It says that from the very moment of fertilization, a woman has no rights to speak of. A State can force her to bring a pregnancy to term, even at the steepest personal and familial costs. An abortion restriction, the majority holds, is permissible whenever rational, the lowest level of scrutiny known to the law. And because, as the Court has often stated, protecting fetal life is rational, States will feel free to enact all manner of restrictions. The Mississippi law at issue here bars abortions after the 15th week of pregnancy. Under the majority's ruling, though, another State's law could do so after ten weeks, or five or three or one—or, again, from the moment of fertilization. States have already passed such laws, in anticipation of today's ruling. More will follow. Some States have enacted laws extending to all forms of abortion procedure, including taking medication in one's own home. They have passed laws without any exceptions for when the woman is the victim of rape or incest. Under those laws, a woman will have to bear her rapist's child or a young girl her father's—no matter if doing so will destroy her life. So too, after today's ruling, some States may compel women to carry to term a fetus with severe physical anomalies—for example, one afflicted with Tay-Sachs disease, sure to die within a few years of birth. States may even argue that a prohibition on abortion need make no provision for protecting a woman from risk of death or physical harm. Across a vast array of circumstances, a State will be able to impose its moral choice on a woman and coerce her to give birth to a child.

Enforcement of all these draconian restrictions will also be left largely to the States' devices. A State can of course impose criminal penalties on abortion providers, including lengthy prison sentences. But some States will not stop there. Perhaps, in the wake of today's decision, a state law will criminalize the woman's conduct too, incarcerating or fining her for daring to seek or obtain an abortion. And as Texas has recently shown, a State can turn neighbor against neighbor, enlisting fellow citizens in the effort to root out anyone who tries to get an abortion, or to assist another in doing so.

The majority tries to hide the geographically expansive effects of its holding. Today's decision, the majority says, permits "each State" to address abortion as it pleases. *Ante*, at 79. That is cold comfort, of course, for the poor woman who cannot get the money to fly to a distant State for a procedure. Above all others, women lacking financial resources will suffer from today's decision. In any event, interstate restrictions will also soon be in the offing. After this decision, some States may block women from traveling out of State to obtain abortions, or even from receiving abortion medications from out of State. Some may criminalize efforts, including the provision of information or funding, to help women gain access to other States' abortion services. Most threatening of all, no language in today's decision stops the Federal Government from prohibiting abortions nationwide, once again from the moment of conception and without exceptions for rape or incest. If that happens, "the views of [an individual State's] citizens" will not matter. *Ante*, at 1. The challenge for a woman will be to finance a trip not to "New York [or] California" but to Toronto. *Ante*, at 4 (KAVANAUGH, J., concurring).

Whatever the exact scope of the coming laws, one result of today's decision is certain: the curtailment of women's rights, and of their status as free and equal citizens. Yesterday, the Constitution guaranteed that a woman confronted with an unplanned pregnancy could (within reasonable limits) make her own decision about whether to bear a child, with all the life-transforming consequences that act involves. And in thus safeguarding each woman's reproductive freedom, the Constitution also protected "[t]he ability of women to participate equally in [this Nation's] economic and social life." *Casey*, 505 U.S., at 856. But no longer. As of today, this Court holds, a State can always force a woman to give birth, prohibiting even the earliest abortions. A State can thus transform what, when freely undertaken, is a wonder into what, when forced, may be a nightmare. Some women, especially women of means, will find ways around the State's assertion of power. Others—those without money or childcare or the ability to take time off from work—will not be so fortunate. Maybe they will try an unsafe method of abortion, and come to physical harm, or even die. Maybe they will undergo pregnancy and have a child, but at significant personal or familial cost. At the least, they will incur the cost of losing control of their lives. The Constitution will, today's majority holds, provide no shield, despite its guarantees of liberty and equality for all.

And no one should be confident that this majority is done with its work. The right *Roe* and *Casey* recognized does not stand alone. To the contrary, the Court has linked it for decades to other settled freedoms involving bodily integrity, familial relationships, and procreation. Most obviously, the right to terminate a pregnancy arose straight out of the right to purchase and use contraception. See *Griswold* v. *Connecticut*, 381 U.S. 479

(1965); *Eisenstadt* v. *Baird*, 405 U.S. 438 (1972). In turn, those rights led, more recently, to rights of same-sex intimacy and marriage. See *Lawrence* v. *Texas*, 539 U.S. 558 (2003); *Obergefell* v. *Hodges*, 576 U.S. 644 (2015). They are all part of the same constitutional fabric, protecting autonomous decisionmaking over the most personal of life decisions. The majority (or to be more accurate, most of it) is eager to tell us today that nothing it does "cast[s] doubt on precedents that do not concern abortion." *Ante*, at 66; cf. *ante*, at 3 (THOMAS, J., concurring) (advocating the overruling of *Griswold*, *Lawrence*, and *Obergefell*). But how could that be? The lone rationale for what the majority does today is that the right to elect an abortion is not "deeply rooted in history": Not until *Roe*, the majority argues, did people think abortion fell within the Constitution's guarantee of liberty. *Ante*, at 32. The same could be said, though, of most of the rights the majority claims it is not tampering with. The majority could write just as long an opinion showing, for example, that until the mid-20th century, "there was no support in American law for a constitutional right to obtain [contraceptives]." *Ante*, at 15. So one of two things must be true. Either the majority does not really believe in its own reasoning. Or if it does, all rights that have no history stretching back to the mid-19th century are insecure. Either the mass of the majority's opinion is hypocrisy, or additional constitutional rights are under threat. It is one or the other.

One piece of evidence on that score seems especially salient: The majority's cavalier approach to overturning this Court's precedents. *Stare decisis* is the Latin phrase for a foundation stone of the rule of law: that things decided should stay decided unless there is a very good reason for change. It is a doctrine of judicial modesty and humility. Those qualities are not evident in today's opinion. The majority has no good reason for the upheaval in law and society it sets off. *Roe* and *Casey* have been the law of the land for decades, shaping women's expectations of their choices when an unplanned pregnancy occurs. Women have relied on the availability of abortion both in structuring their relationships and in planning their lives. The legal framework *Roe* and *Casey* developed to balance the competing interests in this sphere has proved workable in courts across the country. No recent developments, in either law or fact, have eroded or cast doubt on those precedents. Nothing, in short, has changed. Indeed, the Court in *Casey* already found all of that to be true. *Casey* is a precedent about precedent. It reviewed the same arguments made here in support of overruling *Roe*, and it found that doing so was not warranted. The Court reverses course today for one reason and one reason only: because the composition of this Court has changed. *Stare decisis*, this Court has often said, "contributes to the actual and perceived integrity of the judicial process" by ensuring that decisions are "founded in the law rather than in the proclivities of individuals." *Payne* v. *Tennessee*, 501 U.S. 808, 827 (1991); *Vasquez* v. *Hillery*, 474 U.S. 254, 265 (1986). Today, the proclivities of individuals rule. The Court departs from its obligation to faithfully and impartially apply the law. We dissent. . . .

I

B

The majority makes this change based on a single question: Did the reproductive right recognized in *Roe* and *Casey* exist in "1868, the year when the Fourteenth Amendment was ratified"? *Ante*, at 23. The majority says (and with this much we agree) that the answer to this question is no: In 1868, there was no nationwide right to end a pregnancy, and no thought that the Fourteenth Amendment provided one. . . .

The majority's core legal postulate, then, is that we in the 21st century must read the Fourteenth Amendment just as its ratifiers did. And that is indeed what the majority emphasizes over and over again. See *ante*, at 47 ("[T]he most important historical fact [is] how the States regulated abortion when the Fourteenth Amendment was adopted"); see also *ante*, at 5, 16, and n. 24, 23, 25, 28. If the ratifiers did not understand something as central to freedom, then neither can we. Or said more particularly: If those people did not understand reproductive rights as part of the guarantee of liberty conferred in the Fourteenth Amendment, then those rights do not exist.

As an initial matter, note a mistake in the just preceding sentence. We referred there to the "people" who ratified the Fourteenth Amendment: What rights did those "people" have in their heads at the time? But, of course, "people" did not ratify the Fourteenth Amendment. Men did. So it is perhaps not so surprising that the ratifiers were not perfectly attuned to the importance of reproductive rights for women's liberty, or for their capacity to participate as equal members of our Nation. Indeed, the ratifiers—both in 1868 and when the original Constitution was approved in 1788—did not understand women as full members of the community embraced by the phrase "We the People." In 1868, the first wave of American feminists were explicitly told—of course by men—that it was not their time to seek constitutional protections. (Women would not get even the vote for another half-century.) To be sure, most women in 1868 also had a foreshortened view of their rights: If most men could not then imagine giving women control over their bodies, most women could not imagine having that kind of autonomy. But that takes away nothing from the core point. Those responsible for the original Constitution, including the Fourteenth Amendment, did not perceive women as equals, and did not recognize women's rights. When the majority says that we must read our foundational charter as viewed at the time of ratification (except that we may also check it against the Dark Ages), it consigns women to second-class citizenship.

Casey itself understood this point, as will become clear. See *infra*, at 23–24. It recollected with dismay a decision this Court issued just five years after the Fourteenth Amendment's ratification, approving a State's decision to deny a law license to a woman and suggesting as well that a woman had no legal status apart from her husband. See 505 U.S., at 896–897 (majority opinion) (citing *Bradwell* v. *State*, 16 Wall. 130 (1873)). "There was a time," *Casey* explained, when the Constitution did not protect "men and women alike."

505 U.S., at 896. But times had changed. A woman's place in society had changed, and constitutional law had changed along with it. The relegation of women to inferior status in either the public sphere or the family was "no longer consistent with our understanding" of the Constitution. *Id.*, at 897. Now, "[t]he Constitution protects all individuals, male or female," from "the abuse of governmental power" or "unjustified state interference." *Id.*, at 896, 898.

So how is it that, as *Casey* said, our Constitution, read now, grants rights to women, though it did not in 1868? How is it that our Constitution subjects discrimination against them to heightened judicial scrutiny? How is it that our Constitution, through the Fourteenth Amendment's liberty clause, guarantees access to contraception (also not legally protected in 1868) so that women can decide for themselves whether and when to bear a child? How is it that until today, that same constitutional clause protected a woman's right, in the event contraception failed, to end a pregnancy in its earlier stages?

The answer is that this Court has rejected the majority's pinched view of how to read our Constitution. "The Founders," we recently wrote, "knew they were writing a document designed to apply to ever-changing circumstances over centuries." *NLRB* v. *Noel Canning*, 573 U.S. 513, 533–534 (2014). Or in the words of the great Chief Justice John Marshall, our Constitution is "intended to endure for ages to come," and must adapt itself to a future "seen dimly," if at all. *McCulloch* v. *Maryland*, 4 Wheat. 316, 415 (1819). That is indeed why our Constitution is written as it is. The Framers (both in 1788 and 1868) understood that the world changes. So they did not define rights by reference to the specific practices existing at the time. Instead, the Framers defined rights in general terms, to permit future evolution in their scope and meaning. And over the course of our history, this Court has taken up the Framers' invitation. It has kept true to the Framers' principles by applying them in new ways, responsive to new societal understandings and conditions.

Nowhere has that approach been more prevalent than in construing the majestic but open-ended words of the Fourteenth Amendment—the guarantees of "liberty" and "equality" for all. And nowhere has that approach produced prouder moments, for this country and the Court. Consider an example *Obergefell* used a few years ago. The Court there confronted a claim, based on *Washington* v. *Glucksberg*, 521 U.S. 702 (1997), that the Fourteenth Amendment "must be defined in a most circumscribed manner, with central reference to specific historical practices"—exactly the view today's majority follows. *Obergefell*, 576 U.S., at 671. And the Court specifically rejected that view.[4] In doing so, the Court reflected on what the proposed, historically circumscribed approach would have meant for interracial marriage. See *ibid.* The Fourteenth Amendment's ratifiers did not think it gave black and white people a right to marry each other. To the contrary,

---

4. The majority ignores that rejection. See *ante*, at 5, 13, 36. But it is unequivocal: The *Glucksberg* test, *Obergefell* said, "may have been appropriate" in considering physician-assisted suicide, but "is inconsistent with the approach this Court has used in discussing other fundamental rights, including marriage and intimacy." 576 U.S., at 671.

contemporaneous practice deemed that act quite as unprotected as abortion. Yet the Court in *Loving* v. *Virginia*, 388 U.S. 1 (1967), read the Fourteenth Amendment to embrace the Lovings' union. If, *Obergefell* explained, "rights were defined by who exercised them in the past, then received practices could serve as their own continued justification"—even when they conflict with "liberty" and "equality" as later and more broadly understood. 576 U.S., at 671. The Constitution does not freeze for all time the original view of what those rights guarantee, or how they apply. . . .

All that is what *Casey* understood. *Casey* explicitly rejected the present majority's method. "[T]he specific practices of States at the time of the adoption of the Fourteenth Amendment," *Casey* stated, do not "mark[ ] the outer limits of the substantive sphere of liberty which the Fourteenth Amendment protects." 505 U.S., at 848.[5] To hold otherwise—as the majority does today—"would be inconsistent with our law." *Id.*, at 847. Why? Because the Court has "vindicated [the] principle" over and over that (no matter the sentiment in 1868) "there is a realm of personal liberty which the government may not enter"—especially relating to "bodily integrity" and "family life." *Id.*, at 847, 849, 851. *Casey* described in detail the Court's contraception cases. See *id.*, at 848–849, 851–853. It noted decisions protecting the right to marry, including to someone of another race. See *id.*, at 847–848 ("[I]nterracial marriage was illegal in most States in the 19th century, but the Court was no doubt correct in finding it to be an aspect of liberty protected against state interference"). In reviewing decades and decades of constitutional law, *Casey* could draw but one conclusion: Whatever was true in 1868, "[i]t is settled now, as it was when the Court heard arguments in *Roe* v. *Wade*, that the Constitution places limits on a State's right to interfere with a person's most basic decisions about family and parenthood." *Id.*, at 849.

And that conclusion still held good, until the Court's intervention here. It was settled at the time of *Roe*, settled at the time of *Casey*, and settled yesterday that the Constitution places limits on a State's power to assert control over an individual's body and most personal decisionmaking. A multitude of decisions supporting that principle led to *Roe*'s recognition and *Casey*'s reaffirmation of the right to choose; and *Roe* and *Casey* in turn supported additional protections for intimate and familial relations. The majority

---

5. In a perplexing paragraph in its opinion, the majority declares that it need not say whether that statement from *Casey* is true. See *ante*, at 32–33. But how could that be? Has not the majority insisted for the prior 30 or so pages that the "specific practice[]" respecting abortion at the time of the Fourteenth Amendment precludes its recognition as a constitutional right? *Ante*, at 33. It has. And indeed, it has given no other reason for overruling *Roe* and *Casey*. *Ante*, at 15–16. We are not mindreaders, but here is our best guess as to what the majority means. It says next that "[a]bortion is nothing new." *Ante*, at 33. So apparently, the Fourteenth Amendment might provide protection for things wholly unknown in the 19th century; maybe one day there could be constitutional protection for, oh, time travel. But as to anything that was known back then (such as abortion or contraception), no such luck.

has embarrassingly little to say about those precedents. It (literally) rattles them off in a single paragraph; and it implies that they have nothing to do with each other, or with the right to terminate an early pregnancy. See *ante*, at 31–32 (asserting that recognizing a relationship among them, as addressing aspects of personal autonomy, would ineluctably "license fundamental rights" to illegal "drug use [and] prostitution"). But that is flat wrong. The Court's precedents about bodily autonomy, sexual and familial relations, and procreation are all interwoven—all part of the fabric of our constitutional law, and because that is so, of our lives. Especially women's lives, where they safeguard a right to self-determination. . . .

Consider first, then, the line of this Court's cases protecting "bodily integrity." *Casey*, 505 U.S., at 849. "No right," in this Court's time-honored view, "is held more sacred, or is more carefully guarded," than "the right of every individual to the possession and control of his own person." *Union Pacific R. Co.* v. *Botsford*, 141 U.S. 250, 251 (1891); see *Cruzan* v. *Director, Mo. Dept. of Health*, 497 U.S. 261, 269 (1990) (Every adult "has a right to determine what shall be done with his own body"). Or to put it more simply: Everyone, including women, owns their own bodies. So the Court has restricted the power of government to interfere with a person's medical decisions or compel her to undergo medical procedures or treatments. See, *e.g., Winston* v. *Lee*, 470 U.S. 753, 766–767 (1985) (forced surgery); *Rochin* v. *California*, 342 U.S. 165, 166, 173–174 (1952) (forced stomach pumping); *Washington* v. *Harper*, 494 U.S. 210, 229, 236 (1990) (forced administration of antipsychotic drugs).

Casey recognized the "doctrinal affinity" between those precedents and *Roe*. 505 U.S., at 857. And that doctrinal affinity is born of a factual likeness. There are few greater incursions on a body than forcing a woman to complete a pregnancy and give birth. For every woman, those experiences involve all manner of physical changes, medical treatments (including the possibility of a cesarean section), and medical risk. Just as one example, an American woman is 14 times more likely to die by carrying a pregnancy to term than by having an abortion. See *Whole Woman's Health* v. *Hellerstedt*, 579 U.S. 582, 618 (2016). That women happily undergo those burdens and hazards of their own accord does not lessen how far a State impinges on a woman's body when it compels her to bring a pregnancy to term. And for some women, as *Roe* recognized, abortions are medically necessary to prevent harm. See 410 U.S., at 153. The majority does not say—which is itself ominous—whether a State may prevent a woman from obtaining an abortion when she and her doctor have determined it is a needed medical treatment.

So too, *Roe* and *Casey* fit neatly into a long line of decisions protecting from government intrusion a wealth of private choices about family matters, child rearing, intimate relationships, and procreation. See *Casey*, 505 U.S., at 851, 857; *Roe*, 410 U.S., at 152–153; see also *ante*, at 31–32 (listing the myriad decisions of this kind that *Casey* relied on). Those cases safeguard particular choices about whom to marry; whom to have sex with; what family members to live with; how to raise children—and crucially, whether and when to have children. In varied cases, the Court explained that those choices—"the most intimate and personal" a person can make—reflect fundamental aspects of personal identity; they define the very "attributes of personhood." *Casey*, 505 U.S., at 851. And they inevitably shape the nature and future course of a person's life (and often the lives of those closest to her). So, the Court held, those choices belong to the individual, and not the government. That is the essence of what liberty requires.

And liberty may require it, this Court has repeatedly said, even when those living in 1868 would not have recognized the claim—because they would not have seen the person making it as a full-fledged member of the community. Throughout our history, the sphere of protected liberty has expanded, bringing in individuals formerly excluded. In that way, the constitutional values of liberty and equality go hand in hand; they do not inhabit the hermetically sealed containers the majority portrays. Compare *Obergefell*, 576 U.S., at 672–675, with *ante*, at 10–11. So before *Roe* and *Casey*, the Court expanded in successive cases those who could claim the right to marry—though their relationships would have been outside the law's protection in the mid-19th century. See, *e.g.*, *Loving*, 388 U.S. 1 (interracial couples); *Turner* v. *Safley*, 482 U.S. 78 (1987) (prisoners); see also, *e.g.*, *Stanley* v. *Illinois*, 405 U.S. 645, 651–652 (1972) (offering constitutional protection to untraditional "family unit[s]"). And after *Roe* and *Casey*, of course, the Court continued in that vein. With a critical stop to hold that the Fourteenth Amendment protected same-sex intimacy, the Court resolved that the Amendment also conferred on same-sex couples the right to marry. See *Lawrence*, 539 U.S. 558; *Obergefell*, 576 U.S. 644. In considering that question, the Court held, "[h]istory and tradition," especially as reflected in the course of our precedent, "guide and discipline [the] inquiry." *Id.*, at 664. But the sentiments of 1868 alone do not and cannot "rule the present." *Ibid.*

Casey similarly recognized the need to extend the constitutional sphere of liberty to a previously excluded group. The Court then understood, as the majority today does not, that the men who ratified the Fourteenth Amendment and wrote the state laws of the time did not view women as full and equal citizens. See *supra*, at 15. A woman then, *Casey* wrote, "had no legal existence separate from her husband." 505 U.S., at 897. Women were seen only "as the center of home and family life," without "full and independent legal status under the Constitution." *Ibid.* But that could not be true any longer: The State could not now insist on the historically dominant "vision of the woman's role." *Id.*, at 852. And equal citizenship, *Casey* realized, was inescapably connected to reproductive rights. "The ability of women to participate equally" in the "life of the Nation"—in all its economic, social, political, and legal aspects—"has been facilitated by their ability to control their reproductive lives." *Id.*, at 856. Without the ability to decide whether and when to have children, women could not—in the way men took for granted—determine how they would live their lives, and how they would contribute to the society around them.

For much that reason, *Casey* made clear that the precedents *Roe* most closely tracked were those involving contraception. Over the course of three cases, the Court had held that a right to use and gain access to contraception was part of the Fourteenth Amendment's guarantee of liberty. See *Griswold*, 381 U.S. 479; *Eisenstadt*, 405 U.S. 438; *Carey* v.

Population Services Int'l, 431 U.S. 678 (1977). That clause, we explained, necessarily conferred a right "to be free from unwarranted governmental intrusion into matters so fundamentally affecting a person as the decision whether to bear or beget a child." *Eisenstadt*, 405 U.S., at 453; see *Carey*, 431 U.S., at 684–685. *Casey* saw *Roe* as of a piece: In "critical respects the abortion decision is of the same character." 505 U.S., at 852. "[R]easonable people," the Court noted, could also oppose contraception; and indeed, they could believe that "some forms of contraception" similarly implicate a concern with "potential life." *Id.*, at 853, 859. Yet the views of others could not automatically prevail against a woman's right to control her own body and make her own choice about whether to bear, and probably to raise, a child. When an unplanned pregnancy is involved—because either contraception or abortion is outlawed—"the liberty of the woman is at stake in a sense unique to the human condition." *Id.*, at 852. No State could undertake to resolve the moral questions raised "in such a definitive way" as to deprive a woman of all choice. *Id.*, at 850.

Faced with all these connections between *Roe/Casey* and judicial decisions recognizing other constitutional rights, the majority tells everyone not to worry. It can (so it says) neatly extract the right to choose from the constitutional edifice without affecting any associated rights. (Think of someone telling you that the Jenga tower simply will not collapse.) Today's decision, the majority first says, "does not undermine" the decisions cited by *Roe* and *Casey*—the ones involving "marriage, procreation, contraception, [and] family relationships"—"in any way." *Ante*, at 32; *Casey*, 505 U.S., at 851. Note that this first assurance does not extend to rights recognized after *Roe* and *Casey*, and partly based on them—in particular, rights to same-sex intimacy and marriage. See *supra*, at 23.[6] On its later tries, though, the majority includes those too: "Nothing in this opinion should be understood to cast doubt on precedents that do not concern abortion." *Ante*, at 66; see *ante*, at 71–72. That right is unique, the majority asserts, "because [abortion] terminates life or potential life." *Ante*, at 66 (internal quotation marks omitted); see *ante*, at 32, 71–72. So the majority depicts today's decision as "a restricted railroad ticket, good for this day and train only." *Smith* v. *Allwright*, 321 U.S. 649, 669 (1944) (Roberts, J., dissenting). Should the audience for these too-much-repeated protestations be duly satisfied? We think not.

The first problem with the majority's account comes from JUSTICE THOMAS's concurrence—which makes clear he is not with the program. In saying that nothing in today's opinion casts doubt on non-abortion precedents, JUSTICE THOMAS explains, he means

---

6. And note, too, that the author of the majority opinion recently joined a statement, written by another member of the majority, lamenting that *Obergefell* deprived States of the ability "to resolve th[e] question [of same-sex marriage] through legislation." *Davis* v. *Ermold*, 592 U.S. ___, ___ (2020) (statement of THOMAS, J.) (slip op., at 1). That might sound familiar. Cf. *ante*, at 44 (lamenting that *Roe* "short-circuited the democratic process"). And those two Justices hardly seemed content to let the matter rest: The Court, they said, had "created a problem that only it can fix." *Davis*, 592 U.S., at ___ (slip op., at 4).

only that they are not at issue in this very case. See *ante*, at 7 ("[T]his case does not present the opportunity to reject" those precedents). But he lets us know what he wants to do when they are. "[I]n future cases," he says, "we should reconsider all of this Court's substantive due process precedents, including *Griswold, Lawrence,* and *Obergefell.*" *Ante*, at 3; see also *supra*, at 25, and n. 6. And when we reconsider them? Then "we have a duty" to "overrul[e] these demonstrably erroneous decisions." *Ante*, at 3. So at least one Justice is planning to use the ticket of today's decision again and again and again.

Even placing the concurrence to the side, the assurance in today's opinion still does not work. Or at least that is so if the majority is serious about its sole reason for overturning *Roe* and *Casey*: the legal status of abortion in the 19th century. Except in the places quoted above, the state interest in protecting fetal life plays no part in the majority's analysis. To the contrary, the majority takes pride in not expressing a view "about the status of the fetus." *Ante*, at 65; see *ante*, at 32 (aligning itself with *Roe*'s and *Casey*'s stance of not deciding whether life or potential life is involved); *ante*, at 38–39 (similar). The majority's departure from *Roe* and *Casey* rests instead—and only—on whether a woman's decision to end a pregnancy involves any Fourteenth Amendment liberty interest (against which *Roe* and *Casey* balanced the state interest in preserving fetal life).[7]

According to the majority, no liberty interest is present—because (and only because) the law offered no protection to the woman's choice in the 19th century. But here is the rub. The law also did not then (and would not for ages) protect a wealth of other things. It did not protect the rights recognized in *Lawrence* and *Obergefell* to same-sex intimacy and marriage. It did not protect the right recognized in *Loving* to marry across racial lines. It did not protect the right recognized in *Griswold* to contraceptive use. For that matter, it did not protect the right recognized in *Skinner* v. *Oklahoma ex rel. Williamson*, 316 U. S. 535 (1942), not to be sterilized without consent. So if the majority is right in its legal analysis, all those decisions were wrong, and all those matters properly belong to the States too—whatever the particular state interests involved. And if that is true, it is impossible to understand (as a matter of logic and principle) how the majority can say that

---

7. Indulge a few more words about this point. The majority had a choice of two different ways to overrule *Roe* and *Casey*. It could claim that those cases underrated the State's interest in fetal life. Or it could claim that they overrated a woman's constitutional liberty interest in choosing an abortion. (Or both.) The majority here rejects the first path, and we can see why. Taking that route would have prevented the majority from claiming that it means only to leave this issue to the democratic process—that it does not have a dog in the fight. See *ante*, at 38–39, 65. And indeed, doing so might have suggested a revolutionary proposition: that the fetus is itself a constitutionally protected "person," such that an abortion ban is constitutionally *mandated*. The majority therefore chooses the second path, arguing that the Fourteenth Amendment does not conceive of the abortion decision as implicating liberty, because the law in the 19th century gave that choice no protection. The trouble is that the chosen path—which is, again, the solitary rationale for the Court's decision—provides no way to distinguish between the right to choose an abortion and a range of other rights, including contraception.

its opinion today does not threaten—does not even "undermine"—any number of other constitutional rights. *Ante*, at 32.[8]

Nor does it even help just to take the majority at its word. Assume the majority is sincere in saying, for whatever reason, that it will go so far and no further. Scout's honor. Still, the future significance of today's opinion will be decided in the future. And law often has a way of evolving without regard to original intentions—a way of actually following where logic leads, rather than tolerating hard-to-explain lines. Rights can expand in that way. Dissenting in *Lawrence*, Justice Scalia explained why he took no comfort in the Court's statement that a decision recognizing the right to same-sex intimacy did "not involve" same-sex marriage. 539 U.S., at 604. That could be true, he wrote, "only if one entertains the belief that principle and logic have nothing to do with the decisions of this Court." *Id.*, at 605. Score one for the dissent, as a matter of prophecy. And logic and principle are not one-way ratchets. Rights can contract in the same way and for the same reason—because whatever today's majority might say, one thing really does lead to another. We fervently hope that does not happen because of today's decision. We hope that we will not join Justice Scalia in the book of prophets. But we cannot understand how anyone can be confident that today's opinion will be the last of its kind.

Consider, as our last word on this issue, contraception. The Constitution, of course, does not mention that word. And there is no historical right to contraception, of the kind the majority insists on. To the contrary, the American legal landscape in the decades after the Civil War was littered with bans on the sale of contraceptive devices. So again, there seem to be two choices. See *supra*, at 5, 26–27. If the majority is serious about its historical approach, then *Griswold* and its progeny are in the line of fire too. Or if it is not serious, then . . . what *is* the basis of today's decision? If we had to guess, we suspect the prospects of this Court approving bans on contraception are low. But once again, the future significance of today's opinion will be decided in the future. At the least, today's opinion will fuel the fight to get contraception, and any other issues with a moral dimension, out of the Fourteenth Amendment and into state legislatures.[9]

---

8. The majority briefly (very briefly) gestures at the idea that some *stare decisis* factors might play out differently with respect to these other constitutional rights. But the majority gives no hint as to why. And the majority's (mis)treatment of *stare decisis* in this case provides little reason to think that the doctrine would stand as a barrier to the majority's redoing any other decision it considered egregiously wrong. See *infra*, at 30–57.

9. As this Court has considered this case, some state legislators have begun to call for restrictions on certain forms of contraception. See I. Stevenson, After *Roe* Decision, Idaho Lawmakers May Consider Restricting Some Contraception, Idaho Statesman (May 10, 2022), https://www.idahostatesman.com/news/politics-government/state-politics/article261207007.html; T. Weinberg, "Anything's on the Table": Missouri Legislature May Revisit Contraceptive Limits Post-*Roe*, Missouri Independent (May 20, 2022), https://www.missouriindependent.com/2022/05/20/anythings-on-the-table-missouri-legislature-may-revisit-contraceptive-limits-post-roe/.

Anyway, today's decision, taken on its own, is catastrophic enough. As a matter of constitutional method, the majority's commitment to replicate in 2022 every view about the meaning of liberty held in 1868 has precious little to recommend it. Our law in this constitutional sphere, as in most, has for decades upon decades proceeded differently. It has considered fundamental constitutional principles, the whole course of the Nation's history and traditions, and the step-by-step evolution of the Court's precedents. It is disciplined but not static. It relies on accumulated judgments, not just the sentiments of one long-ago generation of men (who themselves believed, and drafted the Constitution to reflect, that the world progresses). And by doing so, it includes those excluded from that olden conversation, rather than perpetuating its bounds.

As a matter of constitutional substance, the majority's opinion has all the flaws its method would suggest. Because laws in 1868 deprived women of any control over their bodies, the majority approves States doing so today. Because those laws prevented women from charting the course of their own lives, the majority says States can do the same again. Because in 1868, the government could tell a pregnant woman—even in the first days of her pregnancy—that she could do nothing but bear a child, it can once more impose that command. Today's decision strips women of agency over what even the majority agrees is a contested and contestable moral issue. It forces her to carry out the State's will, whatever the circumstances and whatever the harm it will wreak on her and her family. In the Fourteenth Amendment's terms, it takes away her liberty. . . .

INDEX

A

Abele v. *Markle*, 32, 35
Abortion Act of 1967, 26–27
abortion jurisprudence, x, xxix(n78), xxxviii–xlix, xlvii–xlviii, 194, 239, 250, 267
Adamson v. *California*, 10, 168
Adkins v. *Children's Hospital*, 198, 311
Adler v. *Board of Education*, 2
admitting-privileges requirement, 260, 262–64, 266, 275, 280
Affordable Care Act, xxxi
Akron v. *Akron Center for Reproductive Health*, xx, xxiii
    cited in *Box* v. *Planned Parenthood*, 272
    cited in *Hodgson* v. *Minnesota*, 162
    cited in *Ohio* v. *Akron Center for Reproductive Health*, 154–55
    cited in *Planned Parenthood of Southeastern Pennsylvania* v. *Casey*, 177–78, 181, 188, 197, 204
    cited in *Simopoulos* v. *Virginia*, 130
    cited in *Stenberg* v. *Carhart*, 230–31, 239
    cited in *Thornburgh* v. *American College of Obstetricians and Gynecologists*, 132–35
    cited in *Webster* v. *Reproductive Health Services*, 138–39, 141, 143, 149–50
    opinion of the Court, 111–27
Alden v. *Maine*, 287
Alito, S. A., xiv, xxix
    on *Dobbs* v. *Jackson Women's Health Organization*, xxxv–xxxviii, xlii, 291–326
    on *Gonzales* v. *Carhart*, 242
    on *June Medical Services, LLC* v. *Russo*, xxxiii–xxxiv, 279
    on *Planned Parenthood of Southeastern Pennsylvania* v. *Casey*, 293–97, 301, 306–8, 312–13, 317–25
    on *Roe* v. *Wade*, 293–97, 300–301, 306–18, 320–21, 323–25
    on *Whole Woman's Health* v. *Hellerstedt*, 260
    on *Whole Woman's Health* v. *Jackson*, 281, 286
Almendarez-Torres v. *United States*, 246
American abortion law, 27–28
American College of Obstetricians and Gynecologists (ACOG), 114, 121, 131, 218–20, 229, 237–39, 251, 253
American Medical Association (AMA), 185, 218–20, 228–29, 232–33, 236, 238
American Public Health Association (APHA), 130–31
ancient views on abortion, 22–23
appropriate medical judgment, xix, xxvii, xxviii, 39, 141, 179, 213, 216–17, 220–21, 223, 231, 247, 252, 314
Aptheker v. *Secretary of State*, 5(n1), 33
Aristotle, 23, 24(n22), 36
Arizona Free Enterprise Club's Freedom Club PAC v. *Bennett*, 277
Arizona v. *California*, 306
Arizona v. *Rumsey*, 153, 173
Armour v. *Indianapolis*, 272
Ashwander v. *TVA*, 40, 63, 67
Association of American Physicians and Surgeons, 218, 236

Augustine, St., 24(n22)
Ayoola, A., 328
Ayotte v. Planned Parenthood of Northern New England, 247, 251

B

Babbitz v. McCann, 32
Baggett v. Bullitt, 3
Baird, W., 16
Baker, J., 316(n51)
Barbier v. Connolly, 17
Barenblatt. v. United States, 3
Barrett, A. C., xiv, xxxiv–xxxv, 286, 291
Barron ex rel. Tiernan v. Mayor of Baltimore, 298
Barrows v. Jackson, 2, 63–64
Barsky v. Board of Regents of Univ. of N. Y., 246
Bates v. Little Rock, 11, 15(n7), 124
Beal v. Doe, 66–69, 73, 100, 112, 124(n8), 135–36, 177
Beare, E., 302
Beck, J., 316(n51)
Bellotti v. Baird, xxi, xxiii, 56, 87–94, 106–7, 107(n17), 115–16, 120, 124(n8), 125, 125(n12), 154–58, 161–62, 162(n31), 165, 178, 188
Bendix Autolite Corp. v. Midwesco Enterprises, Inc., 277
Benz, A., 288
Berlin, I., 299
Biden, J., xxxv, xliii, lii
Black, H. L., 1, 8–9, 11–13
Blackmun, H., xiii, xvi, lii
  on *Akron v. Akron Center for Reproductive Health*, 111
  on *Beal v. Doe*, 66–67, 69
  on *Bellotti v. Baird*, 87
  on *Colautti v. Franklin*, 80–84
  on *Doe v. Bolton*, 42–48
  on *Eisenstadt, Sheriff v. Baird*, 16

  on *Griswold v. Connecticut*, xlvii, xlvii(n149)
  on *Harris v. McRae*, 95, 99
  on *H. L. v. Matheson*, 103, 108
  on *Hodgson v. Minnesota*, 160
  on *Maher v. Roe*, 70, 73, 75
  on *Ohio v. Akron Center for Reproductive Health*, 154
  on *Planned Parenthood of Central Missouri v. Danforth*, 50–57
  on *Planned Parenthood of Kansas City v. Ashcroft*, 128
  on *Planned Parenthood of Southeastern Pennsylvania v. Casey*, 166, 189–94
  on *Poelker v. Doe*, 78
  on *Roe v. Wade*, xix, xxi–xxiv, xxxix, xliii, xlvii, 19–39, 52–54, 143, 145–49, 151–52, 190–94
  on *Simopoulos v. Virginia*, 130
  on *Singleton v. Wulff*, 62–63
  on *Thornburgh v. American College of Obstetricians and Gynecologists*, 132–34
  on *Webster v. Reproductive Health Services*, 138, 141–53
Black's Law Dictionary, xli(n121), 197, 319
Blackstone, W., 25, 302–3, 314
Blue Chip Stamps v. Manor Drug Stores, 66
Board of Education v. Barnette, 3
Board of Trustees of Univ. of Ala. v. Garrett, 326
bodily integrity, xlv, 170, 187, 192, 203, 332, 336–37
Boehm, F., 229–30
Bolling v. Sharpe, 5(n1)
Bork, R., xliii–xliv
Bowers v. Hardwick, 203
Box v. Planned Parenthood, xxxiii, 271–74, 307(n41)

Boyd v. *United States*, 3, 31
Bracton, H., 25, 25(n23), 301, 301(n25), 302, 305, 314
Bradwell v. *Illinois*, 187
Bradwell v. *State*, 256, 334
Brandeis, L. D., 13(n1), 168
Breard v. *Alexandria*, 4
Breed v. *Jones*, 55, 88
Brennan, W. J., xiii, xxii
   on *Akron* v. *Akron Center for Reproductive Health*, 111
   on *Beal* v. *Doe*, 66–67, 69
   on *Bellotti* v. *Baird*, 87
   on *Cohen* v. *Hurley*, 5
   on *Colautti* v. *Franklin*, 80
   on *Doe* v. *Bolton*, 42, 67, 74
   on *Eisenstadt* v. *Baird*, xliii, 16–18
   on *Griswold* v. *Connecticut*, 1, 5
   on *Harris* v. *McRae*, 95, 99–101
   on *H. L.* v. *Matheson*, 103, 108
   on *Hodgson* v. *Minnesota*, 160
   on *Maher* v. *Roe*, 67, 70, 73–76
   on *Planned Parenthood of Kansas City* v. *Ashcroft*, 128
   on *Planned Parenthood of Missouri* v. *Danforth*, 50
   on *Poelker* v. *Doe*, 78–79
   on *Roe* v. *Wade*, 19, 67, 74–76, 99–100
   on *Simopoulos* v. *Virginia*, 130
   on *Singleton* v. *Wulff*, 62
   on *Thornburgh* v. *American College of Obstetricians and Gynecologists*, 132
   on *Webster* v. *Reproductive Health Services*, 138, 145
Breyer, S., xiii
   on *Dobbs* v. *Jackson Women's Health Organization*, xliv, 291, 331–42
   on *Gonzales* v. *Carhart*, 242, 250
   on *June Medical Services, LLC* v. *Russo*, 275
   on *Stenberg* v. *Carhart*, xlviii, 212–23
   on *Whole Woman's Health* v. *Hellerstedt*, 260–66
   on *Whole Woman's Health* v. *Jackson*, xxxv, 281, 286, 288–89
Broadrick v. *Oklahoma*, 232
Brockett v. *Spokane Arcades, Inc.*, 180
Brotherhood of Railroad Trainmen v. *Virginia ex rel. Virginia State Bar*, 11
Brown v. *Board of Education*, xxxix, xl, 99, 198–99, 311, 330
Buchanan, J., 211
Buck v. *Bell*, 32
Bunting v. *Oregon*, 199
Burger, W. E., xiii
   on *Akron* v. *Akron Center for Reproductive Health*, 111
   on *Beal* v. *Doe*, 66
   on *Bellotti* v. *Baird*, 87, 106–7
   on *Colautti* v. *Franklin*, 80, 84
   on *Doe* v. *Bolton*, 42
   on *Eisenstadt* v. *Baird*, 16
   on *Harris* v. *McRae*, 95
   on *H. L.* v. *Matheson*, 103–7
   on *Maher* v. *Roe*, 70
   on *Planned Parenthood of Central Missouri* v. *Danforth*, 50
   on *Planned Parenthood of Kansas City* v. *Ashcroft*, 128
   on *Roe* v. *Wade*, 19
   on *Simopoulos* v. *Virginia*, 130
   on *Singleton* v. *Wulff*, 62
   on *Thornburgh* v. *American College of Obstetricians and Gynecologists*, 132
Burn, R., 303
Burnet v. *Coronado Oil & Gas Co.*, 153, 173, 197
Burt, R., xxxix, xl–xli
Burwell v. *Hobby Lobby Stores, Inc.*, 277
Bush, G. W., xiv, xxviii, 242

Buxton v. Ullman, 10
bypass procedures, xxi, xxvi, 154–58, 161, 165
Byrn v. New York City Health & Hospitals Corp., 35

C

Caban v. Mohammed, 162, 187
Calhoun, J. C., 289–90
Califano v. Goldfarb, 257
California v. Texas, 281
Camden, Lord, 4
Cantwell v. Connecticut, 33
Cardozo, B., 172
Carey v. Population Services International, 124(n8), 169–72, 174, 193, 308, 338–39
Carhart, L., 214, 217–19, 224, 226–27, 229, 231–32
Carlton, S., 287–88
Carrington v. Rash, 5(n1)
Carter v. Carter Coal Co., 126
Catholic Church, xviii(n28), 36, 98
Cheaney v. State, 33, 35
Citizens United v. Federal Election Commission, xxxi–xxxii
City of El Paso v. Simmons, 12
Civil Rights Act, xxxix
Clapper v. Amnesty Int'l USA, 281
Clarkston, P., 287
Clark v. Martinez, 246
Cleveland Bd. of Education v. LaFleur, 163
Clinton, B., xiii, xxv, xxviii
Cohen v. Hurley, 5
Cohn, N., 1
Coke, E., 25, 25(n26), 26, 301, 314
Colautti v. Franklin, xx, 80–86, 116, 119, 122, 141, 143, 217, 245, 317
Collins v. Harker Heights, 299, 327
Collins v. Texas, 248

Committee for Public Education v. Regan, 98
common law, xlvi, 23–24, 24(n21), 25–28, 31, 36, 39, 161, 187, 192, 196, 291, 299–303, 309
Commonwealth v. Allison, 17
Commonwealth v. Baird, 16, 18
Commonwealth v. Corbett, 18
Commonwealth v. Parker, 304
Commonwealth v. Trombetta, 305(n35)
Commonwealth v. Wheeler, 305(n35)
Compassion in Dying v. Washington, 308
constitutional right to abortion
 abortion jurisprudence and, xxxviii–xlix
 future of, xlix–lii
 history of, xv–xxxviii, 300–301, 309–11
contraception for married persons, xviii(n31), xliii–xliv, 10–13, 16–18
contraceptive access, xviii, xliv–xlvi, xlviii, xlix, 4, 16–18, 64, 97, 332, 338, 341, 341(n8)
Cook, C., 238
Cooper v. Aaron, 290
Coppage v. Kansas, 311
copper IUD, xlv
Corfield v. Coryell, 300(n22)
Corkey v. Edwards, 32–33
Cox v. Louisiana, 11
Craig v. Boren, 193
criminal abortion statutes, xlvi, 14(n2), 21, 28, 28(n34), 29–31, 47, 256, 294, 300–301, 301(n24), 302–3, 303(n29), 304, 304(n34), 305, 305(n35), 306, 309
Crossen v. Attorney General, 32
Cross v. Ledford, 158
Cruzan v. Director, Missouri Dept. of Health, 187, 337

Currie, D., 209
Cutter v. Wilkinson, 250

D

Dandridge v. Williams, 72, 326
Daniels v. Williams, 150, 168
Davis v. Ermold, 339(n6)
De Jonge v. Oregon, 3
Dellapenna, J., 302, 304–5
Devins, N., xxx–xxxi
dilation and evacuation (D&E) procedures, xxviii–xxix, 113–14, 114(n24), 121, 130–31, 214–15, 218–22, 224, 226, 228, 232–35, 237, 245–47, 249, 253–54, 254(n5), 255–56, 258
dilation and extraction (D&X) method, xxvii–xxix, 215–22, 224–26, 228–32, 237
disability-selective abortion, 271–72
District of Columbia v. Heller, 303
Dobbs v. Jackson Women's Health Organization, x, xii, xiv–xvi, xxxiv–xlii, xliv, xlviii–lii, 291–342
Doerfler, R. D., lii
Doe v. Beal, 74
Doe v. Bolton, xx, 19, 23, 28, 32, 42–51, 53–54, 56, 62, 65, 67–68, 74–75, 77, 84, 90
Doe v. Rampton, 33, 54, 74
Doe v. Rose, 74
Doe v. Westby, 74
Doe v. Wohlgemuth, 74
Dorland's Illustrated Medical Dictionary, 35
Dougherty v. People, 307
Douglas, W. O., xiii, xviii, 1–4, 16, 19, 42
Douglas v. California, 72(n6)
Dred Scott v. Sandford, li, li(n158), 209, 211

Due Process Clause, xix, xxiii–xxiv, xxxvi, xxxvi(n100), xxxix, xlii, xliv–xlvi, xlviii, 2, 5, 8–9, 11, 13–14, 21, 34, 38, 40, 74, 97, 112, 119, 143–44, 146, 168–70, 190, 195, 293, 296–99, 300(n22), 326–27
Duncan v. Louisiana, 168, 298(n19), 300(n22)
Dunn v. Blumstein, 98(n25)
Dworkin, R., xi, xvi(n23), xlv, xlvii(n149)

E

Edelstein, L, 23
Edward J. DeBartolo Corp. v. Florida Gulf Coast Building & Constr. Trades Council, 245
Edwards v. South Carolina, 15(n7)
Eisenstadt v. Baird, xviii(n31), xliii, 16–18, 21, 31, 33, 35, 54, 54(n11), 64, 64(n5), 148, 169–72, 187, 190, 192, 196, 250, 308, 310, 333, 338–39
Eleventh Amendment, 287
Ellenborough Act, 26–27
English statutory law, 26–27, 301(n25)
Entick v. Carrington, 4
equality argument, xl, xlvi–xlviii, xlix
Equal Protection Clause, xviii(n31), xl, xlvii–xlviii, 15(n7), 17–18, 34, 40, 71, 72(n6), 74, 97, 98(n25), 101, 149, 193, 297
Erie R. Co. v. Tompkins, 197
Erie v. Pap's A. M., 306
Erznoznik v. Jacksonville, 235
eugenics, 273, 273(n2), 274
Everson v. Board of Education, 98
Ex parte Young, 287–88

F

FCC v. Beach Communications, Inc., 326
Federal Election Comm'n v. Wisconsin Right to Life, Inc., 329

Ferguson v. *Skrupa*, 14, 171, 322, 326
fetal disposal, xxxiii, 112, 119, 127, 271, 274, 274(n1)
fetal pain, xvi, xxxiv, xxxviii, 326
fetal viability, ix–x, xiii–xxi, xxv, xxxiv, xxxvii, xlii, 36–38, 51–52, 80–86, 121–22, 122(n5), 123, 129, 140–43, 147, 175–79, 213, 250, 315–16, 316(n51), 317–18
fetus
    as constitutional person, xv–xvi, xv(n19), xvi(n23), xvii, li, 34, 34(n54), 316, 340(n7)
    mediate animation and, 24, 24(n22), 36
    personhood at conception, xi–xii, li, 30, 35
Fifth Amendment, xxxvi(n100), xlvi, 3–4, 5(n1), 8(n6), 13–14, 31, 34, 44, 96, 98, 101, 296
First Amendment, xxxi, 2–3, 5, 8(n6), 11–14, 15(n7), 31, 44, 89, 96, 98, 296, 321
first trimester abortion, xiii, xix, 29, 37, 39, 46, 56, 59–60, 70, 112–13, 121, 123, 124(n8), 213–14
Florida v. *Riley*, 149
Flowers, R. C., xv(n19)
Ford, C. B., xxxiii
Forsythe, C., 314
Foster, D. G., xlix
Fourteenth Amendment
    constitutional right to abortion and, xv–xvi, xxxvi–xxxvii, 334
    Doe v. *Bolton*, 44
    Dred Scott v. *Sandford*, li(n158)
    Due Process Clause, xix, xxiii, xxxvi(n100), xxxix, xlii, 8–9, 13, 88, 168–71, 190, 195, 293, 296–99, 300(n22), 317, 328
    Eisenstadt v. *Baird*, xviii(n31), 17
    Equal Protection Clause, xviii(n31), xlvi, 71, 97, 98(n25), 101, 297, 335–36
    Griswold v. *Connecticut*, 1–2, 5–6
    liberty rights, 223, 294, 296–97, 297(n16), 298–99, 335, 340, 340(n7), 342
    notice statutes, 154–55
    privacy rights, 10–11, 14(n1), 126, 297(n16)
    Roe v. *Wade*, 21, 31, 33–34, 34(n54), 35, 38, 40–41, 293–94, 296–97
Fourth Amendment, 3–4, 12–14, 31, 44, 96, 296
Frankfurter, F., 10, 74, 88
Franklin v. *Fitzpatrick*, 127
Frank v. *Maryland*, 4
Freedom of Choice Act, xxx
Freiman, M., 51
Frisby v. *Schultz*, 157, 180, 235
fundamental rights, xxxvi, 6–8, 10, 33, 46

G

Galen, 23, 24(n22)
Gamble v. *United States*, 328
Garcia v. *San Antonio Metropolitan Transit Authority*, 148, 173, 197
Garland, M., xxxv
Geders v. *United States*, 149
genetic testing, 81, 81(n3)
Gibbons v. *Ogden*, 296
Giboney v. *Empire Storage & Ice Co.*, 11
Gibson v. *Florida Legislative Investigation Committee*, 124
Gilbert v. *Minnesota*, 163
Ginsberg v. *New York*, 55, 89
Ginsburg, R. B., xiii–xiv, xxxiv
    on *Box* v. *Planned Parenthood*, xxxiii, 274
    on *Gonzales* v. *Carhart*, xxix, 242, 250–51

on *June Medical Services, LLC* v. *Russo*, 275
on *Roe* v. *Wade*, xi, xxxix, xl–xli, xlvii
on *Stenberg* v. *Carhart*, xxvi(n72), 212, 223–25
on *Whole Woman's Health* v. *Hellerstedt*, 260
Gitlow v. *New York*, 5
Glidden Co. v. *Zdanok*, 123
Goldberg, J., 1, 5, 11, 14, 18
Goldberg v. *Kelly*, 46
Gonzales v. *Carhart*, xvi, xvii(n26), xxix, xxxii, xlviii, li, 241–59, 261–62, 267, 269–70, 295, 326
Gorsuch, N., xiv, xxxiii, 278(n2), 279, 286–88, 291
Goss v. *Lopez*, 55, 88
Grayned v. *City of Rockford*, 81, 245
Greenhouse, L., xxxv, xliii
Griffin v. *California*, 9
Griffin v. *Illinois*, 72(n6), 74
Griswold, E., 1
Griswold v. *Connecticut*, xxxvi, xlii–xlvi, xlix
cited in *Akron* v. *Akron Center for Reproductive Health*, 124(n8)
cited in *Dobbs* v. *Jackson Women's Health Organization*, 308, 310, 327, 340
cited in *Eisenstadt* v. *Baird*, 18
cited in *Harris* v. *McRae*, 97
cited in *Hodgson* v. *Minnesota*, 163
cited in *Planned Parenthood of Central Missouri* v. *Danforth*, 54
cited in *Planned Parenthood of Southeastern Pennsylvania* v. *Casey*, 169–70, 172, 174, 193
cited in *Roe* v. *Wade*, xliii, xlvii, xlvii(n149), 21, 31, 33, 35
cited in *Singleton* v. *Wulff*, 62, 65
cited in *Thornburgh* v. *American College of Obstetricians and Gynecologists*, 136

cited in *Webster* v. *Reproductive Health Services*, 142, 148
contraceptive access, xviii, xviii(n31), 195, 332, 338, 341
Due Process Clause, 327
opinion of the Court, 1–15
Groppi v. *Wisconsin*, 17
Gulfstream Aerospace Corp. v. *Mayacamas Corp.*, 318
Guttmacher, A., 273

H

Hagans v. *Lavine*, 74
Hale, M., 301–3, 314
Hall, D., 51
Hambleton v. *R. G. Barry Corp.*, 159
Hamilton, A., 6(n4)
Hampton v. *Mow Sun Wong*, 101
Harlan, J. M., 8, 11, 14, 169–70
Harrison v. *NAACP*, 126
Harris v. *McRae*, xx, 95–102, 120, 124(n8), 125, 127, 134, 136, 139–40, 177, 196, 202, 216
Hartigan v. *Zbaraz*, xx, 102, 163
Haskell, M., 227, 229
Heler v. *Doe*, 326
Hellman, L., 121
Hill v. *Colorado*, 240
Hippocratic Oath, 22–23
H. L. v. *Matheson*, xxi, 103–10, 115, 125, 125(n12), 127, 154, 162, 200
Hodgson v. *Minnesota*, xxi, xxiii, 155, 160–65, 177–78, 188–89, 194, 200
Holden v. *Hardy*, 199
Holmes, O. W., 19, 41, 168, 199
Hooper v. *California*, 245
Hope Clinic v. *Ryan*, 225, 230, 237, 259
Hoyt v. *Florida*, 188, 251
Hughes, C. E., 199
Hurtado v. *California*, 168

Hyde Amendment, xxxix, 95–100, 102, 139

I

Illinois ex rel. McCollum v. *Board of Education of School Dist. No. 71, Champaign County*, 149
incest, xxxix, l, 95, 109, 331–32
informed consent, ix, xxiii, xxvi, 107, 112, 116–19, 126, 132–36, 166, 180–81, 189
Ingraham v. *Wright*, 88
in-hospital abortion, xx, 112–14
In re Gault, 55, 88–89
In re Winship, 88
instillation procedures, 114(n24)
in vitro fertilization (IVF), xvii(n24)

J

Jackson, A., 287–88
Jackson Women's Health Org. v. *Currier*, 295
Jacobson v. *Massachusetts*, 18, 32, 231, 248
James v. *Valtierra*, 99
Janus v. *State, County, and Municipal Employees*, xxxvi, 312
Jay Burns Baking Co. v. *Bryan*, 311
Johnson v. *United States*, 327
Joint Commission on Accreditation of Hospitals, 43, 45
Jones v. *United States*, 248
judicial activism, xxxix, xli, xli(n121)
judicial self-restraint, 9, 65, 144
June Medical Services, LLC v. *Russo*, x, xxxiii–xxxiv, 275–80, 282, 318–21

K

Kagan, E., xiv, xxxv, xliv, 260, 275, 281, 286, 288–89, 291, 331–42
Kahler v. *Kansas*, 301

Kansas v. *Hendricks*, 233, 238, 248
Katz v. *United States*, 31, 40
Kavanaugh, B., xiv, xxxiii, 279, 286, 291
Keeler v. *Superior Court*, 35
Kennedy, A., xiii–xiv, xxi, xxiii, xxxiii, xliii
   on *Bellotti* v. *Baird*, 155–58
   on *Gonzales* v. *Carhart*, xxx, 242–49
   on *Hodgson* v. *Minnesota*, 160
   on *Ohio* v. *Akron Center for Reproductive Health*, 154–59
   on *Planned Parenthood of Southeastern Pennsylvania* v. *Casey*, 166, 190
   on *Stenberg* v. *Carhart*, xxvi–xxviii, 212, 226–33
   on *Webster* v. *Reproductive Health Services*, 138
   on *Whole Woman's Health* v. *Hellerstedt*, 260
Kent v. *Dulles*, 5(n1)
Kent v. *United States*, 89
Keown, J., 302
Keyishian v. *Board of Regents*, 81
Kimble v. *Marvel Entertainment, LLC*, 310
Klein v. *Nassau County Medical Center*, 68, 74
Kolender v. *Lawson*, 244
Kovacs v. *Cooper*, 10
Kramer v. *Union Free School District*, 33

L

Labine v. *Vincent*, 201
Lambert v. *Yellowley*, 248
Lanza v. *New York*, 4
Lawrence v. *Texas*, xliv, 256, 308, 310, 327, 333, 338, 340–41
Lee v. *Weisman*, 210
Lehr v. *Robertson*, 162, 187
LeRoy Fibre Co. v. *Chicago, M. & St. P. R. Co.*, 150

Life's Dominion (Dworkin), xvi(n23)
Lindsley v. *Natural Carbonic Gas Co.*, 17
Little Rock Family Planning Servs. v. *Jegley*, 232
Liverpool New York & Philadelphia S. S. Co. v. *Commissioners of Emigration*, 40
Living Infants Fairness and Equality Act, li
Lochner v. *New York*, xxxvi, 2, 14, 19, 41, 198–99, 209, 299, 311
Loving v. *Virginia*, 17(n1), 31, 35, 148, 169–70, 195, 308, 336, 338
Lucas, R., 300(n23)
Luker, K., xv
Lusk, W., 316(n51)

M

MacIntyre, A., xiv
Macnaghten, M., 26
Madison, J., 6, 6(n3), 7, 15
Madsen v. *Women's Health Center, Inc.*, 320
Maher v. *Roe*, xx, xxii, 67, 70–76, 78, 96–97, 99, 101, 120, 123–24, 124(n8), 135–36, 139–40, 177
Mapp v. *Ohio*, 4
Marbury v. *Madison*, 8, 145, 206, 288
marital privacy, 4–5, 10, 18, 31, 54(n11)
marital rape, xlvi, 184–87
Marks v. *United States*, 195, 225
Marrs v. *Motorola, Inc.*, 277
Marshall, T., xiii
  on *Akron* v. *Akron Center for Reproductive Health*, 111
  on *Beal* v. *Doe*, 66–67, 69
  on *Bellotti* v. *Baird*, 87
  on *Colautti* v. *Franklin*, 80
  on *Doe* v. *Bolton*, 42
  on *Eisenstadt* v. *Baird*, 16
  on *Harris* v. *McRae*, 95, 99
  on *H. L.* v. *Matheson*, 103, 108–10
  on *Hodgson* v. *Minnesota*, 160
  on *Maher* v. *Roe*, 70, 73
  on *Ohio* v. *Akron Center for Reproductive Health*, 154
  on *Planned Parenthood of Kansas City* v. *Ashcroft*, 128
  on *Planned Parenthood of Missouri* v. *Danforth*, 50
  on *Poelker* v. *Doe*, 78
  on *Roe* v. *Wade*, xxii, 19
  on *Simopoulos* v. *Virginia*, 130
  on *Singleton* v. *Wulff*, 62
  on *Thornburgh* v. *American College of Obstetricians and Gynecologists*, 132
  on *Webster* v. *Reproductive Health Services*, 138, 145
Marshall v. *United States*, 315
Martin v. *Struthers*, 2
Massachusetts Bd. of Retirement v. *Murgia*, 71
maternal health exception, xiii, xix, xxiv–xxv, xxvii, l, 26–28, 37, 42, 56, 77, 79, 101, 113, 117, 120–22, 217–21, 231, 238, 250–51, 255, 258, 331, 337
maternal life exception, xiii, xix, xxiv–xxvii, xxxix, 30, 38, 77, 95, 112, 152, 217–18, 305, 331
Mayeri, S., xlviii
Maynard v. *Hill*, 54, 162
May v. *Anderson*, 88
Mazurek v. *Armstrong*, 268, 278
McBoyle v. *United States*, 232
McCarthy, K., li
McConnell, M., xxxiii–xxxiv
McCulloch v. *Maryland*, 335
McDonald v. *Board of Election Commissioners*, 17
McDonald v. *Chicago*, xxxvii, 296, 298–99, 300(n22), 327–28

McGarvey v. *Magee-Womens Hospital*, 35
McGowan v. *Maryland*, 98–99
McKeiver v. *Pennsylvania*, 89
McLaughlin v. *Florida*, 11, 15(n7)
McRae, C., 95
McRae v. *Califano*, 96, 102
mediate animation, 24, 24(n22), 36
Medicaid funding of abortions, 62–63, 65–68, 70–71, 73, 77–78, 95–98, 100, 139
medical emergency, 127, 167, 179–80, 183
medication abortion, xlv–xlvi, l, lii, 331–32
Memphis Center for Reproductive Health v. *Slatery*, 307, 325
#MeToo movement, xxxiii
Meyer v. *Nebraska*, 2–3, 5(n1), 6, 10, 31, 35, 65, 110, 163, 169, 308
Michael H. v. *Gerald D.*, 162–63, 168, 195–96
Miller v. *California*, 148
Minersville School Dist. v. *Gobitis*, 312
minors
  constitutional rights, 55, 88
  judicial consent and, xxi, xxvi, 87, 91–92, 92(n28), 93–94, 125, 154–58, 161, 165
  parental consent and, xxi, 55–56, 58, 60–61, 90–92, 92(n28), 93, 112, 114–16, 125, 166, 188–89
  parental notification and, 103–10, 112, 125, 125(n12), 126, 154–56, 160–65, 268
  two-parent notification requirement, 161, 164–65
Minors' Consent to Health Services Act, 161
Minor v. *Happersett*, 98(n25)
Mississippi Gestational Age Act, xxxiv, xlii, 294–95

Mississippi Univ. for Women v. *Hogan*, 193
Missouri abortion statute (*Webster*), xxi–xxii, 138, 140, 143, 146
Mohr, J., 196
Monroe v. *Pape*, 4
Montana v. *Kennedy*, 35
Montana v. *Rogers*, 35
Montejo v. *Louisiana*, 318
Moore v. *East Cleveland*, 88, 110, 163, 170, 175, 299, 308
Moore v. *Texas*, 276
Moose Lodge v. *Irvis*, 39
Morey v. *Doud*, 46
morning-after pill, xlv, 36
Moyn, S., lii
Mugler v. *Kansas*, 168
Muller v. *Oregon*, 199, 256
Murphy v. *United Parcel Service, Inc.*, 277
Murray, M., xlviii
Muskrat v. *United States*, 287
Myers v. *United States*, 8

N

NAACP v. *Alabama*, 2–4, 5(n1), 15(n7), 64
NAACP v. *Button*, 2–3, 11
Nash v. *Meyer*, 306
National Abortion Federation v. *Ashcroft*, 253–54, 254(n5), 255
New Jersey v. *T. L. O.*, 277
New Orleans v. *Dukes*, 326
New York City Health and Hospitals Corp., 95–96
New York Dept. of Soc. Services v. *Dublino*, 67
New York Times Co. v. *Sullivan*, 12, 148
Ninth Amendment, 3, 5–7, 7(n4), 8, 8(n6), 13–15, 31, 44, 96, 296
Nken v. *Holder*, 281
NLRB v. *Noel Canning*, 335

O

Obama, B., xiv, xxx–xxxi, xxxiii, xxxv
Obergefell v. *Hodges*, xliv, 308, 310, 327, 333, 335, 335(n4), 338, 339(n6), 340
O'Connor, S. D., xiii–xiv, xxix
   on *Akron* v. *Akron Center for Reproductive Health*, xxiii, 111, 119–27
   on *Hodgson* v. *Minnesota*, 160
   on *Ohio* v. *Akron Center for Reproductive Health*, 154
   on *Planned Parenthood of Central Missouri* v. *Danforth*, 127
   on *Planned Parenthood of Kansas City* v. *Ashcroft*, 128
   on *Planned Parenthood of Southeastern Pennsylvania* v. *Casey*, 166–90
   on *Roe* v. *Wade*, xxii, 119–25, 144
   on *Simopoulos* v. *Virginia*, 130
   on *Stenberg* v. *Carhart*, xxvi, xxvii, 212, 223–25
   on *Thornburgh* v. *American College of Obstetricians and Gynecologists*, 132
   on *Webster* v. *Reproductive Health Services*, 138, 144
Office of Personnel Management v. *Richmond*, 329
Ohio v. *Akron Center for Reproductive Health*, xxi, 154–59, 162, 190, 201
Olmstead v. *United States*, 31

P

Palko v. *Connecticut*, 9, 31, 195, 298(n19)
Palmer v. *Hoffman*, 180
Papachristou v. *Jacksonville*, 81
parental authority, 56, 107(n17), 110, 162(n31), 163
parental consent for minors, xxi, 55–56, 58, 60–61, 90–92, 92(n28), 93, 106, 112, 114–16, 125, 166, 188–89
parental notification for minors, xx–xxi, xxvi, 103–10, 112, 125, 125(n12), 126, 154–56, 160–65, 268
Parham v. *J. R.*, 162–63
partial-birth abortion, xxvi–xxviii, 213, 216–17, 222, 224–27, 232–38, 243, 246, 253
Partial-Birth Abortion Ban Act, x, xvii–xxviii, li, 242–49, 252, 252(n4), 253–59
Patterson v. *McLean Credit Union*, 173, 318
Pavesich v. *New England Life Ins. Co.*, 13(n1)
Payne v. *Tennessee*, 173–74, 198, 321, 333
Peckham, C. W., 41
Pennsylvania Abortion Control Act, 80, 83, 85–86, 166
People v. *Belous*, 32
Perry v. *Leeke*, 144, 149
personhood, xv, xv(n19), xvi, xvi(n23), xvii, 30, 34, 316, 316(n50)
Petchesky, R., 174
physician standard of care, 80–83
physician's veto, xxi, xxvii, 229
Pierce v. *Society of Sisters*, 2–3, 5(n1), 10, 31, 35, 90, 97, 110, 162, 169–70, 195, 308
Pierce v. *Underwood*, 235
Planned Parenthood Assn. v. *Fitzpatrick*, 119, 127
Planned Parenthood of Central Missouri v. *Danforth*, xx
   cited in *Akron* v. *Akron Center for Reproductive Health*, 112–13, 115–18, 121–22, 124, 124(n8), 125, 127
   cited in *Bellotti* v. *Baird*, 90–91
   cited in *Colautti* v. *Franklin*, 82, 84–85
   cited in *Gonzales* v. *Carhart*, 248, 252

Planned Parenthood of Central Missouri v.
    Danforth (Continued)
  cited in *H. L.* v. *Matheson*, 107
  cited in *Hodgson* v. *Minnesota*, 162
  cited in *Maher* v. *Roe*, 75
  cited in *Ohio* v. *Akron Center for Reproductive Health*, 154–55
  cited in *Planned Parenthood of Southeastern Pennsylvania* v. *Casey*, 180–81, 188–89, 200–202
  cited in *Singleton* v. *Wulff*, 65
  cited in *Stenberg* v. *Carhart*, 217, 237
  cited in *Thornburgh* v. *American College of Obstetricians and Gynecologists*, 132
  cited in *Webster* v. *Reproductive Health Services*, 141–42, 150
  opinion of the Court, 50–61
Planned Parenthood of Indiana and Kentucky, Inc. v. *Commissioner of Indiana State Dept. of Health*, 271
Planned Parenthood of Kansas City v. *Ashcroft*, xx, 111, 128–30, 154–57, 165, 204
Planned Parenthood of Southeastern Pennsylvania v. *Casey*, xxxi
  altering of *Roe* v. *Wade* in, xiv–xxv, xxviii
  cited in *Box* v. *Planned Parenthood*, 271
  cited in *Dobbs* v. *Jackson Women's Health Organization*, 292–97, 301, 306–8, 312–13, 317–25, 328–36, 336(n5), 337–40, 340(n7)
  cited in *Gonzales* v. *Carhart*, 244, 246, 250–52, 256–59
  cited in *June Medical Services, LLC* v. *Russo*, 276–80
  cited in *Stenberg* v. *Carhart*, 212, 216, 220–21, 224–25, 227–28, 230, 233, 236–37, 239–41
  cited in *Whole Woman's Health* v. *Hellerstedt*, 260–62, 267–70

  opinion of the Court, 166–211
  overturning of, xvi, xxviii–xxxiv, xxxvi–xxxviii, xlii, xliv, 293, 330
  personal liberty and, 251(n2)
  stare decisis doctrine, xxiv, xlvii, 294, 296
  undue-burden standard, x, xxiii, xxv–xxvii, xxix–xxx, xxxii–xxxiii, 258, 261, 267–68, 278(n2), 293, 318–20
Planned Parenthood of Wis. v. *Doyle*, 232
Plessy v. *Ferguson*, xxxix, 198–99, 311–12
plurality opinion, vii(n4), viii
Poelker v. *Doe*, 69, 77–79, 139–40, 177
Poe v. *Gerstein*, 54
Poe v. *Menghini*, 32, 46
Poe v. *Ullman*, 3, 9, 112, 163, 168, 170
Pointer v. *Texas*, 5, 9
Posters 'N' Things, Ltd. v. *United States*, 244–45
Powell, L. F., xiii, xliii
  on *Akron* v. *Akron Center for Reproductive Health*, 111–19
  on *Beal* v. *Doe*, 66–67
  on *Bellotti* v. *Baird*, 87–94, 115, 125(n12), 165
  on *Colautti* v. *Franklin*, 80
  on *Doe* v. *Bolton*, 42
  on *Eisenstadt* v. *Baird*, 16
  on *Harris* v. *McRae*, 95
  on *H. L.* v. *Matheson*, 103
  on *Maher* v. *Roe*, 70–73
  on *Planned Parenthood of Central Missouri* v. *Danforth*, 50, 115–18, 162
  on *Planned Parenthood of Kansas City* v. *Ashcroft*, 128–29
  on *Roe* v. *Wade*, 19, 111–14, 117
  on *Simopoulos* v. *Virginia*, 130–31
  on *Singleton* v. *Wulff*, 62–65, 75
  on *Thornburgh* v. *American College of Obstetricians and Gynecologists*, 132

Index

Presidential Commission on the Supreme Court, xxxv, lii
Prince v. *Massachusetts*, 10, 31, 55, 89, 110, 162–63, 171
Pritchard, J., 121
privacy rights, xviii–xxxix, xliii–xlv, xlvii, 3–5, 5(n1), 12, 13(n1), 15, 31–33, 35, 40, 75, 111–12, 192–93, 196, 297(n16), 307
private civil-enforcement lawsuits, xxxv, 282–83, 332
Proprietary v. *Mitchell*, 304
prostaglandin abortion method, 56, 59–60
psychological abuse, 185–86
public facilities for abortion, 138–40
Public Utilities Comm'n v. *Pollak*, 4
Pulliam v. *Allen*, 287

Q

quickening, xviii, 23–24, 24(n21), 25–26, 31, 36, 301, 301(n24), 302–4, 306, 309, 314
Quilloin v. *Walcott*, 187

R

race-selective abortion, 271–72
Railway Express Agency v. *New York*, 17
Ramos v. *Louisiana*, 312, 320–21, 328
rape, xxxix, l, 42, 42(n5), 95, 134, 185, 331–32
Reagan, R., xliii
Red Lion Broadcasting Co. v. *FCC*, 67
Reed v. *Reed*, 17, 17(n1)
Regents of Univ. of Mich. v. *Ewing*, 299
Rehnquist, W. H., xiii–xiv, xxiv, xxix
  on *Akron* v. *Akron Center for Reproductive Health*, 111, 119
  on *Beal* v. *Doe*, 66
  on *Bellotti* v. *Baird*, 87
  on *Colautti* v. *Franklin*, 80, 84
  on *Doe* v. *Bolton*, 42, 48–49
  on *Eisenstadt* v. *Baird*, 16
  on *Harris* v. *McRae*, 95
  on *H. L.* v. *Matheson*, 103
  on *Hodgson* v. *Minnesota*, 160
  on *Maher* v. *Roe*, 70
  on *Ohio* v. *Akron Center for Reproductive Health*, 154
  on *Planned Parenthood of Central Missouri* v. *Danforth*, 50, 57
  on *Planned Parenthood of Kansas City* v. *Ashcroft*, 128
  on *Planned Parenthood of Southeastern Pennsylvania* v. *Casey*, 166, 194–202, 225, 320
  on *Roe* v. *Wade*, xvii(n25), xxi, 19, 39–41, 57, 194–98
  on *Simopoulos* v. *Virginia*, 130
  on *Singleton* v. *Wulff*, 62–63
  on *Stenberg* v. *Carhart*, 212, 225–33
  on *Thornburgh* v. *American College of Obstetricians and Gynecologists*, 132, 134
  on *Webster* v. *Reproductive Health Services*, 138–44
Reno v. *Flores*, 327
reproductive justice, xlix
Rex v. *Bourne*, 26
Reynolds v. *Sims*, 9, 15(n8), 98(n25)
Reynolds v. *United States*, 11–12
Richmond Medical Center for Women v. *Gilmore*, 230
Richmond v. *J. A. Croson Co.*, 144
right of assembly, 3
right of association, 3, 15(n7)
Roberts, J., xiv, xxix, xxxvi
  on *Dobbs* v. *Jackson Women's Health Organization*, xxxiv, xli–xlii, 291, 328–31
  on *Gonzales* v. *Carhart*, 242
  on *June Medical Services, LLC* v. *Russo*, xxxiii, 276

Roberts, J. (*Continued*)
   on *Planned Parenthood of Southeastern Pennsylvania* v. *Casey*, 328–30
   on *Roe* v. *Wade*, 328–30
   on *Whole Woman's Health* v. *Hellerstedt*, 260
   on *Whole Woman's Health* v. *Jackson*, xxxv, 286, 288
Roberts v. *United States Jaycees*, 163
Rochin v. *California*, 9, 170, 192, 308, 337
Rodgers v. *Danforth*, 50
Roe v. *Norton*, 68, 71(n3), 73
Roe v. *Wade*
   cited in *Akron* v. *Akron Center for Reproductive Health*, 111–14, 117, 119–25
   cited in *Beal* v. *Doe*, 67–69
   cited in *Bellotti* v. *Baird*, 90
   cited in *Colautti* v. *Franklin*, 82, 84–85
   cited in *Dobbs* v. *Jackson Women's Health Organization*, 291–97, 300–301, 305–18, 320–21, 323–25, 328–34, 336, 336(n5), 337–40, 340(n7)
   cited in *Doe* v. *Bolton*, 42, 44, 46
   cited in *Gonzales* v. *Carhart*, 250–51, 259
   cited in *Harris* v. *McRae*, 96, 99–100, 102
   cited in *Maher* v. *Roe*, 72–76
   cited in *Planned Parenthood of Central Missouri* v. *Danforth*, 50, 52–58, 60–61
   cited in *Planned Parenthood of Southeastern Pennsylvania* v. *Casey*, 166–67, 169, 172–78, 190–98, 202–3, 206–10
   cited in *Poelker* v. *Doe*, 77, 79
   cited in *Singleton* v. *Wulff*, 62–63
   cited in *Stenberg* v. *Carhart*, 212, 216, 223
   cited in *Thornburgh* v. *American College of Obstetricians and Gynecologists*, 134–36
   cited in *Webster* v. *Reproductive Health Services*, 138–49, 151–52
   cited in *Whole Woman's Health* v. *Hellerstedt*, 261
   codification of, xxx, xxxvi
   constitutional right to abortion and, x–xi, xv, xviii, xix–xx, xxiii, xxxv, xxxix, 152, 167–68, 192, 197
   equality argument, xlvii–xlviii
   impact of *Casey* decision, xxiv, xxvii–xxviii
   judicial critique of, xi, xiii, xxxix, xl–xlii
   jurisprudential foundations for, ix
   overturning of, x, xii–xvii, xxxi, xxxiv, xxxvii, xl–xli, xliv, xlvi, l–lii, 293, 330
   personal liberty and, 168, 172, 251(n2)
   privacy rights and, xliii, xlv, xlvii, 192, 196, 307
   stare decisis doctrine, 111(n1), 191, 196–98, 202, 206, 259
   Supreme Court case, 19–41
   trimester approach in, xxi–xxii, 142, 147–49, 176–77, 179, 197, 318
   undue-burden standard, 124(n8)
   viability of fetus in, 142, 147–48, 167, 175–76, 179
Roman Catholic Diocese of Brooklyn v. *Cuomo*, 281
Romer, N. G., 238
Roosevelt, F. D., 198
Rosenberg, G., xl
Rosen v. *Louisiana State Board of Medical Examiners*, 32
Royster Guano Co. v. *Virginia*, 17

S

saline amniocentesis, 56, 59–60, 214, 248
Salve Regina College v. *Russell*, 254
same-sex marriage, xliv, 310, 327, 333, 339(n6). *See also Obergefell*
San Antonio Independent School District v. *Rodriguez*, 71, 124, 326
Sanger, M., 273
Santosky v. *Kramer*, 158
S. B. 8 (Texas), 282–90
Scalia, A., xiii–xiv, xxxiii
   on *Gonzales* v. *Carhart*, 242, 250
   on *Hodgson* v. *Minnesota*, 160
   on *Lawrence* v. *Texas*, 341
   on *Ohio* v. *Akron Center for Reproductive Health*, 154
   on originalists and non-originalists, viii
   on *Planned Parenthood of Southeastern Pennsylvania* v. *Casey*, 194, 202–11, 318
   on *Roe* v. *Wade*, xi–xxiii, 144–45, 202–3, 206–10, 241
   on *Stenberg* v. *Carhart*, xxviii, 212, 233, 239–41
   on *Webster* v. *Reproductive Health Services*, 138, 144–45
Schware v. *Board of Bar Examiners*, 3, 5(n1), 11
Second Amendment, 298
second physician approval, 43, 48
second physician attendance, 128–29
second trimester abortion, xiii, xxvii, 60, 113–14, 114(n22), 114(n24), 120–21, 125, 130–31, 149, 214, 224–25, 248
second trimester hospitalization, 113, 120–21, 125, 130–31, 149
severe fetal abnormality, xxxiv, l, 42, 81, 81(n3), 272

sex-selective abortion, 271–72
Sex Selective and Disability Abortion Ban, 272
sexual assault, xxxiii, 183, 185–86, 200, 256(n8). *See also* rape
Shafer, B. P., 236
Shapiro, I., ix, x
Shapiro, S., 286
Shapiro v. *Thompson*, 17(n1), 33
Shelley v. *Kracmer*, 64
Shelton v. *Tucker*, 11, 15(n7)
Sherbert v. *Verner*, 33
Siegel, R., xliii, xlviii
Sierra Club v. *Morton*, 39
Simopoulos v. *Virginia*, xx, 111, 130–31, 149–50
Singer, P., 316(n50)
Singleton v. *Wulff*, 62–65, 75
Sixth Amendment, 144, 149
Skinner v. *Oklahoma*, 4, 10–11, 18, 31, 35, 148, 170, 195, 201, 308, 340
Sloan v. *Lemon*, 126
Smith v. *Allwright*, 123, 197, 339
Smith v. *Gaffard*, 304
Smith v. *Goguen*, 81
Smith v. *State*, 304
Smith v. *Texas*, 290
Snyder v. *Massachusetts*, 5, 41, 195, 298(n19)
Sosna v. *Iowa*, 162
Sotomayor, S., xiv
   on *Box* v. *Planned Parenthood*, 272
   on *Dobbs* v. *Jackson Women's Health Organization*, xliv, 291, 331–42
   on *June Medical Services, LLC* v. *Russo*, 275
   on *United States* v. *Texas*, 284–85
   on *Whole Woman's Health* v. *Hellerstedt*, 260
   on *Whole Woman's Health* v. *Jackson*, xxxv, 281–83, 286, 288–90

Souter, D., xiii, xiv, xxiii
  on *Gonzales* v. *Carhart*, 242, 250
  on *Planned Parenthood of Southeastern Pennsylvania* v. *Casey*, 166, 190
  on *Stenberg* v. *Carhart*, 212
sovereign immunity, 287–88
Spears v. *State*, 33
spousal abuse, xxvi, 183–87, 256(n8)
spousal consent, 53–55, 57–58, 75–76, 188, 200
spousal notification, xx, xxv, xxvi, 166, 183–84, 186–87, 191, 200–202, 268–69
Standards for Obstetric-Gynecologic Services (ACOG), 114, 121, 131
Stanley v. *Georgia*, 18, 31, 35, 134
Stanley v. *Illinois*, 58, 162, 187, 338
stare decisis doctrine, xxiv, xxxvi, xxxix, xlii, xlvii, 111, 111(n1), 122–23, 152–53, 165, 173, 175, 190–91, 196–98, 202, 206, 276, 280, 294, 296, 323–25, 328, 333, 341(n8)
Starkloff Hospital, 77
State v. *Ausplund*, 306
State v. *Barquet*, 32
State v. *Brandenberg*, 305(n35)
State v. *Carpenter*, 235
State v. *Cooper*, 304
State v. *Gedicke*, 29(n42), 307
State v. *Griswold*, 11
State v. *Miller*, 306
State v. *Moore*, 307
State v. *Munson*, 33
State v. *Nelson*, 11
State v. *Tippie*, 307
Steinberg v. *Brown*, 33
Steinbock, B., 316(n50)
Stenberg v. *Carhart*, xxvi–xxvii, xxix, xlviii, 212–46, 248–50, 252, 254–55, 258, 267
Stevens, J. P., xii–xiv
  on *Akron* v. *Akron Center for Reproductive Health*, 111
  on *Beal* v. *Doe*, 66
  on *Bellotti* v. *Baird*, 87
  on *Colautti* v. *Franklin*, 80
  on *Gonzales* v. *Carhart*, 242, 250
  on *Harris* v. *McRae*, 95, 100–102
  on *H. L.* v. *Matheson*, 103
  on *Hodgson* v. *Minnesota*, 160–65
  on *Maher* v. *Roe*, 70, 75
  on *Ohio* v. *Akron Center for Reproductive Health*, 154
  on *Planned Parenthood of Kansas City* v. *Ashcroft*, 128
  on *Planned Parenthood of Missouri* v. *Danforth*, 50
  on *Planned Parenthood of Southeastern Pennsylvania* v. *Casey*, 166, 190, 278
  on *Roe* v. *Wade*, 102, 190
  on *Simopoulos* v. *Virginia*, 130
  on *Singleton* v. *Wulff*, 62
  on *Stenberg* v. *Carhart*, 212, 223, 225
  on *Thornburgh* v. *American College of Obstetricians and Gynecologists*, 132, 150–51
  on *Webster* v. *Reproductive Health Services*, 138
Stewart, P., xiii
  on *Beal* v. *Doe*, 66
  on *Bellotti* v. *Baird*, 87
  on *Colautti* v. *Franklin*, 80
  on *Doe* v. *Bolton*, 42
  on *Eisenstadt* v. *Baird*, 16
  on *Griswold* v. *Connecticut*, 1, 5(n1), 8–9, 11, 13–15
  on *Harris* v. *McRae*, 95–99
  on *H. L.* v. *Matheson*, 103
  on *Maher* v. *Roe*, 70
  on *Planned Parenthood of Central Missouri* v. *Danforth*, 50, 162

on *Roe v. Wade*, 19, 40
on *Singleton v. Wulff*, 62–63
Story, J., 7, 296
Stubblefield, P., 214, 230, 232
Sturgis v. Attorney General, 18
surgical-center requirement, 260, 264–66
Sweezy v. New Hampshire, 3
Swift & Co. v. Wickham, 173
Swint v. Chambers County Comm'n, 286

T

Tenth Amendment, 7(n4), 7(n5), 8(n6), 15
Terry v. Ohio, 31
Texas Heartbeat Act (S. B. 8), xxxv, 282–290
Texas v. Johnson, 171, 324
Third Amendment, 3
third trimester abortion, xiii, xxiii, 128–29
Thirteenth Amendment, li(n158)
Thomas, C., xiii, xiv
  on *Box v. Planned Parenthood*, xxxiii, 272–74
  on *Dobbs v. Jackson Women's Health Organization*, xliv, xlv, 291, 326–28, 339
  on *Gonzales v. Carhart*, 242, 250
  on *Griswold v. Connecticut*, 340
  on *June Medical Services, LLC v. Russo*, xxxiii, 279
  on *Lawrence v. Texas*, 340
  on *Obergefell v. Hodges*, 340
  on *Planned Parenthood of Southeastern Pennsylvania v. Casey*, 166, 194, 202, 250
  on *Roe v. Wade*, 250
  on *Stenberg v. Carhart*, xxviii, 212, 217, 233–39
  on *Whole Woman's Health v. Hellerstedt*, xxxii, 260, 267–70
  on *Whole Woman's Health v. Jackson*, 286

Thomas, K., 287–88
Thompson, J. J., xvi(n23)
Thornburgh v. Abbott, 150
Thornburgh v. American College of Obstetricians and Gynecologists, 132–37, 142, 151, 175–77, 181, 196–97, 202, 204, 217, 246, 313, 315, 320
Tileston v. Ullman, 1, 10
Timbs v. Indiana, xxxvii, 298–99
Tinker v. Des Moines School Dist., 55
Tooley, M., 316(n50)
Trent v. State, 306
Tribe, L., 315
trimester approach, xix, xxi–xxiii, xl, 120–23, 147–50, 176–77, 179, 197, 318
Truax v. Raich, 2
Trubek v. Ullman, 10
Trump, D., xiv, xxxiii–xxxiv
Tucker, S. G., 303
Turnaway Study, xlix
Turner Broadcasting System, Inc. v. FCC, 306
Turner v. Safley, 169, 308, 338
Twelfth Amendment, 34
Twenty-second Amendment, 34
two-parent notification requirement, 161, 164–65

U

undue-burden standard, x, xxiii, xxv–xxvi, xxviii, xxix–xxx, xxxii–xxxiii, 123–24, 124(n8), 125, 178–79, 181–83, 194–95, 203–6, 212, 224, 240, 258, 260–61, 264, 266–70, 275–76, 278, 293, 318–20
Uniform Abortion Act, 46
Union Pacific R. Co. v. Botsford, 31, 192, 337
United Public Workers v. Mitchell, 8(n6)

United States v. *Carlton*, 327
United States v. *Carolene Products Co.*, 326
United States v. *Darby*, 14
United States v. *Harriss*, 81, 119
United States v. *Nixon*, 286
United States v. *O'Brien*, 306
United States v. *Peters*, 288
United States v. *Richardson*, 63
United States v. *Salerno*, 200
United States v. *Scott*, 197
United States v. *Texas*, 284–85, 289
United States v. *Title Ins. & Trust Co.*, 173
United States v. *Vaello Madero*, 327
United States v. *Virginia*, 256–57
United States v. *Vuitch*, 35, 38, 49

V

vacuum aspiration, 214–15, 224
Vasquez v. *Hillery*, 153, 321, 333
viability. *See* fetal viability
Viemester v. *White*, 231
Virginia Office for Protection and Advocacy v. *Stewart*, 282

W

waiting period, xx, xxvi, 112, 119, 126–27, 161, 166, 182, 237
Walker, L., 185
Warren, E., 13(n1)
Warren, M., 316(n50)
Washington State Grange v. *Washington State Republican Party*, 329
Washington v. *Glucksberg*, xiv, xxx, xxxvii, 228, 246–47, 271, 293, 298–99, 305, 309, 326, 335, 335(n4)
Washington v. *Harper*, 170, 308, 337
Weber v. *Aetna Casualty & Surety Co.*, 40
Webster v. *Reproductive Health Services*, xxi–xxiv, 138–53, 157, 177, 190, 194, 210, 315, 330
Wesberry v. *Sanders*, 9

Westby v. *Doe*, 67
West Coast Hotel Co. v. *Parrish*, 198–99, 209, 311, 313, 330
West Virginia State Bd. of Education v. *Barnette*, 171, 197, 312, 330
Whalen v. *Roe*, 72, 117
White, B.
   on *Akron* v. *Akron Center for Reproductive Health*, xiii, xxi, xxvi(n72), 111, 119
   on *Beal* v. *Doe*, 66
   on *Bellotti* v. *Baird*, 87
   on *Colautti* v. *Franklin*, 80, 84–86
   on *Doe* v. *Bolton*, 42, 48–49
   on *Eisenstadt* v. *Baird*, 16
   on *Griswold* v. *Connecticut*, 10–11, 14
   on *Harris* v. *McRae*, 95
   on *H. L.* v. *Matheson*, 103
   on *Hodgson* v. *Minnesota*, 160
   on *Maher* v. *Roe*, 70
   on *Ohio* v. *Akron Center for Reproductive Health*, 154
   on *Planned Parenthood of Central Missouri* v. *Danforth*, 57–61
   on *Planned Parenthood of Kansas City* v. *Ashcroft*, 128
   on *Planned Parenthood of Southeastern Pennsylvania* v. *Casey*, 166, 194, 202
   on *Roe* v. *Wade*, 19, 57, 134–36, 292
   on *Simopoulos* v. *Virginia*, 130
   on *Singleton* v. *Wulff*, 62
   on *Thornburgh* v. *American College of Obstetricians and Gynecologists*, 132, 134–37, 313
   on *Webster* v. *Reproductive Health Services*, 138
Whitney v. *California*, 168
Whole Woman's Health v. *Hellerstedt*, xxxii–xxxiv, 260–70, 274, 275–80, 319–21, 337

Whole Woman's Health v. *Jackson*, xxxv, 286–90
Whole Woman's Health v. *Jackson* Injunctive Relief Application, 281–83
Wieman v. *Updegraff*, 2
Williams Obstetrics (Hellman & Pritchard), 36(n59), 36(n60), 121
Williamson v. *Lee Optical Co.*, 40, 125, 146, 171, 261, 326
Winston v. *Lee*, 170, 192, 308, 337
Winter v. *Natural Resources Defense Council, Inc.*, 281
Wisconsin v. *Constantineau*, 46
Wisconsin v. *Yoder*, 90, 110, 163
Wolfe v. *Schroering*, 54, 57, 60
Wulff v. *Singleton*, 74, 77

Y

Yick Wo v. *Hopkins*, 11
Young, C., 288, 288(n3)
YWCA v. *Kugler*, 29(n42), 32

Z

Zemel v. *Rusk*, 11
Ziegler, M., xii(n5), xxxi(n84), xxxiii(n90), lii
Zorach v. *Clauson*, 149